DOCTRINAL NEW TESTAMENT COMMENTARY

Volume III

COLOSSIANS — REVELATION

DOCTRINAL NEW TESTAMENT COMMENTARY

Volume III

COLOSSIANS – REVELATION

By

Bruce R. McConkie

Salt Lake City, Utah

19TH PRINTING, 1994

Lithographed in the United States of America
PUBLISHERS PRESS
Salt Lake City, Utah

Preface

Peter said: "Be ready always to give an answer to every man that asketh you a reason of the hope that is in you."

Many of the answers and much of the inspired reasoning needed by the saints to comply with this counsel is found in the New Testament.

Peter himself recorded his testimony and preserved in writing his doctrinal explanations so "that ye may be able after my decease to have these things always in remembrance."

There is a crying need in the Church today for more real gospel scholarship, for a knowledge of the doctrines of salvation.

We need to know the doctrines found in the Standard Works, to instil into our souls the inspired teachings of Holy Writ.

Volume III of this *Doctrinal New Testament Commentary* is designed to help fulfil these needs. The New Testament contains a blueprint of the gospel; it charts a course leading to eternal life in God's kingdom. The Lord has preserved it for us so that we may enjoy the words of eternal life in this world and be led toward eternal glory in the next.

Since the New Testament was written to the saints, to members of the Church, to those who knew and understood the doctrines of salvation, there is no way to absorb its teachings except to have the background knowledge and the personal revelation possessed by the saints. Accordingly, this volume, which begins with Colossians and continues through the Book of Revelation, analyzes doctrinal truths in the light of latter-day revelation.

This work is not a church publication; I alone am responsible for the interpretations and views set forth.

As with the two previous volumes, I find it difficult to overstate how greatly I am indebted to Velma Harvey, my very able and conscientious secretary. She has performed indispensable and superior service.

—Bruce R. McConkie

Salt Lake City, Utah
December 1, 1972

ABBREVIATIONS

Scriptural references are abbreviated in a standard self-identifying way. Other books are cited by author and title, except the following:

Commentary I	— Bruce R. McConkie, *Doctrinal New Testament Commentary*, Volume I, The Gospels
Commentary II	— Bruce R. McConkie, *Doctrinal New Testament Commentary*, Volume II, Acts - Philippians
Dummelow	— J. R. Dummelow, *The One Volume Bible Commentary*
I. V.	— Joseph Smith, *Inspired Version of Bible*, First Edition
Jamieson	— Robert Jamieson, A. R. Fausset, and David Brown, *Commentary on the Whole Bible*
Mormon Doctrine	— Bruce R. McConkie, *Mormon Doctrine*, Second Edition
Teachings	— Joseph Fielding Smith, *Teachings of the Prophet Joseph Smith*

Index — Scriptural Passages

Scriptural Passage	Subject	Page
	COLOSSIANS	
1:1-12	Gospel Brings Hope, Blessings, Salvation	21
1:13-19	Christ, The Firstborn, Created All Things	24
1:20-29	Gospel Preached to Every Creature	26
2:1-9	Fulness of Godhead Dwelleth in Christ	28
2:10-23	Mosaic Ordinances Nailed to Cross of Christ	32
3:1-4	Some Lives are Hid with Christ in God	34
3:5-17	Saints Exhorted to be Holy	35
3:18-25; 4:1-18	Saints Exhorted to be Wise in All Things	38
	FIRST THESSALONIANS	
1:1-10	Gospel Comes in Word and Power	41
2:1-12	True Ministers Preach in a Godly Manner	44
2:13-20	Converts are the Glory and Joy of Missionaries	45
3:1-13	"Perfect That Which Is Lacking in Your Faith"	47
4:1-8	Be Holy; Sanctify Yourselves	48
4:9-12	"Work with Your Own Hands"	50
4:13-18	Saints Saved at Second Coming	51
5:1-11	Saints Know Season of Second Coming	53
5:12-28	Live as Becometh Saints	57

Scriptural Passage	Subject	Page
	SECOND THESSALONIANS	
1:1-12	Ungodly Damned at Second Coming	59
2:1-12	Apostasy to Precede Second Coming	61
2:13-17	Gospel Prepares Men for Eternal Glory	64
3:1-5	Pray for Triumph of Gospel Cause	65
3:6	Saints Withdraw Fellowship from Apostates	65
3:7-12	Paul Preacheth the Gospel of Work	66
3:13-18	"Be Not Weary In Well Doing"	67
	FIRST TIMOTHY	
1:1-11	Teach True Doctrine Only	70
1:12-17	Christ Came to Save Repentant Sinners	71
1:18-20	Apostates Delivered Unto Satan	74
2:1-7	Christ Ordained to be a Mediator	77
2:8-15	Paul Speaks About Dress of Women	79
3:1-7	Paul Speaketh of Bishops	80
3:8-13	Paul Speaketh of Deacons	81
3:14-16	"Great Is the Mystery of Godliness"	83
4:1-6	Paul Gives Signs of Latter-day Apostasy	84
4:7-11	Christ Brings Two Kinds of Salvation	86
4:12-16	"Be Thou An Example of the Believers"	87
5:1-18	Saints Commanded to Care for Worthy Poor	88
5:19-25; 6:1-6	Paul Names Divers Church Policies	91
6:7-10	"The Love of Money Is the Root of All Evil"	93
6:11-19	"Fight the Good Fight of Faith"	94

INDEX — SCRIPTURAL PASSAGES

Scriptural Passage	Subject	Page
6:20-21	Does Science Destroy Faith?	95
	SECOND TIMOTHY	
1:1-12	Christ Brought Immortality and Eternal Life	98
1:13-18; 2:1-7	Be Strong in the Faith	101
2:8-13	Christ Giveth Eternal Glory to the Elect	103
2:14-26	Shun Contention, Seek Godliness	104
3:1-13	Paul Describes Apostate Christendom	106
3:14-17	Scriptures Guide Man to Salvation	112
4:1-5	"Preach the Word"	114
4:6-22	Paul and All Saints Assured of Exaltation	115
	TITUS	
1:1-4	Paul Foreordained to Gain Eternal Life	119
1:5-16	Sound Doctrine Makes Men Sound in the Faith	120
2:1-15	Live Righteously, Deny Ungodliness, Seek the Lord	123
3:1-15	How to Live After Baptism	125
	PHILEMON	
1-25	Gospel Changes a Servant into a Brother	129
	HEBREWS	
1:1-4	God has a Body of Flesh and Bones	135
1:5-14	Christ Is God; Angels are Ministering Spirits	139
2:1-9	Jesus Made a Little Lower than Elohim	142

Scriptural Passage	Subject	Page
2:10-18	Christ Became Mortal to Save Man	143
3:1-6	Christ Is the Great High Priest and Apostle	146
3:7-19	"Now Is the Time and the Day of Your Salvation"	147
4:1-2	Gospel Offered to Ancient Israel	149
4:3-11	How to Enter into the Rest of the Lord	150
4:12-13	Word of God Pierces the Soul of Man	152
4:14-16; 5:1-3	"Come Boldly unto the Throne of Grace"	153
5:4-14	Even Christ Called to Holy Priesthood	154
6:1-3	"Let Us Go on unto Perfection"	159
6:4-9	Sons of Perdition Crucify Christ Afresh	160
6:10-20	God Swears Faithful Shall be Saved	162
7:1-3	Melchizedek Priesthood Brings Exaltation	165
7:4-10	Both Gospel and Mosaic Law Require Tithes	168
7:11-14	Melchizedek Priesthood Administereth the Gospel	169
7:15-17	Melchizedek Priesthood Is Power of an Endless Life	171
7:18-22	Melchizedek Priesthood Given with Oath and Covenant	172
7:23-28	Salvation Comes Through Intercession of Christ	174
8:1-5	Christ Offered Himself a Sacrifice for Sin	175
8:6-13	God Promised to Make a New Covenant with Israel	177
9:1-14	Mosaic Ordinances Prefigure Christ's Ministry	179

INDEX — SCRIPTURAL PASSAGES

Scriptural Passage	Subject	Page
9:15-28	Christ Is the Mediator of the New Covenant	181
10:1-18	"By the Blood Ye are Sanctified"	185
10:19-39	Those Who Fall from Grace are Damned	189
11:1-3	By Faith the Worlds were Made	192
11:4	Why was Abel's Sacrifice Accepted?	195
11:5-6	What Is the Doctrine of Translation?	198
11:7	Faith Saved Noah Temporally and Spiritually	200
11:8-16	Abraham Sought a Heavenly City	200
11:17-19	Why was Abraham Commanded to Sacrifice Isaac?	206
11:20-22	Patriarchal Blessings Come by Faith	208
11:23-31	Faith of Ancients Centered in Christ	210
11:32-35a	Faith and Miracles Go Together	214
11:35b-40	Faith Enables Men to Endure Sufferings	218
12:1-8	"Whom the Lord Loveth He Chasteneth"	221
12:9-10	Paul Speaketh of Pre-existence and Exaltation	224
12:11-17	To See God Follow Peace and Holiness	226
12:18-24	Exalted Saints Belong to Church of the Firstborn	228
12:25-29	"Our God Is a Consuming Fire"	232
13:1-3	"Some have Entertained Angels Unawares"	234
13:4-7	"Marriage Is Honourable in All"	236
13:8	Christ Is the Same Everlastingly	238
13:9-25	How Christians Offer Sacrifices	240

Scriptural Passage	Subject	Page
	JAMES	
1:1-7	Ask God for Wisdom	244
1:8-16	Resist Temptation and Gain Salvation	247
1:17-21	Every Good Gift Cometh from God	249
1:22-25	"Be Ye Doers of the Word"	250
1:26-27	How to Recognize Pure Religion	253
2:1-9	We Commit Sin if We Respect Persons	254
2:10-13	Salvation Gained by Keeping Whole Law	255
2:14-26	"Faith Without Works Is Dead"	257
3:1-13	Tame Thy Tongue to Perfect Thy Soul	261
3:14-18	Envy and Strife are of the Devil	262
4:1-3	Why and Whence Wars Come	263
4:4-6	Who are the Enemies of God?	264
4:7-12	How to Become a Friend of God	265
4:13-17	What Is Sin?	266
5:1-6	Misery Awaits the Wanton Rich	268
5:7-11	Await the Lord's Coming with Patience	270
5:12-20	Elders Anoint and Heal the Sick	272
	FIRST PETER	
1:1-16	Salvation Comes by Faith in Christ	282
1:17-21	Christ Foreordained to be the Redeemer	287
1:22-25; 2:1-3	Converts are Newborn Babes in Christ	288
2:4-8	Christ Is the Chief Cornerstone	290
2:9-10	What Is the Royal Priesthood?	293
2:11-12	Why There are Fleshly Lusts	295

Scriptural Passage	Subject	Page
2:13-25	Be in Subjection to Laws of Man	297
3:1-7	Husbands and Wives Should Honor Each Other	301
3:8-17	"Be Followers of that Which Is Good"	303
3:18-22; 4:1-6	Christ Preached Gospel to Spirits in Prison	305
4:7-11	"Speak as an Oracle of God"	316
4:12-19	Saints to be Tried in All Things	317
5:1-4	Elders to Feed the Flock of God	319
5:5-14	"Be Thou Humble"	321

SECOND PETER

Scriptural Passage	Subject	Page
1:1-19	"Make Your Calling and Election Sure"	323
1:20-21	Prophecy Comes by Power of Holy Ghost	355
2:1-9	False Teachers are Damned	357
2:10-22	Lustful Saints Perish in Own Corruption	358
3:1-9	Latter-day Scoffers Deny Second Coming	363
3:10-18	Elements to Melt at Second Coming	367

FIRST JOHN

Scriptural Passage	Subject	Page
1:1-7	How to Find Fellowship with God	372
1:8-10; 2:1-2	Gospel Offers Confession, Forgiveness, Propitiation	375
2:3-6	How Saints Can Know God and Christ	376
2:7-14	How Saints Can Abide in the Light	377
2:15-17	"Love Not the World"	379
2:18-26	Antichrists Shall Come in the Last Days	380

Scriptural Passage	Subject	Page
2:27-29	Holy Ghost Leads Saints to All Truth	383
3:1-3	Sons of God Shall be Like Christ	384
3:4-9	Why Saints Need Not Continue in Sin	385
3:10-18	Love the Brethren and Gain Eternal Life	387
3:19-24	How to Gain Answers to Prayers	390
4:1-6	"Try the Spirits"	392
4:7-21	"God Is Love"	397
5:1-5	Who Is Born of God?	401
5:6-9	Water, Blood, and Spirit Testify of Christ	403
5:10-21	Believe in Christ and Gain Eternal Life	405

SECOND JOHN

1:1-6	"Bring Up Your Children in Light and Truth"	409
1:7-13	Do Not Aid and Assist False Teachers	411

THIRD JOHN

1:1-14	Aid and Help Those Who Love the Truth	412

JUDE

1:1-5	"Contend For the Faith"	415
1:6	Certain Angels Kept Not Their First Estate	418
1:7-13	Michael Disputed About Body of Moses	419
1:14-16	Enoch Prophesieth of Second Coming	424
1:17-25	"Keep Yourselves in the Love of God"	426

INDEX — SCRIPTURAL PASSAGES

Scriptural Passage	Subject	Page
	REVELATION	
1:1-6	Christ Maketh Kings and Priests Unto God	433
1:7-8	Christ, the Almighty, Shall Come Again	438
1:9-11	Ancient Saints Worshiped on Sunday	439
1:12-20	John Seeth the Risen Lord	441
2:1-7	Overcome and Gain Eternal Life	444
2:8-11	"He that Overcometh Shall not be Hurt of the Second Death"	447
2:12-17	Overcome and Inherit Celestial Kingdom	449
2:18-29	Overcome and Rule Many Kingdoms	451
3:1-6	Overcome and Stay in the Book of Life	453
3:7-13	Overcome and Gain Godhood	455
3:14-22	Overcome and Sit on God's Throne	459
4:1-11	All Created Things Worship the Lord	463
5:1-14	"Worthy Is the Lamb"	469
6:1-2	Enoch Ministers During First Seal	476
6:3-4	War Rageth During Second Seal	478
6:5-6	Famine Stalks the Earth During Third Seal	479
6:7-8	Death, Hell, War, Famine Prevail During Fourth Seal	480
6:9-11	Christian Martyrs Slain During Fifth Seal	482
6:12-17	Signs of the Times Manifest in Sixth Seal	485
7:1	Gospel Restored During Sixth Seal	489
7:2-8	Elias to Seal 144,000 During Sixth Seal	490
7:9-17	John Seeth the Hosts of the Exalted from All Nations	495

Scriptural Passage	Subject	Page
8:1-13	Fire and Desolation Poured out During Seventh Seal	497
9:1-21	War and Plagues Poured out During Seventh Seal	500
10:1-11	John to Participate in Restoration of All Things	504
11:1-14	Two Prophets Shall be Slain in Jerusalem	507
11:15-19	Christ Shall Reign Over All the Earth	511
12:1-17	Satan Maketh War in Heaven and on Earth	513
13:1-10	Satan Governs Earthly Kingdoms	519
13:11-18	Church of Devil Worketh Miracles	523
14:1-5	"The Lamb Shall Stand Upon Mount Zion"	524
14:6-7	Gospel Restored by Angelic Ministrants	527
14:8-11	Eternal Torment Awaits the Wicked	531
14:12-13	"Blessed are the Dead which Die in the Lord"	533
14:14-20	Son of Man Harvests the Earth	534
15:1-4	Exalted Saints Praise God Forever	537
15:5-8; 16:1-12	God Poureth out Plagues Upon the Wicked	538
16:13-16	Nations Assemble for Armageddon	541
16:17-21	Christ Comes, Islands Flee, Mountains Cease	542
17:1-18	Devil Formeth a Great and Abominable Church	544
18:1-24	"Babylon the Great Is Fallen, Is Fallen"	556

INDEX — SCRIPTURAL PASSAGES

Scriptural Passage	Subject	Page
19:1-9a	Come Unto the Marriage Supper of the Lamb	562
19:9b-10	"The Testimony of Jesus Is the Spirit of Prophecy	564
19:11-16	Christ Is King of Kings and Lord of Lords	566
19:17-21	"Come . . . Unto the Supper of the Great God"	568
20:1-3	Satan Bound During Millennium	569
20:4-6	Saints Live and Reign During Millennium	571
20:7-10	Devil and His Armies Cast out Eternally	574
20:11-15	Dead are Judged According to Their Works	575
21:1-6a	Earth Receiveth its Paradisiacal Glory	580
21:6b-7	Overcome and Become a Son of God	583
21:8	What Is the Second Death?	583
21:9-27	Earth Attains Its Celestial Glory	584
22:1-5	Saints Reign as Gods in Celestial Splendor	588
22:6-16	Christ Cometh and His Reward Is with Him	589
22:17-21	"Come Unto Christ"	592

The Epistle of Paul the Apostle to the Colossians

As with other congregations of the Lord's saints in time's meridian, false doctrine reared its ugly head among the members of the kingdom in Colosse. These church members were faced with the usual Jewish concepts about the law of Moses with all its performances and rites. But they also seem to have been subjected to the idea that a great concourse of angels ministered between God and man. These angels were supposed to govern in mortal affairs and thereby became the recipients of that worship which is properly reserved for God only.

Accordingly, with true apostolic zeal, Paul wrote to remind the Colossian Saints that true worship centers in Christ and his Father and that the Mosaic system has long since been replaced by the gospel. His statements, among others, that Christ is the Firstborn, the Creator, the Head of the Church, in whom the fulness of the Godhead dwells, are inspired writing of superlative quality. His handling of the Mosaic problem falls into his usual pattern, and his then appended comments about seeking holiness and conforming to gospel standards are wise and appropriate.

GOSPEL BRINGS HOPE, BLESSINGS, SALVATION

COLOSSIANS 1:1-12.

1 Paul, an apostle of Jesus Christ by the will of God, and Timotheus *our* brother,

2 To the saints and faithful brethren in Christ which are at Colosse: Grace *be* unto you, and peace, from God our Father and the Lord Jesus Christ.

3 We give thanks to God and the Father of our Lord Jesus Christ, praying always for you,

4 Since we heard of your faith in Christ Jesus, and of the love *which ye have* to all the saints,

5 For the hope which is laid up for you in heaven, whereof ye heard before in the word of the truth of the gospel;

6 Which is come unto you, as *it is* in all the world; and bringeth forth fruit, as *it doth* also in you, since the day ye heard *of it*, and knew the grace of God in truth:

7 As ye also learned of Epaphras our dear fellowservant, who is for you a faithful minister of Christ;

8 Who also declared unto us your love in the Spirit.

9 For this cause we also, since the day we heard *it*, do not cease to pray for you, and to desire that ye might be filled with the knowledge of his will in all wisdom and spiritual understanding;

10 That ye might walk worthy of the Lord unto all pleasing, being fruitful in every good work, and increasing in the knowledge of God;

11 Strengthened with all might, according to his glorious power, unto all patience and longsuffering with joyfulness;

12 Giving thanks unto the Father, which hath made us meet to be partakers of the inheritance of the saints in light:

I.V. COLOSSIANS 1:4, 6.

4 Since we heard of your faith in Christ Jesus, and of **your** love to all the saints,

6 Which is come unto you, as **in all generations of** the world; and bringeth forth fruit, as it doth also in you, since the day ye heard of it, and knew the grace of God in truth;

The gospel consists of those laws, ordained by God the Father, whereby progression and advancement come. Accordingly, every good thing in time and in eternity grows out of and flows from the gospel. There is no blessing, no knowledge, no power, might or dominion, no grace or good thing that will or can be withheld from those who live the gospel. Temporarily God's saints may lack health or wealth or power or influence or many desirable things, but eventually all things shall be theirs, for they are Christ's and Christ is God's. (D. & C. 76:50-70.)

1. **An apostle]** See *Commentary II*, pp. 130-131, 328-333.

2. **Saints]** See *Commentary II*, pp. 525-529.

God our Father] Elohim the Father of our spirits. See *Commentary II*, pp. 154-162.

3. The Father of our Lord Jesus Christ] Elohim the Father of the mortal body of Christ, his Only Begotten in the flesh.

4. Faith in Christ] See Heb. 11:1-3.

5. Hope which is laid up for you in heaven] See *Commentary II*, pp. 262-265. **Gospel]** See *Commentary II*, pp. 213-216.

I. V. 6. In all generations] In all dispensations; that is, the same gospel now preached by Paul and accepted by the Colossians had been among the saints in generations past. See *Commentary II*, pp. 491-493.

K. J. 6. The Grace of God] See *Commentary II*, pp. 233-238.

8. Love in the Spirit] Love is of God. It is shed forth by the Light of Christ upon all mankind. But when it is perfected in the lives of righteous saints it comes as a gift of the Spirit, by the power of the Holy Ghost.

9. Filled with the knowledge of his will] We can learn the mind and will of the Lord in general — in the general sense of obedience to the basic laws of universal application — by reference to the recorded revelations which God has given. But we can only know the Lord's will where our specific and personal affairs are concerned by personal revelation. Hence, when we conform to the divine will calling for baptism and admission to the kingdom of God on earth, we then receive the gift of the Holy Ghost and are entitled to continuing revelation. Then we can be filled with the knowledge of God's will concerning our personal affairs.

Wisdom] See Jas. 1:1-7.

Spiritual understanding] This is what sets the saints apart from the world. Others may equal or excel them in scientific knowledge, in philosophical comprehension, or in any of the things of the world, but only the saints of God do or can understand the things of God, for these come by revelation. For instance, only the saints understand the atonement, comprehend the doctrines of salvation, enjoy the gifts of the Spirit, receive the spiritual rebirth, exercise faith unto life and salvation, and have a sure hope of eternal life.

10. Walk worthily unto the Lord] 'Remember who you are. Honor the name of Christ, which was placed upon you in the waters of baptism. Keep the commandments.'

Fruitful in every good work] Abounding in righteousness; those who keep the commandments thereby work the works of righteousness and do good continually.

11. Patience] See Jas. 5:7-11.

12. The inheritance of the saints] The kingdom of God on earth, which is the Church, and the kingdom of God in heaven, which is the celestial kingdom; hence, peace in this life and eternal life in the world to come.

CHRIST, THE FIRSTBORN, CREATED ALL THINGS

COLOSSIANS 1:13-19.

13 Who hath delivered us from the power of darkness, and hath translated *us* into the kingdom of his dear Son:

14 In whom we have redemption through his blood, *even* the forgiveness of sins:

15 Who is the image of the invisible God, the firstborn of every creature:

16 For by him were all things created, that are in heaven, and that are in earth, visible and invisible, whether *they be* thrones, or dominions, or principalities, or powers: all things were created by him, and for him:

17 And he is before all things, and by him all things consist.

18 And he is the head of the body, the church: who is the beginning, the firstborn from the dead; that in all *things* he might have the preeminence.

19 For it pleased *the Father* that in him should all fulness dwell;

13. [God] hath delivered us from the power of darkness] He has delivered his saints from the world where spiritual darkness reigns. The world is in darkness, the saints are in the light. "The whole world lieth in sin, and groaneth under darkness and under the bondage of sin." (D. & C. 84:49.)

Hath translated us] 'Hath changed us from our fallen and carnal state to a state of righteousness; hath transformed us from natural men to saints of God.' (Mosiah 3:19.)

The kingdom of his dear Son] The Church and kingdom of God on earth.

14. Redemption] See Rev. 5:1-14.

15. The image of the invisible God] Christ is the image of the Father physically and spiritually, in person and in personality. Physically the Resurrected Lord — who ate and drank with his disciples after he attained immortality, and whose body of flesh and bones they felt and handled — is in "the express image of his [Father's] person." (Heb. 1:3.) They look alike; in appearance one could pass for the other. Spiritually our Lord is "in the form of God" (Philip. 2:6); he has acquired all of the attributes of godliness in their perfection; as it is with the Father, so it is with him; he is the embodiment of justice, mercy and truth, of faith, hope and charity, of wisdom, virtue and knowledge, and of every good thing; thus he is in the likeness of and a projection of the personality of the Father.

The firstborn of every creature] God is the Father, Christ in the Son — in pre-existence. He is our Elder Brother, the first of the spirit children born to his exalted Parent. "I was in the beginning with the Father," he said, "and am the Firstborn." (D. & C. 93:21.) In that spirit sphere he advanced and progressed until he became "like unto God" (Abra. 3:24) in power and intelligence, and it was then that he was chosen and foreordained to be the Redeemer. When he, as a Spirit Being, appeared to the Brother of Jared, he said: "This body, which ye now behold, is the body of my spirit; . . . and even as I appear unto thee to be in the spirit will I appear unto my people in the flesh." (Ether 3:16.) See *Commentary I*, pp. 70-71.

16-17. Christ created the universe and all things that in it are, but in doing so he acted in the power, might, and omnipotence of the Father. "Worlds without number have I created," is God's language, "and by the Son I created them, which is mine Only Begotten." (Moses 1:33.) "By him, and through him, and of him, the worlds are and were created, and the inhabitants thereof are begotten sons and daughters unto God." (D. & C. 76:24; John 1:1-3; Heb. 1:2.)

18. Head of the . . . church] Whenever there is a true Church on earth, it is Christ's. He is its Author and Creator. He ordains and establishes it. By his power it shall triumph. He acts as directed by his Fathers. And he is the One who said: "Every plant, which my heavenly Father hath not planted, shall be rooted up." (Matt. 15:13.)

18. Firstborn from the dead] Firstfruits of the resurrection; first person to be resurrected.

19. Fulness] See Col. 2:1-9.

GOSPEL PREACHED TO EVERY CREATURE

COLOSSIANS 1:20-29.

20 And, having made peace through the blood of his cross, by him to reconcile all things unto himself; by him, *I say*, whether *they be* things in earth, or things in heaven.

21 And you, that were sometime alienated and enemies in *your* mind by wicked works, yet now hath he reconciled

22 In the body of his flesh through death, to present you holy and unblameable and unreproveable in his sight:

23 If ye continue in the faith grounded and settled, and *be* not moved away from the hope of the gospel, which ye have heard, *and* which was preached to every creature which is under heaven; whereof I Paul am made a minister;

24 Who now rejoice in my sufferings for you, and fill up that which is behind of the afflictions of Christ in my flesh for his body's sake, which is the church:

25 Whereof I am made a minister, according to the dispensation of God which is given to me for you, to fulfil the word of God;

26 *Even* the mystery which hath been hid from ages and from generations, but now is made manifest to his saints:

27 To whom God would make known what *is* the riches of the glory of this mystery among the Gentiles; which is Christ in you, the hope of glory:

28 Whom we preach, warning every man, and teaching every man in all wisdom; that we may present every man perfect in Christ Jesus:

29 Whereunto I also labour, striving according to his working, which worketh in me mightily.

20-23. Through the atonement of Christ, coupled with obedience to the laws and ordinances of the gospel, men are reconciled to God and to Christ. **Reconciliation]** See *Commentary II*, pp. 421-423.

20. Reconciliation comes by the shedding of Christ's blood and is between God in heaven and man on earth.

21. Even wicked men (through repentance!) are reconciled to God through Christ.

22. Those who are reconciled become clean; they are pure and blameless; their sins are forgiven.

23. But the reconciliation remains in force only on the condition of continued obedience.

Gospel] See *Commentary II*, pp. 213-216.

Which was preached to every creature which is under heaven] What Paul probably wrote was that the gospel shall be preached to every creature which is under heaven. This is what we commonly say today to emphasize the importance of the gospel message and the universality of its application. However, two truths are known with reference to who has and who will hear the gospel: 1. Every living soul did hear the gospel in pre-existence, and 2. Every living soul shall hear the gospel again, either in this life or in the spirit world before the day of resurrection and judgment.

The gospel is the plan of salvation. It consists of the laws, ordinances, and eternal truths by conformity to which the spirit children of God can progress and advance until they become like their Eternal Parent. It is centered in Christ, whose atoning sacrifice guarantees immortality to all men and offers eternal life to all who obey its laws. The gospel was first revealed in the pre-mortal life; it was known to all the spirit hosts of heaven in that day when Christ was chosen and foreordained to be the Redeemer. Those who then rejected it were cast out with Lucifer and his angels.

This same gospel was revealed to Adam and to all of the saints of old. Christ restored it in the meridian of time. Paul and the ancient apostles preached it to the extent of their strength and abilities. And it has been restored again, for the last time, through Joseph Smith, in this final dispensation. With its restoration has come the decree that it shall be preached in every nation and among every people before the Second Coming of Christ. All men however will not hear it while in mortality. Rather, untold hosts will hear the message in the spirit world, for the eternal decree is that "there is no eye that shall not see, neither ear that shall not hear, neither heart that shall not be penetrated." (D. & C. 1:2.)

24-25. Paul was a minister of the gospel, sent to teach those truths dispensed to him by revelation.

26-29. His preaching was the mystery of Christ; that is, his teachings were incomprehensible to the carnal mind; they could not be understood by worldly power, only by revelation from God.

28. Warning every man] True ministers always raise the voice of warning — a voice which invites men to flee from the desolation awaiting the world and come to the safety and security of the gospel. (D. & C. 1:4; 38:41; 63:37, 58; 88:81.)

FULNESS OF GODHEAD DWELLETH IN CHRIST

COLOSSIANS 2:1-9.

1 For I would that ye knew what great conflict I have for you, and *for* them at Laodicea, and *for* as many as have not seen my face in the flesh;

2 That their hearts might be comforted, being knit together in love, and unto all riches of the full assurance of understanding, to the acknowledgment of the mystery of God, and of the Father, and of Christ;

3 In whom are hid all the treasures of wisdom and knowledge.

4 And this I say, lest any man should beguile you with enticing words.

5 For though I be absent in the flesh, yet am I with you in the spirit, joying and beholding your order, and the stedfastness of your faith in Christ.

6 As ye have therefore received Christ Jesus the Lord, *so* walk ye in him:

7 Rooted and built up in him, and stablished in the faith, as ye have been taught, abounding therein with thanksgiving.

8 Beware lest any man spoil you through philosophy and vain deceit, after the tradition of men, after the rudiments of the world, and not after Christ.

9 For in him dwelleth all the fulness of the Godhead bodily.

I.V. COLOSSIANS 2:2.

2 That their hearts might be comforted, being knit together in love, and unto all riches of the full assurance of understanding, to the acknowledgment of the mystery of God **and of Christ, who is of God, even the Father;**

2. The mystery of God] The things about God that cannot be learned by reason, but must be revealed, such as that he is a personal being, and that Christ is his Son, into whose hands he has given all things. Men can reason that, because there is order in the universe, there must be some power which is called God. And though such a conclusion is true, it has no saving power. Salvation comes through that knowledge of God which comes by revelation, and which therefore remains forever a mystery to the carnal mind.

3. 'The Father and the Son have all wisdom and all knowledge.'

5-7. 'Endure to the end; keep the commandments; live the gospel.'

8. Philosophy] See *Commentary II*, pp. 154-162.

9. Godhead] "Three glorified, exalted, and perfected personages comprise the Godhead or supreme presidency of the universe. (*Doctrines of Salvation*, vol. 1, pp. 1-55.) They are: God the Father; God the Son; God the Holy Ghost. (First Article of Faith.) 'Everlasting covenant was made between three personages' the

Prophet said, 'before the organization of this earth, and relates to their dispensation of things to men on the earth; these personages, according to Abraham's record, are called God the first, the Creator; God the second, the Redeemer; and God the third, the witness or Testator.' (*Teachings*, p. 190.)

"Though each God in the Godhead is a personage, separate and distinct from each of the others, yet they are 'one God' (Testimony of Three Witnsses in Book of Mormon), meaning that they are united as one in the attributes of perfection. For instance, each has the fulness of truth, knowledge, charity, power, justice, judgment, mercy, and faith. Accordingly they all think, act, speak, and are alike in all things and yet they are three separate and distinct entities. Each occupies space and is and can be in but one place at one time, but each has power and influence that is everywhere present. The oneness of the Gods is the same unity that should exist among the saints. (John 17; 3 Ne. 28:10-11.)

"Perhaps no better statement defining the Godhead and showing the relationship of its members to each other has been written in this dispensation than that given by the Prophet Joseph Smith in the Lectures on Faith. 'There are two personages who constitute the great, matchless, governing, and supreme, power over all things, by whom all things were created and made, that are created and made, whether visible or invisible, whether in heaven, on earth, or in the earth, under the earth, or throughout the immensity of space. They are the Father and the Son — the Father being a personage of spirit [meaning that he has a spiritual body which by revealed definition is a resurrected body of flesh and bones (1 Cor. 15:44-45; D. & C. 88:27)], glory, and power, possessing all perfection and fulness; the Son, who was in the bosom of the Father, a personage of tabernacle, made or fashioned like unto man, or being in the form and likeness of man, or rather man was formed after his likeness and in his image, he is also the express image and likeness of the personage of the Father, possessing all the fulness of the Father, or the same fulness with the Father; being begotten of him, and ordained from before the foundation of the world to be a propitiation for the sins of all those who should believe on his name, and is called the Son because of the flesh, and descended in suffering below that which man can suffer; or, in other words, suffered greater sufferings, and was exposed to more powerful contradictions than any man can be.

" 'But, notwithstanding all this, he kept the law of God, and remained without sin, showing thereby that it is in the power of man to keep the law and remain also without sin; and also, that by him a righteous judgment might come upon all flesh, and that all who walk not in the law of God may justly be condemned by the law, and have no excuse for their sins.

" 'And he being the Only Begotten of the Father, full of grace and truth, and having overcome, received a fulness of the glory of the Father, possessing the same mind with the Father, which mind is the Holy Spirit, that bears record of the Father and the Son, and these three are one; or in other words, these three constitute the great, matchless, governing and supreme, power over all things; by whom all things were created and made that were created and made, and these three consitute the Godhead, and are one; the Father and the Son possessing the same mind, the same wisdom, glory, power, and fulness — filling all in all; the Son being filled with the fulness of his mind, glory, and power; or, in other words, the spirit, glory, and power, of the Father, possessing all knowledge and glory, and the same kingdom, sitting at the right hand of power, in the express image and likeness of the Father, mediator for man, being filled with the fulness of the mind of the Father; or, in other words, the Spirit of the Father, which Spirit is shed forth upon all who believe on his name and keep his commandments.

" 'And all those who keep his commandments shall grow up from grace to grace, and become heirs of the heavenly kingdom, and joint-heirs with Jesus Christ; possessing the same mind, being transformed into the same image or likeness, even the express image of him who fills all in all; being filled with the fulness of his glory, and become one in him, even as the Father, Son and Holy Spirit are one.' (*Lectures on Faith* pp. 50-51.)" (*Mormon Doctrine*, 2nd ed., pp. 319-321.) See *Commentary I*, pp. 75-77.

MOSAIC ORDINANCES NAILED TO CROSS OF CHRIST

COLOSSIANS 2:10-23.

10 And ye are complete in him, which is the head of all principality and power:

11 In whom also ye are circumcised with the circumcision made without hands, in putting off the body of the sins of the flesh by the circumcision of Christ:

12 Buried with him in baptism, wherein also ye are risen with *him* through the faith of the operation of God, who hath raised him from the dead.

13 And you, being dead in your sins and the uncircumcision of your flesh, hath he quickened together with him, having forgiven you all trespasses;

14 Blotting out the handwriting of ordinances that was against us, which was contrary to us, and took it out of the way, nailing it to his cross;

15 *And* having spoiled principalities and powers, he made a show of them openly, triumphing over them in it.

16 Let no man therefore judge you in meat, or in drink, or in respect of an holyday, or of the new moon, or of the sabbath *days:*

17 Which are a shadow of things to come; but the body *is* of Christ.

18 Let no man beguile you of your reward in a voluntary humility and worshipping of angels, intruding into those things which he hath not seen, vainly puffed up by his fleshly mind,

19 And not holding the Head, from which all the body by joints and bands having nourishment ministered, and knit together, increaseth with the increase of God.

20 Wherefore if ye be dead with Christ from the rudiments of the world, why, as though living in the world, are ye subject to ordinances,

21 (Touch not; taste not; handle not;

22 Which all are to perish with the using;) after the commandments and doctrines of men?

23 Which things have indeed a show of wisdom in will worship, and humility, and neglecting of the body; not in any honour to the satisfying of the flesh.

I.V. COLOSSIANS 2:21-22.

21 **Which are after the doctrines and commandments of men, who teach you to touch not; taste not; handle not; all those things which are to perish with the using?**

22 Which things have indeed a show of wisdom in will-worship, and humility, and neglecting the body **as to the satisfying the flesh, not in any honour to God.**

10. Ye are complete in him] Men receive all they need for salvation through Christ and his gospel. They need not add thereto the learning of the world, the philosophies of men, or the so-called wisdom of the ages. Salvation is in Christ and his gospel. However beneficial it may be to be learned in the things of the world, still spiritual blessings come through revealed knowledge. The knowledge that saves is the knowledge of God.

11. Circumcision of Christ] A spiritual circumcision, which consists in accepting Christ and living his gospel, of cutting away, not a part of the body, but one's whole carnal nature. The contrast is with carnal or literal circumcision, which had in times past been a symbol of conformity to the law of carnal commandments which God gave Moses to remind Israel of her duties.

12. Buried with him in baptism] See *Commentary II*, pp. 248-250.

13. By baptism those who are dead in sins, who are spiritually uncircumcised, gain a forgiveness of their sins.

14-15. Christ fulfilled the law of Moses, thereby blotting out its ordinances and performances, symbolically nailing them to his cross.

16. 'Accordingly, do not be misled by following the rituals and restrictions of the law of Moses.'

17. 'These performances were only a type and a shadow of Christ and his gospel, and we now have the substance itself rather then the shadow.' (Mosiah 13:27-31.)

18. 'Neither turn aside to worship angels, nor to be puffed up in the things of the world.'

19. 'But be steadfast in Christ, from whom true nourishment and increase come.'

20-23. 'If, with Christ, you have left the world, why should you longer be subject to its false doctrines? Rather, forsake them, not so much as touching, tasting, or handling those things which satisfy the flesh.'

23. Will Worship] Worship devised by the will of man; man-made worship; any system of religion which does not come from God. Among some of the Colossians it included the worship of angels, among some modern Christians, the worship of relics or "saints."

Circumcision and the law of Moses] See *Commentary II*, pp. 134-145.

SOME LIVES ARE HID WITH CHRIST IN GOD

COLOSSIANS 3:1-4.

1 If ye then be risen with Christ, seek those things which are above, where Christ sitteth on the right hand of God.

2 Set your affection on things above, not on things on the earth.

3 For ye are dead, and your life is hid with Christ in God.

4 When Christ, *who is* our life, shall appear, then shall ye also appear with him in glory.

1. Risen with Christ] Risen to a newness of life, through baptism. See *Commentary II*, pp. 248-250.

Christ sitteth on the right hand of God] They are two exalted, perfected, and glorified men.

3. Ye are dead] Dead to sin.

Your life is hid with Christ in God] 'Your calling and election has been made sure; you have been sealed up unto eternal life; the Lord has said unto you, "Son thou shalt be exalted"; you have received the more sure word of prophecy.'

On May 16, 1843, Joseph Smith gave the following interpretation of Paul's phrase: "Putting my hand," the Prophet said, "on the knee of William Clayton, I said: 'Your life is hid with Christ in God, and so are many others. Nothing but the unpardonable sin can prevent you from inheriting eternal life for you are sealed up by the power of the priesthood unto eternal life, having taken the step necessary for that purpose.'" (*History of the Church,* vol. 5, p. 391.)

4. Those whose callings and elections have been made sure shall appear with Christ in glory at his Second Coming.

Calling and election sure] See 2 Pet. 1:1-19.

SAINTS EXHORTED TO BE HOLY

COLOSSIANS 3:5-17.

5 Mortify therefore your members which are upon the earth; fornication, uncleanness, inordinate affection, evil concupiscence, and covetousness, which is idolatry:

6 For which things' sake the wrath of God cometh on the children of disobedience:

7 In the which ye also walked sometime, when ye lived in them.

8 But now ye also put off all these: anger, wrath, malice, blasphemy, filthy communication out of your mouth.

9 Lie not one to another, seeing that ye have put off the old man with his deeds;

10 And have put on the new *man,* which is renewed in knowledge after the image of him that created him:

11 Where there is neither Greek nor Jew, circumcision nor uncircumcision, Barbarian, Scythian, bond *nor* free: but Christ *is* all, and in all.

12 Put on therefore, as the elect of God, holy and beloved, bowels of mercies, kindness, humbleness of mind, meekness, longsuffering;

13 Forbearing one another, and forgiving one another, if any man have a quarrel against any: even as Christ forgave you, so also *do* ye.

14 And above all these things *put on* charity, which is the bond of perfectness.

15 And let the peace of God rule in your hearts, to the which also ye are called in one body; and be ye thankful.

16 Let the word of Christ dwell in you richly in all wisdom; teaching and admonishing one another in psalms and hymns and spiritual songs, singing with grace in your hearts to the Lord.

17 And whatsoever ye do in word or deed, *do* all in the name of the Lord Jesus, giving thanks to God and the Father by him.

Holiness becometh the saints of the Lord! "Be ye holy," saith the Lord. (Lev. 20:7.) There is no substitute for personal righteousness, for cleansing and sanctifying the human soul. Holy beings are saved beings. And so we now find Paul telling even those who are sealed up unto eternal life that they must press forward, forsaking all evil and cleaving unto all good.

Enduring to the end] See *Commentary II*, pp. 42-44.

Obedience] Jas. 1:22-25.

5. Mortify . . . your members] 'Deaden and control your carnal desires; discipline your appetites; control your worldly desires.'

Fornication] See *Commentary II*, pp. 337-340.

Uncleanness] See *Commentary II*, pp. 482-484.

Inordinate affection] An excessive and unrestrained display of affection which exceeds the bounds of propriety or decency.

Evil concupiscence] Evil and lustful sexual desires.

Covetousness, which is idolatry] Those strong and inordinate desires for the possessions or things of another which make up covetousness are here equated with idolatry, which is the excessive love or veneration of anything other than Deity. See *Commentary II*, pp. 337-340.

6. Wrath of God] The angry and indignant outpouring of divine justice upon the wicked; the meting out of just punishment to those who rebel against God and his laws.

Children of disobedience] See *Commentary II*, pp. 497-500.

8. Anger] See *Commentary II*, pp. 514-517.

Wrath] See *Commentary II*, pp. 482-484.

Malice] See *Commentary II*, pp. 514-517.

Blasphemy] "Blasphemy consists in either or both of the following: 1. Speaking irreverently, evilly, abusively, or scurrilously against God or sacred things; or 2. Speaking profanely or falsely about Deity.

"Among a great host of impious and sacrilegious speaking that constitute blasphemy are such things as: Taking the name of God in vain; evil-speaking about the Lord's annointed; belittling sacred temple ordinances, or patriarchal blessings, or sacramental administrations; claiming unwarranted divine authority; and promulgating with profane piety a false system of salvation." (*Mormon Doctrine*, 2nd ed., p. 90.)

Filthy Communications] Obscene, pornographic, or vulgar pictures, speech, or writing. See *Commentary II*, pp. 514-517.

9. Lie not] Lying is worldly, perfect honesty is saintly. Liars shall be damned, the perfectly honest shall be saved. (*Mormon Doctrine*, 2nd ed., pp. 440-441.)

The old man] The natural man, the man of sin, who lives after the manner of the world.

10. The new man] The saint of God, the man of righteousness, whose life is now patterned after Christ's.

12. Elect of God] Those foreordained persons who believe in Christ, accept his gospel, gain the blessings of the temple, and thereafter continue to walk in paths of truth and righteousness. (*Mormon Doctrine*, 2nd ed., pp. 217-218.) See *Commentary II*, pp. 271-278.

Bowels] The seat of such feelings as compassion, tenderness, pity, and kindness.

Mercies] Manifestations of such things as compassion, forgiveness, clemency, charity, and benevolence.

Kindness] Acts embodying such things as good will, sympathy, tenderness, or benevolence, which show forth an interest in the welfare of others.

Humbleness of mind] Freedom from pride and arrogance; an unassuming attitude.

Meekness] See *Commentary II*, pp. 482-484.

Longsuffering] See *Commentary II*, pp. 482-484.

13. "Ye ought to forgive one another; for he that forgiveth not his brother his trespasses standeth condemned before the Lord;

for there remaineth in him the greater sin. I, the Lord, will forgive whom I will forgive, but of you it is required to forgive all men." (D. & C. 64:9-10.)

14. "And above all things, clothe yourselves with the bond of charity, as with a mantle, which is the bond of perfectness and peace." (D. & C. 88:125.) See *Commentary II*, pp. 377-380.

15. Be ye thankful] "Thou shalt thank the Lord thy God in all things." (D. & C. 59:7.)

16. Let the word of Christ dwell in you] 'Feast upon the words of Christ; let the doctrines of salvation sink into your soul.'

Teaching and admonishing one another] "Teach one another the doctrine of the kingdom." (D. & C. 88:77.) **Singing with grace in your hearts to the Lord]** "My soul delighteth in the song of the heart," the Lord says, "yea, the song of the righteous is a prayer unto me, and it shall be answered with a blessing upon their heads." (D. & C. 25:12.)

17. Any word which cannot be spoken in the name of Christ should be left unsaid, any deed that cannot properly bear our Lord's name should be left undone.

SAINTS EXHORTED TO BE WISE IN ALL THINGS

COLOSSIANS 3:18-25; 4:1-18.

18 Wives, submit yourselves unto your own husbands, as it is fit in the Lord.

19 Husbands, love *your* wives, and be not bitter against them.

20 Children, obey *your* parents in all things; for this is wellpleasing unto the Lord.

21 Fathers, provoke not your children *to anger*, lest they be discouraged.

22 Servants, obey in all things *your* masters according to the flesh; not with eye-service, as menpleasers; but in singleness of heart, fearing God:

23 And whatsoever ye do, do *it* heartily, as to the Lord, and not unto men;

24 Knowing that of the Lord ye shall receive the reward of the inheritance; for ye serve the Lord Christ.

25 But he that doeth wrong shall receive for the wrong which he hath done: and there is no respect of persons.

1 Masters, give unto *your* servants that which is just and equal; knowing that ye also have a Master in heaven.

2 Continue in prayer, and watch in the same with thanksgiving;

3 Withal praying also for us, that God would open unto us a door of utterance, to speak the mystery of Christ, for which I am also in bonds:

4 That I may make it manifest, as I ought to speak.

5 Walk in wisdom toward them that are without, redeeming the time.

6 Let your speech *be* alway with grace, seasoned with salt, that ye may know how ye ought to answer every man.

7 All my state shall Tychicus declare unto you, *who* is a beloved brother, and a faithful minister and fellowservant in the Lord:

8 Whom I have sent unto you for the same purpose, that he might know your estate, and comfort your hearts;

9 With Onesimus, a faithful and beloved brother, who is *one* of you. They shall make known unto you all things which *are done* here.

10 Aristarchus my fellow prisoner saluteth you, and Marcus, sister's son to Barnabas, (touching whom ye received commandments: if he come unto you, receive him;)

11 And Jesus, which is called Justus, who are of the circumcision. These only *are my* fellowworkers unto the kingdom of God, which have been a comfort unto me.

12 Epaphras, who is *one* of you, a servant of Christ, saluteth you, always labouring fervently for you in prayers, that ye may stand perfect and complete in all the will of God.

13 For I bear him record, that he hath a great zeal for you, and them *that are* in Laodicea, and them in Hierapolis.

14 Luke, the beloved physician, and Demas, greet you.

15 Salute the brethren which are in Laodicea, and Nymphas, and the church which is in his house.

16 And when this epistle is read among you, cause that it be read also in the church of the Laodiceans; and that ye likewise read the *epistle* from Laodicea.

17 And say to Archippus, Take heed to the ministry which thou hast received in the Lord, that thou fulfil it.

18 The salutation by the hand of me Paul. Remember my bonds. Grace *be* with you. Amen.

I.V. COLOSSIANS 4:11.

11 And Jesus, which is called Justus, who are of the circumcision. These only are my fellow-workers **in** the kingdom of God, which have been a comfort unto me.

3:18-19. See *Commentary II*, pp. 518-520.

20-21. See *Commentary II*, pp. 520-522.

22-25; 4:1. See *Commentary II*, pp. 522-523.

4:2. Prayer] See 1 John 3:19-24.

5. Church members have a special obligation to conduct themselves in such a way that others, seeing their good works, will be led to accept the gospel. When Corianton, for instance, consorted with an harlot, the Zoramites, seeing his conduct, would not believe the gospel teachings of Alma. (Alma 39:1-14.)

10, 16. Reference appears to be made in these verses to a previous epistle to the Colossians and to an epistle to the Laodiceans, both of which are now lost and unknown.

The First Epistle of Paul the Apostle to the Thessalonians

Many doors of gospel investigation are opened by Paul in this first epistle to the Thessalonians. Supposed to be one of his earliest writings, he takes occasion in it to remind his beloved associates in Thessalonica of the coming of our Lord, of the power resident in his gospel, of how diligent they must be in walking as becometh saints, and of summarizing many church and ministerial duties. His explanations relative to the Second Coming contain what is probably the best approach in any inspired writing to an interpretation of when the signs of the times shall be fulfilled.

GOSPEL COMES IN WORD AND POWER

I THESSALONIANS 1:1-10.

1 Paul, and Silvanus, and Timotheus, unto the church of the Thessalonians *which is* in God the Father and *in* the Lord Jesus Christ: Grace *be* unto you, and peace, from God our Father, and the Lord Jesus Christ.

2 We give thanks to God always for you all, making mention of you in our prayers;

3 Remembering without ceasing your work of faith, and labour of love, and patience of hope in our Lord Jesus Christ, in the sight of God and our Father;

4 Knowing, brethren beloved, your election of God.

5 For our gospel came not unto you in word only, but also in power, and in the Holy Ghost, and in much assurance; as ye know what manner of men we were among you for your sake.

6 And ye became followers of us, and of the Lord, having received the word in much affliction, with joy of the Holy Ghost:

7 So that ye were ensamples to all that believe in Macedonia and Achaia.

8 For from you sounded out the word of the Lord not only in

Macedonia and Achaia, but also in every place your faith to Godward is spread abroad; so that we need not to speak any thing.

9 For they themselves show of us what manner of entering in we had unto you, and how ye turned to God from idols to serve the living and true God;

10 And to wait for his Son from heaven, whom he raised from the dead, *even* Jesus, which delivered us from the wrath to come.

I.V. I THESSALONIANS 1:1-2.

1 Paul, and Silvanus, and Timotheus, **servants of God the Father and the Lord Jesus Christ, unto the church of the Thessalonians;** grace unto you, and peace from God our Father, and the Lord Jesus Christ.

2 **We give thanks always, making mention of you all, in our prayers to God for you.**

4. Your election of God] See *Commentary II*, pp. 271-278.

5. This one verse smashes to smithereens the sectarian claim of having saving truth, for the true gospel consists of two things: The Word, and The Power. Anyone can have the word; the books in which it is written are universally available. But the power must come from God; it is and must be dispensed according to his mind and his will to those who abide the law entitling them to receive it.

The word of the gospel is the spoken or written account of what men must do to be saved. It is a record of the plan of salvation. It is a recitation that men must have faith, repent, be baptized, receive the Holy Ghost and endure in righteousness to the end. It is not the enjoyment of the gift of the Holy Ghost, but the explanation that this gift must be received if a human soul is to be saved.

This word is in the Bible, and in the Doctrine and Covenants, and in the Book of Mormon, and for that matter, it is in many books which are not themselves canonized as Holy Writ. Our revelations say that the Book of Mormon "contains . . . the fulness of the gospel of Jesus Christ" (D. & C. 20:9), meaning that it contains a record of God's dealings with a people who had the fulness of the gospel, meaning that in it is recorded the things men must do to be saved, meaning that it contains a summary of what the plan of salvation is. If men will do what the Book of Mormon counsels, they will be saved in the celestial heaven. The same is true of the Bible, and of the Doctrine and Covenants, and of other books.

But actual salvation comes only when the power of God is received and used; and this power is the power of the priesthood and the power of the Holy Ghost. These must operate in the lives of men; otherwise their souls cannot be cleansed; they cannot be born again; they cannot become new creatures of the Holy Ghost; they cannot put off the natural man and become saints; they cannot be sanctified by the Spirit. In this sense the gospel cannot be written, except in the bones and sinews and tissues of a human body. When it is so written, the record is then found in the Book of Life of the converted believer. And it will be out of what is written in this Book of Life that men shall be judged. (Rev. 20:12-13.)

Anyone can claim to have the gospel and can in fact have it in the intellectual sense of knowing what the doctrines of salvation are. But only those who receive the power of God in their lives have the fulness of the gospel; they only are candidates for salvation. To identify this power, God has ordained that certain signs and gifts shall follow those that believe. By faith they cast out devils, heal the sick, raise the dead, work miracles, gain testimonies, receive revelations, entertain angels, and view the visions of eternity. Where these signs are, there is the power of the gospel; and where the power is, there is the fulness of the everlasting gospel. (Mark 16:16-20; Morm. 9:7-27.)

Gospel] See *Commentary II*, pp. 213-216.

Much assurance] Much testimony; repeated promptings from the Holy Spirit that the gospel is true and consists of such and such things.

6. Received the word . . . of the Holy Ghost] No one ever receives the gospel until he gains a revelation from the Holy Ghost; the gospel is a spiritual matter and comes only by the power of the Spirit.

10. The wrath to come] The gospel is "to prepare the saints for the hour of judgment which is to come; That their souls may escape the wrath of God, the desolation of abomination which awaits the wicked, both in this world and in the world to come." (D. & C. 88:84-85.)

TRUE MINISTERS PREACH IN A GODLY MANNER

I THESSALONIANS 2:1-12.

1 For yourselves, brethren, know our entrance in unto you, that it was not in vain:

2 But even after that we had suffered before, and were shamefully entreated, as ye know, at Philippi, we were bold in our God to speak unto you the gospel of God with much contention.

3 For our exhortation *was* not of deceit, nor of uncleanness, nor in guile:

4 But as we were allowed of God to be put in trust with the gospel, even so we speak; not as pleasing men, but God, which trieth our hearts.

5 For neither at any time used we flattering words, as ye know, nor a cloak of covetousness; God *is* witness:

6 Nor of men sought we glory, neither of you, nor *yet* of others, when we might have been burdensome, as the apostles of Christ.

7 But we were gentle among you, even as a nurse cherisheth her children:

8 So being affectionately desirous of you, we were willing to have imparted unto you, not the gospel of God only, but also our own souls, because ye were dear unto us.

9 For ye remember, brethren, our labour and travail: for labouring night and day, because we would not be chargeable unto any of you, we preached unto you the gospel of God.

10 Ye *are* witnesses, and God *also*, how holily and justly and unblameably we behaved ourselves among you that believe:

11 As ye know how we exhorted and comforted and charged every one of you, as a father *doth* his children,

12 That ye would walk worthy of God, who hath called you unto his kingdom and glory.

TRUE MINISTERS PREACH IN A GODLY MANNER

The manner in which the Lord's ministers carry their message to the world is one of the great identifying characteristics of the truth. Paul here recites the valiance and devotion, the uprightness and gentleness, the fairness and holiness that attended his missionary efforts and those of his companions. He and they manifest the same spirit and course which the Lord set for his latter-day ministers in these words: "No one can assist in this work except he shall be humble and full of love, having faith, hope, and charity, being temperate in all things, whatsoever shall be entrusted to his care." (D. & C. 12:8.)

Contrast this Christ-like preaching of the word with the forced spread of an apostate religion — through civil war in England, through the Inquisition in Spain, through the sale of indulgences in all Europe, through the sword of Cortez in Mexico, and so on.

2. The gospel of God] See *Commentary II*, pp. 213-216.

With much contention] 9. Labouring night and day] "Contend thou, therefore, morning by morning; and day after day let thy warning voice go forth; and when the night cometh let not the inhabitants of the earth slumber, because of thy speech." (D. & C. 112:5.)

12. God . . . hath called you unto his kingdom and glory] 'You were foreordained to join the Church and to receive eternal life.' See 2 Pet. 1:1-19.

CONVERTS ARE THE GLORY AND JOY OF MISSIONARIES

I THESSALONIANS 2:13-20.

13 For this cause also thank we God without ceasing, because, when ye received the word of God which ye heard of us, ye received *it* not *as* the word of men, but as it is in truth, the word of God, which effectually worketh also in you that believe.

14 For ye, brethren, became followers of the churches of God which in Judaea are in Christ Jesus: for ye also have suffered like things of your own country-

men, even as they *have* of the Jews:

15 Who both killed the Lord Jesus, and their own prophets, and have persecuted us; and they please not God, and are contrary to all men:

16 Forbidding us to speak to the Gentiles that they might be saved, to fill up their sins alway: for the wrath is come upon them to the uttermost.

17 But we, brethren, being taken from you for a short time in presence, not in heart, endeavoured the more abundantly to see your face with great desire.

18 Wherefore we would have come unto you, even I Paul, once and again; but Satan hindered us.

19 For what *is* our hope, or joy, or crown of rejoicing? *Are* not even ye in the presence of our Lord Jesus Christ at his coming?

20 For ye are our glory and joy.

No man can conceive how great is the worth of souls. One soul saved which would have been lost means added kingdoms and worlds, added spirit children born to exalted beings, added hosts of intelligent beings going forward everlastingly in eternal progression. Is it any wonder that Paul gloried and rejoiced in his converts? Is it any wonder that the Lord himself said: "And if it so be that you should labor all your days in crying repentance unto this people, and bring, save it be one soul unto me, how great shall be your joy with him in the kingdom of my Father! And now, if your joy will be great with one soul that you have brought unto me into the kingdom of my Father, how great will be your joy if you should bring many souls unto me!" (D. & C. 18:15-16.)

14-16. Why should the Jews seek to prevent the spread of the gospel, not alone among themselves and their kindred, but among the Gentiles also? Is not this very manifestation of hatred and venom an evidence of the divinity of the work? How could so much hatred and bitterness against the truth be kept alive unless Satan was stirring them up, using persecution as a tool to fight the truth?

14. Churches of God . . . in Christ Jesus] Congregations of God's people comprising the Church of Jesus Christ.

16. Wrath is come upon them to the uttermost] Soon the Jews, incident to the destruction of Jerusalem, as a nation and as a people, were to suffer such tribulation and desolation as never before or since has ever befallen their house. (Matt. 24:15-22; Jos. Sm. 1:12-20.)

Missionary work] See *Commentary II*, pp. 111-113, 146-147.

Glorying in the Lord] See *Commentary II*, pp. 436-439.

"PERFECT THAT WHICH IS LACKING IN YOUR FAITH"

I THESSALONIANS 3:1-13.

1 Wherefore when we could no longer forbear, we thought it good to be left at Athens alone;

2 And sent Timotheus, our brother, and minister of God, and our fellowlabourer in the gospel of Christ, to establish you, and to comfort you concerning your faith:

3 That no man should be moved by these afflictions: for yourselves know that we are appointed thereunto.

4 For verily, when we were with you, we told you before that we should suffer tribulation; even as it came to pass, and ye know.

5 For this cause, when I could no longer forbear, I sent to know your faith, lest by some means the tempter have tempted you, and our labour be in vain.

6 But now when Timotheus came from you unto us, and brought us good tidings of your faith and charity, and that ye have good remembrance of us always, desiring greatly to see us, as we also *to see* you:

7 Therefore, brethren, we were comforted over you in all our affliction and distress by your faith:

8 For now we live, if ye stand fast in the Lord.

9 For what thanks can we render to God again for you, for all the joy wherewith we joy for your sakes before our God;

10 Night and day praying exceedingly that we might see your face, and might perfect that which is lacking in your faith?

11 Now God himself and our Father, and our Lord Jesus Christ, direct our way unto you.

12 And the Lord make you to increase and abound in love one toward another, and toward all *men*, even as we *do* toward you:

13 To the end he may stablish your hearts unblameable in holiness before God, even our Father, at the coming of our Lord Jesus Christ with all his saints.

When converts, as we are pleased to call them, join the Church, they thereby get on the path leading to eternal life. (2 Ne. 31:17-21.) Before entering the gate of repentance and baptism to start their course toward salvation, they gain a testimony of the truth and divinity of the work. But after joining the Church, they must press forward until they are converted in the full sense (Luke 22:32), until they are sanctified in Christ, until they become inheritors of all things. Hence Paul's counsel to members of the Church to perfect that which is lacking in their faith.

By way of illustration, this means that those who believe in part must give their whole hearts to the Lord; those whose minds are yet entangled in false educational philosophies must purge their thinking; those who give lip service must now serve with all their might, mind, and strength; those who are lukewarm must reach the boiling point; those with a meager knowledge of the doctrines of eternal truth must treasure up the words of life. When faith is perfected, salvation is assured.

3-4. Christ's ministers are appointed to suffer persecution and affliction.

5. The tempter] Satan.

8. Stand fast in the Lord] 'Keep the commandments. Endure to the end. Live the gospel.'

Enduring to the end] See *Commentary II*, pp. 42-44.

Obedience] See Jas. 1:22-25.

Perfection] See Heb. 6:1-3.

BE HOLY; SANCTIFY YOURSELVES

I THESSALONIANS 4:1-8.

1 Furthermore then we beseech you, brethren, and exhort *you* by the Lord Jesus, that as ye have received of us how ye ought to walk and to please God, *so* ye would abound more and more.

2 For ye know what commandments we gave you by the Lord Jesus.

3 For this is the will of God, *even* your sanctification, that ye should abstain from fornication:

4 That every one of you should know how to possess his vessel in sanctification and honour;

5 Not in the lust of concupiscence, even as the Gentiles which know not God:

6 That no *man* go beyond and defraud his brother in *any* matter: because that the Lord *is* the avenger of all such, as we also have forewarned you and testified.

7 For God hath not called us unto uncleanness, but unto holiness.

8 He therefore that despiseth, despiseth not man, but God, who hath also given unto us his holy Spirit.

1-2. Keep the commandments.

3. Sanctification] "To be sanctified is to become clean, pure, and spotless; to be free from the blood and sins of the world; to become a new creature of the Holy Ghost, one whose body has been renewed by the rebirth of the Spirit. Sanctification is a state of saintliness, a state attained only by conformity to the laws and ordinances of the gospel. The plan of salvation is the system and means provided whereby men may sanctify their souls and thereby become worthy of a celestial inheritance.

"Sanctification is a basic doctrine of the gospel (D. & C. 20:31-34); indeed, the very reason men are commanded to believe, repent, and be baptized is so they 'may be sanctified by the reception of the Holy Ghost,' and thereby be enabled to stand spotless before the judgment bar of Christ. (2 Ne. 27:19-21.)

"Moroni summarized the plan of salvation in these words: Come unto Christ, and be perfected in him, and deny yourselves of all ungodliness; and if ye shall deny yourselves of all ungodliness, and love God with all your might, mind and strength, then is his grace sufficient for you, that by his grace ye may be perfect in Christ; and if by the grace of God ye are perfect in Christ, ye can in nowise deny the power of God. And again, if ye by the grace of God are perfect in Christ, and deny not his power, then are ye sanctified in Christ by the grace of God, through the shedding of the blood of Christ, which is in the covenant of the

Father unto the remission of your sins, that ye become holy, without spot.' (Moro. 10:32-33.)" (*Mormon Doctrine*, 2nd ed., p. 675.)

Fornication] See *Commentary II*, pp. 337-340.

4. Possess his vessel in sanctification] 'Possess his body in holiness.'

5. Lust of concupiscence] See Col. 3:5-17.

6. The Lord is the avenger of all such] 'The Lord will heap vengeance upon those who commit sex sin.'

7. "Ye shall be holy: for I the Lord your God am holy." (Lev. 19:2.)

Enduring to the end] See *Commentary II*, pp. 42-44.

Obedience] See Jas. 1:22-25.

Sanctified by the blood of Christ] See Heb. 10:1-18.

"WORK WITH YOUR OWN HANDS"

I THESSALONIANS 4:9-12.

9 But as touching brotherly love ye need not that I write unto you: for ye yourselves are taught of God to love one another.

10 And indeed ye do it toward all the brethren which are in all Macedonia: but we beseech you, brethren, that ye increase more and more;

11 And that ye study to be quiet, and to do your own business, and to work with your own hands, as we commanded you;

12 That ye may walk honestly toward them that are without, and *that* ye may have lack of nothing.

9. Love one another] See *Commentary II*, p. 297; 1 John 2:7-14.

11. Be quiet] Avoid disturbances. **Do your own business]** Don't meddle in other people's affairs. **Work with your own hands]** Paul was a tent maker, Peter a fisherman; Adam farmed, David herded sheep; Brigham Young was a glazier, Jesus a carpenter.

Labor is a part of life; physical work is honorable. "In the sweat of thy face shalt thou eat bread, till thou return unto the ground." (Gen. 3:19.) Every man should labor physically as well as mentally.

12. Them that are without] See Col. 3:18-25; 4:1-18.

The gospel of work] See 2 Thess. 3:7-12.

SAINTS SAVED AT SECOND COMING

I THESSALONIANS 4:13-18.

13 But I would not have you to be ignorant, brethren, concerning them which are asleep, that ye sorrow not, even as others which have no hope.

14 For if we believe that Jesus died and rose again, even so them also which sleep in Jesus will God bring with him.

15 For this we say unto you by the word of the Lord, that we which are alive *and* remain unto the coming of the Lord shall not prevent them which are asleep.

16 For the Lord himself shall descend from heaven with a shout, with the voice of the archangel, and with the trump of God: and the dead in Christ shall rise first:

17 Then we which are alive *and* remain shall be caught up together with them in the clouds, to meet the Lord in the air: and so shall we ever be with the Lord.

18 Wherefore comfort one another with these words.

I.V. I THESSALONIANS 4:15, 17.

15 For this we say unto you by the word of the Lord, **that they who are alive at** the coming of the Lord, shall not prevent **them who remain unto the coming of the Lord, who are asleep.**

17 Then **they who** are alive, shall be caught up together **into the clouds with them who remain,** to meet the Lord in the air; and so shall we **be ever** with the Lord.

Salvation is given the saints — all of them, both the living and the dead — at the Second Coming. The living are caught up to meet their returning Lord, and with him they shall return to live on this earth, which will then be changed and receive its paradisiacal glory. (Tenth Article of Faith.) When the living arrive at the age of a tree, 100 years, they shall be changed from mortality to immortality in the twinkling of an eye and shall then reign as kings and priests in exalted glory. (D. & C. 101:23-31.)

Also at our Lord's return, the righteous dead shall come forth from their graves with celestial bodies to meet their God. They, then, as kings and priests, shall live and reign with Christ on earth in resurrected glory for a thousand years. (Rev. 5:10.) Thus the saints, whether they sleep in the Lord or live in the flesh until he comes, shall inherit glory and honor and salvation at his Coming. The formal, shall we even say ritualistic judgment, when all stand before his bar, shall not take place until after the millennium, after all have come forth from their graves. (2 Ne. 9:15-16.)

13. Them which are asleep] 14. Which sleep in Jesus] The righteous saints who have died, whose spirits are in the paradise of God, awaiting the day of a glorious resurrection.

16-17. "A trump shall sound both long and loud, even as upon Mount Sinai, and all the earth shall quake, and they shall come forth — yea, even the dead which died in me, to receive a crown of righteousness, and to be clothed upon, even as I am, to be with me, that we may be one." (D. & C. 29:13.) "And the saints that are upon the earth, who are alive, shall be quickened and be caught up to meet him. And they who have slept in their graves shall come forth, for their graves shall be opened; and they also shall be caught up to meet him in the midst of the pillar of heaven — They are Christ's, the first fruits, they who shall descend with him first, and they who are on the earth and in their graves, who are first caught up to meet him; and all this by the voice of the sounding of the trump of the angel of God." (D. & C. 88:96-98.)

16. The dead in Christ shall rise first] The righteous dead shall come forth in the resurrection of the just; wicked men shall rise "second," in the resurrection of the unjust. The catching up of the living saints shall take place at the same time the righteous dead are resurrected.

Second Coming of Christ] See *Commentary II*, pp. 27-29.

Judgment at the Second Coming] See Rev. 22:6-16; *Commentary I*, pp. 395-397.

Ungodly damned at Second Coming] See 2 Thess. 1:1-12.

End of the world] See 1 John 2:15-17.

Abiding the day of the Second Coming] See Rev. 6:12-17.

Harvest of the earth] See Rev. 14:14-20.

Sequence in the resurrection] See *Commentary II*, pp. 393-395.

First and second resurrections] See Rev. 20:4-6.

SAINTS KNOW SEASON OF SECOND COMING

I THESSALONIANS 5:1-11.

1 But of the times and the seasons, brethren, ye have no need that I write unto you.

2 For yourselves know perfectly that the day of the Lord so cometh as a thief in the night.

3 For when they shall say, Peace and safety; then sudden destruction cometh upon them, as travail upon a woman with child; and they shall not escape.

4 But ye, brethren, are not in darkness, that that day should overtake you as a thief.

5 Ye are all the children of light, and the children of the day: we are not of the night, nor of darkness.

6 Therefore let us not sleep, as *do* others; but let us watch and be sober.

7 For they that sleep sleep in the night; and they that be drunken are drunken in the night.

8 But let us, who are of the day, be sober, putting on the breastplate of faith and love; and for an helmet, the hope of salvation.

9 For God hath not appointed us to wrath, but to obtain salvation by our Lord Jesus Christ,

10 Who died for us, that, whether we wake or sleep, we should live together with him.

11 Wherefore comfort yourselves together, and edify one another, even as also ye do.

Do we know when Christ shall come again, to take vengeance on the ungodly and to reign on earth in love and peace for the space of a thousand years? It is generally assumed we do not have any such information as this, that such has not and will not be revealed. The fact is, we do know — that is, we know in general when his coming shall be. We do not know the day nor the hour, and for that matter neither do the angels of God in heaven (Matt. 24:36), but we do know the time and the season; that is, we know the approximate time, shall we say, the generation of his return.

Paul's illustration here is perfect. The Second Coming is compared to a woman about to give birth to a child. She does not know the hour or the minute of the child's arrival, but she does know the approximate time. There are signs which precede and presage the promised arrival. And so it is with our Lord's coming. He shall come as a thief in the night, unexpectedly and without warning, to the world, to those who are in spiritual darkness, to those who are not enlightened by the power of the Spirit. But his coming shall not overtake the saints as a thief, for they know and understand the signs of the times. An extended consideration of these signs, of the events which must occur between the first and second comings of our Lord, is found in *Mormon Doctrine*, 2nd ed., pp. 687-698 and in *Commentary I*, pp. 634-686. Let us here simply list some of them by name:

1. There is to be an era of total apostasy from the truth; universal spiritual darkness is to blanket the earth.

2. Then there is to be an age of restoration, a period in which God shall restore again all the saving truths ever revealed in any time or day.

3. In this period of restoration, the fulness of the everlasting gospel is to be given again to men on earth.

4. This restored gospel shall then be preached in all the world, in all nations, among every kindred and people, before our Lord's return.

5. The promised restitution of all things is to include the coming forth of the Book of Mormon and its promulgation among all peoples.

6. The Church and kingdom of God is to be set up again on earth in all its glory, beauty, and perfection.

7. Many of the scattered remnants of ancient Israel are to be gathered into the fold of Christ, come to the knowledge of their true Messiah, and be assembled again to the lands of their inheritance.

8. That age known as the times of the Gentiles is to end; that is, the period of earth's history in which the gospel goes to the Gentiles on a preferential basis shall end.

9. Elijah is to come again, restoring the keys of the sealing power.

10. There is to be a messenger before the face of the Lord, preparing the way before him.

11. The Lord is to make various preliminary appearances in his temples.

12. Desolations, evil, abominations, wars, and signs both in heaven and on earth shall be shown forth, including the sending again upon Jerusalem of the abomination of desolation.

13. Many of the Jews shall again be assembled in Jerusalem their city of old.

14. The Lord will come to Adam-ondi-Ahman to receive a report from all those who have held the keys of his kingdom on earth, and to take back from the Ancient of Days the keys and powers needed to reign personally on earth during the Millennial Era.

15. Then shall come the great and dreadful day, the day of vengeance and burning, the day when all nations shall be gathered at Armageddon, the day of "the battle of that great day of God Almighty," the day when the vineyard shall be burned and every corruptible thing consumed, the day when peace and prosperity shall prevail for a thousand years.

When shall this promised generation be? It is clear that nearly all of the foregoing has already transpired, and our revelation says that "the great and dreadful day of the Lord is near, even at the doors." (D. & C. 110:16.)

"True it is that the day and hour of our Lord's coming are and will remain unknown, such being an incentive to all to watch and be ready at all times. But true it also is that those who watch for that great and dread day are expected to read the signs of the times so as to know the approximate time of his coming. President Wilford Woodruff taught that we do know the generation when he will come. (G. Homer Durham, *Discourses of Wilford Woodruff*, p. 253.)

" 'I was once praying very earnestly to know the time of the coming of the Son of Man,' the Prophet Joseph Smith recorded on April 2, 1843, 'when I heard a voice repeat the following: Joseph, my son, if thou livest until thou art eighty-five years old, thou shalt see the face of the Son of Man; therefore let this suffice, and trouble me no more on this matter.

" 'I was left thus, without being able to decide whether this coming referred to the beginning of the millennium or to some previous appearing, or whether I should die and thus see his face. I believe the coming of the Son of Man will not be any sooner than that time.' (D. & C. 130:14-17.)

"Four days later, April 6, 1843, at the General Conference of the Church, while the Spirit rested upon him, the Prophet said: 'Were I going to prophesy, I would say the end would not come in 1844, 5, or 6, or in forty years. There are those of the rising generation who shall not taste death till Christ comes.'

"The rising generation is the one that has just begun. Thus, technically, children born on April 6, 1843, would be the first members of the rising generation, and all children born, however many years later, to the same parents would still be members of that same rising generation. It is not unreasonable to suppose that many young men had babies at the time of this prophecy and also had other children as much as 50 or 75 years later, assuming for instance that they were married again to younger women. This very probable assumption would bring the date up to, say, the 2nd decade in the 20th century — and the children so born would be members of that same rising generation of which the Prophet spoke. Now if these children lived to the normal age of men generally, they would be alive well past the year 2000 A.D.

"This reasoning takes on added significance when considered in connection with the revelation which states categorically that Christ will come 'in the beginning of the seventh thousand years' of the earth's temporal continuance. (D. & C. 77:6, 12.) We, of course, do not know exactly how many years elapsed between Adam and the birth of Christ, but suppose it to have been 4004; nor can we be certain, from historical sources, how many years have passed since. But reading these inspired statements in connection with the signs of the times which we can interpret, it is plain that the day of the coming of the Son of Man is not far distant." (*Mormon Doctrine*, 2nd ed., pp. 692-693.)

1. Times and seasons] Age or era or generation in which Christ shall come.

2. As a thief in the night] Unexpectedly, without warning.

5. The children of light] Members of the Church of Jesus Christ, those who have forsaken the world and come unto the light of the gospel, those who enjoy the gift and guidance of the Holy Ghost, those who can read the signs of the times.

8. Breastplate . . . helmet] Part of the armor of God considered in Ephesians 6:10-24.

9-10. Christ . . . died for us] Salvation comes because of the atoning sacrifice of Christ.

LIVE AS BECOMETH SAINTS,

I THESSALONIANS 5:12-28.

12 And we beseech you, brethren, to know them which labour among you, and are over you in the Lord, and admonish you;

13 And to esteem them very highly in love for their work's sake. *And* be at peace among yourselves.

14 Now we exhort you, brethren, warn them that are unruly, comfort the feebleminded, support the weak, be patient toward all *men.*

15 See that none render evil for evil unto any *man;* but ever follow that which is good, both among yourselves, and to all *men.*

16 Rejoice evermore.

17 Pray without ceasing.

18 In every thing give thanks:

for this is the will of God in Christ Jesus concerning you.

19 Quench not the Spirit.

20 Despise not prophesyings.

21 Prove all things; hold fast that which is good.

22 Abstain from all appearance of evil.

23 And the very God of peace sanctify you wholly; and *I pray God* your whole spirit and soul and body be preserved blameless unto the coming of our Lord Jesus Christ.

24 Faithful *is* he that calleth you, who also will do *it*.

25 Brethren, pray for us.

26 Greet all the brethren with an holy kiss.

27 I charge you by the Lord that this epistle be read unto all the holy brethren.

28 The grace of our Lord Jesus Christ *be* with you. Amen.

I.V. I THESSALONIANS 5:26.

26 Greet all the brethren with **a holy salutation.**

Paul's cry to the saints, as is that of every true minister, is always and everlastingly that they should keep the commandments and live as becometh those who have forsaken the world and taken upon them the name of Jesus Christ.

12-13. Bishops, and quorum and church officers in general, should be esteemed highly for their ministerial labors.

14-15. Church officers are appointed to warn, comfort, support, teach, and help their brethren. "Be faithful; stand in the office which I have appointed unto you; succor the weak. lift up the hands which hang down, and strengthen the feeble knees." (D. & C. 81:5.)

14. Feebleminded] Better, 'fainthearted.'

19. Quench not the Spirit] In the true Church there will always be powerful manifestations of the Spirit of God. Inclinations to bridle and submerge these is of the world.

20. Despise not prophesyings] In the true Church is found the gift of prophecy. "Deny not the spirit of revelation, nor the spirit of prophecy, for wo unto him that denieth these things." (D. & C. 11:25.)

The Second Epistle of Paul the Apostle to the Thessalonians

Paul here picks up again the main theme of his previous letter to his beloved Thessalonian friends — that of the Second Coming of the Son of Man. In pointed language he reveals that there can be no return of the Lord Jesus until after the era of apostasy when the Man of Sin shall have control over all the earth. To this great gospel concept he then adds his views on the gospel of work and some other practical Christian virtues.

UNGODLY DAMNED AT SECOND COMING

II THESSALONIANS 1:1-12.

1 Paul, and Silvanus, and Timotheus, unto the church of the Thessalonians in God our Father and the Lord Jesus Christ:

2 Grace unto you, and peace, from God our Father and the Lord Jesus Christ.

3 We are bound to thank God always for you, brethren, as it is meet, because that your faith groweth exceedingly, and the charity of every one of you all toward each other aboundeth;

4 So that we ourselves glory in you in the churches of God for your patience and faith in all your persecutions and tribulations that ye endure:

5 Which is a manifest token of the righteous judgment of God, that ye may be counted worthy of the kingdom of God, for which ye also suffer:

6 Seeing *it is* a righteous thing with God to recompense tribulation to them that trouble you;

7 And to you who are troubled rest with us, when the Lord Jesus shall be revealed from heaven with his mighty angels,

8 In flaming fire taking vengeance on them that know not God, and that obey not the gospel of our Lord Jesus Christ:

9 Who shall be punished with everlasting destruction from the presence of the Lord, and from the glory of his power;

10 When he shall come to be glorified in his saints, and to be admired in all them that believe (because our testimony among you was believed) in that day.

11 Wherefore also we pray always for you, that our God would count you worthy of *this* calling, and fulfil all the good pleasure of *his* goodness, and the work of faith with power:

12 That the name of our Lord Jesus Christ may be glorified in you, and ye in him, according to the grace of our God and the Lord Jesus Christ.

I.V. II THESSALONIANS 1:1, 9.

1 Paul, and Sylvanus, and Timotheus, **the servants** of God **the** Father and **our** Lord Jesus Christ, unto the church of the Thessalonians;

9 Who shall be punished with destruction from the presence of the Lord, and from the glory of his **everlasting** power;

3-6. Justice demands both rewards and penalties. Thus, salvation and damnation both come from God; blessings and cursings both flow from him. If he rewards the righteous, he must punish the wicked. If he blesses those who suffer persecution for righteousness' sake, he must condemn those who act as the persecutors.

4. The churches of God] The congregations of God's people comprising the Church of Jesus Christ.

5. The kingdom of God] The celestial kingdom.

7-10. Our Lord's Second Coming will be a day of vengeance, burning, and destruction — a great and dreadful day — for the wicked, for those who rebel against his gospel. But for the righteous, it will be a day of redemption, blessing, and salvation, a glorious day of peace and righteousness. At that day, "Every corruptible thing . . . shall be consumed" (D. & C. 101:24), with those only who are worthy being able to abide the day. And in that day, "His voice shall be heard: I have trodden the winepress alone, and have brought judgment upon all people; and none were with me; And I have trampled them in my fury, and I did tread upon them in mine anger, and their blood have I sprinkled upon my garments, and stained all my raiment; for this was the day of vengeance which was in my heart. And now the year of my redeemed is come; and they shall mention the loving kindness of their Lord, and all that he has bestowed upon them according to his goodness, and according to his loving kindness, forever and ever." (D. & C. 133:50-52.)

8. In flaming fire] In that day the "element shall melt with fervent heat." (D. & C. 101:25.) See 2 Pet. 3:10-18.

9. Destruction] Spiritual death, which is to be cast out of the presence of God and to die as pertaining to the things of righteousness.

11. This calling] The saints are called to glory and honor, to be glorified in Christ at his coming, to inherit eternal life with him in his kingdom.

Second Coming of Christ] See *Commentary, II* pp. 27-29; Rev. 1:7-8.

Judgment at Second Coming] See Rev. 22:6-16; *Commentary I*, pp. 395-396.

End of the world] See 1 John 2:15-17.

Harvest of the Earth] See Rev. 14:14-20.

APOSTASY TO PRECEDE SECOND COMING

II THESSALONIANS 2:1-12.

1 Now we beseech you, brethren, by the coming of our Lord Jesus Christ, and *by* our gathering together unto him,

2 That ye be not soon shaken in mind, or be troubled, neither by spirit, nor by word, nor by letter as from us, as that the day of Christ is at hand.

3 Let no man deceive you by any means: for *that day shall not come*, except there come a falling away first, and that man of sin be revealed, the son of perdition;

4 Who opposeth and exalteth himself above all that is called God, or that is worshipped; so that he as God sitteth in the temple of God, showing himself that he is God.

5 Remember ye not, that, when I was yet with you, I told you these things?

6 And now ye know what withholdeth that he might be revealed in his time.

7 For the mystery of iniquity doth already work: only he who now letteth *will let*, until he be taken out of the way.

8 And then shall that Wicked be revealed, whom the Lord shall consume with the spirit of his mouth, and shall destroy with the brightness of his coming:

9 *Even him*, whose coming is after the working of Satan with all power and signs and lying wonders,

10 And with all deceivableness of unrighteousness in them that perish; because they received not the love of the truth, that they might be saved.

11 And for this cause God shall send them strong delusion, that they should believe a lie:

12 That they all might be damned who believed not the truth, but had pleasure in unrighteousness.

I.V. II THESSALONIANS 2:2-3, 7, 9.

2 That ye be not soon shaken in mind, or be troubled **by letter, except ye receive it from us;** neither by spirit, nor by word, as that the day of Christ is at hand.

3 Let no man deceive you by any means; for **there shall** come a falling away first, and that man of sin be revealed, the son of perdition;

7 For the mystery of iniquity doth already work, **and he it is who now worketh, and Christ suffereth him to work,** until **the time is fulfilled that he shall be** taken out of the way.

9 **Yea, the Lord, even Jesus,** whose coming is **not until after there cometh a falling away, by** the working of Satan with all power, and signs and lying wonders,

In his previous epistle to the Thessalonians, Paul wrote of the times and seasons relative to the Second Coming. Our Lord's glorious return, he taught, was not destined to overtake the children of light as a thief in the night. They, as a woman in travail, would recognize the signs of the times. Now the Apostle takes occasion to name one of these signs. It is that before our Lord's return there was to be a falling away from the true faith; there was to be a universal apostasy, a complete loss of that pure and perfect Christianity revealed by Jesus and the ancient apostles. In other words, between the first and second personal ministries of the Lord Jesus on planet earth, the gospel was to be lost, darkness was to cover the earth, and Satan was to have control and dominion over the hearts and minds of men. See *Commentary I*, pp. 645-648.

Apostasy] See 2 Tim. 3:1-13.

Second Coming of Christ] See *Commentary II*, pp. 27-29.

Times and seasons] See 1 Thess. 5:1-11.

3. **Man of sin]** "Lucifer is the man of sin, spoken of by Paul who was to be revealed in the last days before the Second Coming of our Lord. (2 Thess. 2:1-12.) He is the one of whom men shall say: 'Is this the man that made the earth to tremble, that did shake kingdoms; That made the world as a wilderness, and destroyed the cities thereof; that opened not the house of his prisoners?' (Isa. 14:12-20.)

"Joseph Smith, by revelation, inserted into Paul's account about the man of sin, these words: 'He it is who now worketh, and Christ suffereth him to work, until the time is fulfilled that he shall be taken out of the way.' (*Inspired Version*, 2 Thess. 2:7.) That is, Satan was then committing havoc among men, and he would continue to do so until the ushering in of the millennial era when he would be bound.

"Paul's promise that the man of sin must be revealed before our Lord could return for the millennial era has been abundantly fulfilled. Lucifer's wicked plans, purposes, and works have been revealed or manifest from time to time, from the day of Paul to the present. At a conference of the Church held June 3, 1831, 'the man of sin was revealed,' in that some of the brethren were overcome by devils whom the Prophet rebuked and cast out. (*History of the Church*, vol. 1, p. 175.)" (*Mormon Doctrine*, 2nd ed., pp. 467-468.)

6 and 8 **Revealed]** Manifested.

8. **Destroy]** Cast out from the presence of the Lord, which is spiritual death or destruction.

9. **All power and signs and lying wonders]** Satan has power to imitate the truth, to lead men astray, to perform false miracles.

(Rev. 16:14.) The magicians in the court of Pharaoh imitated some of the miracles of Moses and Aaron. (Ex. 7:10-11, 20-22; 8:6-7.)

10. All deceivableness of unrighteousness] All doctrines, views, philosophies, and concepts, in whatever field, which lead away from God and salvation in his kingdom.

11. God shall send them strong delusion] God shall permit them to believe false doctrines, as the vagaries of sectarianism which say, for instance, that God is a Spirit, that revelation and miracles have ceased, and that men are saved by lip service only without the works of righteousness.

Believe a lie] Believe false doctrines.

GOSPEL PREPARES MEN FOR ETERNAL GLORY

II THESSALONIANS 2:13-17.

13 But we are bound to give thanks alway to God for you, brethren beloved of the Lord, because God hath from the beginning chosen you to salvation through sanctification of the Spirit and belief of the truth:

14 Whereunto he called you by our gospel, to the obtaining of the glory of our Lord Jesus Christ.

15 Therefore, brethren, stand fast, and hold the traditions which ye have been taught, whether by word, or our epistle.

16 Now our Lord Jesus Christ himself, and God, even our Father, which hath loved us, and hath given *us* everlasting consolation and good hope through grace,

17 Comfort your hearts, and stablish you in every good word and work.

13. God hath from the beginning chosen you to salvation] Members of the Church were foreordained to be saved in the celestial kingdom; they were chosen in the pre-existence to gain eternal life. **Calling and election]** See *Commentary II*, pp. 267-269, 271-278.

14. Obtaining the glory of our Lord Jesus Christ] All who live the whole gospel law become sons of God and joint-heirs with Christ; they inherit glory, power, might, and dominion with him.

They become "like him" (1 John 3:2), and they have eternal life. His glory is their glory. Is it possible for anyone to obtain more than this?

15-17. Hence: Keep the commandments.

PRAY FOR TRIUMPH OF GOSPEL CAUSE

II THESSALONIANS 3:1-5.

1 Finally, brethren, pray for us, that the word of the Lord may have *free* course, and be glorified, even as *it is* with you:

2 And that we may be delivered from unreasonable and wicked men: for all *men* have not faith.

3 But the Lord is faithful, who shall stablish you, and keep *you* from evil.

4 And we have confidence in the Lord touching you, that ye both do and will do the things which we command you.

5 And the Lord direct your hearts into the love of God, and into the patient waiting for Christ.

How often Paul prays for the saints and implores them to unite their prayers for him and the Cause! Prayer has a sanctifying effect; it unites the Church; and it causes the blessings of heaven to be poured out upon the heads of the saints. We should pray for the success and triumph of all the programs of the Lord's earthly kingdom, and we should then suit our actions to our words.

Prayer] See 1 John 3:19-24.

2. All men have not faith] Indeed, few men do; and without faith it is impossible to be saved.

SAINTS WITHDRAW FELLOWSHIP FROM APOSTATES

II THESSALONIANS 3:6.

6 Now we command you, brethren, in the name of our Lord Jesus Christ, that ye withdraw yourselves from every brother that walketh disorderly, and not after the tradition which he received of us.

It is one thing to extend the hand of prospective fellowship to those who seek the truth and who are living according to the best light and knowledge they have, but it is quite another to clasp an enemy to the bosom of the Church. "Public meetings, which are held before the world," are open to anyone. Non-members "who are earnestly seeking the kingdom" are welcome in sacrament meetings. (D. & C. 46:3-5.) However, those who have known the truth, and who have rebelled and become enemies of the Church, are in a different category. Those who sin and remain unrepentant are cast out of the Church. (D. & C. 42:20-28.) Excommunicated and disfellowshiped persons have definite restrictions placed upon them. Even God cast one-third of the hosts of heaven out for rebellion.

Enemies from within, traitors to the Cause, cultists who pervert the doctrines and practices which lead to salvation, often draw others away with them, and added souls lose their anticipated inheritance in the heavenly kingdom. When cultists and enemies become fixed in their opposition to the Church, and when they seek to convert others to their divisive positions, the course of wisdom is to avoid them, as Paul here directs, and to leave them in the Lord's hands.

Cultists] See *Commentary II*, pp. 177-178.

6. The tradition which he received of us] 'The gospel, the teachings and doctrines both oral and written, which he received from us.'

PAUL PREACHETH THE GOSPEL OF WORK

II THESSALONIANS 3:7-12.

7 For yourselves know how ye ought to follow us: for we behaved not ourselves disorderly among you;

8 Neither did we eat any man's bread for nought; but wrought with labour and travail night and day, that we might not be chargeable to any of you:

9 Not because we have not power, but to make ourselves an ensample unto you to follow us.

10 For even when we were with you, this we commanded you, that

if any would not work, neither should he eat.

11 For we hear that there are some which walk among you disorderly, working not at all, but are busybodies.

12 Now them that are such we command and exhort by our Lord Jesus Christ, that with quietness they work, and eat their own bread.

Temporal work is essential to salvation. Man cannot be saved in idleness. It is not enough simply to believe the great spiritual realities. We could do that as spirits in pre-existence. But we are now placed on a temporal earth, to gain the experiences of mortality, with the command: "In the sweat of thy face shalt thou eat bread, till thou return unto the ground." (Gen. 3:19.) Work, as such, is an essential part of eternal progression. Hence: "The idler shall be had in remembrance before the Lord." (D. & C. 68:30.) And: "The idler shall not have place in the church, except he repent and mend his ways." (D. & C. 75:29.)

7-9. Even Paul and his ministerial associates, who were in fact entitled to temporal help from the saints, chose to set an example of self-support. There are perils in a paid ministry. Of the elders of the Church in general the Lord says: "Let the residue of the elders watch over the churches, and declare the word in the regions round about them; and let them labor with their own hands that there be no idolatry nor wickedness practised." (D. & C. 52.39.)

10-12. Work is a commandment of the Lord. "Thou shalt not be idle; for he that is idle shall not eat the bread nor wear the garments of the laborer." (D. & C. 42:42.)

Work with your own hands] See 1 Thess. 4:9-12.

"BE NOT WEARY IN WELL DOING"

II THESSALONIANS 3:13-18.

13 But ye, brethren, be not weary in well doing.

14 And if any man obey not our word by this epistle, note that man, and have no company with him, that he may be ashamed.

15 Yet count *him* not as an enemy, but admonish *him* as a brother.

16 Now the Lord of peace himself give you peace always by all means. The Lord *be* with you all.

17 The salutation of Paul with mine own hand, which is the token in every epistle: so I write.

18 The grace of our Lord Jesus Christ *be* with you all. Amen.

The saints are expected to try and better their circumstances in temporal and spiritual matters, in social and governmental affairs, and in all things. Initiative in choosing and advocating proper causes is essential to salvation. "It is not meet that I should command in all things," the Lord says, "for he that is compelled in all things, the same is a slothful and not a wise servant; wherefore he receiveth no reward. Verily I say, men should be anxiously engaged in a good cause, and do many things of their own free will, and bring to pass much rightousness; For the power is in them, wherein they are agents unto themselves. And inasmuch as men do good they shall in nowise lose their reward. But he that doeth not anything until he is commanded, and receiveth a commandment with doubtful heart, and keepeth it with slothfulness, the same is damned." (D. & C. 58:26-29.)

14-15. Compare 2 Thess. 3:6.

The First Epistle of Paul the Apostle to Timothy

Who was Timothy?

Paul calls him his dearly beloved son in the gospel, and it is clear he was born with a heritage of faith. He became the companion, confidant, and missionary associate of the Apostle. At the time he received this first epistle, he must have held some major position of church supervision and administration, for Paul instructs him in the calling of bishops and other church officers and directs him to tell other ministers what and how to preach.

Could he have been the equivalent of a stake president, or at least the presiding officer over a number of wards or their equivalents? At the time Paul sent him the second epistle he was, of course, a patriarch, perhaps giving blessings over a large area and to members of many congregations. For that matter, was he also one of the Council of the Twelve to whom a senior officer was giving counsel and direction? In any event he was a faithful saint, a trusted church administrator, and a friend of one of the greatest theologians of any dispensation.

In this first epistle we find his friend Paul counseling him on church organization and on the imperative need to teach sound doctrine, with some severe comments interwoven relative to apostasy and false teaching. As was Paul's wont, he also interspersed his counsel with numerous doctrinal gems about Christ, salvation, and obedience to gospel law.

TEACH TRUE DOCTRINE ONLY

I TIMOTHY 1:1-11.

1 Paul, an apostle of Jesus Christ by the commandment of God our Saviour, and Lord Jesus Christ, *which is* our hope;

2 Unto Timothy, *my* own son in the faith: Grace, mercy, *and* peace, from God our Father and Jesus Christ our Lord.

3 As I besought thee to abide still at Ephesus, when I went into Macedonia, that thou mightest charge some that they teach no other doctrine,

4 Neither give heed to fables and endless genealogies, which minister questions, rather than godly edifying which is in faith: *so do.*

5 Now the end of the commandment is charity out of a pure heart, and *of* a good conscience, and *of* faith unfeigned:

6 From which some having swerved have turned aside unto vain jangling;

7 Desiring to be teachers of the law; understanding neither what they say, nor whereof they affirm.

8 But we know that the law *is* good, if a man use it lawfully;

9 Knowing this, that the law is not made for a righteous man, but for the lawless and disobedient, for the ungodly and for sinners, for unholy and profane, for murderers of fathers and murderers of mothers, for manslayers,

10 For whoremongers, for them that defile themselves with mankind, for menstealers, for liars, for perjured persons, and if there be any other thing that is contrary to sound doctrine;

11 According to the glorious gospel of the blessed God, which was committed to my trust.

I.V. I TIMOTHY 1:1.

1 Paul, an apostle of Jesus Christ by the commandment of God and the Lord Jesus Christ, **our Saviour and our hope;**

1. An apostle of Jesus Christ] See *Commentary II*, pp. 130-131, 328-333.

2. My own son in the faith] 'My own convert, my own gospel son, who has received spiritual life through my teachings.'

3-4. Teachers in the Church represent the Lord in their teaching. The Church is the Lord's; the doctrine is the Lord's.

Teachers speak at the invitation of the Lord and are appointed to say what he wants said, nothing more and nothing less. There is no freedom to teach or speculate contrary to the revealed will. Those who desire to express views contrary to gospel truth are at liberty to find other forums or to organize churches of their own. But in God's Church, the only approved doctrine is God's doctrine.

The Church is not a debating society; it is not searching for a system of salvation; it is not a forum for social or political philosophies. It is, rather, the Lord's kingdom with a commission to teach his truths for the salvation of men. Anything contrary to or short of this standard in not of God. "I give unto you a commandment," he says, "that you shall teach one another the doctrine of the kingdom. Teach ye diligently and my grace shall attend you, that you may be instructed more perfectly in theory, in principle, in doctrine, in the law of the gospel, in all things that pertain unto the kingdom of God, that are expedient for you to understand." (D. & C. 88:77-78.)

4. **Fables]** See 2 Tim. 4:1-5.

Endless genealogies] See Titus 3:1-15.

5-7. **False teachers]** See *Commentary II*, pp. 456-460.

5. **The end of the commandment is charity]** The result of gospel obedience is to acquire charity, which is the pure love of Christ.

10. **Them that defile themselves with mankind]** Those who commit homosexual acts.

11. **The glorious gospel of the blessed God]** See *Commentary II*, pp. 213-216.

CHRIST CAME TO SAVE REPENTANT SINNERS

I TIMOTHY 1:12-17.

12 And I thank Christ Jesus our Lord, who hath enabled me, for that he counted me faithful, putting me into the ministry;

13 Who was before a blasphemer, and a persecutor, and injurious: but I obtained mercy, because I did *it* ignorantly in unbelief.

14 And the grace of our Lord
was exceeding abundant with faith
and love which is in Christ Jesus.

15 This *is* a faithful saying,
and worthy of all acceptation, that
Christ Jesus came into the world
to save sinners; of whom I am
chief.

16 Howbeit for this cause I
obtained mercy, that in me first
Jesus Christ might show forth all
longsuffering, for a pattern to
them which should hereafter believe
on him to life everlasting.

17 Now unto the King eternal,
immortal, invisible, the only wise
God, *be* honour and glory for ever
and ever. Amen.

It is a continuing marvel to Paul — as it should be to all believers — that Christ saves repentant sinners!

What hope of salvation would any of us have if Christ had not come? How could we be redeemed, either temporally or spiritually, from the effects of Adam's fall, except it be through the atoning sacrifice of our Lord? How could we become free from the bondage of sin, except by the grace of God and the blood of Christ?

Truly, without Christ, there would be neither immortality nor eternal life. How glorious it is to know that Christ came to save sinners!

Repentance] See *Commentary II*, pp. 108-110.

13. I obtained mercy] "In the gospel sense, mercy consists in our Lord's forebearance, on certain specified conditions, from imposing punishments that, except for his grace and goodness, would be the just reward of man. . . .

"No cry of thanksgiving and relief seems to come more gratefully from the prophetic voice than the comforting exclamation, 'His mercy endureth for ever!' (1 Chron. 16:34, 41; 2 Chron. 5:13; 7:3, 6; Ezra 3:11; Ps. 106:1; 107:1; 118:1-4; 136; Jer. 33:11.) Certainly his mercy is manifest in all his doings — his creative enterprises and his hand-dealings in all ages with all people. (Ps. 136.)

"The atoning sacrifice of our Lord, upon which all things rest, came because of his infinite mercy. (D. & C. 29:1.) Through his condescension, grace, and mercy he has visited the children of men and given great promises to them. (2 Ne. 4:26; 9:53.) . . .

"But mercy is not showered promiscuously upon mankind, except in the general sense that it is manifest in the creation and peopling of the earth and in the granting of immortality to all men as a free gift. Rather, mercy is granted (because of the grace, love, and condescension of God), as it is with all blessings to those who comply with the law upon which its receipt is predicated. (D. & C. 130:20-21.) That law is the law of righteousness; those who sow righteousness, reap mercy. (Hos. 10:12.) There is no promise of mercy to the wicked; rather, as stated in the Ten Commandments, the Lord promises to show mercy unto thousands of them that love him and keep his commandments. (Ex. 20:6; Dan. 9:4; D. & C. 70:18.)

"The great Sinaitic proclamation, from the Lord's own mouth, announced: 'The Lord, The Lord God, merciful and gracious, longsuffering, and abundant in goodness and truth, Keeping mercy for thousands, forgiving iniquity and transgression and sin, and that will by no means clear the guilty; visiting the iniquity of the fathers upon the chilren, and upon the children's children, unto the third and to the fourth generation.' (Ex. 34:6-7.)

"Mercy is a gift the Lord reserves for his saints and their weaknesses (D. & C. 38:14; 50:16; 64:4); it is reserved for the meek, they who are the god-fearing and the righteous (D. & C. 97:2); because of it, they will be remembered in the day of wrath. (D. & C. 101:9.) Because of mercy men are enabled to repent (D. & C. 3:10), and when the elders of Israel 'confess their sins with humble hearts,' a merciful God forgives them of those sins. (D. & C. 61:2.) Indeed, the Lord's people may well ask themselves, 'What doth the Lord require of thee, but to do justly, and to love mercy, and to walk humbly with thy God?' (Mic. 6:8.)

"Justice demands that for every broken law a penalty must be paid, for 'How could there be a law save there was a punishment?' And since all men have sinned, all are in the grasp of justice. Accordingly, all men must pay the penalty for their transgressions unless they can find a supervening power which will wash away their sins and free them from the penalty, unless someone else pays a ransom for them. That ransom is offered to all men in and through the atoning sacrifice of Christ." (*Mormon Doctrine*, 2nd ed., pp. 483-486.)

15. "For, behold, the Lord your Redeemer suffered death in the flesh; wherefore he suffered the pain of all men, that all men might repent and come unto him. And he hath risen again from the dead, that he might bring all men unto him, on conditions of repentance." (D. & C. 18:11-12.)

16. A pattern to them which should hereafter believe] Christ is of course the perfect Prototype, the great Exemplar, the true Pattern for all men. In a lesser sense all of the prophets, and all of the elders of the kingdom, and all of the saints of God, should be living examples to the world of the truth and divinity of the Lord's great work of salvation. But where among all the prophets and apostles, among all the saints and righteous persons of all the ages, can one find a better pattern, save Jesus only, than Paul? Here is a man who fought the truth, who persecuted the saints, on whose hands was found the blood of martyrs. And yet he repented and became one of the most valiant defenders of the faith of all the ages. And yet he enjoyed the gifts of the Spirit, worked out his salvation, made his calling and election sure, and has gone on to eternal exaltation in the mansions which are prepared. In effect, he is saying to Timothy, and through him to all of us, 'If a blasphemer and perjurer, such as I, can be saved, what stands in your way?'

APOSTATES DELIVERED UNTO SATAN

I TIMOTHY 1:18-20.

18 This charge I commit unto thee, son Timothy, according to the prophecies which went before on thee, that thou by them mightest war a good warfare;

19 Holding faith, and a good conscience; which some having put away concerning faith have made shipwreck:

20 Of whom is Hymenaeus and Alexander; whom I have delivered unto Satan, that they may learn not to blaspheme.

18. The prophecies which went before on thee] At some prior time, quite possibly in a patriarchal blessing, inspired declarations had been made relative to the work and ministry of Timothy. And these prophetic utterances, as is the case with the inspired statements found in patriarchal blessings in general, were intended and designed to encourage him to meet the standards, do the work, and achieve the rewards referred to in them.

19-20. Apostates exhibit varying degrees of indifference and of rebellion, and their punishment, in time and in eternity, is based on the type and degree of apostasy which is involved. Those who become indifferent to the Church, who simply drift from the course of righteousness to the way of the world, are not in the same category with traitors who fight the truth, and with those whose open rebellion destines them to eternal damnation as sons of perdition. All apostates are turned over to the buffetings of Satan in one degree or another, with the full wrath of Satan reserved for those who are cast into outer darkness with him in that kingdom devoid of glory.

In this dispensation, those saints who broke the covenant of consecration by which they were bound in the united order were turned over to the buffetings of Satan. (D. & C. 78:3-12; 82:15-24; 104:1-10.) Those whose callings and elections have been made sure, and who then rebel against the truth, are so assigned, "that they might be saved in the day of the Lord Jesus." They are "sealed by the spirit of Elijah unto the damnation of hell until the day of the Lord, or revelation of Jesus Christ." (*Teachings*, pp. 338-339; 301; D. & C. 132:26.) Those whose traitorous conduct causes them to become sons of perdition are so cursed eternally. (*Teachings*, p. 128.)

With reference to the nature and course of apostates and the need to exclude them from the fellowship of the saints, the Prophet Joseph Smith said: "The Messiah's kingdom on earth is of that kind of government, that there has always been numerous apostates, for the reason that it admits of no sins unrepented of without excluding the individual from its fellowship. Our Lord said, 'Strive to enter in at the strait gate: for many, I say unto you, will seek to enter in, and shall not be able.' And again, many are called, but few are chosen. Paul said to the elders of the Church at Ephesus, after he had labored three years with them, that he knew that some of their own number would turn away from the faith, and seek to lead away disciples after them. None, we presume, in this generation will pretend that he has the experience of Paul in building up the Church of Christ and yet, after his departure from the Church at Ephesus, many, even of the elders turned away from the truth; and what is almost always the case, sought to lead away disciples after them.

"Strange as it may appear at first thought, yet it is no less strange than true, that notwithstanding all the professed determination to live godly, apostates after turning from the faith of Christ, unless they have speedily repented, have sooner or later fallen into the snares of the wicked one, and have been left destitute of the Spirit of God, to manifest their wickedness in the eyes of multitudes.

"From apostates the faithful have received the severest persecutions. Judas, was rebuked and immediately betrayed his Lord into the hands of his emenies, because Satan entered into him. There is a superior intelligence bestowed upon such as obey the gospel with full purpose of heart, which, if sinned against, the apostate is left naked and destitute of the Spirit of God, and he is, in truth, nigh unto cursing, and his end is to be burned. When once that light which was in them is taken from them, they become as much darkened as they were previously enlightened, and then, no marvel, if all their power should be enlisted against the truth, and they, Judas like, seek the destruction of those who were their greatest benefactors.

"What nearer friend on earth, or in heaven, had Judas than the Savior? And his first object was to destroy him. Who, among all the saints in these last days, can consider himself as good as our Lord? Who is as perfect? Who is as pure? Who is as holy as he was? Are they to be found? He never transgressed or broke a commandment or law of heaven — no deceit was in his mouth, neither was guile found in his heart. And yet one that ate with him, who had often drunk of the same cup, was the first to lift up his heel against him. Where is one like Christ? He cannot be found on earth. Then why should his followers complain, if from those whom they once called brethren, and considered as standing in the nearest relation in the everlasting covenant they should receive persecution?

"From what source emanated the principle which has ever been manifested by apostates from the true Church to persecute with double diligence, and seek with double perseverance, to destroy those whom they once professed to love, with whom they once communed, and with whom they once covenanted to strive with every power in righteousness to obtain the rest of God? Perhaps our brethren will say the same that caused Satan to seek to overthrow the kingdom of God, because he himself was evil, and God's kingdom is holy." (*Teachings*, pp. 66-68.)

Apostasy] See 2 Tim. 3:1-13.

Cultists] See *Commentary II*, pp. 177-178.

Sons of perdition] See Heb. 6:4-9.

CHRIST ORDAINED TO BE A MEDIATOR

I TIMOTHY 2:1-7.

1 I exhort therefore, that, first of all, supplications, prayers, intercessions, *and* giving of thanks, be made for all men;

2 For kings, and *for* all that are in authority; that we may lead a quiet and peaceable life in all godliness and honesty.

3 For this *is* good and acceptable in the sight of God our Saviour;

4 Who will have all men to be saved, and to come unto the knowledge of the truth.

5. For *there is* one God, and one mediator between God and men, the man Christ Jesus;

6 Who gave himself a ransom for all, to be testified in due time,

7 Whereunto I am ordained a preacher, and an apostle, (I speak the truth in Christ, *and* lie not;) a teacher of the Gentiles in faith and verity.

I.V. I TIMOTHY 2:4.

4 Who **is willing to have** all men to be saved, and to come unto the knowledge of the truth **which is in Christ Jesus, who is the only Begotten Son of God, and ordained to be a Mediator between God and man; who is one God, and hath power over all men.**

1. **Prayers]** See 1 John 3:19-24.

2. **A quiet and peaceable life in all godliness and honesty]** An apt summary of the purpose of life while in mortality, a state possible only when there is peace among men and nations.

3. **God our Saviour]** Christ.

I. V. 4. Ordained to be a Mediator] As Moses was the mediator of the old covenant or testament, so Jesus is the Mediator of the new covenant or testament. (D. & C. 76:69; 107:19.) "Look to the great Mediator," Lehi said, "and hearken unto his great commandments; and be faithful unto his words, and choose eternal life, according to the will of his Holy Spirit." (2 Ne. 2:28.) "Our Lord's mission was to bring to pass 'the great mediation of all men,' meaning that in his capacity as Mediator he had power to intervene between God and man and effect a reconciliation. This mediation or reconciliation was affected through his atoning sacrifice, a sacrifice by means of which sinful men — by the proper use of agency — can wash away their guilt and place themselves in harmony with God. Men 'are free to choose liberty and eternal life, through the great mediation of all men, or to choose captivity and death, according to the captivity and power of the devil.' (2 Ne. 2:27.) Those choosing obedience receive the Holy Ghost, are reconciled to God in this world, and continue in his presence in the world to come." (*Mormon Doctrine*, 2nd ed., p. 472.)

Intercession] See *Commentary II*, pp. 269-271.

6. **Gave himself a ransom]** See *Commentary II*, pp. 241-248.

7. **An apostle]** See *Commentary II*, pp. 130-131, 328-333.

PAUL SPEAKS ABOUT DRESS OF WOMEN

I TIMOTHY 2:8-15.

8 I will therefore that men pray every where, lifting up holy hands, without wrath and doubting.

9 In like manner also, that women adorn themselves in modest apparel, with shame-facedness and sobriety; not with broided hair, or gold, or pearls, or costly array;

10 But (which becometh women professing godliness) with good works.

11 Let the woman learn in silence with all subjection.

12 But I suffer not a woman to teach, nor to usurp authority over the man, but to be in silence.

13 For Adam was first formed, then Eve.

14 And Adam was not deceived, but the woman being deceived was in the transgression.

15 Notwithstanding she shall be saved in childbearing, if they continue in faith and charity and holiness with sobriety.

I.V. I TIMOTHY 2:12, 15.

12 **For** I suffer not a woman to teach, nor to usurp authority over the man, but to be in silence.

15 Notwithstanding **they** shall be saved in child-bearing, if they continue in faith and charity and holiness with sobriety.

9-10. Worldly styles and fashions in women's dress, whatever they may happen to be at any moment, being of the world, which those who join the Church are commanded to forsake, are improper and to be avoided. Almost always the apparel so involved is excessively costly, with those who wear it being lifted up in the pride of their hearts. The Nephite prophets repeatedly indentified the wearing of costly clothing with apostasy and failure to live by gospel standards. (Jac. 2:13; Alma 1:6, 32; 4:6; 5:53; 31:27-28; 4 Ne. 24; Morm. 8:36-37.) The love of precious clothing is one of the desires of the great and abominable church. (1 Ne. 13:7-8.) In this dispensation, the Lord has commanded: "Thou shalt not be proud in thy heart; let all thy garments be plain, and their beauty the beauty of the work of thine own hands." (D. & C. 42:40.)

11-12. In the true order of government, man — not woman — is the head of the house and of the Church. She is and should be in subjection to her husband. In Paul's day the social custom extended this rule to the point of keeping women from teaching in the Church. See *Commentary II*, pp. 359-362.

PAUL SPEAKETH OF BISHOPS

I TIMOTHY 3:1-7.

1 This *is* a true saying, If a man desire the office of a bishop, he desireth a good work.

2. A bishop then must be blameless, the husband of one wife, vigilant, sober, of good behaviour, given to hospitality, apt to teach;

3 Not given to wine, no striker, not greedy of filthy lucre; but patient, not a brawler, not covetous;

4 One that ruleth well his own house, having his children in subjection with all gravity;

5 (For if a man know not how to rule his own house, how shall he take care of the church of God?)

6 Not a novice, lest being lifted up with pride he fall into the condemnation of the devil.

7 Moreover he must have a good report of them which are without; lest he fall into reproach and the snare of the devil.

1. Bishop] "One of the ordained offices in the Aaronic Priesthood is that of bishop. (D. & C. 20:67.) Those so ordained and set apart to serve either in the Presiding Bishopric or as ward bishops are called to preside over the Aaronic Priesthood. A ward bishop is the president of the Aaronic Priesthood in his ward and is also the president of the priests quorum. (D. & C. 107:87-88.) The office of a bishop is also an appendage 'belonging unto the high priesthood.' (D. & C. 84:29.)

"In his Aaronic Priesthood capacity a bishop deals primarily with temporal concerns (D. & C. 107:68); as the presiding high priest in his ward, however, he presides over all ward affairs and members. A bishop is a common judge in Israel (D. & C. 107:74);

it is his right to have the gift of discernment, the power to discern all other spiritual gifts, 'lest there shall be any among you professing and yet be not God.' (D. & C. 46:27.)" (*Mormon Doctrine*, 2nd ed., pp. 89-90.)

2. Husband of one wife] From the day of Adam to the present, and from this hour to the end of the peopling of the world, the law of God has been, is, and shall be that man should have one wife at a time and one wife only, except when God by revelation specifically directs otherwise. Thus in March of 1831, the Lord said to Joseph Smith: "It is lawful that he should have one wife, and they twain shall be one flesh, and all this that the earth might answer the end of its creation; And that it might be filled with the measure of man, according to his creation before the world was made." (D. & C. 49:16-17.) Thus also "the word of the Lord" in the day of Nephi was: "There shall not any man among you have save it be one wife; and concubines he shall have none; For I, the Lord God, delight in the chastity of women. And whoredoms are an abomination before me; thus saith the Lord of Hosts . . . For if I will, saith the Lord of Hosts, raise up seed unto me, I will command my people; otherwise they shall hearken unto these things." (Jac. 2:27-30.) At proper and appointed times the Lord has, of course, given the revelation and issued the command directing certain persons to enter plural marriage in the new and everlasting covenant. (D. & C. 132.)

Hospitality] See 1 Pet. 4:7-11.

PAUL SPEAKETH OF DEACONS

I TIMOTHY 3:8-13.

8 Likewise *must* the deacons *be* grave, not double-tongued, not given to much wine, not greedy of filthy lucre;

9 Holding the mystery of the faith in a pure conscience.

10 And let these also first be proved; then let them use the office of a deacon, being *found* blameless.

11. Even so *must their* wives *be* grave, not slanderers, sober, faithful in all things.

12 Let the deacons be the husbands of one wife, ruling their children and their own houses well.

13 For they that have used the office of a deacon well purchase to themselves a good degree, and great boldness in the faith which is in Christ Jesus.

8. Deacons] "One of the ordained offices in the Aaronic Priesthood is that of a deacon. (D. & C. 20:60.) This office, the lowest in the priesthood heirarchy(D. & C. 88:127), is an appendage to the lesser priesthood. (D. & C. 84:30.) Deacons are 'appointed to watch over the church, to be standing ministers unto the church.' (D. & C. 84:111.) They are to assist the teachers in all their duties (which includes home teaching), and are 'to warn, expound, exhort, and teach, and invite all to come unto Christ,' although they can neither 'baptize, administer the sacrment, or lay on hands.' (D. & C. 20:57-60.) Among other things, it is the practice of the Church to assign them to pass the sacrament, perform messenger service, act as ushers, keep church facilities in good repair, go home teaching, and perform special assignments at the direction of the bishopric. Many of their assigned functions are comparable to those performed by the Levites of old. (*Doctrines of Salvation*, vol. 3, pp. 111-114.)

"It is the practice of the Church in this dispensation — a practice dictated by the needs of the present day ministry and confirmed by the inspiration of the Spirit resting upon those who hold the keys of the kingdom — to confer the Aaronic Priesthood upon worthy young men who are 12 years of age and to ordain them to the office of a deacon in that priesthood. Notwithstanding the fact that this is the lowest priesthood office, it is yet a high and holy one in God's kingdom. In the meridian of time the needs of the ministry were such that adult brethren were ordained deacons." (*Mormon Doctrine*, 2nd ed., p. 183.)

9. Mystery of the faith] Since the things of God are and can be known only by the power of the Spirit, they remain forever hidden, unknown, and mysterious to the carnal mind, to the mind enlightened by reason but not by revelation.

12. One wife] See 1 Tim. 3:1-7.

"GREAT IS THE MYSTERY OF GODLINESS"

I TIMOTHY 3:14-16.

14 These things write I unto thee, hoping to come unto thee shortly:

15 But if I tarry long, that thou mayest know how thou oughtest to behave thyself in the house of God, which is the church of the living God, the pillar and ground of the truth.

16 And without controversy great is the mystery of godliness: God was manifest in the flesh, justified in the Spirit, seen of angels, preached unto the Gentiles, believed on in the world, received up into glory.

I.V. I TIMOTHY 3:15-16.

15 But if I tarry long, that thou mayest know how thou oughtest to behave thyself in the house of God, which is the church of the living God.

16 **The pillar and ground of the truth is,** (and without controversy, great is the mystery of godliness,) God was manifest in the flesh, justified in the Spirit, seen of angels, preached unto the Gentiles, believed on in the world, received up into glory.

Why is it that many men do not believe and accept the gospel? Why are there so few, among the many, who actually know and understand the doctrines of salvation? How is it that only a handful out of the billions of earth's inhabitants know the truth about God and his laws? Why is religion a hidden mystery to mankind generally?

One of the main reasons is that religion is not a matter of reason alone; it is not based on or comprehended by the power of intellectuality. Because a man has a bright mind, because he is a profound scholar, because he knows or has discovered great truths in any of a hundred fields, does not mean he knows or understands religious truths.

True religion comes from God by revelation. It is manifest to and understood by those with a talent for spirituality. It is hidden, unknown, and mysterious to all others. To comprehend the things of the world, one must be intellectually enlightened; to know and understand the things of God, one must be spiritually enlightened. One of the great fallacies of modern Christendom is turning for religious guidance to those who are highly endowed intellectually, rather than to those who comprehend the things of the Spirit, to those who receive personal revelation from the Holy Ghost.

True religion, for instance, embraces the verity that God is a Holy Man, that we are his spirit offspring, that his Firstborn in the spirit was his Only Begotten in the flesh, that through faith men may become like Christ, that eternal life is gained through the continuation of the family unit in eternity. None of these truths are born of reason alone; all spring from revelation. None sinks into the heart of a true believer because of intellectual capacity; all have the ring of truth to those who are spiritually endowed, who are born again, who are alive to the things of the Spirit.

Godliness] See 2 Tim. 2:14-26.

PAUL GIVES SIGNS OF LATTER-DAY APOSTASY

I TIMOTHY 4:1-6.

1 Now the Spirit speaketh expressly, that in the latter times some shall depart from the faith, giving heed to seducing spirits, and doctrines of devils;

2 Speaking lies in hypocrisy; having their conscience seared with a hot iron;

3 Forbidding to marry, *and commanding* to abstain from meats, which God hath created to be received with thanksgiving of them which believe and know the truth.

4 For every creature of God *is* good, and nothing to be refused, if it be received with thanksgiving:

5 For it is sanctified by the word of God and prayer.

6 If thou put the brethren in remembrance of these things, thou shalt be a good minister of Jesus Christ, nourished up in the words of faith and of good doctrine, whereunto thou hast attained.

I.V. I TIMOTHY 4:2.

2 Speaking lies in hypocrisy; having their conscience seared **as** with a hot iron;

1. The Spirit speaketh expressly] Revelation does not always come with the same force and power. In recording an express and powerful impression from the Spirit, for instance, Joseph Smith wrote: "Thus saith the still small voice, which whispereth through and pierceth all things, and often times it maketh my bones to quake while it maketh manifest." (D. & C. 85:6.)

In the latter times] In later times, in a day then future, in the whole era of spiritual darkness which covered the earth from the loss of primitive Christianity to the restoration of the gospel, and also in the period of restoration itself, as far as most of the inhabitants of the earth are concerned.

Some shall depart from the faith] Some shall fall away beginning in Timothy's day; some other shall forsake the truth after it has been restored in our day, with this difference: The apostasy from the primitive Church shall, in due course, be universal; spiritual darkness will cover the earth and envelop all peoples; but in the day of restoration, though individuals and groups shall fall away, the Church itself shall remain to prepare a people for the Second Coming of the Son of Man. **Apostasy]** See 2 Tim. 3:1-13.

Seducing spirits] Devils, evil spirits who lead men astray; also, the fanatical crazes and false spirits which sweep through whole nations and peoples, as the spirit of false zeal which led to the Crusades, or the spirit which unites and impels a whole nation to invade and plunder its neighbor.

Doctrines of devils] False doctrines in which there is no salvation; doctrines that lead men away from the truths of salvation; doctrines which are contrary to the mind and will of God and which are encouraged and sponsored by Satan, as for instance: That God is an immaterial Spirit essence filling all immensity; that revelation, gifts, and miracles ceased with the apostles; that infants must be baptized to be saved.

3. Forbidding to marry] The practice of celibacy is an illustration of this. Since eternal life grows out of marriage, anything Satan can do to pervert or prevent the creation and continuance of this holy union is in his interest. "Whoso forbiddeth to marry is not ordained of God, for marriage is ordained of God unto man." (D. & C. 49:15.)

Commanding to abstain from meats] "Whoso forbiddeth to abstain from meats, that man should not eat the same, is not ordained of God; For, behold, the beasts of the field and the fowls of the air, and that which cometh of the earth, is ordained for the use of man for food and for raiment, and that he might have in abundance." (D. & C. 49:18-19.)

5. God has removed the Mosaic restrictions where the eating of certain meats and foods are concerned. These are now clean (sanctified, as it were); there are no longer any ceremonially unclean or forbidden foods.

CHRIST BRINGS TWO KINDS OF SALVATION

I TIMOTHY 4:7-11.

7 But refuse profane and old wives' fables, and exercise thyself *rather* unto godliness.

8 For bodily exercise profiteth little: but godliness is profitable unto all things, having promise of the life that now is, and of that which is to come.

9 This *is* a faithful saying and worthy of all acceptation.

10 For therefore we both labour and suffer reproach, because we trust in the living God, who is the Saviour of all men, specially of those that believe.

11 These things command and teach.

7. Fables] See 2 Tim. 3:1-13.

Godliness] See 2 Tim. 2:14-26.

10. Salvation is a study in contrasts. There is a salvation for all men, meaning resurrection. They are thus saved from death, hell, the devil, and endless torment, while at the same time they are damned when their state is contrasted with that of those who are saved in the kingdom of God. (2 Ne. 9:17-27.) One salvation consists of immortality, which comes as a free gift to all men; the other consists of immortality, coupled with eternal life, which comes only to those who obey the laws and ordinances of the gospel.

Immortality and eternal life] See 2 Tim. 2:1-12.

Salvation] See 1 Pet. 1:1-16.

"BE THOU AN EXAMPLE OF THE BELIEVERS"

I TIMOTHY 4:12-16.

12 Let no man despise thy youth; but be thou an example of the believers, in word, in conversation, in charity, in spirit, in faith, in purity.

13 Till I come, give attendance to reading, to exhortation, to doctrine.

14 Neglect not the gift that is in thee, which was given thee by prophecy, with the laying on of the hands of the presbytery.

15 Meditate upon these things; give thyself wholly to them; that thy profiting may appear to all.

16 Take heed unto thyself, and unto the doctrine; continue in them: for in doing this thou shalt both save thyself, and them that hear thee.

12. Youth] Age has very little to do with spirituality. Spiritual talents are developed primarily in pre-existence. Joseph Smith was 14 when he saw the Father and the Son; Samuel was but a boy when he heard the voice of the Lord. Nephi was a young man when he received revelations and saw visions; Jesus confounded the doctors when 12.

Be thou an example] Christ is the Great Exemplar. Every minister of Christ, walking and acting in the place and stead of his Master, is expected to be a living example of personal righteousness. As Christ was perfect in word and deed, so should his ministers seek to be. Their lives become Christianity in operation.

14. The gift that is in thee] The gift of the Holy Ghost, which is the right to the constant companionship of that member of the Godhead based on faithfulness. The actual enjoyment of this gift is the greatest gift man can possess in mortality.

Laying on of the hands] The prescribed procedure for conferring the gift of the Holy Ghost.

Presbytery] Elders.

16. Those who minister with zeal and devotion to their Lord's errand thereby save both themselves and others. (D. & C. 4.)

Obedience] See Jas. 1:22-25.

Enduring to the end] See *Commentary II*, pp. 42-44.

SAINTS COMMANDED TO CARE FOR WORTHY POOR

I TIMOTHY 5:1-18.

1 Rebuke not an elder, but intreat *him* as a father; *and* the younger men as brethren;

2 The elder women as mothers; the younger as sisters, with all purity.

3 Honour widows that are widows indeed.

4 But if any widow have children or nephews, let them learn first to show piety at home, and to requite their parents: for that is good and acceptable before God.

5 Now she that is a widow indeed, and desolate, trusteth in God, and continueth in supplications and prayers night and day.

6 But she that liveth in pleasure is dead while she liveth.

7 And these things give in charge, that they may be blameless.

8 But if any provide not for his own, and specially for those of his own house, he hath denied the faith, and is worse than an infidel.

9 Let not a widow be taken into the number under three-score years old, having been the wife of one man.

10 Well reported of for good works; if she have brought up children, if she have lodged strangers, if she have washed the saints' feet, if she have relieved the afflicted, if she have diligently followed every good work.

11 But the younger widows refuse: for when they have begun to wax wanton against Christ, they will marry;

12 Having damnation, because they have cast off their first faith.

13 And withal they learn *to be* idle, wandering about from house to house; and not only idle, but tattlers also and busybodies, speaking things which they ought not.

14 I will therefore that the younger women marry, bear children, guide the house, give none occasion to the adversary to speak reproachfully.

15 For some are already turned aside after Satan.

16 If any man or woman that believeth have widows, let them relieve them, and let not the church be charged; that it may relieve them that are widows indeed.

17 Let the elders that rule well be counted worthy of double honour, especially they who labour in the word and doctrine.

18 For the scripture saith, Thou shalt not muzzle the ox that treadeth out the corn. And, The labourer *is* worthy of his reward.

I.V. I TIMOTHY 5:10.

10 Well reported of for good works; if she have brought up children, if she have lodged strangers, if she have washed the saints' **clothes**, if she have relieved the afflicted, if she have diligently followed every good work.

1-2. Treat all saints with Christian charity.

3-16. A gospel that cannot save men temporally cannot save them spiritually. Temporal concerns are part and portion of the gospel of Christ. Hence, in every dispensation provision is made for the temporal needs of the people. The Church Welfare Plan, as administered in our day, is that part of the gospel which is designed under our present economic circumstances to care for the temporal needs of the saints on the basis of gospel principles. In the early days of this dispensation attempts were made to practice the United Order. Some form of this system operated among some of the early Christians. See *Commentary II*, pp. 56-57.

When the United Order was set up in modern times the Lord said: "It is my purpose to provide for my saints, for all things are mine. But it must needs be done in mine own way; and behold this is the way that I, the Lord, have decreed to provide for my saints, that the poor shall be exalted, in that the rich are made low. For the earth is full, and there is enough and to spare; yea, I prepared all things, and have given unto the children of men to be agents unto themselves. Therefore, if any man shall take of the abundance which I have made, and impart not his portion, according to the law of my gospel, unto the poor and the needy, he shall, with the wicked, lift up his eyes in hell, being in torment." (D. & C. 104:15-18.) Also: "Thou wilt remember the poor, and consecrate of thy properties for their support that which thou hast to impart unto them, with a covenant and a deed which cannot be broken. And inasmuch as ye impart of your substance unto the poor, ye will do it unto me; and they shall be laid before the bishop of my church and his counselors, two of the elders, or high priests, such as he shall appoint or has appointed and set apart for that purpose." (D. & C. 42:30-31.)

Since the principles upon which the Lord operates are eternal, the concepts set forth in these revelations would have been operative in Paul's day. The mechanics and the arrangements would have been such as to suit the needs and circumstances of the people. In any event, Paul is here directing Timothy on how to conduct whatever system of welfare administration was in operation to care for the poor among them, particularly for the widows.

3-5. Widows that are widows indeed] Widows who had no means of support except from the Church.

4, 8, 16. Gospel standards provide that members of the Church should work and support themselves. When this fails, they are to gain temporal assistance from their family, including children and grandchildren. Only when these resources do not suffice is there justification for calling on the Church itself for temporal assistance.

4. Nephews] Rather, grandchildren.

6. Members of the Church who live after the manner of the world are dead spiritually and so remain, unless and until they repent and live again as becometh saints.

9-16. To qualify for church assistance, under the welfare system then in operation, widows were: To be in need; to be without children or relatives who could support them; to be 60 years of age: to have been faithful to their husbands; to have lived the gospel in general, as shown by the fact of rearing children, of lodging strangers, of washing the clothes of the saints, of relieving the afflicted, and of general proper living. Young widows were counseled to marry again and raise families.

17-18. There are times when elders, spending their full time in the ministry, should receive temporal help from the Church, especially for their families. "It is the duty of the church," for instance, the Lord says, "to assist in supporting the families of those, and also to support the families of those who are called and must needs be sent unto the world to proclaim the gospel unto the world." (D. & C. 75:24.)

PAUL NAMES DIVERS CHURCH POLICIES

I TIMOTHY 5:19-25; 6:1-6.

19 Against an elder receive not an accusation, but before two or three witnesses.

20 Them that sin rebuke before all, that others also may fear.

21 I charge *thee* before God, and the Lord Jesus Christ, and the elect angels, that thou observe these things without preferring one before another, doing nothing by partiality.

22 Lay hands suddenly on no man, neither be partaker of other men's sins: keep thyself pure.

23 Drink no longer water, but use a little wine for thy stomach's sake and thine often infirmities.

24 Some men's sins are open beforehand, going before to judgment; and some *men* they follow after.

25 Likewise also the good works *of some* are manifest beforehand; and they that are otherwise cannot be hid.

1 Let as many servants as are under the yoke count their own masters worthy of all honour, that the name of God and *his* doctrine be not blasphemed.

2 And they that have believing masters, let them not despise *them*, because they are brethren; but rather do *them* service, because they are faithful and beloved, partakers of the benefit. These things teach and exhort.

3 If any man teach otherwise, and consent not to wholesome words, *even* the words of our Lord Jesus Christ, and to the doctrine which is according to godliness;

4 He is proud, knowing nothing, but doting about questions

and strifes of words, whereof cometh envy, strife, railings, evil surmisings.

5 Perverse disputings of men of corrupt minds, and destitute of the truth, supposing that gain is godliness: from such withdraw thyself.

6 But godliness with contentment is great gain.

I.V. I TIMOTHY 5:23-25.

23 Some men's sins are open beforehand, going before to judgment; and some men they follow after.

24 Likewise also the good works of some are manifest beforehand; and they that are otherwise cannot be hid.

25 Drink no longer water, but use a little wine for thy stomach's sake and thine often infirmities.

5:19. Christ's ministers should not be condemned on hearsay and gossip. Formal charges should be made through the court system of the Church.

20. Public sins should be dealt with publicly. "And if thy brother or sister offend many, he or she shall be chastened before many. And if any one offend openly, he or she shall be rebuked openly, that he or she may be ashamed." (D. & C. 42:90-91.)

21. The elect angels] Those angels, as Moroni and Elijah, who inherit exaltation in celestial glory. "Then shall the angels be crowned with the glory of his might, and the saints shall be filled with his glory, and receive their inheritance and be made equal with him." (D. & C. 88:107.)

Doing nothing by partiality] God is no respecter of persons; let his ministers be as he is.

22. Lay hands suddenly on no man] Brethren should be seasoned, tried, and found worthy before they are ordained and set apart to serve in positions of power and influence in the Church.

23. Wine] "The fermented, or, loosely, the unfermented, juice of any fruit or plant used as a beverage; as, currant wine." (*Webster's New Collegiate Dictionary.*) Having knowledge of Timothy's physical infirmities, Paul is probably here counseling him that fruit juices will be more healthful than water. It is not reasonable to suppose that Timothy was being told to drink an alcoholic beverage, unless such was under limited medicinal circumstances.

24-25. Concerning those to be ordained to priestly office (verse 22): 'Some are known to bc unworthy when considered for ordination; the unworthiness of others is revealed later. Some are recognized as worthy in advance; the fitness and qualifications of others is manifest later.'

6:1. Servants . . . 2. Masters] See *Commentary II*, pp. 522-523.

3. Wholesome words] The words of Christ and his servants, words of truth and righteousness, words which teach sound doctrine, words that edify.

4-5. How aptly these descriptive phrases of Paul's describe apostate religionists! And how universal is their application!

"THE LOVE OF MONEY IS THE ROOT OF ALL EVIL"

I TIMOTHY 6:7-10.

7 For we brought nothing into *this* world, *and it is* certain we can carry nothing out.

8 And having food and raiment let us be therewith content.

9 But they that will be rich fall into temptation and a snare, and *into* many foolish and hurtful lusts, which drown men in destruction and perdition.

10 For the love of money is the root of all evil: which while some coveted after, they have erred from the faith, and pierced themselves through with many sorrows.

One of the great purposes of this mortal probation is to allow men to choose between the riches of the world and the riches of eternity. Those who set their hearts on the things of this world lose their souls. "Wo unto the rich, who are rich as to the things of the world. For because they are rich they despise the poor, and they persecute the meek, and their hearts are upon their treasures; wherefore, their treasure is their God. And behold, their treasure shall perish with them also." (2 Ne. 9:30.) "For what shall it profit a man, if he shall gain the whole world, and lose his own soul? Or what shall a man give in exchange for his soul?" (Mark 8:36-37.) Those who set their hearts on the things of the Spirit inherit eternal riches which consist of eternal life.

Effect of riches] See Jas. 5:1-5.

"FIGHT THE GOOD FIGHT OF FAITH"

I TIMOTHY 6:11-19.

11 But thou, O man of God, flee these things; and follow after righteousness, godliness, faith, love, patience, meekness.

12 Fight the good fight of faith, lay hold on eternal life, whereunto thou art also called, and hast professed a good profession before many witnesses.

13 I give thee charge in the sight of God, who quickeneth all things, and *before* Christ Jesus, who before Pontius Pilate witnessed a good confession;

14 That thou keep *this* commandment without spot, unrebukeable, until the appearing of our Lord Jesus Christ:

15 Which in his times he shall show, *who is* the blessed and only Potentate, the King of kings, and Lord of lords;

16 Who only hath immortality, dwelling in the light which no man can approach unto; whom no man hath seen, nor can see: to whom *be* honour and power everlasting. Amen.

17 Charge them that are rich in this world, that they be not highminded, nor trust in uncertain riches, but in the living God, who giveth us richly all things to enjoy;

18 That they do good, that they be rich in good works, ready to distribute, willing to communicate;

19 Laying up in store for themselves a good foundation against the time to come, that they may lay hold on eternal life.

I.V. I TIMOTHY 6:15-16.

15 Which in his times he shall show, who is the blessed and only Potentate, the King of kings, and Lord of lords, **to whom be honour and power everlasting;**

16 **Whom no man hath seen, nor can see, unto whom no man can approach, only he who hath the light and the hope of immortality dwelling in him.**

11-14. Keep the commandments.

12. Eternal life, whereunto thou are also called] The saints are foreordained to receive eternal life.

15. King of kings, and Lord of lords] See Rev. 19:11-16.

16. Who only hath immortality] Here is an obvious error in the King James Version of the Bible. To assert that Christ only has immortality is to run counter to the whole doctrine of the resurrection, which is that unnumbered hosts of resurrected persons have attained immortality. And here also is a marvelous illustration of the inspiration attending the Prophet's Biblical revisions. By the simple expedient of rearranging some phrases and adding a few words, verses 15 and 16 shed a flood of gospel light where before there was darkness and confusion.

17-19. See 1 Tim. 6:7-10.

Seeing God] See Heb. 12:11-17.

DOES SCIENCE DESTROY FAITH?

I TIMOTHY 6:20-21.

20 O Timothy, keep that which is committed to thy trust, avoiding profane *and* vain babblings, and oppositions of science falsely so called:

21 Which some professing have erred concerning the faith. Grace *be* with thee. Amen.

"Is there a conflict between science and religion? The answer to this basic query depends entirely upon what is meant by and accepted as science and as religion. It is common to say there is no such conflict, meaning between true science and true religion — for one truth never conflicts with another, no matter what fields or categories the truths are put in for purposes of study. But there most certainly is a conflict between science and religion, if by science is meant (for instance) the theoretical guesses and postulates of some organic evolutionists, or if by religion is meant the false creeds and dogmas of the sectarian and pagan worlds.

'Oppositions of science falsely so called' were causing people to err 'concerning the faith' even in the days of Paul. (1 Tim. 6:20-21.)

"There is, of course, no conflict between revealed religion as it has been restored in our day and those scientific realities which have been established as ultimate truth. The mental quagmires in which many students struggle result from the acceptance of unproven scientific theories as ultimate facts, which brings the student to the necessity of rejecting conflicting truths of revealed religion. If, for example, a student accepts the untrue theory that death has been present on the earth for scores of thousands or millions of years, he must reject the revealed truth that there was no death either for man or animals or plants or any form of life until some 6000 years ago when Adam fell.

"As a matter of fact, from the eternal perspective, true science is part of the gospel itself; in its broadest signification the gospel embraces all truth. When the full blessings of the millennium are poured out upon the earth and its inhabitants, pseudo-science and pseudo-religion will be swept aside, and all supposed conflicts between science and religion will vanish away." (*Mormon Doctrine*, 2nd ed., p. 681.)

The Second Epistle of Paul the Apostle to Timothy

In the four short chapters of Second Timothy, our friend Paul — literary craftsman and master theologian that he is — teaches, exhorts, prophesies and testifies as few but he have ever done.

Here we find him making the announcement that He who is the Resurrection and the Life hath abolished death and brought life and immortality to light through the gospel.

Here we read the comforting assurances that Christ hath called his saints with an holy calling, and shall yet call them to reign with him in eternal glory.

Here we find persuasive pleas to be strong in the faith, to keep the commandments, to shun contention, to seek godliness, to come off victorious in the war with the world.

And as to apostate Christendom, who but Paul could have summarized, in words as few, the great spiritual desolation that covers the earth in the dispensation of the fulness of times?

Plain words are also found as to the need and purpose of holy writ, together with a solemn charge that God's ministers teach therefrom.

And then the Apostle testifies that he himself shall have eternal life, as well as all saints who believe and obey.

Truly the word of God "is quick and powerful, sharper than a two-edged sword" (D. & C. 6:2) — all to the end that men shall give proper heed thereto.

CHRIST BROUGHT IMMORTALITY AND ETERNAL LIFE

II TIMOTHY 1:1-12.

1 Paul, an apostle of Jesus Christ by the will of God, according to the promise of life which is in Christ Jesus,

2 To Timothy, *my* dearly beloved son: Grace, mercy, *and* peace, from God the Father and Christ Jesus our Lord.

3 I thank God, whom I serve from *my* forefathers with pure conscience, that without ceasing I have remembrance of thee in my prayers night and day;

4 Greatly desiring to see thee, being mindful of thy tears, that I may be filled with joy;

5 When I call to remembrance the unfeigned faith that is in thee, which dwelt first in thy grandmother Lois, and thy mother Eunice; and I am persuaded that in thee also.

6 Wherefore I put thee in remembrance that thou stir up the gift of God, which is in thee by the putting on of my hands.

7 For God hath not given us the spirit of fear; but of power, and of love, and of a sound mind.

8 Be not thou therefore ashamed of the testimony of our Lord, nor of me his prisoner: but be thou partaker of the afflictions of the gospel according to the power of God;

9 Who hath saved us, and called *us* with an holy calling, not according to our works, but according to his own purpose and grace, which was given us in Christ Jesus before the world began,

10 But is now made manifest by the appearing of our Saviour Jesus Christ, who hath abolished death, and hath brought life and immortality to light through the gospel:

11 Whereunto I am appointed a preacher, and an apostle, and a teacher of the Gentiles.

12 For the which cause I also suffer these things: nevertheless I am not ashamed: for I know whom I have believed, and am persuaded that he is able to keep that which I have committed unto him against that day.

1. Apostle] See *Commentary II*, pp. 130-131, 328-333.

The promise of life which is in Christ Jesus] The promise of eternal life, given in pre-existence, that the obedient saints shall be saved because of our Lord's atoning sacrifice.

2. **My dearly beloved son]** See 1 Tim. 1:1-11.

3. **God, whom I serve from my forefathers with pure conscience]** Paul had always served God according to the best light and knowledge he had. In this sense his conscience was clear. Unlike those who believe the false creeds of modern Christendom, he did not have to change his allegiance from a spirit essence that fills the immensity of space to a personal God when he received the gospel. He had inherited from his fathers the knowledge that God was his Father and that Israel was the Lord's chosen people. His problem was to learn and to do the will of God. First he falsely assumed this meant persecuting Christ and the Christians. On the Damascus Road the Lord called him to defend those whom he had persecuted. But he had always been zealous; he was religiously inclined by instinct. And as with all misguided zealots his problem was one of finding the truth and directing his zeal where the Lord of Heaven would have it centered.

5. Faith runs in families. In general, though not invariably, the Lord sends a faith-endowed spirit into a household of faith.

6. **Stir up the gift of God, which is in thee]** It is not enough to have hands laid on our heads for the gift of the Holy Ghost; thereafter we must seek the Spirit until we actually enjoy the companionship and guidance of that member of the Godhead. See 1 Tim. 4:12-16.

7. **The spirit of fear]** See 1 John 4:7-21.

8. **The testimony of our Lord]** The knowledge, received by revelation from the Holy Ghost, that Jesus is the Christ, the Son of the living God. Those endowed with this heaven-born knowledge are witnesses, appointed to testify and warn the world. Salvation is for those who are valiant in the testimony of Jesus.

The afflictions of the gospel] Afflictions imposed upon the saints by wicked, worldly, and ungodly people. These were exceedingly severe in Paul's dispensation — a dispensation of persecution and martyrdom.

9. God's saints have the promise of eternal life, not because of great achievements in mortality, but because of what they did

before the world began. That is, while they yet dwelt in God's presence as spirits, he foreordained them to receive the gospel and all its blessings including eternal life.

10. Jesus Christ hath abolished death! What wonder, what miracle, what inconceivable glory attends this transcendent truth! Death ceaseth because Christ liveth! There are two deaths and Adam is father of them both — first, the temporal or natural death, which consists in the separation of body and spirit and the return of the body to the dust from whence it came; second, the spiritual death, which consists in being cast out of the presence of the Lord and of dying as pertaining to the things of righteousness or the things of the Spirit. In spiritual death existence continues, but the awareness of spiritual realities ceases. Our Lord's atoning sacrifice redeems men from the effects of both deaths. Temporal death is replaced with temporal life, and spiritual death with spiritual life. That is, all men are raised from the natural death to a state of immortality, and those who believe and obey the fulness of gospel law attain eternal life also.

Jesus said: "I am the resurrection, and the life." (John 11:25.) That is: 'By me immortality and eternal life come, for I have abolished death.' But resurrection and life are not one and the same thing; immortality and eternal life are distinct but associated states. "Immortality is to live forever in the resurrected state with body and spirit inseparably connected. The Lord's work and glory is to bring to pass both the immortality and the eternal life of man (Moses 1:39): all are resurrected to a state of immortality, those who believe and obey the gospel plan go on 'in immortality unto eternal life.' (D. & C. 29:42-43.) Immortality is a free gift which comes by grace alone without works on man's part; eternal life, 'the greatest of all the gifts of God' (D. & C. 14:7), results from 'obedience to the laws and ordinances of the Gospel.' (Third Article of Faith; 1 Cor. 15:42-54; 2 Tim. 1:10; *Doctrines of Salvation*, vol. 2, pp. 4-10, 24, 309-310.)" (*Mormon Doctrine*, 2nd ed., pp. 376-377.)

"Eternal life is the name given to the kind of life that our Eternal Father lives. The word eternal, as used in the name eternal life, is a noun and not an adjective. It is one of the formal names of Deity (Moses 1:3; 7:35; D. & C. 19:11) and has been chosen by him as the particular name to identify the kind of life that he lives. He being God, the life he lives is God's life; and his name (in the noun sense) being Eternal, the kind of life he lives is eternal life. Thus: God's life is eternal life; eternal life is God's life — the expressions are synonymous.

"Accordingly, eternal life is not a name that has reference only to the unending duration of a future life; immortality is to live forever in the resurrected state, and by the grace of God all men will gain this unending continuance of life. But only those who obey the fulness of the gospel law will inherit eternal life. (D. & C. 29: 43-44.) It is 'the greatest of all gifts of God' (D. & C. 14:7), for it is the kind, status, type, and quality of life that God himself enjoys. Thus those who gain eternal life receive exaltation; they are sons of God, joint-heirs with Christ, members of the Church of the Firstborn; they overcome all things, have all power, and receive the fulness of the Father. They are gods." (*Mormon Doctrine*, 2nd ed., p. 237.)

12. That day] The Second Coming, the day of judgment, the day of vengeance, the day when every man's works shall be tried by fire.

Jesus gained power over death from his Father] See *Commentary I*, pp. 486-487.

Jesus glorified by gaining eternal life] See *Commentary I*, pp. 759-762.

BE STRONG IN THE FAITH

II TIMOTHY 1:13-18; 2:1-7.

13 Hold fast the form of sound words, which thou hast heard of me, in faith and love which is in Christ Jesus.

14 That good thing which was committed unto thee keep by the Holy Ghost which dwelleth in us.

15 This thou knowest, that all they which are in Asia be turned away from me; of whom are Phygellus and Hermogenes.

16 The Lord give mercy unto the house of Onesiphorus; for he oft refreshed me, and was not ashamed of my chain:

17 But, when he was in Rome, he sought me out very diligently, and found *me*.

18 The Lord grant unto him that he may find mercy of the Lord in that day: and in how many things he ministered unto me at Ephesus, thou knowest very well.

1 Thou therefore, my son, be strong in the grace that is in Christ Jesus.

2 And the things that thou hast heard of me among many witnesses, the same commit thou to faithful men, who shall be able to teach others also.

3 Thou therefore endure hardness, as a good soldier of Jesus Christ.

4 No man that warreth entangleth himself with the affairs of *this* life; that he may please him who hath chosen him to be a soldier.

5 And if a man also strive for masteries, *yet* is he not crowned, except he strive lawfully.

6 The husbandman that laboureth must be first partaker of the fruits.

7 Consider what I say; and the Lord give thee understanding in all things.

1:13. Sound words] True doctrine.

14. That good thing] The gospel.

The Holy Ghost which dwelleth in us] "The Holy Ghost has not a body of flesh and bones, but is a personage of Spirit. Were it not so, the Holy Ghost could not dwell in us." (D. & C. 130:22.) That is, the Holy Ghost is a Spirit Man, an individual, an entity, who because of his spirit state has power to speak to the spirit within man, thus dwelling in man in the sense of conveying truth to the human heart.

16-18. God grants mercy to the merciful; those who succor the saints temporally shall receive rich spiritual rewards from the Lord.

2:1. Be strong] Be valiant and courageous in the war with sin. Keep the commandments.

2. Paul was one of many witnesses. And he now hopes that the truth shall go from witness to witness until all the world is warned.

3. Endure hardness] Rather, 'Suffer hardship with me.'

Soldier of Jesus Christ] There is war on earth, as there was in heaven; Christ's ministers are soldiers in the war with sin.

4-5. Only the valiant warriors are saved.

6. The reward of eternal life is for the minister first and the convert second. Those who labor in the Lord's vineyard bring salvation to their own souls first and then to the souls of those who believe and obey their witness of the truth. (D. & C. 4.) "He that reapeth receiveth wages, and gathereth fruit unto life eternal." (John 4:36.)

Valiance] See Rev. 3:14-22.

Salvation] See 1 Pet. 1:1-16.

CHRIST GIVETH ETERNAL GLORY TO THE ELECT

II TIMOTHY 2:8-13.

8 Remember that Jesus Christ of the seed of David was raised from the dead according to my gospel:

9 Wherein I suffer trouble, as an evil doer, *even* unto bonds; but the word of God is not bound.

10 Therefore I endure all things for the elect's sakes, that they may also obtain the salvation which is in Christ Jesus with eternal glory.

11 *It is* a faithful saying: For if we be dead with *him*, we shall also live with *him:*

12 If we suffer, we shall also reign with *him:* if we deny *him*, he also will deny us:

13 If we believe not, *yet* he abideth faithful: he cannot deny himself.

I.V. II TIMOTHY 2:8, 11.

8 Remember that Jesus Christ of the seed of David was raised from the dead, according to **the** gospel;

11 **For this** is a faithful saying, If we be dead with him, we shall also live with him;

8. Jesus Christ . . . was raised from the dead] See *Commentary* II, pp. 390-392.

9. The word of God is not bound] The gospel cannot be put in prison; the truth of heaven cannot be locked in a jail cell.

10. Christ's ministers suffer persecution in order to make the truths of salvation available to the saints.

The salvation which is in Christ] See 1 Pet. 1:1-16.

Eternal glory] Exaltation; eternal life; the fulness of salvation in the highest heaven of the celestial world.

11. Dead with him] Dead to sin. **Live with him]** Live in exaltation in his kingdom.

12. Reign with him] Stand with him as kings and priests, ruling and reigning over kingdoms and dominions forever.

SHUN CONTENTION, SEEK GODLINESS

II TIMOTHY 2:14-26.

14 Of these things put *them* in remembrance, charging *them* before the Lord that they strive not about words to no profit, *but* to the subverting of the hearers.

15 Study to show thyself approved unto God, a workman that needeth not to be ashamed, rightly dividing the word of truth.

16 But shun profane *and* vain babblings: for they will increase unto more ungodliness.

17 And their word will eat as doth a canker: of whom is Hymenaeus and Philetus;

18 Who concerning the truth have erred, saying that the resurrection is past already; and overthrow the faith of some.

19 Nevertheless the foundation of God standeth sure, having this seal, The Lord knoweth them that are his. And, Let every one that nameth the name of Christ depart from iniquity.

20 But in a great house there are not only vessels of gold and of silver, but also of wood and of earth; and some to honour, and some to dishonour.

21 If a man therefore purge himself from these, he shall be a vessel unto honour, sanctified, and meet for the master's use, *and* prepared unto every good work.

22 Flee also youthful lusts: but follow righteousness, faith, char-

ity, peace, with them that call on the Lord out of a pure heart.

23 But foolish and unlearned questions avoid, knowing that they do gender strifes.

24 And the servant of the Lord must not strive; but be gentle unto all *men*, apt to teach, patient.

25 In meekness instructing those that oppose themselves; if God peradventure will give them repentance to the acknowledging of the truth;

26 And *that* they may recover themselves out of the snare of the devil, who are taken captive by him at his will.

14. Strive not about words] 16. Shun profane and vain babblings] 23. Foolish and unlearned questions avoid] 24. The servant of the Lord must not strive] Contention and division are of the devil. Agreement and unity are of God. Since true religion comes by revelation, man's sole purpose in trying to understand and interpret gospel principles should be to find out what the Lord means in any given revelation. This knowledge can be gained only by the power of the Spirit. Hence, there is no occasion to debate, to argue, to contend, to champion one cause as against another. "Those who have the Spirit do not hang doggedly to a point of doctrine or philosophy for no other reason than to come off victorious in a disagreement. Their purpose, rather, is to seek truth by investigation, research, and inspiration. 'Cease to contend one with another,' the Lord has commanded. (D. & C. 136:23; Tit. 3:9.)" (*Mormon Doctrine*, 2nd ed., p. 161.)

"There shall be no disputations among you," the Lord commanded the Nephites, "For verily, verily I say unto you, he that hath the spirit of contention is not of me, but is of the devil, who is the father of contention, and he stirreth up the hearts of men to contend with anger, one with another. Behold, this is not my doctrine, to stir up the hearts of men with anger, one against another; but this is my doctrine, that such things should be done away." (3 Ne. 11:28-30.)

15. Rightly dividing the word of truth] Not all truth is of equal value. Some scientific truths may benefit men in this life only; the truths of revealed religion will pour out blessings upon them now and forever. But even revealed truth is not all of the same worth. Some things apply only to past dispensations, as the performances of the Mosaic system; others are binding in all ages, as the laws pertaining to baptism and celestial marriage.

16. Ungodliness] Disobedience, wickedness, conduct that offends God.

18. The resurrection is past] Satan's ministers delight in spiritualizing away the prophecies and doctrines of the gospel. Probably what was here involved was the allegorical teaching that the resurrection consisted in imparting new life to the soul through acceptance of the gospel. Such a view is on a par with the sectarian heresy that the Second Coming is past, meaning that the Lord already has returned to dwell in the hearts of the faithful.

19. The Lord knoweth them that are his] "My sheep hear my voice, and I know them, and they follow me." (John 10:27.)

Let every one that nameth the name of Christ depart from iniquity] 'Let everyone who has taken upon him the name of Christ in the waters of baptism, and then again by partaking of the sacrament, keep the commandments.'

20-21. 'In the Church there are people of all kinds: good and evil, clean and unclean, righteous and wicked. So live that you shall be numbered with the sanctified who shall thereby gain salvation.'

22. Follow righteousness] How often, how emphatically, how persuasively Paul exhorts men to keep the commandments! The salvation he everlastingly preaches is not one of grace alone, but of grace coupled with good works!

26. Snare of the devil] All ungodliness. In this case it was teaching false doctrine.

PAUL DESCRIBES APOSTATE CHRISTENDOM

II TIMOTHY 3:1-13.

1 This know also, that in the last days perilous times shall come.

2 For men shall be lovers of their own selves, covetous, boasters, proud, blasphemers, disobedient to parents, unthankful, unholy,

3 Without natural affection, trucebreakers, false accusers, incontinent, fierce, despisers of those that are good,

4 Traitors, heady, high-minded, lovers of pleasures more than lovers of God;

5 Having a form of godliness, but denying the power thereof: from such turn away.

6 For of this sort are they which creep into houses, and lead captive silly women laden with sins, led away with divers lusts,

7 Ever learning, and never able to come to the knowledge of the truth.

8 Now as Jannes and Jambres withstood Moses, so do these also resist the truth: men of corrupt minds, reprobate concerning the faith.

9 But they shall proceed no further: for their folly shall be manifest unto all *men*, as their's also was.

10 But thou hast fully known my doctrine, manner of life, purpose, faith, long-suffering, charity, patience,

11 Persecutions, afflictions, which came unto me at Antioch, at Iconium, at Lystra; what persecutions I endured: but out of *them* all the Lord delivered me.

12 Yea, and all that will live godly in Christ Jesus shall suffer persecution.

13 But evil men and seducers shall wax worse and worse, deceiving, and being deceived.

Paul speaks here of the direful spiritual darkness that covers the earth in the dispensation of the fulness of times, the seeds of which were even then sprouting among the meridian Christians. This apostasy, spawned by Satan and nurtured in lust, has increased and abounded for two millenniums—until it is universal and all pervading; until God himself has quoted Paul's very words in describing it; until the perilous times following the restoration of the gospel; until this final period of the earth's temporal continuance in which we now live; and it shall continue until the cup of iniquity overflows; until the Lord shall return to take vengeance on the wicked; until he shall come to destroy and burn and consume every ungodly thing and to usher in his own era of millennial righteousness.

The Book of Mormon prophets also, guided by the same Spirit that enlightened Paul, testified in some detail of the damning iniquities of the last days. Moroni, for instance, said: "There shall be great pollutions upon the face of the earth; there shall be murders, and robbing, and lying, and deceivings, and whoredoms, and all manner of abominations." (Morm. 8:31.)

But thanks be to God, the First Vision rent the veil of darkness; the restored gospel became a standard to rally the righteous; and there is hope again for those who now choose to serve God and keep his commandments, though the whole world and all hell oppose them.

Apostasy to precede Second Coming] See *Commentary I*, pp. 645-648; 2 Thess. 2:1-12.

Apostates] 1 Tim. 1:18-20.

Cultists] See *Commentary II*, pp. 177-178.

Fables] 2 Tim. 4:1-5.

1. In the last days perilous times shall come] In the days incident to and after the restoration of the gospel; in the days when the Lord winds up his premillennial work; in the age when the forces of freedom and of slavery align themselves for the great conflict which shall be in progress when the Son of Man returns; in the day when the tares are being bound into bundles for the burning and the righteous are fleeing from Babylon; in this day in which we now live—in this day both the temporal and spiritual well-being of all men shall be in peril.

"In the last days, or in the days of the Gentiles—yea, behold all the nations of the Gentiles and also the Jews, both those who shall come upon this land and those who shall be upon other lands, yea, even upon all the lands of the earth, behold, they will be drunken with iniquity and all manner of abominations." (2 Ne. 27:1.)

2. Lovers of their own selves] Self-centered, withholding from God and their fellowmen the love and appreciation due them; hence, devoid of the incentive and desire to serve God or their fellow beings.

Covetous] Money-loving. See *Commentary II*, pp. 337-340.

Boasters] The sin of boasting consists of self-exultation, of proclaiming or exaggerating one's own accomplishments, of exhibiting pride in those things achieved by the arm of flesh.

Proud] "As spoken of in the revelations, pride is the opposite of humility. It is inordinate self-esteem arising because of one's position, achievements, or possessions; and it has the effect of centering a person's heart on the things of the world rather than the things of the Spirit. (1 John 2:15-17.) As humility, which is an attribute of godliness possessed by true saints, leads to salvation, so pride, which is of the devil, leads to damnation. (2 Ne. 28:15.) 'God resisteth the proud, but giveth grace unto the humble.' (Jas. 4:6; 1 Pet. 5:5.)

"Latter-day prevalence of pride in the hearts of men is one of the sure proofs that apostasy and unrighteousness prevail on the earth. (Rom. 1:28-32; 2 Tim. 3:1-7; 2 Ne. 28-10-15; Morm. 8:28-36.) The Lord hates 'a proud look.' (Prov. 6:16-19.) 'Pride goeth before destruction, and an haughty spirit before a fall.' (Prov. 16:18.) Pride among the inhabitants of Sodom was one of the chief reasons for her destruction. (Ezek. 16:49.) Pride is wickedness, and those who are proud are living a telestial law and will be utterly destroyed at the Second Coming of Christ. (Isa. 2:12; Mal. 4:1; 1 Ne. 22:15; 3 Ne. 25:1; D. & C. 29:9; 64:24; 133:64.)

"Pride is such a gross evil that the scriptures abound in counsels against it. 'Be not proud.' (Jer. 13:15.) 'Beware of pride.' (D & C. 23:1; 25:14; 38:39.) Repent of pride. (D. & C. 56:8.) Cease from pride. (D. & C. 88:121.) 'Thou shalt not be proud in thy heart.' (D. & C. 42:40.)" (*Mormon Doctrine*, 2nd ed., p. 593.)

Blasphemers] See Col. 3:5-17.

Disobedient to parents] In the last days, among the ungodly, children shall refuse to obey their parents.

Unthankful] The sin of ingratitude.

Unholy] Evil; wicked.

3. Without natural affection] An inevitable result of demeaning the family unit so that it is no longer deemed to be the basic unit of society.

Trucebreakers] Rather, *implacable,* as in Romans 1:31.

False accusers] Slanderers.

Incontinent] Without self-control; failing to restrain appetites and passions, especially sexual appetites.

Fierce] Cruel and inhuman to others.

Despisers of those that are good] Not merely neutral and indifferent where the truths of salvation are concerned, but affirmatively against God and his laws.

4. Traitors] Apostates, enemies of God who have violated their allegiance to the gospel and betrayed the trust placed in them by the Lord and his servants.

Heady] Rash and violent; precipitate in action and passion.

High-minded] Arrogant, puffed up with pride.

Lovers of pleasures more than lovers of God] Following worldliness rather than godliness; serving Satan, who is the god of worldly pleasures, rather than the Lord, who commands men to forsake and overcome the world with its tinsel and pleasures.

5. Time—The Spring of 1820.

Place—A grove of trees near Palmyra in Western New York.

Scene—Joseph Smith bows in humble reverence before the great God who created the universe, by whose side stands his Only Begotten Son.

Question — of transcendent import to Joseph Smith and all who seek salvation — Which of all the sects is right and which should the young boy join.

A Voice Speaks—It is the voice of the Son of God; he joins Paul's language with that of Isaiah (Isa. 29:13) to answer the Prophet's query: Join none of them; they are all wrong; all their creeds are an abomination in his sight; those professors are all corrupt; "they draw near to me with their lips, but their hearts are far from me, they teach for doctrines the commandments of men, having a form of godlines, but they deny the power thereof." (Jos. Smith 2:19.)

A form of godliness without saving power! A hollow shell shattered into many fragments! An illusive image without substance! An imitation of what God had aforetime revealed through Peter and Paul! A system of so-called Christianity which worshiped a God without power, a God who gave no revelations, unfolded no visions, worked no miracles, and had forgotten the unchangeable pattern of the past! All Christendom wallowing in the mire and filth of apostasy! As the *Homily on the Perils of Idolatry* of the Church of England had recited in the Sixteenth Century: "Laity and clergy, learned and unlearned, all ages, sects and degrees of men, women, and children of whole Christendom—an horrible and most dreadful thing to think—have been at once drowned in abominable idolatry; of all other vices most detested by God, and most damnable to man; and that by the space of eight hundred years and more." (Cited, James E. Talmage, *Articles of Faith*, p. 202.) And the idolatry of that Catholicism of which the Church of England spoke was but part of the darkness which would blind men in the perilous "last days."

6. Signs of the apostasy were evident even in Paul's day, so that false teachers found it easy to lead away the unwary and the unstable.

Lead captive silly women laden with sins] Sin-laden souls are easily led from the truth. For instance: In their carnal state they find it easier to believe their sins are removed simply by confessing the Lord Jesus with their lips, or through the performance of some act of penitence, rather than by following the hard and rugged course of seeking repentance in tears and anguish.

7. Ever learning the philosophies of men, but not receiving the saving truths of revealed religion! Ever learning intellectual abstractions which purport to show the whence, why, and whither of life, but not turning to God and his prophets to find the simple saving truths! Salvation is not found in much learning; it has little to do with educational degrees and intellectual power. The truths that save are gospel truths whose source is revelation, revelation to spiritual people who may or may not also be intellectual.

8. Jannes and Jambres] According to Jewish tradition, the magicians who opposed Moses in Pharaoh's court. (Ex. 7:11-22.)

12. Persecution is the heritage of the faithful. See *Commentary II*, pp. 62-64.

13. The millennium will not be ushered in because men repent and turn to God, or because mankind generally becomes more upright and wholesome. Sin and evil shall increase from day to day until the Lord comes; every form of corruption shall exceed its counterpart of the past, until the cup of iniquity shall be full. Then the Lord shall return to cleanse the vineyard and the wicked shall be destroyed.

SCRIPTURES GUIDE MAN TO SALVATION

II TIMOTHY 3:14-17.

14 But continue thou in the things which thou hast learned and hast been assured of, knowing of whom thou hast learned *them;*

15 And that from a child thou hast known the holy scriptures, which are able to make thee wise unto salvation through faith which is in Christ Jesus.

16 All scripture *is* given by inspiration of God, and *is* profitable for doctrine, for reproof, for correction, for instruction in righteousness:

17 That the man of God may be perfect, throughly furnished unto all good works.

I.V. II TIMOTHY 3:16.

16 And all scripture given by inspiration of God, is profitable for doctrine, for reproof, for correction, for instruction in righteousness;

"Any message, whether written or spoken, that comes from God to man by the power of the Holy Ghost is scripture. If it is written and accepted by the Church, it becomes part of the scriptures or standard works and ever thereafter may be read and studied with profit. Much of what is in the scriptures was given orally in the first instance and was thereafter recorded either by the uttering prophet or an inspired scribe. Other portions of what is in holy writ were written by the inspired authors by way of revelation and commandment.

"The elders of the Church are sent forth 'to proclaim the everlasting gospel, by the Spirit of the living God,' and they are commanded to 'speak as they are moved upon by the Holy Ghost. And whatsoever they shall speak when moved upon by the Holy Ghost shall be scripture, shall be the will of the Lord, shall be the mind of the Lord, shall be the word of the Lord, shall be the voice of the Lord, and the power of God unto salvation.' (D. & C. 68:1-4.)" (*Mormon Doctrine*, 2nd ed., p. 682.)

14. Endure to the end.

15. The holy scriptures] The canonized, recognized, officially approved inspired writings; to Timothy this meant the Old Testament only; now it includes also the New Testament, Book of Mormon, Doctrine and Covenants, and Pearl of Great Price. The Holy Scriptures contain that portion of the law of the Lord which he has chosen to be a continuing guide to his people and to all men to lead them back into his eternal presence. (Ps. 19:7-11.) The burden of the scriptures is that God is our Creator and Father, that Christ is our Savior and Redeemer, and that salvation comes by obedience to the laws and ordinances of his everlasting gospel.

16. All scripture] Since scripture includes all inspired utterances, it embraces much more than the standard works standing alone. Indeed, it is the spoken testimony, the oral scripture, which makes the fire of conversion burn in the human soul with an unquenchable flame. (2 Ne. 33:1.) Much of our instruction, doctrine, and reproof comes from this source; hence, the need for living prophets to guide the Church and warn the world. But in the eternal sense even oral scripture "is recorded in heaven for the angels to look upon." (D. & C. 62:3.)

Prophecy] See *Commentary II*, pp. 385-388.

"PREACH THE WORD"

II TIMOTHY 4:1-5.

1 I charge *thee* therefore before God, and the Lord Jesus Christ, who shall judge the quick and the dead at his appearing and his kingdom;

2 Preach the word; be instant in season, out of season; reprove, rebuke, exhort with all longsuffering and doctrine.

3 For the time will come when they will not endure sound doctrine; but after their own lusts shall they heap to themselves teachers, having itching ears;

4 And they shall turn away *their* ears from the truth, and shall be turned unto fables.

5 But watch thou in all things, endure afflictions, do the work of an envangelist, make full proof of thy ministry.

What message do the Lord's ministers bear? What should they preach? The gospel of Jesus Christ! The word! The truths of salvation as recorded in the revelations! How sobering is Paul's charge! In God's holy name the command is to preach doctrine, sound doctrine, saving doctrine, the doctrine of Christ!

"These shall be their teachings," the Lord commands in this day: "Teach the principles of my gospel, which are in the Bible and the Book of Mormon," and in "the fulness of my scriptures." (D. & C. 42:12-15.)

2. Preach the word] In sending forth his latter-day ministers, the Lord commanded: "Let them journey from thence preaching the word by the way, saying none other things than that which the prophets and apostles have written, and that which is taught them by the Comforter through the prayer of faith." (D. & C. 52:9.)

3. They will not endure sound doctrine] See 2 Tim. 3:1-13.

4. Fables] "All false doctrines are fables. That is, they are stories which have been imagined, fabricated, and invented as opposed to the gospel which is real and true. (2 Pet. 1:16.) Apostasy consists in turning from true doctrine to fables." (*Mormon Doctrine*, 2nd ed., p. 261.)

5. An evangelist] See *Commentary II*, pp. 508-512.

Teach true doctrine only] See 1 Tim. 1:1-11.

Preach by the Spirit] See *Commentary II*, pp. 317-319.

Take no thought beforehand] 1 Pet. 4:7-11.

PAUL AND ALL SAINTS ASSURED OF EXALTATION

II TIMOTHY 4:6-22.

6 For I am now ready to be offered, and the time of my departure is at hand.

7 I have fought a good fight, I have finished *my* course, I have kept the faith:

8 Henceforth there is laid up for me a crown of righteousness, which the Lord, the righteous judge, shall give me at that day: and not to me only, but unto all them also that love his appearing.

9 Do thy diligence to come shortly unto me:

10 For Demas hath forsaken me, having loved this present world, and is departed unto Thessalonica; Crescens to Galatia, Titus unto Dalmatia.

11 Only Luke is with me. Take Mark, and bring him with thee: for he is profitable to me for the ministry.

12 And Tychicus have I sent to Ephesus.

13 The cloak that I left at Troas with Carpus, when thou comest, bring *with thee*, and the books, *but* especially the parchments.

14 Alexander the coppersmith did me much evil: the Lord reward him according to his works:

15 Of whom be thou ware also; for he hath greatly withstood our words.

16 At my first answer no man stood with me, but all *men* forsook me: *I pray God* that it may not be laid to their charge.

17 Notwithstanding the Lord stood with me, and strengthened me; that by me the preaching might be fully known, and *that* all the Gentiles might hear: and I was delivered out of the mouth of the lion.

18 And the Lord shall deliver me from every evil work, and will preserve *me* unto his heavenly kingdom: to whom *be* glory for ever and ever. Amen.

19 Salute Prisca and Aquila, and the household of Onesiphorus.

20 Erastus abode at Corinth: but Trophimus have I left at Miletum sick.

21 Do thy diligence to come before winter. Eubulus greeteth thee, and Pudens, and Linus, and Claudia, and all the brethren.

22 The Lord Jesus Christ *be* with thy spirit. Grace *be* with you. Amen.

I.V. II TIMOTHY 4:22.

22 The Lord Jesus Christ be with **you, and** grace be with you **all.** Amen.

6-8. Paul's calling and election had been made sure. He was sealed up unto eternal life. He had kept the commandments, been tried at all hazards, and the Lord had given him the promise: "Son, Thou shalt be exalted." And since no man is or can be exalted alone, this is one of the crowning reasons why we know Paul was married.

Calling and election sure] See 1 Pet. 1:1-19.

6. Ready to be offered] Paul is ready to lay down his life for the testimony of Jesus. **Martyrdom]** See Rev. 6:9-11.

7. I have fought a good fight] This life is a continuation of the war in heaven. In it Satan makes war with the saints, "which keep the commandments of God, and have the testimony of Jesus." (Rev. 12:17.) Those saints who overcome the world thereby triumph over Satan and gain the victory. Of King Mosiah, for instance, the Book of Mormon account records, after he had "gone the way of all the earth," that he had "warred a good warfare, walking uprightly before God." (Alma 1:1.)

8. A crown of righteousness] Eternal life.

10. Demas . . . loved this present world] Satan gained the victory; Demas was overcome by the world.

11. Mark . . . is profitable to me for the ministry] Paul and Mark had once been missionary companions. (Acts 12:25.) Then amid the tensions and trials of that early day sharp contention arose between them and they went their separate ways. (Acts 15:37-40.) That thereafter they reconciled their differences and again shared the full confidence and love of each other is evident from Mark's association with Paul in Rome when the epistle to the Colossians was written (Col. 4:10) and from this present expression of commendation which flowed from the pen of Paul.

14-16. "And ye ought to say in your hearts — let God judge between me and thee, and reward thee according to thy deeds." (D. & C. 64:11.)

18. Paul knew he had a sure inheritance of eternal life in the highest heaven of the celestial world.

The Epistle of Paul to Titus

Titus is the epistle of obedience. Writing in his old age, Paul seems increasingly impressed by the Spirit to counsel his beloved Titus, and through him all the saints, of the overpowering need to walk in paths of truth and righteousness.

True, he affirms, as everlastingly he must in a day when the doctrine of Christ is being introduced anew to a pagan world, that salvation comes by God's grace. But his emphasis is upon what the saints must do after baptism to gain the glory that comes by grace.

Titus is written to and for the saints. It is a sermon of practical exhortation to those in the fold, a common sense approach to the problem of living in the world without being of the world. Paul is thus writing, in effect, to the saints today, and as is the never failing effect of the words of the great theologian-apostle, his words are as new and living now as when first recorded on the parchments of antiquity.

PAUL FOREORDAINED TO GAIN ETERNAL LIFE

TITUS 1:1-4.

1 Paul, a servant of God, and an apostle of Jesus Christ, according to the faith of God's elect, and the acknowledging of the truth which is after godliness;

2 In hope of eternal life, which God, that cannot lie, promised before the world began;

3 But hath in due times manifested his word through preaching, which is committed unto me according to the commandment of God our Saviour;

4 To Titus, *mine* own son after the common faith: Grace, mercy, *and* peace, from God the Father and the Lord Jesus Christ our Saviour.

1. An apostle of Jesus Christ] See *Commentary II*, pp. 130-131, 328-333.

The faith of God's elect] The gospel of Jesus Christ.

2. As one of a host of faithful spirits in pre-existence, all of whom received a like blessing, Paul was foreordained to gain eternal life, included within which is the fact he was foreordained to believe the gospel, to be baptized, to receive the Melchizedek Priesthood, to be married for eternity, and to make his calling and election sure — all of which he did.

Foreordination] See *Commentary II*, pp. 267-269, 490-491.

Election] See *Commentary II*, pp. 271-278.

Foreordination of Israel] See *Commentary II*, pp. 283-285.

2. Manifested his word through preaching] God offers salvation to man through "the foolishness of preaching." (1 Cor. 1:21.) Those who respond to this seeming "foolishness" are saved; those who reject it are damned.

God our Saviour] Jesus Christ. "The Lord is God, and beside him there is no Savior." (D. & C. 76:1.)

4. Mine own son] 'My convert, my disciple, my follower, my pupil.'

The common faith] The gospel of Jesus Christ, the faith shared equally by all believers — a faith, with its attendant rewards, which is not reserved for apostles and prophets only, but which blesses equally the lives of all who believe and obey.

SOUND DOCTRINE MAKES MEN SOUND IN THE FAITH

TITUS 1:5-16.

5 For this cause left I thee in Crete, that thou shouldest set in order the things that are wanting, and ordain elders in every city, as I had appointed thee:

6 If any be blameless, the husband of one wife, having faithful children not accused of riot or unruly.

7 For a bishop must be blameless, as the steward of God; not

selfwilled, not soon angry, not given to wine, no striker, not given to filthy lucre;

8 But a lover of hospitality, a lover of good men, sober, just, holy, temperate;

9 Holding fast the faithful word as he hath been taught, that he may be able by sound doctrine both to exhort and to convince the gainsayers.

10 For there are many unruly and vain talkers and deceivers, specially they of the circumcision:

11 Whose mouths must be stopped, who subvert whole houses, teaching things which they ought not, for filthy lucre's sake.

12 One of themselves, *even* a prophet of their own, said, The Cretians *are* alway liars, evil beasts, slow bellies.

13 This witness is true. Wherefore rebuke them sharply, that they may be sound in the faith;

14 Not giving heed to Jewish fables, and commandments of men, that turn from the truth.

15 Unto the pure all things *are* pure: but unto them that are defiled and unbelieving *is* nothing pure; but even their mind and conscience is defiled.

16 They profess that they know God; but in works they deny *him*, being abominable, and disobedient, and unto every good work reprobate.

I.V. TITUS 1:15.

15 Unto the pure, **let** all things **be** pure; but unto them **who** are defiled and unbelieving, nothing **is** pure; but even their mind and conscience is defiled.

5. Elders] See *Commentary II*, pp. 113-115.

6. Husband of one wife] See 1 Tim. 3:1-7.

7. A bishop] See 1 Tim. 3:1-7.

9. Sound doctrine] 13. Sound in the faith] Godly conduct grows out of gospel teachings. Ethical practices are born of true gospel principles. Revealed truth begets righteous living. Right living is the child of true teachings.

And conversely: False doctrine breeds conduct that is not of God. Belief in false principles results in practices based on error. Man-made doctrine has no saving power.

Thus: Sound doctrine is essential to salvation; and sound doctrine comes from God by revelation. Those who believe the gospel are the only ones who will or can live its laws. Men are baptized, married for eternity, and conform to every divine law because they believe the truth.

11. Teaching . . . for filthy lucre's sake] How true (and sad!) it is that almost all false teachers are motivated more by money than by a desire to make the word of God available freely, without money and without price. A paid ministry has already received its reward. Truly, "the laborer in Zion shall labor for Zion; for if they labor for money they shall perish." (2 Ne. 26:31.) **Priestcrafts]** See *Commentary II*, pp. 171-174. **Preaching]** See 2 Tim. 4:1-5.

12. A prophet of their own] Epimenides who lived about 600 B. C., and who — as "a witness or teacher," as a professing "preacher of righteousness," who did not have "the spirit of prophecy, which is the testimony of Jesus" (*Teachings*, p. 269) — was therefore a false prophet. See *Commntary I*, pp. 251-153; Rev. 19:9b-10.

The Cretians are always liars] As the Corinthians were renowned for dissolute living, so the Cretians were famed for dishonesty. Their most well-known false belief — the truth of which even their own "prophets" ridiculed — was that Zeus was buried in Crete.

Slow bellies] Indulgent, fat people, who become so by making gluttony their god.

14. Jewish fables] That whole body of Jewish belief and practice which leads men away from that salvation which is in Christ. See 2 Tim. 4:1-5.

15. The pure] The saints, those whose sins have been washed away in the waters of baptism, who are keeping the commandments, and who enjoy the companionship of that Holy Spirit, which will not dwell in an unclean tabernacle.

Them that are defiled and unbelieving] Those who either reject or depart from the truth, choosing rather to live after the manner of the world with all its carnality, sensuality, and devilishness.

16. Since God can be known only by revelation from the Holy Ghost, and since this Holy Spirit can be received only as a result of righteousness, it follows that those who are disobedient to God's laws do not and cannot know him.

LIVE RIGHTEOUSLY, DENY UNGODLINESS, SEEK THE LORD

TITUS 2:1-15.

1 But speak thou the things which become sound doctrine:

2 That the aged men be sober, grave, temperate, sound in faith, in charity, in patience.

3 The aged women likewise, that *they be* in behaviour as becometh holiness, not false accusers, not given to much wine, teachers of good things;

4 That they may teach the young women to be sober, to love their husbands, to love their children,

5 *To be* discreet, chaste, keepers at home, good, obedient to their own husbands, that the word of God be not blasphemed.

6 Young men likewise exhort to be sober minded.

7 In all things showing thyself a pattern of good works: in doctrine *showing* uncorruptness, gravity, sincerity,

8 Sound speech, that cannot be condemned; that he that is of the contrary part may be ashamed, having no evil thing to say of you.

9 *Exhort* servants to be obedient unto their own masters, *and* to please *them* well in all *things;* not answering again;

10 Not purloining, but showing all good fidelity; that they may adorn the doctrine of God our Saviour in all things.

11 For the grace of God that bringeth salvation hath appeared to all men.

12 Teaching us that, denying ungodliness and worldly lusts, we should live soberly, righteously, and godly, in this present world;

13 Looking for that blessed hope, and the glorious appearing of the great God and our Saviour Jesus Christ;

14 Who gave himself for us, that he might redeem us from all iniquity, and purify unto himself

a peculiar people, zealous of good works.

15 These things speak, and exhort, and rebuke with all authority. Let no man despise thee.

I.V. TITUS 2:11.

11 For the grace of God **which bringeth salvation to all men, hath appeared;**

Paul's doctrine — here and everywhere recorded — is this: Salvation comes by obedience to the laws and ordinances of the gospel!

To the saints his everlasting counsel is: Obey, obey, obey; keep the commandments; earn the attributes of godliness — and then, and then only, cometh salvation!

Enduring to the end] See *Commentary II*, pp. 42-44.

Obedience] See Jas. 1:22-26.

2. "Be patient; be sober; be temperate; have patience, faith, hope and charity." (D. & C. 6:19.)

Sober, grave] A certain soberness, solemnity, and gravity of demeanor becometh the saints, for they have received things of deep and eternal import which affect their eternal salvation.

3-5. The mature women in the Church, those with faith and spiritual stature, are to teach the younger women to live the gospel, to acquire the attributes of godliness, and to care for their families.

6-8. Young men should receive similar teaching from their brethren in the Church.

9-10. And those saints who are slaves are to be so taught that their lives will be patterns of Christian living.

God our Saviour] The Lord Jesus Christ through whom salvation comes.

11. 'Salvation comes by the grace of God and is offered to all men.' See *Commentary II*, pp. 497-500.

12. The whole gospel system is designed to enable men to turn from evil and attain righteousness by obedience to the Lord's law. Salvation is free only in the sense that it is freely available; every blessing, other than the fact of resurrection, must be earned by obedience. "Deny yourselves of all ungodliness and love God with all your might, mind and strength," is the eternal counsel of all the prophets of all the ages. (Moro. 10:32.)

13. That blessed hope] The Second Coming of the Messiah which, seemingly, the Meridian Saints assumed was near at hand.

The great God and our Saviour Jesus Christ] 'Our great God and Savior, Jesus Christ.' It is the Son — not the Father, and not both of them — who shall return at the consummation of "that blessed hope."

14. Redeem us from all iniquity] Redemption from the spiritual fall, which comes on conditions of repentance. (D. & C. 18:10-12; 29:43-45.)

A peculiar people] See 1 Pet. 2:9-10.

HOW TO LIVE AFTER BAPTISM

TITUS 3:1-15.

1 Put them in mind to be subject to principalities and powers, to obey magistrates, to be ready to every good work,

2 To speak evil of no man, to be no brawlers, *but* gentle, shewing all meekness unto all men.

3 For we ourselves also were sometimes foolish, disobedient, deceived, serving divers lusts and pleasures, living in malice and envy, hateful, *and* hating one another.

4 But after that the kindness and love of God our Saviour toward man appeared,

5 Not by works of righteousness which we have done, but according to his mercy he saved us, by the washing of regeneration, and renewing of the Holy Ghost;

6 Which he shed on us abundantly through Jesus Christ our Saviour;

7 That being justified by his grace, we should be made heirs according to the hope of eternal life.

8 *This is* a faithful saying, and these things I will that thou affirm constantly, that they which have believed in God might be careful to maintain good works. These things are good and profitable unto men.

9 But avoid foolish questions, and genealogies, and contentions, and strivings about the law; for they are unprofitable and vain.

10 A man that is an heretic after the first and second admonition reject;

11 Knowing that he that is such is subverted, and sinneth, being condemned of himself.

12 When I shall send Artemas unto thee, or Tychicus, be diligent to come unto me to Nicopolis: for I have determined there to winter.

13 Bring Zenas the lawyer and Apollos on their journey diligently, that nothing be wanting unto them.

14 And let our's also learn to maintain good works for necessary uses, that they be not unfruitful.

15 All that are with me salute thee. Greet them that love us in the faith. Grace *be* with you all. Amen.

1. Them] Those who have joined the Church and who are thus under covenant to live as becometh saints.

Principalities . . . powers . . . magistrates] "We believe in being subject to kings, presidents, rulers, and magistrates, in obeying, honoring, and sustaining the law." (Twelfth Article of Faith.)

Every good work] To be saved, the saints — after baptism! —must keep the commandments.

Endure to the end] See *Commentary II*, pp. 42-44.

Obedience] See Jas. 1:22-25.

2. Brawlers] Those who quarrel or fight noisily.

3-7. 'Before we joined the Church, we lived after the manner of the world. But through the kindness, love, and mercy of Christ, he made salvation available to us through baptism and the cleansing power of the Holy Ghost so that we through righteousness and obedience — after baptism! — shall gain eternal life.'

3. We ourselves] The saints.

4. God our Saviour] "Jesus Christ our Saviour." (Verse 6.)

5. Not by works of righteousness] There is no salvation in good works as such. That is: There are no good works which men may do which — standing alone — will cause them to be resurrected or to gain eternal life. Immortality and eternal life come through the atonement of Christ, the one being a free gift, the other being offered freely to all who will be baptized and who then keep the commandments.

Washing of regeneration] Baptism in water, so named to signify that baptized converts are regenerated; that is, they become new again spiritually; they become like little children, alive in Christ and without sin.

Renewing of the Holy Ghost] Receiving anew that childlike state of purity wherein the Holy Spirit, who dwelleth not in unclean tabernacles, can again dwell in the saints, they thus becoming "new creatures" of the Holy Ghost. (Mosiah 27:24-27.)

7. **Justified by his grace]** See *Commentary II*, pp. 229-233.

Heirs] See *Commentary II*, pp. 261-262.

8. 'Keep the commandments after baptism!'

This is a faithful saying] The summary of the plan of salvation in verses 4 to 7, which being so designated indicates that the saints in that day understood the gospel so well that its basic provisions were almost axiomatic.

9. There is no converting power in debate and contention. Christ's ministers are to teach, not to argue. Missionaries go forth, for instance, to "declare glad tidings," with this restriction: "Of tenets thou shalt not talk" (D. & C. 19:20-31), meaning they are to teach and explain the basic doctrines of salvation and not engage in contentions and strivings about the doctrines of sectarianism.

Genealogies] Linked here with contentions and strivings about the Law of Moses, these refer to the false Jewish tradition that salvation was for the chosen seed as such was known by genealogical recitations. In this dispensation, the Lord has commanded genealogical research as an essential requisite in making salvation available to those who do not have opportunity to receive the gospel in this life.

Salvation for the dead] See 1 Pet. 3:18-22; 4:1-6.

10-11. There comes a time when it is wise to shun and avoid those who rebel against the light and whose hearts are set on promulgating false and damning doctrines. A modern illustration of such is those cultists who leave the Church to advocate and practice plural marriage in a day when the President of the Church has withdrawn from all men the power to perform these marriages.

14. Maintain good works] Keep the commandments after baptism!

The Epistle of Paul to Philemon

Here we have the imprisoned Paul writing a personal letter to his convert-friend Philemon to plead the cause of Onesimus a runaway slave. It appears that Philemon was a rich and faithful member of the Church; that his slave Onesimus chose to escape, apparently robbing his master in the process; that the slave was thereafter converted by and ministered to the needs of Paul; and that the Apostle sent Onesimus back to his master with a plea that he be received mercifully and fellowshipped as one of the saints.

The epistle is tactfully and sweetly written and does more to reveal the personal feelings of its author than to contribute to the body of Christian doctrine.

GOSPEL CHANGES A SERVANT INTO A BROTHER

PHILEMON 1-25.

1 Paul, a prisoner of Jesus Christ, and Timothy *our* brother, unto Philemon our dearly beloved, and fellowlabourer,

2 And to *our* beloved Apphia, and Archippus our fellowsoldier, and to the church in thy house:

3 Grace to you, and peace, from God our Father and the Lord Jesus Christ.

4 I thank my God, making mention of thee always in my prayers,

5 Hearing of thy love and faith, which thou hast toward the Lord Jesus, and toward all saints;

6 That the communication of thy faith may become effectual by the acknowledging of every good thing which is in you in Christ Jesus.

7 For we have great joy and consolation in thy love, because the bowels of the saints are refreshed by thee, brother.

8 Wherefore, though I might be much bold in Christ to enjoin thee that which is covenient,

9 Yet for love's sake I rather beseech *thee*, being such an one as Paul the aged, and now also a prisoner of Jesus Christ.

10 I beseech thee for my son Onesimus, whom I have begotten in my bonds;

11 Which in time past was to thee unprofitable, but now profitable to thee and to me:

12 Whom I have sent again: thou therefore receive him, that is, mine own bowels:

13 Whom I would have retained with me, that in thy stead he might have ministered unto me in the bonds of the gospel:

14 But without thy mind would I do nothing; that thy benefit should not be as it were of necessity, but willingly.

15 For perhaps he therefore departed for a season, that thou shouldest receive him for ever;

16 Not now as a servant, but above a servant, a brother beloved, specially to me, but how much more unto thee, both in the flesh, and in the Lord?

17 If thou count me therefore a partner, receive him as myself.

18 If he hath wronged thee, or oweth *thee* ought, put that on mine account;

19 I Paul have written *it* with mine own hand, I will repay *it:* albeit I do not say to thee how thou owest unto me even thine own self besides.

20 Yea, brother, let me have joy of thee in the Lord: refresh my bowels in the Lord.

21 Having confidence in thy obedience I wrote unto thee, knowing that thou wilt also do more than I say.

22 But withal prepare me also a lodging: for I trust that through your prayers I shall be given unto you.

23 There salute thee Epaphras, my fellowprisoner in Christ Jesus;

24 Marcus, Aristarchus, Demas, Lucas, my fellowlabourers.

25 The grace of our Lord Jesus Christ *be* with your spirit. Amen.

I.V. PHILEMON 25.

25 The grace of our Lord Jesus Christ be with **you.** Amen.

God is no respecter of persons, and few things are of lesser consequence than social caste or status. Rather, "he inviteth them all to come unto him and partake of his goodness; and he denieth none that come unto him, black and white, bond and free, male and female; and he remembereth the heathen; and all are alike unto God." (2 Ne. 26:33.) See *Commentary II*, pp. 522-523.

1. A prisoner of Jesus Christ] Imprisoned because of the testimony of Christ and the work of the ministry.

2. The church in thy house] A branch or ward of the Church apparently met in the home of one of the members, as is not infrequently the case where small congregations are involved.

5. All saints] All members of the Church. See *Commentary II*, pp. 525-529.

7. The bowels of the saints are refreshed] A part of the body is assumed, figuratively, to be the center of emotions. We would say: 'The hearts of the saints are refreshed.'

The Epistle of Paul the Apostle to the Hebrews

Speaking from the standpoint of uninspired Biblical research, one of the so far unsolved mysteries of sectarian scholarship is: Who wrote the Epistle to the Hebrews?

It is variously attributed to Paul, Barnabas, Apollos, Clement of Rome, Luke, and even the female Priscilla. "Origen, the most learned of the early teachers, concluded his examination of the question with the words, 'Who wrote the Epistle God only knows.' " (*Dummelow*, p. 1012.) So uncertain are the scholars that sometimes even Latter-day Saints choose to attribute quotations from it to, "the author of the Epistle to the Hebrews," rather than to Paul the apostle.

But the Prophet Joseph Smith says this Epistle was written "by Paul . . . to the Hebrew brethren" (*Teachings*, p. 59), and repeatedly in his sermons he attributes statements from it to Paul. Peter, himself a Hebrew, whose ministry and teachings were directed in large part to his own people, seems to be identifying its authorship when he writes, "Our beloved brother Paul . . . according to the wisdom given unto him hath written *unto you* [the Hebrews]; As *also* in *all his* [other] *epistles*, . . . some things hard to be understood." (2 Pet. 3:15-16.) In any event, Paul did write Hebrews, and to those who accept Joseph Smith as an inspired witness of truth, the matter is at rest.

However, the principles set forth in the Epistle are more important than the personage who recorded them; an understanding of the doctrines taught is of greater worth than a knowledge of their earthly authorship. In the final analysis they are the Lord's teachings; they were written by the power of the Holy Ghost; and they are superlative.

Paul is at his theological best in Hebrews. There are other epistles, notably Romans, in which he expounds more excellently the doctrine of the atoning sacrifice and the salvation which comes by God's grace. There are other places as in First Corinthians, where the gifts of the Spirit and the wonders of the resurrection are more extensively taught; and there are other writings, as Ephesians, where church organization and the world wide nature of the message of salvation are more explicitly delineated. But in Hebrews, as an inspired theologian, Paul takes the revelations of the past, the dead letter of the ancient law, and ties it into the living Christianity of the present. He shows how the gospel grew out of the preparatory law which prevailed in Israel and which in fact had as its purpose the preparing of the way before the coming of that Prophet who led Israel of old and was the Author of both covenants.

Above all, this Epistle — as seems natural when addressed to a people who had looked forward to the delivering might of their Messiah; a people who had great difficulty in accepting Jesus as their promised Redeemer — above all, this Epistle is a witness of the divine Sonship of Him of whom the Jews had said: "Is not this the carpenter's son?" (Matt. 13:55.)

And so we find Paul teaching that the Great God, the Almighty Elohim, has a body of flesh and bones, and that his Son, the Lord Jehovah, was in very deed born among men as the Son of God.

We find him teaching that Christ, who was born in Bethlehem, was the same personage who appeared as the Lord Jehovah on Sinai.

In Hebrews we learn that Jesus was made a little lower than Elohim; that he has precedence over the angels; that he took upon himself mortality to bring salvation to man.

In Hebrews our understanding is refreshed with the knowledge that salvation is available through his intercession; that he sacrificed himself for the sins of the world; that by his blood the saints are sanctified.

In it we are taught that the Mosaic ordinances prefigured his ministry; that his gospel was offered to ancient Israel; that he is the Mediator of the new covenant.

There is no other Biblical source for detailed knowledge of the Holy Priesthood; of Christ's status as the great High Priest and the Apostle of our profession; of the oath which God swore that his Son would be a priest forever after the order of Melchizedek.

And nowhere else in the Bible do we find the oath and covenant of the priesthood set forth; or that through this priesthood the gospel is administered; or that it is the power whereby eternal life is gained.

And what of the heroes of faith! From Abel to Samuel they are named — all of them men whose mighty works were wrought by faith in that same being, the Lord Jehovah, whose power enabled Peter to say to the man, lame from his mother's womb, "In the name of Jesus Christ of Nazareth rise up and walk." (Acts 3:6.)

And so this Epistle stands — giving doctrine and glory and knowledge; adding immeasurably to the understanding of the faithful. Interestingly, it did not find immediate and universal acceptance as a canonized work. "Rome, in the person of Clement of Rome, originally received this Epistle. Then followed a period in which it ceased to be received by the Roman churches. Then, in the fourth century, Rome retracted her error . . . As far as Rome is concerned, the Epistle to the Hebrews was not only lost for three centuries, but never would have been recovered at all but for the Eastern churches." (*Jamieson*, p. 440.)

Think of the gospel knowledge that would not be available in the Christian world, if we did not have the Epistle of Paul the apostle to his Hebrew brethren! Truly the Lord has preserved this priceless treasure for our blessing and benefit!

GOD HAS A BODY OF FLESH AND BONES

HEBREWS 1:1-4.

1 God, who at sundry times and in divers manners spake in time past unto the fathers by the prophets,

2 Hath in these last days spoken unto us by *his* Son, whom he hath appointed heir of all things, by whom also he made the worlds;

3 Who being the brightness of *his* glory, and the express image of his person, and upholding all things by the word of his power, when he had by himself purged our sins, sat down on the right hand of the Majesty on high;

4 Being made so much better than the angels, as he hath by inheritance obtained a more excellent name than they.

Seldom, in words as few, and with logic as persuasive, does Holy Writ set forth so clearly the nature and kind of Being that God is. As all the meridian saints knew, the Lord Jesus rose from the dead with a body of flesh and bones. "Handle me, and see," he said to his affrighted disciples after his resurrection, "for a spirit hath not flesh and bones, as ye see me have." (Luke 24:39.) To show the material nature of his resurrected body, he ate and drank with them, as a resurrected Man, and they felt the nail marks in his hands and feet and thrust their hands into his wounded side. (Luke 24:36-43; John 20:24-29; Acts 10:39-41.)

Now Paul is saying that the resurrected Christ is in the express image of his Father's person, which is to say that the Father also has a body of flesh and bones; or, as latter-day revelation — equally blunt, equally succinct, equally plain — says simply: "The Father has a body of flesh and bones as tangible as man's; the Son also; but the Holy Ghost has not a body of flesh and bones, but is a personage of Spirit." (D. & C. 130:22.) See *Commentary II*, pp. 154-162.

1. God . . . 2. His Son] Two personages of tabernacle, and a third personage of Spirit, constitute the Eternal Godhead. God the Eternal Father is here separated from his Son as a personage, an entity, a holy and exalted man. Indeed, "in the langauge of Adam, Man of Holiness is his name, and the name of his Only Begotten is the Son of Man, even Jesus Christ, a righteous Judge, who shall come in the meridian of time." (Moses 6:57.)

1. At sundry times] 'At various times.' God does not reveal himself at all times to all peoples in the literal sense of the word. He is or should be known to all people in all ages through the workmanship of his hands, but the actual revelation of himself and his laws is reserved for those who live by faith and seek him with all their hearts.

In divers manners] How does God reveal himself? Though the ways may be infinite, the perfect and crowning way is by direct revelation, by visions, by personal visitations. According to the laws of mediation and intercession which the Father himself ordained, he has chosen to reveal himself through the Son, ordaining that all revelation shall come through the Son, though that holy personage frequently speaks in the Father's name by divine investiture of authority; that is, he speaks in the first person as though he were the Father, because the Father has placed his name upon the Son. The sole reason for the personal appearance of the Father is to introduce the Son, as is illustrated by the appearance of the Father and the Son at the commencement of this dispensation. (Jos. Smith 2:12-20.) And hence the Biblical statement: "No man hath seen God at any time, except he hath borne record of the Son." (*Inspired Version*, John 1:19.) Christ the Son is, of course, the God of Israel through whom the will of the Father was manifest to that chosen people.

2. Spoken unto us by his Son] The perfect revelation of God came in the meridian of time. Whereas in previous ages he had been known by revelation to the holy prophets, in time's meridian he sent his Son into the world so that all men, seeing the Son, could envision perfectly who and what the Father is. The four Gospels contain the most comprehensive revelation of God the Father of any scriptures because they show forth what kind of a being the Son is, and men knowing the Son thereby know the Father. Our Lord said: "He that hath seen me hath seen the Father" (John 14:9), for God was in Christ revealing himself to the world.

Heir of all things] As his Son, Christ is the natural heir of the Father. "All things that the Father hath are mine," he said. (John 16:15.) In similar vein, those who through faith are adopted into the Family of God the Father become "joint-heirs with Christ" (Rom. 8:17), and receive our Lord's promise, "all that my Father hath shall be given" unto them. (D. & C. 84:38.)

By whom also he made the worlds] Christ, under the Father, is the Creator of all things. The word of the Father, spoken to Moses by the Son in accordance with the principle of divine investiture of authority, states: "Worlds without number have I created; and I also created them for mine own purpose; and by the Son I created them, which is mine Only Begotten." (Moses 1: 33.)

3. The brightness of his glory . . . his power] In pre-existence Christ was "like unto God" (Abra. 3:24), thus possessing the power and glory of the Father. While yet dwelling in his pre-mortal sphere, he was "the Lord Omnipotent who reigneth, who was, and is from all eternity to all eternity." (Mosiah 3:5.) And now, raised in glorious immortality, he has attained the state for which he prayed in the great Intercessory Prayer: "O Father, glorify thou me with thine own self with the glory which I had with thee before the world was" (John 17:5), thus being able to affirm anew, "All power is given unto me in heaven and in earth." (Matt. 28:18.)

The express image of his person] What more need be said? God the Eternal Father is the Father; the Son of God is the Son. A father is a father, and a son is a son. The Father begets; the Son is begotten; they are Parent and Child; Sire and Son look alike, so much so that they are the express image of each other's persons. The substance composing the body of one is identical in appearance to that composing the body of the other. What could be plainer?

Purged our sins] Through his atoning sacrifice, coupled with repentance and baptism on our part. That is to say: "The Almighty God gave his Only Begotten Son, as it is written in those scriptures which have been given of him. He suffered temptations but gave no heed unto them. He was crucified, died, and rose again the third day; And ascended into heaven, to sit down on the right hand of the Father, to reign with almightly power according to the will of the Father; That as many as would believe and be baptized in his holy name, and endure in faith to the end, should be saved." (D. & C. 20:21-25.)

Sat down on the right hand of the Majesty on high] Stephen, "being full of the Holy Ghost, looked up stedfastly into heaven, and saw the glory of God, and Jesus standing on the right hand of God, And said, Behold, I see the heavens opened, and the Son of man standing on the right hand of God." (Acts 7:55-56.) Joseph Smith said: "I saw two Personages, whose brightness and glory defy all description, standing above me in the air. One of them spake unto me, calling me by name and said, pointing to the other — This is My Beloved Son. Hear Him!" (Jos. Smith 2:17.)

4. The angels] Other members of the family of God the Father who have a lower status and a lesser rank than Christ. They include the spirits in pre-existence, translated beings, and resurrected personages. See *Commentary II*, pp. 96-98.

CHRIST IS GOD; ANGELS ARE MINISTERING SPIRITS

HEBREWS 1:5-14.

5 For unto which of the angels said he at any time, Thou art my Son, this day have I begotten thee? And again, I will be to him a Father, and he shall be to me a Son?

6 And again, when he bringeth in the first begotten into the world, he saith, And let all the angels of God worship him.

7 And of the angels he saith, Who maketh his angels spirits, and his ministers a flame of fire.

8 But unto the Son *he saith*, Thy throne, O God, *is* for ever and ever: a sceptre of righteousness *is* the sceptre of thy kingdom.

9 Thou hast loved righteousness, and hated iniquity; therefore God, *even* thy God, hath anointed thee with the oil of gladness above thy fellows.

10 And, Thou, Lord, in the beginning hast laid the foundation of the earth; and the heavens are the works of thine hands:

11 They shall perish; but thou remainest; and they all shall wax old as doth a garment;

12 And as a vesture shalt thou fold them up, and they shall be changed: but thou art the same, and thy years shall not fail.

13 But to which of the angels said he at any time, Sit on my right hand, until I make thine enemies thy footstool?

14 Are they not all ministering spirits, sent forth to minister for them who shall be heirs of salvation?

I.V. HEBREWS 1:6-7.

6 And again, when he bringeth in the first-begotten into the world, he saith, And let all the angels of God worship him, **who maketh his ministers as a flame of fire.**

7 And of the angels he saith, **Angels are ministering spirits.**

To gain the full impact of Paul's inspired reasoning about Christ and angels, scriptural exegetes must first know, as did those Hebrew Saints to whom the words were originally addressed, that:

1. There is an eternal and infinite family in heaven and on earth to whom all beings of every rank, status, and position belong.

2. God the Eternal Father, the Almighty Elohim, is the Parent and Father of all.

3. Christ is the Firstborn spirit Son in the eternal family, and while yet in pre-existence he advanced and progressed and became like the Father in power and intelligence; that is, he became a God.

4. As contrasted with the power, glory, and dominion of Christ, all the other spirit children in the eternal family are or were angels of God, most of whom obeyed the Father and served Christ, but one-third of whom rebelled, followed Lucifer, and were cast down to earth without tangible bodies, to remain forever as angels of the Devil.

5. Mortal men, though spirit children of God, are temporarily housed in tabernacles of clay; and Christ our Lord, dwelling in mortality, was the Only Begotten in the flesh; that is, he was the only spirit offspring of the Father who was born into mortality with God as his earthly Father.

6. Translated and resurrected beings continue to serve as angels, pending that day when some of them will "be crowned with the glory of his might, and . . . be made equal with" Christ. (D. & C. 88:107.)

7. Angels serve the Father and the Son and minister on their errand, whether such angels are spirit beings, as Gabriel who came to Zacharias (Luke 1:11-20); or translated beings, as Moses and Elijah who appeared on the Mount of Transfiguration (Matt. 17:1-7); or resurrected beings, as Moroni who ministered to Joseph Smith. (Jos. Smith 2:20-50.)

Angels] See *Commentary II*, pp. 96-98.

5. Thou art my Son, this day have I begotten thee] Quoted from Psalm 2:7, meaning: 'Thou art my Son: my Firstborn in the spirit, my Only Begotten in the flesh.'

Begotten] Begotten means begotten; it means Christ's mortal body was procreated by an Eternal Sire; it means God is the Father of Christ, "after the manner of the flesh." (1 Ne. 11:18.)

I will be to him a Father, and he shall be to me a Son] These words, first given as the Lord's promise to bless Solomon in building a temple, were in fact a Messianic prophecy concerning Him whose "throne shall be established for ever." (2 Sam. 7:12-16.)

6. And let all the angels of God worship him] Quoted from Deut. 32:43 of the Septuagint, and not found in the King James Version of the Bible, the nearest equivalent being, "Worship him, all ye gods." (Psalm 97:7.)

7. This quotation is from Psalm 104:4, which whole Psalm recites that the Lord God, who is Christ, is "very great," and gives as one of the proofs his dominion over and the power he gives to his angels.

8-9. These majestic words are quoted from Psalm 45:6-7 where the Messianic prophecy also describes our Lord as "fairer than the children of men" (verse 2), and then gives inspired intimations of his family relationship.

10-12. Recorded in Psalm 102:25-26 relative to the Lord, thus showing (as do the quotations of this type) that the Lord of the Old Testament is the Christ of the New Testament.

13. Recorded in Psalm 110:1, with the introductory phrase, "The Lord said unto my Lord," thus showing (as do other quotations of this type) that the Old Testament prophets understood there were two Lords, who were the Father and the Son.

14. Ministering spirits] That this term embraces all angelic ministrants, whether spirit beings or resurrected personages, is seen from the fact that the inhabitants of the telestial kingdom shall be ministered to by those from the terrestial kingdom, by "angels who are appointed to minister for them, or who are appointed to be ministering spirits for them; for they shall be heirs of salvation." (D. & C. 76:87-88.)

JESUS MADE A LITTLE LOWER THAN ELOHIM

HEBREWS 2:1-9.

1 Therefore we ought to give the more earnest heed to the things which we have heard, lest at any time we should let *them* slip.

2 For if the word spoken by angels was stedfast, and every transgression and disobedience received a just recompence of reward;

3 How shall we escape, if we neglect so great salvation; which at the first began to be spoken by the Lord, and was confirmed unto us by them that heard *him;*

4 God also bearing *them* witness, both with signs and wonders, and with divers miracles, and gifts of the Holy Ghost, according to his own will?

5 For unto the angels hath he not put in subjection the world to come, whereof we speak.

6 But one in a certain place testified, saying, What is man, that thou art mindful of him? or the son of man, that thou visitest him?

7 Thou madest him a little lower than the angels; thou crownedst him with glory and honour, and didst set him over the works of thy hands:

8 Thou hast put all things in subjection under his feet. For in that he put all in subjection under him, he left nothing *that is* not put under him. But now we see not yet all things put under him.

9 But we see Jesus, who was made a little lower than the angels for the suffering of death, crowned with glory and honour; that he by the grace of God should taste death for every man.

1-4. The argument here is: 'The law was given anciently "by the disposition of angels" (Acts 7:53), and Moses "was ordained by the hand of angels to be a mediator of this first covenant, (the law)." (*Inspired Version*, Gal. 3:19.)

'But the gospel came in the meridian of time from the Lord himself who ordained apostles to bear witness of his name, and their witness has been confirmed with signs and miracles.

'Now, if our fathers were condemned for transgressing and disobeying the law which came from angels through Moses, how much greater shall be our condemnation if we fail to live that gospel which came from the Lord himself through apostles and prophets.'

5. Angels hold positions of power and authority in the world to come. Thus, those who gain eternal life, must "pass by the angels, and the gods, which are set there," if they are to gain "their exaltation and glory." (D. & C. 132:19.)

6-8. The marginal reading of this quotation from Psalm 8:4-6 recites that man is made, not a little lower than the angels, but a little lower than Elohim, which means that all God's offspring, Jesus included, as children in his family, are created subject to him, with the power to advance until all things are "in subjection" to them. Of those who gain eternal life, it is written: "Then shall they be above all, because all things are subject unto them. Then shall they be gods, because they have all power, and the angels are subject unto them." (D. & C. 132:20.)

9. The only sense in which either men or Jesus are lower than the angels is in that mortal restrictions limit them for the moment; and for that matter, angels themselves become mortals and then in the resurrection attain again their angelic status.

CHRIST BECAME MORTAL TO SAVE MAN

HEBREWS 2:10-18.

10 For it became him, for whom *are* all things, and by whom *are* all things, in bringing many sons unto glory, to make the captain of their salvation perfect through sufferings.

11 For both he that sanctifieth and they who are sanctified *are* all of one: for which cause he is not ashamed to call them brethren.

12 Saying, I will declare thy name unto my brethren, in the midst of the church will I sing praise unto thee.

13 And again, I will put my trust in him. And again, Behold I and the children which God hath given me.

14 Forasmuch then as the children are partakers of flesh and blood, he also himself likewise took part of the same; that through death he might destroy him that had the power of death, that is, the devil;

15 And deliver them who through fear of death were all their lifetime subject to bondage.

16 For verily he took not on *him the nature of* angels; but he took on *him* the seed of Abraham.

17 Wherefore in all things it behoved him to be made like unto *his* brethren, that he might be a merciful and faithful high priest in things *pertaining* to God, to make reconciliation for the sins of the people.

18 For in that he himself hath suffered being tempted, he is able to succour them that are tempted.

I.V. HEBREWS 2:16.

16 For verily, he took not on him the **likeness** of angels; but he took on him the seed of Abraham.

10. Him, for whom are all things] The Father.

Many sons] The sons of God who, as such, are joint-heirs with Christ. See *Commentary II*, pp. 261-262.

Captain of their salvation] Christ who, as the Captain or Leader, both engages himself in the warfare whereby the saving victory is won and also leads others to the same triumph.

Perfect through suffering] See Heb. 5:4-14.

11. He that sanctifieth] Christ, through the shedding of whose blood men may be sanctified. "For by the water ye keep the commandment; by the Spirit ye are justified, and by the blood ye are sanctified." (Moses 6:60.)

They who are sanctified] Faithful members of the Church. See 1 Thess. 4:1-8; Heb. 10:1-18.

Are all of one] 'Are all the spirit children of God the Eternal Father.'

Pre-existence] See Heb. 12:9-10.

Brethren] Christ is our Elder Brother; all men are brothers and sisters in the spirit; all have the same Eternal Father.

12. As found in our Bible, the Messianic prophecy here quoted, reads: "I will declare thy name unto my brethren: in the midst of the congregation will I praise thee." (Psalm 22:22.) Interestingly, the Old Testament expression, "congregation," is quoted by Paul as, "church," thus indicating that he knew, as the Book of Mormon also testifies, that there was an organized Church in Old Testament times. (1 Ne. 4:24-27.)

13. I will put my trust in him] This is a paraphrase of a part of a great declaration by David about the Lord Jehovah, the use of which here equates Jehovah and Christ as one and the same. "The Lord is my rock, and my fortress, and my deliverer; The God of my rock; in him will I trust; he is my shield, and the horn of my salvation, my high tower, and my refuge, my saviour; thou savest me from violence. I will call on the Lord, who is worthy to be praised: so shall I be saved from mine enemies." (2 Sam. 22:2-4.)

I and the children which God hath given me] Quoted from Isaiah 8:18, to show that when God gives children to men on earth, he is simply sending to them his own spirit offspring.

14-18. 'The spirit children of the Father leave pre-existence and come to earth to take bodies of flesh and blood; Christ also became mortal that through his death he might ransom his brethren from the bondage of death. He came not as an angelic ministrant, but was born in the lineage of Abraham, that in all things he might be like his brethren. Thus he knew by personal experience the temptations of mortality and could guide his brethren more perfectly in reconciling their lives to God.'

Christ came into the world to die, and through his atoning death to ransom men from effects of Adam's fall. Had he come as an angel or as an immortal personage he could not have performed his mission. Our Lord's atoning sacrifice was possible, not alone because God as his Father bequeathed to him the power of immortality, but also because Mary as his mother bequeathed to him the power of mortality. As a mortal he could die; and having the power of immortality he could rise from the dead. His own death was an essential part of his mission.

Plan of salvation] See *Commentary II,* pp. 40-42. **Reconciliation]** See *Commentary II,* pp. 421-423.

CHRIST IS THE GREAT HIGH PRIEST AND APOSTLE

HEBREWS 3:1-6.

1 Wherefore, holy brethren, partakers of the heavenly calling, consider the Apostle and High Priest of our profession, Christ Jesus;

2 Who was faithful to him that appointed him, as also Moses *was faithful* in all his house.

3 For this *man* was counted worthy of more glory than Moses, inasmuch as he who hath builded the house hath more honour than the house.

4 For every house is builded by some *man;* but he that built all things *is* God.

5 And Moses verily *was* faithful in all his house, as a servant, for a testimony of those things which were to be spoken after;

6 But Christ as a son over his own house; whose house are we, if we hold fast the confidence and the rejoicing of the hope firm unto the end.

1. Wherefore . . . consider] In the light of all that is said in the first two chapters of Hebrews — that Christ is the Son; that he is pre-eminent over the angels; that he became mortal to work out the infinite and eternal atonement; and that through him man is reconciled to God — let us now consider him and his doctrine.

Holy brethren] Faithful members of the Church who, as the subsequent presentations show, held the Melchizedek Priesthood.

The heavenly calling] The Melchizedek Priesthood, which is the "calling" from God through which eternal life is gained. (D. & C. 84:33-41.)

The Apostle] Christ, who was and is his own chief witness, who testifies plainly to the faithful of all ages: "I am the Son of God."

High Priest] "Christ is the Great High Priest; Adam next." (*Teachings*, p. 158.) That is, Christ is the chief minister of salvation for men on earth, in that through his atoning sacrifice salvation itself comes. See Heb. 5:4-14.

Our profession] 'Our faith; our gospel; our priesthood.'

2-6. As the Hebrew Saints knew, the Lord's house anciently was his people, his congregation, his saints, concerning which he said: "My servant Moses . . . is faithful in all mine house." (Num. 12:7.) Now Paul is saying that the Meridian Saints are the Lord's house, among whom is Christ the Lord who excels even Moses in glory and greatness. Moses was the servant in the house for his day and age, but Christ is the Son who made the house and whose it is.

"NOW IS THE TIME AND THE DAY OF YOUR SALVATION"

HEBREWS 3:7-19.

7 Wherefore (as the Holy Ghost saith, To day if ye will hear his voice,

8 Harden not your hearts, as in the provocation, in the day of temptation in the wilderness:

9 When your fathers tempted me, proved me, and saw my works forty years.

10 Wherefore I was grieved with that generation, and said, They do alway err in *their* heart; and they have not known my ways.

11 So I sware in my wrath, They shall not enter into my rest.)

12 Take heed, brethren, lest there be in any of you an evil heart of unbelief, in departing from the living God.

13 But exhort one another daily, while it is called To day;

lest any of you be hardened through the deceitfulness of sin.

14 For we are made partakers of Christ, if we hold the beginning of our confidence stedfast unto the end;

15 While it is said, To day if ye will hear his voice, harden not your hearts, as in the provocation.

16 For some, when they had heard, did provoke: howbeit not all that came out of Egypt by Moses.

17 But with whom was he grieved forty years? *was it* not with them that had sinned, whose carcases fell in the wilderness?

18 And to whom sware he that they should not enter into his rest, but to them that believed not?

19 So we see that they could not enter in because of unbelief.

7-11. Quoted from Psalm 95:7-11, these verses testify that when the Lord offers his saving truths to a people, such is the day and time of their salvation, the day and time when they can do the things necessary to assure themselves of a celestial inheritance. If they reject the proffered saving truths, as did ancient Israel, they fall short of the glory and reward which otherwise would have been theirs. **No Second Chance for Salvation]** See *Commentary II*, pp. 423-424.

7. As the Holy Ghost saith] The Holy Ghost revealed the Psalms to their various authors. God's word is given by the Holy Ghost, and the very passage here quoted, though originally revealed by the Holy Ghost to David, is spoken in the first person as the voice of the Lord. Similarly, the scripture says of one of the great spiritual experiences of the first man: "And in that day the Holy Ghost fell upon Adam, which beareth record of the Father and the Son, saying: I am the Only Begotten of the Father from the beginning, henceforth and forever." (Moses 5:9.)

11. I sware in my wrath] See Heb. 4:1-2.

12. An evil heart of unbelief] For the saints to fail to believe the truths offered to them is sin.

13. Exhort one another daily] All people need encouragement to righteousness every day.

While it is called To day] The period during which the gospel is offered to a people. In our day the Lord says: "Now it is called today until the coming of the Son of Man." (D. & C. 64:23.)

14. Partakers of Christ] Partakers of the full gospel blessings on a par with our Lord, thus having "the mind of Christ" (1 Cor. 2:16), and being "joint-heirs" with him (Rom. 8:17), and finally being "made equal with him." (D. & C. 88:107.)

16-19. Ancient Israel failed to enter into the rest of the Lord because of unbelief. See Heb. 4:1-2.

GOSPEL OFFERED TO ANCIENT ISRAEL

HEBREWS 4:1-2.

1 Let us therefore fear, lest, a promise being left *us* of entering into his rest, any of you should seem to come short of it.

2 For unto us was the gospel preached, as well as unto them: but the word preached did not profit them, not being mixed with faith in them that heard *it*.

I.V. HEBREWS 4:2.

2 For unto us was the **rest** preached, as well as unto them; but the word preached did not profit them, not being mixed with faith in them that heard it.

God gave the fulness of the gospel to Israel, but they rejected this perfect law of liberty and progression and were left with the preparatory gospel only. Moses in righteous anger at the false worship of Israel broke the first "tables of testimony" which were "written with the finger of God." (Ex. 31:18; 32:19.) Thereafter, "the Lord said unto Moses, Hew thee two other tablets of stone, like unto the first, and I will write upon them also, the words of the law, according as they were written at the first on the tables which thou brakest; but it shall not be according to the first, for I will take away the priesthood out of their midst; therefore my holy order, and the ordinances thereof, shall not go before them; for my presence shall not go up in their midst, lest I destroy them. But I will give unto them the law as at the first, but it shall be after the law of a carnal commandment; for I have sworn in my wrath, that they shall not enter into my presence, into my rest, in the days of their pilgrimage." (*Inspired Version*, Ex. 34:1-2.)

From latter-day revelation we learn that Moses taught Israel "plainly" the things they must do to sanctify themselves, to gain the full blessings of the gospel, and to see the face of God. "But they hardened their hearts and could not endure his presence; therefore, the Lord in his wrath, for his anger was kindled against them, swore that they should not enter into his rest while in the wilderness, which rest is the fulness of his glory. Therefore, he took Moses out their midst, and the Holy Priesthood also; And the lesser priesthood continued, which priesthood holdeth the key of the ministering of angels and the preparatory gospel; Which gospel is the gospel of repentance and of baptism, and the remission of sins, and law of carnal commandments, which the Lord in his wrath caused to continue with the house of Aaron among the children of Israel until John." (D. & C. 84:24-27.)

2. The gospel] See *Commentary II*, pp. 213-216. **Dispensations]** See *Commentary II*, pp. 491-493.

HOW TO ENTER INTO THE REST OF THE LORD

HEBREWS 4:3-11.

3 For we which have believed do enter into rest, as he said, As I have sworn in my wrath, if they shall enter into my rest: although the works were finished from the foundation of the world.

4 For he spake in a certain place of the seventh *day* on this wise, And God did rest the seventh day from all his works.

5 And in this *place* again, If they shall enter into my rest.

6 Seeing therefore it remaineth that some must enter therein, and they to whom it was first preached entered not in because of unbelief:

7 Again, he limiteth a certain day, saying in David, To day, after so long a time; as it is said, To day if ye will hear his voice, harden not your hearts.

8 For if Jesus had given them rest, then would he not afterward have spoken of another day.

9 There remaineth therefore a rest to the people of God.

10 For he that is entered into his rest, he also hath ceased from

his own works, as God *did* from his.

11 Let us labour therefore to enter into that rest, lest any man fall after the same example of unbelief.

I.V. HEBREWS 4:3, 5.

3 For we who have believed do enter into rest, as he said, As I have sworn in my wrath, **If they harden their hearts they shall not enter into my rest; also, I have sworn, If they will not harden their hearts,** they shall enter into my rest; although the works **of God** were **prepared,** or finished,) from the foundation of the world.

5 And in this place again, **If they harden not their hearts** they shall enter into my rest.

3. We which have believed do enter into rest] "True saints enter into the rest of the Lord while in this life, and by abiding in the truth, they continue in that blessed state until they rest with the Lord in heaven. (Moro. 7:3; D. & C. 84:17-25; Matt. 11:28-30; Heb. 3:7-19; 4:1-11.) The rest of the Lord, where mortals are concerned, is to gain a perfect knowledge of the divinity of the great latter-day work. 'It means entering into the knowledge and love of God, having faith in his purpose and in his plan, to such an extent that we know we are right, and that we are not hunting for something else; we are not disturbed by every wind of doctrine, or by the cunning and craftiness of men who lie in wait to deceive.' It is 'rest from the religious turmoil of the world; from the cry that is going forth, here and there — lo, here is Christ; lo, there is Christ.' (*Gospel Doctrine*, 5th ed., pp. 58, 125-126.) The rest of the Lord, in eternity, is to inherit eternal life, to gain the fulness of the Lord's glory. (D. & C. 84:24.)" (*Mormon Doctrine*, 2nd ed., p. 633.)

4, 10. The Sabbath Day is the sign and symbol of the rest of the Lord. Those who have entered into gospel rest keep the Sabbath Day holy as part of their righteous conduct and true worship. On that day they rest from their worldly labors, as God did from his creative enterprises, as a sign and testimony that they have entered into the rest of the Lord in this life, have testimonies of the gospel, and look forward to that rest of the Lord "which rest is the fulness of his glory" hereafter. (D. & C. 84:24.)

6-9. Israel was offered gospel rest, but they failed to gain it. Thereafter, through David, the Lord again promised that they as a people should yet obtain this rest which Moses and Joshua had not been able to give them. Now, finally, the promised day has come, with the restoration of the gospel by the Lord Jesus.

8. Jesus] Joshua.

11. Let us labour therefore to enter into that rest] Only the faithful members of the Church enter into the rest of the Lord. This rest is the companion of a pure testimony of the divinity of the Lord's work and carries with it the hope of eternal life in the world to come. To his obedient saints the Lord promises, "I will give you rest . . . Ye shall find rest unto your souls." (Matt. 11: 28-29.)

WORD OF GOD PIERCES THE SOUL OF MAN

HEBREWS 4:12-13.

12 For the word of God *is* quick, and powerful, and sharper than any twoedged sword, piercing even to the dividing asunder of soul and spirit, and of the joints and marrow, and *is* a discerner of the thoughts and intents of the heart.

13 Neither is there any creature that is not manifest in his sight: but all things *are* naked and opened unto the eyes of him with whom we have to do.

I.V. HEBREWS 4:12.

12 For the word of God is quick, and powerful, and sharper than any two-edged sword, piercing even to the dividing asunder of **body** and spirit, and of the joints and marrow, and is a discerner of the thoughts and intents of the heart.

The Holy Ghost is a personage of spirit, a spirit being, and when he speaks to the spirit within man, knowledge and truth are conveyed with absolute surety. These whisperings of the Spirit are called the still small voice as is shown by the experience of Elijah on Mount Horeb. When that Prophet sought instructions from the Lord, "behold, the Lord passed by, and a great and strong wind rent the mountains, and brake in pieces the rocks before the Lord; but the Lord was not in the wind: and after the wind an earthquake; but the Lord was not in the earthquake: And after the earthquake a fire; but the Lord was not in the fire: and after the fire a still small voice." (1 Kings 19:11-12.) Then by the whisperings of the Spirit Elijah learned what the Lord wanted him to do. That these spiritual impressions can sink into the heart with a power transcending anything earthly is shown from Joseph Smith's statement: "Thus saith the still small voice, which whispereth through and pierceth all things, and often times it maketh my bones to quake while it maketh manifest." (D. & C. 85:6.)

12. This same language is used by the Lord in latter-day revelation (D. & C. 11:2; 33:1.)

Discerner of the thoughts and intents of the heart] "There is none else save God that knowest thy thoughts and the intents of thy heart." (D. & C. 6:16.)

13. All things are naked and opened unto the eyes of him] In effect there is an all-seeing eye. God sees and knows all things.

"COME BOLDLY UNTO THE THRONE OF GRACE"

HEBREWS 4:14-16; 5:1-3.

14 Seeing then that we have a great high priest, that is passed into the heavens, Jesus the Son of God, let us hold fast *our* profession.

15 For we have not an high priest which cannot be touched with the feeling of our infirmities; but was in all points tempted like as *we are, yet* without sin.

16 Let us therefore come boldly unto the throne of grace, that we may obtain mercy, and find grace to help in time of need.

1 For every high priest taken from among men is ordained for men in things *pertaining* to God, that he may offer both gifts and sacrifices for sins:

2 Who can have compassion on the ignorant, and on them that are out of the way; for that he himself also is compassed with infirmity.

3 And by reason hereof he ought, as for the people, so also for himself, to offer for sins.

Why does Christ intercede for his erring brethren with such infinite compassion? Because he knows by experience the anguish and pain of mortal suffering and the severity of Lucifer's temptations; because he can put himself in the position of feeble man and then feel the infinite joy of the soul who overcomes the world and feels himself reconciled to Him who is perfect and Almighty.

14. Great high priest] See Heb. 3:1-6.

Our profession] See Heb. 3:1-6.

15. In all points tempted like as we are] Jesus worked out his own salvation, suffered pain of body, was tempted, and overcame the world, thereby learning by experience the temptations and agonies which are the common lot of all men.

Yet without sin] Our Lord was perfect; he kept the whole law, without deviation in any respect. Of all men he alone is the Sinless One.

16. All men should seek forgiveness with all their hearts, but only those who keep the commandments can obtain that self assurance which enables them to approach the throne of grace with boldness. **Forgiveness]** See *Commentary II*, pp. 410-413.

5:1. Sacrifices for sins] The priests in Israel offered sacrifices for the sins of the people. See Heb. 8:1-5; *Commentary I*, pp. 716-725.

3. Christ sacrificed himself for the sins of the people; sins are forgiven in and through his atoning sacrifice and in no other way.

EVEN CHRIST CALLED TO HOLY PRIESTHOOD

HEBREWS 5:4-14.

4 And no man taketh this honour unto himself, but he that is called of God, as *was* Aaron.

5 So also Christ glorified not himself to be made an high priest; but he that said unto him, Thou art my Son, to day have I begotten thee.

6 As he saith also in another *place*, Thou *art* a priest for ever after the order of Melchisedec.

7 Who in the days of his flesh, when he had offered up prayers and supplications with strong crying and tears unto him that was able to save him from death, and was heard in that he feared;

8 Though he were a Son, yet learned he obedience by the things which he suffered;

9 And being made perfect, he became the author of eternal salvation unto all them that obey him;

10 Called of God an high priest after the order of Melchisedec.

11 Of whom we have many things to say, and hard to be uttered, seeing ye are dull of hearing.

12 For when for the time ye ought to be teachers, ye have need that one teach you again which *be* the first principles of the oracles of God; and are become such as have need of milk, and not of strong meat.

13 For every one that useth milk *is* unskillful in the word of righteousness: for he is a babe.

14 But strong meat belongeth to them that are of full age, *even* those who by reason of use have their senses exercised to discern both good and evil.

4. When men are called of God they receive priesthood. To be ministers of the gospel, ambassadors of the Lord Jesus Christ, representatives of the Almighty, holders of divine authority, men must possess priesthood because priesthood is the power and authority of God delegated to men on earth to minister in all things for the salvation of men.

Men cannot ordain themselves, nor can they be ordained by other men unless those so acting possess the power of God and are authorized by Deity to confer that power upon others. Men cannot choose to be ministers and by virtue of that choice, without more, assume they have divine authority. Power from on high comes by the will of God and not of men. To his apostles Jesus said: "Ye have not chosen me, but I have chosen you, and ordained you." (John 15:16.) The choosing is done by the Lord, not by those who would like to serve; and the conferral of authority comes from the Lord under the hands of his legal administrators.

"We believe that a man must be called of God, by prophecy, and by the laying on of hands, by those who are in authority, to preach the Gospel and administer in the ordinances thereof." (Fifth Article of Faith.)

As was Aaron] "To Aaron goes the honor — as a perpetual memorial through all generations — of having his name used to identify the lesser, Levitical, or Aaronic Priesthood. (D. & C. 84:18-27; 107:1, 20.) As a possessor of the Melchizedek Priesthood, Aaron held a position of prominence and leadership among the elders. (Ex. 18:12; John Taylor, *Items on Priesthood*, p. 5.) Indeed, with Moses, Nadab, Abihu, and 70 of the elders of Israel, Aaron saw the God of Israel before the existence of the Aaronic order; and when 'Moses went up into the mount of God,' Aaron and Hur were left in a position of presidency over the other elders. (Ex. 24.) But when the law of carnal commandments was 'added' to the gospel 'because of transgressions,' then Aaron and his sons were chosen to bear that priesthood by which the lesser law was administered. (Gal. 3.) Aaron's position then became comparable to that of the Presiding Bishop of the Church. (John Taylor, *Items on Priesthood*, pp. 5-6.)

"Also before the institution of the Levitical Priesthood, Aaron was chosen by the Lord to act as a minister with and a spokesman for Moses, his younger brother. (Ex. 4; 5; 6; 7; 8; 9; 10; 11; 12; 16.) After the beginning of the Aaronic order, Aaron and his sons after him were anointed priests unto Israel. (Ex. 28; 29; 30; Num. 3; 4.)

"Aaron's call to the Levitical ministry stands as the perfect example of the choosing of legal administrators to do the Lord's work; ever since that day, the legality of priestly administration has been determined by whether the professing minister was 'called of God, as was Aaron' (Heb. 5:4; D. & C. 27:8; 132:59), that is, by revelation and ordination, and with the full approval of the body of the Lord's true worshipers." (*Mormon Doctrine*, 2nd ed., p. 9.)

5. Christ . . . made an high priest] "The priesthood is an everlasting principle, and existed with God from eternity, and will to eternity, without beginning of days or end of years." (*Teachings*, p. 157.) Christ and others held the priesthood in pre-existence.

Adam, the Prophet says, "obtained it in the creation, before the world was formed." (*Teachings*, p. 157.)

But as pertaining to his mortal ministry, Christ our Lord received the Melchizedek Priesthood here on earth, and was ordained to the office of a high priest therein, thus setting an example for others and being in all things the Prototype of salvation. With reference to the mortal receipt of that holy order which is his, and which he had afore used to create this and an infinite number of other worlds, and which he had in fact given to Melchizedek in the first instance, the Prophet says: "If a man gets a fulness of the priesthood of God he has to get it in the same way that Jesus Christ obtained it, and that was by keeping all the commandments and obeying all the ordinances of the house of the Lord." (*Teachings*, p. 308.)

6. See Heb. 7:18-22.

7-10. These verses make clear reference to Christ and his mortal ministry and are in complete harmony with other scriptures which bear on the same matters, as also with the sermons of the early brethren of this dispensation who quote them as applying to our Lord.

However, there is a footnote in the Inspired Version which says, "The 7th and 8th verses allude to Melchizedek, and not to Christ." Standing alone, and because it is only part of the picture, this footnote gives an erroneous impression. The fact is verses 7 and 8 apply to both Melchizedek and to Christ, because Melchizedek was a prototype of Christ and that prophet's ministry typified and foreshadowed that of our Lord in the same sense that the ministry of Moses did. (Deut. 18:15-19; Acts 3:22-23; 3 Ne. 30:23; Jos. Smith 2:40.) Thus, though the words of these verses, and particularly those in the 7th verse, had original application to Melchizedek, they apply with equal and perhaps even greater force to the life and ministry of him through whom all the promises made to Melchizedek were fulfilled. **Melchizedek a Prototype of Christ]** See Heb. 7:1-3.

7. Since Melchizedek was the one to whom Paul is later to refer (Heb. 11:33-34) as having "stopped the mouths of lions, and quenched the violence of fire" (*Inspired Version*, Gen. 14:26), it may well be that such were the occasions when that prophet sought the Lord to save him from death.

Prayers and supplications] In the case of Jesus, these words probably have particular reference to his prayers and agony in Gethsemane when he took upon himself the sins of the world.

To save him from death] As applied to Jesus, these words mean our Lord himself was saved from eternal death through the atonement, which salvation is also the common inheritance of all men.

8. Yet learned he obedience] To gain the eternal fulness destined for him, our Lord needed the experiences of mortality. He was thus subjected by his Father to the same learning processes which apply to all men, and accordingly we have the revealed record "that he received not of the fulness at the first, but received grace for grace; And he received not of the fulness at first, but continued from grace to grace, until he received a fulness." (D. & C. 93:12-13.)

9. Being made perfect] Christ always was perfect in that he obeyed the whole law of the Father at all times and was everlastingly the Sinless One. See Heb. 4:14-16; 5:1-3. But on the other hand he was made perfect, through the sufferings and experiences of mortality, in the sense that he thereby died and was resurrected in glorious immortality. In that perfected state, possessing at long last a body of flesh and bones, he then had the same eternal perfection possessed by his Father. Hence his pronouncement, after the resurrection, that all power was given him in heaven and in earth. (Matt. 28:18.)

The author of eternal salvation] God the Father is the author of the plan of salvation, meaning that he ordained the plan whereby his spirit children, Christ included, might have power to advance and progress and become like him. But Christ is the author in the sense that he adopted it and made it his own, in the sense that through his atoning sacrifice he caused its terms and conditions to have eternal efficacy.

10. See Heb. 7:18-22.

11-14. Christ's ministers should advance beyond the milk of the work and be qualified to teach deep and hard doctrine.

"LET US GO ON UNTO PERFECTION"

HEBREWS 6:1-3.

1 Therefore leaving the principles of the doctrine of Christ, let us go on unto perfection; not laying again the foundation of repentance from dead works, and of faith toward God,

2 Of the doctrine of baptisms, and of laying on of hands, and of resurrection of the dead, and of eternal judgment.

3 And this will we do, if God permit.

I.V. HEBREWS 6:1-3.

1 Therefore **not** leaving the principles of the doctrine of Christ, let us go on unto perfection; not laying again the foundation of repentance from dead works, and of faith toward God.

2 Of the doctrine of baptisms, of laying on of hands, and of **the** resurrection of the dead, and of eternal judgment.

3 And **we will go on unto perfection** if God permit.

1. The doctrine of Christ] The whole gospel plan, the whole system of salvation, the total arrangement whereby man can gain perfection and be like God is five things: 1. Faith in the Lord Jesus Christ; 2. Repentance; 3. Baptism; 4. Receiving the Holy Ghost; and 5. Enduring in righteousness and devotion to the end. After setting this forth in detail, with especial emphasis upon pressing forward in steadfastness and devotion after baptism, Nephi says: "And now, behold, this is the doctrine of Christ, and the only and true doctrine of the Father, and of the Son, and of the Holy Ghost." (2 Ne. 31:21.)

Let us go on unto perfection] The goals of the saints are, finite perfection here and now, and infinite perfection in the mansions on high. See *Commentary I*, pp. 231-232.

2. Baptisms] Of water and of the Spirit.

SONS OF PERDITION CRUCIFY CHRIST AFRESH

HEBREWS 6:4-9.

4 For *it is* impossible for those who were once enlightened, and have tasted of the heavenly gift, and were made partakers of the Holy Ghost,

5 And have tasted the good word of God, and the powers of the world to come,

6 If they shall fall away, to renew them again unto repentance; seeing they crucify to themselves the Son of God afresh, and put *him* to an open shame.

7 For the earth which drinketh in the rain that cometh oft upon it, and bringeth forth herbs meet for them by whom it is dressed, receiveth blessing from God:

8 But that which beareth thorns and briers *is* rejected, and *is* nigh unto cursing; whose end *is* to be burned.

9 But, beloved, we are persuaded better things of you, and things that accompany salvation, though we thus speak.

I.V. HEBREWS 6:4, 6-8.

4 For **he hath made it** impossible for those who were once enlightened, and have tasted of the heavenly gift, and were made partakers of the Holy Ghost,

6 If they shall fall away, to **be renewed** again unto repentance; seeing they crucify **unto** themselves the Son of God afresh, and put him to an open shame.

7 For **the day cometh that** the earth which drinketh in the rain that cometh oft upon it, and bringeth forth herbs meet for them **who dwelleth thereon,** by whom it is dressed, **who now** receiveth blessings from God, **shall be cleansed with fire.**

8 **For** that which beareth thorns and briers is rejected, and is nigh unto cursing; **therefore they who bring not forth good fruits, shall be cast into the fire; for their** end is to be burned.

4-5. Lucifer is Perdition and the one-third of the hosts of heaven who followed him are sons of perdition. "Those in this life who gain a perfect knowledge of the divinity of the gospel cause, a knowledge that comes only by revelation from the Holy Ghost, and who then link themselves with Lucifer and come out in open rebellion, also become sons of perdition. Their destiny, following their resurrection, is to be cast out with the devil and his angels, to inherit the same kingdom in a state where 'their worm dieth not, and the fire is not quenched.' (D. & C. 76:32-49; 29:27-30; Heb. 6:4-8; 2 Pet. 2:20-22; 2 Ne. 9:14-16; *Doctrines of Salvation*, vol. 1, pp. 47-49; vol. 2, pp. 218-225.)" (*Mormon Doctrine*, 2nd ed., p. 746.)

6. Sons of Perdition commit the unpardonable sin. "Commission of the unpardonable sin consists in crucifying unto oneself the Son of God afresh and putting him to open shame. (Heb. 6:4-8; D. & C. 76:34-35.) To commit this unpardonable crime a man must receive the gospel, gain from the Holy Ghost by revelation the absolute knowledge of the divinity of Christ, and then deny 'the new and everlasting covenant by which he was sanctified, calling it an unholy thing, and doing despite to the Spirit of grace.' (*Teachings*, p. 128.) He thereby commits murder by assenting unto the Lord's death, that is, having a perfect knowledge of the truth he comes out in open rebellion and places himself in a position wherein he would have crucified Christ knowing perfectly the while that he was the Son of God. Christ is thus crucified afresh and put to open shame. (D. & C. 132:27.)

" 'What must a man do to commit the unpardonable sin?' the Prophet asked. 'He must receive the Holy Ghost, have the heavens opened unto him, and know God, and then sin against him. After a man has sinned against the Holy Ghost, there is no repentance for him. He has got to say that the sun does not shine while he sees it; he has got to deny Jesus Christ when the heavens have been opened unto him, and to deny the plan of salvation with his eyes open to the truth of it; and from that time he begins to be an enemy. This is the case with many apostates of The Church of Jesus Christ of Latter-day Saints.

" 'When a man begins to be an enemy to this work he hunts me, he seeks to kill me, and never ceases to thirst for my blood. He gets the spirit of the devil — the same spirit that they had who crucified the Lord of Life — the same spirit that sins against the Holy Ghost. You cannot save such persons; you cannot bring them to repentance; they make open war, like the devil, and awful is the consequence.' (*Teachings*, p. 358.)" (*Mormon Doctrine*, 2nd ed., pp. 816-817.)

7-8. "Their torment is as a lake of fire and brimstone, whose flame ascendeth up forever and ever and has no end." (2 Ne. 9:16.)

GOD SWEARS FAITHFUL SHALL BE SAVED

HEBREWS 6:10-20.

10 For God *is* not unrighteous to forget your work and labour of love, which ye have showed toward his name, in that ye have ministered to the saints, and do minister.

11 And we desire that every one of you do show the same diligence to the full assurance of hope unto the end:

12 That ye be not slothful, but followers of them who through faith and patience inherit the promises.

13 For when God made promise to Abraham, because he could swear by no greater, he sware by himself,

14 Saying, Surely blessing I will bless thee, and multiplying I will multiply thee.

15 And so, after he had patiently endured, he obtained the promise.

16 For men verily swear by the greater: and an oath for confirmation *is* to them an end of all strife.

17 Wherein God, willing more abundantly to show unto the heirs of promise the immutability of his counsel, confirmed *it* by an oath:

18 That by two immutable things, in which *it was* impossible for God to lie, we might have a strong consolation, who have fled for refuge to lay hold upon the hope set before us:

19 Which *hope* we have as an anchor of the soul, both sure and stedfast, and which entereth into that within the veil;

20 Whither the forerunner is for us entered, *even* Jesus, made an high priest for ever after the order of Melchisedec.

I.V. HEBREWS 6:10.

10 For God is not unrighteous, **therefore he will not** forget your work and labor of love, which ye have showed toward his name, in that ye have ministered to the saints, and do minister.

10. God remembers and rewards the work of his ministers.

11-12. 'Endure to the end, as did the saints of old, and ye shall have eternal life.'

12. The promises] The repeated promise of eternal life which God gives to his saints — when they receive his everlasting covenant (D. & C. 132:6), in connection with their baptism (2 Ne. 31:11-21), through magnifying priesthood callings (D. & C. 84:31-41), as part of celestial marriage (D. & C. 132:19), as part of patriarchal blessings (D. & C. 124:91-93, 124), and when their calling and election is made sure. (D. & C. 131:5; 132:19.)

13. God made promise to Abraham] For all his seed, plus all who by obedience are adopted into his house, Abraham is the prototype of salvation. Abraham received the promise of eternal life and eternal increase. "This promise is yours also," the Lord says to all who obey the full gospel law, "because ye are of Abraham, and the promise was made unto Abraham; and by this law is the continuation of the works of my Father, wherein he glorifieth himself. Go ye, therefore, and do the works of Abraham; enter ye into my law and ye shall be saved." (D. & C. 132:31-32.)

13. He sware] 16. An oath for confirmation] "In ancient dispensations, particularly the Mosiac, the taking of oaths was an approved and formal part of the religious lives of the people. These oaths were solemn appeals to Deity, or to some sacred object or thing, in attestation of the truth of a statement or of a sworn determination to keep a promise. These statements, usually made in the name of the Lord, by people who valued their religion and their word above their lives, could be and were relied upon with absolute assurance. (Num. 30.)

"Oaths were common among the Nephites, prior to the ministry of the resurrected Lord among them. Nephi guaranteed the freedom of Zoram, for instance, by using in his oath the solemn language, 'as the Lord liveth, and as I live.' (1 Ne. 4:32-33; Alma 44.) Abraham took an oath of his servant to gain assurance that a proper wife would be selected for Isaac. (Gen. 24.) Joseph bound the children of Israel with an oath to carry his bones out of Egypt. (Gen. 50:24-26.)" (*Mormon Doctrine*, 2nd ed., pp. 537-538.)

He sware by himself] "By myself have I sworn, saith the Lord," was the language used by Deity in giving the promise of eternal life "unto Abraham." (Gen. 22:15-16.) That is, God swore with an oath in his own name that Abraham would be saved, which divine assertion absolutely guaranteed the eventuality. Abraham's calling and election was thus made sure.

14. The Lord's oath to Abraham was: "In blessing I will bless thee, and in multiplying I will multiply thy seed as the stars of the heaven, and as the sand which is upon the sea shore. . . . And in thy seed shall all the nations of the earth be blessed." (Gen. 22:17-18.) By way of interpretation, the Lord said to Joseph Smith: "Abraham received promises concerning his seed, and of the fruit of his loins — from whose loins ye are, namely, my servant Joseph — which were to continue so long as they were in the world; and as touching Abraham and his seed, out of the world they should continue; both in the world and out of the world should they continue as innumerable as the stars; or, if ye were to count the sand upon the seashore ye could not number them." (D. & C. 132:30.)

15. He obtained the promise] He gained eternal life. "Abraham . . . hath entered into his exaltation and sitteth upon his throne." (D. & C. 132:29.)

17. Heirs of promise] Abraham's seed, the house of Israel, the children of the prophets, those who are natural inheritors of the promises made to Abraham. (3 Ne. 20:25-26.) These heirs have the "right" to the priesthood. Speaking of this the Lord said to Abraham concerning his seed: "I give unto thee a promise that this right shall continue in thee, and in thy seed after thee (that is to say, the literal seed, or the seed of the body) shall all the families of the earth be blessed, even with the blessings of the Gospel, which are the blessings of salvation, even of life eternal." (Abra. 2:11.)

The immutability of his counsel] God never varies; under the same circumstances he always acts in the same way. Hence, his decree: "I, the Lord, am bound when ye do what I say; but when ye do not what I say, ye have no promise." (D. & C. 82:10.) And his promise is that if the saints will do the works of Abraham, they shall inherit the reward of Abraham.

18. By two immutable things] God swore a dual oath; that is, twice in the same promise he swore in his own name that Abraham and his seed should be blessed.

We might have a strong consolation] As heirs of promise, the saints find great comfort in the promises the Lord made to them through Abraham their father.

Fled for refuge] Fled from Babylon; forsook the world; joined the Church.

The hope set before us] Eternal life, the promise made to Abraham and his seed.

19-20. As the high priest in Israel passed through the veil into the holy of holies on the day of atonement, as part of the cleansing rites which freed Israel from sin (Lev. 16), so Jesus has entered into heaven to prepare the way for those who through obedience to his laws become clean and pure.

20. An high priest forever] See Heb. 7:18-22.

MELCHIZEDEK PRIESTHOOD BRINGS EXALTATION

HEBREWS 7:1-3.

1 For this Melchisedec, king of Salem, priest of the most high God, who met Abraham returning from the slaughter of the kings, and blessed him;

2 To whom also Abraham gave a tenth part of all; first being by interpretation King of righteousness, and after that also King of Salem, which is, King of peace;

3 Without father, without mother, without descent, having neither beginning of days, nor end of life; but made like unto the Son of God; abideth a priest continually.

I.V. HEBREWS 7:3.

3 **For this Melchisedec was ordained a priest after the order of the Son of God, which order was** without father, without mother,

without descent, having neither beginning of days, nor end of life. **And all those who are ordained unto this priesthood are** made like unto the Son of God, abiding a priest continually.

1-2. "To the man Melchizedek goes the honor of having his name used to identify the Holy Priesthood after the Order of the Son of God, thus enabling men 'to avoid the too frequent repetition' of the name of Deity. (D. & C. 107:2-4.) Of all God's ancient high priests 'none were greater.' (Alma 13:19.) His position in the priestly hierarchy of God's earthly kingdom was like unto that of Abraham (Heb. 7:4-10), his contemporary whom he blessed (Gen. 14:18-20; Heb. 7:1; *Inspired Version*, Gen. 14:17-40), and upon whom he conferred the priesthood. (D. & C. 84:14.)

"Indeed, so exalted and high was the position of Melchizedek in the eyes of the Lord and of his people that he stood as a prototype of the Son of God himself, the Son who was to arise 'after the similitude of Melchisedec.' (Heb. 7:15.) Both bore the titles, Prince of Peace and King of Heaven — meaning King of Peace (Alma 13:18; *Inspired Version*, Gen. 14:33, 36) — and both were joint-heirs of the Father's kingdom." (*Mormon Doctrine*, 2nd ed., pp. 474-475.)

"Now this Melchizedek was a king over the land of Salem; and his people had waxed strong in iniquity and abomination; yea, they had all gone astray; they were full of all manner of wickedness; But Melchizedek having exercised mighty faith, and received the office of the high priesthood according to the holy order of God, did preach repentance unto his people. And behold, they did repent; and Melchizedek did establish peace in the land in his days; therefore he was called the prince of peace, for he was the king of Salem; and he did reign under his father." (Alma 13:17-18.)

2. A tenth part of all] See Heb. 7:4-10.

I. V. 3. The order of the Son of God] The Melchizedek Priesthood, so named to avoid the too frequent repetition of the name of Deity. This priesthood is the power and authority of God whereby the worlds were made and by which this earth and all things incident thereto are governed. It is the supreme governing authority in the kingdom of God on earth in all ages and is designed and intended to prepare men for exaltation in the kingdom of God. (*Mormon Doctrine*, 2nd ed., pp. 475-483.)

"Every one being ordained after this order and calling should have power, by faith, to break mountains, to divide the seas, to dry up waters, to turn them out of their course; To put at defiance the armies of nations, to divide the earth, to break every band, to stand in the presence of God; to do all things according to his will, according to his command, subdue principalities and powers; and this by the will of the Son of God which was from before the foundation of the world." (*Inspired Version*, Gen. 14:30-31.)

3. Without father, without mother, without descent] "As compared to the Aaronic Priesthood, as administered in ancient Israel, the order of Melchizedek did not come 'by descent from father and mother.' (*Teachings*, p. 323.) That is, the right to this higher priesthood was not inherited in the same way as was the case with the Levites and sons of Aaron. Righteousness was an absolute requisite for the conferral of the higher priesthood. This 'order came, not by man, nor the will of man; neither by father nor mother; neither by beginning of days nor end of years; but of God; And it was delivered unto men by the calling of his own voice, according to his own will, unto as many as believed on his name.' (*Inspired Version*, Gen. 14:28-29; Heb. 7:1-3.)" (*Mormon Doctrine*, 2nd ed., p. 478.)

Like unto the Son of God] Christ is the perfect Prototype of salvation. As he was baptized to gain his inheritance in his own eternal kingdom (2 Ne. 31:5-11), so must men be born of water and of the Spirit to enter the kingdom of God. (John 3:5; 2 Ne. 31:12-21.) And as he received the Melchizedek Priesthood to prepare himself to inherit the fulness of the Father in glorious exaltation in that eternal world, so must all those who attain joint-heirship with him.

Abideth a priest continually] See Heb. 7:18-22.

BOTH GOSPEL AND MOSAIC LAW REQUIRE TITHES

HEBREWS 7:4-10.

4 Now consider how great this man *was*, unto whom even the patriarch Abraham gave the tenth of the spoils.

5 And verily they that are of the sons of Levi, who receive the office of the priesthood, have a commandment to take tithes of the people according to the law, that is, of their brethren, though they come out of the loins of Abraham:

6 But he whose descent is not counted from them received tithes of Abraham, and blessed him that had the promises.

7 And without all contradiction the less is blessed of the better.

8 And here men that die receive tithes; but there he *receiveth them*, of whom it is witnessed that he liveth.

9 And as I may so say, Levi also, who receiveth tithes, payed tithes in Abraham.

10 For he was yet in the loins of his father, when Melchisedec met him.

Melchizedek was the presiding authority of God on earth in the day of Abraham, and as such the great patriarch paid tithes to and was blessed by Melchizedek. This fact and apparently a good many other things involving Melchizedek, which are unknown to us, seem to have been well known to the Hebrew Saints. Hence, without amplifying his concepts, but simply by way of analogy and symbolism, Paul is able to set forth for his initial readers some historical allusions which will remind them everlastingly that Melchizedek's authority was superior to Aaron's. The argument used is far more meaningful to a people indoctrinated with the concept of a hereditary priesthood than it is for us today who think only of personal worthiness, without reference to lineage, where both Aaronic and Melchizedek authority are concerned.

4-7. "And he lifted up his voice, and he blessed Abram, being the high priest, and the keeper of the storehouse of God; Him whom God had appointed to receive tithes for the poor. Wherefore, Abram paid unto him tithes of all that he had, of all the riches which he possessed, which God had given him more than that which he had need. And it came to pass, that God blessed Abram, and gave unto him riches, and honor, and lands for an everlasting possession; according to the covenant which he had made and according to the blessing wherewith Melchisedek had blessed him." (*Inspired Version*, Gen. 14:37-40.)

5. **Tithes]** Whenever the Lord has had a people on earth, he has commanded them to keep the law of tithing, unless as in Enoch's day they were called upon to consecrate their all to the Lord's purposes. See *Commentary I*, pp. 618-619.

8. The Lord receives the tithes paid to the Church by the saints. It is as though the monies or properties were given to him personally, rather than to his agents, the bishops.

MELCHIZEDEK PRIESTHOOD ADMINISTERETH THE GOSPEL

HEBREWS 7:11-14.

11 If therefore perfection were by the Levitical priesthood, (for under it the people received the law,) what further need *was there* that another priest should rise after the order of Melchisedec, and not be called after the order of Aaron?

12 For the priesthood being changed, there is made of necessity a change also of the law.

13 For he of whom these things are spoken pertaineth to another tribe, of which no man gave attendance at the altar.

14 For *it is* evident that our Lord sprang out of Juda; of which tribe Moses spake nothing concerning priesthood.

11-12. "Without the Melchizedek Priesthood salvation in the kingdom of God would not be available for men on earth, for the ordinances of salvation — the laying on of hands for the gift of the Holy Ghost, for instance — could not be authoritatively performed. Thus, as far as all religious organizations now existing are concerned, the presence or the absence of this priesthood establishes the divinity or falsity of a professing church. It 'continueth in the church of God in all generations,' and it 'administereth the gospel and holdeth the key of the mysteries of the kingdom, even the key of the knowledge of God' (D. & C. 84:17-19), whom to know is eternal life. (John 17:3.) If there is no Melchizedek Priesthood on earth, the true Church is not here and the gospel of Christ is not available to men. But where the Melchizedek Priesthood is, there is the kingdom, the Church, and the fulness of the gospel." (*Mormon Doctrine*, 2nd ed., pp. 479-480.)

11. 'If a man could gain eternal life through the power of the Aaronic Priesthood, why did God promise to send the Melchizedek Pristehood?' To the Hebrew Saints this argument was absolute and conclusive; for them there could be no turning back to their old law.

Order of Melchisedec] The Melchizedek Priesthood. See Heb. 7:1-3.

Order of Aaron] The Aaronic Priesthood; the Levitical Priesthood. "And the Lord confirmed a priesthood also upon Aaron and his seed, throughout all their generations, which priesthood also continueth and abideth forever with the priesthood which is after the holiest order of God." (D. & C. 84:18.) See Heb. 5:4-14.

12. 'A change in priesthood changes the laws and ordinances.' The Aaronic Priesthood administered the law of carnal commandments or preparatory gospel; the Melchizedek Priesthood administers the fulness of the gospel. "All men are liars," the Prophet said, "who say they are of the true Church without the revelations of Jesus Christ and the Priesthood of Melchizedek, which is after the order of the Son of God." (*Teachings*, p. 375.)

Also: "If there is no change of ordinances, there is no change of priesthood. Wherever the ordinances of the gospel are administered, there is the priesthood." (*Teachings*, p. 158.) This matter of changing gospel ordinances is conclusive proof of the universal apostasy which necessitated the restoration of the gospel with the original ordinances. Since the ordinances of the sectarian world are different from those described in the Bible, Joseph Smith used this change to establish the fact of an apostasy in these words:

"Where there is no change of priesthood, there is no change of ordinances, Paul says. If God has not changed the ordinances and the priesthood, [then] howl, ye sectarians! If he has, when and where has he revealed it? Have ye turned revelators? Then why deny revelation?" (*Teachings*, p. 308).

MELCHIZEDEK PRIESTHOOD IS POWER OF AN ENDLESS LIFE

HEBREWS 7:15-17.

15 And it is yet far more evident: for that after the similitude of Melchisedec there ariseth another priest,

16 Who is made, not after the law of a carnal commandment, but after the power of an endless life.

17 For he testifieth, Thou *art* a priest for ever after the order of Melchisedec.

15. After the similitude of Melchisedec] Melchizedek was the prototype of Christ. See Heb. 7:1-3.

16. The power of an endless life] The Melchizedek Priesthood is the power by which men gain eternal life. Where this priesthood is, there men can work out their own salvation and gain a celestial fulness; and where this priesthood is not, there can be no full inheritance in the kingdom of God.

The Melchizedek Priesthood brings to pass the conferral of the gift of the Holy Ghost and the baptism of fire, without which none can enter the celestial kingdom. (Matt. 3:11; John 3:5; Acts 19:1-7.) By its power worthy persons are married for eternity, without which they cannot attain the highest heaven of the celestial world. (D. & C. 131:1-4.) Through this priesthood men become sons of God and joint-heirs with Christ, thus receiving, inheriting, and possessing all things. (D. & C. 76:50-70.) Indeed, the Prophet says that "the power of the Melchizedek Priesthood is to have the power of 'endless lives.' . . . That priesthood . . . stands as God to give laws to the people, administering endless lives to the sons and daughters of Adam." (*Teachings*, p. 322.) Endless lives consists of "a continuation of the seeds forever and ever," of a "continuation of the lives," of "eternal lives" (D. & C. 132:19-24), that is it consists of having spirit children in the resurrection and therefore of having exaltation.

17. See Heb. 7:18-22.

MELCHIZEDEK PRIESTHOOD GIVEN WITH OATH AND COVENANT

HEBREWS 7:18-22.

18 For there is verily a disannulling of the commandment going before for the weakness and unprofitableness thereof.

19 For the law made nothing perfect, but the bringing in of a better hope *did;* by the which we draw nigh unto God.

20 And inasmuch as not without an oath *he was made priest:*

21 (For those priests were made without an oath; but this with an oath by him that said unto him, The Lord sware and will not repent, Thou *art* a priest for ever after the order of Melchisedec:)

22 By so much was Jesus made a surety of a better testament.

I.V. HEBREWS 7:19-21.

19 For **the law was administered without an oath and** made nothing perfect, but **was only** the bringing in of a better hope; by the which we draw nigh unto God.

20 Inasmuch as **this high priest was not without an oath, by so much was Jesus made the surety of a better testament.**

21 (For those priests were made without an oath; but this with an oath by him that said unto him, The Lord sware and will not repent, Thou art a priest for ever after the order of Melchizedek;)

18. 'The law of carnal commandments is abolished because it did not have the power to enable men to gain eternal life.'

19. 'Perfection comes, not through the law, but through the gospel.'

20. 'Callings in the Aaronic Priesthood are conferred without an oath.'

21. God swore an oath that Christ should be a priest forever; that is, though our Lord had possessed the priesthood in pre-existence, he would receive it anew in mortality and would have it forever — in time and in eternity. And this sets the pattern for all who become sons of God and joint-heirs with Christ.

"Every person upon whom the Melchizedek Priesthood is conferred receives his office and calling in this higher priesthood with an oath and a covenant. The covenant is to this effect: 1. Man on his part solemnly agree to magnify his calling in the priesthood, to keep the commandments of God, to live by every word that proceedeth forth from the mouth of Deity, and to walk in paths of righteousness and virtue; and 2. God on his part agrees to give such persons an inheritance of exaltation and godhood in his everlasting presence. The oath is the solemn attestation of Deity, his sworn promise, that those who keep their part of the covenant shall come forth and inherit all things according to the promise." (*Mormon Doctrine*, 2nd ed., p. 480.)

In revealing the terms and conditions of the oath and covenant of the priesthood in this dispensation, the Lord said: "For whoso is faithful unto the obtaining these two priesthoods of which I have spoken, and the magnifying their calling, are sanctified by the Spirit unto the renewing of their bodies. They become the sons of Moses and of Aaron and the seed of Abraham, and the church and kingdom, and the elect of God. And also all they who receive this priesthood receive me, saith the Lord; For he that receiveth my servants receiveth me; And he that receiveth me receiveth my Father; And he that receiveth my Father receiveth my Father's kingdom; therefore all that my Father hath shall be given unto him. And this is according to the oath and covenant which belongeth to the priesthood. Therefore, all those who receive the priesthood, receive this oath and covenant of my Father, which he cannot break, neither can it be moved. But whoso breaketh this covenant after he hath received it, and altogether turneth therefrom, shall not have forgiveness of sins in this world nor in the word to come. And wo unto all those who come not unto this priesthood which ye have received, which I now confirm upon you who are present this day, by mine own voice out of the heavens; and even I have given the heavenly hosts and mine angels charge concerning you. And I now give unto you a commendment to beware concerning yourselves, to give diligent heed to the words of eternal life. For you shall live by every word that proceedeth forth from the mouth of God." (D. & C. 84:33-44.)

22. Testament] See Heb. 9:15-28.

SALVATION COMES THROUGH INTERCESSION OF CHRIST

HEBREWS 7:23-28.

23 And they truly were many priests, because they were not suffered to continue by reason of death:

24 But this *man*, because he continueth ever, hath an unchangeable priesthood.

25 Wherefore he is able also to save them to the uttermost that come unto God by him, seeing he ever liveth to make intercession for them.

26 For such an high priest became us, *who is* holy, harmless, undefiled, separate from sinners, and made higher than the heavens;

27 Who needeth not daily, as those high priests, to offer up sacrifice, first for his own sins, and then for the people's: for this he did once, when he offered up himself.

28 For the law maketh men high priests which have infirmity; but the word of the oath, which was since the law, *maketh* the Son, who is consecrated for evermore.

I.V. HEBREWS 7:25-26.

25 For such an high priest became us, who is holy, harmless, undefiled, separate from sinners, and made **ruler over** the heavens;

26 **And not as those high priests who offered up sacrifice daily,** first for **their** own sins, and then for the **sins of** the **people; for he needeth not offer sacrifice for his own sins, for he knew no sins; but for the sins of the people. And** this he did once, when he offered up himself.

The contrast — in their ministries of intercession — between the Levitical priests and the great high priest is striking.

They were many, he but one. They served during their mortal lives, he continues to plead in immortality.

They (as all men are) were sinners: unholy, carnal, defiled; he (and he only) was separate from sinners: holy, harmless, undefiled.

They offered daily sacrifices of animals for their own sins and for the sins of the people; he knew no sin, but offered himself once for the sins of the world.

They had infirmities, he was perfect. They served as priests, without an oath, under the law; theirs was the Aaronic Priesthood. But he brought the gospel, held the Melchizedek Priesthood, and took his supreme position to intercede forever for his brethren because God swore with an oath that he should be consecrated forevermore.

25. Save them to the uttermost] Give them exaltation in the highest heaven of the celestial world, where they also shall rule and reign as priests forever in his Father's kingdom.

Come unto God by him] "No man shall come unto the Father but by me or by my word, which is my law, saith the Lord." (D. & C. 132:12.)

Intercession] See *Commentary II*, pp. 269-271.

28. The word of the oath, which was since the law] The law, administered by the lesser priesthood, came through Moses; over 400 years later, through David, the Lord swore that his Son would have the higher priesthood, which administers the gospel and therefore supplants the law.

CHRIST OFFERED HIMSELF A SACRIFICE FOR SIN

HEBREWS 8:1-5.

1 Now of the things which we have spoken *this is* the sum: We have such an high priest, who is set on the right hand of the throne of the Majesty in the heavens;

2 A minister of the sanctuary, and of the true tabernacle, which the Lord pitched, and not man.

3 For every high priest is ordained to offer gifts and sacrifices: wherefore *it is* of necessity that this man have somewhat also to offer.

4. For if he were on earth, he should not be a priest, seeing that there are priests that offer gifts according to the law:

5 Who serve unto the example and shadow of heavenly things, as Moses was admonished of God when he was about to make the tabernacle: for, See, saith he, *that* thou make all things according to the pattern showed to thee in the mount.

I.V. HEBREWS 8:4.

4 **Therefore while he was on the earth, he offered for a sacrifice his own life for the sins of the people. Now every priest under the law, must needs offer gifts, or sacrifices,** according to the law.

Christ offered himself as a sacrifice for the sins of the world, thus fulfilling the law of sacrifice which had been in active operation for 4000 years. "Sacrifice was first instituted on earth as a gospel ordinance to be performed by the authority of the priesthood, to typify the coming sacrifice of the Son of God for the sins of the world. From the day of Adam to the death of Christ, sacrifice was practiced by the saints.

"The form of the ordinance was always so arranged as to point attention to our Lord's sacrifice. The sacrificial offering made in connection with the Passover, the killing of the Paschal Lamb, for instance, was so arranged that a male lamb of the first year, one without spot or blemish, was chosen; in the offering the blood was spilled and care was taken to break no bones — all symbolical of the manner of Christ's death. (Ex. 12.) Many sacrificial details were added to the law as it operated in the Mosaic dispensation, but the basic principles governing sacrifices are part of the gospel itself and preceded Moses and the lesser order which came through him." (*Mormon Doctrine*, 2nd ed., pp. 664-665.) See *Commentary I*, pp. 716-725.

Sacrifice] See *Commentary II*, pp. 537-540.

1. 'We have an high priest, through whom salvation comes, who is Christ the Son, who now sits on the right hand of the Father.'

2-5 Everything connected with the law — all its sacrifices, rites, ordinances, and performances — everything, without any exception, was so designed and so done as to bear record of Christ who was to come and of his atoning sacrifice. "All these things," Abinadi says, "were types of things to come." (Mosiah 13:31.)

GOD PROMISED TO MAKE A NEW COVENANT WITH ISRAEL

HEBREWS 8:6-13.

6 But now hath he obtained a more excellent ministry, by how much also he is the mediator of a better covenant, which was established upon better promises.

7 For if that first *covenant* had been faultless, then should no place have been sought for the second.

8 For finding fault with them, he saith, Behold, the days come, saith the Lord, when I will make a new covenant with the house of Israel and with the house of Judah:

9 Not according to the covenant that I made with their fathers in the day when I took them by the hand to lead them out of the land of Egypt; because they continued not in my covenant, and I regarded them not, saith thc Lord.

10 For this *is* the covenant that I will make with the house of Israel after those days, saith the Lord; I will put my laws into their mind, and write them in their hearts: and I will be to them a God, and they shall be to me a people:

11 And they shall not teach every man his neighbour, and every man his brother, saying, Know the Lord: for all shall know me, from the least to the greatest.

12 For I will be merciful to their unrighteousness, and their sins and their iniquities will I remember no more.

13 In that he saith, A new *covenant*, he hath made the first old. Now that which decayeth and waxeth old *is* ready to vanish away.

After Israel had been subject to the law for nearly 900 years, the Lord, through Jeremiah, promised to make a new and better covenant with them, a gospel covenant, a covenant which would bring them into his presence so that all might know him. In using this prophecy of Jeremiah to show that Christ brought the new gospel covenant, Paul is doing the same thing in principle as the Mormon Elders do in quoting Biblical passages about the restoration of the gospel in the latter-days.

6. The mediator] 7. The first covenant] See 1 Tim. 2:1-7.

6. Better covenant] 8. A new covenant] "God's covenant of salvation is the fulness of the gospel. (D. & C. 39:11; 45:9; 66:2; 133:57.) When men accept the gospel, they thereby agree or covenant to keep the commandments of God, and he promises or covenants to give them salvation in his kingdom.

"The gospel is the everlasting covenant because it is ordained by Him who is Everlasting and also because it is everlastingly the same. In all past ages salvation was gained by adherence to its terms and conditions, and that same compliance will bring the same reward in all future ages. Each time this everlasting covenant is revealed it is new to those of that dispensation. Hence the gospel is the new and everlasting covenant." (*Mormon Doctrine*, 2nd ed., pp. 529-530.)

8-12. Jeremiah's promised covenant was offered to Israel in Jesus' day, but found no enduring acceptance. It has been offered anew in this dispensation and is now beginning to be accepted, with the assurance that in due course, in the millennial era, complete fulfilment shall be brought to pass.

Speaking of this promise made through Jeremiah, the Prophet Joseph Smith said: "This covenant has never been established with the house of Israel, nor with the house of Judah, for it requires two parties to make a covenant, and those two parties must be agreed, or no covenant can be made.

"Christ, in the days of his flesh, proposed to make a covenant with them, but they rejected him and his proposals, and in consequence thereof, they were broken off, and no covenant was made with them at that time. But their unbelief has not rendered the promise of God of none effect: no, for there was another day limited in David, which was the day of his power; and then his people, Israel, should be a willing people; and he would write his law in their hearts, and print it in their thoughts; their sins and their iniquities he would remember no more.

"Thus after this chosen family had rejected Christ and his proposals, the heralds of salvation said to them, 'Lo we turn unto the Gentiles;' and the Gentiles received the covenant, and were grafted in from whence the chosen family were broken off: but the Gentiles have not continued in the goodness of God, but have departed from the faith that was once delivered to the Saints, and have broken the covenant in which their fathers were established (see Isaiah 24:5); and have become high-minded, and have not feared; therefore, but few of them will be gathered with the chosen family." (*Teachings*, pp. 14-15.)

That the glorious and full effect of the covenant promised through Jeremiah will come to pass during the millennium, is shown by the following statement of the Prophet about making one's calling and election sure: "This principle ought (in its proper place) to be taught, for God hath not revealed anything to Joseph, but what he will make known unto the Twelve, and even the least saint may know all things as fast as he is able to bear them, for the day must come when no man need say to his neighbor, Know ye the Lord; for all shall know him (who remain) from the least to the greatest. How is this to be done? It is to be done by this sealing power, and the other Comforter spoken of, which will be manifest by revelation." (*Teachings*, p. 149.)

MOSAIC ORDINANCES PREFIGURE CHRIST'S MINISTRY

HEBREWS 9:1-14.

1 Then verily the first *covenant* had also ordinances of divine service, and a worldly sanctuary.

2 For there was a tabernacle made; the first, wherein *was* the candlestick, and the table, and the shewbread; which is called the sanctuary.

3 And after the second veil, the tabernacle which is called the Holiest of all;

4 Which had the golden censer, and the ark of the covenant overlaid round about with gold, wherein *was* the golden pot that had manna, and Aaron's rod that budded, and the tables of the covenant;

5 And over it the cherubim of glory shadowing the mercy-seat; of which we cannot now speak particularly.

6 Now when these things were thus ordained, the priests went always into the first tabernacle, accomplishing the service *of God.*

7 But into the second *went* the high priest alone once every year, not without blood, which he of-

fered for himself, and *for* the errors of the people:

8 The Holy Ghost this signifying, that the way into the holiest of all was not yet made manifest, while as the first tabernacle was yet standing:

9 Which *was* a figure for the time then present, in which were offered both gifts and sacrifices, that could not make him that did the service perfect, as pertaining to the conscience;

10 *Which stood* only in meats and drinks, and divers washings, and carnal ordinances, imposed *on them* until the time of reformation.

11 But Christ being come an high priest of good things to come, by a greater and more perfect tabernacle, not made with hands, that is to say, not of this building;

12 Neither by the blood of goats and calves, but by his own blood he entered in once into the holy place, having obtained eternal redemption *for us*.

13 For if the blood of bulls and of goats, and the ashes of an heifer sprinkling the unclean, sanctifieth to the purifying of the flesh:

14 How much more shall the blood of Christ, who through the eternal Spirit offered himself without spot to God, purge your conscience from dead works to serve the living God?

I.V. HEBREWS 9:10.

10 Which **consisted** only in meats and drinks, and divers washings, and carnal ordinances, imposed on them until the time of reformation.

Since these Hebrew Saints are theologians who have a working knowledge of the Lord's dealings with ancient Israel, Paul takes occasion to show them that the whole system of Mosaic laws, ordinances, and performances was so designed and ordained as to typify and bear record of Christ. Speaking similarly to his Nephite brethren, Abinadi says, "that all these things were types of things to come." (Mosiah 13:31.) That is, for more than 1400 years the Lord required Israel to perform rites and ordinances in such a way as to point attention forward to Christ and his atonement. Thus to a people indoctrinated with the performances of the past, their fulfilment in Christ was the consummation of a glorious hope. And it was certainly faith promoting to have these realities of revealed religion set forth as persuasively as Paul is here doing.

1-10. Israel had her tabernacle (a portable temple!) — with its altar, ark, veil, and holy of holies — in which sacrifices and cleansing ordinances were performed, which the Holy Ghost signified were in similitude of the coming ministry of the Son of God. Through these ordinances the people gained forgiveness of sins because of their faith in the future coming of their Lord.

11-14. But now Christ has come and shed his own blood to redeem us, has entered into the eternal holy of holies, and has given us freedom from sin if we will but serve the living God.

CHRIST IS THE MEDIATOR OF THE NEW COVENANT

HEBREWS 9:15-28.

15 And for this cause he is the mediator of the new testament, that by means of death, for the redemption of the transgressions *that were* under the first testament, they which are called might receive the promise of eternal inheritance.

16 For where a testament *is*, there must also of necessity be the death of the testator.

17 For a testament *is* of force after men are dead: otherwise it is of no strength at all while the testator liveth.

18 Whereupon neither the first *testament* was dedicated without blood.

19 For when Moses had spoken every precept to all the people according to the law, he took the blood of calves and of goats, with water, and scarlet wool, and hyssop, and sprinkled both the book, and all the people,

20 Saying, This *is* the blood of the testament which God hath enjoined unto you.

21 Moreover he sprinkled with blood both the tabernacle, and all the vessels of the ministry.

22 And almost all things are by the law purged with blood; and without shedding of blood is no remission.

23 *It was* therefore necessary that the patterns of things in the heavens should be purified with these; but the heavenly things themselves with better sacrifices than these.

24 For Christ is not entered into the holy places made with

hands, *which are* the figures of the true; but into heaven itself, now to appear in the presence of God for us:

25 Nor yet that he should offer himself often, as the high priest entereth into the holy place every year with blood of others;

26 For then must he often have suffered since the foundation of the world: but now once in the end of the world hath he appeared to put away sin by the sacrifice of himself.

27 And as it is appointed unto men once to die, but after this the judgment:

28 So Christ was once offered to bear the sins of many; and unto them that look for him shall be appear the second time without sin unto salvation.

I.V. HEBREWS 9:15-18, 20-21, 26, 28.

15 And for this cause he is the mediator of the new **covenant,** that by means of death, for the redemption of the transgressions that were under the first **covenant,** they which are called might receive the promise of eternal inheritance.

16 For where a **covenant** is, there must also of necessity be the death of the **victim.**

17 For a **covenant** is of force after **the victim is** dead; otherwise it is of no strength at all while the **victim** liveth.

18 Whereupon neither the first **covenant** was dedicated without blood.

20 Saying, This is the blood of the **covenant** which God hath enjoined unto you.

21 Moreover he sprinkled **likewise** with blood both the tabernacle, and all the vessels of the ministry.

26 For then must he often have suffered since the foundation of the world; but now once in the **meridian of time** hath he appeared to put away sin by the sacrifice of himself.

28 So Christ was once offered to bear the sins of many; and he shall appear the second time, without sin unto salvation **unto them that look for him.**

From the beginning to the end, from Father Adam to the last man, salvation is in Christ and in him only. "Salvation was, and is, and is to come, in and through the atoning blood of Christ, the Lord Omnipotent." (Mosiah 3:18.)

Thus Moses taught faith in Christ and prefigured — in the

multitudinous rites and performances of his day — the shedding of our Lord's blood, through which alone salvation comes.

And thus Moses mediated between Israel and Jehovah, pleading with Deity on their behalf and offering sacrifices for sin in similitude of the coming sacrifice of God's Son. But Christ himself mediates between his saints and the Father, offering them remission of sins and salvation through his own infinite and eternal sacrifice. The law of Moses is the old covenant; the gospel is the new. Moses is the mediator of the old covenant; Jesus, of the new.

15-17. "In legal usage, a testator is one who leaves a valid will or testament at his death. The will or testament is the written document wherein the testator provides for the disposition of his property. As used in the gospel sense, a testament is a covenant. Jesus is the Mediator of the new covenant or testament, that is of the gospel which came to replace the law of Moses." (*Mormon Doctrine*, 2nd ed., pp. 784-785.)

In these verses, Paul uses both the legal and the gospel definition of terms and teaches that it is through Christ's death that gifts are willed to men. "In other words, Christ had to die to bring salvation. The testament or covenant of salvation came in force because of the atonement worked out in connection with that death. Christ is the Testator. His gift, as would be true of any testator, cannot be inherited until his death. Christ died that salvation might come; without his death, he could not have willed either immortality or eternal life." (*Mormon Doctrine*, 2nd ed., p. 785.)

15. Mediator of the new testament] See 1 Tim. 2:1-7.

New Testament] New covenant, the gospel as restored by Jesus when contrasted with the Old Testament or old covenant which was revealed to Moses.

By means of death] Christ came to die for the sins of the world; his mission was to suffer for all men in Gethsemane and then to be lifted up upon the cross. His death and resurrection are the crowning events of his ministry. It is through death that life comes.

The redemption of the transgressions that were under the first testament] Christ's death saved men in Moses' day. The atonement was retroactive; it was for all men of all ages; its effect was past, present, and future. To King Benjamin an angel declared that Christ's "blood atoneth for the sins of those who have fallen by the transgression of Adam," and that if "the children of men" who lived before our Lord's mortal ministry "should believe that Christ should come, the same might receive remission of their sins, and rejoice with exceeding great joy, even as though he had already come among them." (Mosiah 3:11-13.)

First testament] In contrast with the gospel, the law of Moses was the first covenant of salvation and the gospel was the second; in fact, the gopsel covenant was "first" given to Adam and was enjoyed by all the faithful saints who preceded Moses and that lesser law given to him.

They which are called] See *Commentary II*, pp. 267-269.

Eternal inheritance] Eternal life, which is inherited through Christ's will, the legal "document" through which life's greatest blessings are bequeathed upon the death of the testator.

18-22. In offering sacrifices Moses shed and used the blood of animals, in similitude of the future shedding of the blood of Christ and its use in the plan of redemption.

22. Almost all things are by the law purged with blood] There is forgiveness for almost all sins through the blood of Christ. There is, however, no forgiveness for those guilty of the unpardonable sin, those who crucify unto themselves the Son of God afresh. Joseph Smith said, "the power of Elijah cannot seal against this sin, for this is a reserve made in the seals and power of the priesthood." (*Teachings*, p. 339.)

Without shedding of blood is no remission] In setting forth his laws for ancient Israel in connection with sacrificial rites, the Lord said: "For the life of the flesh is in the blood: and I have given it to you upon the altar to make an atonement for your souls: for it is the blood that maketh an atonement for the soul." (Lev. 17:11.) That is, through faith in Christ, who was to come, and by prefiguring the shedding of his blood in their sacrifices and the rites incident thereto, those in ancient Israel were making atonement for their sins. Through their revealed system of rites and performances, they were being reminded that forgiveness and redemption comes through the shedding of the blood of Christ.

23-28. Mosiac sacrifices, in which the blood of animals was shed, and in which the high priest entered into the holy of holies on the day of atonement, typified the death of Christ and his entering into heaven. But whereas the Mosaic ordinances, being imperfect — that is, not of themselves having saving power — were performed every year, our Lord's sacrifice, being perfect, was made once and has saving power forever. In this connection, the Book of Mormon account records that "the Lord God . . . appointed unto" Israel "a law, even the law of Moses. And many signs, and wonders, and types, and shadows showed he unto them, concerning his coming," and also that "the law of Moses availeth nothing except it were through the atonement of his blood." (Mosiah 3:14-15.)

27. Once to die] Reincarnation is a false doctrine. Men are born, die, and are judged once.

28. Christ came once to free men from sin; he shall come again to give salvation, made possible through his atoning blood, to all who are thus free.

"BY THE BLOOD YE ARE SANCTIFIED"

HEBREWS 10:1-18.

1 For the law having a shadow of good things to come, *and* not the very image of the things, can never with those sacrifices which they offered year by year continually make the comers thereunto perfect.

2 For then would they not have ceased to be offered? because that the worshippers once purged should have had no more conscience of sins.

3 But in those *sacrifices there is* a remembrance again *made* of sins every year.

4 For *it is* not possible that the blood of bulls and of goats should take away sins.

5 Wherefore when he cometh into the world, he saith, Sacrifice

and offering thou wouldest not, but a body hast thou prepared me:

6 In burnt offerings and *sacrifices* for sin thou hast had no pleasure.

7 Then said I, Lo, I come (in the volume of the book it is written of me,) to do thy will, O God.

8 Above when he said, Sacrifice and offering, and burnt offerings and *offering* for sin thou wouldest not, neither hadst pleasure *therein;* which are offered by the law;

9 Then said he, Lo, I come to do thy will, O God. He taketh away the first, that he may establish the second.

10 By the which will we are sanctified through the offering of the body of Jesus Christ once *for all.*

11 And every priest standeth daily ministering and offering oftentimes the same sacrifices, which can never take away sins:

12 But this man, after he had offered one sacrifice for sins for ever, sat down on the right hand of God;

13 From henceforth expecting till his enemies be made his footstool.

14 For by one offering he hath perfected for ever them that are sanctified.

15 *Whereof* the Holy Ghost also is a witness to us: for after that he had said before,

16 This *is* the covenant that I will make with them after those days, saith the Lord, I will put my laws into their hearts, and in their minds will I write them;

17 And their sins and iniquities will I remember no more.

18 Now where remission of these *is, there is* no more offering for sin.

I.V. HEBREWS 10:1, 10, 13.

1 For the law having a shadow of good things to come, and not the very image of the things, can never with those sacrifices, which they offered **continually** year by year make the comers thereunto perfect.

10 By which will we are sanctified through the offering **once** of the body of Jesus Christ.

13 From henceforth **to reign until** his enemies be made his footstool.

As he now concludes this portion of his presentation, Paul summarizes his teachings on the law of sacrifice in this way:

1. Salvation is in Christ, and comes through the shedding of

his blood; men are sanctified through his blood and in no other way.

2. The sacrifices of the Mosaic law were types and shadows of our Lord's atoning sacrifice and were to point Israel's attention forward to that transcendent event.

3. Animal sacrifices, standing alone of themselves without more, were imperfect and neither remitted sins nor brought salvation; rather, they had efficacy and virtue only because of Christ's sacrifice.

4. Sacrifices are now done away in Christ.

5. And thus is fulfilled the Lord's promise through Jeremiah that in a day subsequent to the law of Moses, God would give a new covenant which would abolish the sins and iniquities of the people.

1-3. See Heb. 9:15-28.

4. "It is expedient that there should be a great and last sacrifice; yea, not a sacrifice of man, neither of beast, neither of any manner of fowl; for it shall not be a human sacrifice; but it must be an infinite and eternal sacrifice. Now there is not any man that can sacrifice his own blood which will atone for the sins of another." (Alma 34:10-11.) See Heb. 8:1-5.

5-9. Paul quotes Psalm 40:6-8, as found in the Septuagint rather than the King James Version, which Messianic prophecy proclaims, in thought content, that when the Lord comes into mortality to dwell in the body prepared for him, sacrifices and burnt offerings will be done away. This was affirmed, in plain words, to the Nephites by the risen Lord: "Ye shall offer up unto me no more the shedding of blood; yea, your sacrifices and your burnt offerings shall be done away, for I will accept none of your sacrifices and your burnt offerings. And ye shall offer for a sacrifice unto me a broken heart and a contrite spirit." (3 Ne. 9:19-20.)

5. A body hast thou prepared me] This phrase is not found in the prophecy as it is recorded in the King James Version, but is found in the same prophecy in the Septuagint. Paul's use of it certifies to its verity, and it is certainly an expressive and clear pronouncement relative to our Lord's birth into mortality.

9. He taketh away the first, that he may establish the second] The law of sacrifice is done away in Christ; he took away the rites required in the Mosaic system that he might establish the pre-eminence of his own atoning sacrifice.

10. We are sanctified through the offering of the body of Jesus Christ] The atonement of Christ is the rock foundation upon which all things rest which pertain to salvation and eternal life. Hence the Lord said to Adam: "By the blood ye are sanctified" (Moses 6:60), although the usual scriptural pronouncement is that men are "sanctified by the reception of the Holy Ghost." (3 Ne. 27:20.) The meaning is that although men are sanctified by the power of the Holy Ghost, such sanctifying process is effective and operative because of the shedding of the blood of Christ. Thus Moroni says that the faithful saints are "sanctified in Christ by the grace of God, through the shedding of the blood of Christ, which is in the covenant of the Father unto the remission" of their sins, that they become holy and without spot. (Moro. 10:33.)

Sanctification] See 1 Thess. 4:1-8.

11-14. "It is expedient that there should be a great and last sacrifice; and then shall there be, or it is expedient there should be, a stop to the shedding of blood; then shall the law of Moses be fulfilled; yea, it shall be all fulfilled; every jot and tittle, and none shall have passed away. And behold, this is the whole meaning of the law, every whit pointing to that great and last sacrifice; and that great and last sacrifice will be the Son of God, yea, infinite and eternal. And thus he shall bring salvation to all those who shall believe on his name; this being the intent of this last sacrifice, to bring about the bowels of mercy, which overpowereth justice, and bringeth about means unto men that they may have faith unto repentance." (Alma 34:13-15.)

11. Sacrifices, which can never take away sins] Of themselves they cannot; the law of Moses alone is not enough; forgiveness comes through the atonement of Christ; but the faithful compliance of ancient Israel with the laws of the Lord, did sanctify them before him, because of the atonement which was to be.

15-18. This argument is persuasive: Since the new covenant, coming after the law of Moses, was to free men from sin, why then continue the old covenant to do what is now accomplished by the new?

THOSE WHO FALL FROM GRACE ARE DAMNED

HEBREWS 10:19-39.

19 Having therefore, brethren, boldness to enter into the holiest by the blood of Jesus,

20 By a new and living way, which he hath consecrated for us, through the veil, that is to say, his flesh;

21 And *having* an high priest over the house of God;

22 Let us draw near with a true heart in full assurance of faith, having our hearts sprinkled from an evil conscience, and our bodies washed with pure water.

23 Let us hold fast the profession of *our* faith without wavering; (for he *is* faithful that promised;)

24 And let us consider one another to provoke unto love and to good works:

25 Not forsaking the assembling of ourselves together, as the manner of some *is;* but exhorting *one another:* and so much the more, as ye see the day approaching.

26 For if we sin wilfully after that we have received the knowledge of the truth, there remaineth no more sacrifice for sins,

27 But a certain fearful looking for of judgment and fiery indignation, which shall devour the adversaries.

28 He that despised Moses' law died without mercy under two or three witnesses:

29 Of how much sorer punishment, suppose ye, shall he be thought worthy, who hath trodden under foot the Son of God, and hath counted the blood of the covenant, wherewith he was sanctified, an unholy thing, and hath done despite unto the Spirit of grace?

30 For we know him that hath said, Vengeance *belongeth* unto me, I will recompense, saith the Lord. And again, The Lord shall judge his people.

31 *It is* a fearful thing to fall into the hands of the living God.

32 But call to remembrance the former days, in which, after ye were illuminated, ye endured a great fight of afflictions;

33. Partly, whilst ye were made a gazingstock both by reproaches and afflictions; and partly, whilst ye became companions of them that were so used.

34 For ye had compassion of me in my bonds, and took joyfully the spoiling of your goods, knowing in yourselves that ye have in heaven a better and an enduring substance.

35 Cast not away therefore your confidence, which hath great recompense of reward.

36. For ye have need of patience, that, after ye have done the will of God, ye might receive the promise.

37 For yet a little while, and he that shall come will come, and will not tarry.

38 Now the just shall live by faith: but if *any man* draw back, my soul shall have no pleasure in him.

39 But we are not of them who draw back unto perdition; but of them that believe to the saving of the soul.

19-25. 'Ye saints of God: Since Christ our Lord has redeemed us by his blood; since he has made salvation available through the new gospel covenant; since he, as the high priest over the Church, now opens to us the door to his kingdom; since we have cast off the sins of the world, through his blood, and are now clean before him — let us keep the commandments; let us hold fast to the Church; let us lead and guide each other to do good works; let us meet together often and exhort each other in the Cause of Righteousness.'

19-20. Atonement for sin is no longer made by the high priest in Israel when he passes through the veil of the temple into the holy of holies. (Lev. 16.) See Heb. 6:19-20. Now there is a new way, a living way, for the veil of the old temple was rent with the crucifixion. (Matt. 27:50-51.) Now Jesus has passed through the veil into heaven itself. While he lived, his mortal flesh stood between him and the eternal holy of holies, for "flesh and blood cannot inherit the kingdom of God" (1 Cor. 15:50), but now he has, at it were, rent the veil of his flesh through death and entered into the fulness of his Father's kingdom through resurrection.

21. **An high priest over the house of God]** An high priest over the Church, both on earth and in heaven. "Christ is the Great High Priest" (*Teachings*, p. 158), whose atoning sacrifice was the culmination of all the sacrifices of all the high priests in Israel from the beginning of their nation to the day he hung on the cross.

22. **Hearts sprinkled . . . bodies washed]** An apparent allusion to those ordinances whereby the saints of the new covenant are made clean through conformity to the Lord's law (D. & C. 88:74-75; 124:37-40), even as Aaron and his sons were washed in the days of the old covenant. (Ex. 29:4.) See *Commentary II*, pp. 518-520.

24. **Provoke]** Stimulate.

25. **Exhorting one another]** The saints have an obligation to exhort and teach one another. (D. & C. 88:77.) **The day]** The Second Coming.

26-31. **Sons of perdition]** See Heb. 6:4-9.

26-27. There is no forgiveness for those who receive a perfect knowledge of the truth and who then sin wilfully and defy the truth. (D. & C. 76:31-49.)

29. Every member of the Church must live as becometh a saint or suffer the consequences, for "there is a possibility that man may fall from grace and depart from the living God; Therefore let the church take heed and pray always, lest they fall into temptation; Yea, and even let those who are sanctified take heed also." (D. & C. 20:32-34.)

Even though a person has his calling and election made sure and is sealed up unto eternal life, he still has his agency; he can still fall; he can still choose to serve Satan; but if he does — having had a perfect knowledge of the truth and now choosing to defy God; to trample his Son under foot; and to do despite to the Spirit of grace — he is damned eternally as a son of perdition.

Joseph Smith said: "If men have received the good word of God, and tasted of the powers of the world to come, if they shall fall away, it is impossible to renew them again, seeing they have crucified the Son of God afresh, and put him to an open shame; so there is a possibility of falling away; you could not be renewed again, and the power of Elijah cannot seal against this sin, for this is a reserve made in the seals and power of the priesthood." (*Teachings*, p. 339.)

31. 'It is a fearful thing to suffer the wrath of God, with the devil and his angels in eternity; to be cast into the lake of fire; to die the second death; to go away into eternal and everlasting punishment; to be tormented where their worm dieth not and the fire is not quenched — to become a son of perdition.'

32. Illuminated] Enlightened; received the gospel.

33. Reproaches and afflictions] Such are the common lot of all the saints in all ages; none can forsake the world without being reproached and afflicted by those who are worldly.

39. Them who draw back unto perdition] Those who turn from righteousness, serve Satan, and become his sons, sons of perdition.

BY FAITH THE WORLDS WERE MADE

HEBREWS 11:1-3.

1 Now faith is the substance of things hoped for, the evidence of things not seen.

2 For by it the elders obtained a good report.

3 Through faith we understand that the worlds were framed by the word of God, so that things which are seen were not made of things which do appear.

I.V. HEBREWS 11:1.

1 Now faith is the **assurance** of things hoped for, the evidence of things not seen.

Paul now launches into one of his greatest pieces of inspired writing, as he defines and illustrates that law of faith by which the worlds are and by which salvation comes; that faith which is the power of God himself; that faith which has preserved the saints of all ages and which will raise the righteous to be like God and to sit with Christ on his throne. (Rev. 3:21.)

Faith: what it is and how to gain it] See *Commentary I*, pp. 523-525; *Mormon Doctrine*, 2nd ed., pp. 261-267.

Belief] See *Commentary II*, pp. 150-152.

1. Paul's American counterpart, Alma, defined faith in these words: "Faith is not to have a perfect knowledge of things; therefore if ye have faith ye hope for things which are not seen, which are true." (Alma 32:21.) And Moroni said simply: "Faith is things which are hoped for and not seen." (Ether 12:6.)

2. The elders] The ancients, whose good deeds Paul is now going to report approvingly. Since the brethren named all held the Melchizedek Priesthood, they each carried also the priestly title of "elder."

3. Through faith . . . the worlds were framed] Faith is power, the power of God, the power by which the worlds are and were created. "To create is to organize. It is an utterly false and uninspired notion to believe that the world or any other thing was created out of nothing or that any created thing can be destroyed in the sense of annihilation. 'The elements are eternal.' (D. & C. 93:33.)

"Joseph Smith, in the King Follett sermon, said: 'You ask the learned doctors why they say the world was made out of nothing; and they will answer, "Doesn't the Bible say He created the world?" And they infer, from the word create, that it must have been made out of nothing. Now, the word create came from the word *baurau*, which does not mean to create out of nothing; it means to organize; the same as a man would organize materials and build a ship. Hence we infer that God had materials to organize the world out of chaos — chaotic matter, which is element, and in which dwells all the glory. Element had an existence from the time he had. The pure principles of element are principles which can never be destroyed; they may be organized and reorganized, but not destroyed. They had no beginning, and can have no end.' (*Teachings*, pp. 350-352.)

"Christ, acting under the direction of the Father, was and is the Creator of all things. (D. & C. 38:1-4; 76:22-24; John 1:1-3; Col. 1:16-17; Heb. 1:1-3; Moses 1; 2; 3.) That he was aided in the creation of this earth by 'many of the noble and great' spirit children of the Father is evident from Abraham's writings. Unto these superior spirits Christ said: 'We will go down, for there is space there, and we will take of these materials, and we will make an earth whereon these may dwell.' (Abra. 3:22-24.) Michael or Adam was one of these. Enoch, Noah, Abraham, Moses, Peter, James, and John, Joseph Smith, and many other 'noble and great' ones played a part in the great creative enterprise. (*Doctrines of Salvation,* vol. 1, pp. 74-75.)

"This earth was not the first of the Lord's creations. An infinite number of worlds have come rolling into existence at his command. Each is an earth; many are inhabited with his spirit children; each abides the particular law given to it; and each will play its part in the redemption, salvation, and exaltation of that infinite host of the children of an Almighty God. The Lord has said that his work and glory is to bring to pass immortality and eternal life for his children on all the inhabited worlds he has created. (Moses 1:27-40; 7:29-36; D. & C. 88:17-26.)

"Such details of the creative process and of the order of events in it as have been revealed pertain only to this earth. (Moses 1:35.) In the temple we receive the clearest understanding of what took place and how it was accomplished. Abraham has left us an account of the planning and decisions of the Creators 'at the time that they counseled among themselves to form the heavens and the earth.' (Abra. 4; 5.)

"In the books of Moses and Genesis we have revealed accounts of the actual physical creation of the earth. The 2nd chapter of Moses and the 1st chapter of Genesis give the events which occurred on the successive creative days. (Ex. 20:8-11.) Then the 3rd chapter of Moses and the 2nd chapter of Genesis — by way of interpolation, amplification, and parenthetical explanation — recount the added truth that all things were created spiritually 'before they were naturally upon the face of the earth.'

"There is no revealed account of the spirit creation, only this explanatory interpolation that all things had been created in heaven at a previous time. That this prior spirit creation occurred long before the temporal or natural creation is evident from the fact that spirit men, men who themselves were before created spiritually, were participating in the natural creation. (*Doctrines of Salvation*, vol. 1, pp. 72-78.)" (*Mormon Doctrine*, 2nd ed., pp. 169-170)

Things which are seen were not made of things which do appear] A difficult and obscure passage? Not really. Paul is simply saying that created things were not made of or by "things" which are seen. That is: All created things, this earth and all that is thereon — all things were and are made, not by man's power, not by some undirected forces of nature or of the universe. There was no happenstance in creation, no chance creation of life in primordial swamps, no development up from one species to another by evolutionary processes. The creation was planned, organized, and controlled. It came by God's power — by faith! It came by a power that does not appear and is not seen and understood by the carnal mind or the scientific intellect. The creation is God's doing. Things came into being by forces which do not appear to man and can in fact be known only by revelation. And as God created all things by faith, even so his created handiwork can be known and understood only by that same power, the power which is faith.

WHY WAS ABEL'S SACRIFICE ACCEPTED?

HEBREWS 11:4.

4 By faith Abel offered unto God a more excellent sacrifice than Cain, by which he obtained witness that he was righteous, God testifying of his gifts: and by it he being dead yet speaketh.

The story of Cain and Abel, two sons born somewhere down the line after Adam and Eve began to multiply and provide bodies for the spirit children of the Father, is one of the most dramatic but least understood of all the Old Testament accounts.

From the scriptural records available to us, from the sermons of the Prophet, and from a knowledge of the revealed requisites for becoming a son of perdition, we know that Cain was a liar and a rebel in pre-existence; that, like Lucifer, he had power and influence there; that in this life he was taught the gospel, received the priesthood, and knew of the divinity of the Lord's work; that he then came out in open rebellion against God; that he in fact loved Satan more than God, choosing to worship and serve that evil one rather than the Lord; and that he offered false sacrifices at Satan's behest and slew Abel because the devil directed him so to do. (Gen. 4; Moses 5:16-55.)

Abel on the other hand was a righteous and obedient man who walked in holiness before the Lord. He was the head of the Adamic dispensation, and he believed in Christ and offered sacrifices, as directed by the Lord, in similitude of the coming sacrifice of the Son of God.

To show how to reason from the scriptures, let us quote the inspired interpretations of Joseph Smith, as he analyzed the doings of Cain and Abel:

"From time to time these glad tidings [the plan of salvation] were sounded in the ears of men in different ages of the world down to the time of Messiah's coming. By faith in this atonement or plan of redemption, Abel offered to God a sacrifice that was accepted, which was the firstlings of the flock. Cain offered of the fruit of the ground, and was not accepted, because he could not do it in faith, he could have no faith, or could not exercise faith contrary to the plan of heaven. It must be shedding the blood of the Only Begotten to atone for man; for this was the plan of redemption; and without the shedding of blood was no remission; and as the sacrifice was instituted for a type, by which man was to discern the great Sacrifice which God had prepared; to offer a sacrifice contrary to that, no faith could be exercised, because redemption was not purchased in that way, nor the power of atonement instituted after that order; consequently Cain could have no faith; and whatsoever is not of faith, is sin.

WHY WAS ABEL'S SACRIFICE ACCEPTED?

"But Abel offered an acceptable sacrifice, by which he obtained witness that he was righteous, God himself testifying of his gifts. Certainly, the shedding of the blood of a beast could be beneficial to no man, except it was done in imitation, or as a type, or explanation of what was to be offered through the gift of God himself; and this performance done with an eye looking forward in faith on the power of that great sacrifice for a remission of sins.

"But however various may have been, and may be at the present time, the opinions of men respecting the conduct of Abel, and the knowledge which he had on the subject of atonement, it is evident in our minds, that he was instructed more fully in the plan than what the Bible speaks of, for how could he offer a sacrifice in faith, looking to God for a remission of his sins in the power of the great atonement, without having been previously instructed in that plan? And further, if he was accepted of God, what were the ordinances performed further than the offering of the firstlings of the flock?

"It is said by Paul in his letter to the Hebrew brethren, that Abel obtained witness that he was righteous, God testifying of his gifts. To whom did God testify of the gifts of Abel, was it to Paul? We have very little on this important subject in the forepart of the Bible. But it is said that Abel himself obtained witness that he was righteous. Then certainly God spoke to him: indeed, it is said that God talked with him; and if he did, would he not, seeing that Abel was righteous deliver to him the whole plan of the gospel. And is not the gospel the news of the redemption?

"How could Abel offer a sacrifice and look forward with faith on the Son of God for a remission of his sins, and not understand the gospel? The mere shedding of the blood of beasts or offering anything else in sacrifice, could not procure a remission of sins, except it were performed in faith of something to come; if it could, Cain's offering must have been as good as Abel's. And if Abel was taught of the coming of the Son of God, was he not taught also of his ordinances? We all admit that the gospel has ordinances, and if so, had it not always ordinances, and were not its ordinances always the same?" (*Teachings*, pp. 58-59.)

If we may be permitted to reason, as the Prophet here did, and if Cain could not exercise faith contrary to the plan of heaven, then how can anyone exercise faith in any false ordinances? Thus, if infant baptism or any of a hundred unscriptural or pagan-originated practices are contrary to the plan of heaven, how can anyone have faith in their efficacy? And if faith is not present in religious rites, can we reach any other conclusion, with reference to them, than that whatsoever is not of faith is sin? Is not God's rejection of Cain for offering a false sacrifice a type of what his decree is and shall be relative to all false ordinances?

4. He being dead yet speaketh] "How doth he yet speak?" the Prophet asked. His answer: "Why he magnified the priesthood which was conferred upon him, and died a righteous man, and therefore has become an angel of God by receiving his body from the dead, holding still the keys of his dispensation; and was sent down from heaven unto Paul to minister consoling words, and to commit unto him a knowledge of the mysteries of godliness.

"And if this was not the case, I would ask, how did Paul know so much about Abel, and why should he talk about his speaking after he was dead? Hence, that he spoke after he was dead must be by being sent down out of heaven to administer." (*Teachings*, p. 169.)

Law of sacrifice] See Heb. 8:1-5.

Sacrifice] See *Commentary II*, pp. 537-540.

WHAT IS THE DOCTRINE OF TRANSLATION?

HEBREWS 11:5-6.

5. By faith Enoch was translated that he should not see death; and was not found, because God had translated him: for before his translation he had this testimony, that he pleased God.

6 But without faith *it is* impossible to please *him:* for he that cometh to God must believe that he is, and *that* he is a rewarder of them that diligently seek him.

5. Enoch] Joseph Smith said that Enoch held "the presidency of a dispensation" of the gospel, and that Paul was "acquainted" with him "and received instructions from him," meaning that Enoch, by then a resurrected being (D. & C. 133:54-55), ministered unto Paul. (*Teachings*, p. 170.) **Ministry of Enoch]** See Jude 14-15.

Gospel] See *Commentary II*, pp. 213-216.

Translation] "And Enoch walked with God: and he was not; for God took him" (Gen. 5:24), as he did also the whole city of Zion. (Moses 7:18-21.) That is, Enoch and the righteous saints were translated or taken into heaven without tasting death. "Now this Enoch," the Prophet said—and it applies also to all the inhabitants of the holy city founded by him—"God reserved unto himself, that he should not die at that time, and appointed unto him a ministry unto terrestrial bodies, of whom there has been but little revealed."

Then of the matter of translation itself, the Prophet said: "Many have supposed that the doctrine of translation was a doctrine whereby men were taken immediately into the presence of God, and into an eternal fulness, but this is a mistaken idea. Their place of habitation is that of the terrestrial order, and a place prepared for such characters he held in reserve to be ministering angels unto many planets, and who as yet have not entered into so great a fulness as those who are resurrected from the dead." (*Teachings*, p. 170.)

"During the first 2200 or so years of the earth's history—that is, from the fall of Adam to the ministry of Melchizedek — it was a not uncommon occurrence for faithful members of the Church to be translated and taken into the heavenly realms without tasting death. Since that time there have been occasional special instances of translation, instances in which a special work of the ministry required it. . . .

"It is from the account of the translation of the Three Nephites that we gain most of our knowledge of the present ministry among men of translated beings. It is very evident that such persons 'never taste of death; . . . never endure the pains of death'; that they have undergone a change in their bodies, 'that they might not suffer pain nor sorrow save it were for the sins of the world'; that they were holy men, 'sanctified in the flesh'; 'that the powers of the earth could not hold them'; that 'they are as the angels of God,' ministering to whomsoever they will; that they 'shall be changed in the twinkling of an eye from mortality to immortality' at the Second Coming; and that they shall then inherit exaltation in the kingdom of God. (3 Ne. 28.)" (*Mormon Doctrine*, 2nd ed., pp. 804-807.)

6. Without faith it is impossible to please him] By faith men are born again; they become new creatures of the Holy Ghost; their souls are sanctified; they are "purified"; they become "clean" and spotless and are candidates for celestial glory—and such are the only ones with whom God is "well pleased." (D. & C. 38:8-10.)

FAITH SAVED NOAH TEMPORALLY AND SPIRITUALLY

HEBREWS 11:7.

7 By faith Noah, being warned of God of things not seen as yet, moved with fear, prepared an ark to the saving of his house; by the which he condemned the world, and became heir of the righteousness which is by faith.

7. Noah] "Noah, who is Gabriel," the Prophet said, "stands next in authority to Adam," and is "the father of all living in this day." (*Teachings*, p. 157.) He received the same keys, covenants, powers, and glories possessed originally by Adam; presided over a gospel dispensation; and proclaimed its truths to the people of his day. (*Teachings*, p. 171; Moses 8.)

Gospel] See *Commentary II*, pp. 213-216.

Flood of Noah] See 1 Pet. 3:18-22; 4:1-6.

ABRAHAM SOUGHT A HEAVENLY CITY

HEBREWS 11:8-16.

8. By faith Abraham, when he was called to go out into a place which he should after receive for an inheritance, obeyed; and he went out, not knowing whither he went.

9 By faith he sojourned in the land of promise, as *in* a strange country, dwelling in tabernacles

with Isaac and Jacob, the heirs with him of the same promise:

10 For he looked for a city which hath foundations, whose builder and maker *is* God.

11 Through faith also Sara herself received strength to conceive seed, and was delivered of a child when she was past age, because she judged him faithful who had promised.

12 Therefore sprang there even of one, and him as good as dead, *so many* as the stars of the sky in multitude, and as the sand which is by the sea shore innumerable.

13 These all died in faith, not having received the promises, but having seen them afar off, and were persuaded of *them*, and embraced *them*, and confessed that they were strangers and pilgrims on the earth.

14 For they that say such things declare plainly that they seek a country.

15 And truly, if they had been mindful of that *country* from whence they came out, they might have had opportunity to have returned.

16 But now they desire a better *country*, that is, an heavenly: wherefore God is not ashamed to be called their God: for he hath prepared for them a city.

What was the highest point of spiritual perfection ever attained among mortal men? When did hosts of living saints ascend those heights of spiritual knowledge and personal righteousness which made them as near one with Deity as men can be and yet remain in mortality?

True, Our Lord was perfect and some prophets have walked with God in perfect faith, but they are isolated examples of men standing virtually alone in a godless world; and true, a whole nation of Nephite Saints so lived that not one soul was lost, all were saved in the kingdom of God. (3 Ne. 27:30-31.) But only in Enoch's day and among the inhabitants of his city was that perfection found which caused the Lord himself to come down, dwell "with his people," and then take them from this mortal sphere into his heavenly realms. (Moses 7:16-21.) Surely life in the City of Zion reached the highest spiritual pinnacle of the ages.

Is it any wonder, then, that righteous people of succeeding generations looked back with longing for like blessings, and for that matter that God commanded them so to do? To Abraham the Lord said: "Remember the covenant which I make with thee; for it shall be an everlasting covenant; and thou shalt remember the days of Enoch thy father." (*Inspired Version*, Gen. 13:13.) And remember them he did, as he and his children after him sought an habitation in that greatest of all cities—the City of Zion.

Biblical chronologists, Ussher in particular, place the translation of Enoch at 3017 B.C., the flood at 2348 B.C., the death of Noah at 1998 and the birth of Abraham at 1996. Abraham lived until 1822 B.C., Isaac until 1716 and Jacob until 1689. Abraham lived in the days of Melchizedek and was taught, blessed, and ordained by him. (D. & C. 84:14.)

"Enoch and his people were translated, probably just a few years after Adam's death. (Moses 7:18-21, 31, 63, 69; D. & C. 38:4; 45:11-14; 84:99-100; Gen. 5:22-24; Heb. 11:5.) It is apparent from the abbreviated account of the Lord's dealings with Enoch and his people that Zion was a very great and populous city, having perhaps many thousands or even millions of inhabitants. (Moses 7.) Methuselah, the son of Enoch, was not translated, 'that the covenants of the Lord might be fulfilled, which he made to Enoch; for he truly covenanted with Enoch that Noah should be of the fruit of his loins.' (Moses 8:2.) But during the nearly 700 years from the translation of Enoch to the flood of Noah, it would appear that nearly all of the faithful members of the Church were translated, for 'the Holy Ghost fell on many, and they were caught up by the powers of heaven into Zion.' (Moses 7:27.)

"That this process of translating the righteous saints and taking them to heaven was still going on after the flood among the people of Melchizedek is apparent from the account in the Inspired Version of the Bible. Speaking of the faith and righteousness of those holding the Melchizedek Priesthood in that day, the account says: 'And men having this faith, coming up into this order of God, were translated and taken up into heaven. And now, Melchizedek was a priest of this order, therefore he obtained peace in Salem, and was called the Prince of peace. And his people wrought rightousness, and obtained heaven, and sought for the city of Enoch which God had before taken, separating it from the earth, having reserved it unto the latter days, or the end of the world.' (*Inspired Version*, Gen. 14:32-34.)

"As far as we know, instances of translation since the day of Melchizedek and his people have been few and far between. After recording that Enoch was translated, Paul says that Abraham, Isaac, and Jacob, and their seed after them (they obviously knowing what had taken place as pertaining to the people of Melchizedek and others) 'looked for a city which hath foundations, whose builder and maker is God' (Heb. 11:5-10), that is, they 'sought for the city of Enoch which God had before taken.' (*Inspired Version*, Gen. 14:34.) But as Paul said, and as the Lord confirmed by latter-day revelation, even these 'holy men . . . found it not because of wickedness and abominations; And confessed they were strangers and pilgrims on the earth; But obtained a promise that they should find it and see it in their flesh.' (D. & C. 45:11-14; Heb. 11:11-16.)" (*Mormon Doctrine*, 2nd ed., pp. 804-805.)

This promise that the City of Zion shall return, and that holy men of all ages, in their resurrected state, shall dwell therein, will have millennial fulfilment. Of that glorious day, "the Lord said unto Enoch: Then shalt thou and all thy city meet them there, and we will receive them into our bosom, and they shall see us; and we will fall upon their necks, and they shall fall upon our necks, and we will kiss each other; And there shall be mine abode, and it shall be Zion, which shall come forth out of all the creations which I have made; and for the space of a thousand years the earth shall rest." (Moses 7:63-64.)

In giving revealed direction to Noah, the Lord said: "Remember the everlasting covenant, which I made unto thy father Enoch; that, when men should keep all my commandments, Zion should again come on the earth, the city of Enoch, which I have caught up unto myself. And this is mine everlasting covenant, that when thy posterity shall embrace the truth, and look upward, then shall Zion look downward, and all the heavens shall shake with gladness, and the earth shall tremble with joy; And the general assembly of the church of the first-born shall come down out of heaven, and possess the earth, and shall have place until the end come. And this is mine everlasting covenant, which I made with thy father Enoch." (*Inspired Version*, Gen. 9:21-23.)

Translated Beings] See Heb. 11:5-6.

8. Abraham] The friend of God and father of the faithful, one of the noble and great in pre-existence (Abra. 3:22-23), he received a dispensation of the gospel, held the priesthood, married for eternity, saw God, and received the promise that his literal seed after him should have the right to all gospel blessings, and that all others who received the gospel would be adopted into his family and accounted his seed. (Abra. 2:8-11.) Included in the covenant of God with Abraham was the promise that he and his seed after him should possess the land of Canaan. See *Commentary II*, p. 71.

Dispensation of Abraham] See *Commentary II*, pp. 465-470.

9. Dwelling in tabernacles] Dwelling in tents.

9. Heirs with him of the same promise] 14. The promises] What were the promises given, each in turn, to Abraham, Isaac, and Jacob? And for that matter, to Sarah, Rebekah, and Rachel, and to their other wives, for "neither is the man without the woman, neither the woman without the man, in the Lord"? (1 Cor. 11:11.)

In an initial and preliminary sense, they deal with lands and temporal seed. They and their children after them are to inherit the land of Canaan, and their posterity (figuratively) is to be as innumerable as the sands upon the sea shore and the stars of heaven. (Gen. 12:1-3; 17:1-22; 22:15-18; 24:60; 26:2-5; 28:1-15.)

But in a fuller and more complete sense, the promises deal with celestial marriage, with the continuation of the family unit in eternity, with eternal increase, with having spirit children forever so that (literally) they will outnumber the particles of the earth and the near infinite number of stars in all the galaxies of the sidereal heavens. And in this greater and more important sense, all of these same blessings become the inheritance of all saints who live the law of Abraham and enter into the same order of matrimony which blessed his life and that of Isaac and Jacob. (D. & C. 132:29-32.)

10. Looked for a city] 14. Seek a country] Abraham, Isaac, and Jacob sought an inheritance in the City of Zion, as had all the righteous saints from Enoch to Melchizedek—an inheritance which would have been but prelude to gaining exaltation in the Celestial Zion where God and Christ are the judge of all. Since it is no longer the general order for the saints to be translated—their labors in the next sphere now being to preach the gospel to the spirits in prison, rather than to act as ministering servants in other fields—today's saints seek a heavenly country and a celestial city in the sense of striving for an inheritance in the Celestial City of exalted beings.

11. Sarah's initial reaction to the divine promise that she, though well stricken in years and past childbearing age, would bear a son, was one of incredulity and doubt. (Gen. 18:9-15.) But—and it is ever thus!—the promise came to pass by faith. Sarah, on more mature consideration, believed God and thereby reaped the blessing.

13. Not having received the promises] Not having received that portion of the promises which dealt with gaining the City of Zion, or even of having a secure and permanent inheritance in Canaan. These promises were to them "afar off"—that is, first, in a distant millennial day, and then again in that celestial day when "it is decreed that the poor and the meek of the earth shall inherit it." (D. & C. 88:17.)

Strangers and pilgrims on the earth] Those who seek salvation—here described as a place in a heavenly city—account themselves as strangers and pilgrims on earth. They know their eternal home is with God; that they lived and dwelt in his presence in preexistence; that they have come here into mortality to sojourn and gain experience for the moment; that life is a pilgrimage to a place far removed from the home eternal; and that if they fulfil their appointed journey well they shall return home to the place of beginning, where they are no longer strangers, but have full knowledge of that city and country which, amid all the turmoil and strife of life, they have nonetheless sought with full purpose of heart.

15-16. As Abraham left Ur for a better country, so the saints desire, when they leave mortality, to gain a better country, even an inheritance in a heavenly city.

16. God is not ashamed to be called their God] Is God ashamed to be called the God of those who break his laws and reject his eternal truths? If men draw near him with their lips, but remove their hearts far from him, is he ashamed to own them? Will the Son of Man be ashamed to own those who have lived worldly lives when he comes in all the glory of his Father's kingdom? (Mark 8:38.) But here the promise is that God shall not be ashamed of his own. Indeed what greater endorsement could he have given of the righteousness of Abraham, Isaac, and Jacob than to say to Moses that Deity himself should be identified unto the children of Israel as: "The Lord God of your fathers, the God of Abraham, the God of Isaac, and the God of Jacob," and that "this is my name for ever, and this is my memorial unto all generations." (Ex. 3:15.)

WHY WAS ABRAHAM COMMANDED TO SACRIFICE ISAAC?

HEBREWS 11:17-19.

17 By faith Abraham, when he was tried, offered up Isaac: and he that had received the promises offered up his only begotten *son,*

18 Of whom it was said, That in Isaac shall thy seed be called:

19 Accounting that God *was* able to raise *him* up, even from the dead; from whence also he received him in a figure.

In all history there is scarcely a more soul-wrenching moment than that on Mount Moriah nearly 4000 years ago when faithful Abraham, at God's command, raised his knife to slay Isaac, "his only begotten son." (Gen 22:1-19.) Who can conceive of a more severe test of faith than the heaven-sent order to sacrifice the heir of promise, the heir whom God must then raise from the dead that his promises concerning Isaac might be fulfilled. (Gen. 21:12.) Is it any wonder that in all succeeding generations the seed of Abraham have looked back with awe and reverence upon a scene which tested mortal man almost beyond mortal power to obey?

Why did Deity devise such a test? Certainly it was for Abraham's blessing and benefit. There can be no question that the harder the test, the higher the reward for passing it. And here Abraham laid his all on the altar, thus proving himself worthy of that exaltation which he has now received. (D. & C. 132:29.) And immediately following his conformity to the divine will, he received a heavenly manifestation of the glory and honor reserved for him and his seed. (Gen. 22:15-18.)

Certainly, also, Abraham's willingness to sacrifice Issac was intended to be an example forever of that perfect obedience which the Lord expects of all the heirs of promise. "Abraham," the Lord said to Joseph Smith, "was commanded to offer his son Isaac; nevertheless, it was written: Thou shalt not kill. Abraham, however, did not refuse, and it was accounted unto him for righteousness." (D. & C. 132:36.) And in principle, the Lord tests and tries all his saints to see if they "will abide in" his "covenant, even unto death," that they "may be found worthy." (D. & C. 98:14.) "They must needs be chastened and tried, even as Abraham, who was commanded to offer up his only son. For all those who will not endure chastening, but deny me, cannot be sanctified." (D. & C. 101:4-5.) And for those whose sacrifices are acceptable, the Lord provides an escape, a ram in the thicket, so that they and their righteous works are preserved. (Gen. 22:13; D. & C. 132:50.)

But in Abraham's case the Lord did something more than provide a supreme test of faith by which the Father of the Faithful was able to sanctify his soul; he did more than create an example of perfect faith and obedience. In addition he established a "figure," a "similitude," to typify the future sacrifice of his Only Begotten Son. As Jacob expressed it, "Abraham" was "obedient unto the commands of God in offering up his son Isaac, which is a similitude of God and his Only Begotten Son." (Jacob 4:5.) And thus for all generations of time whenever men think of Abraham's test on Mount Moriah, they think also that God himself gave his Only Begotten Son as an infinite and eternal sacrifice for the sins of the world.

Sacrifice] See *Commentary II*, pp. 537-540.

17. The promises] See Heb. 11:8-16.

His only begotten son] Isaac. Abraham in fact was the father of Ishmael by Hagar the bondwoman, but Isaac was the only son in the royal lineage, the lineage through which the promises were to come. (Gen. 16; 21:1-21.)

19. Even as God would yet raise his Only Begotten Son from death to glorious immortality, so Abraham knew that if he slew Isaac at the Lord's command, that same God would have to raise Isaac again to mortal life that the promise might be fulfilled: "In Isaac shall thy seed be called." (Gen 21:12.)

PATRIARCHAL BLESSINGS COME BY FAITH

HEBREWS 11:20-22.

20 By faith Isaac blessed Jacob and Esau concerning things to come.

21 By faith Jacob, when he was a dying, blessed both the sons of Joseph; and worshipped, *leaning* upon the top of his staff.

22 By faith Joseph, when he died, made mention of the departing of the children of Israel; and gave commandment concerning his bones.

Priesthood is the power and authority of God delegated to man on earth to act in all things for the salvation of men. And since salvation is a family affair and consists, in its fullest signification, in the continuation of the family unit in eternity, it follows that the priesthood is especially designed to bless families.

When the priesthood organization is in perfect operation, it functions on a family or patriarchal basis; it operates as a patriarchal order. It is the power to bless, to bless mankind generally and to bless the household of faith specifically. Hence, formal provision is made in the gospel for patriarchal blessings —

blessings given by a patriarch to his family in the power and authority of the holy priesthood.

Patriarchal blessings began with Father Adam. He gave his descendants blessings which included prophetic utterances of "whatsoever should befall his posterity unto the latest generation." (D. & C. 107:39-57.) And when Jacob blessed all his sons, along with Ephraim and Manasseh, the sons of Joseph, he was but following the pattern of the past. (Gen. 48 and 49.)

"As inheritors of the blessings of Jacob, it is the privilege of the gathered remnant of Jacob to receive their own patriarchal blessings and, by faith, to be blessed equally with the ancients. Patriarchal blessings may be given by natural patriarchs, that is by fathers in Israel who enjoy the blessings of the patriarchal order, or they may be given by ordained patriarchs, specially selected brethren who are appointed to bless worthy church members. (*Doctrines of Salvation*, vol. 3, pp. 169-172; *Gospel Kingdom*, p. 146.)

"The First Presidency (David O. McKay, Stephen L Richards, J. Reuben Clark, Jr.), in a letter to all stake presidents, dated June 28, 1957, gave the following definition and explanation: 'Patriarchal blessings contemplate an inspired declaration of the lineage of the recipient, and also where so moved upon by the Spirit, an inspired and prophetic statement of the life mission of the recipient, together with such blessings, cautions, and admonitions as the patriarch may be prompted to give for the accomplishment of such life's mission, it being always made clear that the realization of all promised blessings is conditioned upon faithfulness to the gospel of our Lord, whose servant the patriarch is. All such blessings are recorded and generally only one such blessing should be adequate for each person's life. The sacred nature of the patriarchal blessing must of necessity urge all patriarchs to most earnest solicitation of divine guidance for their prophetic utterances and superior wisdom for cautions and admonitions.' " (*Mormon Doctrine*, 2nd ed., p. 558.)

20. Isaac blessed Jacob] Jacob's blessing — for himself personally and for his posterity after him, as a nation and as a people — included this inspired utterance: "Let people serve thee, and nations bow down to thee: be lord over thy brethren, and let thy mother's sons bow down to thee: cursed be every one that curseth thee, and blessed be he that blesseth thee." (Gen. 27:29.)

21. Jacob . . . blessed . . . the sons of Joseph] In doing so, Jacob adopted them as his own, elevated them to the status of separate tribes in Israel, promised that a multitude of nations should flow from them, and set Ephraim (the younger) before Manasseh (the older). (Gen. 48.)

22. The fact that Joseph elicited a promise from his posterity that they would carry his bones to Canaan, kept dramatically before them, generation after generation, the fact that they as a people would yet return to and inherit their promised land. And when they went out of Egyptian bondage, "Moses took the bones of Joseph with him." (Ex. 13:19.)

FAITH OF ANCIENTS CENTERED IN CHRIST

HEBREWS 11:23-31.

23 By faith Moses, when he was born, was hid three months of his parents, because they saw *he was* a proper child; and they were not afraid of the king's commandment.

24 By faith Moses, when he was come to years, refused to be called the son of Pharaoh's daughter;

25 Choosing rather to suffer affliction with the people of God, than to enjoy the pleasures of sin for a season;

26 Esteeming the reproach of Christ greater riches than the treasures in Egypt: for he had respect unto the recompense of the reward.

27 By faith he forsook Egypt, not fearing the wrath of the king: for he endured, as seeing him who is invisible.

28 Through faith he kept the passover, and the sprinkling of blood, lest he that destroyed the firstborn should touch them.

29 By faith they passed through the Red sea as by dry *land:* which the Egyptians assaying to do were drowned.

30 By faith the walls of Jericho fell down, after they were compassed about seven days.

31 By faith the harlot Rahab perished not with them that believed not, when she had received the spies with peace.

I.V. HEBREWS 11:23-24.

23 By faith Moses, when he was born, was hid three months of his parents, because they saw that he was a **peculiar** child; and they were not afraid of the king's commandment.

24 By faith Moses, when he was come to years **of discretion,** refused to be called the son of Pharaoh's daughter;

Faith unto life and salvation centers in Christ. The first principle of the gospel is faith in the Lord Jesus Christ. It matters not who has faith or what age of the earth's history is involved, faith has been, is now, and everlastingly shall be in the Son of God.

When Paul says Abraham, Isaac, and Jacob gained favor with God by faith, he is saying that they believed in Christ and worshiped the Father in his name the same as all the prophets of all the ages have always done. Every miracle ever performed has been done in the name of Christ the Lord. Contrary to the vagaries of sectarian speculation, Christ and his gospel laws have been known from the beginning, not just from the meridian of time, and no man has or ever will be saved except through faith in his holy name.

Christ is the God of Israel] See *Commentary II*, pp. 354-357.

23-31. Moses lived by faith, as did all the prophets. Their righteous acts were guided by the Lord. Old Testament accounts that seem to be historical recitations only are in fact the stories of men and women who by faith prevailed upon the Lord to intervene miraculously in the affairs of his people. With clear spiritual insight, Paul ties these Old Testament happenings to faith in Christ, thus making them ensamples to all who learn of them.

23. Amram and Jochebed, the parents of Moses (Ex. 6:20), having faith in Christ, defied the decree of Pharaoh which dealt death to all the male children in Israel (Ex. 1:15-22), and the life of Israel's future lawgiver was miraculously preserved. (Ex. 2:1-10.)

24-26. Reared and taught amid all the wealth, splendor, and influence of Pharaoh's court; having at his command the prestige and power of the royal household; knowing he was assured of a life of ease and affluence — yet Moses, because of faith in Christ, chose to suffer with slaves and bondsmen of his own race rather than to accept the honors, wealth, and power of the greatest nation then on earth.

25. The people of God] Israel the chosen race, the people who, though slaves to Egyptian overlords, were chosen by Deity out of all the earth to be a nation of priests and kings.

The pleasure of sin for a season] There is no enduring pleasure in unrighteousness. "Wickedness never was happiness." (Alma 41:10.)

26. Reproach of Christ] The scorn and contempt in which the saints are always held by worldly people.

27. By faith he forsook Egypt] Israel went out from Egypt amid an overwhelming display of divine power. Pharaoh and the overlords whom they served were momentarily softened and made amenable to the departure of their bondsmen by a series of ten plagues, which were climaxed by the death of the firstborn in the homes of all the Egyptians. (Ex. 7, 8, 9, 10, 11, 12.)

That the hand of the Almighty was manifest in the freeing of his people is evident to all. But how came the plagues? What power brought them forth? What power turned the waters that were in the river to blood? How came the frogs, the lice, the flies, and the locust? What caused the death of the cattle, the thunder and hail and the fire that ran along the ground, and the three days of thick darkness? And the death of "all the firstborn in the land of Egypt . . . from the firstborn of Pharaoh that sitteth upon his throne, even unto the firstborn of the maidservant that is behind the mill; and all the firstborn of beasts" (Ex 11:5) — what power brought all this to pass?

And what caused six hundred thousand men, plus women and children, (Ex. 12:37), to unite as one man, leave the fleshpots of Egypt, and go forth into an unknown wilderness at the command of the Lord by the mouth of Moses?

How inspired Paul is when he teaches that all this and much more was wrought by faith in the Lord Jesus Christ! It leaves us to wonder how much fasting and prayer and humble pleading there was for surcease from the burdens of slavery; how many meetings were held to teach the people what they should do; how many testimonies were born of the need to do the things they were commanded? Long intervals may have elapsed between each of the plagues while the people pled anew with the Lord for relief and were strengthened in their faith that they might qualify for manifestations of divine power. But sure it is that Moses and his Israelitish brethren went forth, free from Egyptian bondage, by that power which is named faith.

Signs and miracles] See *Commentary II*, pp. 373-377.

28. The passover] "To commemorate Israel's deliverance from Egyptian bondage, the Lord commanded his people to keep the feast of the passover, a celebration pointing particularly to the fact that the angel of destruction passed over the homes of the faithful sons of Jacob, when the firstborn in all the families of Egypt were slain. (Ex. 12.)" (*Mormon Doctrine*, 2nd ed., p. 556.) See *Commentary I*, pp. 703-705.

Let it be known that it was by the power of faith that the Israelitish homes were spared! And if they of the chosen seed had not believed in their hearts that the Lord Jehovah would spare their firstborn sons, the angel of death would have taken them as he did the firstborn of Pharaoh and all the families of Egypt.

29. What but the power of God (which is named faith) could cause the waters of the Red Sea to divide, so that the children of Israel could pass through on "dry ground," while "the waters were a wall unto them on their right hand, and on their left." (Ex. 14:21-22.) What miracle is like unto causing "the floods" to stand "upright as an heap," and the waters to be "congealed in the heart of the sea"? (Ex. 15:8.) Is it any wonder that ever thereafter in Israel, and particularly among the Nephites, this transcendent event was used as an illustration of faith and power, with various of the prophets teaching that if God parted the Red Sea, leading Israel through on dry ground, a fact known to and accepted by all Israel, why then question other miraculous things? (1 Ne. 4:2; 17:26-27; Mosiah 7:19; Alma 36:28; Hela. 8:11-12.)

30. Why did the hosts of Israel march around Jericho in silence, once each day for six days, with only the seven priests blowing their trumpets? Why did they go around seven times on the seventh day and then amid the trumpet blasts give forth with a tumultuous shout? What was there in this ritualistic performance that caused the walls to fall down flat so that the armies of Israel could go straight into the city and utterly destroy all that was therein, save Rahab and her household? Surely, as Paul says, it was the faith in the hearts of the people, the faith that if they did as Joshua commanded, the city would be theirs. (Josh. 6.)

31. What saved Rahab, "and her father's household, and all that she had," and caused them to be adopted into Israel? (Josh. 6:25.) Faith, yes; which, however, presupposes acceptance of Christ as the God of Israel and consequent repentance — an illustration which shows that salvation is available for all who turn to the Lord with full purpose of heart.

FAITH AND MIRACLES GO TOGETHER

HEBREWS 11:32-35a.

32 And what shall I more say? for the time would fail me to tell of Gedeon, and *of* Barak, and *of* Samson, and *of* Jephthae; *of* David also, and Samuel, and *of* the prophets:

33 Who through faith subdued kingdoms, wrought righteousness, obtained promises, stopped the mouths of lions,

34 Quenched the violence of fire, escaped the edge of the sword, out of weakness were made strong, waxed valiant in fight, turned to flight the armies of the aliens.

35a Women received their dead raised to life again:

FAITH AND MIRACLES GO TOGETHER

Miracles and faith go together; they are inseparable. Where faith is found, miracles abound; where miracles are wrought, faith dwells in the hearts of men. Miracles are the fruit of faith. "No man since the world was had faith without having something along with it," the Prophet said. (*Teachings*, p. 270.)

By the mouth of Mormon, the Lord said: "It is by faith that miracles are wrought" (Moro. 7:37), and Moroni taught: "Yea, and even all they who wrought miracles wrought them by faith, even those who were before Christ and also those who were after." (Ether 12:16.) See *Commentary I*, pp. 723-734; *Commentary II*, pp. 373-377.

32. Moroni makes a similar listing of the torchbearers of faith among the Nephites. "It was the faith of Alma and Amulek that caused the prison to tumble to the earth," he says. "Behold, it was the faith of Nephi and Lehi that wrought the change upon the Lamanites, that they were baptized with fire and with the Holy Ghost. Behold, it was the faith of Ammon and his brethren which wrought so great a miracle among the Lamanites . . . . And it was by faith that the three disciples obtained a promise that they should not taste of death; and they obtained not the promise until after their faith. And neither at any time hath any wrought miracles until after their faith; wherefore they first believed in the Son of God." (Ether 12:13-18.)

But why does Paul list Gideon, Barak, Samson, Jephthah, and David as illustrations of that faith which flows from righteousness? Why not continue in the channel already charted and link with Enoch, Abraham, Moses and the others such names as Elijah, who sealed the heavens, called down fire from heaven on his enemies, raised the dead, and was taken by a chariot of fire into the realms of translated beings? (1 Kings 17, 18, 19 and 21; 2 Kings 1 and 2.)

Or Elisha who parted the waters of Jordan with the mantle of Elijah; healed the waters of Jericho, as also the pottage for the sons of the prophets; multiplied oil in the widow's vessel, as also the bread and corn in Gilgal; cured Naaman of his leprosy and then caused it to fall upon greedy Gehazi; caused the iron ax to swim; and smote the Syrian army with blindness? (2 Kings 2, 3, 4, 5 and 6.)

Or Isaiah who, as a sign to Hezekiah, lengthened the day? (2 Kings 19: Isa. 38.) Or Daniel whose faith saved him in the lion's den? (Dan. 6.) Or Shadrach, Meshach, and Abednego "upon whose bodies the fire had no power, nor was an hair of their head singed, neither were their coats changed," as they walked in the midst of the fiery furnace? (Dan. 3.) Or any of the host of prophets and righteous men whose deeds were legend in the households of the Hebrews?

Obviously Paul was doing no more than to illustrate to the Hebrew Saints the great reservoir of faith found among their forbears. And having named such worthies as Enoch and the patriarchs, he lists some of those whose lives were not all they should have been, to show that even they ministered and labored and worked miracles by that same eternal power which is faith. His choice of those who "put at defiance the armies of nations" and who were able to "subdue principalities and powers" (*Inspired Version*, Gen. 14:31), drives home the reality that faith does more than heal the sick, raise the dead, and work in the realm of spiritual things. It is also the power whereby wars are won, kingdoms are governed, and the Lord's purposes come off triumphant among the nations of men.

Gedeon] Gideon, by whose hand the Lord delivered Israel from the Midianites and the Amalekites. On one occasion, using but 300 warriors, he put to flight hosts that were "like grasshoppers for multitude; and their camels were without number, as the sand by the sea side for multitude." (Judges 6, 7 and 8.)

Barak] A leader of the armies of Israel who, as guided by the prophetess Deborah, utterly routed the Canaanites in the days of the Judges. (Judges 4 and 5.)

Samson] One of the Judges in Israel who in spite of his marriage to a Philistine woman and his numerous acts of rebellion and unrighteousness, had periods of faith and devotion during which the Lord used his great physical strength to perform almost superhuman feats for the deliverance of his people. (Judges 13, 14, 15 and 16.)

Jephthae] Jephthah. Of all Paul's illustrations, that of using Jephthah as an example of great faith is the most difficult to understand. That this captain of Israelitish hosts was guided by Deity in his triumphs over the armies of the Ammonites is not open to question. Born the son of an harlot, Jephthah had nonetheless grown to that spiritual maturity where "the Spirit of the Lord came upon" him and where, by faith, he was led of the Lord in "a very great slaughter" of the people of Ammon. But his rash vow to offer as a burnt offering whatever should first come forth and meet him after his victories, and the resultant sacrifice of his only daughter, is either gross and unbelievable wickedness or the Old Testament account is false. In view of Paul's use of this one of Israel's Judges as an example of faith, the presumption is that there is something amiss in the Old Testament record, as we have it, and that Jephthah's vow and sacrifice were of a different nature than our present record indicates. (Judges 11 and 12; 1 Sam. 12:11.)

David] In his youth and until near the end of a long reign, David was a man after the Lord's own heart. (1 Sam. 13:14; Acts 13:22.) Amid blood and fury and the desolation of war, he delivered Israel and prepared the way for the erection of the temple and the peace of Solomon's reign. But even David, the great king, having taken the virtue of Bathsheba and the life of Uriah (2 Sam. 11), lost his high standing with the Lord and "hath fallen from his exaltation." (D. & C. 132:39.)

Samuel, and . . . the prophets] All these — in all ages, and under all those circumstances where righteousness prevailed — worked by faith. And surely, even with the fragmentary accounts available either to Paul or to us, "time would fail" to tell of the miracles and mighty works wrought by them by that power which is faith.

33-34. In one degree or another these fruits of faith were manifest in the lives of all of the prophets and righteous men of old. The Judges in Israel, whom Paul has just named, were among those who had subdued kingdoms, waxed valiant in fight and turned to flight the armies of their enemies; Daniel had stood unharmed in a den of lions; and Israel's hosts, on many occasions, had escaped the edge of the sword while that God who "is a man of war" (Ex. 15:3) fought their battles. But Paul also must have known what the revelations say about Melchizedek, for in part he paraphrased the account of the works of that mighty prophet as these were revealed anew in this day to Joseph Smith: "Now Melchizedek was a man of faith, who wrought righteousness; and when a child he feared God, and stopped the mouths of lions, and quenched the violence of fire." (*Inspired Version*, Gen. 14:26.)

35a. Old Testament instances known to us of the dead being raised include only the son of the widow of Zarephath, whom Elijah raised (1 Kings 17), and the son of a Shunammite woman, whom Elisha returned to life. (2 Kings 4.) There may, of course, have been other instances known to Paul and the Hebrew Saints of his day. Other prophets who have raised the dead include the Lord Jesus (*Commentary I*, pp. 256, 314-317; 527-534), Peter (*Commentary II*, pp. 94-95), Paul himself (*Commentary II*, pp. 174-175), and Nephi, the disciple. (3 Ne. 7:18-20.)

FAITH ENABLES MEN TO ENDURE SUFFERINGS

HEBREWS 11:35b-40.

35b And others were tortured, not accepting deliverance; that they might obtain a better resurrection:

36 And others had trial of *cruel* mockings and scourgings, yea, moreover of bonds and imprisonment:

37 They were stoned, they were sawn asunder, were tempted, were slain with the sword: they wandered about in sheepskins and goatskins; being destitute, afflicted, tormented;

38 (Of whom the world was not worthy:) they wandered in deserts, and *in* mountains and *in* dens and caves of the earth.

39 And these all, having obtained a good report through faith, received not the promise:

40 God having provided some better thing for us, that they without us should not be made perfect.

I.V. HEBREWS 11:35, 39-40.

35 Women received their dead raised to life again; and others were tortured, not accepting deliverance; that they might obtain **the first** resurrection;

39 And these all, having obtained a good report through faith, received not the **promises;**

40 God having provided some better **things for them through their sufferings, for without sufferings they could** not be made perfect.

It is by faith that the saints of God of all ages endure the sufferings and persecutions heaped upon them by the wicked and ungodly. Those who through faith have a hope of eternal life choose to be mocked, scourged, tortured and slain rather than to deny the testimony of Jesus, without which no man can gain the riches of eternity. Those who through faith gain a knowledge of the plan of salvation are willing to suffer and sacrifice to receive the promised reward. They live not for this life alone and for the blessings that come to them here. But with the eye of faith they forsee the wonders of their eternal home in that celestial city where God shall wipe away all tears, and where suffering and sorrow shall be but a memory of mortality.

35b. Paul has already set forth that Abraham and the patriarchs sought an inheritance in the heavenly city; that is, they sought to be translated and to join the city of Enoch, as had those who became saints during the nearly 700 years from the translation of Enoch to the flood of Noah. See Heb. 11:8-16.

Joseph Smith, in discussing the doctrine of translation, after setting forth the fact that those who are resurrected have a higher state than those who are translated, quoted Hebrews 11:35, and said: "Now it was evident that there was a better resurrection, or else God would not have revealed it unto Paul. Wherein then, can it be said a better resurrection? This distinction is made between the doctrine of the actual resurrection and translation: translation obtains deliverance from the tortures and sufferings of the body, but their existence will prolong as to the labors and toils of the ministry, before they can enter into so great a rest and glory.

"On the other hand, those who were tortured, not accepting deliverance, received an immediate rest from their labors. 'And I heard a voice from heaven, saying, Blessed are the dead who die in the Lord, for from henceforth they do rest from their labors and their works do follow them.' (See Revelation 14:13.)

"They rest from their labors for a long time, and yet their work is held in reserve for them, that they are permitted to do the same work, after they receive a resurrection for their bodies." (*Teachings*, pp. 170-171.)

Resurrection] See *Commentary II*, pp. 388-390. **Obedience brings a better resurrection]** See *Commentary II*, pp. 396-397.

39. Received not the promise] See Heb. 11:8-16, especially verse 13.

40. Salvation, which is eternal life, consists in the continuation of the family unit in the highest heaven of the celestial world. (D. & C. 131:1-4; 132:1-32.) In that blessed realm a perfect patriarchal order will exist with Adam at the head and every saved person in his proper genealogical place. Hence, the salvation of the saints of all ages and dispensations is tied together. In this sense, those who lived in the first dispensation cannot be perfect without those in the last. The perfected families of all ages will take their places in the great patriarchal chain of saved beings. Thus in his great epistle on salvation for the dead, the Prophet Joseph Smith wrote concerning the ancestors of the Latter-day Saints who died without a knowledge of the gospel: "These are principles in relation to the dead and the living that cannot be lightly passed over, as pertaining to our salvation. For their salvation is necessary and essential to our salvation, as Paul says concerning the fathers — that they without us cannot be made perfect — neither can we without our dead be made perfect." (D. & C. 128:15).

Thereafter in one of his sermons, the Prophet expanded upon this doctrine in these words: "What promises are made in relation to the subject of the salvation of the dead? and what kind of characters are those who can be saved, although their bodies are mouldering and decaying in the grave? When his commandments teach us, it is in view of eternity; for we are looked upon by God as though we were in eternity. God dwells in eternity, and does not view things as we do.

"The greatest responsibility in this world that God has laid upon us is to seek after our dead. The Apostle says, 'They without us cannot be made perfect' (Hebrews 11:40); for it is necessary that the sealing power should be in our hands to seal our children and our dead for the fulness of the dispensation of times — a dispensation to meet the promises made by Jesus Christ before the foundation of the world for the salvation of man.

"Now, I will speak of them. I will meet Paul half way. I say to you, Paul, you cannot be perfect without us. It is necessary that those who are going before and those who come after us should have salvation in common with us; and thus hath God made it obligatory upon man." (*Teachings*, p. 356.)

"WHOM THE LORD LOVETH HE CHASTENETH"

HEBREWS 12:1-8.

1 Wherefore seeing we also are compassed about with so great a cloud of witnesses, let us lay aside every weight, and the sin which doth so easily beset *us*, and let us run with patience the race that is set before us,

2 Looking unto Jesus the author and finisher of *our* faith; who for the joy that was set before him endured the cross, despising the shame, and is set down at the right hand of the throne of God.

3 For consider him that endured such contradiction of sinners against himself, lest ye be wearied and faint in your minds.

4 Ye have not yet resisted unto blood, striving against sin.

5 And ye have forgotten the exhortation which speaketh unto you as unto children, My son, despise not thou the chastening of the Lord, nor faint when thou art rebuked of him:

6 For whom the Lord loveth he chasteneth, and scourgeth every son whom he receiveth.

7 If ye endure chastening, God dealeth with you as with sons; for what son is he whom the father chasteneth not?

8 But if ye be without chastisement, whereof all are partakers, then are ye bastards, and not sons.

1-4. Taking as his text, "the just shall live by faith" (Heb. 10:38), Paul taught the law of faith (Heb. 11), and now he exhorts the Hebrew Saints to live as their Israelitish forbears did. Life, he says, is a race. The saints are in the stadium running toward the goal of salvation. The witnesses of the past won the race in their day. Those who look to Christ and run as he ran shall gain the victory as he did.

1. A cloud of witnesses] All the faithful saints of the past bear witness by their lives that men — faced with every trial and temptation to which mortals are heir — can yet keep the faith, work righteousness, and gain the blessings of heaven.

Lay aside every weight] Get in condition for the race of life; take off the excess weight, the sins of the flesh.

2. Looking unto Jesus] Christ is the Prototype, the Great Exemplar; pattern after him; run the race as he did.

The author and finisher of our faith] The Leader and Perfecter of our faith. In Heb. 2:10 the word for *author* is translated *captain.* It is the Father, not the Son, who is the *author* in the sense of *originator.* The gospel originated with God; it is his plan of salvation which we and Christ accepted in pre-existence. See *Commentary II,* pp. 213-216.

4. Resisted unto blood] This our Lord did in his warfare with sin. In the Garden of Gethsemane, when he took upon himself the sins of the world, he sweat "great drops of blood" (Luke 22:44), and his suffering caused him "to bleed at every pore." (D. & C. 19:118.) Paul's reasoning is: If he was steadfast to the faith under his great burdens, how much more so should we be with the lesser weights we carry.

5-6. The quotation is from Proverbs 3:11-12. "My son, despise not the chastening of the Lord; neither be weary of his correction: For whom the Lord loveth he correcteth; even as a father the son in whom he delighteth." Paul's rendition, both in thought content and in doctrinal presentation, is superior to the original.

5. The chastening of the Lord] "By a process of chastening the Lord helps prepare his saints for salvation. It is one of his ways of turning erring souls to paths of righteousness. As varying situations require, chastening may include rebukes for misconduct or subjection to trials and afflictions. It may even take the form of chastisement, meaning corporal punishment.

"Men are chastened for their sins (D. & C. 58:60; 61:8; 64:8; 75:7; 93:50; 97:6; 103:4; 105:6; 1 Ne. 16:25), to bring them to repentance (D. & C. 1:27; 98:21), because the Lord loves them. (D. & C. 95:1-2; Hela. 15:3; Rev. 3:19.) Chastening is designed to try the faith and patience of the saints (Mosiah 23:21), and those who endure it well gain eternal life. . . .

"Chastening is both mental and physical. The Lord and his prophets may rebuke and counsel people for their benefit. (1 Ne. 16:39.) And the Lord may send calamities upon the people to soften their hearts so they will become more receptive to his will. 'Except the Lord doth chasten his people with many afflictions, yea, except he doth visit them with death and with terror, and with famine and with all manner of pestilence, they will not remember him.' (Hela. 12:3; D. & C. 87:6.) 'And my people must needs be chastened until they learn obedience, if it must needs be, by the things which they suffer.' (D. & C. 101:6.)

" 'Verily I say unto you, concerning your brethren who have been afflicted, and persecuted, and cast out from the land of their inheritance' — the Lord is speaking of those driven from their homes in Jackson County by the mobs — 'I, the Lord, have suffered the affliction to come upon them, wherewith they have been afflicted, in consequence of their transgressions; Yet I will own them, and they shall be mine in that day when I shall come to make up my jewels. Therefore, they must needs be chastened and tried, even as Abraham, who was commanded to offer up his only son. For all those who will not endure chastening, but deny me, cannot be sanctified.' (D. & C. 101:1-5.)" (*Mormon Doctrine*, 2nd ed., pp. 122-123.)

6. Scourgeth every son whom he receiveth] Christ our Lord, being without sin, was yet scourged before Pilate. (Matt. 27:26.) How much more ought we — being burdened with sin and needing whatever it takes to guide us to repentance and righteousness —

bow humbly before our God and bear up under his chastening rod? And for our good he uses that rod, in one way or another, the more devoted and faithful saints oftentimes being subjected to greater trials and sufferings than any others, as witness the very ones named by Paul in his discourse on faith.

8. **Bastards]** "Since a bastard is an illegitimate child, one born out of wedlock, Paul aptly and pointedly uses the term to describe those who are not sons of God, who have not been adopted into the family of God as joint-heirs with Christ. (Heb. 12:5-8.) According to his terminology there are sons on the one hand and bastards on the other. The sons inherit the fulness of the Father's kingdom; the bastards — never having been born of God — are cast out of the eternal family as though they were illegitimate; they become 'servants, to minister for those who are worthy of a far more, and an exceeding, and an eternal weight of glory.' (D. & C. 132:16.)" (*Mormon Doctrine*, 2nd ed., p. 74.)

Sons] See *Commentary II*, pp. 474-475.

PAUL SPEAKETH OF PRE-EXISTENCE AND EXALTATION

HEBREWS 12:9-10.

9 Furthermore we have had fathers of our flesh which corrected *us*, and we gave *them* reverence: shall we not much rather be in subjection unto the Father of spirits, and live?

10 For they verily for a few days chastened *us* after their own pleasure; but he for *our* profit, that *we* might be partakers of his holiness.

"Pre-existence is the term commonly used to describe the pre-mortal existence of the spirit children of God the Father. Speaking of this prior existence in a spirit sphere, the First Presidency of the Church (Joseph F. Smith, John R. Winder, and Anthon H. Lund) said: 'All men and women are in the similitude of the universal Father and Mother, and are literally the sons and daughters of Deity'; as spirits they were the 'offspring of celestial parentage.' (*Man: His Origin and Destiny*, pp. 351, 355.) These spirit beings, the offspring of exalted parents, were men and women, appearing in all respects as mortal persons do, excepting only that their spirit bodies were made of a more pure and refined substance than the elements from which mortal bodies are made. (Ether 3:16; D. & C. 131:7-8.)

"To understand the doctrine of pre-existence two great truths must be accepted: 1. That God is a personal Being in whose image man is created, an exalted, perfected, and glorified Man of Holiness (Moses 6:57), and not a spirit essence that fills the immensity of space; and 2. That matter or element is self-existent and eternal in nature, creation being merely the organization and reorganization of that substance which 'was not created or made, neither indeed can be.' (D. & C. 93:29.) Unless God the Father was a personal Being, he could not have begotten spirits in his image, and if there had been no self-existent spirit element, there would have been no substance from which those spirit bodies could have been organized.

"From the time of their spirit birth, the Father's pre-existent offspring were endowed with agency and subjected to the provisions of the laws ordained for their government. They had power to obey or disobey and to progress in one field or another. 'The first principles of man are self-existent with God,' the Prophet said. 'God himself, finding he was in the midst of spirits and glory, because he was more intelligent, saw proper to institute laws whereby the rest could have a privilege to advance like himself.' (*Teachings*, p. 354.)

"The pre-existent life was thus a period — undoubtedly an infinitely long one — of probation, progression and schooling. The spirit hosts were taught and given experiences in various administrative capacities. Some so exercised their agency and so conformed to law as to become 'noble and great'; these were foreordained before their mortal births to perform great missions for the Lord in this life. (Abra. 3:22-28.) Christ, the Firstborn, was the mightiest of all the spirit children of the Father. (D. & C. 93:21-23.) Mortal progression and testing is a continuation of what began in pre-existence." (*Mormon Doctrine*, 2nd ed., pp. 589-590.)

Be in subjection unto the Father of spirits, and live] Serve the Father, in the name of the Son, and gain eternal life.

10. Partakers of his holiness] "Ye shall be holy: for I the Lord your God am holy." (Lev. 19:2.) The whole purpose of the gospel and of creation itself is to enable men to become like God; to be perfect as is their Father in heaven (Matt. 5:58); to be like Deity when he appears (1 John 3:1-3); to "be partakers of the divine nature" (2 Pet. 1:4); to be gods themselves. (D. & C. 132:20.)

TO SEE GOD FOLLOW PEACE AND HOLINESS

HEBREWS 12:11-17.

11 Now no chastening for the present seemeth to be joyous, but grievous: nevertheless afterward it yieldeth the peaceable fruit of righteousness unto them which are exercised thereby.

12 Wherefore lift up the hands which hang down, and the feeble knees;

13 And make straight paths for your feet, lest that which is lame be turned out of the way; but let it rather be healed.

14 Follow peace with all *men*, and holiness, without which no man shall see the Lord:

15 Looking diligently lest any man fail of the grace of God; lest any root of bitterness springing up trouble *you*, and thereby many be defiled;

16 Lest there *be* any fornicator, or profane person, as Esau, who for one morsel of meat sold his birthright.

17 For ye know how that afterward, when he would have inherited the blessing, he was rejected: for he found no place of repentance, though he sought it carefully with tears.

I.V. HEBREWS 12:12.

12 Wherefore lift up the hands which hang down, and **strengthen** the feeble knees;

11. Those saints who yield in the true spirit to chastening increase in personal righteousness.

12. It is the duty of those who serve in the Church to: "Succor the weak, lift up the hands which hang down, and strengthen the feeble knees." (D. & C. 81:5.)

13. **That which is lame]** The spiritually lame, those who are weak in the faith and who need to be healed spiritually.

14. Jesus said: "Blessed are the pure in heart: for they shall see God" (Matt. 5:8), meaning that every person who perfects his life shall see God, here and now, while he yet dwells in the flesh, and that if he continues in grace, he shall also see and dwell with him everlastingly in the realms of immortal glory.

As revealed to Joseph Smith, the divine law enabling man to see Deity is couched in these words: "Verily, thus saith the Lord: It shall come to pass that every soul who forsaketh his sins and cometh unto me, and calleth on my name, and obeyeth my voice, and keepeth my commandments, shall see my face and know that I am." (D. & C. 93:1.)

Through Joseph Smith the Lord also said to all those who hold his holy priesthood: "It is your privilege, and a promise I give unto you that have been ordained unto this ministry, that inasmuch as you strip yourselves from jealousies and fears, and humble yourselves before me, for ye are not sufficiently humble, the veil shall be rent and you shall see me and know that I am — not with the carnal neither natural mind, but with the spiritual. For no man has seen God at any time in the flesh, except quickened by the Spirit of God." (D. & C. 67:10-11.) And the revelation on priesthood says that without "the power of godliness," which is righteousness, "no man can see the face of God, even the Father, and live." (D. & C. 84:21-22.)

The Prophet also taught: "It is the privilege of every Elder to speak of the things of God; and could we all come together with one heart and one mind in perfect faith the veil might as well be rent today as next week, or any other time, and if we will but cleanse ourselves and covenant before God, to serve him, it is our privilege to have an assurance that God will protect us at all times." (*Teachings*, p. 9.)

In his appearances to men, as in all things, the Lord conforms to the eternal laws which he has ordained. Thus, Moroni in telling of the great vision of the Brother of Jared, says: "Because of the knowledge of this man he could not be kept from beholding within the veil; . . . therefore he saw Jesus; and he did minister unto him." (Ether 3:19-20.)

15. 'Keep the commandments, lest through bitterness members of the Church are led astray.' And how true it is that bitterness toward church officers or members leads to loss of faith and devotion and to eventual defilement!

17. This verse is poorly written. What Esau sought "carefully with tears" was, not repentance, but the blessings of the birthright, which he had given up for a mess of pottage. (Gen. 25:29-34.) All men, Esau included, who have not sinned unto death, thereby becoming sons of perdition (Heb. 6:1-8), can of course repent.

EXALTED SAINTS BELONG TO CHURCH OF THE FIRSTBORN

HEBREWS 12:18-24.

18 For ye are not come unto the mount that might be touched, and that burned with fire, nor unto blackness, and darkness, and tempest,

19 And the sound of a trumpet, and the voice of words; which *voice* they that heard intreated that the word should not be spoken to them any more:

20 (For they could not endure that which was commanded, And if so much as a beast touch the mountain, it shall be stoned, or thrust through with a dart:

21 And so terrible was the sight, *that* Moses said, I exceedingly fear and quake:)

22 But ye are come unto mount Sion, and unto the city of the living God, the heavenly Jerusalem, and to an innumerable company of angels,

23 To the general assembly and church of the firstborn, which are written in heaven, and to God the Judge of all, and to the spirits of just men made perfect,

24 And to Jesus the mediator of the new covenant, and to the blood of sprinkling, that speaketh better things than *that* of Abel.

What God did for Moses, in the sight of all Israel, was a type and shadow of what he will do for all the faithful saints when they, through the sanctifying power that is in Christ, become as Moses their prophet and prototype.

Before all Israel, attended by a display of omnipotence that defies description, the Lord Jehovah came down upon mount Sinai and spoke audibly so that all the assembled millions of the chosen people heard his voice. By way of preparation, the people had cleansed their clothing and sanctified their souls. Then as his harbinger the Lord sent "thunders and lightenings, and a thick cloud upon the mount, and the voice of the trumpet exceeding loud." In this setting, and while the mount quaked and was wholly on fire, with the smoke ascending as from a furnace, "the Lord came down upon mount Sinai," appearing and speaking to Moses.

It was then that the great lawgiver received the Ten Commandments and other glorious revelations. But the people themselves went not up upon the mountain lest they be consumed by the glory of God's presence. So strict was the command that they not partake of more than they were prepared to receive spiritually, that any living thing, whether man or beast, that overstepped the prescribed bounds was slain. (Ex. 19:9-25; 20:1-23.)

To all of this, well known to his Hebrew brethren, Paul alluded and then drew his doctrinal conclusions. No longer is there a restraining barrier to keep the people from seeing and communing with their God. The mountain is no longer Sinai but Zion. And all those who have cleansed and perfected their souls, shall be welcomed on the heavenly mountain, and in the heavenly city, the new Jerusalem, the city of exalted beings. And there, in that heavenly realm, where the saints shall see and know, as Moses alone did in Israel, shall be found such might, display, splendor and omnipotence, that the doings of Jehovah on Sinai, incomprehensibly glorious as they were, shall be but a blurred image in comparison.

22-24. In the Vision of the degrees of glory, those who gain exaltation in the highest heaven of the celestial world are described, among other ways, as: "These are they who are come unto Mount Zion, and unto the city of the living God, the heavenly place, the holiest of all. These are they who have come to an innumerable company of angels, to the general assembly and church of Enoch, and of the Firstborn. These are they whose names are written in heaven, where God and Christ are the judge of all. These are they who are just men made perfect through Jesus the mediator of the new covenant, who wrought out this perfect atonement through the shedding of his own blood." (D. & C. 76:66-69.)

22. Mount Sion] Literally, the mount adjoining Jerusalem in Palestine and also the area of the New Jerusalem in Jackson County, Missouri; the place where the Lord shall stand with his exalted associates when he comes again to reign on earth a thousand years. (D. & C. 84:2, 32; 133:18, 56; Isa. 24:23; Joel 2:32; Obad. 21; Rev. 14:1.)

An innumerable company of angels] How many people by actual number shall be saved and exalted in the heavenly Jerusalem? Though the gate is strait and the way narrow and though comparatively few of earth's present inhabitants shall be so rewarded, yet the total number who actually do so obtain shall be large beyond comprehension. John speaks in one place of "ten thousand times ten thousand, and thousands of thousands," which is a hundred million, plus unspecified millions (Rev. 5:11), and in another of "a great multitude, which no man could number." (Rev. 7:9.) It should be remembered that this host shall include the millions of children who have died before they arrived at the years of accountability as well as the unnumbered hosts who pass through their mortal probation in that millennial day when "children shall grow up without sin unto salvation." (D. & C. 45:58.)

23. Church of the firstborn] This is the Church which exists among exalted beings in the celestial realm. But it has its beginning here on earth. "Members of The Church of Jesus Christ of Latter-day Saints who so devote themselves to righteousness that they receive the higher ordinances of exaltation become members of the Church of the Firstborn. Baptism is the gate to the Church itself, but celestial marriage is the gate to membership in the Church of the Firstborn, the inner circle of faithful saints who are heirs of exaltation and the fulness of the Father's kingdom. (D. & C. 76:54, 67, 71, 94, 102; 77:11; 78:21; 88:1-5; Heb. 12:23.)

"The Church of the Firstborn is made up of the sons of God, those who have been adopted into the family of the Lord, those who are destined to be joint-heirs with Christ in receiving all that the Father hath. 'If you keep my commandments you shall receive of his fulness, and be glorified in me as I am in the Father; . . . And all those who are begotten through me are partakers of the glory of the same, and are the church of the Firstborn.' (D. & C. 93:20-22; *Doctrines of Salvation,* vol. 2, pp. 9, 41-43.)" (*Mormon Doctrine,* 2nd ed., pp. 139-140.)

Spirits of just men made perfect] These are in the paradise of God awaiting the day of their resurrection and final inheritance among exalted beings. "There are two kinds of beings in heaven," the Prophet wrote, naming the first as "resurrected personages, having bodies of flesh and bones," and the second as: "The spirits of just men made perfect, they who are not resurrected, but inherit the same glory. When a messenger comes saying he has a message from God, offer him your hand and request him to shake hands with you. If he be an angel he will do so, and you will feel his hand. If he be the spirit of a just man made perfect he will come in his glory; for that is the only way he can appear—Ask him to shake hands with you, but he will not move, because it is contrary to the order of heaven for a just man to deceive; but he will still deliver his message." (D. & C. 129:1-7.)

24. Jesus the mediator of the new covenant] See 1 Tim. 2:1-7.

The blood of sprinkling] The blood of Christ, so described because of the similitude set forth in the Passover of the children of Israel by the angel of death; even as the firstborn in the Israelitish homes were saved because the blood of a lamb was sprinkled on the lintel and side posts of their doors (Ex. 12), so all men may be saved by the blood of that Lamb who was slain from the foundation of the world.

That speaketh better things than that of Abel] Is Paul here alluding to the ancient heresy that the blood of Abel was shed for the remission of sins? Had this false doctrine lingered among some of the Hebrews of that day? As the first gospel martyr (Gen. 4:1-

10; Moses 5:17-35), the shedding of Abel's blood had gained great significance among the descendants of Adam. By the time of Abraham, however, the true understanding of Abel's sacrifice and martyrdom had been so lost and perverted that Deity felt disposed to say to the Father of the Faithful: "My people have gone astray from my precepts, and have not kept mine ordinances, which I gave unto their fathers; And they have not observed mine anointing, and the burial, or baptism wherewith I commanded them; But have turned from the commandment, and taken unto themselves the washing of children, and the blood of sprinkling; And have said that the blood of the righteous Abel was shed for sins; and have not known wherein they are accountable before men." (*Inspired Version*, Gen. 17:4-7.)

But whatever the then prevailing views of the Hebrews may have been, Paul is here teaching: "The blood of righteous Abel" (Matt. 23:35), together "with the innocent blood of all the martyrs under the altar that John saw" (D. & C. 135:7; Rev. 6:9-11) cries unto the Lord for vengeance against the wicked; the blood of Christ, on the other hand, was poured out as a propitiation for sins, and through it men are empowered to repent and be reconciled to God. Thus the voice of Abel's blood is one of death and separation and sorrow; the voice of our Lord's blood is one of life and reunion and eternal joy. Truly his blood speaketh better things than that of Abel!

"OUR GOD IS A CONSUMING FIRE"

HEBREWS 12:25-29.

25 See that ye refuse not him that speaketh. For if they escaped not who refused him that spake on earth, much more *shall not* we *escape*, if we turn away from him that *speaketh* from heaven:

26 Whose voice then shook the earth: but now he hath promised, saying, Yet once more I shake not the earth only, but also heaven.

27 And this *word*, Yet once more, signifieth the removing of those things that are shaken, as

of things that are made, that those things which cannot be shaken may remain.

28 Wherefore we receiving a kingdom which cannot be moved, let us have grace, whereby we may serve God acceptably with reverence and godly fear:

29 For our God *is* a consuming fire.

25-26. 'Do not reject the blessings offered through the blood of Christ. If our fathers felt his wrath when they disobeyed the law he gave out of the darkness and clouds of Sinai, how much more shall we be cursed for rejecting his word, preached to us openly and in plainness in that day when he dwelt among us. If his voice—the voice of the Lord Jehovah—shook Sinai in ancient times, leaving Israel atremble, how much more shall the wicked fear before him when he returns in all the glory of his Father's kingdom to shake not only the earth but the heavens also.'

26. As is his standard practice, Paul here attributes the words of Jehovah to Christ. Before his birth into mortality, and with reference to his Second Coming, our Lord said to the Prophet Haggai: "Yet once, it is a little while, and I will shake the heavens, and the earth, and the sea, and the dry land; And I will shake all nations, and the desire of all nations shall come. . . . I will shake the heavens and the earth; And I will overthrow the throne of kingdoms." (Hag. 2:6, 22.) Seated on the Mount of Olives, some five hundred years later, the same Jehovah, then dwelling in mortality as the Son of Mary, said to his disciples of his Second Coming: "Then shall the Lord set his foot upon this mount, and it shall cleave in twain, and the earth shall tremble, and reel to and fro, and the heavens also shall shake." (D. & C. 45:48.)

27. At the Second Coming, "every corruptible thing . . . shall be consumed" (D. & C. 101:24); "and there shall be a new heaven and a new earth" (D. & C. 29:23) "wherein dwelleth righteousness" (2 Pet. 3:13), and that only shall remain which meets Millennial standards.

29. Our God is a consuming fire] Joseph Smith taught that those who gain exaltation shall "Dwell in everlasting burnings in immortal glory" (*Teachings*, p. 347), and that "God Almighty himself dwells in eternal fire; flesh and blood cannot go there, for all corruption is devoured by the fire. . . . When our flesh is quickened by the Spirit, there will be no blood in this tabernacle." (*Teachings*, p. 367.)

And Paul applies the truth here involved to the Second Coming when the Lord's earthly vineyard shall be burned, when "the elements shall melt with fervent heat" (2 Pet. 3:10), when the earth itself shall "burn as an oven; and all the proud, yea, and all that do wickedly, shall be stubble." (Mal. 4:1.)

Celestial globe] See Rev. 21:9-27.

"SOME HAVE ENTERTAINED ANGELS UNAWARES"

HEBREWS 13:1-3.

1 Let brotherly love continue.

2 Be not forgetful to entertain strangers: for thereby some have entertained angels unawares.

3 Remember them that are in bonds, as bound with them; *and* them which suffer adversity, as being yourselves also in the body.

2. Strangers] Church members from other places, of whom Paul had already spoken, saying that the Lord blesses those who "have ministered to the saints, and do minister." (Heb. 6:10.)

Some have entertained angels unawares] Does this mean that the saints may unknowingly entertain — that is, provide food, clothing, lodging and sociality—for the angels of God in heaven, for spirit beings, or for immortal or translated personages? Such a thought scarcely seems logical, although the disciples did provide food for the resurrected Lord (Luke 24), and according to Genesis 18 and 19, angels ministered to both Abraham and Lot and were banqueted and otherwise cared for by them.

However the Inspired Version marvelously clarifies the experiences of Abraham and of Lot. It appears that as Abraham "sat in his tent door, . . . three men stood by him"; he addressed them as, "My brethren," provided them with food and drink, and was blessed by one of them. They are specifically called "angels," and they spoke of the journey upon which the Lord had sent them. They said they had a message for Sodom and that the Lord had told them that unless they delivered it the sins of that city would be upon their "heads." Then the record says: "And the angels which were holy men, and were sent forth after the order of God, turned their faces from thence and went toward Sodom." (*Inspired Version*, Gen. 18.)

As to Lot's experience, these "three angels" came to Sodom where Lot "made them a feast," and they became the cause of great contention between Lot and the wicked inhabitants of the city. In due course "the angels called upon the name of the Lord for brimstone and fire from the Lord out of heaven. And thus they overthrew those cities [Sodom and Gomorrah] and all the plain." And again the record says that "the angels of God . . . were holy men." (*Inspired Version*, Gen. 19.)

Thus, among those who serve God as angels, that is as his ministers and messengers, are righteous mortal men. And so Paul, with perfect propriety, counsels the Hebrew Saints to entertain other saints who may be serving on the Lord's errand as his messengers, his ministers, his angels.

It would be interesting to know who the angels were who ministered to Abraham and then to Lot and who were in turn entertained by these brethren. Obviously they were great and mighty men for the Lord himself was personally present in connection with their appearance to Abraham. We know that "one of them blessed Abraham" (*Inspired Version*, Gen. 18:9), and also from other sources that Abraham was blessed by and received the priesthood from Melchizedek. (Gen. 14:17-20; Heb. 7:6-10; D. & C. 84:14.) Could it be that one of these angels was Melchizedek and that the three of them together comprised the First Presidency of the Church in their day?

Ministering of angels] See *Commentary II*, pp. 96-98.

"MARRIAGE IS HONOURABLE IN ALL"

HEBREWS 13:4-7.

4 Marriage *is* honourable in all, and the bed undefiled: but whoremongers and adulterers God will judge.

5 *Let your* conversation *be* without covetousness; *and be* content with such things as ye have: for he hath said, I will never leave thee, nor forsake thee.

6 So that we may boldly say, The Lord *is* my helper, and I will not fear what man shall do unto me.

7 Remember them which have the rule over you, who have spoken unto you the word of God: whose faith follow, considering the end of *their* conversation:

I.V. HEBREWS 13:5.

5 Let your **consecrations** be without covetousness; and be content with giving such things as ye have; for he hath said, I will never leave thee, nor forsake thee.

4. Marriage is honourable in all] Celibacy is not of God. Normal men and women of adult age should marry if they have proper opportunity so to do. To deliberately refrain from assuming marital or parental obligation is to fail the most important test of this mortal probation. The whole plan of salvation and exaltation centers in and revolves around the family unit. "Whoso forbiddeth to marry is not ordained of God, for marriage is ordained of God unto man." (D. & C. 49:15.) "The most important things that any member of The Church of Jesus Christ of Latter-day Saints ever does in this world are: 1. To marry the right person, in the right place, by the right authority; and 2. To keep the covenant made in connection with this holy and perfect order of matrimony — thus assuring the obedient persons of an inheritance of exaltation in the celestial kingdom." (*Mormon Doctrine*, 2nd ed., p. 118.)

Marriage] See *Commentary I*, pp. 544-549; 602-608; *Commentary II*, pp. 340-347.

The bed undefiled] Sexual intercourse between a man and woman married to each other is pure and proper.

Whoremongers and adulterers God will judge] Unless they repent, they shall be damned. Their home in the spirit world shall be hell (2 Ne. 9:36), and their inheritance in eternity the lowest kingdom God has provided for men. (D. & C. 76:103-106.) "For I, the Lord God, delight in the chastity of women. And whoredoms are an abomination before me; thus saith the Lord of Hosts." (Jacob 2:28.)

I. V. 5. Let your consecrations be without covetousness] It is not enough simply to pay tithing or otherwise contribute to the building up of the kingdom. True saints make their contributions freely and willingly to the Lord without coveting what they have chosen to return to Him who gave them all. Thus the Lord said to Martin Harris: "I command thee that thou shalt not covet thine own property, but impart it freely to the printing of the Book of Mormon, which contains the truth and the word of God." (D. & C. 19:26.)

K. J. 5. Be content with such things as ye have] Inordinate longing or striving for unneeded worldly possessions is contrary to the spirit of the gospel; the saints should seek instead the riches of eternity and have a lesser concern about temporalities.

I will never leave thee, nor forsake thee] This is an adage in Israel, a universal promise to all the Lord's people in all ages. He gave it to Jacob (Gen. 28:15), to Joshua (Joshua 1:5), to Solomon (1 Chron. 28:20), to all Israel (Deut. 31:6, 8), and it applies in principle to all who love his law and keep his word. "He that seeketh me early shall find me," he said to Joseph Smith, "and shall not be forsaken." (D. & C. 88:83.) The Lord is with his people!

6. "The Lord is on my side; I will not fear: what can man do unto me?" (Psalm 118:6.)

7. 'Follow the counsel of the Brethren; give heed to the General Authorities; take direction from the bishop and stake president; pattern your faith after theirs; and follow their righteous examples.'

CHRIST IS THE SAME EVERLASTINGLY

HEBREWS 13:8.

8 Jesus Christ the same yesterday, and to day, and for ever.

Jesus Christ is the Son of God — the Firstborn in the spirit, the Only Begotten in the flesh. While yet in the spirit he progressed and advanced until he became like his Father, under whose direction he became the Creator of all things and was chosen to be the Redeemer of the world and to work out the infinite and eternal atonement. He came to earth to work out his own salvation and to do the will of the Father in making salvation available to all men. After his resurrection he gained all power in heaven and on earth and became like his Father in all things.

Thus he is the same yesterday, today, and forever; he is a being in whom there is no variableness, neither shadow of turning; and he is from everlasting to everlasting. In the vision of the degrees of glory, he said of himself: "The Lord is God, and beside him there is no Savior. Great is his wisdom, marvelous are his ways, and the extent of his doings none can find out. His purposes fail not, neither are there any who can stay his hand. From eternity to eternity he is the same, and his years never fail." (D. & C. 76:1-4.)

Christ is the same yesterday, today, and forever, meaning that he never varies his course; that he always operates by law; that he is no respecter of persons and always bestows the same blessings as a reward for the same obedience. For instance, he is a God of miracles, and therefore there are always miracles where there is faith. The lame walk and the dead are raised, mountains move, the sun stands still, the Red Sea parts, fire comes down from heaven, wonderous things without end occur — whenever and wherever there is faith and to whomsoever possesses this precious power. No better analysis of this principle is found in Holy Writ than that given by Moroni in these words:

CHRIST IS THE SAME EVERLASTINGLY

"I speak unto you who deny the revelations of God, and say that they are done away, that there are no revelations, nor prophecies, nor gifts, nor healing, nor speaking with tongues, and the interpretation of tongues; Behold I say unto you, he that denieth these things knoweth not the gospel of Christ; yea, he has not read the scriptures; if so, he does not understand them. For do we not read that God is the same yesterday, today, and forever, and in him there is no variableness neither shadow of changing? And now if ye have imagined up unto yourselves a god who doth vary, and in whom there is shadow of changing, then have ye imagined up unto yourselves a god who is not a God of miracles. But behold, I will show unto you a God of miracles, even the God of Abraham, and the God of Isaac, and the God of Jacob; and it is that same God who created the heavens and the earth, and all things that in them are . . . . And who shall say that Jesus Christ did not many mighty miracles? And there were many mighty miracles wrought by the hands of the apostles. And if there were miracles wrought then, why has God ceased to be a God of miracles and yet be an unchangeable Being? And behold, I say unto you he changeth not; if so he would cease to be God; and he ceaseth not to be God, and is a God of miracles." (Morm. 9:7-11, 18-19.)

Christ is the same from eternity to eternity, meaning that from his pre-existent state on into his immortal state his course is one eternal round; meaning that from one pre-existence to the next, his laws are the same, and that the people of the past eternity were saved by the same course of obedience that will bring eternal life to the people of future eternities.

And all who follow their Prototype and gain a like exaltation with him, as joint-heirs in his Father's kingdom, shall be unchangeable and eternal beings who are the same yesterday, today, and forever. "Then shall they be gods, because they have no end; therefore shall they be from everlasting to everlasting because they continue." (D. & C. 132:20.)

God] See *Commentary II*, pp. 154-162.

Exaltation] See 1 John 3:1-3.

HOW CHRISTIANS OFFER SACRIFICES

HEBREWS 13:9-25.

9 Be not carried about with divers and strange doctrines. For *it is* a good thing that the heart be established with grace; not with meats, which have not profited them that have been occupied therein.

10 We have an altar, whereof they have no right to eat which serve the tabernacle.

11 For the bodies of those beasts, whose blood is brought into the sanctuary by the high priest for sin, are burned without the camp.

12 Wherefore Jesus also, that he might sanctify the people with his own blood, suffered without the gate.

13 Let us go forth therefore unto him without the camp, bearing his reproach.

14 For here have we no continuing city, but we seek one to come.

15 By him therefore let us offer the sacrifice of praise to God continually, that is, the fruit of *our* lips giving thanks to his name.

16 But to do good and to communicate forget not: for with such sacrifices God is well pleased.

17 Obey them that have the rule over you, and submit yourselves: for they watch for your souls, as they that must give account, that they may do it with joy, and not with grief: for that *is* unprofitable for you.

18 Pray for us: for we trust we have a good conscience, in all things willing to live honestly.

19 But I beseech *you* the rather to do this, that I may be restored to you the sooner.

20 Now the God of peace, that brought again from the dead our Lord Jesus, that great Shepherd of the sheep, through the blood of the everlasting covenant,

21 Make you perfect in every good work to do his will, working in you that which is wellpleasing in his sight, through Jesus Christ; to whom *be* glory for ever and ever. Amen.

22 And I beseech you, brethren, suffer the word of exhortation: for I have written a letter unto you in few words.

23 Know ye that *our* brother Timothy is set at liberty; with whom, if he come shortly, I will see you.

24 Salute all them that have the rule over you, and all the saints. They of Italy salute you.

25 Grace *be* with you all. Amen.

9-16. Paul now exhorts the Hebrew Saints to leave completely the dead letter of Mosaic performances and come to the living power that is in Christ. Verses 9 to 16 condense, summarize, and allude to a wealth of gospel knowledge and have the following sense and meaning:

9. 'Do not be deceived; there is no salvation in the sacrifices offered upon the altars of Israel; what counts is not the eating of the meat of sacrificial animals, but the sacrifice of a broken heart and a contrite spirit.'

10. 'However, we Christians have an altar, the cross of Christ, whereon he offered himself for the sins of the world; but the full blessings of this atoning sacrifice are reserved for members of the Church; they do not come to those without the fold, those who serve the tabernacle, those who put their trust in the dead ordinances of the Mosaic Law; such persons do not, as it were, partake of the meat sacrificed on the Christian Altar; they do not partake of the sacrament of the Lord's Supper to renew the covenants made in the waters of baptism.'

11-12. 'Even as the high priests in Israel on the Day of Atonement burned the bodies of the sacrificial animals without the camp and brought only their blood into the holy of holies, that thereby the people might be freed from sin (Lev. 16), so Christ our Lord was sacrificed without the gate of Jerusalem, that through the shedding of his blood he might cleanse and perfect his people and admit them to celestial exaltation in the heavenly holy of holies.'

13. 'Let us therefore leave the camp of Judaism, the camp peopled with nonmembers of the kingdom, the camp where trust is placed in animal sacrifices, and come unto Christ and the blessings of his blood, even though by so doing we bear the same reproach placed upon him.'

14. 'And why should we worry about any temporal loss entailed by such a course; the things of this world are fleeting and transitory anyway; what we seek, through Christ, is eternal and enduring; it is an inheritance in the heavenly city.'

15-16. 'What then are the sacrifices of the true Christian? They are unending praise and thankgiving to the Father who gave his Only Begotten Son as a ransom for our sins; they are everlasting praise to the Son for the merits and mercies and grace of his atoning sacrifice; they are obedience to the laws of the Lord; these are the sacrifices that please God. Or as it was said by the Lord himself to his other sheep: "Ye shall offer up unto me no more the shedding of blood; yea, your sacrifices and your burnt offerings shall be done away, for I will accept none of your sacrifices and your burnt offerings. And ye shall offer for a sacrifice unto me a broken heart and a contrite spirit. And whoso cometh unto me with a broken heart and a contrite spirit, him will I baptize with fire and with the Holy Ghost." ' (3 Ne. 9:19-20.)

Law of sacrifice] See Heb. 8:1-5.

17. They that must give account] Christ's ministers are accountable for the sins of those over whom they preside and to whom they are sent. "I have set thee a watchman unto the house of Israel," the Lord said to Ezekiel; "therefore thou shalt hear the word at my mouth, and warn them from me. When I say unto the wicked, O wicked man, thou shalt surely die; if thou dost not speak to warn the wicked from his way, that wicked man shall die in his iniquity; but his blood will I require at thine hand. Nevertheless, if thou warn the wicked of his way to turn from it; if he do not turn from his way, he shall die in his iniquity; but thou hast delivered thy soul." (Ezek. 33:7-9.)

20-21. Perfection and salvation are available "by the grace of God, through the shedding of the blood of Christ, which is in the covenant of the Father unto the remission of your sins, that ye become holy, without spot." (Moro. 10:33.)

The General Epistle of James

To have a book written by the Lord's brother is akin to having one penned by the Master himself. And in this General Epistle we find the son of Joseph, often in language reminiscent of that used by the Son of Mary, setting forth the practical operation of the doctrines taught by his Elder Brother.

James—religious by nature; schooled in the strict Judaism of the day; converted after our Lord's resurrection; and said to have died a martyr's death—took upon himself the awesome responsibility to write an epistle to the saints in the dispensation of the fulness of times.

Paul wrote to the saints of his own day, and if his doctrine and counsel blesses us of later years, so much the better. But James addressed himself to those of the twelve scattered tribes of Israel who belonged to the Church; that is, to a people yet to be gathered, yet to receive the gospel, yet to come into the fold of Christ; and if his words had import to the small cluster of saints of Judah and Benjamin who joined the Church in the meridian of time, so much the better.

He it was who chose the words—"If any of you lack wisdom, let him ask of God, that giveth to all men liberally"—which led Joseph Smith to his knees in the Sacred Grove in the Spring of 1820, when the dispensation of the fulness of times was ushered in by the personal appearance of the Supreme Rulers of the Universe.

And then he it was who proceeded to tell the yet-to-be-gathered remnants of the Lord's people how to live after they believed the restored message of salvation. The gospel had to become a living reality in their lives. They must bridle the tongue, cultivate patience, rise above envy and strife, resist evil, avoid respect of persons, use money wisely, cleave unto every good gift—in effect, endure to the end in keeping the commandments of Him whose household James had shared in his youth.

In addition to his ethical teachings and to the memorable 5th verse of the 1st chapter of his writings, James teaches two doctrines with a clarity and perfection not equaled by any Biblical author. He shows, with inspiration and logic beyond question, that faith itself, the very beginning of righteousness, does not and cannot exist unless works are present. And he sets forth the Lord's order where the anointing and healing of the sick in the household of faith is concerned.

Truly our understanding of God and his laws is enriched because James was guided by the Holy Ghost to pen this brief epistle!

ASK GOD FOR WISDOM

JAMES 1:1-7.

1 James, a servant of God and of the Lord Jesus Christ, to the twelve tribes which are scattered abroad, greeting.

2 My brethren, count it all joy when ye fall into divers temptations;

3 Knowing *this*, that the trying of your faith worketh patience.

4 But let patience have *her* perfect work, that ye may be perfect and entire, wanting nothing.

5 If any of you lack wisdom, let him ask of God, that giveth to all *men* liberally, and upbraideth not; and it shall be given him.

6 But let him ask in faith, nothing wavering. For he that wavereth is like a wave of the sea driven with the wind and tossed.

7 For let not that man think that he shall receive any thing of the Lord.

I.V. JAMES 1:2.

2 My brethren, count it all joy when ye fall into **many afflictions;**

1-3. Our author is addressing himself to the members of the Church; he calls them brethren and speaks of the trial of their faith, which can only mean their faith in the Lord Jesus Christ. And yet he names them as the twelve tribes scattered abroad, meaning the dispersed members of the house of Israel. With the conceivable exception of a few isolated individuals, the whereabouts of the Ten Tribes was unknown to James or any of the meridian saints. The resurrected Lord told the Nephites that his "people at Jerusalem" did not know the location of the "other tribes" because of unbelief. (3 Ne. 16:4.)

Thus, to address an epistle to them is one thing; to put it in their hands for perusal is quite another. It would appear that there is no way to make this delivery until their location is discovered, which may well mean that James was addressing himself in large measure to a people who were yet, and that in a distant day, to be gathered to the fold of Christ. Certainly the memorable fifth verse of this first chapter had more of an effect upon Joseph Smith and the destiny of the Lord's latter-day work than it did upon any person or group in the meridian of time.

It is worthy of note that the Prophet Mormon took a similar approach to his message. Isolated from most of Israel, hidden away as it were on the American Continent, he yet recorded: "I write unto all the ends of the earth; yea, unto you, twelve tribes of Israel, who shall be judged according to your works." (Morm. 3:18.) Clearly the message of James and of Mormon can only be delivered in full measure in that future day when the Lord makes known the identity of the whole house of Israel. So far, again with the exception of a few isolated individuals, the work is going forward among selected tribes.

1. James] The author of this General Epistle is not known for certain. It is generally believed by Biblical scholars that he is that James who is identified as being the Lord's brother.

2-4. Afflictions and trials are a necessary part of mortality; without them we could not be tried and tested, and one of the main purposes of earth life would be lost.

5. That wisdom which leads to salvation comes from God by revelation. Every person on earth, in or out of the Church, can gain wisdom from the Lord, who is the source and font of all truth and righteousness. Those outside the Church who diligently seek will be led to the gospel of salvation where perfect wisdom resides; those in the Church, when they seek righteousness with all their hearts, will be led along the path of truth and revelation until they know all things and have all wisdom.

God's counsel to all men is: "Ask, and ye shall receive; knock, and it shall be opened unto you." (D. & C. 4:7.) Through Brigham Young, he said: "Let him that is ignorant learn wisdom by humbling himself and calling upon the Lord his God, that his eyes may be opened that he may see, and his ears opened that he may hear." (D. & C. 136:32.)

The perfect illustration of how this principle operates is shown forth in the experience of Joseph Smith in the ushering in of this dispensation. In the midst of that war of words and tumult of opinions which made up the great religious revival in Western New York in the Spring of 1820, the young Joseph read and pondered the sobering words of James. "Never did any passage of scripture come with more power to the heart of man than this did at this time to mine," he said. "It seemed to enter with great force into every feeling of my heart. I reflected on it again and again, knowing that if any person needed wisdom from God, I did; for how to act I did not know, and unless I could get more wisdom than I then had, I would never know; for the teachers of religion of the different sects understood the same passages of scripture so differently as to destroy all confidence in settling the question by an appeal to the Bible.

"At length I came to the conclusion that I must either remain in darkness and confusion, or else I must do as James directs, that is, ask of God. I at length came to the determination to 'ask of God,' concluding that if he gave wisdom to them that lacked wisdom, and would give liberally, and not upbraid, I might venture." (Joseph Smith 2:12-13.)

Then followed the most glorious vision of which we have record in the entire history of God's dealings with men—the personal appearance of the Father and the Son, and the consequent ushering in of the greatest of all dispensations, the dispensation of the fulness of times. The long awaited mission and ministry of that prophet who was to do more, "save Jesus only, for the salvation of men in this world, than any other man that ever lived in it" had commenced. (D. & C. 135:3.)

Thus, this single verse of scripture has had a greater impact and a more far reaching effect upon mankind than any other single sentence ever recorded by any prophet in any age. It might well be said that the crowning act of the ministry of James was not his martyrdom for the testimony of Jesus, but his recitation, as guided by the Holy Ghost, of these simple words which led to the opening of the heavens in modern times.

And it might well be added that every investigator of revealed truth stands, at some time in the course of his search, in the place where Joseph Smith stood. He must turn to the Almighty and gain wisdom from God by revelation if he is to gain a place on that strait and narrow path which leads to eternal life.

Personal revelation] See *Commentary II*, pp. 320-322.

6. Let him ask in faith] "Without faith shall not anything be shown forth except desolations upon Babylon." (D. & C. 35:11.) "For without faith no man pleaseth God." (D. & C. 63:11.)

RESIST TEMPTATION AND GAIN SALVATION

JAMES 1:8-16.

8 A double minded man *is* unstable in all his ways.

9 Let the brother of low degree rejoice in that he is exalted:

10 But the rich, in that he is made low: because as the flower of the grass he shall pass away.

11 For the sun is no sooner risen with a burning heat, but it withereth the grass, and the flower thereof falleth, and the grace of the fashion of it perisheth: so also shall the rich man fade away in his ways.

12 Blessed *is* the man that endureth temptation: for when he is tried, he shall receive the crown of life, which the Lord hath promised to them that love him.

13 Let no man say when he is tempted, I am tempted of God: for God cannot be tempted with evil, neither tempteth he any man:

14 But every man is tempted, when he is drawn away of his own lust, and enticed.

15 Then when lust hath conceived, it bringeth forth sin: and sin, when it is finished, bringeth forth death.

16 Do not err, my beloved brethren.

I.V. JAMES 1:12.

12 Blessed is the man that **resisteth** temptation; for when he is tried, he shall receive the crown of life, which the Lord hath promised to them that love him.

8. A double minded man] A fickle, wavering man, as contrasted with one who is constant and firm, who always sustains the cause of righteousness. A member of the Church who tries both to forsake and to follow the world and who does not serve the Lord with an eye single to his glory.

9. 'Let faithful saints who labor in menial positions in this life rejoice, for they shall inherit thrones and kingdoms in the world to come.'

10-11. 'Let wealthy saints who are stripped of their goods because of their allegiance to the gospel also rejoice, for worldly riches are fleeting and not to be compared with the riches of eternity. Or, let them rejoice when, through trials, they become lowly in spirit and no longer trust in those things which wither and die in the day's heat.'

Riches] See Jas. 5:1-6. **Love of money]** See 1 Tim. 6:7-10.

12-16. "Overcoming temptation is an essential and necessary part of working out one's salvation. Mortal man is by nature carnal, sensual, and devilish (Alma 42:10), meaning that he has an inherent and earthly inclination to succumb to the lusts and passions of the flesh. This life is the appointed probationary estate in which it is being determined whether he will fall captive to temptations or rise above the allurement of worldly things so as to merit the riches of eternity.

"Christ himself 'was in all points tempted like as we are, yet [he remained] without sin.' (Heb. 4:15; D. & C. 20:22; Mosiah 3:7.) Adam was 'tempted of the devil,' and yielding thereto found himself cast out of the Garden of Eden. (D. & C. 29:36-40.) And all accountable men since his day, in greater or lesser degree, have been overcome by temptation and become sinners. (1 John 1:7-10.) The atonement, the gospel, and the plan of salvation are designed to free men from past sins and give them power to resist temptation in the future.

"Temptation—though its existence is essential to God's plan—is not of God, but is of the Devil. (Alma 34:39; 3 Ne. 6:17.) . . .

"The saints should pray always lest they enter into temptation. (3 Ne. 18:18; D. & C. 61:39.) The meaning of the petition, 'Lead us not into temptation, but deliver us from evil' (Matt. 6:13; Luke 11:4; 3 Ne. 13:12), is: Suffer us not to be led into greater temptation than we can bear, but deliver us from evil.

"Little children are without sin because 'power is not given unto Satan to tempt little children, until they begin to become accountable before me.' (D. & C. 29:47.) The Three Nephites, having overcome and being 'sanctified in the flesh,' are beyond the power of Satan, and he cannot tempt them. (3 Ne. 28:39.) Similarly, when the righteous saints go to paradise, they will no longer be tempted, but the wicked in hell are subject to the control and torments of Lucifer. (D. & C. 132:26.)" (*Mormon Doctrine*, 2nd ed., pp. 781-782.)

12. 'Blessed are those saints who resist temptation and overcome the world for they shall receive eternal life.'

13. God permits temptation to occur; man was placed on earth to be tried and tested in all things (Abra. 3:25); but temptation itself originates with Lucifer who is the Tempter.

EVERY GOOD GIFT COMETH FROM GOD

JAMES 1:17-21.

17 Every good gift and every perfect gift is from above, and cometh down from the Father of lights, with whom is no variableness, neither shadow of turning.

18 Of his own will begat he us with the word of truth, that we should be a kind of first-fruits of his creatures.

19 Wherefore, my beloved brethren, let every man be swift to hear, slow to speak, slow to wrath:

20 For the wrath of man worketh not the righteousness of God.

21 Wherefore lay apart all filthiness and superfluity of naughtiness, and receive with meekness the engrafted word, which is able to save your souls.

I.V. JAMES 1:21.

21 Wherefore lay **aside** all filthiness and superfluity of naughtiness, and receive with meekness, the engrafted word, which is able to save your souls.

17. God is the source of all that is good, Satan of all that is evil. "All things which are good cometh of God," Mormon taught; "and that which is evil cometh of the devil; for the devil is an enemy unto God, and fighteth against him continually, and inviteth and enticeth to sin, and to do that which is evil continually. But behold, that which is of God inviteth and enticeth to do good continually; wherefore, every thing which inviteth and enticeth to do good, and to love God, and to serve him, is inspired of God." (Moro. 7:12-13.)

The means used by Deity to send forth his gifts is the Spirit of Christ or the Light of Christ, "Which light proceedeth forth from the presence of God to fill the immensity of space." (D. & C. 88:12.) Even the gifts of the Spirit, which are the crowning gifts granted to men by the Lord, are transmitted "by the Spirit of Christ." (Moro. 10:17.)

18. Of his own will begat he us with the word of truth] We are born again because of Christ and his everlasting gospel.

A kind of firstfruits] An initial and beginning harvest of souls; saints in whose souls the gospel seed has sprouted, grown, and brought forth the fruits of the gospel.

20. Man's anger and unrighteousness do not further the cause of righteousness.

21. The engrafted word] The gospel, placed in our very souls.

"BE YE DOERS OF THE WORD"

JAMES 1:22-25.

22 But be ye doers of the word, and not hearers only, deceiving your own selves.

23 For if any be a hearer of the word, and not a doer, he is like unto a man beholding his natural face in a glass:

24 For he beholdeth himself, and goeth his way, and straightway forgetteth what manner of man he was.

25 But whoso looketh into the perfect law of liberty, and continueth *therein,* he being not a forgetful hearer, but a doer of the work, this man shall be blessed in his deed.

"BE YE DOERS OF THE WORD"

Paul is the apostle of good works, of personal righteousness, of keeping the commandments, of working out one's own personal salvation by obedience to the laws and ordinances of the gospel.

Paul is the great expounder of the doctrine that through God's grace salvation is available to those who keep the commandments after baptism.

No apostle of old, no ancient prophet, no person of former days of whom we have record, has ever recorded so emphatically, so repetitiously, with such vigor and plainness, that salvation comes only to those saints who endure to the end, as has our beloved brother Paul.

In this *Commentary*, the following portions, among others, contain and analyze scriptures in which Paul deals with obedience; pure, diamond, unadulterated obedience; obedience to the whole law of God; not a presumptuous, self-serving hope that salvation comes through Christ, without more on man's part than a whispered confession of belief; but obedience, obedience, obedience:

Commentary II

Live As Becometh Saints, pp. 293-295
Righteousness Leads to Salvation, pp. 297-298
The Unrighteous Shall Not Be Saved, pp. 337-340
"Stand Fast in the Faith," pp. 404-406
"Examine Yourselves, Whether Ye Be in the Faith," pp. 451-453
'Stand Fast Lest Ye Fall from Grace,' pp. 479-480
Crucify the Flesh and Walk in the Spirit, pp. 482-484
'As Ye Sow, So Shall Ye Reap,' pp. 486-487
"By Grace Are Ye Saved Through Faith," pp. 497-500
Christ's People Live Righteously, pp. 512-513
Walk Uprightly As Children of Light, pp. 514-517
"Put On the Whole Armour of God," pp. 523-524
Be of One Spirit and One Mind, pp. 529-530
"Work Out Your Own Salvation," pp. 535-536
"Stand Fast in the Lord," pp. 541-542

Commentary III

Saints Exhorted to Be Holy, pp. 35-38
"Perfect That Which Is Lacking in Your Faith," pp. 47-48
Be Holy; Sanctify Yourselves, pp. 48-50
Live As Becometh Saints, pp. 57-58
"Be Not Weary in Well Doing," pp. 67-68
"Fight the Good Fight of Faith," pp. 94-95
Be Strong in the Faith, pp. 101-102
Shun Contention, Seek Godliness, pp. 104-106
Live Righteously, Deny Ungodliness, Seek the Lord, pp. 123-125
How to Live After Baptism, pp. 125-128
"Let Us Go On Unto Perfection," p. 159

But with it all, it remained for James to crystallize the doctrine in headline form—"Be ye doers of the word, and not hearers only" —and to couple faith and works together with a band that cannot be broken (Jas. 2:14-25), thereby recording the texts for countless sermons in that portion of Christendom where sound understanding is found.

In other parts, as was stated, with fire and vehemence, to this present author, by a prominent minister representing one of the largest denominations: "I was saved two thousand years ago, and there is nothing I can do about it one way or the other now." (No works, no righteousness, no obedience, no keeping of the commandments, no nothing—just the Cross of Christ and the blood that flowed from his riven side!)

But: "Let us hear the conclusion of the whole matter: Fear God, and keep his commandments: for this is the whole duty of man." (Eccles. 12:13.)

Obedience to the whole law] See Jas. 2:1-13

23-24. To hear and not do—to seek salvation solely through the goods works of Christ, without personal conformity to his laws — is to see a glimpse of what salvation is in a mirror without ever receiving the real thing.

25. The perfect law of liberty] The fulness of the everlasting gospel, which is founded on the eternal principle of agency, the principle that men are free to choose their own course, "to choose liberty and eternal life, through the great mediation of all men, or to choose captivity and death, according to the captivity and power of the devil." (2 Ne. 2:27.)

Also: Freedom comes by obedience to law; "the truth shall make you free" (John 8:32); and those who are in bondage are bound by the chains of their own sins, from which they may be freed through the gospel law of liberty.

HOW TO RECOGNIZE PURE RELIGION

JAMES 1:26-27.

26 If any man among you seem to be religious, and bridleth not his tongue, but deceiveth his own heart, this man's religion *is* vain.

27 Pure religion and undefiled before God and the Father is this, To visit the fatherless and widows in their affliction, *and* to keep himself unspotted from the world.

I.V. JAMES 1:27.

27 Pure religion and undefiled before God and the Father is this, To visit the fatherless and widows in their affliction, and to keep himself unspotted from the **vices of** the world.

James is speaking to members of the Church who have already come to a knowledge of God and who know the truths of salvation. To them pure religion is to put into living operation the principles they have espoused.

"True religion is the true and revealed worship of the true God; all other systems of religion are false. In its pure and perfect form religion is found only among those members of the Church who practice their professions, who live the gospel, who walk uprightly before the Lord, who conform their lives to gospel standards, who sanctify their souls, and who thereby gain peace in this life and have a sure hope of eternal life hereafter." (*Mormon Doctrine*, 2nd ed., p. 626.)

To gain true religion men must first believe the gospel, repent of their sins, be baptized by a legal administrator, and receive the gift of the Holy Ghost. Then they must become doers of the received word; the gospel must live in their lives. "Wash you, make you clean; put away the evil of your doings from before mine eyes; cease to do evil; Learn to do well; seek judgment; relieve the oppressed, judge the fatherless, plead for the widow." (Isa. 1:16-17.)

Is there more than one true Church?] See *Commentary II*, pp. 506-508.

26. Bridleth not his tongue] See Jas. 3:1-13.

This man's religion is vain] There is no salvation in believing the truth unless you also keep the commandments.

WE COMMIT SIN IF WE RESPECT PERSONS

JAMES 2:1-9.

1 My brethren, have not the faith of our Lord Jesus Christ, *the Lord* of glory, with respect of persons.

2 For if there come unto your assembly a man with a gold ring, in goodly apparel, and there come in also a poor man in vile raiment;

3 And ye have respect to him that weareth the gay clothing, and say unto him, Sit thou here in a good place; and say to the poor, Stand thou there, or sit here under my footstool:

4 Are ye not then partial in yourselves, and are become judges of evil thoughts?

5 Hearken, my beloved brethren, Hath not God chosen the poor of this world rich in faith, and heirs of the kingdom which he hath promised to them that love him?

6 But ye have despised the poor. Do not rich men oppress you, and draw you before the judgment seats?

7 Do not they blaspheme that worthy name by the which ye are called?

8 If ye fulfil the royal law according to the scripture, Thou shalt love thy neighbour as thyself, ye do well:

9 But if ye have respect to persons, ye commit sin, and are convinced of the law as transgressors.

I.V. JAMES 2:1, 4.

1 My brethren, **ye cannot have** the faith of our Lord Jesus Christ, the Lord of glory, **and yet have** respect **to** persons.

4 Are ye not then **in yourselves partial judges, and become evil in your thoughts?**

1. 'If you have respect of persons, you are not living your religion.'

2-4. It is an evil thing to show partiality to men. The gospel calls for equity, justice and fairness in dealing with all. Favoritism and bias are not part of the divine standard.

5-7. Riches are a curse and not a blessing when they lead men to live after the manner of the world and to treat others with partiality. See Jas. 5:1-6.

7. That worthy name by which ye are called] The name of Christ which all saints take upon themselves in the waters of baptism. "There is no other name given whereby salvation cometh; therefore, I would that ye should take upon you the name of Christ, all you that have entered into the covenant with God that ye should be obedient unto the end of your lives. And it shall come to pass that whosoever doeth this shall be found at the right hand of God, for he shall know the name by which he is called; for he shall be called by the name of Christ." (Mosiah 5:8-9.)

8-9. Those who obey the royal law to love their neighbor as themselves are free from the sin of partiality.

SALVATION GAINED BY KEEPING WHOLE LAW

JAMES 2:10-13.

10 For whosoever shall keep the whole law, and yet offend in one *point*, he is guilty of all.

11 For he that said, Do not commit adultery, said also, Do not kill. Now if thou commit no adultery, yet if thou kill, thou art become a transgressor of the law.

12 So speak ye, and so do, as they that shall be judged by the law of liberty.

13 For he shall have judgment without mercy, that hath showed no mercy; and mercy rejoiceth against judgment.

I.V. JAMES 2:10.

10 For whosoever shall, **save in one point, keep the whole law,** he is guilty of all.

10-11. Salvation comes by obedience to the whole law of the whole gospel. Joseph Smith said: "Any person who is exalted to the highest mansion has to abide a celestial law, and the whole law too." (*Teachings*, p. 331.) Thus, a man may be damned for a single sin. He may have a testimony, serve on a mission, pay his tithing, have integrity in his business dealings, keep the Sabbath Day holy, and on and on through all the standards of personal righteousness, but if he commits adultery, he loses his soul. A sinner may, of course, repent and get in harmony again, if he has not sinned unto death, but the fact is that one sin, without repentance, damns, whereas obedience to the whole law is required for salvation. "For he who is not able to abide the law of a celestial kingdom cannot abide a celestial glory." (D. & C. 88:22.)

One of the saddest stories in all sacred writing is that of King David. Through long years of devotion and obedience he lived as a man after the Lord's own heart, and then came "the case of Uriah and his wife," and as a consequence, "he hath fallen from his exaltation," and shall not attain the celestial inheritance that otherwise would have been his. (D. & C. 132:39.)

Obedience] See *Commentary I*, pp. 253-255; 551-556; Jas. 1:22-25.

12. The law of liberty] See Jas. 1:25.

13. "The Lord shall come to recompense unto every man according to his work, and measure to every man according to the measure which he has measured to his fellow man." (D. & C. 1:10.)

Mercy rejoiceth against judgment] Those who have been merciful shall rejoice in the day of judgment for they shall have mercy restored unto them again. (Alma 41:12-15.)

"FAITH WITHOUT WORKS IS DEAD"

JAMES 2:14-26.

14 What *doth it* profit, my brethren, though a man say he hath faith, and have not works? can faith save him?

15 If a brother or sister be naked, and destitute of daily food,

16 And one of you say unto them, Depart in peace, be *ye* warmed and filled; notwithstanding ye give them not those things which are needful to the body; what *doth it* profit?

17 Even so faith, if it hath not works, is dead, being alone.

18 Yea, a man may say, Thou hast faith, and I have works: show me thy faith without thy works, and I will show thee my faith by my works.

19 Thou believest that there is one God; thou doest well: the devils also believe, and tremble.

20 But wilt thou know, O vain man, that faith without works is dead?

21 Was not Abraham our father justified by works, when he had offered Isaac his son upon the altar?

22 Seest thou how faith wrought with his works, and by works was faith made perfect?

23 And the scripture was fulfilled which saith, Abraham believed God, and it was imputed unto him for righteousness: and he was called the Friend of God.

24 Ye see then how that by works a man is justified, and not by faith only.

25 Likewise also was not Rahab the harlot justified by works, when she had received the messengers, and had sent *them* out another way?

26 For as the body without the spirit is dead, so faith without works is dead also.

I.V. JAMES 2:14-20.

14 What **profit is it,** my brethren, **for a** man **to** say he hath faith, and **hath** not works? can faith save him?

15 **Yea, a man may say, I will show thee I have faith without works; but I say, Show me thy faith without works, and I will show thee my faith by my works.**

16 **For if a brother or sister be naked and destitute, and one of you say, Depart in peace, be warmed and filled; notwithstanding he give not those things which**

are needful to the body; what profit is your faith unto such?

17 **Even so faith, if it have not works is dead, being alone.**

18 **Therefore wilt thou know, O vain man, that faith without works is dead and cannot save you?**

19 **Thou believest there is one God; thou doest well; the devils also believe, and tremble; thou hast made thyself like unto them, not being justified.**

20 Was not Abraham our father justified by works, when he had offered Isaac his son upon the altar?

Question: Is it possible to have faith without works?

Answer: Emphatically and unequivocally — No!

Come now, and let us reason together on this issue.

First, faith is power; it is action, the moving cause of all action in intelligent beings; it is, in effect, the occurrence of certain eventualities as a result of the prior assurance that they shall surely come to pass — such is Joseph Smith's inspired explanation. (*Commentary I*, pp. 523-525.) Thus a man who has no power from God, no power to perform the works of the Lord, has no faith.

Next, Jesus said that certain signs shall follow those that believe. That is, whenever and wherever there is faith, the gifts of the Spirit will be found. (Mark 16:16-20.) Thus in the absence of healings, tongues, prophecies, and all the gifts enjoyed by the ancient saints, there is no faith.

Both Mormon and Moroni taught that miracles always accompany faith and that where there are no miracles there is no faith. (Morm. 9:7-25; Moro. 7:26-39.) And the Prophet taught that the fruits of faith always are present when there is faith, and that "no man since the world was had faith without having something along with it." (*Teachings*, p. 270; *Lectures on Faith*, pp. 70-71.)

Faith then includes signs, miracles, and good works. Unless these are present, there is no faith; there may be the stirring motions of hope or belief or anticipation. There may be something which is falsely called faith. But faith in the Lord Jesus Christ, faith unto life and salvation, presupposes works; it requires miracles. Works are part of the definition of faith and without them there is no faith. If a man says he has faith, but no works attend, his faith is dead, and in reality dead faith does not exist anymore than a dead man lives.

But did not Paul say that salvation came by faith alone, without works? Yes, he most assuredly did; and he also said that the works he was talking about were the performances of the Mosaic Law; and then he said, as guided by the same Holy Spirit who gave utterance to James, that implicit in and as part of faith itself were the works of righteousness. (*Commentary II*, pp. 497-500.)

As a theologian, Paul wrote to Gentiles to unfold to them the nature of the atonement and the deadness of the ancient law of ordinances and performances. James wrote to Israelites who had already forsaken the dead dispensation of the past, who already believed in Christ and understood the atonement, and who needed now to press forward, manifesting their faith in the only way such can be done — through good works. Had their positions been reversed, Paul would have said what James did, and James would have taken up Paul's cudgel. Their approaches were different, but their doctrine was the same. In the ultimate there is no more substantial difference between them than there is when one elder preaches the gospel in Spanish to the Mexicans and another preaches it in Mandarin to the Chinese. The doctrine is the same but is presented according to the needs of hearers.

14. Though a man say] This is only a claim to faith, not the real thing, as for instance the claim of those who think they have faith but falsely suppose they are saved by belief alone without works.

Can faith save him?] Not the false claim to faith, not the presumption that there can be faith without miracles and good works attending.

15-17. A perfect illustration! There is no more power in faith that does not include works than there is strength in food that is not eaten, or warmth in clothes that are not worn.

17. Faith . . . is dead] A dead faith equates with a dead god; dead things do not exist; the language is used here simply for purposes of analysis and comparison — to show the absurdity of claiming faith where there are no works. The true doctrine is: God lives and faith lives; "And signs shall follow living faith, Down to the latest day." (Hymn 46, "Come Listen to a Prophet's Voice!")

18. (I. V. 15). 'So you think you can have faith without works; if so, show it to me; where is it? How does it operate, what power does it have, or is it an ethereal nothingness, like the sectarian concept of God? Can it heal the sick or raise the dead (for these are works!)? Nay, your faith is dead; it does not exist. Come, rather, and I will show you my faith which hath works. Give heed while I say unto Mount Zerin, "Remove," and it shall be removed. (Ether 12:30.) Did not He who said, "By their fruits [works!] ye shall know them" (Matt. 7:20), say also, "If ye have faith as a grain of mustard seed, ye shall say unto this mountain, Remove hence to yonder place; and it shall remove; and nothing shall be impossible unto you"? (Matt. 17:20.) Where are the fruits of your faith?'

19. (I. V. 19). 'It is the doctrine of the devil to believe there can be faith without works; even the devils believe in God; and those who so think, without more, are "like unto them," and are not justified.'

20. (I. V. 18). 'You cannot be saved by faith that has no works.'

21-25. 'Man is justified by works.' For an extended discussion of this doctrine of justification, see *Commentary II*, pp. 224-240.

26. This verse contains the same type of argument which Lehi used to show that if there were no law, there could be no sin, righteousness, happiness, punishment, or misery, no God, no creation, no mortal men, and therefore that "all things must have vanished away." (2 Ne. 2:13.) It is an argument so persuasive in nature that it is an end to all contention. As used by James, it is in effect: 'Without works — faith is dead, the body is dead, God is dead, there is nothing, all things have vanished away.' Or: 'If ye shall say there are no works, ye shall say there is no faith; and if there is no faith, there is no salvation, for salvation comes by faith; and if there is no salvation, there is no redemption; and if these is no redemption, there is no Christ and no God; and if these are not, there is no creation, and we are not and all things have vanished away.'

TAME THY TONGUE TO PERFECT THY SOUL

JAMES 3:1-13.

1 My brethren, be not many masters, knowing that we shall receive the greater condemnation.

2 For in many things we offend all. If any man offend not in word, the same *is* a perfect man, *and* able also to bridle the whole body.

3 Behold, we put bits in the horses' mouths, that they may obey us; and we turn about their whole body.

4 Behold also the ships, which though *they be* so great, and *are* driven of fierce winds, yet are they turned about with a very small helm, whithersoever the governor listeth.

5 Even so the tongue is a little member, and boasteth great things. Behold, how great a matter a little fire kindleth!

6 And the tongue *is* a fire, a world of iniquity: so is the tongue among our members, that it defileth the whole body, and setteth on fire the course of nature; and it is set on fire of hell.

7 For every kind of beasts, and of birds, and of serpents, and of things in the sea, is tamed, and hath been tamed of mankind:

8 But the tongue can no man tame; *it is* an unruly evil, full of deadly poison.

9 Therewith bless we God, even the Father; and therewith curse we men, which are made after the similitude of God.

10 Out of the same mouth proceedeth blessing and cursing. My brethren, these things ought not so to be.

11 Doth a fountain send forth at the same place sweet *water* and bitter?

12 Can the fig tree, my brethren, bear olive berries? either a vine, figs? so *can* no fountain both yield salt water and fresh.

13 Who *is* a wise man and endued with knowledge among you? let him show out of a good conversation his works with meekness of wisdom.

I.V. JAMES 3:1.

1 My brethren, **strive not for the mastery,** knowing that **in so doing** we shall receive the greater condemnation.

The tongue is the mirror of the soul. Spoken words reveal the intents, desires, and feelings of the heart. We shall give an account before the judgment bar for every spoken word, and shall be condemned for our idle, intemperate, profane, and false words. (Matt. 12:34-37; Alma 12:14.) Implicit in this principle of judgment is the fact that we can control what we say. And what better test can there be of a godly self-control than the ability to tame the tongue!

2. Worldly men are often vulgar, profane, and dishonest in speech; even the saints are sometimes harsh, intemperate, and unwise in their conversation.

5-6. A single spark may become a blazing inferno and burn a whole forest, and the tongue that uses improper language is as the igniting spark; it defiles the whole body, and burns the whole being of man.

9-12. Mormon uses this same reasoning to show that "a man being evil cannot do that which is good; . . . For behold, a bitter fountain cannot bring forth good water; neither can a good fountain bring forth bitter water; wherefore, a man being a servant of the devil cannot follow Christ; and if he follow Christ he cannot be a servant of the devil." (Moro. 7:6-11.)

ENVY AND STRIFE ARE OF THE DEVIL

JAMES 3:14-18.

14 But if ye have bitter envying and strife in your hearts, glory not, and lie not against the truth.

15 This wisdom descendeth not from *above*, but is earthly, sensual, devilish.

16 For where envying and

strife *is*, there *is* confusion and every evil work.

17 But the wisdom that is from above is first pure, then peaceable, gentle, *and* easy to be intreated, full of mercy and good fruits, without partiality, and without hypocrisy.

18 And the fruit of righteousness is sown in peace of them that make peace.

14. Envying and strife] Envying (resentment and discontent over the excellence or good fortune of another) and strife (contention for superiority) are of the devil; they lead away from God and his goodness, and estop men from acquiring those attributes which enable them to be like him.

Contention] See 2 Tim. 2:14-18.

15. Wisdom . . . not from above] 17. Wisdom . . . from above] James is here making the same distinction found in the writings of various of the prophets. There is one form of wisdom that is of God, another that is from beneath; one that is true and invaluable, in the eternal perspective, another that is false and counterfeit and leads away from salvation. Jacob speaks of "the wise, and the learned, and they that are rich, who are puffed up because of their learning, and their wisdom, and their riches," and says they are despised by the Lord, and that "the things of the wise and the prudent shall be hid from them forever." (2 Ne. 9:42-43.) Paul is even more explicit. He says the wisdom of the world is foolishness with God and that faith cannot stand on this wisdom of men. "Howbeit we speak wisdom among them that are perfect," he says, "yet not the wisdom of this world, . . . But we speak the wisdom of God in a mystery." (1 Cor. 1:17-31; 2:1-16.)

WHY AND WHENCE WARS COME

JAMES 4:1-3.

1 From whence *come* wars and fightings among you? *come they* not hence, *even* of your lusts that war in your members?

2 Ye lust, and have not: ye

kill, and desire to have, and cannot obtain: ye fight and war, yet ye have not, because ye ask not.

3 Ye ask, and receive not, because ye ask amiss, that ye may consume *it* upon your lusts.

1. Wars come because of a desire to steal, to plunder, to take another man's goods; they come because of a desire for sex immorality, for power, for fame, and for wealth. There are no great international principles at stake; there are no earthshaking reasons for combat. Any such are simply execuses. It is not nations of people and races of men that rise up to battle because of some irresistible need to take up the sword against other nations and kingdoms. Wars are simply quarreling and fighting in a magnified and organized form. They are born of lust and inspired by the devil. Satan is a warrior. In heaven and on earth he rebels and fights because wars destroy souls and hinder the work of righteousness. They are no different in principle from fighting and contention between individuals.

Lust] See 2 Pet. 2:10-22. **Carnality]** See *Commentary II*, pp. 322-324.

2. Men seek to gratify the lusts of the flesh through contention and war, but still do not gain their desires, whereas if they would ask of God, he would give them all that is proper and right.

3. "Whatsoever ye ask the Father in my name it shall be given unto you, that is expedient for you; And if ye ask anything that is not expedient for you, it shall turn unto your condemnation." (D. & C. 88:64-65.)

WHO ARE THE ENEMIES OF GOD?

JAMES 4:4-6.

4 Ye adulterers and adulteresses, know ye not that the friendship of the world is enmity with God? whosoever therefore will be a friend of the world is the enemy of God.

5 Do ye think that the scripture saith in vain, The spirit that dwelleth in us lusteth to envy?

6 But he giveth more grace. Wherefore he saith, God resisteth the proud, but giveth grace unto the humble.

4. Ye adulterers and adulteresses] Literally, those guilty of sex immorality; figuratively, those who have forsaken the Lord. (Isa. 57:3-9; Jer. 3:20; Ezek. 16; Hos. 2.)

The world] See *Commentary I*, pp. 749-752; 1 John 2:15-17.

Enmity with God] The Lord has his friends and his enemies. When people serve him with full purpose of heart, they become his friends (John 15:14-15), and they are the ones he shall take with him into his kingdom, and with whom he shall associate forever. (D. & C. 93:45-46.) His enemies, on the other hand, are those who oppose his work; who fight the truth; who live carnal and sensual lives, and advocate those principles and practices which debase men; who commit sin and live after the manner of the world.

5. The spirit that dwelleth in us lusteth to envy] There is no scripture to this effect in our present Old Testament. As here given, the meaning must be that man in this mortal probation is subject to envy and other lusts.

HOW TO BECOME A FRIEND OF GOD

JAMES 4:7-12.

7 Submit yourselves therefore to God. Resist the devil, and he will flee from you.

8 Draw nigh to God, and he will draw nigh to you. Cleanse *your* hands, *ye* sinners; and purify *your* hearts, *ye* double minded.

9 Be afflicted, and mourn, and weep; let your laughter be turned to mourning, and *your* joy to heaviness.

10 Humble yourselves in the sight of the Lord, and he shall lift you up.

11. Speak not evil one of another, brethren. He that speaketh evil of *his* brother, and judgeth his brother, speaketh evil of the law, and judgeth the law: but if thou judge the law, thou art not a doer of the law, but a judge.

12 There is one lawgiver, who is able to save and to destroy: who art thou that judgest another?

Having warned the saints lest through sin and apostasy they become friends of the world and therefore enemies of God, James now enumerates what they must do to remain in grace and stand as friends of Deity. After accepting the gospel and thereby gaining an introduction, as it were, to the Lord of Heaven, it is simply a matter of earning and acquiring the attributes of godliness so as to feel at ease in the divine Presence. And so James, in language of majestic simplicity, enumerates some of the principles of conduct which grow out of the doctrines of the gospel.

7. Resist the devil, and he will flee from you] 'Resist the devil, and he will have no power over you.' All of the prophets and righteous men, even our Lord himself included, are or were confronted and tempted by Lucifer. It is not until men dwell in celestial burnings that the devil, unable to stand the glory of such a world, flees from them in the true and ultimate sense of the word.

9. Weep, as Jesus did over doomed Jerusalem (Luke 19:41-44), for the sins of men.

11-12. Judging the brethren and evil speaking against the saints is in effect judging the gospel and evil speaking against its laws, for the gospel reserves judgment to the Lord. Thus, those who presume to judge others usurp the prerogatives of Deity, of him only who has power to impose sentence, that is, "to save and to destroy."

WHAT IS SIN?

JAMES 4:13-17.

13 Go to now, ye that say, To-day or to-morrow we will go into such a city, and continue there a year, and buy and sell, and get gain:

14 Whereas ye know not what *shall be* on the morrow. For what *is* your life? It is even a vapour, that appeareth for a little time, and then vanisheth away.

15 For that ye *ought* to say, If the Lord will, we shall live, and do this, or that.

16 But now ye rejoice in your boastings: all such rejoicing is evil.

17 Therefore to him that knoweth to do good, and doeth *it* not, to him it is sin.

WHAT IS SIN?

13-16. Those who have taken upon themselves the name of Christ, who have joined his family, who have chosen him as their Father, are now subject to family discipline. They are no longer free to go and come at will. They must conform to the family pattern of life. Their goings and comings and doings are now subject to the will of the Lord, their new Father. They may plan their own affairs as long as these do not run counter to what the Lord may have in mind. But his preferences prevail. He may want them to go on a proselyting mission, to serve in a bishopric, to preside over an elders quorum. Their obligation is to put first in their lives the things of his kingdom.

17. "What is sin? John said: 'All unrighteousness is sin.' (1 John 5:17.) Also: 'Whosoever committeth sin transgresseth also the law; for sin is the transgression of the law.' (1 John 3:4.) Paul taught: 'Whatsoever is not of faith is sin.' (Rom. 14:23.) James explained: 'To him that knoweth to do good, and doeth it not, to him it is sin.' (Jas. 4:17.) It should be noted that all of these statements were addressed to members of the Church who had received the gospel law.

"Elder Orson F. Whitney made this explanation: 'Sin is the transgression of divine law, as made known through the conscience or by revelation. A man sins when he violates his conscience, going contrary to light and knowledge—not the light and knowledge that has come to his neighbor, but that which has come to himself. He sins when he does the opposite of what he knows to be right. Up to that point he only blunders. One may suffer painful consequences for only blundering, but he cannot commit sin unless he knows better than to do the thing in which the sin consists. One must have a conscience before he can violate it.' (*Saturday Night Thoughts*, p. 239.) 'Where there is no law given there is no punishment; and where there is no punishment there is no condemnation.' (2 Ne. 9:25.) 'He that knoweth not good from evil is blameless.' (Alma 29:5.) (McConkie. Mormon Doct.)

"Sin cannot be committed unless laws are ordained (Alma 42:17) and unless people have knowledge of those laws so that they can violate them. Adam and Eve could not commit sin while in the Garden of Eden, although laws of conduct had already been established, because the knowledge of good and evil had not yet been given them. Unless they had partaken of the fruit of the tree of the knowledge of good and evil 'they would have remained in a state of innocence, having no joy, for they knew no misery; doing no good, for they knew no sin.' (2 Ne. 2:23.)" (*Mormon Doctrine*, 2nd ed., p. 735.)

MISERY AWAITS THE WANTON RICH

JAMES 5:1-6.

1 Go to now, *ye* rich men, weep and howl for your miseries that shall come upon *you.*

2 Your riches are corrupted, and your garments are motheaten.

3 Your gold and silver is cankered; and the rust of them shall be a witness against you, and shall eat your flesh as it were fire. Ye have heaped treasure together for the last days.

4 Behold, the hire of the labourers who have reaped down your fields, which is of you kept back by fraud, crieth: and the cries of them which have reaped are entered into the ears of the Lord of sabaoth.

5 Ye have lived in pleasure on the earth, and been wanton; ye have nourished your hearts, as in a day of slaughter.

6 Ye have condemned *and* killed the just; *and* he doth not resist you.

"As with all men, those who have riches will be judged according to their works and gain either salvation or damnation as they may chance to merit. But the nature of fallen man is such that in the overwhelming majority of cases riches are far more of a hindrance than a help in attaining peace in this world and eternal life in the world to come. Accordingly prophets in all ages have warned against 'the cares of this world, and the deceitfulness of riches' (Mark 4:19; Matt. 13:22; Luke 8:14), lest men love the things of this world more than the riches of eternity and thereby lose their souls." (*Mormon Doctrine*, 2nd ed., p. 652.)

1. Ye rich men] Not all rich men; rather, those whose money is their god, who lay up treasures upon earth only and not in heaven, whose hearts are set upon the things of this world. The righteous rich shall be saved. Relative to them, in counseling the Nephite Saints, Jacob taught: "Think of your brethren like unto yourselves, and be familiar with all and free with your substance, that they may be rich like unto you. But before ye seek for riches, seek ye for the kingdom of God. And after ye have obtained a hope in Christ ye shall obtain riches, if ye seek them; and ye will seek them for the intent to do good—to clothe the naked, and to feed the hungry, and to liberate the captive, and administer relief to the sick and the afflicted." (Jac. 2:17-19.)

Your miseries] Damnation. "Wo unto you rich men, that will not give your substance to the poor, for your riches will canker your souls; and this shall be your lamentation in the day of visitation, and of judgment, and of indignation: The harvest is past, the summer is ended, and my soul is not saved!" (D. & C. 56:16.)

Love of money] See 1 Tim. 6:7-10.

2-3. 'Riches should be used to do good and work righteousness. Treasures heaped up against days of trouble and peril shall perish. They become motheaten and rust away through disuse. Their loss bears witness of the selfishness of those who hoard them, in whose souls the fires of conscience shall burn, consuming, as it were, their very beings.'

4. "Thou shalt not oppress an hired servant that is poor and needy," the Lord told ancient Israel. "Thou shalt give him his hire, neither shall the sun go down upon it, . . . lest he cry against thee unto the Lord, and it be sin unto thee." (Deut. 24:14-15.) And the Lord also said that at his Second Coming he himself would be "a swift witness . . . against those that oppress the hireling in his wages," that they should not be able to "abide the day," but that with the proud and the wicked they should be consumed as stubble. (Mal. 3:2, 5; 4:1.)

Lord of sabaoth] "Christ is the Lord of Sabaoth. (Isa. 1:9; Rom. 9:29; Jas. 5:4; D. & C. 87:7; 88:2; 98:2.) Sabaoth is a Hebrew word meaning hosts or armies; thus, Jehovah Sabaoth means the Lord of Hosts. Also, as revealed to the Prophet, 'The Lord of Sabaoth, . . . is by interpretation, the creator of the first day, the beginning and the end.' (D. & C. 95:7.)" (*Mormon Doctrine*, 2nd ed., pp. 451-452.) James here equates the Lord of Sabaoth with the Lord who shall come at the Second Coming (Jas. 5:7), thereby testifying that Jehovah and Christ are the same person.

5. 'You have lived in pleasure, at the expense of the defrauded poor; you have glutted your souls with temporal things, like beasts who eat to their heart's content right up to their day of slaughter.' (Jer. 12:1-3.)

6. How often do riches, and the worldly power they beget, set the stage for the slaying of the prophets!

The just] Specifically, Christ; generally, all of the martyrs of true religion, all of the innocent blood shed upon the earth, all of the prophets and saints who lay down their lives for the love of God and the testimony of Jesus.

AWAIT THE LORD'S COMING WITH PATIENCE

JAMES 5:7-11.

7 Be patient therefore, brethren, unto the coming of the Lord. Behold, the husbandman waiteth for the precious fruit of the earth, and hath long patience for it, until he receive the early and latter rain.

8 Be ye also patient; stablish your hearts: for the coming of the Lord draweth nigh.

9 Grudge not one against another, brethren, lest ye be condemned: behold, the judge standeth before the door.

10 Take, my brethren, the prophets, who have spoken in the name of the Lord, for an example of suffering affliction, and of patience.

11 Behold, we count them happy which endure. Ye have heard of the patience of Job, and have seen the end of the Lord; that the Lord is very pitiful, and of tender mercy.

7-8. Our Lord's return is like the planting and harvesting of crops by an husbandman. The seeds are sown at his first coming and are watered by the early rains so that they sprout and take root. Then after a long wait, attended by much patience and endurance on the part of the saints, amid the latter rains, the rains that ripen the harvest, he comes again to pluck the fruit of his vineyard and to reign on earth a thousand years with those who have kept the faith.

7. The early and latter rain] The early rain fell at sowing time; the latter rain came to mature the crop for harvest. Thus, the heavens rained righteousness when our Lord ministered among mortal men in time's meridian; and also there shall be a great day of revelation, refreshment, and restoration when "Truth shall spring out of the earth; and righteousness shall look down from heaven" (Psalm 85:11), incident to the Second Coming. As one commentator says: "The latter rain that shall precede the coming spiritual harvest, will probably be another Pentecost-like effusion of the Holy Ghost." (*Jamieson,* p. 493.) And truly it shall be, for it has already begun, and it includes the restoration of the everlasting gospel to prepare a people for the Second Coming of the Son of Man.

8. The coming of the Lord draweth nigh] See 1 Thess. 5:1-11.

9. Grudge not one against another] It is one thing to bear up under the wrongs of the wicked; it sometimes is quite another to rise above the offenses given by one's fellow saints. Hence the counsel: 'Do not murmur or grumble or manifest harsh judgment against the brethren.'

The judge standeth before the door] The Lord's coming is near. When the fig tree puts forth its leaves, and all other signs are shown forth, then the saints shall know that their Lord's return "is near, even at the doors." (Matt. 24:32-33.) And finally, at the set time, passing through the "everlasting doors, . . . the King of glory shall come in." (Psalm 24:7.)

10. Patience] "To fill the full measure and purpose of our mortal probation, we must have patience. This mortal existence is the Lord's sifting sphere, the time when we are subject to trials, testing, and tribulations. Future rewards will be based on our patient endurance of all things.

" 'The patience of the saints' consists in bearing or enduring pains, trials, and persecutions (even unto death), without complaint and with equanimity. (Rev. 13:10; 14:12.) It was the Master himself who said: 'In your patience possess ye your souls' (Luke 21:19), and anyone who yields his whole soul and being to the Lord 'becometh as a child, submissive, meek, humble, patient, full of love, willing to submit to all things which the Lord seeth fit to inflict upon him, even as a child doth submit to his father.' (Mosiah 3:19.)

"Patience, also, involves an exercise of forbearance under provocation as illustrated in the celestial principle, 'whosoever shall smite thee on thy right cheek, turn to him the other also.' (Matt. 5:38-42; 3 Ne. 12:38-42.) Patience in righteousness leads to perfection and eternal life. Thus Paul wrote that 'by patient continuance in well doing' the saints 'seek for glory and honour and immortality, [and] eternal life.' (Rom. 2:7.) And by revelation in our day the Lord commanded: 'Continue in patience until ye are perfected'(D. & C. 67:13); 'And seek the face of the Lord always, that in patience ye may possess your souls, and ye shall have eternal life.' (D. & C. 101:38.)" (*Mormon Doctrine*, 2nd ed., pp. 557-558.)

11. Job] Not a mythical, but a real person, as this reference attests; as also does the Lord's statement to Joseph Smith: "Thou art not yet as Job; thy friends do not contend against thee, neither charge thee with transgression, as they did Job" (D. & C. 121:10); as also does Ezekiel's reference to certain wickedness being so great that though "Noah, Daniel, and Job" were in the land, "they should deliver but their own souls by their righteousness." (Ezek. 14:14, 20.)

The end of the Lord] First, patient endurance of all things; then, "All power . . . in heaven and in earth." (Matt. 28:18.)

ELDERS ANOINT AND HEAL THE SICK

JAMES 5:12-20.

12 But above all things, my brethren, swear not, neither by heaven, neither by the earth, neither by any other oath: but let your yea be yea; and *your* nay, nay; lest ye fall into condemnation.

13 Is any among you afflicted? let him pray. Is any merry? let him sing psalms.

14 Is any sick among you? let him call for the elders of the church; and let them pray over him, anointing him with oil in the name of the Lord:

15 And the prayer of faith shall save the sick, and the Lord shall raise him up; and if he have committed sins, they shall be forgiven him.

16 Confess *your* faults one to another, and pray one for another, that ye may be healed. The effectual fervent prayer of a righteous man availeth much.

17 Elias was a man subject to like passions as we are, and he prayed earnestly that it might not rain: and it rained not on the earth by the space of three years and six months.

18 And he prayed again, and the heaven gave rain, and the earth brought forth her fruit.

19 Brethren, if any of you do err from the truth, and one convert him;

20 Let him know, that he which converteth the sinner from the error of his way shall save a soul from death, and shall hide a multitude of sins.

12. Swear not] See *Commentary I*, pp. 225-227; Heb. 6:10-20; 7:18-22.

14. Is any among you afflicted? let him pray] We must do all we can ourselves to merit the receipt of the Lord's blessings. Before we seek the united faith of others, before we call in the elders to administer to us, before all else—we ourselves importune at the throne of grace, pleading in faith and thanksgiving for health and well-being, pleading for an outpouring of the healing power of the Lord upon us as individuals, pleading for strength and wisdom and guidance according to our needs and circumstances.

Is any merry?] "If thou art merry, praise the Lord with singing, with music, with dancing, and with a prayer of praise and thanksgiving." (D. & C. 136:28.)

14-16. "These words of James aptly summarize the practice of the Church in all ages where administrations are concerned. (D. & C. 42:43-44; 66:9; Mark 5:23; 6:5; 16:18; Luke 4:40-41; 13:11-13; Acts 28:8.) Administrations are of two parts: anointings and sealings; both performances are accompanied by the laying on of hands.

"It is the policy of the Church that administering to the sick should be done at the request of the sick person or someone vitally concerned, so that it will be done in answer to faith. Those called to perform the ordinance should encourage the sick person to rely on the Lord's promise, 'Whatsoever thing ye shall ask the Father in my name, which is good, in faith believing that ye shall receive, behold, it shall be done unto you.' (Moro. 7:26.) If need be the sick person should be encouraged to keep the commandments so that he can have faith and be entitled to the blessings of the Lord.

"In the performance of the administration, one of the elders should anoint the sick person with oil on or near the crown of the head, for the restoration of his health. Ordinarily he should not seal the anointing. Pure olive oil which has been consecrated for the anointing and healing of the sick in the household of faith should be used. Taking consecrated oil internally, or using it for anointing or rubbing afflicted parts of the body, is not part of the ordinance of administering to the sick.

"After the anointing two or more elders should lay their hands on the head of the sick person, and with one of them acting as voice, seal the anointing. The one speaking should offer such prayers, pronounce such blessings, give such promises, say such things, and rebuke the affliction—all as the Spirit of the Lord may dictate.

"Ordinarily one administration is sufficient for one illness, although in serious cases, or where other circumstances seem to dictate the propriety of such, a sick person may be administered to several times during one illness. It is also the common practice, if a sick person has recently been anointed, for those performing a second administration merely to give the sick person a blessing in the authority of the priesthood. In an emergency, where only one elder is present or available, he may either give the sick person a blessing or he can both anoint and seal in a formal administration.

"Ordinances of administration with actual healings resulting therefrom are one of the evidences of the divinity of the Lord's work. Where these are, there is God's kingdom; where these are not, there God's kingdom is not. Sincere investigators must necessarily beware of the devil's substitutes of the true ordinances." (*Mormon Doctrine*, 2nd ed., pp. 22-23.)

15. If he have committed sins, they shall be forgiven him] This is part—indeed, the most glorious part—of the ordinance of administering to the sick. The following explanation sets forth how this principle operates: "It is an axiomatic gospel verity that the Spirit of the Lord will not dwell in an unclean tabernacle. (1 Cor. 3:16-17; 6:19; Mosiah 2:37; Alma 7:21; 34:36; Hela. 4:24.) The Spirit will not come to a man unless and until he is prepared by personal righteousness to have the companionship of that member of the Godhead. Thus to be worthy of baptism men must 'witness before the church that they have truly repented of all their sins' (D. & C. 20:37), and precisely the same thing is involved in their preparation to partake of the sacrament. In other words, as a result of worthy baptism men stand clean before him if they fulfil the full law involved in partaking of the sacrament, for in each instance they are rewarded with the companionship of the Spirit, which companionship they cannot have unless they are cleansed and purified from sin.

"There are also other sacred occasions on which men are privileged to ascend to those spiritual heights where they gain the justifying approval of the Spirit for their conduct and as a consequence are forgiven of their sins. James named the ordinance of administration to the sick as one of these. . . . That is, the person who by faith, devotion, righteousness, and personal worthiness, is in a position to be healed, is also in a position to have the justifying approval of the Spirit for his course of life, and his sins are forgiven him, as witnessed by the fact that he receives the companionship of the Spirit, which he could not have if he were unworthy.

"In principle, what is here stated with reference to the sacrament and the ordinance of administration to the sick, applies to any other course of spiritual preparation which persons undergo, if that course of life is such as to get them in harmony with the Spirit of the Lord. One of the beauties of this doctrine is that in and through it repeated opportunities are given to sinners—and all men are sinners to a greater or lesser degree, whether they are in the Church or out of it—to repent and get their lives in such accord with the divine will that they may become heirs of salvation.

"In the final analysis, men are not saved unless they have struggled and labored through repentance and the attainment of forgiveness to the point that they stand clean and spotless before the judgment bar, for 'no unclean thing can inherit the kingdom of heaven.' (Alma 11:27.)" (*Mormon Doctrine*, 2nd ed., pp. 297-298.)

16. Confess your faults one to another] Not a promiscuous recitation of one's sins and shortcomings; men should, in wisdom, keep their own faults to themselves; but an organized system of confession as part of the law of forgiveness.

"To gain forgiveness all sins must be confessed to the Lord. The sinner must open his heart to the Almighty and with godly sorrow admit the error of his ways and plead for grace. 'I, the Lord, forgive sins unto those who confess their sins before me and ask forgiveness, who have not sinned unto death.' (D. & C. 64:7.)

"Further, those sins which involve moral turpitude—meaning serious sins for which the court procedures of the Church could be instituted so that a person's fellowship or membership might be called in question—such sins must be confessed to the proper church officer. 'To whom should confession be made?' President Stephen L Richards asked. "To the Lord, of course, whose law has been violated. To the aggrieved person or persons, as an essential in making due retribution if that is necessary. And then certainly to the Lord's representative, his appointed judge in Israel, under whose ecclesiastical jurisdiction the offender lives and holds membership in the kingdom.

" 'Is the offender justified in bypassing his immediate church authority and judge, and going to those who do not know him so well to make his confession? Almost universally, I think the answer should be No, for the local tribunals are in position to know the individual, his history and environs far better than those who have not had close contact with him, and in consequence the local authorities have a background which will enable them to pass judgment with more justice, and also mercy, than might be reasonably expected from any other source. It follows that it is the order of the Church for confession to be made to the bishop, which entails heavy and exacting responsibilities on the part of the bishop, the first of which is that every confession should be received and held in the utmost confidence. A bishop who violates such a sacred confidence is himself guilty of an offense before God and the Church. Where it becomes necessary to take counselors into his confidence, as it frequently does, and where it is necessary to organize tribunals, the bishop should inform the confessor, and if possible obtain his permission so to do.

" 'Why is confession essential? First, because the Lord has commanded it, and secondly, because the offender cannot live and participate in the kingdom of God, to receive the blessings therefrom, with a lie in his heart.

" 'Now the confessed offender is not left without hope, for he can obtain forgiveness by following the course outlined, and by forsaking sins comparable to that committed, as well as all other sin, and living before the Church and the Lord in such manner as to win approbation of both. The offender who has brought stigma and affront to the ward, the stake or the mission should seek the forgiveness of those he has thus offended. That may be had at times through the presiding authorities of the various divisions of the Church. At other times it may be appropriate and quite necessary to make amends for public offenses and seek forgiveness before organizations of the people. The judges of Israel will determine this matter.' (Conf. Rep., Apr., 1954, pp. 10-13.)

"It should be clear that bishops and other church officers, when confessions are made to them, do not forgive sins except in the sense that they forgive them as far as the Church is concerned; they remit any penalty which the Church on earth might impose; they adjudge that repentant persons are worthy of full fellowship in the earthly kingdom.

"Normally a period of probation is involved before the earthly agent determines to refrain from instituting the procedures whereunder church penalties are imposed. 'This probation serves a double purpose,' President Richards says. 'First, and perhaps most important, it enables the offender to determine for himself whether he has been able to so master himself as to trust himself in the face of ever-recurring temptation; and secondly, to enable the judges to make a more reliable appraisement of the genuineness of repentance and worthiness for restored confidence.' (Conf. Rep., Apr., 1954, p. 12.)

"Actual and ultimate forgiveness comes only from the Lord in heaven. He of course on occasions forgave sins during his ministry (Matt. 9:2-8), and he has by revelation in modern times announced that certain persons were free from sin. (D. & C. 29:3; 31:5; 36:1; 50:36; 60:7.) The Prophet Enos received a personal revelation telling him his sins were forgiven. (Enos 4-8.) Similar revelations might come at any time to the Lord's earthly agents, in which instances they could and would remit the sins of the repentant persons. But in the true sense it would be the Lord forgiving the sins, though he acted through the agency of his servants the prophets. (D. & C. 132:46-47; John 20:23.)

"Unless practiced and regulated in strict harmony with the divine will, the gospel requirement of confession can easily degenerate into a system which has the practical effect of inviting and enticing men to commit sin. By leaving the impression in men's minds that mere vocal recitation of past sins to the appointed church officer — without the attendant contrition of heart and the future righteousness of life—will suffice to cleanse the sinner, it is obvious that many persons will not be restrained from the commission of sin. Further, this true doctrine and law of confession stands in sharp contrast to the customs and practices found in the world in which churches say to their adherents, as Moroni expressed it: 'Come unto me, and for your money you shall be forgiven of your sins.' (Morm. 8:32.)" (*Mormon Doctrine*, 2nd ed., pp. 292-294.)

Pray for one another, that ye may be healed] The saints pray in faith for their own health and well-being (verses 12-13); they call in the elders of the Church for the prayers and blessings incident to the formal ordinance of administration (verses 14-15); and they also, now and always, pray for one another. It is not just a matter of a formal recitation of prayer-type words, or the mere ritual of administering to the sick; blessings come by faith; and continuing, fervent, pleading prayers increase one's faith and open the door to healings and miracles of all kinds.

17. Elias . . . prayed] The Old Testament account does not say that Elijah prayed, but such is implicit in the miraculous events that attended his word. (I Kings 17 and 18.) The fact is that faith and prayer and mighty pleading with the Lord are the usual and normal accompaniment of miracles.

19-20. By reclaiming an erring brother, we save both him and ourselves. Our sins are hidden (remitted) because we ministered for the salvation and blessing of another member of the kingdom. In principle this special reward for Christ's ministers applies also to those who preach the gospel and bring souls into the kingdom. The minister is rewarded with salvation and, of necessity, in the process, is freed from his own sins. (D. & C. 4:1-4.)

The First Epistle General of Peter

Lo, Peter, the Rock; the senior and chief apostle; the presiding officer in God's earthly kingdom; the one whom Jesus, the Lord, chose as his successor; lo, he now speaketh! And what a message is his; what truths flow from his pen! As Joseph Smith said, having reference to both the doctrines taught and the language used, "Peter penned the most sublime language of any of the apostles." (*Teachings*, p. 301.)

Dummelow, one of the better sectarian commentators, makes two rather excellent summary statements of the teachings and doctrines of First Peter.

One of these recites: "Peter begins by greeting them in the name of the Holy Trinity; reminds them that all events have their source in God's foreknowledge; that this trial is part of his eternal purpose, and that they are therefore sure of his protection; that, if the veil were lifted, as one day it will be, they would see the divine power and glory surrounding them; that Christ's work was done through suffering, and that suffering is the proper state of Christians, and the condition of their happiness and hope, for safety from the perils of this life is a little matter to those who are heirs of eternal safety; that the Holy Spirit, who in times past gave ancient Israel its Messianic hope, is with them still, making them the people of Christ, the manifested Messiah, binding together the whole brotherhood throughout the world for the fulfillment of God's single purpose, and enabling them to live as a consecrated people should."

In the other he summarizes Peter's views by saying: "His speeches, as recorded in Acts, show that he was sustained in those days by the same kind of thoughts as he expresses in this epistle—obedience is the great duty; the sufferings of Christ were appointed by God, and were not the chance triumph of his enemies; they involved humiliation, rejection, and the curse of the tree; they led to the resurrection which was due to the act of the Father, and is the source of Christian hope; now he sits supreme at the right hand of God, and has poured forth upon his people the Holy Spirit of whom he had received the promise from the Father: from thence he shall come at the time of the restoration of all things to judge the quick and dead. Jesus of Nazareth is the Messiah, of whom prophets spoke, and for whom Israel hoped. Forgiveness and repentance come from him, and through faith in his name is safety and salvation. The apostles are his witnesses, and so is the Holy Spirit in his people. All that has happened since he came is the outcome of past history, and there has been no break in the life of the people who are God's peculiar care; among them the believing Gentiles are also reckoned." (*Dummelow*, pp. 1038-1039.)

And yet how can the uninspired exegetists of the world begin to comprehend the import and depth of Peter's teachings? Particularly when he speaks of that faith which raises men to salvation in spiritual places; of our Lord's call and foreordination to be the Savior and Redeemer; of the elect status of all the saints; of their royal priesthood, the priesthood that makes them kings and priests; and of that glorious proclamation that the Lord of glory took the saving truths of his everlasting gospel to the spirits in prison, to the souls of men who were awaiting their resurrection and judgment.

If Peter had never recorded a syllable of scripture except in those verses which tell of salvation for the dead, his name would have been enshrined forever with the greatest of the prophets. And how appropriate it is that such a glorious doctrine should come to us from the mouth of the chief apostle, the chief undershepherd, the one upon whose shoulders the Son of God had laid the burden of his kingdom in the dispensation of persecution and martyrdom.

SALVATION COMES BY FAITH IN CHRIST

I PETER 1:1-16.

1 Peter, an apostle of Jesus Christ, to the strangers scattered throughout Pontus, Galatia, Cappadocia, Asia, and Bithynia,

2 Elect according to the foreknowledge of God the Father, through sanctification of the Spir-

it, unto obedience and sprinkling of the blood of Jesus Christ: Grace unto you, and peace, be multiplied.

3 Blessed *be* the God and Father of our Lord Jesus Christ, which according to his abundant mercy hath begotten us again unto a lively hope by the resurrection of Jesus Christ from the dead,

4 To an inheritance incorruptible, and undefiled, and that fadeth not away, reserved in heaven for you,

5 Who are kept by the power of God through faith unto salvation ready to be revealed in the last time.

6 Wherein ye greatly rejoice, though now for a season, if need be, ye are in heaviness through manifold temptations:

7 That the trial of your faith, being much more precious than of gold that perisheth, though it be tried with fire, might be found unto praise and honour and glory at the appearing of Jesus Christ:

8 Whom having not seen, ye love; in whom, though now ye see *him* not, yet believing, ye rejoice with joy unspeakable and full of glory:

9 Receiving the end of your faith, *even* the salvation of *your* souls.

10 Of which salvation the prophets have enquired and searched diligently, who prophesied of the grace *that should come* unto you:

11 Searching what, or what manner of time the Spirit of Christ which was in them did signify, when it testified beforehand the sufferings of Christ, and the glory that should follow.

12 Unto whom it was revealed, that not unto themselves, but unto us they did minister the things, which are now reported unto you by them that have preached the gospel unto you with the Holy Ghost sent down from heaven; which things the angels desire to look into.

13 Wherefore gird up the loins of your mind, be sober, and hope to the end for the grace that is to be brought unto you at the revelation of Jesus Christ;

14 As obedient children, not fashioning yourselves according to the former lusts in your ignorance:

15 But as he which hath called you is holy, so be ye holy in all manner of conversation;

16 Because it is written, Be ye holy; for I am holy.

I.V. I PETER 1:9-11.

9 Receiving the **object** of your faith, even the salvation of your souls.

10 **Concerning** which salvation the prophets **who prophesied of**

the grace bestowed upon you, inquired and searched diligently;

11 Searching what **time, and what manner of salvation** the Spirit of Christ which was in them did signify, when it testified beforehand the sufferings of Christ, and the glory which should follow.

1. Peter] The senior apostle of God on earth in the dispensation of the meridian of time. With James and John he held the Melchizedek Priesthood, the keys of the kingdom of God on earth, and the keys of the dispensation of the fulness of times, all of which he, in concert with his two associates, conferred upon Joseph Smith and Oliver Cowdery in about June of 1829. (D. & C. 27:12-13; 128:20.)

An apostle] See *Commentary II*, pp. 130-131; 328-333.

Strangers scattered] Pilgrims, travelers on earth; Israelites who are scattered in the named locations and who have joined the Church.

2. The elect are foreordained to be sanctified, by virtue of the blood of Christ, on conditions of gospel obedience.

Elect according to the foreknowledge of God] See *Commentary II*, pp. 267-269; 271-278; 283-285.

Sanctification] See 1 Thess. 4:1-8.

Sprinkling of the blood] See Heb. 12:24.

3-5. The elect are born again and shall be saved if they keep the commandments.

3. Hath begotten us again] See *Commentary II*, pp. 471-473; 1 John 5:1-5.

4. An inheritance incorruptible] Salvation.

5. Kept . . . through faith] Those foreordained to be saved shall be saved if they keep the commandments.

Salvation] With three or four possible exceptions all of the revelations of all the ages speak of salvation as being wholly, completely, and totally synonymous with eternal or everlasting life, with exaltation in the highest heaven of the celestial world, with attaining Godhood and being like God the Eternal Father. The exceptions are given to enable us to gain a complete perspective of the plan of salvation and to have an understanding of the goodness of God even where the wicked and ungodly are concerned. In substance and thought content these exceptions equate salvation with resurrection or immortality only, rather than with immortality coupled with eternal glory. (2 Ne. 9:26; D. & C. 76:40-44; 132:17.)

We may, of course, for purposes of clear understanding create definitions of salvation of our own, as telestial or terrestrial salvation, meaning an inheritance in one or the other of those kingdoms. But the gospel is a gospel of eternal life, of exaltation, of glory and honor, and so the Lord chooses to have his prophets equate salvation with the type and kind of life he lives, rather than with the ultimate inheritance of some lesser being, or of some wicked and rebellious person who rejected the gospel, suffered in hell until the second resurrection, and then came forth to that telestial inheritance whose inhabitants cannot go where God and Christ are worlds without end. (D. & C. 76:109-112.) Amulek, for instance, says that "no unclean thing can inherit the kingdom of heaven," and then asks: "How can ye be saved, except ye inherit the kingdom of heaven." (Alma 11:37.)

Salvation is defined and explained in the *Lectures on Faith* in these words: "Where shall we find a prototype into whose likeness we may be assimilated, in order that we may be made partakers of life and salvation? or, in other words, where shall we find a saved being? for if we can find a saved being, we may ascertain without much difficulty what all others must be in order to be saved. We think that it will not be a matter of dispute, that two beings who are unlike each other cannot be saved; for whatever constitutes the salvation of one will constitute the salvation of every creature which will be saved; and if we find one saved being in all existence, we may see what others must be, or else not be saved.

"We ask, then, where is the prototype? Or where is the saved being? We conclude, as to the answer of this question, there will be no dispute among those who believe the Bible, that it is Christ: all will agree in this, that he is the prototype or standard of salvation; or, in other words, that he is a saved being. And if we should continue our interrogation and ask how it is that he is saved, the answer would be—because he is a just and holy being; and if he were anything different from what he is, he would not be saved; for his salvation depends on his being precisely what he is and nothing else; for if it were possible for him to change, in the least degree, so sure he would fail of salvation and lose all his dominion, power, authority and glory, which constitute salvation; for salvation consists in the glory, authority, majesty, power and dominion which Jehovah possesses and in nothing else; and no being can possess it but himself or one like him."

Then after quoting several Biblical passages, the account continues: "These teachings of the Savior most clearly show unto us the nature of salvation, and what he proposed unto the human family when he proposed to save them—that he proposed to make them like unto himself, and he was like the Father, the great prototype of all saved beings; and for any portion of the human family to be assimilated into their likeness is to be saved; and to be unlike them is to be destroyed; and on this hinge turns the door of salvation." (*Lectures on Faith*, pp. 63-67.)

Immortality and eternal life] See 2 Tim. 1:1-22.

Work out your own salvation] See *Commentary II*, pp. 535-536.

Few saved or many?] See *Commentary I*, pp. 494-497.

Salvation for the dead] See 1 Pet. 3:18-22; 4:1-6.

6. Manifold temptations] 7. The trial of your faith] See 1 Pet. 4:12-19.

10-12. 'All the ancient prophets sought salvation and prophesied of the coming of Christ and his sufferings and atoning sacrifice. They knew beforehand, by the power of the Holy Ghost, what God had in store for the Meridian Saints. And so glorious is the message of redemption that even the angels desire to learn of it.'

11. The Spirit of Christ] The Holy Ghost] The Holy Ghost, a personage of Spirit, is a Revelator. Revelation comes by his power. He is broadcasting all truth out into all immensity all the time. And the Spirit of Christ—the light of Christ, the light that proceedeth forth from the presence of God to fill the immensity of space—is the means and agency used for carrying the revealed word to men, for disseminating eternal truth to mortal hearts. See Jas. 1:17-21.

13-16. Christ is the Prototype of salvation, the great Exemplar, the only one who can say with perfect propriety, and without any reservation or limitation on the language used: "Be holy, for I am holy." (Lev. 11:45.) "What manner of men ought ye to be? Verily I say unto you, even as I am." (3 Ne. 27:27.)

CHRIST FOREORDAINED TO BE THE REDEEMER

I PETER 1:17-21.

17 And if ye call on the Father, who without respect of persons judgeth according to every man's work, pass the time of your sojourning *here* in fear:

18 Forasmuch as ye know that ye were not redeemed with corruptible things, *as* silver and gold, from your vain conversation *received* by tradition from your fathers;

19 But with the precious blood of Christ, as of a lamb without blemish and without spot:

20 Who verily was foreordained before the foundation of the world, but was manifest in these last times for you,

21 Who by him do believe in God, that raised him up from the dead, and gave him glory; that your faith and hope might be in God.

17. When He judges whose judgment is just, it shall be done without respect of persons; every person will receive exactly what he merits, neither adding to nor diminishing from. See Jas. 2:1-9.

Time of your sojourning here] We are pilgrims; we are here on earth on a temporary basis; we traveled from pre-existence and shall return to a spirit sphere when death occurs.

18. Conversation] Manner of life.

19-20. Christ is "the Lamb slain from the foundation of the world." (Rev. 13:8.) That is, he was chosen and ordained to be the Savior of the world and the Redeemer of men in the councils of eternity. When the Father presented the plan of salvation in the pre-mortal life, when he announced the need for one of his spirit sons to be born into mortality as the literal Son of God—thus inheriting from the Father the power to work out the infinite and eternal atonement—Christ answered by saying in substance and thought content: 'Here am I, send me; I will be thy Son; I will follow thy plan; men shall have their agency and those who believe and obey shall be saved; and Father, the honor and the glory be thine forever.' (Moses 4:1-4; Abra. 3:27-28.)

The Father's plan of salvation] See *Commentary II*, pp. 213-216.

Plan of salvation] See *Commentary II*, pp. 40-42.

Plan of redemption] See Heb. 2:10-18.

21. By him . . . believe in God] It is only in and through Christ that men can believe in the Father. God is in Christ manifesting himself to the world. "No man cometh unto the Father" (John 14:6), except through Christ; and belief in the Father begins with belief in the Son. (John 12:44.)

Faith . . . in God] Christ is the door to the Father. The first principle of the gospel is faith in the Lord Jesus Christ. Our faith is centered in him and through him in the Father. Faith in the Father grows out of faith in the Son. "He that will not believe me will not believe the Father who sent me." (Ether 4:12.)

CONVERTS ARE NEWBORN BABES IN CHRIST

I PETER 1:22-25; 2:1-3.

22 Seeing ye have purified your souls in obeying the truth through the Spirit unto unfeigned love of the brethren, *see that ye* love one another with a pure heart fervently:

23 Being born again, not of corruptible seed, but of incorruptible, by the word of God, which liveth and abideth for ever.

24 For all flesh *is* as grass, and all the glory of man as the flower of grass. The grass withereth, and the flower thereof falleth away:

25 But the word of the Lord endureth for ever. And this is the word which by the gospel is

preached unto you.

1 Wherefore laying aside all malice, and all guile, and hypocrisies, and envies, and all evil speakings,

2 As newborn babes, desire the sincere milk of the word, that ye may grow thereby:

3 If so be ye have tasted that the Lord *is* gracious.

22. Purified . . . through the Spirit] Remission of sins comes by the power of the Holy Ghost. The receipt of the Holy Ghost is the baptism of fire, which baptism burns sin and iniquity out of the human soul as though by fire.

Baptism of water and the Spirit] See *Commentary II,* pp. 165-167.

Sanctification] See 1 Thess. 4:1-8.

23. The fruit of earthly harvests is born from seed that dies in the birth process, but the seed which brings spiritual rebirth to the saints is the word of truth found in the gospel, and it liveth and abideth forever.

Born again] See 1 John 5:1-5.

24. The glory of man] What is it? Nothing more than the grass that withereth and the flowers that fade away. (Isa. 40:6-8.) Kings and emperors rule today and are dust tomorrow! And what of their eternal souls, what shall their eternal glory be unless they had also the gospel, out of which salvation comes and which alone endures forever?

25. The gospel is preached] See 2 Tim. 4:1-5.

2:1-3. Baptism is the beginning. Joining the Church starts one out on the path leading to eternal life. (2 Ne. 31:17-21.) Then comes the process of enduring to the end, of working out one's own salvation (Philip. 2:12), of being fellowshiped to the full. "And after they had been received unto baptism, and were wrought upon and cleansed by the power of the Holy Ghost," Moroni said of the converts in Book of Mormon days, "they were numbered among the people of the church of Christ; and their names were taken, that they might be remembered and nourished by the good word of God, to keep them in the right way, to keep them continually watchful unto prayer, relying alone upon the merits of Christ, who was the author and the finisher of their faith." (Moro. 6:4.)

1. Malice . . . evil speakings] See *Commentary II*, pp. 514-517.

Guile] Deceitful cunning, craft and treachery. Guile is of the devil and damns the soul. Those in whose mouths no guile is found, "are without fault before the throne of God" (Rev. 14:5), and they shall have eternal life. Many of the faithful members of the Church are without guile. (D. & C. 41:9-11; 124:20.)

Hypocrisies] Where members of the Church are concerned, "Hypocrisy is to profess religion and not practice it. If a teacher advocates the payment of tithing, but does not himself pay an honest tithing, he is a hypocrite. If a person prays and seeks temporal and spiritual blessings from the Lord, and then turns away the naked and needy and fails to visit the sick and afflicted, he is a hypocrite. He has professed religion, but not practiced it. (Alma 34:17-29.)" (*Mormon Doctrine*, 2nd ed., pp. 371-372.)

Envies] See *Commentary II*, pp. 482-484.

2. Newborn babes] Newly baptized persons are newborn babes in spiritual things. Growth and strength come gradually. The most stable saints and powerful prophets did not attain their high states of spiritual maturity all at once. Even the Lord Jesus "increased in wisdom and stature, and in favour with God and man." (Luke 2:52.) Deity gives his truths to the obedient line upon line and precept upon precept. A student cannot learn calculus until he first knows the basic principles of mathematics, and it is only after the Lord has thoroughly proved a man and found him worthy in all respects that he is prepared to have direct and personal converse with his Maker. (*Teachings*, pp. 149-151.)

CHRIST IS THE CHIEF CORNERSTONE

I PETER 2:4-8.

4 To whom coming, as *unto* a living stone, disallowed indeed of men, but chosen of God, *and* precious.

5 Ye also, as lively stones, are built up a spiritual house, an holy priesthood, to offer up spiritual sacrifices, acceptable to God by Jesus Christ.

6 Wherefore also it is contained in the scripture, Behold, I lay in Sion a chief corner stone, elect, precious: and he that believeth on him shall not be confounded.

7 Unto you therefore which believe *he is* precious: but unto them which be disobedient, the stone which the builders disallowed, the same is made the head of the corner,

8 And a stone of stumbling, and a rock of offence, *even to them* which stumble at the word, being disobedient: whereunto also they were appointed.

I.V. I PETER 2:7-8.

7 Unto you therefore who believe, he is precious; but unto them **who are** disobedient, **who stumble at the word, through disobedience, whereunto they were appointed, a stone of stumbling, and a rock of offense.**

8 **For the stone which the builders disallowed, is become the head of the corner.**

"Christ is the Stone of Israel. (Gen. 49:24.) 'I am the good shepherd, and the stone of Israel. He that buildeth upon this rock shall never fall.' (D. & C. 50:44.) Christ is thus the stone or foundation upon which all men must build. Of him the Psalmist prophesied: 'The stone which the builders refused is become the head stone of the corner.' (Ps. 118:22; Matt. 21:42; Mark 12:10-11; Luke 20:17-18.) Peter used this truth to teach that the saints 'as lively stones' should build 'a spiritual house,' with Christ, the Stone of Israel, as the foundation. (1 Pet. 2:1-9.)" (*Mormon Doctrine*, 2nd ed., p. 768.)

4. A living stone] Christ—who is a living God, a living Redeemer, a living reality, and who has a living Church, "the only true and living church upon the face of the whole earth." (D. & C. 1:30.) There is no power in death; it is to life that we look for growth and advancement and salvation. Christ lives and is the living Stone upon which the living Church rests!

5. Lively stones] Christ the Living Stone giveth life to all who follow him, and they become lively stones in his living kingdom. Christ is "the life," and all those who live in him, as lively stones, "shall never die." (John 11:25-26.)

A spiritual house] The Church of Jesus Christ, either of Latter-day saints or of whatever age of the earth is involved, for in all ages the Church is "built upon the foundation of the apostles and prophets, Jesus Christ himself being the chief corner stone" (Eph. 2:20), and "other foundation can no man lay than that is laid, which is Jesus Christ." (1 Cor. 3:11.)

An holy priesthood] The Melchizedek Priesthood, which "continueth in the church of God in all generations," and "administereth the gospel" (D. & C. 84:17-19), thereby enabling men to obtain that holiness which is of Him who said: "Ye shall be holy: for I the Lord your God am holy." (Lev. 19:2.)

Spiritual sacrifices] The continuing, daily, everlasting sacrifice of a broken heart and a contrite spirit, offered up by those saints who cleave unto the Cause of Righteousness with all their hearts. (3 Ne. 9:19-20.)

6-8. Peter here quotes, combines, and interprets three Messianic prophecies, two from Isaiah and one from the Psalms. "Thus saith the Lord God," Isaiah announced in one of them, "I lay in Zion for a foundation a stone, a tried stone, a precious corner stone, a sure foundation: he that believeth shall not make haste." (Isa. 28:16.)

The clear meaning is: 'Christ our Lord, the promised Messiah, the Stone of Israel—as a precious and tried person—shall come to Israel; and be the foundation upon which they shall build the house of salvation; he shall be the cornerstone of the house and kingdom of God itself; and all they who believe in him and build on the foundation he lays shall be saved.'

The other Isaiah prophecy says that "he shall be for a sanctuary; but for a stone of stumbling and for a rock of offence to both the houses of Israel, for a gin and for a snare to the inhabitants of Jerusalem. And many among them shall stumble, and fall, and be broken, and be snared, and be taken." (Isa. 8:14-15.)

Again the meaning is clear: 'When the stone of Israel comes, he shall be a sanctuary for the righteous; they shall find peace and safety under the shelter of his gospel; but he shall be a Stone of Stumbling and a Rock of Offense (as also a gin and a snare) to the rebellious and disobedient in Jerusalem and in all Israel. They shall stumble and fall because of him; they shall take offense because of his teachings and be condemned and broken and snared and taken for rejecting them.' During his mortal ministry, our Lord discussed this very prophecy with his disciples and said that "on whomsoever this stone shall fall, it shall grind him to powder." (*Commentary I*, pp. 590-595.)

From the Psalmist, Peter quoted the inspired prophecy, "The stone which the builders refused is become the head stone of the corner" (Psalm 118:22), having reference to the rejection by the Jews of their Messiah and his subsequent acceptance by them as the foundation or cornerstone upon which they should build.

It is to the Book of Mormon that we turn to see how the Jews would both reject their Messiah and yet have him as "the head of their corner." Jacob, son of Lehi, foretelling our Lord's mortal ministry said: "I perceive by the workings of the Spirit which is in me, that by the stumbling of the Jews they will reject the stone upon which they might build and have safe foundation. But behold, according to the scriptures, this stone shall become the great, and the last, and the only sure foundation, upon which the Jews can build. And now, my beloved, how is it possible that these, after having rejected the sure foundation, can ever build upon it, that it may become the head of their corner? Behold, my beloved brethren, I will unfold this mystery unto you." (Jacob 4:15-18.)

By way of explanation, he then quotes, from the Prophet Zenos, the allegory of the tame and wild olive tree, and shows how in the latter-days, after a long night of apostasy and darkness and following the restoration of the gospel, the Jews will be led to believe and gain sanctuary with Christ through faith in his name. (Jacob 5 and 6.)

WHAT IS THE ROYAL PRIESTHOOD?

I PETER 2:9-10.

9 But ye *are* a chosen generation, a royal priesthood, an holy nation, a peculiar people; that ye should show forth the praises of him who hath called you out of darkness into his marvellous light:

10 Which in time past *were* not a people, but *are* now the people of God: which had not obtained mercy, but now have obtained mercy.

9. A chosen generation] Not those living in a particular period or age, but a race of people; the progeny of Jacob in all ages; the house of Israel both anciently, in the meridian of time, and now in these latter-days. "But thou, Israel, art my servant, Jacob whom I have chosen, the seed of Abraham my friend. Thou whom I have taken from the ends of the earth, and called thee from the chief men thereof, and said unto thee, Thou art my servant; I have chosen thee, and not cast thee away." (Isa. 41:8-9.)

A royal priesthood] Whenever the Lord has a people on earth he offers to make them a nation of kings and priests—not a congregation of lay members with a priest or a minister at the head—but a whole Church in which every man is his own minister, in which every man stands as a king in his own right, reigning over his own family-kingdom. The priesthood which makes a man a king and a priest is thus a royal priesthood.

To ancient Israel the offer was made in these words: "If ye will obey my voice indeed, and keep my covenant, then ye shall be a peculiar treasure unto me above all people: for all the earth is mine: And ye shall be unto me a kingdom of priests, and an holy nation." (Ex. 19:5-6.) Peter is here telling the Meridian Saints that they have the same promise, and John records that some of them did in fact obtain this royal status and become kings and priests, who should in due course live and reign with Christ on earth. (Rev. 1:6; 5:10; 20:4.) And the same blessings are available to the Latter-day Saints through the ordinances of the house of the Lord.

An holy nation] "For thou art an holy people unto the Lord thy God: the Lord thy God hath chosen thee to be a special people unto himself, above all people that are upon the face of the earth." (Deut. 7:6.)

A peculiar people] Faithful members of the Church who have taken upon themselves the name of Christ and been adopted into his family. "Ye are the children of the Lord your God: . . . For thou art an holy people unto the Lord thy God, and the Lord hath chosen thee to be a peculiar people unto himself, above all the nations that are upon the earth." (Deut. 14:1-2.) Manifestly such a people, as certified by their way of life in the midst of a crooked and perverse generation, are deemed by worldly people to be peculiar.

Called . . . out of darkness] "Darkness covereth the earth, and gross darkness the minds of the people." (D. & C. 112:23.) Thus, every person who accepts the gospel and joins the Church is called out of darkness.

His marvellous light] The Light of Christ, the light of truth, the light of the gospel. "That which is of God is light; and he that receiveth light, and continueth in God, receiveth more light; and that light groweth brighter and brighter until the perfect day." (D. & C. 50:24.)

10. The people of God] Those who join the Church thereby become the Lord's people. They are adopted into his family; they are set apart from the world; they become part of the nation and kingdom of Israel.

Obtained mercy] Justice is for the ungodly, mercy for the penitent. Mercy comes only to those who repent and live the gospel; all others are subject to the law of justice and pay the penalty for their own sins. (Alma 42:22-26.) "Know therefore that the Lord thy God, he is God, the faithful God, which keepeth covenant and mercy with them that love him and keep his commandments to a thousand generations." (Deut. 7:9.)

WHY THERE ARE FLESHLY LUSTS

I PETER 2:11-12.

11 Dearly beloved, I beseech *you* as strangers and pilgrims, abstain from fleshly lusts, which war against the soul:

12 Having your conversation honest among the Gentiles: that, whereas they speak against you as evildoers, they may by *your* good works, which they shall behold, glorify God in the day of visitation.

I.V. I PETER 2:12.

12 Having your **conduct** honest among the Gentiles; that, whereas they speak against you as evil-doers, they may by your good works, which they shall behold, glorify God in the day of visitation.

11. Strangers and pilgrims] See Heb. 11:8-16.

Abstain from fleshly lusts] As part of the Father's plan to enable his spirit children to advance and progress and become like him, two probationary estates are provided—the pre-existent first estate and the second estate of mortality.

In pre-existence we were tested as spirit beings and under circumstances where we walked by sight, knowing who our Father was and having a perfect knowledge that he was the Source and Author of the laws we were counseled to obey. As a result of long association there, the Lord knows exactly how we respond to his will as spirits and when we have a knowledge of him and his laws.

Hence he provided this mortal estate to try and test us under different circumstances, under circumstances in which we would be subject to the lusts of the flesh and when we would walk, not by sight, but by faith. And thus there is an imperative need for fleshly lusts as part of the eternal plan. This very sphere of existence is deliberately designed as one in which all men will be subject to the appetites and passions and lusts of life. The whole issue is whether we as mortals walk in the Spirit, whether we walk by faith as though seeing him who is invisible. The issue is whether we take Peter's counsel and abstain from these fleshly lusts or whether we follow the worldly course of appetite and indulgence.

Probationary estate] See 1 Pet. 4:12-19.

12. 'Set an example of proper conduct to nonmembers, and though they now think evilly of you, perhaps they, seeing your good works, will repent and gain the blessings of the gospel.'

They speak against you as evildoers] It is standard operating procedure for the unrepentant and sin-laden enemies of the truth to accuse the saints of evil-doing. Probably there is no better illustration of this than the charges made by wicked and adulterous persons against the early saints in this dispensation where the practice of plural marriage was concerned.

The day of visitation] The day of judgment, the Second Coming, the day when the Lord comes again to take vengeance upon the wicked and ungodly.

BE IN SUBJECTION TO LAWS OF MAN

I PETER 2:13-25.

13 Submit yourselves to every ordinance of man for the Lord's sake: whether it be to the king, as supreme;

14 Or unto governors, as unto them that are sent by him for the punishment of evildoers, and for the praise of them that do well.

15 For so is the will of God, that with well doing ye may put to silence the ignorance of foolish men:

16 As free, and not using *your* liberty for a cloak of maliciousness, but as the servants of God.

17 Honour all *men*. Love the brotherhood. Fear God. Honour the king.

18 Servants, *be* subject to *your* masters with all fear; not only to the good and gentle, but also to the froward.

19 For this *is* thankworthy, if a man for conscience toward God endure grief, suffering wrongfully.

20 For what glory *is it*, if when ye be buffeted for your faults, ye shall take it patiently? but if, when ye do well, and suffer *for it*, ye take it patiently, this *is* acceptable with God.

21 For even hereunto were ye called: because Christ also suffered for us, leaving us an example, that ye should follow his steps:

22 Who did no sin, neither was guile found in his mouth:

23 Who, when he was reviled, reviled not again; when he suffered, he threatened not; but committed *himself* to him that judgeth righteously:

24 Who his own self bare our sins in his own body on the tree, that we, being dead to sins, should live unto righteousness: by whose stripes ye were healed.

25 For ye were as sheep going astray; but are now returned unto the Shepherd and Bishop of your souls.

13-14. While man dwells in this temporal sphere, and as an essential part of working out his salvation, he must obey the laws of the land in which he lives. The perfect system of government is a theocracy in which God governs in both civil and ecclesiastical fields. Such was the case among the saints from Adam to Noah.

But with the rise of other governments, and the birth of religious climates in which church members were a minority portion of the population of the earth, sharp divisions between the operation of church and state came into being. Abraham, Jacob, Joseph, and Moses were all subject to the Pharaohs while in Egypt. The children of Israel were subject to a partially theocratic governmental arrangement during much of their history.

But in Peter's day, and in ours, the saints are subject to two wholly separate and independent systems of direction — the Church which directs in ecclesiastical matters and the state which governs in civil affairs. And experience gained through conformity to both systems of government is essential to the perfecting of the human soul. Hence Peter's categorical statement that it is the will of the Lord for his saints to submit to civil governments, for the Lord truly renders "unto Caesar the things which are Caesar's." (D. & C. 63:26.)

On August 1, 1831, with reference to the then existent laws in the United States the Lord revealed this same principle to Joseph Smith in these words: "Let no man break the laws of the land, for he that keepeth the laws of God hath no need to break the laws of the land. Wherefore, be subject to the powers that be, until he reigns whose right it is to reign, and subdues all enemies under his feet." (D. & C. 58:21-22.)

Similarly the Lord justifies those saints who live under the American constitutional system "in befriending that law which is the constitutional law of the land." (D. & C. 98:6.) And in its "Declaration of Belief regarding Governments and Laws in General." the Church affirms: "We believe that all men are bound to sustain and uphold the respective governments in which they reside, while protected in their inherent and inalienable rights by the laws of such governments; and that sedition and rebellion are unbecoming every citizen thus protected, and should be punished accordingly; and that all governments have a right to enact such laws as in their own judgments are best calculated to secure the public interest; at the same time, however, holding sacred the freedom of conscience." (D. & C. 134:5.)

It is true that instances may arise when the rulers of men may issue decrees which are counter to the mind and will of the

Lord, as when Peter and John — having healed the man lame from his mother's womb, and having caused some 5000 men to believe in Christ and his resurrection, to the great consternation of the Jewish priests and Sadducees — were commanded "not to speak at all or teach in the name of Jesus." (Acts 3; 4:1-22.) In such cases, when God so reveals and commands, his people are expected to reject the civil law and follow the course announced from on high. Otherwise his saints are expected to conform to the civil law, and they are never justified in opposing it unless such a course is marked out for them by revelation.

16. As free] It is the will of the Lord that all men should be free, and governments are or should be designed to aid them in preserving their freedoms. Speaking to the saints in America in the early days of this dispensation, he said: "I, the Lord God, make you free, therefore ye are free indeed; and the law — ['the constitutional law of the land'] — maketh you free." The "principle of freedom" on which this law is based, he said, "belongs to all mankind." (D. & C. 98:5-7.) And further: Laws based on these principles of freedom "should be maintained for the rights and protection of all flesh, according to just and holy principles; That every man may act in doctrine and principle pertaining to futurity, according to the moral agency which I have given unto him, that every man may be accountable for his own sins in the day of judgment." (D. & C. 101:77-78.)

Not using your liberty for a cloak of maliciousness] Though ungodly men may turn freedom into license, "the servants of God" are to exercise their liberty according to gospel standards.

17. Honour all men] "We believe that every man should be honored in his station, rulers and magistrates as such, being placed for the protection of the innocent and the punishment of the guilty." (D. & C. 134:6.)

Love the brotherhood] 'Love the Church, the congregation of the saints, the priesthood brethren, the elect who have forsaken the world and whom the Lord loves because they keep his commandments.'

Fear God] Worship the Lord with reverential awe. See *Commentary II*, pp. 154-162.

Honour the king] Honor is shown forth by obedience. "We believe in being subject to kings, presidents, rulers, and magistrates, in obeying, honoring, and sustaining the law." (Twelfth Article of Faith.)

18-20. It is when the saints endure undeserved buffetings that they develop those godly characteristics and attributes which perfect their souls.

18. Servants] See *Commentary II*, pp. 522-523.

21. Christ also suffered for us] "Which suffering caused myself, even God, the greatest of all, to tremble because of pain, and to bleed at every pore, and to suffer both body and spirit — and would that I might not drink the bitter cup, and shrink." (D. & C. 19:18.)

Follow his steps] "Christ is the great Exemplar. With reference to 'all covenants, contracts, bonds, obligations, oaths, vows, performances, connections, associations, or expectations' (D. & C. 132:7) — that is, in all things — he leads the way and sets an example for his brethren. 'Follow thou me,' is his cry. (2 Ne. 31:10.) 'What manner of men ought ye to be?' he asked; and then answered: 'Verily I say unto you, even as I am.' (3 Ne. 27:27.)" (*Mormon Doctrine*, 2nd ed., p. 259.)

22. Who did no sin] Christ was sinless.

24. Bare our sins] "On conditions of repentance" (D. & C. 18:10-12); on conditions of obedience; on conditions of complete compliance to his laws; otherwise men pay the penalty for their own sins. (D. & C. 19:4-20.)

On the tree] On the cross, speaking loosely; actually, our Lord took upon himself the sins of the world in the Garden of Gethsemane, when he bled great drops of blood from every pore and suffered beyond mortal endurance in both body and spirit. (D. & C. 19:16-18; Luke 22:44.)

By whose stripes ye were healed] The sole New Testament instance in which Isaiah's great Messianic prophecy is quoted:

"And with his stripes we are healed." (Isa. 53:5.) Literally, stripes are the strokes given by a scourge or rod, as when Jesus was scourged before Pilate (Matt. 27:24-26), but as applied to his atoning sacrifice, they symbolize the whole wounding, scarring, suffering steps by which he took upon himself the sins of repentant mankind.

25. The Shepherd and Bishop] Christ as the Chief Pastor and Overseer of the flock of God.

HUSBANDS AND WIVES SHOULD HONOR EACH OTHER

I PETER 3:1-7.

1 Likewise, ye wives, *be* in subjection to your own husbands; that, if any obey not the word, they also may without the word be won by the conversation of the wives;

2 While they behold your chaste conversation *coupled* with fear.

3 Whose adorning let it not be that outward *adorning* of plaiting the hair, and of wearing of gold, or of putting on of apparel;

4 But *let it be* the hidden man of the heart, in that which is not corruptible, *even the ornament* of a meek and quiet spirit, which is in the sight of God of great price.

5 For after this manner in the old time the holy women also, who trusted in God, adorned themselves, being in subjection unto their own husbands.

6 Even as Sara obeyed Abraham, calling him lord: whose daughters ye are, as long as ye do well, and are not afraid with any amazement.

7 Likewise, ye husbands, dwell with *them* according to knowledge, giving honour unto the wife, as unto the weaker vessel, and as being heirs together of the grace of life; that your prayers be not hindered.

I.V. I PETER 3:1-3.

1 Likewise, ye wives, be in subjection to your own husbands; that, if any obey not the word, they also may without the word be won by the **conduct** of the wives;

2 While they behold your chaste **conduct** coupled with fear.

3 Let your adorning be not that outward adorning of plaiting the hair, and wearing of gold, or putting on of apparel;

1-2. Nonmember husbands may be led to accept the gospel by the good works of their wives.

1. Wives, be in subjection to your own husbands] God Almighty placed man at the head and created woman to be his helpmeet (Gen. 2:18), and there is nothing, in the Lord's eternal providences, that either one of them can do about it one way or the other. By divine law women are commanded to be in subjection to their husbands and to abide by their righteous counsel.

3. Outward adorning] Gospel standards call for modest and conservative dress. See 1 Tim. 2:8-15.

4. The ornament of a meek and quiet spirit] Such adorning — not the fashions and jewels of the rich and worldly — constitutes the true ornament of the saints! In the eternal wisdom of God, what covering is to be compared with the robes of righteousness?

5. Holy women] The Lord never sends apostles and prophets and righteous men to minister to his people without placing women of like spiritual stature at their sides. Adam stands as the great high priest, under Christ, to rule as a natural patriarch over all men of all ages, but he cannot rule alone; Eve, his wife, rules at his side, having like caliber and attainments to his own. Abraham is tested as few men have been when the Lord commands him to offer Isaac upon the altar (Gen. 22:1-19); and Sarah struggles with like problems when the Lord directs that she withhold from the Egyptians her status as Abraham's wife. (Abra. 2:21-25; Gen. 12:7-20.) Isaac gains from the Lord the promise that his seed shall "multiply as the stars of heaven" (Gen. 26:1-4); and Rebekah, his wife, receives a blessing of her own in which she is promised that she shall be "the mother of thousands of millions." (Gen. 24:59-60.) And so it goes, in all dispensations and at all times when there are holy men there are also holy women. Neither stands alone before the Lord. The exaltation of the one is dependent upon that of the other.

6. Whose daughters ye are] Brethren in the Church become "the seed of Abraham" by faith. (D. & C. 84:34.) That is, they believe what Abraham believed; they worship as Abraham worshiped; they are one with him in spiritual things — and are therefore considered to be his followers and sons, for "if ye be Christ's, then are ye Abraham's seed, and heirs according to the promise." (Gal. 3:29.) Thus, to identify the women in the Church as the daughters of Sarah is to testify that Sarah, and Abraham her husband, were also followers of Christ and believers in the same truths of salvation revealed anew in the Christian dispensation. See *Commentary II*, pp. 465-475.

7. Honour unto the wife] See *Commentary II*, pp. 518-520.

Heirs together] Neither men or women are saved alone. Salvation is a family affair. The fulness of the blessings of the gospel come to men and women together; they grow out of the new and everlasting covenant of marriage.

"BE FOLLOWERS OF THAT WHICH IS GOOD"

I PETER 3:8-17.

8 Finally, *be ye* all of one mind, having compassion one of another, love as brethren, *be* pitiful, *be* courteous:

9 Not rendering evil for evil, or railing for railing: but contrariwise blessing; knowing that ye are thereunto called, that ye should inherit a blessing.

10 For he that will love life, and see good days, let him refrain his tongue from evil, and his lips that they speak no guile:

11 Let him eschew evil, and do good; let him seek peace, and ensue it.

12 For the eyes of the Lord *are* over the righteous, and his ears *are open* unto their prayers: but the face of the Lord *is* against them that do evil.

13 And who *is* he that will harm you, if ye be followers of that which is good?

14 But and if ye suffer for righteousness' sake, happy *are ye:* and be not afraid of their terror, neither be troubled;

15 But sanctify the Lord God in your hearts: and *be* ready always to *give* an answer to every man that asketh you a reason of the hope that is in you with meekness and fear:

16 Having a good conscience; that, whereas they speak evil of you, as of evildoers, they may be ashamed that falsely accuse your good conversation in Christ.

17 For *it is* better, if the will of God be so, that ye suffer for well doing, than for evil doing.

I.V. I PETER 3:15-16.

15 But sanctify the Lord God in your hearts; and be ready always to give an answer **with meekness and fear** to every man that asketh of you a reason **for** the hope that is in you:

16 Having a good conscience; that, whereas they speak evil of you, as of evil-doers, they may be ashamed that falsely accuse your good **conduct** in Christ.

Christian virtues and godly conduct abound in the lives of the Lord's people. Compassion, love, courtesy, and the spirit of blessing are but the beginning of the attributes of Deity which they possess. Where these heaven-patterned virtues are, there are the true saints; where these are not, true religion has not taken hold of the souls of men, however devout they may otherwise appear to be. See *Commentary II*, pp. 542-544.

8. Be ye all of one mind] Perfect unity prevails among the true saints. There are no divisions among them; they all believe and think and speak alike, because they — by the power of the Holy Ghost — have the mind of Christ. (1 Cor. 2:16.) "Be one; and if ye are not one ye are not mine." (D. & C. 38:27.)

9. 'Render good for evil and the Lord will bless you.'

10-12. Peter here quotes — more accurately, perhaps, paraphrases — the cry of David when the ancient Psalmist, feeling troubled and persecuted, sought salvation in the midst of perilous circumstances, and was assured that those who trust in the Lord shall triumph. "The angel of the Lord encampeth round about them that fear him, and delivereth them," David said; and then: "What man is he that desireth life, and loveth many days, that he may see good? Keep thy tongue from evil, and thy lips from speaking guile. Depart from evil, and do good; seek peace, and pursue it. The eyes of the Lord are upon the righteous, and his ears are open unto their cry. The face of the Lord is against them that do evil, to cut off the remembrance of them from the earth." (Psalm 34:7, 12-16.) How often it is that the problems of one generation are those of another, and that the solution of them is for the Lord's saints to trust in him and keep his commandments!

13-14a. 'Ordinarily the saints are not harmed for doing that which is good; but if they are, so be it; and blessed are they who are persecuted for righteousness' sake.'

14b-15a. Speaking of worldly people and influences, Isaiah said to the saints in ancient Israel: "Neither fear ye their fear, nor be afraid. Sanctify the Lord of hosts himself; and let him be your fear, and let him be your dread. And he shall be for a sanctuary." (Isa. 8:12-14.) Then he comes forth with his great Messianic prophecy that Israel's Redeemer shall be a stone of stumbling and a rock of offense to many among whom he shall minister. By applying Isaiah's counsel to the saints of his day, Peter, among other things, is equating the Lord of hosts with the Lord Jesus. He is directing the meridian Christians to sanctify in their hearts Christ as the Lord.

15. Give an answer to every man] The true saints are an informed people. They know the doctrines of salvation and rejoice in the privilege of presenting them to their Father's other children.

17. 'If occasion requires, it is better for persecution to come upon you because of your good conduct than for you to suffer for your sins.'

CHRIST PREACHED GOSPEL TO SPIRITS IN PRISON

I PETER 3:18-22; 4:1-6.

18 For Christ also hath once suffered for sins, the just for the unjust, that he might bring us to God, being put to death in the flesh, but quickened by the Spirit:

19 By which also he went and preached unto the spirits in prison;

20 Which sometime were disobedient, when once the long-suffering of God waited in the days of Noah, while the ark was a preparing, wherein few, that is, eight souls were saved by water.

21 The like figure whereunto *even* baptism doth also now save us (not the putting away of the

filth of the flesh, but the answer of a good conscience toward God,) by the resurrection of Jesus Christ:

22 Who is gone into heaven, and is on the right hand of God; angels and authorities and powers being made subject unto him.

1 Forasmuch then as Christ hath suffered for us in the flesh, arm yourselves likewise with the same mind: for he that hath suffered in the flesh hath ceased from sin:

2 That he no longer should live the rest of *his* time in the flesh to the lusts of men, but to the will of God.

3 For the time past of *our* life may suffice us to have wrought the will of the Gentiles, when we walked in lasciviousness, lusts, excess of wine, revellings, banquetings, and abominable idolatries:

4 Wherein they think it strange that ye run not with *them* to the same excess of riot, speaking evil of *you:*

5 Who shall give account to him that is ready to judge the quick and the dead.

6 For for this cause was the gospel preached also to them that are dead, that they might be judged according to men in the flesh, but live according to God in the spirit.

I.V. I PETER 3:18-20; 4:2-4, 6.

18 For Christ also once suffered for sins, the just for the unjust, **being put to death in the flesh, but quickened by the Spirit, that he might bring us to God.**

19 **For which cause** also, he went and preached unto the spirits in prison;

20 **Some of whom were disobedient in the days of Noah, while the long-suffering of God waited,** while the ark was preparing, wherein few, that is, eight souls were saved by water.

2 **For you who have suffered in the flesh should cease from sin, that you no longer the rest of your time in the flesh, should live to the lusts of men,** but to the will of God.

3 For the time past of life may suffice to have wrought the will of the Gentiles, when **ye** walked in lasciviousness, lusts, excess of wine, revellings, banquetings, and abominable idolatries;

4 Wherein **they speak evil of you, thinking it strange that you run not with them to the same excess of riot;**

6 **Because of this, is** the gospel preached to them **who** are dead, that they might be judged according to men in the flesh, but live **in the spirit according to the will of God.**

Peter patterned his presentation of one of the most glorious of all doctrines, that of salvation for the dead, after the approach used by Isaiah to acclaim the divine Sonship of the Lord Jesus.

In the midst of a long and somewhat intricate commentary about some warlike intrigue then in progress, Isaiah prophesies that "a virgin shall conceive, and bear a son, and shall call his name Immanuel," using this Messianic utterance as "a sign" of the assured eventuality where the local war and intrigue were concerned. (Isa. 7.) Our interest in the ancient contention is nominal, but the almost incidental proclamation about the future birth of the Son of God is of transcendent worth.

Continuing his counsel about local political circumstances, and after decrying the course of those in Israel who would make "a confederacy" with other nations, Isaiah burst forth with his great prophecy that the promised Messiah would be "a stone of stumbling" and "a rock of offense" in the day of his mortal ministry. (Isa. 8.) And then as he spoke of still other unrelated matters. Israel's Messianic seer wove in the fact that when Christ came, the people that walked in darkness should see a great light, and that the child who should be born as Israel's King should be the mighty God, who should reign on David's throne over an endless and eternal kingdom. (Isa. 9.) And so it has been with a host of the Messianic utterances and of other matters of infinite worth — they have been presented in an almost casual and offhand way.

And so Peter is here engaged in a persuasive presentation of the sufferings endured by the saints at the hands of wicked men; he is counseling the members of the Church to bear up under these unjust burdens; and he uses Christ and his suffering as the crowning illustration of enduring the sharp daggers of infamy for righteousness' sake. Then, almost incidentally, he adds that this suffering of the Just One resulted in his death and subsequent ministry among departed souls, who hearing the gospel in the spirit prison would then be judged on the same basis as is the case with men in the flesh. And what a glorious doctrine this is! There is scarcely another gospel teaching — save our Lord's very atonement itself — to compare with it! To think that in the mercy and wisdom of God, every living soul shall have a fair and a just opportunity for salvation and exaltation regardless of the time and circumstances of his probation!

"The great principles and procedures whereby the saving truths of the gospel are offered to, accepted by, and made binding upon the departed dead, comprise the doctrine of salvation for the dead. Pursuant to this doctrine the principles of salvation are taught in the spirit world, leaving the ordinances thereof to be performed in this life on a vicarious-proxy basis. By accepting the gospel in the spirit world, and because the ordinances of salvation and exaltation are performed vicariously in this world, the worthy dead can become heirs of the fulness of the Father's kingdom. Salvation for the dead is the system whereunder those who would have accepted the gospel in this life had they been permitted to hear it, will have the chance to accept it in the spirit world, and will then be entitled to all the blessings which passed them by in mortality. (*Doctrines of Salvation*, vol. 2 pp. 100-196.)" (*Mormon Doctrine*, 2nd ed., p. 673.) See *Commentary I*, pp. 193-194, 518-523, 622-624.

18. Christ . . . suffered for sins] The most severe and intense suffering ever undergone by any person in all eternity was borne by the Son of God in Gethsemane when he took upon himself the sins of all men on conditions of repentance. "Behold, I , God, have suffered these things for all, that they might not suffer if they would repent; But if they would not repent they must suffer even as I; Which suffering caused myself, even God, the greatest of all, to tremble because of pain, and to bleed at every pore, and to suffer both body and spirit—and would that I might not drink the bitter cup, and shrink." (D. & C. 19:16-18.)

The just for the unjust] The righteous Lord, who was without sin (1 Pet. 2:22), suffered for us men who are sinners. "For all have sinned, and come short of the glory of God." (Rom. 3:23.)

That he might bring us to God] It is only in and through the atonement of Christ that men are or can be brought to God. If there had been no atonement, all men would have remained everlastingly in the grave, without temporal redemption; and all men, having been cast out of the presence of God and being in the bondage of sin, would have become "angels to a devil," without spiritual redemption. (2 Ne. 9:6-9.)

Being put to death in the flesh, but quickened by the Spirit] "The Holy Messiah . . . layeth down his life according to the flesh, and taketh it again by the power of the Spirit." (2 Ne. 2:8.) That is, having inherited the power of mortality, which is the power to die, from a mortal mother, he voluntarily laid down his life; and having inherited the power of immortality, which is the power to live, from an Immortal Father, he was able to take up his body again in glorious immortality.

19. He went and preached unto the spirits in prison] In the realm of departed spirits there are two divisions — paradise, where the spirits of the righteous go to await the day when they shall come forth in the resurrection of the just; and hell, where the spirits of the wicked go to be buffeted and tormented until that day when they shall come forth in the resurrection of the unjust. Our Lord did not go in person to the spirits in hell, which is the spirit prison as such. His ministry in the spirit world was among the righteous in paradise, but even these considered their disembodied state as one of bondage. Thus the designation *spirit prison* may be said to have two meanings — *hell,* which is the prison proper; and the *whole spirit world,* in the sense that all who are therein are restricted and cannot gain a fulness of joy until after their resurrection. (D. & C. 93:33-34.)

In President Joseph F. Smith's vision of the redemption of the dead, the Lord revealed this detailed account of what actually transpired when the slain Lord ministered to the spirits in prison: "The eyes of my understanding were opened," President Smith said, "and I saw the hosts of the dead, both small and great. And there were gathered together in one place an innumerable company of the spirits of the just, who had been faithful in the testimony of Jesus while they lived in mortality, and who had offered sacrifice in the similitude of the great sacrifice of the Son of God, and had suffered tribulation in their Redeemer's name. All these had departed the mortal life, firm in the hope of a glorious resurrection, through the grace of God the Father and his Only Begotten Son, Jesus Christ.

"I beheld that they were filled with joy and gladness, and were rejoicing together because the day of their deliverance was at hand. They were assembled awaiting the advent of the Son of God into the spirit world, to declare their redemption from the bands of death. Their sleeping dust was to be restored unto its perfect frame, bone to his bone, and the sinews and the flesh upon them, the spirit and the body to be united never again to be divided, that they might receive a fulness of joy.

"While this vast multitude waited and conversed, rejoicing in the hour of their deliverance from the chains of death, the Son of God appeared, declaring liberty to the captives who had been faithful, and there he preached to them the everlasting gospel, the doctrine of the resurrection and the redemption of mankind from the fall, and from individual sins on conditions of repentance. But unto the wicked he did not go, and among the ungodly and the unrepentant who had defiled themselves while in the flesh, his voice was not raised, neither did the rebellious who rejected the testimonies and the warnings of the ancient prophets behold his presence, nor look upon his face. Where these were, darkness reigned, but among the righteous there was peace, and the saints rejoiced in their redemption, and bowed the knee and acknowledged the Son of God as their Redeemer and Deliverer from death and the chains of hell. Their countenances shone and the radiance from the presence of the Lord rested upon them and they sang praises unto his holy Name.

"I marveled, for I understood that the Savior spent about three years in his ministry among the Jews and those of the house of Israel, endeavoring to teach them the everlasting gospel and call them unto repentance; and yet, notwithstanding his mighty works and miracles and proclamation of the truth in great power and authority, there were but few who hearkened to his voice and rejoiced in his presence and received salvation at his hands. But his ministry among those who were dead was limited to the brief time intervening between the crucifixion and his resurrection; and I wondered at the words of Peter wherein he said that the Son of God preached unto the spirits in prison who sometime were disobedient, when once the longsuffering of God waited in the days of Noah, and how it was possible for him to preach to those spirits and perform the necessary labor among them in so short a time.

"And as I wondered, my eyes were opened, and my understanding quickened, and I perceived that the Lord went not in person among the wicked and the disobedient who had rejected the truth, to teach them; but behold, from among the righteous he organized his forces and appointed messengers, clothed with power and authority, and commissioned them to go forth and carry the light of the gospel to them that were in darkness, even to all the spirits of men. And thus was the gospel preached to the dead. And the chosen messengers went forth to declare the acceptable day of the Lord, and proclaim liberty to the captives who were bound; even unto all who would repent of their sins and receive the gospel. Thus was the gospel preached to those who had died in their sins, without a knowledge of the truth, or in transgression, having rejected the prophets. These were taught faith in God, repentance from sin, vicarious baptism for the remission of sins, the gift of the Holy Ghost by the laying on of hands, and all other principles of the gospel that were necessary for them to know in order to qualify themselves that they might be judged according to men in the flesh, but live according to God in the Spirit.

"And so it was made known among the dead, both small and great, the unrighteous as well as the faithful, that redemption had been wrought through the sacrifice of the Son of God upon the cross. Thus was it made known that our Redeemer spent his time during his sojourn in the world of spirits instructing and preparing the faithful spirits of the prophets who had testified of him in the flesh, that they might carry the message of redemption unto all the dead unto whom he could not go personally because of their rebellion and transgression, that they through the ministration of his servants might also hear his words."

Then President Smith named some of the noble and great ones whom he saw in the great assemblage in the spirit world and said that they and the whole "vast assembly . . . waited for their deliverance, for the dead had looked upon the long absence of their spirits from their bodies as a bondage. These the Lord taught, and gave them power to come forth, after his resurrection from the dead, to enter into his Father's kingdom, there to be crowned with immortality and eternal life, and continue thenceforth their labors as had been promised by the Lord, and be partakers of all blessings which were held in reserve for them that love him."

"I beheld that the faithful elders of this dispensation," he also said, "when they depart from mortal life, continue their labors in the preaching of the gospel of repentance and redemption, through the sacrifice of the Only Begotten Son of God, among those who are in darkness and under the bondage of sin in the great world of the spirits of the dead." (*Gospel Doctrine*, 5th ed., pp. 472-476.)

Hell] See Rev. 20:11-15.

Paradise] See *Commentary I*, pp. 823-825.

20. These particular spirits, the souls of those who lived in Noah's day were taught the gospel during their mortal probation. (Moses 8:19-24.) Their opportunity to believe and obey the truths of salvation came while they yet dwelt in mortality. Hence, even assuming they accept the truth in the spirit world, the highest inheritance available to them is the terrestrial kingdom; they are forever barred from that eternal life found only in the celestial kingdom of heaven. This limitation on the doctrine of salvation for the dead was revealed to Joseph Smith in the vision of the degrees of glory. Speaking of the terrestrial world, the Lord said: These are "they who are the spirits of men kept in prison, whom the Son visited, and preached the gospel unto them, that they might be judged according to men in the flesh; Who received not the testimony of Jesus in the flesh, but afterwards received it." (D. & C. 76:73-74.)

Thus: "There is no such thing as a second chance to gain salvation by accepting the gospel in the spirit world after spurning, declining, or refusing to accept it in this life. It is true that there may be a second chance to hear and accept the gospel, but those who have thus procrastinated their acceptance of the saving truths will not gain salvation in the celestial kingdom of God.

"Salvation for the dead is the system by means of which those who 'die without a knowledge of the gospel' (D. & C. 128:5) may gain such knowledge in the spirit world and then, following the vicarious performance of the necessary ordinances, become heirs of salvation on the same basis as though the gospel truths had been obeyed in mortality. Salvation for the dead is limited expressly to those who do not have opportunity in this life to accept the gospel but who would have taken the opportunity had it come to them.

" 'All who have died without a knowledge of this gospel,' the Lord said to the Prophet, 'who would have received it if they had been permitted to tarry, shall be heirs of the celestial kingdom of God; also all that shall die henceforth without a knowledge of it, who would have received it with all their hearts, shall be heirs of that kingdom, for I, the Lord, will judge all men according to their works, according to the desire of their hearts.' (*Teachings*, p. 107.)

"This is the only revealed principle by means of which the laws pertaining to salvation for the dead can be made effective in the lives of any persons. There is no promise in any revelation that those who have a fair and just opportunity in this life to accept the gospel, and who do not do it, will have another chance in the spirit world to gain salvation. On the contrary, there is the express stipulation that men cannot be saved without accepting the gospel in this life, if they are given opportunity to accept it.

" 'Now is the time and the day of your salvation,' Amulek said. 'For behold, this life is the time for men to prepare to meet God; yea, behold the day of this life is the day for men to perform their labors . . . . For after this day of life, which is given us to prepare for eternity, behold, if we do not improve our time while in this life, then cometh the night of darkness wherein there can be no labor performed.' (Alma 34:31-35; 2 Ne. 9:27; 3 Ne. 28:34; Luke 9:62.)

"An application of this law is seen in the words of the resurrected Christ to the Nephites. 'Therefore come unto me and be ye saved,' he said in repeating with some variations the Sermon on the Mount he had previously given the Jews, 'for verily

I say unto you, that except ye shall keep my commandments, which I have commanded you at this time, ye shall in no case enter into the kingdom of heaven.' (3 Ne. 12:20.) Thus salvation was forever denied those Nephites unless they gained it by virtue of their obedience during mortality. On the same basis, there is no such thing as salvation for the dead for the Latter-day Saints who have been taught the truths of salvation and had a fair and just opportunity to live them." (*Mormon Doctrine* 2nd ed., pp. 685-686.)

Eight souls were saved by water] They were saved temporally in that they did not drown with the rest of the inhabitants of the earth.

"In the days of Noah the Lord sent a universal flood which completely immersed the whole earth and destroyed all flesh except that preserved on the ark. (Gen. 6; 7; 8; 9; Moses 7:38-45; 8; Ether 12:2.) 'Noah was born to save seed of everything, when the earth was washed of its wickedness by the flood.' (*Teachings*, p. 12.) This flood was the baptism of the earth; before it occured the land was all in one place, a condition that will again prevail during the millennial era. (D. & C. 133:23-24.)" (*Mormon Doctrine*, 2nd ed., p. 289.)

And, although Peter is not here alluding to this more important fact, they were saved spiritually in that each of them had been baptized by immersion under the hands of a legal administrator, had received the gift of the Holy Ghost, and been thereafter obedient to the Lord's decree that they build an ark and keep all his commandments. (Moses 8:9-30.)

21. The temporal salvation that came to Noah's family because they had faith to build and use the ark is a symbol of the spiritual salvation available to all men who, through faith, are baptized and use the principles of the gospel in their lives.

Baptism . . . not the putting away of the filth of the flesh, but the answer of a good conscience toward God] Baptism does not wash away the sins of men unless they have repented. It is not immersion in water alone that saves; it is baptism plus personal righteousness. If those who are baptized "are just and true" (D.

& C. 76:53), that is, if they have complied with the law of repentance which qualifies them for the blessings of baptism, then the ordinance so performed will be sealed by the Holy Spirit of promise and will remit their sins on earth and in heaven. (D. & C. 132:7.)

By the resurrection of Jesus Christ] Baptism is efficacious because of the atonement and resurrection of Christ; without this most transcendent of all things, none of the terms and conditions of the plan of salvation would have any efficacy, virtue, or force whatever.

Salvation] See 1 Pet. 1:1-16.

4:1-2. 'Even as Christ, the Prototype of salvation, suffered for us in the flesh, so should we, following his example, submit to suffering in the cause of righteousness. Those who are faithful when persecuted for righteousness' sake thereby show they have overcome the lusts of men and are walking in the Spirit.'

1. Arm yourself . . . with the same mind] Gain the mind of Christ (1 Cor. 2:16), thereby thinking what he thought, saying what he said, and doing what he did—which course of life will stand as a defense against the evils of the world.

3-5. 'Before we received the gospel we walked in wickedness, and worldly people think it strange that we no longer consort with them in their evil doings, for which evils, however, they shall give account at the judgment bar.'

6. Nothing shows forth more perfectly the complete justice, equity, and mercy of God's dealings with men than the doctrine of salvation for the dead. Salvation is not limited to those who are born in a favored lineage. It is not reserved for people who chance to live in a day when there are prophets and apostles on earth who have authority from the Almighty to teach the doctrines and perform the ordinances of salvation. It is not for those only who learn of Christ and his laws in this life. It is available for all men, in all ages, and in all places. In the infinite wisdom of Him who knoweth all things and who seeks the salvation of all his children, it was ordained in the councils of eternity, before the foundations of this earth were laid, that every living soul, either in mortality or in the spirit world, would have a fair, a just, and an equitable opportunity to believe and obey those laws which lead to eternal life. The Lord be praised!

"SPEAK AS AN ORACLE OF GOD"

I PETER 4:7-11.

7 But the end of all things is at hand: be ye therefore sober, and watch unto prayer.

8 And above all things have fervent charity among yourselves: for charity shall cover the multitude of sins.

9 Using hospitality one to another without grudging.

10 As every man hath received the gift, *even so* minister the same one to another, as good stewards of the manifold grace of God.

11 If any man speak, *let him speak* as the oracles of God; if any man minister, *let him do it* as of the ability which God giveth: that God in all things may be glorified through Jesus Christ, to whom be praise and dominion for ever and ever. Amen.

I.V. I PETER 4:7-8, 11.

7 But **to you,** the end of all things is at hand; be ye therefore sober, and watch unto prayer.

8 And above all things have fervent charity among yourselves; for charity **preventeth a** multitude of sins.

11 If any man speak, let him speak as **an oracle** of God; if any man minister, let him do it as of the ability which God giveth; that God in all things may be glorified through Jesus Christ; to whom be praise and dominion for ever and ever. Amen.

I. V. 7. To you, the end of all things is at hand] In every dispensation, to gain salvation the saints must overcome the world and endure manfully whatever persecution is heaped upon them. And as each faithful saint approaches the day of his departure to the paradise of God, it is as though he were prepared for the Lord's Second Coming; it is as though the end of the world had come in his day. Luke 12:35-48, as marvelously expanded and clarified by the Prophet Joseph Smith in the Inspired Version, sets forth the concept that the Lord comes, in effect, in every watch of the night, so that his saints of all ages must watch and be ready. See *Commentary I*, pp. 670-677.

Be . . . sober] "Be sober." (Alma 38:15.) "Cast away your idle thoughts and your excess of laughter far from you." (D. & C. 88:69.) "Let the solemnities of eternity rest upon your minds." (D. & C. 43:34.)

K. J. 8. Charity] See *Commentary II*, pp. 377-380.

9-10. Anciently a hospital was a place for the shelter or entertainment of travelers, strangers, or other guests, and hospitality was the treatment given such persons. Since all that we have comes as a gift from God, and is a manifestation of his hospitality to us, it follows that we are to minister from our means to the needs of our fellowmen. Hospitality to each other thus automatically becomes the mark of a true saint and shall ever remain so, although in our modern society it is sometimes considered to be more a matter of showing forth the social graces than of providing food, clothing, and shelter to the needy traveler. In the true Church, hospitality is one of the characteristics of the members and officers, as for instance a bishop. (1 Tim. 3:1-3.)

I. V. 11. Speak as an oracle] 'Speak by inspiration, not of yourself, but simply as a medium through whom the mind and will of the Lord is revealed.' This is an absolute requisite of a true minister. They must preach by the power of the Spirit. See *Commentary II*, pp. 317-319. Unless they do so they cannot minister life and salvation to the children of men. Hence the divine counsel that the Lord's servants are to treasure up in their minds continually the words of life; to rely upon the Holy Spirit; and then, without taking thought beforehand, to speak forth what the Lord wants them to say, at the very moment of their preaching. (D. & C. 84:85.)

Preaching] See 2 Tim. 4:1-5.

SAINTS TO BE TRIED IN ALL THINGS

I PETER 4:12-19.

12 Beloved, think it not strange
concerning the fiery trial which is
to try you, as though some strange
thing happened unto you:

13 But rejoice, inasmuch as ye

are partakers of Christ's sufferings; that, when his glory shall be revealed, ye may be glad also with exceeding joy.

14 If ye be reproached for the name of Christ, happy *are ye;* for the spirit of glory and of God resteth upon you: on their part he is evil spoken of, but on your part he is glorified.

15 But let none of you suffer as a murderer, or *as* a thief, or *as* an evildoer, or as a busybody in other men's matters.

16 Yet if *any man suffer* as a Christian, let him not be ashamed; but let him glorify God on this behalf.

17 For the time *is come* that judgment must begin at the house of God: and if *it* first *begin* at us, what shall the end *be* of them that obey not the gospel of God?

18 And if the righteous scarcely be saved, where shall the ungodly and the sinner appear?

19 Wherefore let them that suffer according to the will of God commit the keeping of their souls *to him* in well doing, as unto a faithful Creator.

12. The fiery trial which is to try you] 16. Suffer as a Christian] Mortality itself is a probationary estate (Alma 42), a time of trial and testing for all men. With reference to his eternal plan to send all the pre-existent hosts to earth, the Lord said: "We will prove them herewith, to see if they will do all things whatsoever the Lord their God shall command them." (Abra. 3:25.) But the greatest trials of life are reserved for the saints. They are the ones whom the world hates (Matt. 10:22), and they must overcome the world, if they are to gain the Lord's approval. They face all that the world faces in the way of mortal difficulties — sickness, disease, calamities, famine, pain, sorrow, death — and in addition their faith in Christ and his work is tested to see if they will serve the Lord at all hazards. "I will prove you in all things," the Lord says to his saints, "whether you will abide in my covenant, even unto death, that you may be found worthy. For if ye will not abide in my covenant ye are not worthy of me." (D. & C. 98:14-15.) "Blessed are they which are persecuted for righteousness' sake: for theirs is the kingdom of heaven." (Matt. 5:10.)

17. When men are slain and destroyed for their sins, let it "begin at my sanctuary," saith the Lord (Ezek 9:6), for where there is more light, there is greater condemnation. (D. & C. 82:3.) "Behold, vengeance cometh speedily upon the inhabitants of the earth, a day of wrath, a day of burning, a day of desolation, of weeping, of mourning, and of lamentation; and as a whirlwind it shall come upon all the face of the earth, saith the Lord. And upon my house shall it begin, and from my house shall it go forth, saith the Lord; First among those among you, saith the Lord, who have professed to know my name and have not known me, and have blasphemed against me in the midst of my house, saith the Lord." (D. & C. 112:24-26.)

18. "If the fire can scathe a green tree for the glory of God, how easy it will burn up the dry trees to purify the vineyard of corruption." (D. & C. 135:6.)

ELDERS TO FEED THE FLOCK OF GOD

I PETER 5:1-4.

1 The elders which are among you I exhort, who am also an elder, and a witness of the sufferings of Christ, and also a partaker of the glory that shall be revealed:

2 Feed the flock of God which is among you, taking the oversight *thereof*, not by constraint, but willingly; not for filthy lucre, but of a ready mind;

3 Neither as being lords over *God's* heritage, but being ensamples to the flock.

4 And when the chief Shepherd shall appear, ye shall receive a crown of glory that fadeth not away.

1. Elders] See *Commentary II*, pp. 113-115.

Who am also an elder] "An apostle is an elder" (D. & C. 20:38), and so is every person who holds the Melchizedek Priesthood. By classing himself with his high apostolic calling as an elder, Peter dramatizes the pre-eminence of the priesthood over the offices in the priesthood — a principle which dignifies the status of all brethren who hold the holy priesthood and raises them, as it were, to apostolic stature.

"The priesthood is greater than any of its offices. No office adds any power, dignity, or authority to the priesthood. . . .

"An elder has all the priesthood he needs to qualify for exaltation in the highest heaven of the celestial world. . . .

"Joseph Smith and Oliver Cowdery were ordained elders on April 6, 1830, thus obtaining the first ordained offices in the Church in this dispensation. Peter, James, and John had conferred the Melchizedek Priesthood upon them in June, 1829, but there were no offices in the priesthood until after the organization of the Church. It is not possible to hold an office in an organization that does not exist. Later, other offices came as the needs of the ministry required. *Doctrines of Salvation,* vol. 3, pp. 147-149.) Ordinations to offices must conform to the law of common consent. (D. & C. 20:65.)

"Those receiving priesthood offices have the obligation to labor with zeal and energy in their particular callings. (D. & C. 84:109-110; 107:99-100.) It is by magnifying one's calling in the higher priesthood that men obtain exaltation in the eternal worlds. (D. & C. 84:33-41.) Priesthood offices exist in time and in eternity, and those who magnify their callings in this life will continue on as ministers of Christ holding offices in the priesthood in the realms to come. (Rev. 4; D. & C. 77; 124:130; *Gospel Kingdom,* pp. 182-184.)" (*Mormon Doctrine,* 2nd ed., pp. 595-597.)

A partaker of the glory that shall be revealed] Peter's calling and election had been made sure; he had already received the promise of eternal life in the Father's kingdom. See 2 Pet. 1:1-19.

2. Feed the flock of God] "The elders, priests and teachers of this church shall teach the principles of my gospel, which are in the Bible and the Book of Mormon, in the which is the fulness of the gospel. And they shall observe the covenants and church articles to do them, and these shall be their teachings, as they shall be directed by the Spirit." (D. & C. 42:12-13.)

4. The chief Shepherd] The Lord Jesus Christ himself. See *Commentary I,* pp. 482-485.

A crown of glory] Eternal life.

"BE THOU HUMBLE"

I PETER 5:5-14.

5 Likewise, ye younger, submit yourselves unto the elder. Yea, all *of you* be subject one to another, and be clothed with humility: for God resisteth the proud, and giveth grace to the humble.

6 Humble yourselves therefore under the mighty hand of God, that he may exalt you in due time:

7 Casting all your care upon him; for he careth for you.

8 Be sober, be vigilant; because your adversary the devil, as a roaring lion, walketh about, seeking whom he may devour:

9 Whom resist stedfast in the faith, knowing that the same afflictions are accomplished in your brethren that are in the world.

10 But the God of all grace, who hath called us unto his eternal glory by Christ Jesus, after that ye have suffered a while, make you perfect, stablish, strengthen, settle *you*.

11 To him *be* glory and dominion for ever and ever. Amen.

12 By Silvanus, a faithful brother unto you, as I suppose, I have written briefly, exhorting, and testifying that this is the true grace of God wherein ye stand.

13 The *church that is* at Babylon, elected together with *you*, saluteth you; and *so doth* Marcus my son.

14 Greet ye one another with a kiss of charity. Peace *be* with you all that are in Christ Jesus. Amen.

I.V. I PETER 5:13.

13 **They** at Babylon, elected together with you, saluteth you; and so doth Marcus my son.

5. Ye younger, submit yourselves unto the elder] The divine plan calls for the young and rising generation to take counsel from their elders, to submit to parental guidance, to conform to the revealed pattern. Rebellion, dissension, and disobedience are anti-Christ.

Humility] "All progress in spiritual things is conditioned upon the prior attainment of humility. Pride, conceit, haughtiness, and vainglory are of the world and stand as a bar to the receipt of spiritual gifts.

"We are commanded to be humble. (D. & C. 105:23; 112:10; 124:97, 103; Jas. 4:6, 10.) 'Always retain in remembrance, the greatness of God, and your own nothingness, and his goodness and long-suffering towards you, unworthy creatures,' King Benjamin taught, 'and humble yourselves even in the depths of humility, calling on the name of the Lord daily, and standing steadfastly in the faith.' (Mosiah 4:11.)

"Humility must accompany repentance to qualify a person for baptism (D. & C. 20:37); it is required of all engaged in gospel service (D. & C. 12:8); is an essential attribute for all who embark in the service of God (D. & C. 4:6); precedes the acquiring of wisdom from the Spirit (D. & C. 136:32-33); is needed to qualify the righteous to see God (D. & C. 67:10); and without it no one can gain entrance to the kingdom of God hereafter. (2 Ne. 9:42.)" (*Mormon Doctrine*, 2nd ed., p. 370.)

"Be thou humble; and the Lord thy God shall lead thee by the hand, and give thee answer to thy prayers." (D. & C. 112:10.)

8. **Your adversary the devil]** See Rev. 12:1-17.

10. **God . . . hath called us unto his eternal glory]** See 2 Pet. 1:1-19.

13. **Marcus my son]** Probably John Mark, Peter's friend and companion, who wrote the gospel account which bears his name.

The Second Epistle General of Peter

In his Second Epistle, the Chief Apostle discusses three doctrines of transcendent import:

1. Making our calling and election sure;

2. False teachers in the Church, who shall be damned for their heretical doctrines; and

3. Our Lord's glorious return, amid the fires of heaven, whose heat shall melt the mountains and cleanse the vineyard of corruption.

Peter knew the doctrines of his Lord and had a blunt, rugged, emphatic way of presenting them that is marvelous to behold.

Nowhere else in ancient writ do we find the door so frankly opened to a knowledge of the course men must pursue to have their calling and election made sure; nowhere else in Biblical teachings is found such a plain, unvarnished recitation of the burning of the Lord's vineyard at his return to earth. And as for false teachers — how better can they be rebuked than to equate their course with the madness of Balaam, whose dumb ass spoke out to rebuke his iniquity?

"MAKE YOUR CALLING AND ELECTION SURE"

II PETER 1:1-19.

1 Simon Peter, a servant and an apostle of Jesus Christ, to them that have obtained like precious faith with us through the righteousness of God and our Saviour Jesus Christ:

2 Grace and peace be multiplied unto you through the knowledge of God, and of Jesus our Lord,

3 According as his divine power hath given unto us all things that *pertain* unto life and godliness, through the knowledge of him that hath called us to glory and virtue:

4 Whereby are given unto us exceeding great and precious promises: that by these ye might be partakers of the divine nature, having escaped the corruption that is in the world through lust.

5 And beside this, giving all diligence, add to your faith virtue; and to virtue knowledge;

6 And to knowledge temperance; and to temperance patience; and to patience godliness;

7 And to godliness brotherly kindness; and to brotherly kindness charity.

8 For if these things be in you, and abound, they make *you that ye shall* neither *be* barren nor unfruitful in the knowledge of our Lord Jesus Christ.

9 But he that lacketh these things is blind, and cannot see afar off, and hath forgotten that he was purged from his old sins.

10 Wherefore the rather, brethren, give diligence to make your calling and election sure: for if ye do these things, ye shall never fall:

11 For so an entrance shall be ministered unto you abundantly into the everlasting kingdom of our Lord and Saviour Jesus Christ.

12 Wherefore I will not be negligent to put you always in remembrance of these things, though ye know *them*, and be established in the present truth.

13 Yea, I think it meet, as long as I am in this tabernacle, to stir you up by putting *you* in remembrance;

14 Knowing that shortly I must put off *this* my tabernacle, even as our Lord Jesus Christ hath showed me.

15 Moreover I will endeavour that ye may be able after my decease to have these things always in remembrance.

16 For we have not followed cunningly devised fables, when we made known unto you the power and coming of our Lord Jesus Christ, but were eyewitnesses of his majesty.

17 For he received from God the Father honour and glory, when there came such a voice to him from the excellent glory, This is my beloved Son, in whom I am well pleased.

18 And this voice which came from heaven we heard, when we were with him in the holy mount.

19 We have also a more sure word of prophecy; whereunto ye do well that ye take heed, as unto a light that shineth in a dark place, until the day dawn, and the day star arise in your hearts:

I.V. II PETER 1:19.

19 We have **therefore** a more sure **knowledge** of the word of prophecy, **to which word of prophecy** ye do well that ye take heed, as unto a light **which** shineth in a dark place, until the day-dawn, and the day-star arise in your hearts;

"MAKE YOUR CALLING AND ELECTION SURE"

Among those who have received the gospel, and who are seeking diligently to live its laws and gain eternal life, there is an instinctive and determined desire to make their calling and election sure. Because they have tasted the good things of God and sipped from the fountain of eternal truth, they now seek the divine presence, where they shall know all things, have all power, all might, and all dominion, and in fact be like Him who is the great Prototype of all saved beings — God our Heavenly and Eternal Father. (D. & C. 132:20.) This is the end objective, the chief goal of all the faithful, and there is nothing greater in all eternity, "for there is no gift greater than the gift of salvation." (D. & C. 6:13.)

It is little wonder then that the Prophet Joseph Smith, particularly during the latter and crowning years of his mortal ministry, repeatedly exhorted the saints to press forward with that steadfastness in Christ which would enable them to make their calling and election sure. "I am going on in my progress for eternal life," he said of himself; and then in fervent pleading to all the saints, he exclaimed: "Oh! I beseech you to go forward, go forward and make your calling and your election sure." (*Teachings*, p. 366.)

As a prelude to analyzing Peter's words on this subject — and they rank in spiritual grandeur and insight with those in the Vision of the degrees of glory and the sermons of the Lord himself — as a prelude to this analysis, let us define and outline what is involved in having one's calling and election made sure, taking cautious heed the while to anchor each thought and concept to the revealed word and the prophetic utterances.

Of necessity we must define some words and phrases in most pointed terms. Unless we know what they mean, in their scriptural contexts, we cannot comprehend what the Holy Spirit was teaching by the mouths of the prophets as he inspired those preachers of righteousness to use them. And since there is so much misunderstanding and misinformation where these glorious concepts are concerned, it will not be amiss to approach the subject in an organized and intelligent manner, building our house of understanding, brick upon brick, precept upon precept. The fact is that the doctrinal concepts in this field are fully set forth in the revelations, and all that is needed is to put the whole subject together in one well built structure, so that it becomes clear how each separate part fits into the one united whole. One brick or one window by itself does not show forth what the whole house is like; but each part fitly framed together with its fellow parts soon becomes a marvelous mansion which is gratifying to behold.

What is meant by calling? And who are the called of God?

To be called is to be a member of the Church and kingdom of God on earth; it is to be numbered with the saints; it is to accept the gospel and receive the everlasting covenant; it is to have part and lot in the earthly Zion; it is to be born again, to be a son or a daughter of the Lord Jesus Christ; to have membership in the household of faith; it is to be on the path leading to eternal life and to have the hope of eternal glory; it is to have a conditional promise of eternal life; it is to be an inheritor of all of the blessings of the gospel, provided there is continued obedience to the laws and ordinances thereof.

Within this over-all framework, there are individual calls to positions of trust and responsibility, but these are simply assignments to labor on the Lord's errand, in particular places, for a time and a season. The call itself is to the gospel cause; it is not reserved for apostles and prophets or for the great and mighty in Israel; it is for all the members of the kingdom.

The call originates with God, is available because of his grace and goodness, and is offered to various peoples and nations according to his will and on his divine timetable. From the day of Jacob to the coming of Christ the house of Israel was the called and chosen people of the Lord. During the day of his mortal ministry our Lord limited the call to the lost sheep of the house of Israel. (Matt. 10:5-7.) After his resurrection he commanded his ministers to make the call available to all men. (Mark 16:15-16.) But only those who actually receive the gospel, who make the everlasting covenant, who cleave unto the truth and strive to live in harmony with the revealed word, only these are numbered among those whom the scriptures name as the called of the Lord.

Thus we find hosts of statements in holy writ telling who is called and what they have and may yet receive as a result thereof. For instance: On the day of Pentecost itself, as he began the ministry which would take the gospel from the house of Israel to the ends of the earth, Peter announced that the repentant, baptized converts "shall receive the gift of the Holy Ghost. For," said he, "the promise is unto you, and to your children, and to all that are afar off, even as many as the Lord our God shall call." (Acts 2:37-39.)

Later the chief apostle told members of the Church that they had been "called . . . out of darkness" into the "marvellous light" of the gospel (1 Pet. 2:9); that they were "called" to suffer in the cause of righteousness, that thereby they "should inherit a blessing" (1 Pet. 2:21; 3:9); that their call came from God, by his grace, through "Christ Jesus," and was a call unto "eternal glory." (1 Pet. 5:10.) And accordingly Peter exhorted the saints to be holy "as he which hath called you is holy." (1 Pet. 1:15.)

Our friend Paul proclaims the same principles. He speaks of members of the Church as "the called of Jesus Christ," as those who are "called to be saints" (Rom. 1:6-7; 1 Cor. 1:2); he says they are "called . . . into the grace of Christ" (Gal. 1:6); "called unto liberty" (Gal. 5:13); "called . . . to peace" (1 Cor. 7:15, 17); "called" to "the fellowship" of "Jesus Christ" (1 Cor. 1:9); "called" to "holiness" (1 Thess. 4:7; Heb. 3:1); "called" to the Lord's "kingdom and glory" (1 Thess. 2:12); and that all these calls come by "grace." (Gal. 1:15.)

Like Peter he teaches that the saints are called to "eternal life" (1 Tim. 6:12), called to "the promise of eternal inheritance" (Heb. 9:15), but he explains also that the Lord's calls are the result of foreordination and grow out of faithfulness in pre-existence. (2 Tim. 1:8-9.) "God hath from the beginning," that is, from before the foundations of the world, "chosen you [his saints] to salvation through sanctification of the Spirit and belief of the truth: Whereunto he called you by our gospel, to the obtaining of the glory of our Lord Jesus Christ." (2 Thess. 2:13-14.) That is, the saints were foreordained in the councils of eternity to believe the truth, to be sanctified, and to save their souls; and then in this life they are called to that gospel whereby these eternal promises can be fulfilled.

In another glorious passage, Paul says: "We know that all things work together for good to them that love God, to them who are the called according to his purpose." That is, the Lord's hand governs and controls in the lives of those whom he, in his infinite foreknowledge, hath called to be his people. And then: "For whom he did foreknow, he also did predestinate to be conformed to the image of his Son, that he might be the firstborn among many brethren," which is to say that God in his infinite wisdom foreordained the noble and great spirits in pre-existence to become like Christ, to gain glory, power and might like unto the Son of God, so that the Son becomes the firstborn, as it were, among many exalted sons. And then in glorious conclusion: "Moreover whom he did predestinate [foreordain], them he also called: and whom he called, them he also justified: and whom he justified, them he also glorified." (Rom. 8. 28-30.) Thus "the noble and great ones," who were chosen before they were born (Abra. 3:22-23), who were foreordained to have exaltation, are the ones whom God hath called in this life to be glorified through the gospel in due course.

With such a glorious hope before them, surely the saints should be encouraged to gain the promised rewards, and so Paul joins Peter in using the doctrine of calling as an occasion for exhortation. Let all the saints so "work" as to be "worthy of this calling," he says, in that day when the Lord "shall come to be glorified in his saints" (2 Thess. 1:10-11), and even of such a great one as himself he says: "I press toward the mark for the prize of the high calling of God in Christ Jesus." (Philip. 3:14.)

In modern revelation the Lord confirms the doctrine of his ancient apostles, speaks of our "calling and election in the church" (D. & C. 53:1; 55:1), of the fact we "are called" to his "everlasting gospel" (D. & C. 101:39), and names the elders of his Church as among those "whom he hath called and chosen in these last days." (D. & C. 52:1; 41:2.)

Since men are foreordained to gain exaltation, and since no

man can be exalted without the priesthood, it is almost self-evident that worthy brethren were foreordained to receive the priesthood. And so we find Alma teaching that those who hold the Melchizedek Priesthood in this life were "called and prepared from the foundation of the world according to the foreknowledge of God." (Alma 13:1-12.) And Joseph Smith said, "Every man who has a calling to minister to the inhabitants of the world," and this includes all who hold the Melchizedek Priesthood, "was ordained to that very purpose in the Grand Council of heaven before this world was. I suppose that I was ordained to this very office in that Grand Council." (*Teachings,* p. 365.)

Now what is meant by making a calling sure?

All blessings promised in connection with the callings of God are conditional; they are offered to men provided they obey the laws upon which their receipt is predicated. (D. & C. 130:20-21.) "For all who will have a blessing at my hands," the Lord says, "shall abide the law which was appointed for that blessing, and the conditions thereof, as were instituted from before the foundation of the world." (D. & C. 132:5.)

It follows, then, that when the law has been lived to the full, the promised blessing is guaranteed. "I, the Lord, am bound when ye do what I say; but when ye do not what I say, ye have no promise." (D. & C. 82:10.) Accordingly, when a man lives the law that qualifies him for eternal life, the Lord is bound by his own law to confer that greatest of all gifts upon him. And if by a long course of trial and obedience, while yet in this life, a man proves to the Lord that he has and will abide in the truth, the Lord accepts the exhibited devotion and issues his decree that the promised blessings shall be received. The calling, which up to that time was provisional, is then made sure. The receipt of the promised blessings are no longer conditional; they are guaranteed. Announcement is made that every gospel blessing shall be inherited.

What is meant by election? Who are the elect of God? To what have they been elected? And why?

Election is akin to and synonymous with calling, and in a general sense the elect comprise the whole house of Israel. (Isa.

45:4; 65:9.) Jesus and Paul and Peter speak of the elect as the saints, as the faithful believers, as those who love the Lord and are seeking righteousness. (Matt. 24:22; Mark 13:20; Luke 18:7; Col. 3:12; 2 Tim. 2:10; Titus 1:1.) And the Lord in our day has promised to gather and save his elect. (D. & C. 29:7; 33:6; 35:20.) Paul speaks of the elect along with the called, setting forth that they are foreordained to be like Christ, that their conduct here is justified, and that they shall be glorified hereafter. (Rom. 8:28-30.) Peter specifies that their high status is "according to the foreknowledge of God the Father" (1 Pet. 1:2), and Isaiah assures us that great blessings shall flow to them during the Millennial Era. (Isa. 65:22.)

But in the most express and proper usage of terms, "The elect of God comprise a very select group, an inner circle of faithful members of the Church. . . . They are the portion of church members who are striving with all their hearts to keep the fulness of the gospel law in this life so that they can become inheritors of the fulness of gospel rewards in the life to come.

"As far as the male sex is concerned, they are the ones, the Lord says, who have the Melchizedek Priesthood conferred upon them and who thereafter magnify their callings and are sanctified by the Spirit. In this way, 'They become the sons of Moses and of Aaron and the seed of Abraham, and the church and kingdom, and the elect of God.' " (*Mormon Doctrine*, 2nd ed., p. 217.) See *Commentary II*, pp. 267-269, 271-278, 283-285.

What is meant by making an election sure?

It is with election as with calling: the chosen of the Lord are offered all of the blessings of the gospel on condition of obedience to the Lord's laws; and they, having been tried and tested and found worthy in all things, eventually have a seal placed on their election which guarantees the receipt of the promised blessing.

What is meant by having one's calling and election made sure?

To have one's calling and election made sure is to be sealed up unto eternal life; it is to have the unconditional guarantee of exaltation in the highest heaven of the celestial world; it is to receive the assurance of godhood; it is, in effect, to have the day of judgment advanced, so that an inheritance of all the glory and honor of the Father's kingdom is assured prior to the day when the faithful actually enter into the divine presence to sit with Christ in his throne, even as he is "set down" with his "Father in his throne." (Rev. 3:21.)

What is the relationship between baptism and having one's calling and election made sure?

Baptism is the beginning of personal righteousness; it opens the door to celestial exaltation; it puts us on the path leading to eternal life. As Nephi expressed it, when we enter "the gate" of "repentance and baptism" and receive "a remission" of our sins "by fire and by the Holy Ghost," we are then on the "straight and narrow path which leads to eternal life."

Nephi then asks if we have thereby done all that is necessary to gain that glorious reward, and answers with an emphatic, No! "Ye must press forward with a steadfastness in Christ," he says, "having a perfect brightness of hope, and a love of God and of all men. Wherefore, if ye shall press forward, feasting upon the word of Christ, and endure to the end, behold, thus saith the Father: Ye shall have eternal life." (2 Ne. 31:17-21.)

That is to say, after baptism, after being called out of darkness into the light of the gospel; after having been numbered with the elect of God, we must receive the guarantees to which we have been called, and the assurances that appertain to our election, and which are given on a conditional basis only in baptism. We must have our calling and election made sure, and this high achievement grows out of and is the crowning reward of baptism.

What is the relationship between celestial mariage and having one's calling and election made sure?

In the same sense that baptism opens the door and starts repentant persons traveling on the path leading to eternal life, so also does celestial marriage. This holy order of matrimony also opens a door leading to celestial exaltation. "In the celestial glory there are three heavens or degrees; And in order to obtain the highest, a man must enter into this order of the priesthood [meaning the new and everlasting covenant of marriage]; And if he does not, he cannot obtain it. He may enter into the other, but that is the end of his kingdom; he cannot have an increase." (D. & C. 131:1-4.)

As everyone who has been married in the temple knows, those so united — by the power and authority of the holy priesthood and by virtue of the sealing power restored by Elijah — are promised an inheritance of glory, honor, power, and dominion in the kingdom of God. But, as with baptism, all the promises are conditional; they are specifically and pointedly stated as being contingent upon the subsequent faithfulness of the participating parties. If they keep the commandments after celestial marriage, their union continues in the life to come; if they do not conform to the standards of personal righteousness involved, their marriage is not of force when they die and they revert to their separate and single status.

Unfortunately some are confused on this point because of a misunderstanding of some of the truths revealed in the revelation on marriage. Because no person can gain exaltation or eternal life alone; because exaltation includes the continuation of the family unit in eternity; because the whole thrust of revealed religion is to perfect and center everything in the family; and because having one's calling and election made sure is the receipt of a guarantee of eternal life — it was the most natural thing in the world for the Lord to reveal both the doctrine of eternal marriage and the doctrine of being sealed up unto eternal life (meaning having one's calling and election made sure) in one and the same revelation. In effect one grows out of the other. The one is a conditional promise of eternal life; the other is an unconditional promise.

Thus in Section 132, verse 19 begins by talking of celestial marriage in these words: "If a man marry a wife by my word, which is my law, and by the new and everlasting covenant, and it is sealed unto them by the Holy Spirit of promise, by him who is anointed, unto whom I have appointed this power and the keys of this priesthood," but then proceeds to consider the matter of having their callings and elections made sure by saying: "and it shall be said unto them [meaning that in addition to the marriage sealing, it shall be said unto them] — Ye shall come forth in the first resurrection; . . . and shall inherit thrones, kingdoms, principalities, and powers, dominions, all heights and depths — then . . . they shall pass by the angels, and the gods, which are set there, to their exaltation and glory in all things, as hath been sealed upon their heads, which glory shall be a fulness and a continuation of the seeds forever and ever."

That is to say, after celestial marriage; after entering into sacred covenants in the house of the Lord; after receiving the conditional promise of the continuation of the family unit in eternity; after receiving power to gain kingdoms and thrones — we must so live as to receive the guarantees to which we have thus been called, and the assurances that appertain to our election, and which are given on a conditional basis only in celestial marriage. As with baptism, so with celestial marriage; after the glorious promise of eternal life that is part of each of these covenants, we must press forward in righteousness until our calling and election is made sure; and this high achievement grows out of and is the crowning reward of celestial marriage.

What is the relationship between holding the holy Melchizedek Priesthood and having one's calling and election made sure?

The Melchizedek Priesthood is conferred with an oath and a covenant — a covenant on man's part that he will receive the priesthood and magnify his calling therein, and an oath on God's part that man shall, as a consequence, be "made like unto the Son of God, abiding a priest continally." (*Inspired Version*, Heb. 7:3; D. & C. 84:33-44.) See Heb. 7:1-3; 7:18-22. In other words, those who magnify their callings shall gain eternal life. But one cannot keep a covenant before it is made; a calling in the priesthood cannot be magnified until it is received. The covenant is the contract which sets forth the terms and conditions by obedience to which eternal life may be won; the obedience comes after the call; and when it is whole and complete, the worthy son has his calling and election made sure, and he inherits the promised reward.

Is having one's calling and election made sure the same as being sealed by the Holy Spirit of Promise?

The Holy Ghost is the Holy Spirit; he is the Holy Spirit

promised the saints at baptism, or in other words the Holy Spirit of Promise, this exalted name-title signifying that the promised receipt of the Holy Spirit, as on the day of Pentecost, is the greatest gift man can receive in mortality.

The gift of the Holy Ghost is the right to the constant companionship of that member of the Godhead based on faithfulness; it is bestowed with a promise that we shall receive revelation and be sanctified if we are true and faithful and so live as to qualify for the companionship of that Holy Spirit who will not dwell in an unclean temple. (1 Cor. 3:16-17; 6:19; Mosiah 2:37; Hela. 4:24.) The receipt of the promise is conditional! If after we receive the promise, we then keep the commandment, we gain the companionship of this member of the Godhead, and not otherwise.

One of the functions assigned and delegated to the Holy spirit is to seal, and the following expressions are identical in thought content:

To be sealed by the Holy Spirit of Promise;
To be justified by the Spirit;
To be approved by the Lord; and
To be ratified by the Holy Ghost.

Accordingly, any act which is sealed by the Holy Spirit of Promise is one which is justified by the Spirit, one which is approved by the Lord, one which is ratified by the Holy Ghost. One of Paul's great concerns was that the saints in his day should be justified by faith, through grace, because of the shedding of the blood of Christ. (*Commentary II*, pp. 224-240.) In other words, he sought to perfect the lives of those souls put into his care and custody so that, as a result of good works, all their acts would have divine approval and be sealed by the Holy Spirit of Promise.

As revealed to Joseph Smith, the Lord's law in this respect is: "All covenants, contracts, bonds, obligations, oaths, vows, performances, connections, associations, or expectations, that are not made and entered into and sealed by the Holy Spirit of promise, of him who is anointed, both as well for time and for all eternity, and that too most holy, by revelation and commandment through the medium of mine anointed, whom I have appointed on the earth to hold this power (and I have appointed unto my servant Joseph to hold this power in the last days, and there is never but one on the earth at a time on whom this power and the keys of this priesthood are conferred), are of no efficacy, virtue, or force in and after the resurrection from the dead; for all contracts that are not made unto this end have an end when men are dead." (D. & C. 132:7.)

By way of illustration, this means that baptism, partaking of the sacrament, administering to the sick, marriage, and every covenant that man ever makes with the Lord — plus all other "contracts, bonds, obligations, oaths, vows, performances, associations, or expectations" — must be performed in righteousness by and for people who are worthy to receive whatever blessing is involved, otherwise whatever is done has no binding and sealing effect in eternity.

Since "the Comforter knoweth all things" (D. & C. 42:17), it follows that it is not possible "to lie to the Holy Ghost" and thereby gain an unearned or undeserved blessing, as Ananias and Sapphira found out to their sorrow. (Acts 5:1-11.) And so this provision that all things must be sealed by the Holy Spirit of Promise, if they are to have "efficacy, virtue, or force in and after the resurrection from the dead" (D. & C. 132:7), is the Lord's system for dealing with absolute impartiality with all men, and for giving all men exactly what they merit, neither adding to nor diminishing from. See *Commentary II*, pp. 493-495.

When the Holy Spirit of Promise places his ratifying seal upon a baptism, or a marriage, or any covenant, except that of having one's calling and election made sure, the seal is a conditional approval or ratification; it is binding in eternity only in the event of subsequent obedience to the terms and conditions of whatever covenant is involved.

But when the ratifying seal of approval is placed upon someone whose calling and election is thereby made sure — because there are no more conditions to be met by the obedient person — this act of being sealed up unto eternal life is of such transcendent import that of itself it is called being sealed by the Holy Spirit of Promise, which means that in this crowning sense, being so sealed is the same as having one's calling and election made sure. Thus, to be sealed by the Holy Spirit of Promise is to be sealed up unto eternal life; and to be sealed up unto eternal life is to be sealed by the Holy Spirit of Promise. And of this usage of terms, a usage which is wholly misunderstood unless the whole concept of the sealing power of the Spirit is understood, the scriptures and other prophetic utterances bear repeated witness.

Thus Joseph Smith says that when Peter "exhorts us to make our calling and election sure," it is the same thing as "the sealing power spoken of by Paul in other places." (*Teachings*, p. 149.) The illustrative quotation from Paul which the Prophet then quotes is: "In whom ye also trusted, after that ye heard the word of truth, the gospel of your salvation: in whom also after that ye believed, ye were sealed with that holy Spirit of promise, Which is the earnest of our inheritance until the redemption of the purchased possession, unto the praise of his glory," that we may be sealed up unto the day of redemption. (Eph. 1:13-14.) That is, the calling and election of Ephesian Saints had been made sure because they were sealed by the Holy Spirit of Promise.

Those who gain exaltation in the celestial kingdom are described in the Vision of the degrees of glory in these words: "They are they who received the testimony of Jesus, and believed on his name and were baptized after the manner of his burial, being buried in the water in his name, and this according to the commandment which he has given — That by keeping the commandments they might be washed and cleansed from all their sins, and receive the Holy Spirit by the laying on of the hands of him who is ordained and sealed unto this power; And who overcome by faith, and are sealed by the Holy Spirit of promise, which the Father sheds forth upon all those who are just and true." (D. & C. 76:51-53.) That is, they first believed the gospel, received all the conditional promises of eternal life, including the gift of the Holy Ghost, and then having "overcome by faith," having kept the commandments, having proved themselves worthy, they finally had their calling and election made sure.

"This principle" — that of having one's calling and election made sure and of being sealed with that Holy Spirit of Promise — "ought (in its proper place) to be taught," the Prophet said, "for God hath not revealed anything to Joseph, but what he will make known unto the Twelve, and even the least saint may know all things as fast as he is able to bear them, for the day must come when no man need say to his neighbor, know ye the Lord; for all shall know him (who remain) from the least to the greatest. How is this to be done? It is to be done by this sealing power, and the other Comforter spoken of, which will be manifest by revelation." (*Teachings*, p. 149.)

The scriptural passage alluded to by the Prophet in this statement is from Jeremiah and is as follows: "Behold, the days come, saith the Lord, that I will make a new covenant with the house of Israel, and with the house of Judah: Not according to the covenant that I made with their fathers in the day that I took them by the hand to bring them out of the land of Egypt; which my covenant they brake, although I was an husband unto them, saith the Lord: But this shall be the covenant that I will make with the house of Israel; After those days, saith the Lord, I will put my law in their inward parts, and write it in their hearts; and will be their God, and they shall be my people. And they shall teach no more every man his neighbour, and every man his brother, saying, Know the Lord: for they shall all know me, from the least of them unto the greatest of them, saith the Lord: for I will forgive their iniquity, and I will remember their sin no more." (Jer. 31:31-34.) Complete realization of the blessings here promised is Millennial, and the knowledge of God spoken of shall be manifest by the receipt of the Second Comforter, as the Prophet then proceeds to state, and as we shall now consider.

Is having one's calling and election made sure the same as receiving the Second Comforter?

It is the privilege of those who have their calling and election made sure, meaning those who are sealed up unto eternal life, meaning those who are "sealed with that holy Spirit of promise" (Eph. 1:13), to receive the Second Comforter.

"There are two Comforters spoken of," says the Prophet in one of his most profound and enlightening discourses. "One of these is the Holy Ghost, the same as given on the day of Pentecost, and that all saints receive after faith, repentance, and baptism. The first Comforter or Holy Ghost has no other effect than pure intelligence. It is more powerful in expanding the mind, enlightening the understanding, and storing the intellect with present knowledge, of a man who is of the literal seed of Abraham, than one that is a Gentile, though it may not have half as much visible effect upon the body; for as the Holy Ghost falls upon one of the literal seed of Abraham, it is calm and serene; and his whole soul and body are only exercised by the pure spirit of intelligence; while the effect of the Holy Ghost upon a Gentile, is to purge out the old blood, and make him actually of the seed of Abraham. That man that has none of the blood of Abraham (naturally) must have a new creation by the Holy Ghost. In such a case, there may be more of a powerful effect upon the body, and visible to the eye, than upon an Israelite, while the Israelite at first might be far before the Gentile in pure intelligence.

"The other Comforter spoken of is a subject of great interest, and perhaps understood by few of this generation. After a person has faith in Christ, repents of his sins, and is baptized for the remission of his sins and receives the Holy Ghost, (by the laying on of hands), which is the first Comforter, then let him continue to humble himself before God, hungering and thirsting after righteousness, and living by every word of God, and the Lord will soon say unto him, Son, thou shalt be exalted. When the Lord has thoroughly proved him, and finds that the man is determined to serve him at all hazards, then the man will find his calling and his election made sure, then it will be his privilege to receive the other Comforter, which the Lord hath promised the saints, as is recorded in the testimony of St. John, in the 14th chapter, from the 12th to the 27th verses." (*Teachings*, p. 149-150.) The Prophet then quotes verses 16, 17, 18, 21, and 23, and asks that they be noted in particular.

In a revelation to certain selected saints in this dispensation, the Lord said that the alms of their prayers were "recorded in the book of the names of the sanctified, even them of the celestial world" (D. & C. 88:2), which is to say that they were among those who had "overcome by faith," and were "sealed by the Holy Spirit of promise, which the Father sheds forth upon all those who are just and true." (D. & C. 76:53.)

"Wherefore," the Lord said to them, "I now send upon you another Comforter, even upon you my friends, that it may abide in your hearts, even the Holy Spirit of promise; which other Comforter is the same that I promised unto my disciples, as is recorded in the testimony of John. This Comforter is the promise which I give unto you of eternal life, even the glory of the celestial kingdom; Which glory is that of the church of the Firstborn, even of God, the holiest of all, through Jesus Christ his Son." (D. & C. 88:3-5.)

These saints, like their Ephesian Brethren before them, had been called and chosen "before the foundation of the world" that they "should be holy and without blame" before the Lord, through baptism and obedience (Eph. 1:4-7), which is the sole course by which men can sanctify their souls (3 Ne. 27:19-20), thereby qualifying to have their names recorded "in the book of the names of the sanctified." (D. & C. 88:2.) They had then earned the right by faith and devotion to have the seal of divine acceptance placed on the conditional promises which they had theretofore made. They now had the sure "promise . . . of eternal life" (D. & C. 88:4), which eternal life is the name of the kind of life which God our Heavenly and Eternal Father lives, and they were prepared to receive the Second Comforter.

As set forth by the Lord Jesus himself to the ancient Twelve, in one of his most loving and gracious sermons, the doctrine of the Second Comforter, noting particularly the verses quoted by the Prophet, is this:

Verse 16: "And I will pray the Father, and he shall give you another Comforter, that he may abide with you for ever." That is, in their case they are going to receive a Comforter in addition to the Holy Ghost already promised, and this Comforter will abide with them forever, for they shall have membership in the Church of the Firstborn in celestial exaltation.

Verse 17: "Even the Spirit of truth; whom the world cannot receive, because it seeth him not, neither knoweth him: but ye know him; for he dwelleth with you, and shall be in you." All that is said in this verse, if taken out of context, could apply to the Holy Ghost, whom the world cannot receive, and who figuratively dwells in the hearts of the righteous, for the title, "Spirit of truth," applies to this Spirit member of the Godhead. (John 16:13.)

But as spoken by Jesus, as recorded by the Beloved John, and as interpreted by the Prophet Joseph Smith, the verse has application to Jesus himself. "I am the Spirit of truth," is his latter-day declaration (D. & C. 93:26), which is but another of the many instances in which the same name-title applies to more than one member of the Godhead. Thus the Lord Jesus is telling his ancient apostles that he will dwell in them in the figurative sense stated three sentences later in the same sermon: "I am in the Father, and ye in me, and I in you." (Verse 20.)

Verse 18: "I will not leave you comfortless: I will come to you." I will come! The Lord Jesus Christ himself will do it! He will appear to them and be with them! And what an eternal comfort it will be, in days and years to come, to see the face of their Beloved Lord! And verses 19 and 20 then reaffirm that when the world no longer sees him, yet because he continues to live in glorious immortality, his beloved disciples shall continue to see him — "Yet a little while, and the world seeth me no more; but ye see me: because I live, ye shall live also. At that day ye shall know that I am in my Father, and ye in me, and I in you."

Verse 21: "He that hath my commandments, and keepeth them, he it is that loveth me: and he that loveth me shall be loved of my Father, and I will love him, and will manifest myself to him." Again the Master Teacher affirms that because of love and obedience he personally will hereafter manifest himself to his disciples. And then, one of the Twelve, hearing the words but not comprehending the deep spiritual truths they convey, asks Jesus: "Lord, how is it that thou wilt manifest thyself unto us, and not unto the world?" (Verse 22.)

Verse 23: "Jesus answered and said unto him, If a man love me, he will keep my words: and my Father will love him, and we will come unto him, and make our abode with him." Can this be possible that the Father and the Son, as resurrected, glorified persons, will come to and make their abode with those who love and serve God with all their hearts? (D. & C. 93:1.) Such seems almost beyond comprehension, but so gracious and infinite is God's grace that such is verily the case, and so we find the Prophet, writing by the spirit of prophecy and revelation: "John 14:23 — The appearing of the Father and the Son, in that verse is a personal appearance; and the idea that the Father and the Son dwell in a man's heart is an old sectarian notion, and is false." (D. & C. 130:3.)

Having thus set forth the doctrine that he and his Father will manifest themselves to those who are sealed up unto eternal life — and for that matter, why should they not come to such persons, since all who gain eternal life shall dwell in their presence and be like them? — having so taught, Jesus says: "These things have I spoken unto you, being yet present with you. But the Comforter, which is the Holy Ghost" — the First Comforter, the initial Comforter, the one "that all saints receive after faith, repentance, and baptism," the one that "has no other effect than pure intelligence" (*Teachings*, p. 149) — this Comforter, "whom the Father will send in my name, he shall teach you all things, and bring all things to your remembrance, whatsoever I have said unto you." (Verses 25 and 26.)

After quoting the named verses from the 14th chapter of John, the Prophet continues his own inspired analysis: "Now what is this other Comforter?" he asks. "It is no more nor less than the Lord Jesus Christ himself; and this is the sum and substance of the whole matter; that when any man obtains this last Comforter, he will have the personage of Jesus Christ to attend him, or appear unto him from time to time, and even he will manifest the Father unto him, and they will take up their abode with him, and the visions of the heavens will be opened unto him, and the Lord will teach him face to face, and he may have a perfect knowledge of the mysteries of the Kingdom of God; and this is the state and place the ancient saints arrived at when they had such glorious visions — Isaiah, Ezekiel, John upon the Isle of Patmos, St. Paul in the three heavens, and all the saints who held communion with the general assembly and Church of the Firstborn." (*Teachings*, pp. 150-151.)

Speaking in November, 1831, to those whose calling and election would in due course be made sure, and whose "privilege" it would then be to receive the Second Comforter, the Lord said: "Verily I say unto you that it is your privilege, and a promise I give unto you that have been ordained unto this ministry, that inasmuch as you strip yourselves from jealousies and fears, and humble yourselves before me, for ye are not sufficiently humble, the veil shall be rent and you shall see me." (D. & C. 67:10-14.)

What if those whose calling and election has been made sure thereafter commit grievous sins? Suppose they backslide and walk in the ways of wickedness? Or fight the truth and rebel against God — what then?

That all men commit sin, before and after baptism, and for that matter, before and after their calling and election is made sure, is self-evident. There has been only one Sinless One — the Lord Jesus who was God's own Son.

Thus in the revelation announcing the setting up of the restored church in this day, the Lord says: "There is a possibility that man may fall from grace and depart from the living God; Therefore let the church take heed and pray always, lest they fall into temptation; Yea, and even let those who are sanctified take heed also." (D. & C. 20:32-34.)

The prophets and apostles from Adam and Enoch down, and all men, whether cleansed and sanctified from sin or not, are yet subject to and do in fact commit sin. This is the case even after men have seen the visions of eternity and been sealed by that Holy Spirit of Promise which makes their calling and election sure. Since these chosen ones have the sure promise of eternal life, and since "no unclean thing can enter into" the Father's "kingdom" (3 Ne. 27:19), "or dwell in his presence" (Moses 6:57), what of sins committed after being sealed up into eternal life?

Obviously the laws of repentance still apply, and the more enlightened a person is, the more he seeks the gift of repentance, and the harder he strives to free himself from sin as often as he falls short of the divine will and becomes subject in any degree to the Master of Sin who is Lucifer. It follows that the sins of the godfearing and the righteous are continually remitted because they repent and seek the Lord anew every day and every hour.

And as a matter of fact, the added blessing of having one's calling and election made sure is itself an encouragement to avoid sin and a hedge against its further commission. By that long course of obedience and trial which enabled them to gain so great a blessing the sanctified saints have charted a course and developed a pattern of living which avoids sin and encourages righteousness. Thus the Lord said: "I give unto you Hyrum Smith to be a patriarch unto you, to hold the sealing blessings of my church, even the Holy Spirit of promise, whereby ye are sealed up unto the day of redemption, that ye may not fall notwithstanding the hour of temptation that may come upon you." (D. & C. 124: 124.)

But suppose such persons become disaffected and the spirit of repentance leaves them — which is a seldom and almost unheard of eventuality — still, what then? The answer is — and the revelations and teachings of the Prophet Joseph Smith so recite! — they must then pay the penalty of their own sins, for the blood of Christ will not cleanse them. Or if they commit murder or adultery, they lose their promised inheritance because these sins are exempt from the sealing promises. Or if they commit the unpardonable sin, they become sons of perdition.

As we have already seen, making one's calling and election sure comes after and grows out of celestial marriage. Eternal life does not and cannot exist for a man or a woman alone, because in its very nature it consists of the continuation of the family unit in eternity. Thus the revelation on marriage speaks both of celestial marriage (in which the conditional promises of eternal life are given) and of making one's calling and election sure (in which the unconditional promise of eternal life are given) in one and the same sentence — which sentence also says that those who commit sins (except "murder whereby to shed innocent blood") after being sealed up unto eternal life shall still gain exaltation. This is the language: "Then" — that is, after their calling and election has been made sure — "shall it be written in the Lamb's Book of

Life, that he shall commit no murder whereby to shed innocent blood, and if ye abide in my covenant, and commit no murder whereby to shed innocent blood, it shall be done unto them in all things whatsoever my servant hath put upon them, in time, and through all eternity; and shall be of full force when they are out of the world; and they shall pass by the angels, and the gods, which are set there, to their exaltation and glory in all things, as hath been sealed upon their heads, which glory shall be a fulness and a continuation of the seeds forever and ever. Then shall they be gods," because they have eternal life. (D. & C. 132:19-20.)

Then the revelation speaks of that obedience out of which eternal life grows, and still speaking both of celestial marriage and of making one's calling and election sure says: "Verily, verily, I say unto you, if a man marry a wife according to my word, and they are sealed by the Holy Spirit of promise, according to mine appointment" — that is, if they are both married and have their calling and election made sure — "and he or she shall commit any sin or transgression of the new and everlasting covenant whatever, and all manner of blasphemies, and if they commit no murder wherein they shed innocent blood, yet they shall come forth in the first resurrection, and enter into their exaltation; but they shall be destroyed in the flesh, and shall be delivered unto the buffetings of Satan unto the day of redemption, saith the Lord God." (D. & C. 132:26.)

This matter of being destroyed in the flesh and delivered over to the buffetings of Satan until the day of redemption is the doctrine of blood atonement, whereunder those here involved are not cleansed by the blood of Christ, but must pay the penalty for their own sins. This principle can only operate in a day, as that of Moses, when there is no separation of Church and state and when the Church has power to take life. Of conditions in our day, and as to how this law applies to us, President Joseph Fielding Smith says: "We cannot destroy men in the flesh, because we do not control the lives of men and do not have power to pass sentences upon them which involve capital punishment. In the days when there was a theocracy on the earth, then this decree was enforced. What the Lord will do in lieu of this, because we cannot destroy in the flesh, I am unable to say, but it will have to be made up in some other way." (*Doctrines of Salvation*, vol. 2, p. 97.)

As to the shedding of innocent blood, within the meaning of this revelation, the Lord says: "The blasphemy against the Holy Ghost, which shall not be forgiven in the world nor out of the world, is in that ye commit murder wherein ye shed innocent blood, and assent unto my death, after ye have received my new and everlasting covenant, saith the Lord God; and he that abideth not this law can in nowise enter into my glory, but shall be damned, saith the Lord." (D. & C. 132:27.) That is, the innocent blood is that of Christ; and those who commit blasphemy against the Holy Ghost, which is the unpardonable sin (Matt. 12:31-32), thereby "crucify to themselves the Son of God afresh, and put him to an open shame." (Heb. 6:6.) They are, in other words, people who would have crucified Christ, having the while a perfect knowledge that he was the Son of God.

Following the pattern set by the Lord of speaking both of celestial marriage and of being sealed up unto eternal life in the same context, Joseph Smith said: "Putting my hand on the knee of William Clayton, I said: Your life is hid with Christ in God, and so are many others. Nothing but the unpardonable sin can prevent you from inheriting eternal life for you are sealed up by the power of the priesthood unto eternal life, having taken the step necessary for that purpose. Except a man and his wife enter into an everlasting covenant and be married for eternity, while in this probation, by the power and authority of the Holy Priesthood, they will cease to increase when they die; that is, they will not have any children after the resurrection. But those who are married by the power and authority of the priesthood in this life, and continue without committing the sin against the Holy Ghost, will continue to increase and have children in the celestial glory. The unpardonable sin is to shed innocent blood, or be accessory thereto. All other sins will be visited with judgment in the flesh, and the spirit being delivered to the buffetings of Satan until the day of the Lord Jesus." (*History of Church*, vol. 5, pp. 391-392.)

Perhaps this matter of being "visited with judgment in the flesh" — whatever it may be in an individual case — is the Lord's way of handling things when it is not possible for a person to be "destroyed in the flesh." (D. & C. 132:26.) In this connection, also — and having in mind that the sealing power was given by Elijah to Peter, James, and John on the Mount of Transfiguration (*Teachings*, p. 158), and again to Joseph Smith and Oliver Cowdery in the Kirtland Temple (D. & C. 110:13-16) — we should note these words of the Prophet: "This spirit of Elijah was manifest in the days of the Apostles, in delivering certain ones to the buffetings of Satan, that they might be saved in the day of the Lord Jesus. They were sealed by the spirit of Elijah unto the damnation of hell until the day of Lord, or revelation of Jesus Christ." (*Teachings*, p. 338.)

As to the fact that the sealing power cannot seal a man up so as to keep him from being a son of perdition, if that is the course he chooses to follow, the Prophet says: "The doctrine that the Presbyterians and Methodists have quarreled so much about — once in grace, always in grace, or falling away from grace, I will say a word about. They are both wrong. Truth takes a road between them both, for while the Presbyterian says: 'Once in grace, you cannot fall;' the Methodist says: 'You can have grace today, fall from it tomorrow, next day have grace again; and so follow on, changing continually.' But the doctrine of the scriptures and the spirit of Elijah would show them both false, and take a road between them both; for, according to the scripture, if men have received the good word of God, and tasted of the powers of the world to come, if they shall fall away, it is impossible to renew them again, seeing they have crucified the Son of God afresh, and put him to an open shame; so there is a possibility of falling away; you could not be renewed again, and the power of Elijah cannot seal against this sin, for this is a reserve made in the seals and power of the priesthood." (*Teachings*, pp. 338-339.) Thus, even though a man's calling and election has been made sure, if he then commits blasphemy against the Holy Ghost, he becomes a son of perdition, because when he was sealed up unto eternal life it was with a reservation. The sealing was not to apply in the case of the unpardonable sin.

As to the fact that the sealing power cannot seal a man up unto eternal life if he thereafter commits murder and thereby sheds innocent blood (not in this case the blood of Christ, but the blood of any person slain unlawfully and with malice) the Prophet says: "A murderer, for instance, one that sheds innocent blood, cannot have forgiveness. David sought repentance at the hand of God carefully with tears, for the murder of Uriah; but he could only get it through hell; he got a promise that his soul should not be left in hell.

"Although David was a king, he never did obtain the spirit and power of Elijah and the fullness of the priesthood; and the priesthood that he received, and the throne and kingdom of David is to be taken from him and given to another by the name of David in the last days, raised up out of his lineage." (*Teachings*, p. 339.) Thus, even though a man's calling and election has been made sure, if he then commits murder, all of the promises are of no effect, and he goes to a telestial kingdom (Rev. 21:8; D. & C. 76:103), because when he was sealed up unto eternal life, it was with a reservation. The sealing was not to apply in the case of murder.

And as to the fact that the sealing power cannot seal a man up unto eternal life if he thereafter commits adultery, the Prophet says: "If a man commit adultery, he cannot receive the celestial kingdom of God. Even if he is saved in any kingdom, it cannot be the celestial kingdom." (*History of the Church*, vol. 6, p. 81.) Thus, even though a man's calling and election has been sure, if he then commits adultery, all of the promises are of no effect, and he goes to a telestial kingdom, because when he was sealed up unto eternal life, it was with a reservation. The sealing was not to apply in the case of subsequent adultery. In other cases, through repentance, there is forgiveness for this sin which is second only to murder in the category of personal sins. (1 Cor. 6:9-11; 3 Ne. 30; D. & C. 42:24-26.)

Who has had their calling and election made sure and how can they be identified?

In the providences of the Lord, there is no question that many of the saints of all ages and dispensations have attained this high status, a fact which can be known in individual cases by applying the principles above set forth to the individual situation.

In this present discussion we have named Isaiah, Ezekiel, John the Revelator, Paul, William Clayton and "many others" of the Prophet's day, the Ephesian Saints, and "all the saints who held communion with the general assembly and Church of the Firstborn." (*Teachings*, p. 151.)

For our day, the Prophet Joseph Smith is the classical example of one who was sealed up unto eternal life. Of him the revelation states: "I am the Lord thy God, and will be with thee even unto the end of the world, and through all eternity; for verily I seal upon you your exaltation, and prepare a throne for you in the kingdom of my Father, with Abraham your father." (D. & C. 132:49.)

Obviously if it applies to Isaiah and Ezekiel, it applies also to Jeremiah, Samuel, Moses, Joshua and all of the prophets; if it applies to Joseph Smith and William Clayton and "many others" in the Prophet's day, certainly a great many of the later worthies of this dispensation are also included; and if a sizeable number of the Ephesian Saints were so classifed, then surely the same applies to like groups of the saints in Rome, Corinth, Galatia, Philippi, Colosse, Thessalonica, and in all the places where the Meridian Saints were congregated. If Paul and John are part of the group, so also are Peter, James, Titus, Jude, Matthew, the other apostles, and many of the preachers of righteousness of that ancient day.

And can there be any question that the same was true among the Nephites? And Jaredites? That it included all of the City of Zion and those who were thereafter caught up to heaven to dwell with Enoch and his translated brethren? And if this glorious principle has always operated in days past, is it beyond reason that it is still sealing blessings upon the heads of the Latter-day Saints? Verily, such is the case now — a situation which we anticipate shall be increasingly so as the Millennium approaches, during which period the sealing power and all its attendant blessings will abound on every side.

As with all the blessings of the gospel, the glorious reality of having one's calling and election made sure is within the power of the faithful saints to obtain, including both men and women.

How many of the saints have or shall make their calling and election sure?

There is no more an answer to this question than there was to the query put to Jesus: "Lord, are there few that be saved?" to which he answered: "Strive to enter in at the strait gate: for many, I say unto you, will seek to enter in, and shall not be able" (Luke 13:23-24), by which he meant to teach that though the total saved will be many they are few as compared to the masses of men. And so it is among the saints with reference to being sealed up unto eternal life: though many shall so obtain, they will be few compared to the total population of the Church.

It is in this sense that Jesus used the enigmatic expression, "Many are called, but few are chosen." (Matt. 22:14.) Called to what? Chosen for what? Called into the Church, called to the holy priesthood, called to receive all of the blessings of the gospel, including the crowning blessing of eternal life. Chosen to inherit the blessings offered through the gospel and the priesthood; chosen for eternal life and exaltation. Called to the Church, but chosen to be sealed up unto eternal life and to have one's calling and election made sure.

"How many will be able to abide a celestial law, and go through and receive their exaltation," the Prophet said, "I am unable to say, as many are called, but few are chosen." (*Teachings*, p. 331.)

And from the Lord himself we have these words: "There are many who have been ordained among you, whom I have called but few of them are chosen. They who are not chosen have sinned a very grievious sin, in that they are walking in darkness at noon-day. . . . If you keep not my commandments, the love of the Father shall not continue with you, therefore you shall walk in darkness." (D. & C. 95:5-6, 12.) Also: "There has been a day of calling, but the time has come for a day of choosing; and let those be chosen that are worthy. And it shall be manifest unto my servant, by the voice of the Spirit, those that are chosen; and they shall be sanctified." (D. & C. 105:35-36.)

And, finally, as to reason why so few of the saints shall be saved, we have this great and inspired utterance of the Prophet: "Behold, there are many called, but few are chosen. And why are they not chosen? Because their hearts are set so much upon the things of this world, and aspire to the honors of men, that they do not learn this one lesson — That the rights of the priesthood are inseparably connected with the powers of heaven, and that the powers of heaven cannot be controlled nor handled only upon the principles of righteousness. That they may be conferred upon us, it is true; but when we undertake to cover our sins, or to gratify our pride, our vain ambition, or to exercise control or dominion or compulsion upon the souls of the children of men, in any degree of unrighteousness, behold, the heavens withdraw themselves; the Spirit of the Lord is grieved; and when it is withdrawn, Amen to the priesthood or the authority of that man. Behold, ere he is aware, he is left unto himself, to kick against the pricks, to persecute the saints, and to fight against God. We have learned by sad experience that it is the nature and disposition of almost all men, as soon as they get a little authority, as they suppose, they will immediately begin to exercise unrighteous dominion. Hence many are called, but few are chosen." (D. & C. 121:34-40.)

And now to return to Peter's pleading that the saints make their calling and election sure.

1-19. "There are three grand secrets lying in this chapter," the Prophet said, "which no man can dig out, unless by the light of revelation, and which unlock the whole chapter, as the things that are written are only hints of things which existed in the prophet's mind, which are not written concerning eternal glory. I am going to take up this subject by virtue of the knowledge of God in me, which I have received from heaven." (*Teachings*, p. 304.) And it is these teachings of Joseph Smith which we have essayed to put forth in the foregoing discussion.

These are the three secrets: "1st key: Knowledge is the power of salvation. 2nd key: Make your calling and election sure: 3rd key: It is one thing to be on the mount and hear the excellent voice, etc., and another to hear the voice declare to you, You have a part and lot in that kingdom." (*Teachings* p. 306.)

1. Like precious faith with us] Peter is writing to those who believe as he and the other apostles believe. The doctrines he is about to present are beyond the comprehension of uninspired men; they can only be understood by the power of that Spirit which the saints receive at baptism.

2-10. The Prophet taught: "It is not wisdom that we should have all knowledge at once presented before us; but that we should have a little at a time; then we can comprehend it . . . . Add to your faith knowledge, etc. The principle of knowledge is the principle of salvation. This principle can be comprehended by the faithful and diligent; and every one that does not obtain knowledge sufficient to be saved will be condemned. The principle of salvation is given us through the knowledge of Jesus Christ." (*Teachings*, p. 297.)

Also: "Contend earnestly for the like precious faith with the Apostle Peter, 'and add to your faith virtue,' knowledge, temperance, patience, godliness, brotherly kindness, charity; 'for if these things be in you, and abound, they make you that ye shall neither be barren nor unfruitful in the knowledge of our Lord Jesus Christ.' Another point, after having all these qualifications, he lays this injunction upon the people 'to make your calling and election sure.' He is emphatic upon this subject — after adding all this virtue, knowledge, etc., 'Make your calling and election sure.' What is the secret — the starting point? 'According as his divine power hath given unto us all things that pertain unto life and godliness.' How did he obtain all things? Through the knowledge of him who hath called him. There could not anything be given, pertaining to life and godliness, without knowledge. Woe! woe! woe to Christendom! — especially the divines and priests if this be true.

"Salvation is for a man to be saved from all his enemies; for until a man can triumph over death, he is not saved. A knowledge of the priesthood alone will do this." (*Teachings*, p. 305.)

3. All things that pertain unto life and godliness] The true saints have every doctrine, law, key, and power needed to gain eternal life and become like God.

Called us to glory and virtue] Called us to that eternal life which none but the clean can inherit, for "no unclean thing can enter into his kingdom." (3 Ne. 27:19.)

4. Exceeding great and precious promises] Promises of eternal life, which is "the greatest of all the gifts of God." (D. & C. 14:7.)

Partakers of the divine nature] Become as God is, enjoying to the full every characteristic, perfection, and attribute which he possesses and which dwell in him independently.

5-19. Joseph Smith said: "Now, there is some grand secret here, and keys to unlock the subject. Notwithstanding the apostle exhorts them to add to their faith, virtue, knowledge, temperance, etc., yet he exhorts them to make their calling and election sure. And though they had heard an audible voice from heaven bearing testimony that Jesus was the Son of God; yet he says we have a more sure word of prophecy, whereunto ye do well that ye take heed as unto a light shining in a dark place. Now, wherein could they have a more sure word of prophecy than to hear the voice of God saying, This is my beloved Son.

"Now for the secret and grand key. Though they might hear the voice of God and know that Jesus was the Son of God, this would be no evidence that their election and calling was made sure, that they had part with Christ, and were joint-heirs with him. They then would want that more sure word of prophecy, that they were sealed in the heavens and had the promise of eternal life in the kingdom of God. Then, having this promise sealed unto them, it was an anchor to the soul, sure and steadfast. Though the thunders might roll and lightnings flash, and earthquakes bellow, and war gather thick around, yet this hope and knowledge would support the soul in every hour of trial, trouble and tribulation. Then knowledge through our Lord and Savior Jesus Christ is the grand key that unlocks the glories and mysteries of the kingdom of heaven.

"Compare this principle once with Christendom at the present day, and where are they, with all their boasted religion, piety and sacredness while at the same time they are crying out against prophets, apostles, angels, revelations, prophesying and visions, etc. Why, they are just ripening for the damnation of hell. They will be damned, for they reject the most glorious principle of the Gospel of Jesus Christ and treat with disdain and trample under foot the key that unlocks the heavens and puts in our possession the glories of the celestial world. Yes, I say, such will be damned, with all their professed godliness. Then I would exhort you to go on and continue to call upon God until you make your calling and election sure for yourselves, by obtaining this more sure word of prophecy, and wait patiently for the promise until you obtain it." (*Teachings*, pp. 298-299.)

5-7. The attributes of godliness here listed are the ones which qualify the Lord's ministers for effective service on his errand, and all his saints for eternal life in his kingdom. Salvation must be won, and to go where God is, we must be like him; and to be like him we must possess the character, perfections, and attributes which he possesses. "And faith, hope, charity and love, with an eye single to the glory of God, qualify him for the work. Remember faith, virtue, knowledge, temperance, patience, brotherly kindness, godliness, charity, humility, diligence." (D. & C. 4:5-6.)

5. Faith] See *Commentary I*, pp. 523-525; *Mormon Doctrine*, 2nd ed., pp. 261-267.

Virtue] Moral excellence and rectitude in every field, including personal chastity. To his saints the Lord decrees: "Ye must practise virtue and holiness before me continually." (D. & C. 46:33.)

Knowledge] An understanding of and familiarity with gospel truth; a clear perception of eternal truth; enlightenment and learning about God and his laws. Thus, "A man is saved no faster than he gets knowledge" (*Teachings*, p. 217), of God and his laws; and "It is impossible for a man to be saved in ignorance" (D. & C. 131:6), of Jesus Christ and the saving principles of the gospel. Accordingly, "the word of knowledge" (1 Cor. 12:8) is one of the gifts of the Spirit.

6. Temperance] See *Commentary II*, pp. 482-484.

Patience] See Jas. 5:7-11.

Godliness] See 2 Tim. 2:14-26.

7. Brotherly kindness] "In their pursuit of godly graces the saints are exhorted, 'And be ye kind one to another, tenderhearted, forgiving one another, even as God for Christ's sake hath forgiven you.' (Eph. 4:32; D. & C. 4:6; 121:42.) Kindness embraces an interest in another's welfare and a disposition to be helpful. The kind are tender, gracious, benevolent, well-disposed, and exhibit sympathy and humaneness toward their follow men." (*Mormon Doctrine*, 2nd ed., pp. 413-414.)

Charity] See *Commentary II*, pp. 377-380.

8. None can comprehend the knowledge of God, of Christ, and of the gospel unless he himself possesses the attribbutes of godliness, for the knowledge of spiritual things comes only by revelation, and until a person gains godly attributes he cannot receive the Spirit from whom revelation comes.

9. Purged from his old sins] By baptism and the receipt of the gift of the Holy Ghost.

10. Those who keep the commandments shall be saved; they cannot fall; and every saint who walks continually in paths of truth and righteousness shall have his calling and election made sure.

11. Those saints who keep the commandments shall gain an inheritance in the highest heaven in the celestial kingdom.

13. I am in this tabernacle] 14. Shortly I must put off this tabernacle] Peter is a spirit child of an Eternal Father; the living, intelligent, sentient part of his personality is his spirit; and shortly he shall be slain for the word of truth and the testimony of Jesus. (John 21:18-19.)

16-19. Peter here recounts his experience with James and John on the Mount of Transfiguration when those chosen three were eyewitnesses of our Lord's transfiguration and when they heard the voice of the Father, and then says there is something even greater than this. "And what could be more sure? When he was transfigured on the mount, what could be more sure to them?" the Prophet asks. (*Teachings*, p. 303.) The answer is to gain the personal revelation that one is sealed up unto eternal life.

19. "The more sure word of prophecy means a man's knowing that he is sealed up unto eternal life, by revelation and the spirit of prophecy, through the power of the Holy Priesthood." (D. & C. 131:5.) "The anointing and sealing is to be called, elected and made sure." (*Teachings*, p. 323.) "Let us suppose a case," the Prophet says. "Suppose the great God who dwells in heaven should reveal himself to Father Cutler here, by the opening heavens, and tell him, I offer up a decree that whatsoever you seal on earth with your decree, I will seal it in heaven; you have the power then; can it be taken off? No. Then what you seal on earth, by the keys of Elijah, is sealed in heaven; and this is the power of Elijah, and this is the difference between the spirit and power of Elias and Elijah; for while the spirit of Elias is a forerunner, the power of Elijah is sufficient to make our calling and election sure; and the same doctrine, where we are exhorted to go on to perfection, not laying again the foundation of repentance from dead works, and of laying on of hands, resurrection of the dead, etc. . . . Here is the doctrine of election that the world has quarreled so much about; but they do not know anything about it." (*Teachings*, p. 338.)

Until the day dawn, and the day star arise in your hearts] Until the Second Coming of the Lord; until the Millennial day dawns; until the day when "the root and the offspring of David" who is "the bright and morning star" (Rev. 22:16) shall reign personally on earth and be the companion, confidant, and friend of those whose calling and election is sure and who are thus called forth as "kings and priests" to live and "reign on earth" (Rev. 5:10) with him a thousand years.

PROPHECY COMES BY POWER OF HOLY GHOST

II PETER 1:20-21.

20 Knowing this first, that no prophecy of the scripture is of any private interpretation.

21 For the prophecy came not in old time by the will of man: but holy men of God spake *as they were* moved by the Holy Ghost.

I.V. II PETER 1:20.

20 Knowing this first, that no prophecy of the scriptures is **given of any private will of man.**

Let it be said; let it be written; let it be known — in all places, among every people, in all ages, from creation's morn to all eternity — that all scripture comes from God, by the power of the Holy Ghost, and means only what He who knows all things intended it to mean! There are no private interpretations! This is a basic law of scriptural interpretation!

Unless and until a scripture means to a man what it means to God, man has not caught the vision of the truth taught, or comprehended the doctrine being revealed. Two persons, two groups of theologians, or two churches cannot reach divergent conclusions as to the meaning of any scripture and both of them be right. And be it known, on earth and in heaven, now and forever, that truth only will prevail!

Further: All scripture comes by the power of the Holy Ghost, no matter what age of the earth is involved, and must and can be interpreted only by the same power. A prophet speaks when his mind is filled with the power and glory of God. His hearers and those who later read his words understand and envision the true import of his utterances only when their minds are filled with the same power and glory. "The things of God knoweth no man, but the Spirit of God," and the saints must truly "have the mind of Christ" (1 Cor. 2:11, 16), if they are to gain spiritual knowledge. None can comprehend the true meaning of the scriptures except by revelation from the same Revelator who revealed them in the first instance, who is the Holy Ghost. (D. & C. 50:10-22.)

And so Nephi, writing "by the power of the Holy Ghost, which power he received by faith on the Son of God," set forth this eternal truth: "The Holy Ghost . . . is the gift of God unto all those who diligently seek him, as well in times of old as in the time that he should manifest himself unto the children of men. For he is the same yesterday, today, and forever; and the way is prepared for all men from the foundation of the world, if it so be that they repent and come unto him. For he that diligently seeketh shall find; and the mysteries of God shall be unfolded unto them, by the power of the Holy Ghost, as well in these times as in times of old, and as well in times of old as in times to come; wherefore, the course of the Lord is one eternal round." (1 Ne. 10:17-19.)

20. Prophecy] See *Commentary II*, pp. 385-388.

Scripture] See 2 Tim. 3:14-17.

21. Holy Ghost] See *Commentary II*, pp. 104-107.

FALSE TEACHERS ARE DAMNED

II PETER 2:1-9.

1 But there were false prophets also among the people, even as there shall be false teachers among you, who privily shall bring in damnable heresies, even denying the Lord that bought them, and bring upon themselves swift destruction.

2 And many shall follow their pernicious ways: by reason of whom the way of truth shall be evil spoken of.

3 And through covetousness shall they with feigned words make merchandise of you: whose judgment now of a long time lingereth not, and their damnation slumbereth not.

4 For if God spared not the angels that sinned, but cast *them* down to hell, and delivered *them* into chains of darkness, to be reserved unto judgment;

5 And spared not the old world, but saved Noah, the eighth *person*, a preacher of righteousness, bringing in the flood upon the world of the ungodly;

6 And turning the cities of Sodom and Gomorrha into ashes condemned *them* with an overthrow, making *them* an ensample unto those that after should live ungodly;

7 And delivered just Lot, vexed with the filthy conversation of the wicked:

8 (For that righteous man dwelling among them, in seeing and hearing, vexed *his* righteous soul from day to day with *their* unlawful deeds;)

9 The Lord knoweth how to deliver the godly out of temptations, and to reserve the unjust unto the day of judgment to be punished:

I.V. II PETER 2:1, 3.

1 But there were false prophets also among the people, even as there shall be false teachers among you, who privily shall bring in **abominable** heresies, even denying the Lord that bought them, and bring upon themselves swift destruction.

3 And through covetousness shall they with feigned words make merchandise of you; whose judgment now of a long time lingereth not, and their **destruction** slumbereth not.

1. As Joseph Smith said, a teacher who does not have the testimony of Jesus, which is the spirit of prophecy, is a false prophet. (*Teachings*, p. 269.) And as there were false prophets and teachers in ancient Israel, so there were among the Meridian Saints, and so there are in both the world and in the Church today.

False prophets, . . . false teachers] See *Commentary I*, pp. 251-253; *Commentary II*, pp. 456-460.

Heresies] See *Commentary II*, pp. 362-363.

Denying the Lord that bought them] Our Lord pays the price for the sins of all those who believe in him and obey his laws (D. & C. 19:16-20), thus saving them from spiritual death. Accordingly, those who belong to the Church have been "purchased with his own blood" (Acts 20:28); they have been bought with a price — the life blood of the Lamb. And what more abominable heresy is there than for them to deny the atoning sacrifice of their Lord?

2-3. Many of the early Christians were destined to be led away by false teachers, teachers who would be damned for their "pernicious ways" and teachings.

4-8. If God cast one-third of the hosts of heaven down to eternal damnation, for their rebellion; if in the flood he destroyed all but Noah and his family, for rejecting the divine will; if he rained brimstone and fire upon Sodom and Gomorrah, utterly destroying all, save Lot and his family only, that dwelt therein, for their sins and abominations — why should false prophets and teachers expect to escape the wrath of Him who is no respecter of persons?

4. The angels that sinned] See Rev. 12:1-17.

Hell] See Rev. 20:11-15.

5. Noah the eighth person] Noah and seven others were the only ones saved in the flood. (1 Pet. 3:20.)

LUSTFUL SAINTS PERISH IN OWN CORRUPTION

II PETER 2:10-22.

10 But chiefly them that walk after the flesh in the lust of uncleanness, and despise government. Presumptuous *are they*, selfwilled, they are not afraid to speak evil of dignities.

11 Whereas angels, which are

greater in power and might, bring not railing accusation against them before the Lord.

12 But these, as natural brute beasts, made to be taken and destroyed, speak evil of the things that they understand not; and shall utterly perish in their own corruption;

13 And shall receive the reward of unrighteousness, *as* they that count it pleasure to riot in the day time. Spots *they are* and blemishes, sporting themselves with their own deceivings while they feast with you;

14 Having eyes full of adultery, and that cannot cease from sin; beguiling unstable souls: an heart they have exercised with covetous practices; cursed children:

15 Which have forsaken the right way, and are gone astray, following the way of Balaam *the son* of Bosor, who loved the wages of unrighteousness;

16 But was rebuked for his iniquity: the dumb ass speaking with man's voice forbad the madness of the prophet.

17 These are wells without water, clouds that are carried with a tempest; to whom the mist of darkness is reserved for ever.

18 For when they speak great swelling *words* of vanity, they allure through the lusts of the flesh, *through much* wantonness, those that were clean escaped from them who live in error.

19 While they promise them liberty, they themselves are the servants of corruption: for of whom a man is overcome, of the same is he brought in bondage.

20 For if after they have escaped the pollutions of the world through the knowledge of the Lord and Saviour Jesus Christ, they are again entangled therein, and overcome, the latter end is worse with them than the beginning.

21 For it had been better for them not to have known the way of righteousness, than, after they have known *it*, to turn from the holy commandment delivered unto them.

22 But it is happened unto them according to the true proverb, The dog *is* turned to his own vomit again; and the sow that was washed to her wallowing in the mire.

In plain, blunt language, Peter sets forth what the Holy Ghost thinks of members of the Church who depart from the truth and walk in the ways of wickedness. In the process he tells why people apostatize, showing that in large measure it is a matter of succumbing to the lusts of the flesh. That is, men choose to disbelieve the truth because it condemns their evil deeds; rather than bridle their passions, as the gospel requires, they choose to live carnal and evil lives, with the result that they are worse off than if they had never received the truth in the first instance. "For although a man may have many revelations, and have power to do many mighty works, yet if he boasts in his own strength, and sets at naught the counsels of God, and follows after the dictates of his own will and carnal desires, he must fall and incur the vengeance of a just God upon him." (D. & C. 3:4.)

Apostasy] See 2 Tim. 3:1-13.

Cultists] See *Commentary II*, pp. 177-178.

10. Lust of uncleanness] Illicit sex-centered passions; sinful and sensuous desires.

Despise government . . . speak evil of dignities] Are the problems any different today? Has not Lucifer persuaded great hosts of people, in and out of the Church, to rebel against governmental restraints and to revile those who, in the interest of law and order, seek to administer them.

11. Judgment is the Lord's; he will rebuke and condemn; all others, even including mighty Michael and the host of heaven's angels, are to bring no railing accusation against governments and leaders. (Jude 9.)

12. Natural brute beasts] Backsliding church members who are as creatures without reason. And how often apostasy is born of emotion, not of reason!

13. The reward of unrighteousness] Among church members it is to lose the blessings of the gospel, which are peace in this life and eternal life in the world to come.

To riot in the day time] To engage in open, public, wilful sin; to rebel against the truth without making any effort to hide one's opposition to the cause of righteousness.

Spots they are and blemishes] Spiritually diseased members of the body of the Church, which should be cut away with the surgeon's knife, lest the whole body be overcome with disease.

Sporting themselves with their own deceivings while they feast with you] Proudly displaying themselves in the Church and pretending to feast upon the good word of God, though they are in fact out of harmony with the teachings and practices of the true saints.

14. Eyes full of adultery] "The lust of the eyes" (1 John 2:16), through which they commit adultery in their hearts. (Matt. 5:28.)

Cursed children] Members of the household of faith who reject Christ, their adopted Father, and are thereby rejected by him; contrasted with "obedient children" (1 Pet. 1:14), those members of the Church who, by keeping the faith, honor the new name they have taken upon themselves. (Mosiah 5:7-14.)

15-16. This single, inspired sentence enables us to put in proper perspective the whole story of Balaam the son of Beor who was entreated by Balak to curse Israel and bless Moab. (Num. 22, 23 and 24.) Though Balaam was true to his prophetic trust and delivered the Lord's message of blessing to Israel and cursing to Moab, yet as here shown he "loved the wages of unrighteousness"; that is, he sought the honor and wealth offered him if he would curse the Lord's chosen people. And how often it is that the honors of men and the wealth of the world lead members of the Church away from their duty and cause them to lose their souls!

15. The wages of unrighteousness] In this case, as it so often is, the wages of unrighteousness consist of the honors of men and the wealth of the world. Balak sent this message to Balaam: "I will promote thee unto very great honour, and I will do whatsoever thou sayest unto me: come therefore, I pray thee, curse me this people." Balaam replied: "If Balak would give me his house full of silver and gold, I cannot go beyond the word of the Lord my God, to do less or more." (Num. 22:17-18.) After Balaam had prophesied well of Israel and ill of Moab, Balak in anger cried out: "I thought to promote thee unto great honour; but, lo, the Lord hath kept thee back from honour." (Num. 24:11.)

Madness of the prophet] Could Peter have found stronger language? Surely it is madness, nothing less, to give up the eternal blessings of the Lord for the passing honors and wealth of this life.

17. Wells without water] Delinquent church members, from whom the waters of life should flow freely, but who instead have dried up spiritually, so their teachings can no longer quench the throats of those who "thirst after righteousness." (Matt. 5:6.)

Clouds that are carried with a tempest] Faithless church members, whose duty it is to rain righteousness upon mankind, but who instead are themselves driven about by the tempests of false doctrine.

To whom the mist of darkness is reserved for ever] Having forsaken the effulgent gospel light, they are now overshadowed by the mists of spiritual darkness, in which state they shall remain forever unless they repent. In his dream of the tree of life, Lehi saw "that there arose a mist of darkness; yea, even an exceeding great mist of darkness, insomuch that they who had commenced in the path did lose their way, that they wandered off and were lost." Others, however, as he beheld, "did press forward through the mist of darkness, clinging to the rod of iron, even until they did come forth and partake of the fruit of the tree." (1 Ne. 8:23-24.) And then, by way of interpretation, Nephi said: "The mists of darkness are the temptations of the devil, which blindeth the eyes, and hardeneth the hearts of the children of men, and leadeth them away into broad roads, that they perish and are lost." (1 Ne. 12:17.)

18-19. 'They teach false doctrines that have their roots in the lusts of the flesh, doctrines which promise freedom from church restrictions, but which in fact bring those who accept them into the bondage of sin.' In similar vein, many modern ministers teach, openly and officially and with seeming sincerity, that illicit sexual relations are not always evil; that there are situations in which adultery is not a breach of the divine law; that homosexual perversions between consulting adults carry no divine condemnation; that church members may choose to worship on a week day so as to keep the Sabbath free for hunting, fishing, or other recreational activities; that there will be no Second Coming of the Son of Man at which the wicked shall be destroyed, for he has already come in the hearts of those who believe; and so on and so on through the ten thousand times ten thousand vagaries of the current brand of false religions.

18. Those that were clean escaped] Recent converts, "newborn babes" in Christ (1 Pet. 2:2), those who have but recently come into the fold and who are not yet so secure and grounded in the faith as to be able to resist the sophistry of false teachers.

20-21. "For of him unto whom much is given much is required; and he who sins against the greater light shall receive the greater condemnation." (D. & C. 82:3.)

22. "As a dog returneth to his vomit, so a fool returneth to his folly." (Prov. 26:11.)

LATTER-DAY SCOFFERS DENY SECOND COMING

II PETER 3:1-9.

1 This second epistle, beloved, I now write unto you; in *both* which I stir up your pure minds by way of remembrance:

2 That ye may be mindful of the words which were spoken before by the holy prophets, and of the commandment of us the apostles of the Lord and Saviour:

3 Knowing this first, that there shall come in the last days scoffers, walking after their own lusts,

4 And saying, Where is the promise of his coming? for since the fathers fell asleep, all things continue as *they were* from the beginning of the creation.

5 For this they willingly are ignorant of, that by the word of God the heavens were of old, and the earth standing out of the water and in the water:

6 Whereby the world that then was, being overflowed with water, perished:

7 But the heavens and the earth, which are now, by the same word are kept in store, reserved unto fire against the day of judgment and perdition of ungodly men.

8 But, beloved, be not ignorant of this one thing, that one day *is* with the Lord as a thousand years, and a thousand years as one day.

9 The Lord is not slack concerning his promise, as some men count slackness; but is longsuffering to us-ward, not willing that any should perish, but that all should come to repentance.

I.V. II PETER 3:2-9.

2 That ye may be mindful of the words which were spoken before by the holy prophets, and of the **commandments** of us, the apostles of the Lord and Savior;

3 Knowing this first, that **in the last days there shall come scoffers,** walking after their own lusts.

4 **Denying the Lord Jesus Christ,** and saying, Where is the promise of his coming? for since the fathers fell asleep, all things **must** continue as they **are, and have continued as they are** from the beginning of the creation.

5 For this they willingly are ignorant of, **that of old the heavens, and the earth standing in the water and out of the water, were created by the word of God;**

6 **And by the word of God,** the world that then was, being overflowed with water perished;

7 But the heavens, and the earth which are now, **are kept in store by the same word,** reserved unto fire against the day of judgment and perdition of ungodly men.

8 **But concerning the coming of the Lord,** beloved, **I would not have you ignorant** of this one thing, that one day is with the Lord as a thousand years, and a thousand years as one day.

9 The Lord is not slack concerning his promise **and coming,** as some men count slackness; but long-suffering toward us, not willing that any should perish, but that all should come to repentance.

That our Lord shall come again, to live and reign with men on earth a thousand years, is amply attested in the revelations both ancient and modern. See *Commentary II*, pp. 27-29; 1 Thess. 5:1-11. In "this second epistle," the Chief Apostle both assumes and announces the literal nature of the Second Coming of the Son of Man, with this added proclamation: In the last days, in so-called Christendom (for the doctrine is not so much as an issue in other circles) the fact of our Lord's literal return shall be challenged; false ministers shall mock at such an antiquated view; and the scientists shall scoff at the idea of the burning of the earth as a prelude to a Millennial era when none but the righteous shall dwell on the new earth thus cleansed from its wicked inhabitants. All history, all experience, and all reason, they shall say, negate these old-fashioned doctrines about the Lord living again among men. Surely the scriptures must mean that he shall come as a power or influence to dwell in the hearts of men whenever they gain oneness with him, shall be their cry.

But Peter, whose views came not from reason but by revelation, replies: Which is easier, to believe in a creation (which fact is self-evident) or a Second Coming? To believe in the destruction of the world by water in Noah's day (of which fact there is ample evidence) or the burning of the vineyard in that day when "as it was in the days of Noe, so shall it be also in the days of the Son of man"? (Luke 17:26.)

1-2. Both the ancient prophets and the apostles of Peter's day — as well, for that matter, as all the preachers of righteousness of all ages and places — have taught the same doctrine: a doctrine centered in Christ as the Son of God; a doctrine of his atoning sacrifice, of obedience to his laws, of his personal return to dwell among men on earth in the last days; a doctrine of salvation with him in the kingdom of his Father.

3. In the last days] Now, today; in the Saturday night of time; in the day of restoration preceding our Lord's return.

Scoffers, walking after their own lusts] Here Peter gives the almost invarying reason why men reject and scoff at the truth. It is their entanglements with the world, their failure to overcome the lusts of the flesh. On the other hand, those who walk in righteousness have the companionship of the Holy Spirit and are thereby enabled to see and believe the truth.

I. V. 4. Denying the Lord Jesus Christ] If people — scientists, ministers, supposed Christians, all people — do not believe that Jesus Christ is literally the Son of God; that God, a personal Being, was his Father; that our Lord rose from the dead and now lives, as does his Father, having a tangible body of flesh and bones, why should they believe in his literal return to walk again in the flesh with his brethren on planet earth?

K. J. 4. All things continue as they were from the beginning of the creation] In this simple statement is summarized one of the basic reasons why the wisdom of men cannot interpret the events of creation, redemption, and salvation. The reason: It is false to assume that all things have always been the same. For instance: When the Lord created this earth, it was in a terrestrial state, an Edenic state, a paradisiacal state; death had not then entered the world. Adam and Eve and all created things were in an immortal state. The begetting of offspring had not yet begun. (Moses 5:11.) Then came the fall. And, "if Adam had not transgressed he would not have fallen, but he would have remained in the garden of Eden. And all things which were created must have remained in the same state in which they were after they were created; and they must have remained forever, and had no end. And they would have had no children; wherefore they would have remained in a state of innocence, having no joy, for they knew no misery; doing no good, for they knew no sin. But behold, all things have been done in the wisdom of him who knoweth all things. Adam fell that men might be, and men are, that they might have joy." (2 Ne. 2:22-25.) In due course, when Christ reigns "personall upon the earth," then "the earth will be renewed and receive its paradisiacal glory." (Tenth Article of Faith.) That is, it will return to its terrestrial, Edenic, or paradisiacal state; it will be the new heaven and new earth of which Peter is about to speak. None of these eternal verities are known to or understood by the scientists of the world or the uninspired teachers among men. Without them how can they possibly understand the true import and meaning of the doctrine of the Second Coming of the Son of Man?

6. The world . . . overflowed with water] A literal, universal flood!

7. The heaven and the earth, which are now] This present planet (surrounded by the atmospheric heavens) in its fallen state, its telestial state, a state where carnality and evil can and do dwell upon its face.

Reserved unto fire] The vineyard of the earth shall be burned, literally. "The day cometh, that shall burn as an oven; and all the proud, yea, and all that do wickedly, shall be stubble." (Mal. 4:1.)

The day of judgment and perdition of ungodly man] The Second Coming when the unrighteous shall be destroyed by fire, "for they that come shall burn them, saith the Lord of Hosts, that it shall leave them neither root nor branch." (Jos. Sm. 2:37.)

8. Time is measured by the revolutions of whatever planet or other heavenly body is involved. With reference to "celestial time," the Lord said to Abraham, "that Kolob was after the manner of the Lord, according to its times and seasons in the revolutions thereof; that one revolution was a day unto the Lord, after his manner of reckoning, it being one thousand years according to the time appointed unto that whereon thou standest. This is the reckoning of the Lord's time, according to the reckoning of Kolob." (Abra. 3:4.) Later, with reference to God's decree that in the day Adam partook of the forbidden fruit he should surely die, the record says: "Now I, Abraham, saw that it was after the Lord's time, which was after the time of Kolob, for as yet the Gods had not appointed unto Adam his reckoning." (Abra. 5:13.)

9. It is the will of the Lord that all men should repent and be saved.

ELEMENTS TO MELT AT SECOND COMING

II PETER 3:10-18.

10 But the day of the Lord will come as a thief in the night; in the which the heavens shall pass away with a great noise, and the elements shall melt with fervent heat, the earth also and the works that are therein shall be burned up.

11 *Seeing* then *that* all these things shall be dissolved, what manner *of persons* ought ye to be in *all* holy conversation and godliness,

12 Looking for and hasting unto the coming of the day of God, wherein the heavens being on fire shall be dissolved, and the elements shall melt with fervent heat?

13 Nevertheless we, according to his promise, look for new heavens and a new earth, wherein dwelleth righteousness.

14 Wherefore, beloved, seeing that ye look for such things, be diligent that ye may be found of him in peace, without spot, and blameless.

15 And account *that* the longsuffering of our Lord *is* salvation; even as our beloved brother Paul also according to the wisdom given unto him hath written unto you;

16 As also in all *his* epistles, speaking in them of these things; in which are some things hard to be understood, which they that are unlearned and unstable wrest, as *they do* also the other scriptures, unto their own destruction.

17 Ye therefore, beloved, seeing ye know *these things* before, beware lest ye also, being led away with the error of the wicked, fall from your own stedfastness.

18 But grow in grace, and *in* the knowledge of our Lord and Saviour Jesus Christ. To him *be* glory both now and for ever. Amen.

I.V. II PETER 3:10-13, 15, 17.

10 But the day of the Lord will come as a thief in the night, in the which the heavens shall **shake, and the earth also shall tremble, and the mountains shall melt, and** pass away with a great noise, and the elements shall **be filled** with fervent heat; **the earth also shall be filled, and the corrupitble works which** are therein shall be burned up.

11 **If then all these things shall be destroyed,** what manner of persons ought ye to be in holy **conduct** and godliness,

12 Looking **unto, and preparing for the day of the coming of the Lord** wherein **the corruptible things of** the heavens being on fire, shall be dissolved, and the **mountains** shall melt with fervent heat?

13 Nevertheless, **if we shall endure, we shall be kept** according to his promise. **And we** look for a new heavens, and a new earth wherein dwelleth righteousness.

15. And account, even as our beloved brother Paul also, according to the wisdom given unto him, hath written unto you, **the longsuffering and waiting of our Lord, for salvation.**

17 Ye therefore, beloved, seeing ye know **before the things which are coming,** beware lest ye also being led away with the error of the wicked, fall from your own steadfastness.

10-12. When the Lord comes and the earth is burned, so intense shall be the heat that "the mountains shall melt" and "flow down" at his presence (Isa. 64:1; D. & C. 133:40), and carnal and worldly things shall be destroyed. In a revelation to

Joseph Smith, he said: "Every corruptible thing, both of man, or of the beasts of the field, or of the fowls of the heavens, or of the fish of the sea, that dwells upon all the face of the earth, shall be consumed; And also that of element shall melt with fervent heat." (D. & C. 101:24-25.)

11. If every corruptible thing shall be consumed at our Lord's return, how important it is for us so to live that we can "abide the day of his coming" (Mal. 3:2), for in that day "shall two be in the field; the one shall be taken, and the other left." (Matt. 24:40.)

13. New heavens and a new earth] See Rev. 21:1-6a.

16. Paul is probably the most misinterpreted prophet of whom we have knowledge. And it started in the day of Peter! But, be it known, that all men interpret the scriptures at their peril. As Alma said, "Behold, the scriptures are before you; if ye will wrest them it shall be to your own destruction." (Alma 13:20.) And as Peter, in this very epistle, has taught, there are no approved private interpretations. (2 Pet. 1:20-21.)

The Second Coming of Christ] See *Commentary II*, pp. 27-29.

Ungodly damned at Second Coming] See 2 Thess. 1:1-12.

Abiding the day of the Second Coming] See Rev. 6:12-17.

The First Epistle General of John

The Beloved John — apostle, revelator, historian, supreme literary craftsman, and friend and confidant of God — here gives us his own commentary upon the Gospel of John!

Of all the accounts of the life of our Lord, the Gospel of John is the one which is dearest to the hearts of the saints. In it is the most persuasive testimony of the Divine Sonship; in it is the most elaborate imagery and symbolism; in it are many of the more mature doctrinal concepts. And this later writing — as much a treatise as an epistle — is the Beloved Disciple's explanation of many of the great truths announced more than defined in his Gospel.

Written by the Disciple whom Jesus loved, and who in turn had such great love for his Lord and his fellowmen that he gained permission to remain on earth and seek to save souls until the Second Coming — this Epistle has as its essential theme:

That God is love;

That love is the foundation upon which all personal righteousness rests;

That all the purposes and plans of Deity are based on his infinite and eternal love; and

That if men will personify that love in their lives, they will become like the Lord himself and have eternal life with him.

The doctrines expounded include how to gain fellowship with God; how to know God and Christ; how to become the sons of God; how to abide in the light and love the brethren; how to dwell in God and have him dwell in us; how to be born again and gain eternal life.

As far as the Biblical Dispensation is concerned, this treatise is probably the last recorded inspired writing of which we have record. After it was penned, the long night of apostate darkness descended upon the earth; the heavens were sealed and God no longer communed with men in open vision and by angelic ministration.

"If, as seems likely," Dummelow says, "the Epistle is St. John's latest work, these are, in point of time, the last words of Holy Scripture" (*Dummelow*, p. 1057) — all of which, to Latter-day Saints, singles out the concluding sentence of the Epistle as a message of supreme prophetic insight and warning to all those from John's day forward as long as time shall stand:

"Little children, keep yourselves from idols!"

HOW TO FIND FELLOWSHIP WITH GOD

I JOHN 1:1-7.

1 That which was from the beginning, which we have heard, which we have seen with our eyes, which we have looked upon, and our hands have handled, of the Word of life;

2 (For the life was manifested, and we have seen *it*, and bear witness, and show unto you that eternal life, which was with the Father, and was manifested unto us;)

3 That which we have seen and heard declare we unto you, that ye also may have fellowship with us: and truly our fellowship *is* with the Father, and with his Son Jesus Christ.

4 And these things write we unto you, that your joy may be full.

5 This then is the message which we have heard of him, and declare unto you, that God is light, and in him is no darkness at all.

6 If we say that we have fellowship with him, and walk in darkness, we lie, and do not the truth:

7 But if we walk in the light, as he is in the light, we have fellowship one with another, and the blood of Jesus Christ his Son cleanseth us from all sin.

I.V. I JOHN 1:1.

1 **Brethren, this is the testimony which we give of** that which was from the beginning, which we have heard, which we have seen with our eyes, which we have looked upon, and our hands have handled, of the Word of life;

HOW TO FIND FELLOWSHIP WITH GOD

1-4. In an introduction which closely parallels the one he wrote for the Gospel of John, the Beloved disciple, as an apostle of the Lord Jesus Christ, bears testimony of the divine Sonship. He has heard, seen, looked upon and handled; he is a witness; he knows. The gospel he preaches will bring a fulness of joy. It is true.

1. That which was from the beginning] The Lord Jesus Christ. "In the beginning was the Word, and the Word was with God, and the Word was God." (John 1:1.)

Which we have heard] That he is God's Son, through whose gospel salvation comes.

Seen . . . looked upon . . . our hands have handled] 'We were with him in the upper room, after his resurrection; we saw his person and looked upon his face. We heard him say, "Behold my hands and my feet, that it is I myself"; and we accepted his invitation: "Handle me, and see; for a spirit hath not flesh and bones, as ye see me have." (Luke 24:39.) We know he is the Son of God because he rose from the dead. We are witnesses.'

The Word of life] The Son of God who was in the beginning with the Father; the Messenger of Salvation, who carried the Father's message of eternal life to all the sons of men; the Life of the world.

2. The life was manifested] "In him was life; and the life was the light of men. And the light shineth in darkness; and the darkness comprehended it not." (John 1:4-5.)

That eternal life, which was with the Father] Eternal life is the name of the kind of life lived by God the Eternal Father; eternal life is God's life. This life is "manifested" to all men through the gospel, and is the reward of all who live the whole law of the whole gospel.

3. We have seen and heard] 'We have seen the Risen Lord; we have heard his word; we bear record; "and the record which we bear is the fulness of the gospel of Jesus Christ, who is the Son." ' (D. & C. 76:14.)

Ye also may have fellowship with us] Fellowship connotes a community of interest, activity and feeling; it is the association enjoyed by a group of equals or friends. And in the Church, it is not the apostles only who are to see and hear and know and understand and feel and handle; it is all the saints who have fellowship with them, "for God hath not revealed anything to Joseph, but what he will make known unto the Twelve, and even the least saint may know all things as fast as he is able to bear them, for the day must come when no man need say to his neighbor, Know ye the Lord; for all shall know him (who remain) from the least to the greatest." (*Teachings,* p. 149.)

Our fellowship is with the Father, and with his Son Jesus Christ] John— himself soon to be translated—is in the same state of fellowship with the Lord which was enjoyed by the three soon-to-be translated Nephite disciples, to whom the Lord said: "Ye shall have fulness of joy; and ye shall sit down in the kingdom of my Father; yea, your joy shall be full, even as the Father hath given me fulness of joy; and ye shall be even as I am, and I am even as the Father; and the Father and I are one." (3 Ne. 28:10.) Thus, John is here saying: 'Our fellowship is with the Father and the Son; we are one with them; they accept us as friends; and we shall be "equal in power, and in might, and in dominion" (D. & C. 76:95), in that glorious day when we receive of their fulness and grace.' To have fellowship with the Lord in this life is to enjoy the companionship of his Holy Spirit, which makes us one with him; and to have fellowship with him in eternity is to be like him, having that eternal life of which he is the possessor and originator.

4. That your joy may be full] "Men are, that they might have joy" (2 Ne. 2:25), the final and complete enjoyment of which is reserved for those who have the fellowship of eternal life with exalted beings in the highest heaven of the celestial world.

5. God is light, and in him is no darkness at all] He is the source, the creator, the embodiment, the personification of light —light both temporal and spiritual, that light which is shed forth by the rays of the sun, and that which enlightens the mind; and the Son, who came forth from him, is "the true Light, which lighteth every man that cometh into the world." (John 1:9.) "The light shineth in darkness, and the darkness comprehendeth it not; nevertheless, the day shall come when you shall comprehend even God, being quickened in him and by him. Then shall ye know that ye have seen me, that I am, and that I am the true light that is in you, and that you are in me; otherwise ye could not abound." (D. & C. 88:49-50.) "That which is of God is light; and he that receiveth light, and continueth in God, receiveth more light; and that light groweth brighter and brighter until the perfect day." (D. & C. 50:24.)

6-7. Obedience is the test of true fellowship with God; only the obedient are cleansed from sin by the blood of Christ; only the obedient press forward to that perfect oneness with Deity which is eternal life.

Blood of Christ] See Heb. 10:1-18.

Light of the World] See *Commentary I*, pp. 452-453.

GOSPEL OFFERS CONFESSION, FORGIVENESS, PROPITIATION

I JOHN 1:8-10; 2:1-2.

8 If we say that we have no sin, we deceive ourselves, and the truth is not in us.

9 If we confess our sins, he is faithful and just to forgive us *our* sins, and to cleanse us from all unrighteousness.

10 If we say that we have not sinned, we make him a liar, and his word is not in us.

1 My little children, these things write I unto you, that ye sin not. And if any man sin, we have an advocate with the Father, Jesus Christ the righteous:

2 And he is the propitiation for our sins: and not for our's only, but also for *the sins of* the whole world.

I.V. I JOHN 2:1.

1 My little children, these things write I unto you, that ye sin not. **But** if any man sin **and repent,** we have an advocate with the Father, Jesus Christ the righteous;

8 and 10. All men have sinned; there are no exceptions; Jesus only lived the whole law in perfection. Baptism is for the remission of sins, but all of the saints commit sin after baptism. The processes of being cleansed anew by repentance must go on as long as mortal life lasts.

9. Confess . . . sins] See Jas. 5:12-20.

Forgive us our sins] See *Commentary I*, pp. 175-180, 270-276, 421-423, 818-819; *Mormon Doctrine*, 2nd ed., pp. 292-298.

2:1. An advocate with the Father] "Listen to him who is the advocate with the Father, who is pleading your cause before him — Saying: Father, behold the sufferings and death of him who did no sin, in whom thou wast well pleased; behold the blood of thy Son which was shed, the blood of him whom thou gavest that thyself might be glorified; Wherefore, Father, spare these my brethren that believe on my name, that they may come unto me and have everlasting life." (D. & C. 45:3-5.)

2. Propitiation] "Our Lord's atoning sacrifice brought the provisions of the law of propitiation into full force. That is, he appeased the demands of divine justice and effected a reconciliation between God and man." (*Mormon Doctrine*, 2nd ed., p. 609.)

The sins of the whole world] "Remember the worth of souls is great in the sight of God; For, behold, the Lord your Redeemer suffered death in the flesh; wherefore he suffered the pain of all men, that all men might repent and come unto him. And he hath risen again from the dead, that he might bring all men unto him, on conditions of repentance." (D. & C. 18:10-12.)

Intercession] See *Commentary II*, pp. 269-271.

HOW SAINTS CAN KNOW GOD AND CHRIST

I JOHN 2:3-6.

3 And hereby we do know that we know him, if we keep this commandments.

4 He that saith, I know him, and keepeth not his commandments, is a liar, and the truth is not in him.

5 But whoso keepeth his word, in him verily is the love of God perfected: hereby know we that we are in him.

6 He that saith he abideth in him ought himself also so to walk, even as he walked.

3. We know him, if] That John who recorded in his gospel account the great *Intercessory Prayer*, in which Jesus taught that life eternal consists in knowing the Father and the Son (John 17:3), now announces how it is possible to know God. It is by obedience to the laws and ordinances of the gospel! And in no other way! Which is to say, among other things: There is not one scintilla of spiritual sense in the sectarian supposition that salvation is gained simply by saying: "I accept Jesus as my personal Savior."

Since the very fact of knowing God, in the ultimate and full sense, consists of thinking what he thinks, saying what he says, doing what he does, and of being like him, thus having exaltation or godhood — it follows that saved souls must advance and progress until they acquire his character, perfections, and attributes, until they gain his eternal power, until they themselves become gods.

God and the Godhead] See *Commentary II*, pp. 154-162.

Knowing God] See *Commentary I*, pp. 759-762.

Exaltation] See 1 John 3:1-3.

5. We are in him] See 1 John 4:7-21.

6. 'Those who say they are Christians, that they believe in Christ and have accepted his gospel, should keep his commandments.'

HOW SAINTS CAN ABIDE IN THE LIGHT

I JOHN 2:7-14.

7 Brethren, I write no new commandment unto you, but an old commandment which ye had from the beginning. The old commandment is the word which ye have heard from the beginning.

8 Again, a new commandment I write unto you, which thing is true in him and in you: because

the darkness is past, and the true light now shineth.

9 He that saith he is in the light, and hateth his brother, is in darkness even until now.

10 He that loveth his brother abideth in the light, and there is none occasion of stumbling in him.

11 But he that hateth his brother is in darkness, and walketh in darkness, and knoweth not whither he goeth, because that darkness hath blinded his eyes.

12 I write unto you, little children, because your sins are forgiven you for his name's sake.

13 I write unto you, fathers, because ye have known him *that is* from the beginning. I write unto you, young men, because ye have overcome the wicked one. I write unto you, little children, because ye have known the Father.

14 I have written unto you, fathers, because ye have known him *that is* from the beginning. I have written unto you, young men, because ye are strong, and the word of God abideth in you, and ye have overcome the wicked one.

I.V. I JOHN 2:7-8.

7 Brethren, I write **a** new commandment unto you, but it is **the same** commandment which ye had from the beginning. The old commandment is the word which ye have heard from the beginning.

8 Again, a new commandment I write unto you, which thing **was of old ordained of God; and** is true in him, and in you; because the darkness is past **in you,** and the true light now shineth.

7-8. 'Brethren, I write unto you about the new and everlasting covenant, which is revealed anew unto you, but which is also the same gospel had from the beginning. It was ordained of God for the salvation of his children and is true, as all of you know, for you have passed from the darkness of the world into its true light.'

9-11. 'If we claim to be Christians and to have the light of the gospel in our lives, and yet hate our brethren, we are in fact in darkness. If we live the gospel, we love our brethren and are on the path leading to eternal life. If we hate our brethren, we have strayed onto bye and forbidden paths and are enveloped by mists of darkness which blind us to the truth.' "If therefore the light that is in thee be darkness, how great is that darkness!" (Matt. 6:23.)

12. Little children] Members of the Church, who have taken upon themselves the name of Christ and are accounted as his sons and his daughters (Mosiah 5:7), and who now need to grow to that spiritual maturity inherent in the attainment of eternal life.

Your sins are forgiven you] Through baptism and the cleansing power of the Holy Ghost.

13. I write] 14. I have written] Apparently John is saying: 'I now write you this Epistle, but I have already written you my Gospel.'

"LOVE NOT THE WORLD"

I JOHN 2:15-17.

15 Love not the world, neither the things *that are* in the world. If any man love the world, the love of the Father is not in him.

16 For all that *is* in the world, the lust of the flesh, and the lust of the eyes, and the pride of life, is not of the Father, but is of the world.

17 And the world passeth away, and the lust thereof: but he that doeth the will of God abideth for ever.

I.V. I JOHN 2:16.

16 **For all in the world that is of the lusts** of the flesh, and the lust of the eyes, and the pride of life, is not of the Father, but is of the world.

15. The world] Not the earth or planet upon which we dwell, but "the social conditions created by such of the inhabitants of the earth as live carnal, sensuous, lustful lives, and who have not put off the natural man by obedience to the laws and ordinances of the gospel." (*Mormon Doctrine*, 2nd ed., p. 847.)

The love of the Father is not in him] No man can love God and rebel against him. Love is measured in obedience and service. "If ye love me, keep my commandments," Jesus said. (John 14:15.) It follows that one cannot love both the Lord and the world. It is like trying to serve both God and mammon, "for either he will hate the one, and love the other; or else he will hold to the one, and despise the other." (Matt. 6:24.)

16. The lust of the flesh] Appetites and passions which are carnal, sensual, and devilish; in their most common and evil form they involve unbridled and illicit sexual acts and perversions.

The lust of the eyes] Looking upon carnality, sensuality, and devilishness with approval and desire, as looking upon "a woman to lust after her," thus committing adultery with her in the heart. (Matt. 5:28.)

The pride of life] See 2 Tim. 3:1-13.
17. The world passeth away] See *Commentary I*, pp. 749-752.
Overcoming the world] See Rev. 2:1-7.
Second Coming of Christ] See *Commentary II*, pp. 27-29.
Ungodly damned at Second Coming] See 2 Thess. 1:1-12.
Harvest of the earth] See Rev. 14:14-20.
Judgment at Second Coming] See Rev. 22:6-16.

ANTICHRISTS SHALL COME IN THE LAST DAYS

I JOHN 2:18-26.

18 Little children, it is the last time: and as ye have heard that antichrist shall come, even now are there many antichrists; whereby we know that it is the last time.

19 They went out from us, but they were not of us; for if they had been of us, they would *no doubt* have continued with us: but *they went out*, that they might be made manifest that they were not all of us.

20 But ye have an unction from the Holy One, and ye know all things.

21 I have not written unto you because ye know not the truth, but because ye know it, and that no lie is of the truth.

22 Who is a liar but he that denieth that Jesus is the Christ? He is antichrist, that denieth the Father and the Son.

23 Whosoever denieth the Son, the same hath not the Father: [*but*] *he that acknowledgeth the Son hath the Father also.*

24 Let that therefore abide in you, which ye have heard from the beginning. If that which ye have heard from the beginning shall remain in you, ye also shall continue in the Son, and in the Father.

25 And this is the promise that he hath promised us, *even* eternal life.

26 These *things* have I written unto you concerning them that seduce you.

18. The last time] To the Meridian Saints it seemed as though the last days were upon them because the apostasy destined to occur between the first and second comings of the Lord had already commenced. However, the last days during which their Lord would in fact return were not destined to come to pass until our day.

Antichrist shall come] As an outgrowth of the true Church of Christ established in the meridian of time, there shall come an apostate system of religion, whose professors are all corrupt, because they draw near to the Lord with their lips, but their hearts are far from him, and who "teach for doctrines the commandments of men, having a form of godliness, but they deny the power thereof." (Jos. Sm. 2:19.) In most graphic terms the Book of Mormon account sets forth the rise of this great church which was "most abominable above all other churches," and which was founded and guided by the devil. (1 Ne. 13.)

Many antichrists] "An antichrist is an opponent of Christ; he is one who is in opposition to the true gospel, the true Church, and the true plan of salvation. (1 John 2:19; 4:4-6.) He is one who offers salvation to men on some other terms than those laid down by Christ. Sherem (Jac. 7:1-23), Nehor (Alma 1:2-16), and Korihor (Alma 30:6-60) were antichrists who spread their delusions among the Nephites." (*Mormon Doctrine*, 2nd ed., pp. 39-40.)

20. An unction] An anointing. See 1 John 2:27-29.

21. No lie is of the truth] Everything connected with the Lord's system of revealed religion is true. There is no intermixture of truth and error. It is not a matter of concensus or of mathematical probability. Truth is truth, and when God speaks truth alone flows forth.

Liar] "In the general dealings of men, those who knowingly utter or act out falsehoods are liars. This is also true in the gospel sense. But according to scriptural standards the sin of lying also branches out to include a much larger group of persons. Scripturally, anything that in its nature is untrue and is therefore designed to deceive is a lie. Those who believe in false doctrines are thus guilty of believing a lie, and those who propagate these untruths are guilty of lying.

"For instance: The creeds of apostate Christendom teach untruths about God, and the scriptures say that those who accept these creeds 'have inherited lies.' (Jer. 16:16-21.) Those who accept any of the doctrines of the apostate churches are said to 'believe a lie.' (2 Thess. 2:1-12.) The process of apostasy consists in changing 'the truth of God into a lie.' (Rom. 1:25.) Alma taught that all who do not hearken to the voice of 'the good shepherd' are part of the devil's fold, and then he added, 'whosoever denieth this is a liar.' (Alma 5:38-40.) Sherem confessed, after being smitten, 'I have lied unto God; for I denied the Christ.' (Jac. 7:19; Alma 12:3.) False teachers are liars. (Rev. 2:2.) Conversely, Moroni concluded some of his expositions of the truth by saying, 'I lie not.' (Moro. 10:26-27.) In other words, to teach true doctrine is to tell the truth, and to teach false doctrine is to lie." (*Mormon Doctrine*, 2nd ed., pp. 440-441.) See *Commentary II*, pp. 57-59.

23. The Father and the Son go together; to believe in one is to believe in the other; to reject one is to reject the other; to love one is to love the other. "He that hateth me hateth my Father also." (John 15:23.)

24-25. 'Continue to believe the everlasting gospel so that you shall inherit eternal life.'

25. He hath promised us . . . eternal life] Every member of the Church has the promise of eternal life on the condition of obedience to the laws and ordinances of the gospel. To those who are baptized and who then endure to the end, the Lord says: "Ye shall have eternal life." (2 Ne. 31:20.)

26. Them that seduce you] Those who teach false doctrines and lead the saints away from the paths of truth and righteousness.

HOLY GHOST LEADS SAINTS TO ALL TRUTH

I JOHN 2:27-29.

27 But the anointing which ye have received of him abideth in you, and ye need not that any man teach you: but as the same anointing teacheth you of all things, and is truth, and is no lie, and even as it hath taught you, ye shall abide in him.

28 And now, little children, abide in him; that, when he shall appear, we may have confidence, and not be ashamed before him at his coming.

29 If ye know that he is righteous, ye know that every one that doeth righteousness is born of him.

Our inspired apostolic author, who had aforetime recorded Jesus' promise that the Comforter would teach them all things and bring all things to their remembrance (John 14:26), and that he would guide them into all truth (John 16:13), now announces the fulfillment of the promise. The glorious gift has in reality come to them. "Ye have an unction from the Holy One," he says, and therefore "ye know all things." (1 John 2:20.) This unction, this holy anointing, is the gift of the Holy Ghost, which gives them access to the infinite wisdom of the Father and the Son so that they may know all things as fast as they are able to bear them.

The Holy Ghost and the gift of the Holy Ghost] See *Commentary II*, pp. 104-107.

Receiving revelation from the Holy Ghost] See *Commentary I*, pp. 752-756; *Commentary II*, pp. 320-322.

Anointing] Literally, to pour oil upon one as part of a sacred rite; figuratively, as here, to receive an outpouring of the Holy Spirit; that is, to receive not alone a flash of spiritual insight, as may be the case in the life of any sincere investigator of the truth, but to receive a manifold outpouring of this greatest of all gifts, to actually receive the companionship of this member of the Godhead.

Abideth in you] Figuratively, the Holy Ghost dwells in the hearts of the righteous. (D. & C. 130:22-23.)

Ye need not that any man teach you] "Ye are not sent forth to be taught, but to teach the children of men the things which I have put into your hands by the power of my Spirit; And ye are to be taught from on high." (D. & C. 43:15-16.)

28. Abide in him] Abide in Christ; keep the commandments; work the works of righteousness.

29. By doing what Christ did we partake of his nature, become like him, are transformed into his image, and are thus spiritually born of him.

Born of him] See 1 John 5:1-5.

SONS OF GOD SHALL BE LIKE CHRIST

I JOHN 3:1-3.

1 Behold, what manner of love the Father hath bestowed upon us, that we should be called the sons of God: therefore the world knoweth us not, because it knew him not.

2 Beloved, now are we the sons of God, and it doth not yet appear what we shall be: but we know that, when he shall appear, we shall be like him; for we shall see him as he is.

3 And every man that hath this hope in him purifieth himself, even as he is pure.

"God so loved the world, that he gave his only begotten Son" (John 3:16), to ransom men from the temporal and spiritual death brought into the world through the fall of Adam. None of his spirit children are outside the pale of this redeeming love. But here John speaks of something more, of a special love bestowed upon those who keep his commandments and are adopted into his family as joint-heirs with his natural Son. Their reward is to be like Christ, his natural Son, and to reign in glory with the gods forever.

The Prophet Mormon exhorted his Nephite brethren to seek this special outpouring of divine love. "My beloved brethren," he said, "pray unto the Father with all the energy of heart, that ye may be filled with this love, which he hath bestowed upon all who are true followers of his Son, Jesus Christ; that ye may become the sons of God; that when he shall appear we shall be like him, for we shall see him as he is; that we may have this hope; that we may be purified even as he is pure." (Moro. 7:48.)

Sons of God] See *Commentary II*, pp. 471-475.

The world . . . knew him not] Our Lord, Jesus the Christ "was in the world . . . and the world knew him not." (John 1:10.)

2. Now are we the sons of God] 'We have received Christ and exercised the power given us by him to become his sons. (John 1:12.) And we have been adopted into the family of his Father, so that we are joint-heirs with God's natural Son of all the blessings and exaltations of eternity. (Rom. 8:14-17, 29-30.) It has already happened. We are the sons of God who shall hereafter become gods.' (D. & C. 76:54-60.)

We shall be like him] We shall be like Christ. We shall conform to his image and be glorified as he is. (Rom 8:29.) We shall have exaltation, for that is what he has; and he is like his Father. Thus we also shall be as the Father, which accords with the Prophet's declaration: "God himself, finding he was in the midst of spirits and glory, because he was more intelligent, saw proper to institute laws whereby the rest could have a privilege to advance like himself." (*Teachings*, p. 354.)

3. What greater incentive could there be to live righteously than the promised hope of eternal life with all that is implicit therein? See *Commentary II*, pp. 530-533.

Eternal life] See *Commentary II*, pp. 759-762.

WHY SAINTS NEED NOT CONTINUE IN SIN

I JOHN 3:4-9.

4 Whosoever committeth sin transgresseth also the law: for sin is the transgression of the law.

5 And ye know that he was manifested to take away our sins; and in him is no sin.

6 Whosoever abideth in him sinneth not: whosoever sinneth hath not seen him, neither known him.

7 Little children, let no man deceive you: he that doeth righteousness is righteous, even as he is righteous.

8 He that committeth sin is of the devil; for the devil sinneth from the beginning. For this purpose the Son of God was manifested, that he might destroy the works of the devil.

9 Whosoever is born of God doth not commit sin; for his seed remaineth in him: and he cannot sin, because he is born of God.

I.V. I JOHN 3:6, 8-9.

6 Whosoever abideth in him sinneth not; whosoever **continueth in sin** hath not seen him, neither known him.

8 He that **continueth** in sin is of the devil; for the devil sinneth from the beginning. For this purpose the Son of God was manifested, that he might destroy the works of the devil.

9 Whosoever is born of God doth not **continue in** sin; for **the Spirit of God** remaineth in him; and he cannot **continue in** sin, because he is born of God, **having received that holy Spirit of promise.**

4. Sin] See Jas. 4:13-17.

5. The Sinless One "came into the world to save sinners" (1 Tim. 1:15), "on conditions of repentance." (D. & C. 18:12.)

I. V. 6. Continueth in sin] All men sin, before and after baptism, but those saints who strive to keep the commandments, and are continually repenting and returning to the Lord, no longer continue in that course of sinful rebellion against God and his laws which was their lot before they were baptized for the remission of sins. Church members who do so continue in sin are members in name only; they do not receive the companionship of the Holy Ghost, through whose revelations alone can the Lord be "known."

K. J. 8. The devil sinneth from the beginning] Lucifer rebelled in pre-existence; his wickedness has been accumulating from all eternity; he "sought that which was evil before God" while yet in his presence (2 Ne. 2:17-18); he "was a liar from the beginning." (D. & C. 93:25.)

Destroy the works of the devil] Christ came to overthrow Lucifer, to free men from sin, to abolish death, to bring "life and immortality to light through the gospel" (2 Tim. 1:10), to deliver men from "death and hell, and the devil, and the lake of fire and brimstone, which is endless torment." (2 Ne. 9:26.)

I. V. 9. Sin is of Satan; righteousness is of God. Those saints who overcome the world and gain the companionship of that Holy

Spirit promised the saints at baptism do not continue in sin as long as they walk in the light and enjoy the companionship of the Holy Spirit.

That holy Spirit of promise] See 2 Pet. 1:1-19.

LOVE THE BRETHREN AND GAIN ETERNAL LIFE

I JOHN 3:10-18.

10 In this the children of God are manifest, and the children of the devil: whosoever doeth not righteousness is not of God, neither he that loveth not his brother.

11 For this is the message that ye heard from the beginning, that we should love one another.

12 Not as Cain, *who* was of that wicked one, and slew his brother. And wherefore slew he him? Because his own works were evil, and his brother's righteous.

13 Marvel not, my brethren, if the world hate you.

14 We know that we have passed from death unto life, because we love the brethren. He that loveth not *his* brother abideth in death.

15 Whosoever hateth his brother is a murderer: and ye know that no murderer hath eternal life abiding in him.

16 Hereby perceive we the love *of God*, because he laid down his life for us: and we ought to lay down *our* lives for the brethren.

17 But whoso hath this world's good, and seeth his brother have need, and shutteth up his bowels *of compassion* from him, how dwelleth the love of God in him?

18 My little children, let us not love in word, neither in tongue; but in deed and in truth.

I.V. I JOHN 3:16, 18.

16 Hereby perceive we the love of **Christ,** because he laid down his life for us; and we ought to lay down our lives for the brethren.

18 My little children, let us not love in word, neither in tongue **only;** but in deed and in truth.

10. True saints are known by their works! There neither is nor can be any other standard of judgment. "By their fruits ye shall know them." (Matt. 7:20.) Unless and until they do the works of righteousness they are members of the Church in name only, and the gospel is not a living thing in their lives. And so too are the ungodly known by their works; until they do good and love their fellowmen, they are "not of God."

The children of God] Faithful members of the Church who by spiritual rebirth have been adopted into the family of Jesus Christ. See *Commentary II*, pp. 471-473.

The children of the devil] Rebellious persons who serve Satan by means of their evil deeds, and who thereby attain kinship with him and are figuratively his offspring. Thus Jesus said to certain Jews: "Ye are of your father the devil, and the lusts of your father ye will do" (John 8:44), and Paul in cursing Elymas the sorcerer exclaimed: "O full of all subtilty and all mischief, thou child of the devil, thou enemy of all righteousness, wilt thou not cease to pervert the right ways of the Lord?" (Acts 13:10.)

11. See 1 John 2:7-14.

12-13. Why did Cain slay Abel? Because Cain's works were evil and those of Abel were righteous. Why do worldly people hate the saints? Because the ungodly are living in wickedness and the saints are keeping the commandments. How simple the answers are when we turn to basic principles! Of course the wicked and ungodly oppose the Church; such is implicit in their very way of life, for they are sons of Satan, "children of the devil," followers of him whose whole mission and purpose is to fight against God, to seek "the misery of all mankind" (2 Ne. 2:18), and to stir "up the children of men unto secret combinations of murder and all manner of secret works of darkness." (2 Ne. 9:9.)

14. Those saints who love the brethren have been born again; they have risen from the tomb of spiritual death and are alive in Christ, while those who do not love the brethren abide in that darkness which leaves them dead as pertaining to the things of righteousness.

The brethren] Members of the brotherhood of Christ; those who have taken upon themselves his name and are now brothers in that special sense reserved for the kin of the Lord Jesus. See *Commentary II*, pp. 471-473.

15. Whoso hateth his brother is a murderer] How strong is this doctrine! In the eternal perspective those who hate their fellowmen are murders whether they shed blood in the literal sense or not. They have committed murder in their hearts and will be judged accordingly, even as those who look upon women in lust are numbered with and judged as adulterers. (Matt. 5:28.) The deeds have been done in the heart. And so Jesus said of the devil: "He was a murderer from the beginning" (John 8:44), though that enemy of all righteousness did not personally shed blood either in pre-existence or after being cast down to earth.

No murderer hath eternal life abiding in him] "Murder, the unlawful killing of a human being with malice aforethought or under such circumstances of criminality that the malice is presumed, 'is a sin unto death' (1 John 5:16-17), a sin for which there is 'no forgiveness' (D. & C. 42:79), meaning that a murderer can never gain salvation. 'No murderer hath eternal life abiding in him.' (1 John 3:15.) He cannot join the Church by baptism; he is outside the pale of redeeming grace.

"The call to repentance and baptism which includes murderers (3 Ne. 30) has reference to those who took life while engaged in unrighteous wars, as did the Lamanites, because they were compelled to do so, and not because they in their hearts sought the blood of their fellow men. On the other hand, the Jews on whose hands the blood of Christ was found were not invited to repent and be baptized. (Acts 3:19-21.)

"Murderers are forgiven eventually but only in the sense that all sins are forgiven except the sin against the Holy Ghost; they are not forgiven in the sense that celestial salvation is made available to them. (Matt. 12:31-32; *Teachings*, p. 356-357.) After they have paid the full penalty for their crime, they shall go on to a telestial inheritance. (Rev. 22:15.)" (*Mormon Doctrine*, 2nd ed., p. 520.)

16. 'Even as Christ manifested perfect love for us in voluntarily laying down his life, so we should be willing, through love, so to sacrifice ourselves for each other.'

17-18. 'Does the love of God dwell in the heart of a rich member of the Church who withholds his substance from his poor and needy brethren? Love is more than words; it also requires compassionate service.'

Salvation] See 1 Pet. 1:1-16.

Immortality and eternal life] 2 Tim. 2:1-12.

HOW TO GAIN ANSWERS TO PRAYERS

I JOHN 3:19-24.

19 And hereby we know that we are of the truth, and shall assure our hearts before him.

20 For if our heart condemn us, God is greater than our heart, and knoweth all things.

21 Beloved, if our heart condemn us not, *then* have we confidence toward God.

22 And whatsoever we ask, we receive of him, because we keep his commandments, and do those things that are pleasing in his sight.

23 And this is his commandment, That we should believe on the name of his Son Jesus Christ, and love one another, as he gave us commandment.

24 And he that keepeth his commandments dwelleth in him, and he in him. And hereby we know that he abideth in us, by the Spirit which he hath given us.

19a. One of the chief evidences of the divinity of the gospel, of the true Church, and of the Lord's work on earth is that it improves the lives of men. The proof of the possession of true religion is the wholesome and edifying effect it has in the lives of its adherents. Thus John testifies: 'We know we have true religion because our lives are improved by living its precepts; we love God and our fellowmen in word and in deed, which thing we could not do in full measure if we were yet of the world.'

19b-21. 'If we keep the commandments and have a clear conscience, we gain confidence that the Lord will bless us; if we do not keep the commandments, we have no such assurance, but are condemned by our own conscience and by God who knoweth all things.'

21. Confidence toward God] The assurance, born of living faith, that God will grant us the desires of our hearts in righteousness.

22. How can we be assured that God will in fact answer our prayers and give us those things which we seek from his hands? To his faithful saints he gives this blanket promise; "Ask, and ye shall receive" (D. & C. 4:7; Matt. 7:7-11); and the whole concept of effectual prayer is summarized in his counsel to the Nephites that whatsoever they asked the Father in his name, which was good and right, believing that they should receive, would be given unto them. (3 Ne. 18:20; Moro. 7:26.)

The key, then, is to have faith, to believe that the blessing sought shall be forthcoming. And as Joseph Smith expressed it, one of the things that is "necessary in order that any rational and intelligent being may exercise faith in God unto life and salvation" is: "An actual knowledge that the course of life which he is pursuing is according to his will."

Thus: "Faith is a gift of God bestowed as a reward for personal righteousness. It is always given when righteousness is present, and the greater the measure of obedience to God's laws the greater will be the endowment of faith. Hence the Prophet says that to acquire faith men must gain the actual knowledge 'that the course of life which they pursue is according to the will of God, in order that they may be enabled to exercise faith in him unto life and salvation. This knowledge supplies an important place in revealed religion; for it was by reason of it that the ancients were enabled to endure as seeing him who is invisible. An actual knowledge to any person, that the course of life which he pursues is according to the will of God, is essentially necessary to enable him to have that confidence in God without which no person can obtain eternal life. It was this that enabled the ancient saints to endure all their afflictions and persecutions, and to take joyfully the spoiling of their goods, knowing (not believing merely) that they had a more enduring substance.' (*Lectures on Faith*, p. 57; Heb. 10:34.)" (*Mormon Doctrine*, 2nd ed., pp. 262, 264.)

Accordingly, the secret of gaining answers to prayers is prior obedience to the Lord's law. "If ye will not harden your hearts," he says, but will "ask me in faith, believing that ye shall receive, with diligence in keeping my commandments," (1 Ne. 15:11), then the desired blessing shall be received.

23. Surely all the commandments are summarized in this one decree: Believe in Christ and love one another!

24. Dwelleth in him . . . abideth in us] See 1 John 4:7-21.

The Spirit which he hath given us] The Holy Ghost.

Prayers] See *Commentary I*, pp. 233-237, 763-765. 772-777.

"TRY THE SPIRITS"

I JOHN 4:1-6.

1 Beloved, believe not every spirit, but try the spirits whether they are of God: because many false prophets are gone out into the world.

2 Hereby know ye the Spirit of God: Every spirit that confesseth that Jesus Christ is come in the flesh is of God:

3 And every spirit that confesseth not that Jesus Christ is come in the flesh is not of God: and this is that *spirit* of antichrist, whereof ye have heard that it should come; and even now already is it in the world.

4 Ye are of God, little children, and have overcome them; because greater is he that is in you, than he that is in the world.

5 They are of the world: therefore speak they of the world, and the world heareth them.

6 We are of God: he that knoweth God heareth us; he that is not of God heareth not us. Hereby know we the spirit of truth, and the spirit of error.

"Two spirits are abroad in the earth— one is of God, the other of the devil. The spirit which is of God is one that leads to light, truth, freedom, progress, and every good thing; on the other hand, the spirit which is of Lucifer leads to darkness, error, bondage, retrogression, and every evil thing. One spirit is from above, the other from beneath; and that which is from beneath never allows more light or truth or freedom to exist than it can help. All religion, philosophy, education, science, governmental control — indeed, all things — are influenced and governed by one or the other (in some cases, part by one and part by the other) of these spirits. (Moro. 7.)

"It should be understood that these two influences in the world are manifest through the ministrations of actual spirit personages from the unseen world. The power and influence wielded by Satan is exercised through the host of evil spirits who do his bidding and who have power, according to the laws that exist, to impress their wills upon the minds of receptive mortals. On the other hand, much of the power and influence of Deity is exercised by and manifest through spirit beings who appear and give revelation and guidance as the Lord's purposes may require. In general, the more righteous and saintly a person is, the easier it will be for him to receive communications from heavenly sources; and the more evil and corrupt he is, the easier will it be for evil spirits to implant their nefarious schemes in his mind and heart.

"The problem that most men have is to discern the spirits, so that they may know what is of God and what is not. The gift of discernment, that is the 'discerning of spirits,' is itself one of the gifts of the Spirit which comes from God. (1 Cor. 12:10; D. & C. 46:23.) 'Believe not every spirit,' John counseled, 'but try the spirits whether they are of God: because many false prophets are gone out into the world.' (1 John 4:1.)

"How can we try the spirits? By what tests shall it be known whether they are of God or the devil? If a messenger appears from the unseen world, how shall we know whether he is a good spirit or an evil spirit? When a revelation is received is it one born of light or darkness? When trances, visions, tongues, enchantments, miracles, and related things come to view, are they from above or beneath? When a philosophy is taught, a doctrine preached, a religion proclaimed, an educational theory espoused, how shall we know whether it is true or false?

" 'We may look for angels and receive their ministrations,' the Prophet said, 'but we are to try the spirits and prove them, for it is often the case that men make a mistake in regard to these things.

God has so ordained that when he has communicated, no vision is to be taken but what you see by the seeing of the eye, or what you hear by the hearing of the ear. When you see a vision pray for the interpretation; if you get not this, shut it up; there must be certainty in this matter. An open vision will manifiest that which is more important. Lying spirits are going forth in the earth. There will be great manifestations of spirits, both false and true. . . . Not every spirit, or vision, or singing, is of God.' (*Teachings*, pp. 161-162.)

"As part of a long discussion of true and false spirits, and in explaining how they may be distinguished, the Prophet also said: 'No man can do this without the priesthood, and having a knowledge of the laws by which spirits are governed; for, as no man knows the things of God, but by the Spirit of God, so no man knows the spirit of the devil, and his power and influence, but by possessing intelligence which is more than human, and having unfolded through the medium of the priesthood the mysterious operation of his devices . . . .

" 'A man must have the discerning of spirits before he can drag into daylight this hellish influence and unfold it unto the world in all its soul-destroying, diabolical, and horrid colors; for nothing is a greater injury to the children of men than to be under the influence of a false spirit when they think they have the Spirit of God. Thousands have felt the influence of its terrible power and baneful effects. Long pilgrimages have been undertaken, penances endured, and pain, misery and ruin have followed in their train; nations have been convulsed, kingdoms overthrown, provinces laid waste, and blood, carnage and desolation are habiliments in which it has been clothed.

" 'As we have noticed before, the great difficulty lies in the ignorance of the nature of spirits, of the laws by which they are governed, and the signs by which they may be known; if it requires the Spirit of God to know the things of God; and the spirit of the devil can only be unmasked through that medium, then it follows as a natural consequence that unless some person or persons have a communication, or revelation from God, unfolding to them the operation of the spirit, they must eternally remain ignorant of these principles; for I contend that if one man cannot understand these things but by the Spirit of God, ten thousand men cannot; it is alike out of the reach of the wisdom of the learned, the tongue of the eloquent, the power of the mighty. And we shall at last have to come to this conclusion, whatever we may think of revelation, that without it we can neither know nor understand anything of God, or the devil; and however unwilling the world may be to acknowledge this principle, it is evident from the multifarious creeds and notions concerning this matter that they understand nothing of this principle, and it is equally as plain that without a divine communication they must remain in ignorance.' (*Teachings*, pp. 204-206.)

"It follows that the discerning of spirits is and can be practiced in righteousness only where the true Church and kingdom of God is found. In the final analysis, it takes apostles, prophets, priesthood, the gift of the Holy Ghost, and a knowledge of God's laws and the manner in which he operates, in order to separate the spirits into their two opposing camps. Only where these things are found can error be segregated from truth, because only there are the channels of revelation open." (*Mormon Doctrine*, 2nd ed., pp. 270-273.)

1. Believe not every spirit] 'Do not be misled by false doctrines, political theories, or philosophical concepts; believe only those true principles which are inspired of God.'

Try the spirits] 'Test every doctrine; prove every theory; examine every philosophy — using gospel standards as the measuring rod.'

False prophets] See *Commentary II*, pp. 440-441.

2-3. On the surface John seems to be saying that all Christians, because they have a belief of sorts in Christ, are thereby numbered with the Lord's people, whereas those who do not so believe (meaning non-Christians) are antichrist. In fact he is making no such assertion, and such is far from the truth. The key to an understanding of the great truth here presented is what is meant by the expression, "Jesus Christ is come in the flesh."

For instance: In all Christendom, and in all the world, who is it that believes that God the Father is a personal being in whose image man is created; that he has a body of flesh and bones as tangible as man's; that he is the literal Father of the spirits of all men, with Christ our Lord, the Almighty Jehovah, being the Firstborn among the pre-existent hosts; that in that spirit sphere our Lord became like the Father in power and intelligence; that he was the Lord Omnipotent who created all things; that he was foreordained to be the Savior and Redeemer; that he was born of Mary, in the literal sense, inheriting from her the power of mortality, which is the power to die; that he was born of God, in the literal sense, inheriting from him the power of immortality, which is the power to live; that he worked out the infinite and eternal atonement because God was his Father and Mary his mother; and that he has now ascended, in resurrected immortality, to sit down on the right hand of the Father, where he reigns with almighty power forever? Who is it that believing all this and much more that is implicit in it, thereby classifies as one who confesses with comprehension that Jesus Christ actually "is come in the flesh"? And those who disbelieve and oppose all or part of these glorious truths —are they included with the antichrists of whom John speaks?

4. The true saints have overcome the spirit of antichrist in the world because they believe and know the truth about God and Christ.

5. False prophets, false teachers, advocates of doctrines, or policies, or philosophies, or feelings, or "spirits" that are not of God — all these "are of the world," and so naturally they are accepted by worldly people.

6. To catch the full import of this inspired utterance, apply it to the Lord's people in this day: 'We Latter-day Saints are of God; we alone have the truth; we alone have the gospel; we alone can save men in the celestial kingdom. Unless men hear us and receive our message they shall be damned. What we have is true; what the world has is error; all things are judged by the gospel standard which we have.' How plainly and bluntly John and all the prophets speak as the Holy Ghost rests upon them!

"GOD IS LOVE"

I JOHN 4:7-21.

7 Beloved, let us love one another: for love is of God; and every one that loveth is born of God and knoweth God.

8 He that loveth not knoweth not God; for God is love.

9 In this was manifested the love of God toward us, because that God sent his only begotten Son into the world, that we might live through him.

10 Herein is love, not that we loved God, but that he loved us, and sent his Son *to be* the propitiation for our sins.

11 Beloved, if God so loved us, we ought also to love one another.

12 No man hath seen God at any time. If we love one another, God dwelleth in us, and his love is perfected in us.

13 Hereby know we that we dwell in him, and he in us, because he hath given us of his Spirit.

14 And we have seen and do testify that the Father sent the Son *to be* the Saviour of the world.

15 Whosoever shall confess that Jesus is the Son of God, God dwelleth in him, and he in God.

16 And we have known and believed the love that God hath to us. God is love; and he that dwelleth in love dwelleth in God, and God in him.

17 Herein is our love made perfect, that we may have boldness in the day of judgment: because as he is, so are we in this world.

18 There is no fear in love; but perfect love casteth out fear: because fear hath torment. He that feareth is not made perfect in love.

19 We love him, because he first loved us.

20 If a man say, I love God, and hateth his brother, he is a liar: for he that loveth not his brother whom he hath seen, how can he love God whom he hath not seen?

21 And this commandment have we from him, That he who loveth God love his brother also.

I.V. I JOHN 4:12.

12 No man hath seen God at any time, **except them who believe.** If we love one another, God dwelleth in us, and his love is perfected in us.

7. Love is of God] "Every good gift and every perfect gift is from above, and cometh down from the Father of lights." (Jas. 1:17.) Conversely, hate is of the devil, from whom every evil thing flows.

Every one that loveth is born of God] Gospel love consists of and is manifest through obedience to the laws and ordinances of the gospel (John 14:15; 1 John 5:3), in consequence of which, those who truly love their brethren in full measure are persons who have already been born again; and conversely, as John here states the proposition, those who love their brethren in the full gospel sense thereby show they have been born again.

Every one that loveth . . . knoweth God] As the presence of true gospel love is proof positive that the recipient has been born again, so also, on the same basis, it establishes that he knows God, whom to know is eternal life. (John 17:3.) This knowledge comes only by revelation from the Holy Ghost; and, of course, "He that loveth not knoweth not God." (Verse 8.)

8. God is love] "Our God is a consuming fire." (Heb. 12:29.) "God is light." (1 John 1:5.) Similarly, God is also faith, hope, charity, righteousness, truth, virtue, temperance, patience, humility, and so forth. That is, God is the embodiment and personification of every good grace and godly attribute — all of which dwell in his person in perfection and in fulness. See *Commentary I*, pp. 229-230, 725-727, 746-749; *Commentary II*, p. 297.

9-10. These verses are John's commentary upon Jesus' words: "For God so loved the world, that he gave his only begotten Son, that whosoever believeth in him should not perish, but have everlasting life." (John 3:16.) See *Commentary I*, pp. 143-145.

10. The propitiation for our sins] See 1 John: 1:8-10; 2:1-2.

11. God and Christ are the great Prototypes of all saved beings. They are our Patterns, our Exemplars. To be saved is to be like them. If they manifest perfect and infinite love, such is the goal toward which we must strive.

I. V. 12. No man hath seen God at any time, except them who believe] Who has, and does, and shall see God? Prophets in great number have seen the Lord of Heaven, often receiving such plain and open manifestations that it has been as though they communed with their friends. One of these was John himself who (like Joseph Smith) was able to describe the clothing he wore, the appearance of his hair, eyes, and feet, and the sound of his voice. (Rev. 2:13-15; D. & C. 110:1-3.)

Of one of the appearances of the Lord to Moses the record says: "The Lord talked with Moses . . . . And the Lord spake unto Moses face to face, as a man speaketh unto his friend." (Ex. 33:9-11.) And Abraham recorded his similar experience with the same God in these words: "I, Abraham, talked with the Lord, face to face, as one man talketh with another, . . . and his hand was stretched out." (Abra. 3:11-12.)

"I saw also the Lord sitting upon a throne, high and lifted up, and his train [his skirts] filled the temple," Isaiah said, and the Brother of Jared saw the spirit body of the Lord Jesus in such detail that it appeared even as his mortal and resurrected body would appear. (Ether 3:15-17.) But the most glorious theophany of which we have record is the vision vouchsafed to Joseph Smith when he saw "two Personages" — the Father and the Son — standing above him in glory and brightness which defied all description. (Jos. Sm. 2:16-17.) See Jas. 1:1-7.

And as with the prophets and seers of ancient and modern times, so with all the saints who will obey the same laws, all shall see the Lord, for God is no respecter of persons. "Verily, thus saith the Lord," he decrees: "It shall come to pass that every soul who forsaketh his sins and cometh unto me, and calleth on my name, and obeyeth my voice, and keepeth my commandments, shall see my face and know that I am." (D. & C. 93:1.) And again: "Sanctify yourselves that your minds become single to God, and the days will come that you shall see him; for he will unveil his face unto you, and it shall be in his own time, and in his own way, and according to his own will." (D. & C. 88:68.) See 2 Pet. 1:1-19.

K. J. 12. God dwelleth in us] 16. He that dwelleth in love dwelleth in God, and God in him] God dwells in the hearts of the righteous! Not literally, but by the power of his Spirit! What beautiful imagery this is! How well it teaches the perfect unity that should prevail among all the saints and between God and his people! "Jesus Christ is in you," Paul says of the saints. (2 Cor. 13:5.) How can this be? His answer is simple: "We have the mind of Christ." (1 Cor. 2:16.)

God dwells in the hearts of those who are as he is. "If you wish to go where God is, you must be like God, or possess the principles which God possesses," the Prophet said. (*Teachings*, p. 216.) To "possess the principles which God possesses" is to dwell in God! That is, if we possess love, charity, faith, and every godly attribute as he possesses them, then he dwells in us because we have received those attributes which come from him, and we dwell in him because we have become as he is.

Be one!] See *Commentary I*, pp. 765-767. **Unity]** See *Commentary II*, pp. 320-322.

12. If we love one another, God dwelleth in us] As only those who love their fellowmen are born again and know God (Verse 7), so also, they alone are the ones in whom God dwells. And again the governing principle is that the love involved can be developed only as a result of keeping the commandments.

13. The extent to which the saints receive the companionship and guidance of the Holy Spirit is the extent to which they dwell in God.

15. Those who have testimonies of the gospel and are in fact converted to its eternal truths are the ones in whom God dwells and who also dwell in him.

17. As he is, so are we] We become like God as we acquire the attributes he possesses.

18. Our Lord's message is one of love and joy and the hope of eternal life. Fear plays no part in it. There is no dread or disquiet in the souls of the saints; they are free from apprehension and anxiety with reference to the course of events in this world and their eternal destiny in the world to come. To them their Lord's voice is: "Fear not, little children, for you are mine, and I have overcome the world, and you are of them that my Father hath given me; And none of them that my Father hath given me shall be lost." (D. & C. 50:41-42.)

20-21. How well do we love our fellowmen? Such is the true test and measure of our love of Him who said: "Inasmuch as ye have done it unto one of the least of these my brethren, ye have done it unto me." (Matt. 25:40.)

WHO IS BORN OF GOD?

I JOHN 5:1-5.

1 Whosoever believeth that Jesus is the Christ is born of God: and every one that loveth him that begat loveth him also that is begotten of him.

2 By this we know that we love the children of God, when we love God, and keep his commandments.

3 For this is the love of God, that we keep his commandments: and his commandments are not grievous.

4 For whatsoever is born of God overcometh the world: and this is the victory that overcometh the world, *even* our faith.

5 Who is he that overcometh the world, but he that believeth that Jesus is the Son of God?

1. Whosoever believeth that Jesus is the Christ is born of God] Execpt in miraculous and unusual circumstances, as with Alma (Mosiah 27), spiritual rebirth is a process. It does not occur instantaneously. It comes to pass by degrees. Repentant persons become alive to one spiritual reality after another, until they are wholly alive in Christ and are qualified to dwell in his presence forever. Similarly, conversion is a process and sanctification is a process. They increase in the hearts of the obedient in process of time as they more fully keep the commandments and seek the Lord.

Spiritual rebirth begins and ends with belief in Christ. When repentant souls turn to Christ and seek a new life with him, the processes of rebirth commence. When their belief in the Lord increases until they are able to do the works that he does, "and greater works than these" (John 14:12), their rebirth is perfect, and they are prepared for salvation with him.

Every one that loveth him that begat loveth him also that is begotten of him] Every one that loveth Christ — who begets us spiritually and whose children we become when we are born again — loveth his brethren also, for his brethren have been adopted into the same family with him and have a special, spiritual kinship with him.

Born again] See *Commentary I*, pp. 140-142.

2. The supreme manifestation of our love for our fellowmen is for us to keep the commandments of God, for in so doing we do those things which further the salvation of all our Father's children.

3a. By definition our love of God consists in and is manifest by full obedience to the laws and ordinances of the gospel. "If ye love me, keep my commandments." (John 14:15.)

His commandments are not grievous] Is it easy or hard to keep the commandments? For instance: To believe and repent? To be baptized? To forsake the world? To be morally clean? The answer depends upon us. Tea, coffee, tobacco, and liquor offer no temptation whatever to those who have bridled their passions in these fields. The issue is not the act of sin as such, but the feelings and desires which are uppermost in the heart of the one who is wrestling with whatever appetite of the flesh is involved.

4. How can members of the Church tell if they have been born again? Yes, they have been born of water in the sense of being baptized; yes, they have received the laying on of hands for the gift of the Holy Ghost, meaning they have gained the right to the constant companionship of this member of the Godhead based on their faithfulness. But have the conversion processes actually operated in their lives? Have they become new creatures of the Holy Ghost? Are they truly alive to the things of righteousness and dead to carnal things? Addressing himself to his "brethren of the church," to those who had been baptized and who were on the path leading to eternal life, Alma asked: "Have ye spiritually been born of God? Have ye received his image in your countenances? Have ye experienced this mighty change in your hearts?" Then he proceeds to ask a long list of questions which enable church members to determine whether and to what extent they have overcome the world, which is the exact extent to which they have in fact been born again. (Alma 5:14-30.)

5. Overcometh the world] See Rev. 2:1-7.

WATER, BLOOD, AND SPIRIT TESTIFY OF CHRIST

I JOHN 5:6-9.

6 This is he that came by water and blood, *even* Jesus Christ; not by water only, but by water and blood. And it is the Spirit that beareth witness, because the Spirit is truth.

7 For there are three that bear record in heaven, the Father, the Word, and the Holy Ghost: and these three are one.

8 And there are three that bear witness in earth, the spirit, and the water, and the blood: and these three agree in one.

9 If we receive the witness of men, the witness of God is greater: for this is the witness of God which he hath testified of his Son.

In the midst of a long discussion about being born again, John here names the three elements which are present in both the mortal and spiritual births. This same doctrine, with all the marvelous symbolism that attends it, was revealed by the Lord to Adam in these words: "Inasmuch as ye were born into the world by water, and blood, and the spirit, which I have made, and so become of dust a living soul, even so ye must be born again into the kingdom of heaven, of water, and of the Spirit, and be cleansed by blood, even the blood of mine Only Begotten; that ye might be sanctified from all sin, and enjoy the words of eternal life in this world, and eternal life in the world to come, even immortal glory; For by the water ye keep the commandment; by the Spirit ye are justified, and by the blood ye are sanctified." (Moses 6:59-60.)

That is, just as there can be no mortal birth without:

Water (the viable fetus being immersed in such in its mother's womb); and

Blood (the life of the mortal body is in the blood, without which there is immediate death; and there can be no mortal birth as such without the loss of blood by the mother); and

Spirit (the offspring of God which comes from pre-existence to dwell in the tabernacle of clay formed from the dust of the earth in the womb of the mother);

So there can be no spiritual birth into the kingdom of heaven without:

Water (baptism by immersion under the hands of a legal administrator); and

Spirit (the cleansing power of the Holy Spirit which burns sin and iniquity out of the human soul as though by fire, thus making the soul fit to dwell with holy and pure beings in God's kingdom); and

Blood (the shed blood of Him who poured out his soul unto death so that all of the terms and conditions of the plan of salvation would have force and validity, and so that mortal man might be ransomed from the temporal and spiritual death brought into the world by the fall of Adam).

Thus every birth into this world becomes a visible reminder that the living soul, newly departed from the Celestial Presence and now resident on planet earth, can return to the Eternal Presence only on condition of undergoing a rebirth, a spiritual birth, a birth involving the same elements present in the miraculous advent into mortality.

6. As with all men, Christ himself was born into mortality of water, blood, and spirit; and as with all who are saved, he gained an inheritance in the celestial kingdom through baptism of water and the Spirit and the cleansing power of his own blood (2 Ne. 31) — to all of which the Spirit beareth witness.

Also: The symbolism here used helps center our attention in the atoning sacrifice of the Son. The same elements were there present:

Spirit (in that our Lord voluntarily gave up the Ghost, permitting his spirit to leave the body);

Blood (in that he there completed the act, commenced in Gethsemane, of shedding his own blood for the sins of men); and

Water (in that when "one of the soldiers with a spear pierced his side, . . . forthwith came there out blood and water. And he that saw it [John himself] bare record, and his record is true: and he knoweth that he saith true, that ye might believe.") (John 19:34-35.)

7. These three are one] Jesus said: "The Father, and I, and the Holy Ghost are one." (3 Ne. 11:36.)

9. God himself, in the very nature of that birth into mortality which he has provided for his spirit children, bears witness both of the atonement of his Son and of the essential elements in the plan of salvation itself.

BELIEVE IN CHRIST AND GAIN ETERNAL LIFE

I JOHN 5:10-21.

10 He that believeth on the Son of God hath the witness in himself: he that believeth not God hath made him a liar; because he believeth not the record that God gave of his Son.

11 And this is the record, that God hath given to us eternal life, and this life is in his Son.

12 He that hath the Son hath life; *and* he that hath not the Son of God hath not life.

13 These things have I written unto you that believe on the name of the Son of God; that ye may know that ye have eternal life, and that ye may believe on the name of the Son of God.

14 And this is the confidence that we have in him, that, if we ask any thing according to his will, he heareth us:

15 And if we know that he hear us, whatsoever we ask, we know that we have the petitions that we desired of him.

16 If any man see his brother sin a sin *which is* not unto death, he shall ask, and he shall give him life for them that sin not unto death. There is a sin unto death: I do not say that he shall pray for it.

17 All unrighteousness is sin: and there is a sin not unto death.

18 We know that whosoever is born of God sinneth not; but he that is begotten of God keepeth himself, and that wicked one toucheth him not.

19 *And* we know that we are of God, and the whole world lieth in wickedness.

20 And we know that the Son of God is come, and hath given us an understanding, that we may

know him that is true, and we are in him that is true, *even* in his Son Jesus Christ. This is the true God, and eternal life.

21 Little children, keep yourselves from idols. Amen.

I.V. I JOHN 5:13, 18.

13 These things have I written unto you that believe on the name of the Son of God; that ye may know that ye have eternal life, and that ye may **continue to** believe on the name of the Son of God.

18 We know that whosoever is born of God **continueth not in sin;** but he that is begotten of God **and** keepeth himself, that wicked one **overcometh** him not.

10. 'God testifies by the power of the Holy Ghost that Jesus Christ is his Son. If we reject this witness we call God a liar. But we believe in Christ and know by revelation that he is the Son of God.'

11. God hath given to us eternal life] He hath made eternal life available to us on conditions of obedience to the laws and ordinances of the gospel.

This life is in his Son] Salvation is in Christ. He it is who "hath abolished death, and hath brought life and immortality to light through the gospel." (2 Tim. 1:10.)

12. "He that believeth on the Son hath everlasting life: and he that believeth not the Son shall not see life; but the wrath of God abideth on him." (John 3:36.)

13. Ye have eternal life] "If ye shall press forward, feasting upon the word of Christ, and endure to the end, behold, thus saith the Father: Ye shall have eternal life." (2 Ne. 31:20.)

14-15. This is the absolute ultimate in faith — to know our petitions will be granted because they accord with the mind and will of the Lord.

16. A sin unto death] "Those who turn from the light and truth of the gospel; who give themselves up to Satan; who enlist in his cause, supporting and sustaining it; and who thereby become his children — by such a course sin unto death. For them there is neither repentance, forgiveness, nor any hope whatever of salvation of any kind. As children of Satan, they are sons of perdition. 'Whosoever bringeth forth evil works, the same becometh a child of the devil, for he hearkeneth unto his voice, and doth follow him. And whosoever doeth this must receive his wages of him; therefore, for his wages he receiveth death, as to things pertaining unto righteousness being dead unto all good works.' Alma 5:41-42.) . . .

"In the sense that 'no murderer hath eternal life abiding in him' (1 John 3:15), that is, that none guilty of pre-meditated murder can ever gain the celestial kingdom, murder also is a sin unto death. Such persons can never again enjoy spiritual life. It appears that there are some special circumstances under which adultery, in this sense, is also a sin unto death, as witness the Prophet's declaration: 'If a man commit adultery, he cannot receive the celestial kingdom of God. Even if he is saved in any kingdom, it cannot be the celestial kingdom.' (*History of the Church*, vol. 6, p. 81; *Doctrines of Salvation*, vol. 2, pp. 92-94.) It may be that there are other abominable things which men in certain circumstances, can do which will bar them eternally from the receipt of spiritual life." (*Mormon Doctrine*, 2nd ed., pp. 737-738.)

19. "And the whole world lieth in sin, and groaneth under darkness and under the bondage of sin. And by this you may know they are under the bondage of sin, because they come not unto me. For whoso cometh not unto me is under the bondage of sin. And whoso receiveth not my voice is not acquainted with my voice, and is not of me. And by this you may know the righteous from the wicked, and that the whole world groaneth under sin and darkness even now." (D. & C. 84:49-53.)

The Second Epistle of John and The Third Epistle of John

Why these two brief, personal epistles?

Their doctrinal content and historical recitations are, of course, minimal. But they do add a unique contribution to the revealed word which well pays for their preservation. Their purpose seems to be to give us a glimpse of the private life and problems of the Disciple whom Jesus loved.

We see in them his love for his family, and observe how their acceptance of and conformity to the law of his Lord is his chief concern. We see his intense interest in the spread of gospel truth, his support of those who bring it to pass, and his refusal to fellowship those who oppose the rolling forth of the Cause of Righteousness. And, sadly, we see the vigor of the opposition found in some quarters in the Church itself toward the apostolic witnesses who walked with Christ and were the living oracles for their day and dispensation.

Brief, less significant than some portions of Holy Writ, these two lesser epistles of the Beloved John are yet of eternal worth, and the saints rejoice in the added perspective they give to the Bible as a whole.

"BRING UP YOUR CHILDREN IN LIGHT AND TRUTH"

II JOHN 1:1-6.

1 The elder unto the elect lady and her children, whom I love in the truth; and not I only, but also all they that have known the truth;

2 For the truth's sake, which dwelleth in us, and shall be with us forever.

3 Grace be with you, mercy, *and* peace, from God the Father, and from the Lord Jesus Christ,

the Son of the Father, in truth and love.

4 I rejoiced greatly that I found of thy children walking in truth, as we have received a commandment from the Father.

5 And now I beseech thee, lady, not as though I wrote a new commandment unto thee, but that which we had from the beginning, that we love one another.

6 And this is love, that we walk after his commandments. This is the commandment, That, as ye have heard from the beginning, ye should walk in it.

1. The elder] John, the apostle. "An apostle is an elder." (D. & C. 20:38.) See 1 Pet. 5:1-4.

The elect lady] "An elect lady is a female member of the Church who has already received, or who through obedience is qualified to receive, the fulness of gospel blessings. This includes temple endowments, celestial marriage, and the fulness of the sealing power. She is one who has been elected or chosen by faithfulness as a daughter of God in this life, an heir of God, a member of his household. Her position is comparable to that of the elders who magnify their callings in the priesthood and thereby receive all that the Father hath. (D. & C. 84:38.)

"In the early days of this dispensation Emma Smith, the Prophet's wife, was in such complete harmony with the Lord's program that he forgave her of her sins and addressed her as an elect lady. (D. & C. 25:1-3; *History of the Church*, vol. 4, p. 552.) John the Beloved used a similar salutation to certain chosen women in his day. (2 John 1, 13.) Just as it is possible for the very elect to be deceived, and to fall from grace through disobedience, so an elect lady, by failing to endure to the end, can lose her chosen status." (*Mormon Doctrine*, 2nd ed., p. 217.)

Her children, whom I love in truth] Is John writing a personal letter to a wife and expressing appreciation for their children? It is an acceptable thing for righteous parents to rejoice in the faith and devotion of their children, and to take pleasure in the fact that other members of the Church view the conduct of those same children with approbation.

2. For the truth's sake] Every act of a true saint is performed for the truth's sake; that is, a faithful person chooses to do only those things which guide him to salvation and which further the Lord's work and purposes on earth.

4. Thy children walking in truth] See *Commentary II*, pp. 520-522.

5-6. See 1 John 4:7-21; 5:1-5.

DO NOT AID AND ASSIST FALSE TEACHERS

II JOHN 1:7-13.

7 For many deceivers are entered into the world, who confess not that Jesus Christ is come in the flesh. This is a deceiver and an antichrist.

8 Look to yourselves, that we lose not those things which we have wrought, but that we receive a full reward.

9 Whosoever transgresseth, and abideth not in the doctrine of Christ, hath not God. He that abideth in the doctrine of Christ, he hath both the Father and the Son.

10 If there come any unto you, and bring not this doctrine, receive him not into *your* house, neither bid him God speed:

11 For he that biddeth him God speed is partaker of his evil deeds.

12 Having many things to write unto you, I would not *write* with paper and ink: but I trust to come unto you, and speak face to face, that our joy may be full.

13 The children of thy elect sister greet thee. Amen.

7. The promised day of darkness was already descending upon mankind; the great apostasy had its beginning even in that day when the original apostles walked among men. Is it any wonder that the destined darkness would cover the earth after those living lights ceased to minister among men?

8. 'Keep the faith and endure to the end, lest we lose the hope of salvation.'

9. 'Those who do not live the gospel lose the promised blessings, while those who are faithful have fellowship with the Father and the Son and shall be saved.'

10-11. It is a sin to assist and uphold those who preach false doctrine and who run counter to the divine will; by so doing the saints become partakers of their evil deeds and shall be condemned accordingly. See *Commentary II*, pp. 456-460.

12-13. Is John writing to his family — giving them love, blessings, and counsel — while he is dwelling somewhere else with another family, perhaps that of Gaius, to whom his Third Epistle is addressed?

AID AND HELP THOSE WHO LOVE THE TRUTH

III JOHN 1:1-14.

1 The elder unto the wellbeloved Gaius, whom I love in the truth.

2 Beloved, I wish above all things that thou mayest prosper and be in health, even as thy soul prospereth.

3 For I rejoiced greatly, when the brethren came and testified of the truth that is in thee, even as thou walkest in the truth.

4 I have no greater joy than to hear that my children walk in truth.

5 Beloved, thou doest faithfully whatsoever thou doest to the brethren, and to strangers;

6 Which have borne witness of thy charity before the church: whom if thou bring forward on their journey after a godly sort, thou shalt do well:

7 Because that for his name's sake they went forth, taking nothing of the Gentiles.

8 We therefore ought to receive such, that we might be fellowhelpers to the truth.

9 I wrote unto the church: but Diotrephes, who loveth to have the preeminence among them, receiveth us not.

10 Wherefore, if I come, I will remember his deeds which he doeth, prating against us with malicious words: and not content therewith, neither doth he himself receive the brethren, and forbiddeth them that would, and casteth *them* out of the church.

11 Beloved, follow not that which is evil, but that which is good. He that doeth good is of God: but he that doeth evil hath not seen God.

12 Demetrius hath good report of all *men*, and of the truth itself:

yea, and we *also* bear record; and ye know that our record is true.

13 I had many things to write, but I will not with ink and pen write unto thee:

14 But I trust I shall shortly see thee, and we shall speak face to face. Peace *be* to thee. *Our* friends salute thee. Greet the friends by name.

1-4. Is John writing to his wife and family, expressing love and appreciation to them for walking in the light and keeping the commandments?

1. The elder] John, the apostle. "An apostle is an elder." (D. & C. 20:38.) See 1 Pet. 5:1-4.

Gaius, whom I love] Apparently a wife of John, who with her children is hewing a steadfast course in the Cause of Righteousness.

2-3. Apparently Gaius has been in ill health physically, though it is evident from her conduct that she is a spiritual giant.

4. See 2 John 1:1-6.

5-8. How commendable and weighted with blessings is the help and hospitality rendered by the saints to others of their number who are serving on the Lord's errand. (Matt. 10:40-42.)

7. Taking nothing of the Gentiles] For some unspecified reason, the Lord's servants here involved had declined help from the Gentiles to whom they had been sent. Perhaps it was to avoid the slightest intimation that they were selling the gospel. In any event the normal practice is that the laborer is worthy of his hire, and those to whom missionaries are sent are expected to feed, clothe, and otherwise aid them in their ministry. (D. & C. 84:89-90).

9-10. Truly, "it must needs be, that there is an opposition in all things!" (2 Ne. 2:11.) Here is Diotrephes, a local church officer of prominence and influence: (1) Who refuses to permit the doctrine and instructions of a member of the First Presidency of the Church to be read in his congregation; (2) Who preaches against the apostolic heads of the Church; (3) Who refuses to receive the church representatives sent to him; (4) Who refuses to let others in the congregation care for or give heed to the church authorities; and (5) Who casts out (apparently excommunicates) worthy members of the Church. And except for the recording of his name here on the roll of the infamous, who has ever since heard of him or his cause? So be it eventually with all who oppose and fight the truth!

11. "All things which are good cometh of God; and that which is evil cometh of the devil." (Moro. 7:12.)

13-14. Clearly John is writing to a close and intimate loved one, some person within the circle of his special associates and confidants and for whom he has great respect.

The General Epistle of Jude

Second Peter and Jude are companion epistles; they struggle with the same problem and come forth with the same answer.

Aware of the spirit of apostasy and rebellion within the Church, Peter and then Jude set out to testify that the saints still had the truth; to plead with them to stand true and faithful to their covenants; and to condemn, in severe and curt language, the false teachers within the fold.

Jude, a son of Joseph and Mary and therefore one of the Lord's brothers, may well have had Peter's pointed pronouncements before him as he wrote. In any event, in the process of bearing the same witness and giving the same counsel as did the Chief Apostle, Jude came forth with some illustrations and doctrinal concepts that are uniquely his own.

In the whole Bible, it is Jude only who preserves for us the concept that pre-existence was our first estate and that certain angels failed to pass its tests.

It is to him that we turn for our meager knowledge of the disputation between Michael and Lucifer about the body of Moses.

He alone records Enoch's glorious prophecy about the Second Coming of the Son of Man.

And he is the only inspired writer to express the counsel that the saints should hate even the garments spotted with the flesh.

Jude was a theologian indeed to whom the saints of succeeding days are most deeply indebted!

"CONTEND FOR THE FAITH"

JUDE 1:1-5.

1 Jude, the servant of Jesus
Christ, and brother of James, to
them that are sanctified by God
the Father, and preserved in Jesus
Christ, *and* called:

2 Mercy unto you, and peace, and love, be multiplied.

3 Beloved, when I gave all diligence to write unto you of the common salvation, it was needful for me to write unto you, and exhort *you* that ye should earnestly contend for the faith which was once delivered unto the saints.

4 For there are certain men crept in unawares, who were before of old ordained to this condemnation, ungodly men, turning the grace of our God into lasciviousness, and denying the only Lord God, and our Lord Jesus Christ.

5 I will therefore put you in remembrance, though ye once knew this, how that the Lord, having saved the people out of the land of Egypt, afterward destroyed them that believed not.

I.V. JUDE 1:1.

1 Jude, the servant of **God, called of** Jesus Christ, and brother of James; to them **who** are sanctified **of** the Father; and preserved in Jesus Christ;

1. Jude, the . . . brother of James] Jude (called Judas by Matthew and Juda by Mark) and James were sons of Joseph and Mary and therefore brothers — strictly speaking, half brothers — of the Lord Jesus. (Matt. 13:55-56; Mark 6:3.) With an appropriate sense of reverential awe, neither claimed in their epistles to be brothers of the Lord. After our Lord's resurrection James became one of the Council of the Twelve and attained some prominence in the Church. See *Commentary II*, pp. 134-145. Quite naturally Jude here identifies himself with his better known brother.

To them that are sanctified] Jude is writing to members of the Church, to the saints of God who have been born of water and of the Spirit, who have been cleansed from their sins, who have been "sanctified by the reception of the Holy Ghost." (3 Ne. 27:20.) And only those in whose lives the sanctifying power of the Holy Spirit is found can comprehend in full the meaning and import of his message.

3. The common salvation] Salvation is available to all men, not just a select few. Eternal life is not reserved for apostles and prophets, for the saints in Enoch's day, or for the martyrs of the Christian Dispensation. "All mankind may be saved, by obedience to the laws and ordinances of the Gospel." (Third Article of Faith.)

God is no respecter of persons; "he inviteth them all to come unto him and partake of his goodness; and he denieth none that come unto him, black and white, bond and free, male and female; and he remembereth the heathen; and all are alike unto God, both Jew and Gentile." (2 Ne. 26:33.) The eternal call of the Eternal God is: "Ho, every one that thirsteth, come ye to the waters, and he that hath no money; come ye, buy, and eat; yea, come, buy wine and milk without money and without price" (Isa. 55:1), for "salvation is free!" (2 Ne. 2:4.)

Contend for the faith which was once delivered unto the saints] It is ever thus; Lucifer always has his ministers on earth; wherever the truth is found, there is opposition; in and out of the Church, ungodly men always arise to fight the pure and perfect religion which alone bringeth salvation.

Cain and his descendants rebelled against Adam. Hosts of people opposed Enoch and his teachings. Only Noah's immediate family accepted his testimony. The father of Abraham lived and revelled in idolatry. Even the Son of God himself was rejected, mocked, scourged, and crucified by his own. Is it any wonder that inspired writers and preachers must everlastingly plead with the saints to be true to their covenants and uphold the eternal truths which alone qualify men for salvation with those of ancient times who believed and obeyed the same laws?

Is it any wonder that the Lord's instruction to his ministers is: "Contend thou, therefore, morning by morning; and day after day let thy warning voice go forth; and when the night cometh let not the inhabitants of the earth slumber, because of thy speech." (D. & C. 112:5.)

4. False teachers, in and out of the Church, who assume the prerogative of leading the children of men astray do so because of personal sin; because they have lascivious desires; because "their deeds are evil" (D. & C. 29:45); because they are "corrupt" in spite of their professions of religion. (Jos. Smith 2:19.) Those who keep the commandments and enjoy the companionship of the Holy Spirit do not oppose the truth.

5. Even though the Lord saved Israel from Egyptian bondage he later destroyed many of them because of their unbelief. So it is with members of the Church; even though they escape the world when they come into the Lord's earthly kingdom, many shall be lost because of subsequent unbelief and rebellion.

CERTAIN ANGELS KEPT NOT THEIR FIRST ESTATE

JUDE 1:6.

6 And the angels which kept not their first estate, but left their own habitation, he hath reserved in everlasting chains under darkness unto the judgment of the great day.

Jude's argument here is: Why should the wicked and ungodly think they shall escape damnation when God even cast one-third of the hosts of heaven out for their rebellion? See 2 Pet. 2:1-9.

Implicit in his usage of this illustration is the fact that his readers (members of the Church who had already received the truth!) knew about pre-existence, the war in heaven, and the probationary nature of this mortal estate.

The angels which kept not their first estate] See Rev. 12:1-17.

First estate] "Both Abraham and Jude speak of pre-existence as our first estate, that is, it was the first time we lived as conscious identities. The spirits who were faithful in that first estate earned the right to be born into this world and get mortal bodies, bodies which would become the eternal habitation of the spirit after the resurrection. (Abra. 3:22-28.) But the rebellious pre-existent spirits, 'the angels which kept not their first estate' (Jude 6), have been denied bodies and the probationary experiences of this second estate of mortality." (*Mormon Doctrine*, 2nd ed., p. 282.)

Of our first estate and the eternal plan of salvation there formulated, Joseph Smith says: "At the first organization in heaven we were all present, and saw the Savior chosen and appointed and the plan of salvation made, and we sanctioned it. We came to this earth that we might have a body and present it pure before God in the celestial kingdom. The great principle of happiness consists in having a body. The devil has no body, and herein is his punishment." (*Teachings of the Prophet Joseph Smith*, p. 181.) Also: "They who have tabernacles, have power over those who have not." (*Teachings*, p. 190.) And also: "The spirits in the eternal world are like the spirits in this world. When those have come into this world and received tabernacles, then died and again have risen and received glorified bodies, they will have an ascendency over the spirits who have received no bodies, or kept not their first estate, like the devil. The punishment of the devil was that he should not have a habitation like men." (*Teachings*, pp. 305-306.)

In everlasting chains] Lucifer and one-third of the hosts of heaven are damned forever. For them there is no progression, no advancement, no light — only darkness to all eternity. Of them and of the sons of perdition who shall be added to their number, the Lord says: "I will say unto them — Depart from me, ye cursed, into everlasting fire, prepared for the devil and his angels. And now, behold, I say unto you, never at any time have I declared from mine own mouth that they should return, for where I am they cannot come, for they have no power." (D. & C. 29:28-29.)

Pre-existence] See Heb. 12:9-10.

MICHAEL DISPUTED ABOUT BODY OF MOSES

JUDE 1:7-13.

7 Even as Sodom and Gomorrha, and the cities about them in like manner, giving themselves over to fornication, and going after strange flesh, are set forth for an example, suffering the vengeance of eternal fire.

8 Likewise also these *filthy* dreamers defile the flesh, despise dominion, and speak evil of dignities.

9 Yet Michael the archangel, when contending with the devil he disputed about the body of Moses, durst not bring against him a railing accusation, but said, The Lord rebuke thee.

10 But these speak evil of those things which they know not: but what they know naturally, as brute beasts, in those things they corrupt themselves.

11 Woe unto them! for they

have gone in the way of Cain, and ran greedily after the error of Balaam for reward, and perished in the gainsaying of Core.

12 These are spots in your feasts of charity, when they feast with you, feeding themselves without fear: clouds *they are* without water, carried about of winds; trees whose fruit withereth, without fruit, twice dead, plucked up by the roots;

13 Raging waves of the sea, foaming out their own shame; wandering stars, to whom is reserved the blackness of darkness for ever.

I.V. JUDE 1:11.

11 Woe unto them! for they have gone in the way of Cain, and ran greedily after the error of Balaam for reward, and **shall perish** in the gainsaying of Core.

What is mighty Michael doing disputing with the devil over the body of Moses? Why does the foremost (under Christ) of all the sons of God contend about the passing of a prophet from this scene of action? That he did so, Jude tells us — parenthetically, almost casually — in the course of a severe and near merciless castigation of false teachers in the Church.

If the adulterers and sexual perverts of Sodom and Gomorrah suffer the vengeance of eternal fire, Jude says, why should these filthy dreamers who defile the truth think to escape? In their ignorance, as brute beasts, they corrupt the course of nature. They are condemned with Cain who slew Abel (Gen. 4:1-15), with Balaam who divined for hire (Num. 22, 23 and 24), and with Korah and his band who were slain for their rebellion against Moses and Aaron. (Num. 16.) And yet with it all, no railing accusations are intended, for even the archangel left condemnation to the Lord, as witness the affair about the body of Israel's lawgiver.

What then was this dispute between Michael and Satan all about? As it happens, this is our only scriptural allusion to it, although it seems perfectly clear that Jude had before him some other scriptures bearing on the point. Its use as an illustration here is manifestly intended to clarify rather than confuse the doctrine being taught, and the facts relative thereto must have been known to and understood by the saints of that day.

Commentators assume, and it surely must have been so, that Jude had before him and was quoting from a then current apocryphal book, "The Assumption of Moses," which has been preserved to us in fragmentary form only. This non-canonical work presents the doctrine that Moses was translated and taken up into heaven without tasting death. It appears to deal "with certain revelations made by Moses," and "with his disappearance in a cloud, so that his death was hid from human sight . . . Michael was commissioned to bury Moses. Satan opposed the burial on the ground (a) that he was the lord of matter and that accordingly the body should be rightfully handed over to him; (b) that Moses was a murderer, having slain the Egyptian. Michael having rebutted Satan's accusations proceeded to charge Satan with having instigated the serpent to tempt Eve. Finally, all opposition having been overcome, the assumption took place in the presence of Joshua and Caleb." Another "Hebrew Apocalypse tells of Moses' transformation into the form of a fiery angel and his ascent through the seven heavens." And yet another deals "with the temporary translation of Moses before his death into heaven . . . When translated into heaven the heavenly Jerusalem and the Temple were revealed to him, and he was told these would descend to earth after God had gathered Israel a second time from the ends of the earth." Included in these same works are a number of statements not found in the Bible but known by revelation through Joseph Smith to be true, as the fact of a pre-existence for all men and that "Moses was prepared from the foundation of the world to be the mediator of God's covenant with his people," and that "during his life Moses was Israel's intercessor with God." (R. H. Charles, *The Apocrypha and Pseudepigrapha of the Old Testament,* vol. 2, pp. 407-413.)

That Moses was in fact translated is confirmed by President Joseph Fielding Smith. After quoting, from the Prophet Joseph Smith, these words: "The Savior, Moses, and Elias [Elijah, in other words] gave the keys to Peter, James, and John, on the Mount when they were transfigured before him," President Smith says: "From that we understand why Elijah and Moses were preserved from death: because they had a mission to perform, and it had to be performed before the crucifixion of the Son of God, and it could not be done in the spirit. They had to have tangible bodies. Christ is the firstfruits of the resurrection; therefore if any former prophets had a work to perform preparatory to the mission of the Son of God, or to the dispensation of the meridian of times, it was essential that they be preserved to fulfill that mission in the flesh. For that reason Moses disappeared from among the people and was taken up into the mountain, and the people thought he was buried by the Lord. The Lord preserved him, so that he could come at the proper time and restore his keys, on the heads of Peter, James, and John, who stood at the head of the dispensation of the meridian of time. He reserved Elijah from death that he might also come and bestow his keys upon the heads of Peter, James, and John and prepare them for their ministry.

"But, one says, the Lord could have waited until after his resurrection, and then they could have done it. It is quite evident, due to the fact that it did so occur, that it had to be done before; and there was a reason. There may have been other reasons, but that is one reason why Moses and Elijah did not suffer death in the flesh, like other men do." (Joseph Fielding Smith, *Doctrines of Salvation*, vol. 2, pp. 110-111.)

"Moses, Elijah, and Alma the younger, were translated. The Old Testament account that Moses died and was buried by the hand of the Lord in an unknown grave is an error. (Deut. 34:5-7.) It is true that he may have been 'buried by the hand of the Lord,' if that expression is a figure of speech which means that he was translated. But the Book of Mormon account, in recording that Alma 'was taken up by the Spirit,' says, 'the scriptures saith the Lord took Moses unto himself; and we suppose that he has also received Alma in the spirit, unto himself.' (Alma 45:18-19.) It should be remembered that the Nephites had the Brass Plates, and that they were the 'scriptures' which gave the account of Moses being taken by way of translation. As to Elijah, the account of his being taken in 'a chariot of fire . . . by a whirlwind into heaven,' is majestically set out in the Old Testament. (2 Kings 2.)" (*Mormon Doctrine*, 2nd ed., p. 805.)

It appears, then, that Satan — ever anxious to thwart the purposes of God — "disputed about the body of Moses," meaning that he sought the mortal death of Israel's lawgiver so that he would not have a tangible body in which to come — along with Elijah, who also was taken up without tasting death — to confer the keys of the priesthood upon Peter, James, and John.

Translated beings] See Heb. 11:5-6.

9. **Michael the archangel]** "Our great prince, Michael, known in mortality as Adam, stands next to Christ in the eternal plan of salvation and progression. In pre-existence Michael was the most intelligent, powerful, and mighty spirit son of God, who was destined to come to this earth, excepting only the Firstborn, under whose direction and pursuant to whose counsel he worked. 'He is the father of the human family, and presides over the spirits of all men.' (*Teachings*, p. 157.) The name Michael apparently, and with propriety, means one 'who is like God.'

"In the creation of the earth, Michael played a part second only to that of Christ. When Lucifer rebelled and there was war in heaven, it was Michael who led the hosts of the faithful in casting Satan out. (Rev. 12:7-9.) When the time came to people the earth, the spirit Michael came and inhabited the body formed from the dust of the earth, the living soul thus created being known as Adam. As the first man he filled his foreordained destiny of standing as the presiding high priest (under Christ) over all the earth. It is through him that Christ is revealed, that all revelation comes, that the Lord's affairs on earth are directed during the pre-millennial era. (*Teachings*, pp. 157-159, 167-169.) He holds the keys of salvation for all men of all ages. (D. & C. 78:16.)

"Three years previous to Adam's mortal death he met in the Valley of Adam-ondi-Ahman with his righteous descendants. 'And the Lord appeared unto them, and they rose up and blessed Adam, and called him Michael, the prince, the archangel.' (D. & C. 107:54.) He will sit in council at this same place just prior to the great and dreadful day of the Lord; those of all ages who have served under his direction in the ministry will give an accounting of their stewardships; and the Son of Man will come and receive from Adam and all others a final accounting. (D. & C. 116; Dan. 7:9-14, 21-22, 26-27.)

"Michael contended with the devil over the body of Moses (Jude 9); ministered comfort to the Prophet Daniel (Dan. 10:13, 21); appeared to Joseph Smith to detect 'the devil when he appeared as an angel of light,' and to confer keys and authorities (D. & C. 128:20-21); and will hereafter partake of the sacrament with Christ and other righteous persons on earth. (D. & C. 17:11.)

"We know also that he was with Christ in his resurrection (D. & C. 133:54-55); that 'at the time of the end' he shall fight the battles of the saints (Dan. 11:40; 12:1); that all the dead shall come forth from their graves at the sound of his trump (D. & C. 29:26); that he will lead the armies of heaven against the hosts of hell in the final great battle when Lucifer is cast out eternally (D. & C. 88:110-116); and that he does all things 'under the counsel and direction of the Holy One, who is without beginning of days or end of life.' (D. & C. 78:16.)" (*Mormon Doctrine*, 2nd ed., pp. 491-492.)

12. Spots in your feasts of charity] Hidden rocks, found at sacred spiritual feasts, seeking to shipwreck the saints.

Clouds . . . without water] "Wells without water" (2 Pet. 2:17); ministers without a message.

Twice dead] Once they were the withered and fruitless trees of winter, who came alive with the baptism of Spring; now they were dead again because of apostasy, and hence are destined to be plucked up by the roots and to die permanently.

13. Wandering stars] Comets which show forth a flash of prominence for a moment, but soon burn out and travel off into eternal darkness.

ENOCH PROPHESIETH OF SECOND COMING

JUDE 1:14-16.

14 And Enoch also, the seventh from Adam, prophesied of these, saying, Behold, the Lord cometh with ten thousands of his saints,

15 To execute judgment upon all, and to convince all that are

ungodly among them of all their ungodly deeds which they have ungodly committed, and of all their hard *speeches* which ungodly sinners have spoken against him.

16 These are murmurers, complainers, walking after their own lusts; and their mouth speaketh great swelling *words*, having men's persons in admiration because of advantage.

Few of our Father's children have been greater than Enoch, of whose ministry the King James Version of the Old Testament simply says: "And Enoch walked with God: and he was not; for God took him." (Gen. 5:24.) From the accounts in the 6th and 7th chapters of Moses we learn his life was one of miracles, preaching, visions, and revelations, perhaps without parallel in all history. He and his whole city were translated and taken up into heaven, from whence they shall return when the earth is cleansed and becomes again a fit abode for Him who dwelt personally with his saints in Enoch's ancient Zion. From revelations given to Joseph Smith we know that the Book of Enoch will come forth in due course (D. & C. 107:53-57), and that Enoch personally ministered to Jude and quoted the statement recorded in this epistle. (*Teachings*, p. 170.)

There is also now extant an apocryphal work entitled, "The Book of Enoch," which contains many remarkable and inspired teachings and also considerable trashy nonsense. Among numerous statements about the Second Coming is this rather exceptional dissertation, in which is included a recitation of virtually the same presentation quoted by Jude:

"The Holy Great One will come forth from his dwelling, and the eternal God will tread upon the earth, even on Mount Sinai, and appear from his camp, and appear in the strength of his might from the heaven of heavens. And all shall be smitten with fear, and the watchers shall quake, and great fear and trembling shall seize them unto the ends of the earth. And the high mountains shall be shaken, and the high hills shall be made low, and shall melt like wax before the flame. And the earth shall be wholly rent in sunder, and all that is upon the earth shall perish, and there shall be a judgment upon all men. But with the righteous he will make peace, and will protect the elect, and mercy shall be upon them. And they shall all belong to God, and they shall be prospered, and they shall all be blessed. And he will help them all, and light shall appear unto them, and he will make peace with them. And behold! he cometh with ten thousands of his holy ones to execute judgment upon all, and to destroy all the ungodly: And to convict all flesh of all the works of their ungodliness which they have ungodly committed, and of all the hard things which ungodly sinners have spoken against him." (R. H. Charles, *The Apocrypha and Pseudepigrapha of the Old Testament*, vol. 2, pp. 188-189.)

Enoch] Translated beings] See Heb. 11:5-6.

14. The Lord cometh with ten thousands of his saints] "And the Lord my God shall come, and all the saints with thee." (Zech. 14:5.) See 1 Thess. 4:13-18; 5:1-11; 2 Thess. 1:1-12.

"KEEP YOURSELVES IN THE LOVE OF GOD"

JUDE 1:17-25.

17 But, beloved, remember ye the words which were spoken before of the apostles of our Lord Jesus Christ;

18 How that they told you there should be mockers in the last time, who should walk after their own ungodly lusts.

19 These be they who separate themselves, sensual, having not the Spirit.

20 But ye, beloved, building up yourselves on your most holy faith, praying in the Holy Ghost,

21 Keep yourselves in the love of God, looking for the mercy of our Lord Jesus Christ unto eternal life.

22 And of some have compassion, making a difference:

23 And others save with fear, pulling *them* out of the fire; hating even the garment spotted by the flesh.

24 Now unto him that is able to keep you from falling, and to present *you* faultless before the presence of his glory with exceeding joy,

25 To the only wise God our Saviour, *be* glory and majesty, dominion and power, both now and ever. Amen.

18-19. The basic cause of apostasy is sin. Men leave the Church because they are sensual and carnal. It is not a matter of rejecting gospel doctrine, or preferring a more liberal interpretation or application of revealed truth. These are excuses. The basic reason for rebellion against the truth is a desire to enjoy the lusts of the flesh. The choice is not between doctrinal concepts, but between differing ways of life.

18. Mockers in the last time] See 2 Pet. 3:1-9.

20. Building up yourselves] Keeping the commandments, growing in grace, acquiring the attributes of godliness, working out your salvation; salvation must be earned; it is free only in the sense that it is freely available to all who will pay the price of righteousness.

Your most holy faith] The gospel of Jesus Christ. What is more holy and glorious than the gospel which takes fallen man, carnal and sensual as he is, and changes him, by obedience, because of the atonement, into a son of God.

Praying in the Holy Ghost] Praying by the power of the Holy Ghost, so that all requested petitions are granted, because "it shall be given you what you shall ask." (D. & C. 50:29-30; 101:27.)

21. 'Keep the commandments and abide in the truth so as to be subject to the law of mercy and thereby gain eternal life.' (Alma 42:22-26.)

22. 'Be tender and compassionate toward those who have doubts; teach them correct principles and encourage them in righteousness.'

23. Others save with fear] Preach hell fire and damnation to those who need it. After telling his Nephite brethren of the destruction that awaited them unless they repented, Jacob said: "My brethren, is it expedient that I should awake you to an awful reality of these things? Would I harrow up your souls if your minds were pure? Would I be plain unto you according to the plainness of the truth if ye were freed from sin? Behold, if ye were holy I would speak unto you of holiness; but as ye are not holy, and ye look upon me as a teacher, it must needs be expedient that I teach you the consequences of sin." (2 Ne. 9:47-48.)

Pulling them out of the fire] In the day of judgment, every corruptible thing will be consumed (D. & C. 101:24), and the wicked shall be burned with unquenchable fire. (Mal. 4:1.) If the erring saints are to be saved, they must be pulled, as it were, from the coming fire, even as God said of Israel: "Ye were as a firebrand plucked out of the burning." (Amos 4:11.) "If the fire can scathe a green tree for the glory of God, how easy it will burn up the dry trees to purify the vineyard of corruption." (D. & C. 135:6.) See 2 Pet. 3:10-18.

Hating even the garment spotted by the flesh] To stay the spread of disease in ancient Israel, clothing spotted by contagious diseases was destroyed by burning. (Lev. 13:47-59; 15:4-17.) And so with sin in the Church, the saints are to avoid the remotest contact with it; the very garments, as it were, of the sinners are to be burned with fire, meaning that anything which has had contact with the pollutions of the wicked must be shunned. And so also with those yet in the world who are invited to join the kingdom. To them the call is: Repent, "Save yourselves from this untoward generation, and come forth out of the fire, hating even the garments spotted with the flesh." (D. & C. 36:6.)

The Revelation of St. John the Divine

What think ye of the book of Revelation?

To some it is a mass of confusion, uncertainty and mystery — and this includes many of the otherwise devout and informed truth seekers in today's churches.

To others it is a prime source of "answers" to "prove private and speculative notions, particularly about historical matters and God's dealings with nations and kingdoms — and this includes those religious rabble rousers who specialize in so-called radio ministries and cultish cliques.

Still others have a we-couldn't-care-less attitude, which classes the book along with the legends of mythology and says, in effect, why bother with such symbolism and mystery — and this, unfortunately and in practice, includes much of self-styled Christendom.

Even among those who do give serious consideration to the teachings and doctrine of the book of Revelation, there are widely divergent views as to the true meanings of its admittedly hidden doctrines. "There have been three chief schools of interpretation," Dummelow says. "One school (called the 'Futurist') regards the book as dealing with the end of the world, and with events and persons which will immediately precede that end. The 'Historical' school sees in the book a summary of the Church's history from early days until the end. The 'Preterists' look back to the past, and interpret the book as having to do with the times in which it originated. A fourth method sees in the book symbolical representations of good and evil principles, common to every age, and to be understood spiritually. According to this last method, the New Jerusalem, e.g., would be explained as representing the blessedness, even in this earthly state, of true believers whose lives are hid with Christ in God." (*Dummelow*, p. 1066.)

But among the Latter-day Saints — among those who "shun profane and vain babblings," whose interest is not in striving "about words to no profit," but who seek to establish themselves as workmen who are "approved unto God, . . . rightly dividing the word of truth" (2 Tim. 2:14-16) — unto such the book of Revelation sheds forth a blaze of light and understanding.

The issue, thus, in delving into the doctrines and truths of this great repository of revealed writ is to rightly divide the word of truth; it is to learn what God has revealed and unfolded in these apocalyptic writings and to lay the remainder aside, knowing that in our present state of understanding any speculation is worse than useless; such speculation not only leads to misunderstanding but so often becomes the basis of gospel hobbies which lead away from that sound view and perspective of all eternal truths which is an essential part of working out one's salvation.

That there are some mysterious, hidden and unknown things recorded in the Apocalypse is so obvious that it scarcely needs recitation here. But that such is the case should not trouble us in view of these pronouncements from the Prophet Joseph Smith:

"I make this broad declaration that whenever God gives a vision of an image, or beast, or figure of any kind, he always holds himself responsible to give a revelation or interpretation of the meaning thereof, otherwise we are not responsible or accountable for our belief in it. Don't be afraid of being damned for not knowing the meaning of a vision or figure, if God has not given a revelation or interpretation of the subject." (*Teachings*, p. 291.)

"It is not very essential for the elders to have knowledge in relation to the meaning of beasts, and heads and horns, and other figures made use of in the revelations; still, it may be necessary, to prevent contention and division and do away with suspense. If we get puffed up by thinking that we have much knowledge, we are apt to get a contentious spirit, and correct knowledge is necessary to cast out that spirit.

"The evil of being puffed up with correct (though useless) knowledge is not so great as the evil of contention. Knowledge does away with darkness, suspense and doubt; for these cannot exist where knowledge is." (*Teachings*, pp. 287-288.)

As a matter of fact, we are in a much better position to understand those portions of Revelation which we are expected to understand than we generally realize. Thanks be to the interpretive material found in sections 29, 77, 88, and others of the revelations in the Doctrine and Covenants; plus the revisions given in the Inspired Version of the Bible; plus the sermons of the Prophet; plus some clarifying explanations in the Book of Mormon and other latter-day scripture; plus our over-all knowledge of the plan of salvation — thanks be to all of these things (to say nothing of a little conservative sense, wisdom and inspiration in their application), the fact is that we have a marvelously comprehensive and correct understanding of this otherwise hidden book.

That there are some wise restrictions on its use, however, also goes almost without saying, as witness this pointed statement from the Prophet to the first elders of this dispensation: "Oh, ye elders of Israel, hearken to my voice; and when you are sent into the world to preach, tell those things you are sent to tell; preach and cry aloud, 'Repent ye, for the kingdom of heaven is at hand; repent and believe the gospel.' Declare the first principles, and let mysteries alone, lest ye be overthrown. Never meddle with the visions of beasts and subjects you do not understand. Elder Brown, when you go to Palmyra, say nothing about the four beasts, but preach those things the Lord has told you to preach about — repentance and baptism for the remission of sins." (*Teachings*, p. 292.)

But let us remember that the book of Revelation was written to be understood; true, there are many things in it which we cannot now comprehend; but its true and full meaning will someday be revealed to the faithful and obedient saints; and the more we can learn now, with the interpretive insight already available to us, the better off we are. It was to people in our day that Moroni wrote these prophetic words: "Behold, when ye shall rend that veil of unbelief which doth cause you to remain in your awful state of wickedness, and hardness of heart, and blindness of mind, then shall the great and marvelous things which have been hid up from the foundation of the world from you—yea, when ye shall call upon the Father in my name, with a broken heart and a contrite spirit, then shall ye know that the Father hath remembered the covenant which he made unto your fathers, O house of Israel. And then shall my revelations which I have caused to be written by my servant John be unfolded in the eyes of all the people." (Ether 4:15-16.)

During the long hours of study, pondering and prayer that went into the preparation of this commentary data about the book of Revelation, I came to the considered conclusion, not only that it was one of the most fascinating books of holy writ, but that, in the language of the Prophet and as pertaining to those portions we are now expected to know and understand, it "is one of the plainest books God ever caused to be written." (*Teachings*, p. 290.)

Its apocalyptic imagery and symbolism surpass any such found elsewhere in the revealed word; and when these are properly understood and interpreted, they shed forth an effusion of light in which the scripturally oriented saints love to bask. Obviously it is not a book for the theological novice, nor for the uninspired theological speculators of the world. It is written to the saints who already have a knowledge of the plan of salvation, to say nothing of the interpreting power of the Holy Spirit in their hearts. And as with all scripture—the most simple and easy teachings included—it can be understood only by the power of the Holy Ghost, "For the prophecy came not in old time by the will of man: but holy men of God spake as they were moved by the Holy Ghost." And therefore, "No prophecy of the scripture is of any private interpretation." (2 Pet. 1:20-21.)

One of the indications of the importance of that which is written in the book of Revelation is the fact that other prophets have seen and written the same visions, and that in due course the Lord will bring these accounts forth in plainness and perfection. Indeed, when John first wrote this very book, "the things which were written were plain and pure, and most precious and easy to the understanding of all men." (1 Ne. 14:23.)

Nephi was one prophet who saw the same things, but he was commanded not to write them. "For the Lord God hath ordained the apostle of the Lamb of God that he should write them. And also others who have been, to them hath he shown all things, and they have written them; and they are sealed up to come forth in their purity, according to the truth which is in the Lamb, in the own due time of the Lord, unto the house of Israel. And I, Nephi, heard and bear record, that the name of the apostle of the Lamb was John." (1 Ne. 14:25-27.)

And so it is that in this imperfect day when we still "see through a glass, darkly" (1 Cor. 13:12), we look forward to that perfect day when "the Lord shall . . . reveal all things." (D. & C. 101:32.) We have what we have and glory in it, and hope to be worthy to receive more and more until our light and knowledge shall shine forth with divine perfection. (D. & C. 50:24.)

But even now, how glorious is the apocalyptic voice we hear —

A voice of glory and honor and eternal life;

A voice that guides us in overcoming the world and gaining exaltation;

A voice that reveals the mysteries of the kingdom and the hidden dealings of God with his children;

A voice that tells of the restoration of eternal truth, of the plagues of latter-days, of the paradisiacal and celestial earths;

A voice of a thousand times a thousand other things that save for its cry would be unknown —

The voice of John crying to us from the parchments of the past: such is this holy book of Revelation.

CHRIST MAKETH KINGS AND PRIESTS UNTO GOD

REVELATION 1:1-6.

1 The Revelation of Jesus Christ, which God gave unto him, to show unto his servants things which must shortly come to pass; and he sent and signified *it* by his angel unto his servant John:

2 Who bare record of the word

of God, and of the testimony of Jesus Christ, and of all things that he saw.

3 Blessed *is* he that readeth, and they that hear the words of this prophecy, and keep those things which are written therein: for the time *is* at hand.

4 John to the seven churches which are in Asia: Grace *be* unto you, and peace, from him which is, and which was, and which is to come; and from the seven Spirits which are before his throne;

5 And from Jesus Christ *who is* the faithful witness, *and* the first begotten of the dead, and the prince of the kings of the earth. Unto him that loved us, and washed us from our sins in his own blood,

6 And hath made us kings and priests unto God and his Father; to him *be* glory and dominion for ever and ever. Amen.

I.V. REVELATION 1:1-6.

1 The Revelation **of John, a servant of God, which was given unto him of Jesus Christ,** to show unto his servants things which must shortly come to pass, **that** he sent and signified by his angel unto his servant John,

2 Who **bore** record of the word of God, and of the testimony of Jesus Christ, and of all things that he saw.

3 Blessed **are they who readeth,** and they **who heareth and understandeth** the words of this prophecy, and keep those things which are written therein, for the time **of the coming of the Lord draweth nigh.**

4 **Now this is the testimony** of John to **the seven servants who are over** the seven churches in Asia. Grace unto you, and peace from him **who** is, and **who** was, and **who** is to come; **who hath sent forth his angel from before his throne, to testify unto those who are the seven servants over the seven churches.**

5 **Therefore, I, John, the faithful witness, bear record of the things which were delivered me of the angel, and from Jesus Christ** the first begotten of the dead, and the Prince of the kings of the earth.

6 **And** unto him **who** loved us, **be glory; who** washed us from our sins in his own blood, and hath made us kings and priests unto God, his Father. To him be glory and dominion, for ever and ever. Amen.

I. V. 1. The Revelation of John] This book of scripture was given by Christ to John, the Beloved Disciple, who also authored the Gospel of John and the three epistles which bear his name.

With Peter and James he served in the First Presidency of the Church (D. & C. 81:1-2), and he was the last of the ancient apostles to minister among the saints of his day. See Rev. 10:1-11.

K. J. 1. Unto his servants] This revelation was given to the saints, to the servants of God, to those who have the gift of the Holy Ghost, and who thereby have the spirit of understanding and interpretation. It was given to those whose knowledge of what is involved is not limited to the cold words of the Bible; and these are and shall remain the only people who can understand its doctrines, comprehend its symbolisms, and gain from it the mysteries of the kingdom, which God hath reserved for those who fear him, who honor him, and who serve him in righteousness and in truth all their days. (D. & C. 76:5-10.)

Things which must shortly come to pass] This is one of the great keys which opens the door to an understanding of the Book of Revelation. What is recorded therein is to transpire in the future, mainly in a day subsequent to New Testament times. The revelations promised are to come to the saints of latter-days, not to those in the meridian of time. All the promised events shall transpire "shortly"; they are soon to be in the perspective of Him with whom one day is "as a thousand years, and a thousand years as one day." (2 Pet. 3:8.)

Joseph Smith said: "The things which John saw had no allusion to the scenes of the days of Adam, Enoch, Abraham or Jesus, only so far as is plainly represented by John, and clearly set forth by him. John saw that only which was lying in futurity and which was shortly to come to pass." (*Teachings*, p. 289.) Also: "John had the curtains of heaven withdrawn, and by vision looked through the dark vista of future ages, and contemplated events that should transpire throughout every subsequent period of time, until the final winding up scene." (*Teachings*, p. 247.)

He sent and signified it by his angel] The entire revelation was delivered by an angel upon whom the Lord had placed his name and who acted in the Lord's place and stead. See Rev. 19:9b-10.

2. The testimony of Jesus Christ] See Rev. 19:9b-10.

4. The seven churches . . . in Asia] Special instructions are to be forthcoming for seven congregations situated in Asia. Whether these were branches, wards, stakes, or simply the total body of the saints in the named localities, we have no way of knowing; nor, for that matter, do we know the precise organizational arrangement prevailing in that day. Suffice it to say that John, as one holding the keys of the kingdom of God on earth, had jurisdiction over the whole body of the Church and was properly chosen by Deity to convey his message to his people.

I. V. 4. The seven servants over the seven churches] The Lord's message is to all his saints, and particularly to those whom he has called to preside over the various congregations, for they are responsible for the spiritual well-being of those placed in their charge.

K. J. 5. Washed us from our sins in his own blood] The blood of Christ alone cleanseth repentant souls from sin. "No unclean thing can enter" into the kingdom of God, are the words of Christ, the first begotten from the dead; and none shall gain an inheritance there, "save it be those who have washed their garments in my blood, because of their faith, and the repentance of all their sins, and their faithfulness unto the end." (3 Ne. 27:19.)

6. Hath made us kings and priests] "Holders of the Melchizedek Priesthood have power to press forward in righteousness, living by every word that proceedeth forth from the mouth of God, magnifying their callings, going from grace to grace, until through the fulness of the ordinances of the temple they receive the fulness of the priesthood and are ordained kings and priests. Those so attaining shall have exaltation and be kings, priests, rulers, and lords in their respective spheres in the eternal kingdoms of the great King who is God our Father." (*Mormon Doctrine*, 2nd ed., p. 425.) Those of whom John is here writing had already gained their rank and status as kings and priests, as have many also in the dispensation of the fulness of times. "John said he was a king." (*Teachings*, p. 375.)

Unto God and his Father] In one of the crowning sermons of his ministry, delivered June 16, 1844, just eleven days before his martyrdom, the Prophet Joseph Smith read as a text, Revelation 1:6, and announced: "It is altogether correct in the translation." Then he proceeded with great power to consider the subject of a plurality of Gods. He quoted a number of Biblical passages and used his text verse to show there was "a God above the Father of our Lord Jesus Christ." He said that all the faithful saints shall "come to dwell in unity, and in all the glory and everlasting burning of the Gods; and then we shall see as we are seen, and be as our God and he as his Father. I want to reason a little on this subject. I learned it by translating the papyrus which is now in my house.

"I learned a testimony concerning Abraham, and he reasoned concerning the God of heaven. 'In order to do that,' said he, 'suppose we have two facts: that supposes another fact may exist — two men on the earth, one wiser than the other, would logically show that another who is wiser than the wisest may exist. Intelligences exist one above another, so that there is no end to them.'

"If Abraham reasoned thus — If Jesus Christ was the Son of God, and John discovered that God the Father of Jesus Christ had a Father, you may suppose that he had a Father also. Where was there ever a son without a father? And where was there ever a father without first being a son? Whenever did a tree or anything spring into existence without a progenitor? And everything comes in this way. Paul says that which is earthly is in the likeness of that which is heavenly. Hence if Jesus had a Father, can we not believe that he had a Father also? I despise the idea of being scared to death at such a doctrine, for the Bible is full of it.

"I want you to pay particular attention to what I am saying. Jesus said that the Father wrought precisely in the same way as his Father had done before him. As the Father had done before? He laid down his life, and took it up the same as his Father had done before. He did as he was sent, to lay down his life and take it up again; and then was committed unto him the keys. I know it is good reasoning." (*Teachings*, pp. 369-376.)

What is the royal priesthood?] See 1 Pet. 2:9-10.

Sons of God shall be like Christ] See 1 John 3:1-3.

CHRIST, THE ALMIGHTY, SHALL COME AGAIN

REVELATION 1:7-8.

7 Behold, he cometh with clouds; and every eye shall see him, and they *also* which pierced him: and all kindreds of the earth shall wail because of him. Even so, Amen.

8 I am Alpha and Omega, the beginning and the ending, saith the Lord, which is, and which was, and which is to come, the Almighty.

I.V. REVELATION 1:7-8.

7 **For** behold, he cometh **in the** clouds **with ten thousands of his saints in the kingdom, clothed with the glory of his Father.** And every eye shall see him; and they **who** pierced him, and all kindreds of the earth shall wail because of him. Even so, Amen.

8 **For he saith,** I am Alpha and Omega, the beginning and the ending, the Lord, **who** is, and **who** was, and **who** is to come, the Almighty.

I. V. 7. He cometh in the clouds] As he went up, so shall he return. "From the mount called Olivet," he was "taken up," and "a cloud received him out of their sight." (Acts 1:9-12.) And he shall come again, "in the clouds of heaven with power and great glory" (Matt. 24:30; 26:64; Dan. 7:13), and once again, "he shall stand upon the mount of Olivet." (D. & C. 133:20.)

With ten thousands of his saints] Our Lord ascended alone, but he shall return with the hosts of heaven. See Jude 14-16.

K. J. 7. Every eye shall see him] The Incarnate God was born into the world not in secret, but without the knowledge of his advent being known to men generally. But when he comes again, all men shall know. There will be no question about the transcendent events that are transpiring. Every eye shall see him personally. "The glory of the Lord shall be revealed, and all flesh shall see it together." (Isa. 40:5.) "I will gather all nations and tongues," he says, "and they shall come, and see my glory." (Isa. 66:18; Isa. 52:10; D. & C. 133:3.)

They also which pierced him] "And then shall the Jews look upon me and say: What are these wounds in thine hands and in thy feet? Then shall they know that I am the Lord; for I will say unto them: These wounds are the wounds with which I was wounded in the house of my friends. I am he who was lifted up. I am Jesus that was crucified. I am the Son of God." (D. & C. 45:51-52; Zech. 12:10; 13:6.)

All kindreds of the earth shall wail bccausc of him] When our Lord returns, there shall be — among the wicked and ungodly — such wailing and mourning as has never before been known on earth, for the summer will be over, the harvest past, and their souls not saved. (D. & C. 45:49, 53; Zech. 12:10-14; Matt. 24:30.)

8. Alpha and Omega] "These words, the first and last letters of the Greek alphabet, are used figuratively to teach the timelessness and eternal nature of our Lord's existence, that is, that 'from eternity to eternity he is the same, and his years never fail.' (D. & C. 76:4.)" (*Mormon Doctrine*, 2nd ed., p. 31.)

The beginning and the ending] "These are English words having substantially the same meaning as the Greek Alpha and Omega. The thought conveyed is one of timelessness, of a being who is the Beginning and the End because his 'course is one eternal round, the same today as yesterday, and forever.' (D. & C. 35:1.) He was God 'in the beginning' (John 1:1-3); he is God now; he will be God in the 'end,' that is to all eternity. The beginning is the pre-existent eternity that went before; the end is the immortal eternity that is to come." (*Mormon Doctrine*, 2nd ed., p. 77.)

The Almighty] Christ is the Almighty; he knows all things and has all power, all might, and all dominion; he is omnipotent and both created and rules the universe. He is "the Lord Omnipotent who reigneth, who was, and is from all eternity to all eternity." (Mosiah 3:5.)

ANCIENT SAINTS WORSHIPED ON SUNDAY

REVELATION 1:9-11.

9 I John, who also am your brother, and companion in tribulation, and in the kingdom and patience of Jesus Christ, was in the isle that is called Patmos, for the word of God, and for the testimony of Jesus Christ.

10 I was in the Spirit on the Lord's day, and heard behind me a great voice, as of a trumpet,

11 Saying, I am Alpha and Omega, the first and the last: and, What thou seest, write in a book, and send *it* unto the seven churches which are in Asia; unto Ephesus, and unto Smyrna, and unto Pergamos, and unto Thyatira, and unto Sardis, and unto Philadelphia, and unto Laodicea.

10. The Lord's day] "Pursuant to divine command men are to rest from all temporal work and to worship the Lord one day in particular each week. This day — no matter which day of the week is involved — is called the *Sabbath,* from the Hebrew *shabbath* meaning day of rest. The rest, though important, is incidental to the true keeping of the Sabbath. What is more important is that the Sabbath is an holy day — a day of worship, one in which men turn their whole souls to the Lord, renew their covenants with him, and feed their souls upon the things of the Spirit.

"Sabbath observance is an eternal principle, and the day itself is so ordained and arranged that it bears record of Christ by pointing particular attention to great works he has performed. From the day of Adam to the Exodus from Egypt, the Sabbath commemorated the fact that Christ rested from his creative labors on the 7th day. (Ex. 20:8-11.) From the Exodus to the day of his resurrection, the Sabbath commemorated the deliverance of Israel from Egyptian bondage. (Deut. 5:12-15.) As Samuel Walter Gamble has pointed out in his *Sunday, the True Sabbath of God,* this necessarily means that the Sabbath was kept on a different day each year. From the days of the early apostles to the present, the Sabbath has been the first day of the week, the Lord's Day, in commemoration of the fact that Christ came forth from the grave on Sunday. (Acts 20:7.) The Latter-day Saints keep the first day of the week as their Sabbath, not in imitation of what any peoples of the past have done, but because the Lord so commanded them by direct revelation." (*Mormon Doctrine,* 2nd ed., p. 658.)

The Lord's instructions to his saints of latter-days are: "And that thou mayest more fully keep thyself unspotted from the world, thou shalt go to the house of prayer and offer up thy sacraments upon my holy day; For verily this is a day appointed unto you to rest from your labors, and to pay thy devotions unto the Most High; Nevertheless thy vows shall be offered up in righteousness on all days and at all times; But remember that on this, the Lord's day, thou shalt offer thine oblations and thy sacraments unto the Most High, confessing thy sins unto thy brethren, and before the Lord. And on this day thou shalt do none other thing, only let thy food be prepared with singleness of heart that thy fasting may be perfect, or, in other words, that thy joy may be full. Verily, this is fasting and prayer, or in other words, rejoicing and prayer. And inasmuch as ye do these things with thanksgiving, with cheerful hearts and countenances, not with much laughter, for this is sin, but with a glad heart and a cheerful countenance — Verily I say, that inasmuch as ye do this, the fulness of the earth is yours, the beasts of the field and the fowls of the air, and that which climbeth upon the trees and walketh upon the earth; yea, and the herb, and the good things which come of the earth, whether for food or for raiment, or for houses, or for barns, or for orchards, or for gardens, or for vineyards." (D. & C. 59:9-17.)

11. Alpha and Omega] See Rev. 1:7-8.

The first and the last] "These terms are descriptive of his [our Lord's] eternal timelessness; he is God everlastingly. As the First, the thought is conveyed that he is pre-eminent above all the earth's inhabitants, both from the standpoint of time (he being the Firstborn in the spirit), and from the standpoint of power and dominion (he having become a God in the beginning). As the Last, the concept is revealed that he will go on as God, continuing to enjoy his full pre-eminence, to all eternity, everlastingly without end." (*Mormon Doctrine*, 2nd ed., p. 281.)

JOHN SEETH THE RISEN LORD

REVELATION 1:12-20.

12 And I turned to see the voice that spake with me. And being turned, I saw seven golden candlesticks;

13 And in the midst of the seven candlesticks *one* like unto the Son of man, clothed with a garment down to the foot, and girt about the paps with a golden girdle.

14 His head and *his* hairs *were* white like wool, as white as snow; and his eyes *were* as a flame of fire;

15 And his feet like unto fine brass, as if they burned in a furnace; and his voice as the sound of many waters.

16 And he had in his right hand seven stars: and out of his mouth went a sharp twoedged sword: and his countenance *was* as the sun shineth in his strength.

17 And when I saw him, I fell at his feet as dead. And he laid his right hand upon me, saying unto me, Fear not; I am the first and the last:

18 *I am* he that liveth, and was dead; and, behold, I am alive for evermore, Amen; and have the keys of hell and of death.

19 Write the things which thou hast seen, and the things which are, and the things which shall be hereafter;

20 The mystery of the seven stars which thou sawest in my right hand, and the seven golden candlesticks. The seven stars are the angels of the seven churches: and the seven candlesticks which thou sawest are the seven churches.

I.V. REVELATION 1:12, 16, 20.

12 And I turned to see **from whence the voice came** that spake to me; and being turned, I saw seven golden candlesticks:

16 And he had in his right hand seven stars; and out of his mouth went a sharp two-edged sword; and his countenance was as the sun **shining** in his strength.

20 **This is** the mystery of the seven stars which thou sawest in my right hand, and the seven golden candlesticks. The seven stars are the **servants** of the seven churches; and the seven candlesticks which thou sawest are the seven churches.

12. Seven golden candlesticks] Candlesticks carry light; they do not create it. Their function is to make it available, not to bring it into being. So by using seven candlesticks to portray the seven churches to whom John is now to give counsel, the Lord is showing that his congregations on earth are to carry his light to the world. Christ is the Light of the world. (John 8:12.) "Hold up your light that it may shine unto the world. Behold I am the light which ye shall hold up — that which ye have seen me do." (3 Ne. 18:24; Matt. 5:14-16.) So was it also in ancient Israel, when Moses made "a candlestick of pure gold," which held seven candles, for use in the tabernacle (temple). (Ex. 25:31-40.)

13. In the midst of the seven candlesticks] The Lord is with his people. "I am in your midst and ye cannot see me," he says to his saints. (D. & C. 38:7.)

One like unto] John is receiving instruction from an angel upon whom the Lord has placed his name, and who therefore speaks and acts in the first person as though he were the Lord, so that his words, acts, and appearance are those of the Lord. See Rev. 19:9b-10.

The Son of man] "Christ is the Son of Man, meaning that his Father (the Eternal God!) is a Holy Man. 'In the language of Adam, Man of Holiness' is the name of God, 'and the name of his Only Begotten is the Son of Man, even Jesus Christ, a righteous Judge, who shall come in the meridian of time.' (Moses 6:57.) Thus Christ is the Son of Man of Holiness or more briefly put, the Son of Man. Accordingly, when he asked his disciples, 'Whom do men say that I the Son of man am?' (Matt. 16:13), he was conveying precisely the same thought as he would have done by saying, 'Whom do men say that I the Son of God am?' for that God who is his Father is a Holy Man." (*Mormon Doctrine*, 2nd ed., p. 742.)

A garment . . . a golden girdle] Robes of the holy priesthood, even as it had been with Aaron and others when they ministered in their lesser priestly offices. (Ex. 28:2, 4, 31.)

14-16. There are two other recorded accounts of our Lord's appearance in like glory to men on earth. One, before his mortal birth, was to "Moses, and Aaron, Nadab, and Abihu, and seventy of the elders of Israel: And they saw the God of Israel: and there was under his feet as it were a paved work of a sapphire stone, and as it were the body of heaven in his clearness." (Ex. 24:9-10.) The other, after his resurrection and ascension to eternal power, was to Joseph Smith and Oliver Cowdery in the Kirtland Temple. "We saw the Lord standing upon the breastwork of the pulpit, before us," they testified, "and under his feet was a paved work of pure gold, in color like amber. His eyes were as a flame of fire; the hair of his head was white like pure snow; his countenance shone above the brightness of the sun; and his voice was as the sound of the rushing of great waters, even the voice of Jehovah, saying:

I am the first and the last: I am he who liveth, I am he who was slain; I am your advocate with the Father." (D. & C. 110:2-4.)

16. In his right hand seven stars] The presiding officers of the seven congregations who, as with all his ministers, are in the hands of the Lord. They do not speak or act of themselves; they represent their Master, whose words they speak, whose acts they perform, and in fact whose they are.

Out of his mouth went a sharp twoedged sword] The word of God pierces the soul as a sword. See Heb. 4:12-13.

His countenance was as the sun] There is no way to comprehend or describe the brightness and glory of exalted personages. "I saw a pillar of light exactly over my head, above the brightness of the sun," the Prophet said of his First Vision, and, "When the light rested upon me I saw two Personages, whose brightness and glory defy all description." (Jos. Smith 2:16-17.)

18. The keys of death and hell] Death is the separation of the body and spirit, the body returning to the dust from whence it was taken and the spirit entering the spirit world to await the day of the resurrection. Hell is that part of the spirit world where the wicked go to suffer the torments of the damned until they come forth to be assigned their place in the kingdoms that are prepared. Keys are the controlling power. Our Lord, therefore, governs death and hell. All men live or die at his will; they are cast down to hell or saved therefrom by his decree. All men are in his hands forever; he is supreme, because he holds the keys.

OVERCOME AND GAIN ETERNAL LIFE

REVELATION 2:1-7.

1 Unto the angel of the church of Ephesus write; These things saith he that holdeth the seven stars in his right hand, who walketh in the midst of the seven golden candlesticks;

2 I know thy works, and thy labour, and thy patience, and how thou canst not bear them which are evil: and thou hast tried them which say they are apostles, and are not, and hast found them liars:

3 And hast borne, and hast patience, and for my name's sake hast laboured, and hast not fainted.

4 Nevertheless I have *somewhat* against thee, because thou hast left thy first love.

5 Remember therefore from whence thou art fallen, and repent, and do the first works; or else I will come unto thee quickly, and will remove thy candlestick out of his place, except thou repent.

6 But this thou hast, that thou hatest the deeds of the Nicolaitanes, which I also hate.

7 He that hath an ear, let him hear what the Spirit saith unto the churches; To him that overcometh will I give to eat of the tree of life, which is in the midst of the paradise of God.

I.V. REVELATION 2:1.

1 Unto the **servant** of the church of Ephesus write; These things saith he that holdeth the seven stars in his right hand, who walketh in the midst of the seven golden candlesticks;

Chapters two and three of Revelation contain counsel and commendation to the seven churches in Asia; and what is said applies, in principle, to all congregations of saints in all the world, in all ages. In each instance, the promises given are conditioned upon the requirement that the recipients shall overcome the world.

This mortal life is designed as a time of testing and trial. (Abra. 3:25-26.) The Lord is letting us choose whether we shall succumb to the lusts of the flesh and live after the manner of the world, or whether we shall keep the commandments; put first in our lives the things of his kingdom; develop the character, perfections, and attributes which he possesses; and thereby qualify for eternal life with him in the kingdom of his Father. And he expects us to overcome, to conquer, to come off triumphant, to be victorious, to win the war with sin, even as he himself did. (John 16:33.)

Love not the world] See 1 John 2:15-17.

1. See Rev. 1:12-20.

1. The angel [I. V. servant] of the church] The presiding officer of the Church in Ephesus.

2. I know thy works] Christ is omniscient; he knows all things; the status of all men and of all congregations of his saints is open before him. And as is shown by the direction given to the seven churches in Asia, the various congregations of the saints contain an intermixture of the good and the bad. In the Church on earth, the wheat and tares together grow, and only those saints who overcome the world shall inherit eternal life.

Thou hast tried them which say they are apostles] There are both true and false ministers. See *Commentary II*, pp. 440-441. It is the province and commission of the Church to divide the true from the false. "I, the Lord, have made my church in these last days like unto a judge sitting on a hill, or in a high place, to judge the nations. For it shall come to pass that the inhabitants of Zion shall judge all things pertaining to Zion. And liars and hypocrites shall be proved by them, and they who are not apostles and prophets shall be known." (D. & C. 64:37-39.)

4. Thou hast left thy first love] Faithful as they were, the zeal of the new convert was waning; their love for the Lord was not what it had been in the days past.

5. I . . . will remove thy candlestick out of his place] Any congregation of saints which is not true and faithful shall lose its place in the true Church. The Lord will no longer own them, nor receive them as his in that day when he comes to make up his jewels. And such, of course, was the case in due time with all the congregations established in the meridian of time.

6. Nicolaitanes] Members of the Church who were triyng to maintain their church standing while continuing to live after the manner of the world. They must have had some specific doctrinal teachings which they used to justify their course. In the counsel given to the Church in Pergamos, their doctrine is condemned as severely as that of Balaam who sought to lead Israel astray. (Rev. 2:14-16; 2 Pet. 2:10-22; Num. 22, 23, and 24.) Whatever their particular deeds and doctrines were, the designation has come to be used to identify those who want their names on the records of the Church, but do not want to devote themselves to the gospel cause with full purpose of heart. Thus, on July 8, 1838, the Lord said: "Let my servant Newel K. Whitney be ashamed of the Nicolaitane band and of all their secret abominations, and of all his littleness of soul before me, saith the Lord, and come up to the land of Adam-ondi-Ahman, and be a bishop unto my people, saith the Lord, not in name but in deed, saith the Lord." (D. & C. 117:11.)

7. He that hath an ear, let him hear] In the sense of believing and understanding, only those whose souls are enlightened by the power of the Holy Spirit can hear the word of God. The hearing ear is the ear of faith.

Unto the churches] The message is for all saints and all congregations everywhere in all ages. The faithful saints shall eat of the tree of life.

The tree of life] Figuratively, the tree from which the faithful pick the fruit of eternal life. To eat thereof is to inherit eternal life in the kingdom of God. Of his vision of the tree of life. Lehi said: "I beheld a tree, whose fruit was desirable to make one happy. And it came to pass that I did go forth and partake of the fruit thereof; and I beheld that it was most sweet, above all that I ever before tasted. Yea, and I beheld that the fruit thereof was white, to exceed all the whiteness that I had ever seen. And as I partook of the fruit thereof it filled my soul with exceeding great joy; wherefore, I began to be desirous that my family should partake of it also; for I knew that it was desirable above all other fruit." (1 Ne. 8:10-12.)

The paradise of God] That part of the spirit world inhabited by the righteous as they await the day of a glorious resurrection in which they shall inherit eternal life. See *Commentary I*, pp. 823-825; *Commentary II*, pp. 443-447.

"HE THAT OVERCOMETH SHALL NOT BE HURT OF THE SECOND DEATH"

REVELATION 2:8-11.

8 And unto the angel of the church in Smyrna write; These things saith the first and the last, which was dead, and is alive;

9 I know thy works, and tribulation, and poverty, (but thou art rich) and *I know* the blasphemy of them which say they are Jews, and are not, but *are* the synagogue of Satan.

10 Fear none of those things which thou shalt suffer: behold, the devil shall cast *some* of you into prison, that ye may be tried; and ye shall have tribulation ten days: be thou faithful unto death, and I will give thee a crown of life.

11 He that hath an ear, let him hear what the Spirit saith unto the churches; He that overcometh shall not be hurt of the second death.

I.V. REVELATION 2:8.

8 And unto the **servant** of the church in Smyrna write; These things saith the first and the last, which was dead, and is alive;

8. The angel [I. V. servant] of the Church] The presiding officer of the Church in Smyrna.

The first and the last] See Rev. 1:9-11.

9. I know thy works] See Rev. 2:1-7.

Blasphemy] See Rev. 13:1-10.

The synagogue of Satan] The Jewish congregations in Smyrna which rejected Christ and fought the saints were part of the Church of the Devil. See Rev. 17:1-18.

10. Thou shalt suffer] The Lord intends that his saints shall suffer in his Cause, even as he suffered for them. Such is part of the probationary testing of mortality.

The devil shall cast some of you into prison] Who is it that casts the saints into prison? Who closed the prison doors upon Peter and Paul and Joseph Smith? The devil does it, but he uses his servants and mortal representatives; when any man rises up to persecute the saints of God, or any of his fellowmen for that matter, he is in the service of Satan, his master.

Tribulation ten days] The sufferings and trials of this life are short when compared with the eternal peace and comfort that shall be the lot of those who endure them well.

Be thou faithful unto death, and I will give thee a crown of life] 'Endure to the end and thou shalt be saved; keep the commandments and thou shalt have eternal life.' (D. & C. 98:14.)

11. He that hath an ear, let him hear] See Rev. 2:1-7.

Unto the churches] The message is for all saints and all congregations everywhere in all ages. The faithful saints shall not be hurt of the second death.

He that overcometh] See Rev. 2:1-7.

The second death] Spiritual death. See Rev. 21:8.

OVERCOME AND INHERIT CELESTIAL KINGDOM

REVELATION 2:12-17.

12 And to the angel of the church in Pergamos write; These things saith he which hath the sharp sword with two edges;

13 I know thy works, and where thou dwellest, *even* where Satan's seat *is:* and thou holdest fast my name, and hast not denied my faith, even in those days wherein Antipas *was* my faithful martyr, who was slain among you, where Satan dwelleth.

14 But I have a few things against thee, because thou hast there them that hold the doctrine of Balaam, who taught Balac to cast a stumblingblock before the children of Israel, to eat things sacrificed unto idols, and to commit fornication.

15 So hast thou also them that hold the doctrine of thc Nicolaitanes, which thing I hate.

16 Repent; or else I will come unto thee quickly, and will fight against them with the sword of my mouth.

17 He that hath an ear, let him hear what the Spirit saith unto the churches; To him that overcometh will I give to eat of the hidden manna, and will give him a white stone, and in the stone a new name written, which no man knoweth saving he that receiveth *it*.

I.V. REVELATION 2:12.

12 And to the **servant** of the church in Pergamos write; These things saith he which hath the sharp sword with two edges;

12. The angel [I. V. servant] of the church] The presiding officer of the Church in Pergamos.

He which hath the sharp sword with two edges] Christ. Pergamos was the center of the state religion of Rome, a religion in which the emperor was worshipped, and to which Christians must adhere or suffer death. It was a religion imposed upon them by the sword. Here Christ announces that he — out of whose mouth goeth "a sharp twoedged sword" (Rev. 1:16) — has eternal power, power beyond the life and death dominion of Rome, power which will pierce and slay the wicked as with a sword. See Heb. 4:12-13.

13. I know thy works] See Rev. 2:1-7.

Where Satan's seat is . . . where Satan dwelleth] "Under Augustus a temple was built at Pergamum [Pergamos], probably 29 B.C., and dedicated to Rome and Augustus, and Pergamum became the center of the imperial worship and 'Satan's throne' [seat]." (*Dummelow*, p. 1075.) Thus Satan dwelt in Pergamos and sat upon the throne in his own temple; and in like manner Satan dwells in every place and among every people where he, as the author of sin and the advocate of unrighteousness, finds those who open their hearts to him, who believe his doctrines, and who follow his ways; and similarly he reigns on the throne in every house of worship from which those doctrines flow which damn men and lead them carefully down to hell.

Antipas . . . my faithful martyr] See Rev. 6:9-11.

14. The doctrine of Balaam] To divine for hire; to give counsel contrary to the divine will; to pervert the right way of the Lord — all with a view to gaining wealth and the honors of men. In effect, to preach for money, or to gain personal power and influence. In the very nature of things such a course is a perversion of the right way of the Lord. See 2 Pet. 2:10-22.

Eat things sacrificed unto idols] If this is merely eating such meats without attaching religious significance to the act, it is of little moment one way or the other. See *Commentary II*, pp. 347-349. But if, as here, it is eating such meat as a religious performance, as an act of worship to an idol, it is an abomination before the Lord.

To commit fornication] Literally, sex immorality; figuratively, the worship of false gods — both of which meanings are here involved.

15. The doctrine of the Nicolaitanes] See Rev. 2:1-7.

17. He that hath an ear, let him hear] See Rev. 2:1-7.

Unto the churches] The message is for all saints and all congregations everywhere in all ages. The faithful saints shall eat of the hidden manna and receive a white stone with a new name written thereon.

Him that overcometh] See Rev. 2:1-7.

The hidden manna] The bread of life, the good word of God, the doctrines of Him who is the Bread of Life — all of which is hidden from the carnal mind. Those who eat thereof shall never hunger more; eternal life is their eventual inheritance.

A white stone . . . a new name] When this earth becomes a celestial sphere, "Then the white stone mentioned in Revelation 2:17, will become a Urim and Thummim to each individual who receives one, whereby things pertaining to a higher order of kingdoms will be made known; And a white stone is given to each of those who come into the celestial kingdom, whereon is a new name written, which no man knoweth save he that receiveth it. The new name is the key word." (D. & C. 130:10-11.) See Rev. 21:9-27.

OVERCOME AND RULE MANY KINGDOMS

REVELATION 2:18-29.

18 And unto the angel of the church in Thyatira write; These things saith the Son of God, who hath his eyes like unto a flame of fire, and his feet *are* like fine brass;

19 I know thy works, and charity, and service, and faith, and thy patience, and thy works; and the last *to be* more than the first.

20 Notwithstanding I have a few things against thee, because thou sufferest that woman Jezebel, which calleth herself a prophetess, to teach and to seduce my servants to commit fornication, and to eat things sacrificed unto idols.

21 And I gave her space to repent of her fornication; and she repented not.

22 Behold, I will cast her into a bed, and them that commit adultery with her into great tribulation, except they repent of their deeds.

23 And I will kill her children with death; and all the churches shall know that I am he which searcheth the reins and hearts: and I will give unto every one of you according to your works.

24 But unto you I say, and unto the rest in Thyatira, as many as have not this doctrine, and which have not known the depths of Satan, as they speak; I will put upon you none other burden.

25 But that which ye have *already* hold fast till I come.

26 And he that overcometh, and keepeth my works unto the end, to him will I give power over the nations:

27 And he shall rule them with a rod of iron; as the vessels of a potter shall they be broken to shivers: even as I received of my Father.

28 And I will give him the morning star.

29 He that hath an ear, let him hear what the Spirit saith unto the churches.

I.V. REVELATION 2:18, 22, 26-27.

18 And unto the **servant** of the church in Thyatira write; These things saith the Son of God, who hath his eyes like unto a flame of fire, and his feet are like fine brass;

22 Behold, I will cast her into **hell,** and them that commit adultery with her into great tribulation, except they repent of their deeds.

26 And **to him who** overcometh, and keep my **commandments** unto the end, will I give power over **many kingdoms;**

27 And he shall rule them with **the word of God; and they shall be in his hands as the vessels of clay in the hands of a potter; and he shall govern them by faith, with equity and justice,** even as I received of my Father.

18. The angel [I. V. servant] of the church] The presiding officer of the Church in Thyatira.

19. I know thy works] See Rev. 2:1-7.

20. As Ahab's wife led Israel to sacrifice to Baal and to worship false gods (i. e. to commit fornication), so another self-styled prophetess was leading many in Thyatira in an almost identical course; and the sin of the faithful members of the congregation was that they permitted her to teach her false doctrines.

To commit fornication, and to eat things sacrificed unto idols] See Rev. 2:12-17.

23. I will kill her children with death] Those who follow false teachings shall die spiritually.

26-28. Those who overcome the world and gain eternal life shall be made rulers over many kingdoms — not over the nations of men, which Rome then ruled with a rod of iron, but rulers over kingdoms in eternity, kingdoms patterned after the kingdom of God our Father, kingdoms that will be ruled by his power, by "the word of God," "by faith, with equity and justice." It shall then be with exalted persons as it is with Christ, who is King of kings and Lord of lords. To them the Lord will say: "Come up unto the crown prepared for you, and be made rulers over many kingdoms, saith the Lord God, the Holy One of Zion." (D. & C. 78:15.) All shall then reign in the kingdoms which are prepared.

26. He that overcometh] See Rev. 2:1-7.

28. 'I will give him eternal life; he shall be "even as I am" (3 Ne. 28:10), and I am "the bright and morning star" (Rev. 22:16), the brightest luminary among all the stars of heaven.' See Rev. 12:1-17.

29. He that hath an ear, let him hear] See Rev. 2:1-7.

Unto the churches] The message is for all saints and all congregations everywhere in all ages. The faithful saints shall be made rulers over many kingdoms, and they shall be even as their Great Prototype, "the bright and morning star." (Rev. 22:16.)

OVERCOME AND STAY IN THE BOOK OF LIFE

REVELATION 3:1-6.

1 And unto the angel of the church in Sardis write; These things saith he that hath the seven Spirits of God, and the seven stars; I know thy works, that thou hast a name that thou livest, and art dead.

2 Be watchful, and strengthen the things which remain, that are ready to die: for I have not found thy works perfect before God.

3 Remember therefore how thou hast received and heard, and hold fast, and repent. If therefore thou shalt not watch, I will come on thee as a thief, and thou shalt not know what hour I will come upon thee.

4 Thou hast a few names even in Sardis which have not defiled their garments; and they shall walk with me in white: for they are worthy.

5 He that overcometh, the same shall be clothed in white raiment; and I will not blot out his name out of the book of life, but I will confess his name before my Father, and before his angels.

6 He that hath an ear, let him hear what the Spirit saith unto the churches.

I.V. REVELATION 3:1-2.

1 And unto the **servant** of the church in Sardis, write; These things saith he **who** hath the **seven stars, which are the seven servants of God;** I know thy works, that thou hast a name that thou livest, and art not dead.

2 Be watchful **therefore,** and strengthen **those** who remain, **who** are ready to die; for I have not found thy works perfect before God.

1. The angel [I. V. servant] of the church] The presiding officer of the Church in Sardis.

The seven stars] See Rev. 1:12-20.

I know thy works] See Rev. 2:1-7.

Thou hast a name that thou livest, and art dead] 'You have a reputation for righteousness and spiritual strength, but are in fact spiritually dead.' And how often is it so, both with individuals and congregations, in the eyes of Him who readeth the hearts of men!

2. Things which remain, that are ready to die] Even some of those in Sardis who are yet faithful are not far from spiritual death.

3. I will come on thee as a thief] The faithful saints, reading the signs of the times, shall know the time and the season of our Lord's return; but he shall come as a thief in the night, unexpectedly and without warning, to the wicked and ungodly—rebellious members of the Church included! See 1 Thess. 5:1-11.

4. Their garments] Temple garments, garments of the holy priesthood, symbolical of the robes of righteousness with which the saints must clothe themselves if they are to gain eternal life. Both literally and figuratively, to defile one's garments is to disobey the

Lord's law, and to keep one's garments (Rev. 16:15) is to keep the commandments and qualify for the robes of righteousness that clothe celestial beings. Thus in the revealed prayer, offered at the dedication of the Kirtland Temple, the Prophet pleaded with the Lord for the saints: "That our garments may be pure, that we may be clothed upon with robes of righteousness, with palms in our hands, and crowns of glory upon our heads, and reap eternal joy for all our sufferings." (D. & C. 109:76.)

Walk with me in white] 'Live with me in glory and be "even as I am." ' (3 Ne. 28:10.)

5. He that overcometh] See Rev. 2:1-7.

The book of life] "In a literal sense, the book of life, or Lamb's book of Life, is the record kept in heaven which contains the names of the faithful and an account of their righteous covenants and deeds. (D. & C. 128:6-7; Ps. 69:28; Rev. 3:5; 21:27.) The book of life is the book containing the names of those who shall inherit eternal life; it is the book of eternal life. (Dan. 12:1-4; Heb. 12:23; D. & C. 76:68; 132:19.) It is 'the book of the names of the sanctified, even them of the celestial world.' (D. & C. 88:2.) Names of faithful saints are recorded in the book of life while they are yet in mortality. (Luke 10:20; Philip. 4:3; *Teachings*, p. 9.) But those names are blotted out in the event of wickedness. (Rev. 13:8; 17:8; 22:19.)" (*Mormon Doctrine*, 2nd ed., p. 97.)

6. He that hath an ear, let him hear] See Rev. 2:1-7.

Unto the churches] The message is for all saints and all congregations everywhere in all ages. The faithful saints who defile not their garments shall be clothed in white raiment, in celestial glory, where their names are recorded in the Lamb's Book of Life, the book of the names of those who gain eternal life.

OVERCOME AND GAIN GODHOOD

REVELATION 3:7-13.

7 And to the angel of the church in Philadelphia write; These things saith he that is holy, he that is true, he that hath the key of David, he that openeth, and no man shutteth; and shutteth, and no man openeth;

8 I know thy works: behold, I have set before thee an open door, and no man can shut it: for thou hast a little strength, and hast kept my word, and hast not denied my name.

9 Behold, I will make them of the synagogue of Satan, which say they are Jews, and are not, but do lie; behold, I will make them to come and worship before thy feet, and to know that I have loved thee.

10 Because thou hast kept the word of my patience, I also will keep thee from the hour of temptation, which shall come upon all the world, to try them that dwell upon the earth.

11 Behold, I come quickly: hold that fast which thou hast, that no man take thy crown.

12 Him that overcometh will I make a pillar in the temple of my God, and he shall go no more out: and I will write upon him the name of my God, and the name of the city of my God, *which is* new Jerusalem, which cometh down out of heaven from my God: and *I will write upon him* my new name.

13 He that hath an ear, let him hear what the Spirit saith unto the churches.

I.V. REVELATION 3:7.

7 And to the **servant** of the church in Philadelphia write; These things saith he that is holy, he that is true, he that hath the key of David, he that openeth, and no man shutteth; and shutteth, and no man openeth;

7. The angel [I. V. servant] of the church] The presiding officer of the Church in Philadelphia.

He that is holy] "The Lord, the Holy One of Israel." (Isa. 10:20.) "Ye shall be holy: for I the Lord your God am holy." (Lev. 19:2.) Thus, Christ is the God of Israel, the God of the Old Testament.

The key of David] "From the day of Adam the term *key* has been used by inspired writers as a symbol of power and authority. Keys are the right of presidency, and the one holding them holds the reigns of government within the field and sphere of his appointment. In ancient Israel, David was a man of blood and battle whose word was law and whose very name was also a symbol of power and authority. Accordingly, when Isaiah sought to convey a realization of the supreme, directive control and power resident in our Lord, the Son of David, he spoke these words in the Lord's name: 'And the key of the house of David will I lay upon his shoulder; so he shall open, and none shall shut; and he shall shut, and none shall open.' (Isa. 22:22.) . . . Thus, the key of David is the absolute power resident in Christ whereby his will is expressed in all things both temporal and spiritual." (*Mormon Doctrine*, 2nd ed., p. 409.)

He that openeth, and no man shutteth] For instance: Christ opens the door to the preaching of his gospel and no man can stop the work. "And the voice of warning shall be unto all people, by the mouths of my disciples, whom I have chosen in these last days. And they shall go forth and none shall stay them, for I the Lord have commanded them." (D. & C. 1:4-5.)

And shutteth, and no man openeth] For instance: Our Lord into whose hands the Father has given all judgment (John 5:22), shall cast the wicked, the sons of perdition, into that prison whose doors shall never open again. (D. & C. 29:27-29; 76:44-48.)

8. I know thy works] See Rev. 2:1-7.

I have set before thee an open door] 'I have opened the door so that you may enter my kingdom; no man can shut it against you because you have kept my commandments.'

9. The synagogue of Satan] The Jewish congregations in Philadelphia which rejected Christ and fought the saints were part of the Church of the Devil. See Rev. 17:1-18.

I will make them to come and worship before thy feet] Those who reject the gospel and oppose the saints of God shall some day worship before them and know they were loved and chosen of the Lord. The place and lot of rebellious persons in the realms ahead shall be "to minister for those who are worthy of a far more, and an exceeding, and an eternal weight of glory." (D. & C. 132:16.)

10. Through faith the saints ofttimes escape the trials and desolations that pass upon the wicked and ungodly.

11. I come quickly] See Rev. 22:6-16.

12. Him that overcometh] See Rev. 2:1-7.

A pillar in the temple of my God] 'A personage of stature and eminence in the celestial kingdom of God.' Heaven itself, the house and abode of God, is a temple, the supreme and chief temple of eternity. See Rev. 21:9-27.

He shall go no more out] Saved persons remain in their exalted state forever. They cannot fall, but dwell forever in the celestial city, to go out never more at all. Their lot is "to sit down" in the kingdom of heaven "with Abraham, and Isaac, and with Jacob, and with all our holy fathers, to go no more out." (Hela. 3:30.) Their inheritance is in that realm from which no friend departs and into which no enemy enters. They are as God, and God is as he is from everlasting to everlasting.

I will write upon him the name of my God] God's name is God. To have his name written on a person is to identify that person as a god. How can it be said more plainly? Those who gain eternal life become gods! Their inheritance is both a fulness of the glory of the Father and "a continuation of the seed forever and ever. Then shall they be gods, because they have no end; therefore shall they be from everlasting to everlasting, because they continue; then shall they be above all, because all things are subject unto them. Then shall they be gods, because they have all power, and the angels are subject unto them." (D. & C. 132:19-20.)

In this great King Follett Sermon, the Prophet Joseph Smith taught this doctrine in these words: "Here, then, is eternal life — to know the only wise and true God; and you have got to learn how to be Gods yourselves, and to be kings and priests to God, the same as all Gods have done before you, namely, by going from one small degree to another, and from a small capacity to a great one; from grace to grace, from exaltation to exaltation, until you attain to the resurrection of the dead and are able to dwell in everlasting burnings, and to sit in glory, as do those who sit enthroned in everlasting power . . . . What is it? To inherit the same power, the same glory and the same exaltation, until you arrive at the station of a God, and ascend the throne of eternal power, the same as those who have gone before." (*Teachings*, pp. 346-347.)

The city of my God] See Rev. 21:9-27.

My new name] See Rev. 19:11-16.

13. He that hath an ear, let him hear] See Rev. 2:1-7.

Unto the churches] This message is for all saints and all congregations everywhere in all ages. The faithful saints who gain eternal life shall reign forever in celestial glory, in the celestial city, as gods, having all power and being like their Eternal Father.

OVERCOME AND SIT ON GOD'S THRONE

REVELATION 3:14-22.

14 And unto the angel of the church of the Laodiceans write; These things saith the Amen, the faithful and true witness, the beginning of the creation of God;

15 I know thy works, that thou art neither cold nor hot: I would thou wert cold or hot.

16 So then because thou art lukewarm, and neither cold nor hot, I will spue thee out of my mouth.

17 Because thou sayest, I am rich, and increased with goods, and have need of nothing; and knowest not that thou art wretched, and miserable, and poor, and blind, and naked:

18 I counsel thee to buy of me gold tried in the fire, that thou mayest be rich; and white raiment, that thou mayest be clothed, and *that* the shame of thy nakedness do not appear; and anoint thine eyes with eyesalve, that thou mayest see.

19 As many as I love, I rebuke and chasten: be zealous therefore, and repent.

20 Behold, I stand at the door and knock: if any man hear my voice, and open the door, I will come in to him, and will sup with him, and he with me.

21 To him that overcometh will I grant to sit with me in my throne, even as I also overcame, and am set down with my Father in his throne.

22 He that hath an ear, let him hear what the Spirit saith unto the churches.

I.V. REVELATION 3:14.

14 And unto the **servant** of the church of the Laodiceans write; These things saith the Amen, the faithful and true witness, the beginning of the creation of God;

14. The angel [I. V. servant] of the church] The presiding officer of the Church in Laodicea.

The Amen] Christ is the Truth, "the God of truth" (Isa. 65:16); that is, he is the Amen, the God of Amen — titles signifying "that it is in and through him that the seal of divine affirmation is placed on all the promises of the Father." (*Mormon Doctrine*, 2nd ed., p. 32.) His word is absolute; his promises are sure; when he speaks, all controversy ends; it is amen, or so be it, to whatever is involved.

The faithful and true witness] Our Lord is a witness; he testifies of the truth; his voice is the voice of testimony — thus setting the perfect example for all his ministers. See *Commentary I*, pp. 197-200; *Commentary II*, pp. 102-104.

The beginning of the creation of God] "The firstborn of every creature" (Col. 1:15), the first of all the spirit progeny of Him who could not be a Father unless he had children. "I was in the beginning with the Father, and am the Firstborn." (D. & C. 93:21.)

15. I know thy works] See Rev. 2:1-7.

Lukewarm] Good, upright, decent members of the Church who nonetheless do not put first in their lives the things of God's earthly kingdom. They have testimonies; they know the work is true; but they specialize, as it were, in the social gospel; that is, in that portion of the truth which seems to bless others on pretty much the same basis as people are bettered by any good concepts in any church. Their interests are largely centered in temporal things, in making a living, in the things of this world. They are not wicked and ungodly in the sense of being carnal and evil. But they are not devoting their energies to the spread of truth and the perfecting of the lives of their brethren. They are probably part tithepayers, and they likely go to sacrament meeting and perform church service when it is convenient. They seek the honors of men and the wealth of the world with more zeal than they do the honors of God and the riches of eternity. They are lukewarm and their souls will not be saved. "These are they who are not valiant in the testimony of Jesus; wherefore, they obtain not the crown over the kingdom of our God." (D. & C. 76:79.)

17. 'Lukewarm church members say: "We have testimonies, we have received the gospel, we belong to the Church; surely we shall be saved along with all the rest; what more do we need?" But the fact is (and they know it not!) they are no better off spiritually than many nonmembers of the Church; they are still poor in the things of the Spirit, are blind to the real blessings of the gospel, and have not in fact put on the robes of righteousness.'

Temporal riches] See Jas. 5:1-6.

18. I counsel thee] What counsel is like unto the counsel of God? The Lord Jehovah, now the Risen Christ, whose very name is Wonderful Counsellor (Isa. 9:6), issues that counsel which excels in importance all other: 'Come unto me and be saved!'

Buy of me] "Salvation is free" (2 Ne. 2:4), but it must also be purchased; and the price is obedience to the laws and ordinances of the gospel. Eternal life is available freely, "without money and without price" (Isa. 55:1; 2 Ne. 9:50), but it is gained only by those who buy it at the storehouse of the Great God who pleads with men to purchase his priceless possession.

Gold tried in the fire] Salvation, gained by withstanding the fiery trials of mortality; an inheritance in that city whose streets are paved with "pure gold." (Rev. 21:21.)

That thou mayest be rich] "Behold, he that hath eternal life is rich." (D. & C. 6:7.)

White raiment] The garments of the holy priesthood; the robes of righteousness; the clothing worn by exalted beings. Of the appearance of Moroni to him, the Prophet said: "He had on a loose robe of most exquisite whiteness. It was a whiteness beyond anything earthly I had ever seen; nor do I believe that any earthly thing could be made to appear so exceedingly white and brilliant." (Jos. Smith 2:31.)

Anoint thine eyes with eyesalve] 'Receive the companionship of the Holy Spirit so that your spiritual eyes shall be opened and your whole body filled with light.' (Matt. 6:22.) "The Holy Spirit's unction, like the ancient eyesalve's, first smarts with conviction of sin, then heals." (*Jamieson*, p. 562.)

19. See Heb. 12:1-8.

20. 'The gospel is offered to all men; those who receive it find themselves on terms of friendly intimacy with Him whose saving truth it is.'

21. To him that overcometh] See Rev. 2:1-7.

Sit with me in my throne] In conversation with Deity, Enoch said: "Thou hast made me, and given unto me a right to thy throne." (Moses 7:59.) Thus: "Ye shall be even as I am." (3 Ne. 28:10.) 'Ye shall have eternal life; ye shall have exaltation; ye shall be gods; ye shall rule and reign forever on a heavenly throne.'

I . . . am set down with my Father in his throne] "I am even as the Father." (3 Ne. 28:10.) Speaking of those who are "heirs of God and joint-heirs with Jesus Christ," the Prophet asked, "What is it?" and then answered: "To inherit the same power, the same glory and the same exaltation, until you arrive at the station of a God, and ascend the throne of eternal power, the same as those who have gone before. What did Jesus do? Why; I do the things I saw my Father do when worlds came rolling into existence. My Father worked out his kingdom with fear and trembling, and I must do the same; and when I get my kingdom, I shall present it to my Father, so that he may obtain kingdom upon kingdom, and it will exalt him in glory. He will then take a higher exaltation, and I will take his place, and thereby become exalted myself. So that Jesus treads in the tracks of his Father, and inherits what God did before; and God is thus glorified and exalted in the salvation and exaltation of all his children. It is plain beyond disputation, and you thus learn some of the first principles of the gospel." (*Teachings*, pp. 347-348.) See *Commentary II*, pp. 530-533.

22. He that hath an ear, let him hear] See Rev. 2:1-7.

Unto the churches] This message is for all saints and all congregations everywhere in all ages. The faithful saints who gain eternal life shall sit with Christ on his throne, because they have like glory and exaltation with him, even as he sits on the throne of his Father, because the Father and the Son both possess the fulness of the glory of the Father and have all power, all might, and all dominion forever.

ALL CREATED THINGS WORSHIP THE LORD

REVELATION 4:1-11.

1 After this I looked, and, behold, a door *was* opened in heaven: and the first voice which I heard *was* as it were of a trumpet talking with me; which said, Come up hither, and I will show thee things which must be hereafter.

2 And immediately I was in the spirit: and, behold, a throne was set in heaven, and *one* sat on the throne.

3 And he that sat was to look upon like a jasper and a sardine stone: and *there was* a rainbow round about the throne, in sight like unto an emerald.

4 And round about the throne *were* four and twenty seats: and upon the seats I saw four and twenty elders sitting, clothed in white raiment; and they had on their heads crowns of gold.

5 And out of the throne proceeded lightnings and thunderings and voices: and *there were* seven lamps of fire burning before the throne, which are the seven Spirits of God.

6 And before the throne *there was* a sea of glass like unto crystal: and in the midst of the throne, and round about the throne, *were* four beasts full of eyes before and behind.

7 And the first beast *was* like a lion, and the second beast like a calf, and the third beast had a face as a man, and the fourth beast *was* like a flying eagle.

8 And the four beasts had each of them six wings about *him;* and *they were* full of eyes within: and they rest not day and night, saying, Holy, holy, holy, Lord God Almighty, which was, and is, and is to come.

9 And when those beasts give glory and honour and thanks to him that sat on the throne, who liveth for ever and ever,

10 The four and twenty elders fall down before him that sat on the throne, and worship him that liveth for ever and ever, and cast their crowns before the throne, saying,

11 Thou art worthy, O Lord, to receive glory and honour and power: for thou hast created all things, and for thy pleasure they are and were created.

I.V. REVELATION 4:1, 3-6.

1 After this I looked, and behold, a door was opened **into** heaven; and the first voice which I heard was as it were of a trumpet talking with me; which said, Come

up hither, and I will show thee things which must be hereafter.

3 And he that sat **there** was to look upon like a jasper and a sardine-stone; and there was a rainbow round about the throne, in sight like unto an emerald.

4 And **in the midst** of the throne were four and twenty seats; and upon the seats I saw four and twenty elders sitting, clothed in white raiment, and they had on their heads crowns **like** gold.

5 And out of the throne proceeded lightnings and thunderings and voices; and there were seven lamps of fire burning before the throne, which are the seven **servants** of God.

6 And before the throne there was a sea of glass like unto crystal; and in the midst of the throne **were the four and twenty elders;** and round about the throne, were four beasts full of eyes before and behind.

I. V. 1. A door was opened into heaven] "The heavens were opened." (Ezek. 1:1.) John on earth was permitted to gaze into heaven.

K. J. 1. The first voice which I heard] The voice of the angel (Rev. 1:1), upon whom the Lord had placed his own name, and who was thus commanded to speak in the first person as though he were the Son of God himself. See Rev. 19:9b-10.

Things which must be hereafter] See Rev. 1:1-6.

2. One sat on the throne] God the Eternal Father, the Almighty Elohim.

3. In striving to record for mortal comprehension the grandeur, glory, and beauty of the Almighty of Almighties, John likens his appearance to precious and semi-precious stones. The jasper mentioned is believed by commentators to be a diamond.

A rainbow round about the throne] Encircling the throne. (The author, flying above clouds and storm, has seen in the mists and clouds below, a rainbow forming a perfect circle.) Of the "visions of God" which he saw, Ezekiel wrote: "As the appearance of the bow that is in the cloud in the day of rain, so was the appearance of the brightness round about. This was the appearance of the likeness of the glory of the Lord." (Ezek. 1:28.)

In seeking to describe the splendor of a similar scene, the Prophet Joseph Smith said: "The heavens were opened upon us, and I beheld the celestial kingdom of God, and the glory thereof, whether in the body or out I cannot tell. I saw the transcendent beauty of the gate through which the heirs of that kingdom will enter, which was like unto circling flames of fire; also the blazing throne of God, whereon was seated the Father and the Son. I saw the beautiful streets of that kingdom, which had the appearance of being paved with gold." (*Teachings*, p. 107.)

I. V. 4. In the midst of the throne were four and twenty seats] That is, those who sat thereon were sitting with God on his throne, or in other words, having eternal life they had become as he is. See Rev. 3:14-22.

K. J. 4. Four and twenty elders] "Q. What are we to understand by the four and twenty elders, spoken of by John? A. We are to understand that these elders whom John saw, were elders who had been faithful in the work of the ministry and were dead; who belonged to the seven churches, and were then in the paradise of God." (D. & C. 77:5.) Thus John is seeing what is to be in the future; he is seeing certain elders in celestial splendor who at that time were in their disembodied state in paradise awaiting the day of their resurrection and the receipt of eternal life. In principle it is the same as when Joseph Smith, on January 21, 1836, saw his father and mother — who were then still living in mortality — in the celestial kingdom of heaven. (*Teachings*, p. 107.)

It is worthy of note that these exalted persons who are sitting with God on his throne are elders: not seventies, not high priests, not partriarchs, not apostles, but elders — than which there is no more important priesthood in God's earthly kingdom. Indeed, every elder who magnifies his calling as an elder has the immutable promise of the Father, guaranteed by his personal oath, that he shall gain all that the Father hath, which is eternal life, which is godhood, which is to sit with him on his throne. (D. & C. 84:33-41.)

5. Out of the throne proceeded lightnings and thunderings and voices] How can mortal prophets find language to unveil to the view of their fellow mortals the splendor and transcendent beauty of that eternal world of celestial might and glory? They speak of rainbows and jewels, of circling flames of fires, of burning coals of fire with lightning flashing forth therefrom; they tell of thunders and voices, of the sound of the rushing of many waters, and of majestic displays of might and beauty — all in an attempt to record in mortal words that which can be seen and known only by the power of the Spirit. (Ezek. 1 and 10; Isa. 6.) But the Lord be praised that they have made such attempts so that those who have not seen and heard may gain some meager knowledge of those things hidden behind the windows of heaven.

I. V. 5. The seven servants of God] The presiding officers of each of the seven churches in Asia, to whom the counsel in chapters 3 and 4 was directed, would in due course — for the vision is of the future — join the celestial hosts in glorious exaltation.

K. J. 6. A sea of glass like unto crystal] "Q. What is the sea of glass spoken of by John, 4th chapter, and 6th verse of the Revelation? A. It is the earth, in its sanctified, immortal, and eternal state." (D. & C. 77:1.) See Rev. 21:9-27.

Four beasts] "Q. What are we to understand by the four beasts, spoken of in the same verse? A. They are figurative expressions, used by the Revelator, John, in describing heaven, the paradise of God, the happiness of man, and of beasts, and of creeping things, and of the fowls of the air; that which is spiritual being in the likeness of that which is temporal; and that which is temporal in the likeness of that which is spiritual; the spirit of man in the likeness of his person, as also the spirit of the beast, and every other creature which God has created. Q. Are the four beasts limited to individual beasts, or do they represent classes or orders? A. They are limited to four individual beasts, which were shown to John, to represent the glory of the classes of beings in their destined order or sphere of creation, in the enjoyment of their eternal felicity." (D. & C. 77:2-3.)

In a great sermon about the resurrection and salvation of all forms of life, the Prophet expanded upon these inspired words from Section 77, saying among other things:

"When God made use of the figure of a beast in visions to the prophets he did it to represent those kingdoms which had degenerated and become corrupt, savage and beast-like in their dispositions, even the degenerate kingdoms of the wicked world; but he never made use of the figure of a beast nor any of the brute kind to represent his kingdom."

Then he referred to a statement made by Daniel: "I came near unto one of them that stood by, and asked him the truth of all this." (Dan 7:16-17.)

Continuing his own explanations, the Prophet said: "The angel interpreted the vision to Daniel; but we find, by the interpretation that the figures of beasts had no allusion to the kingdom of God. You there see that the beasts are spoken of to represent the kingdoms of the world. . . .

"There is a grand difference and distinction between the visions and figures spoken of by the ancient prophets, and those spoken of in the revelations of John . . . .

"I am now going to take exceptions to the present translation of the Bible in relation to these matters. Our latitude and longitude can be determined in the original Hebrew with far greater accuracy than in the English version. There is a grand distinction between the actual meaning of the prophets and the present translation. The prophets do not declare that they saw a beast or beasts, but that they saw the image or figure of a beast. Daniel did not see an actual bear or a lion, but the images or figures of those beasts. The translation should have been rendered 'image' instead of 'beast,' in every instance where beasts are mentioned by the prophets. But John saw the actual beast in heaven, showing to John that beasts did actually exist there, and not to represent figures of things on the earth. When the prophets speak of seeing beasts in their visions, they mean that they saw the images, they being types to represent certain things. At the same time they received the interpretation as to what those images or types were designed to represent." (*Teachings*, pp. 289-291.)

6. Full of eyes before and behind] 8. The four beasts had each of them six wings] "Q. What are we to understand by the eyes and wings, which the beasts had? A. Their eyes are a representation of light and knowledge, that is, they are full of knowledge; and their wings are a representation of power, to move, to act, etc." (D. & C. 77:4.) Similar descriptions of the eyes and wings of beasts in heaven were given by Isaiah and Ezekiel. (Isa. 6:2-3; Ezek. 1:18; 10:12.)

7. In the "visions of God" which he saw, Ezekiel also spoke of four beasts who had the faces of a man, a lion, an ox (John says a calf), and an eagle. (Ezek. 1:10.) The presumption is that both prophets were seeing some of the same things.

8. Holy] The Lord our God—meaning either the Father or the Son, as the case may be—is holy. Here it is the Father to whom this salutation of praise is made. When Isaiah "saw also the Lord sitting upon a throne, high and lifted up," and heard the seraphims cry: "Holy, holy, holy, is the Lord of hosts: the whole earth is full of his glory" (Isa. 6:1-4), the Deity involved was the Lord Jehovah; and the words of the Psalmist in acclaiming, "The Lord reigneth" and "is holy" (Psalm 99), have application to both the Father and the Son.

Lord God Almighty, which was, and is, and is to come] Here and in Rev. 11:16-17 this praise is given to the Father; in Rev. 1:4 and 8 the same pronouncement is made relative to the Son.

9-11. See Rev. 5:1-14.

11. Why should all created things, whether men or beasts, give glory and honor to God? Joseph Smith said: "Everlasting covenant was made between three personages before the organization of this earth, and relates to their dispensation of things to men on the earth; these personages, according to Abraham's record, are called God the first, the Creator; God the second, the Redeemer; and God the third, the witness or Testator." (*Teachings*, p. 190.) Accordingly, we here find the four beasts and the four and twenty elders giving glory and honor to the Father—because he created them. Were it not for him, they would not be. And in Rev. 5:8-14, we shall find these same creatures, coupled with an innumerable host of others, giving glory to the Son—because he redeemed them. And were it not for the redemption, the whole purposes of creation would have faded away into nothingness; there would be neither immortality nor eternal life. On the same basis, we should rejoice in the mission of the Holy Ghost, the mission of revealing to men the truths of salvation and of sanctifying their souls when they conform to the revealed word — for without such revelation and sanctifying power there could be no salvation.

For thy pleasure they are and were created] The creative enterprises of Deity are past, present, and future; they go on everlastingly. But why? What is the purpose of creation? Speaking of man, of "the beasts of the field and the fowls of the air, and in fine, all things which are created," Lehi said: "There is a God, and he hath created all things, both the heavens and the earth, and all things that in them are, both things to act and things to be acted upon. And bring about his eternal purposes in the end of man." (2 Ne. 2:14-15.) That is, the purpose of creation is "to bring to pass the immortality and eternal life of man" (Moses 1:39), to say nothing of the salvation of worlds without number and of all created things that on them are. See Rev. 5:1-14. But in its fullest signification, the purpose of creation is to enable men to gain eternal life, so that they being thus glorified and having gained for themselves eternal kingdoms patterned after the kingdom of their Eternal Father, may present their kingdoms to him, "so that he may obtain kingdom upon kingdom, and it will exalt him in glory." (*Teachings*, pp. 347-348.)

Resurrection] See *Commentary II*, pp. 388-404.

Celestial earth] See Rev. 21:9-27.

"WORTHY IS THE LAMB"

REVELATION 5:1-14.

1 And I saw in the right hand of him that sat on the throne a book written within and on the backside, sealed with seven seals.

2 And I saw a strong angel proclaiming with a loud voice, Who is worthy to open the book, and to loose the seals thereof?

3 And no man in heaven, nor in earth, neither under the earth, was able to open the book, neither to look thereon.

4 And I wept much, because no man was found worthy to open and to read the book, neither to look thereon.

5 And one of the elders saith unto me, Weep not: behold, the Lion of the tribe of Juda, the Root of David, hath prevailed to open the book, and to loose the seven seals thereof.

6 And I beheld, and, lo, in the midst of the throne and of the four beasts, and in the midst of the elders, stood a Lamb as it had been slain, having seven horns and seven eyes, which are the seven Spirits of God sent forth into all the earth.

7 And he came and took the book out of the right hand of him that sat upon the throne.

8 And when he had taken the book, the four beasts and four *and* twenty elders fell down before the Lamb, having every one of them harps, and golden vials full of odours, which are the prayers of saints.

9 And they sung a new song, saying, Thou art worthy to take the book, and to open the seals thereof: for thou wast slain, and hast redeemed us to God by thy blood out of every kindred, and tongue, and people, and nation;

10 And hast made us unto our God kings and priests: and we shall reign on the earth.

11 And I beheld, and I heard the voice of many angels round about the throne and the beasts and the elders: and the number of them was ten thousand times ten thousand, and thousands of thousands;

12 Saying with a loud voice, Worthy is the Lamb that was slain to receive power, and riches, and wisdom, and strength, and honour, and glory, and blessing.

13 And every creature which is in heaven, and on the earth, and under the earth, and such as are in the sea, and all that are in them, heard I saying, Blessing, and honour, and glory, and power, *be* unto him that sitteth upon the throne, and unto the Lamb for ever and ever.

14 And the four beasts said, Amen. And the four *and* twenty elders fell down and worshipped him that liveth for ever and ever.

I.V. REVELATION 5:2, 6.

2 And I saw a strong angel, **and heard him** proclaiming with a loud voice, Who is worthy to open the book, and loose the seals thereof?

6 And I beheld, and, lo, in the midst of the throne and of the four beasts, and in the midst of the elders, stood a Lamb as it had been slain, having **twelve** horns and **twelve** eyes, which are the **twelve servants** of God, sent forth into all the earth.

1. Him that sat on the throne] God the Father, the Almighty Elohim.

A book written within and on the backside] A roll of a book, with writing on both sides. "Q. What are we to understand by the book which John saw, which was sealed on the back with seven seals? A. We are to understand that it contains the revealed will, mysteries, and works of God; the hidden things of his economy concerning this earth during the seven thousand years of its continuance, or its temporal existence." (D. & C. 77:6.)

Seven seals] "Q. What are we to understand by the seven seals with which it was sealed? A. We are to understand that the first seal contains the things of the first thousand years and the second also of the second thousand years, and so on until the seventh." (D. & C. 77:7.)

Shortly John is to see and make an extremely brief mention of some of the events which have and will transpire in the successive periods of one thousand years each. That there will be a day when the complete account is revealed for all to know appears from these words revealed to Joseph Smith: "And then shall the first angel again sound his trump in the ears of all living, and reveal the secret acts of men, and the mighty works of God in the first thousand years. And then shall the second angel sound his trump, and reveal the secret acts of men, and thoughts and intents of their hearts, and the mighty works of God in the second thousand years — And so on, until the seventh angel shall sound his trump." (D. & C. 88:108-110.)

2. A strong angel] As with men, so with angels, some are greater than others. There is rank and precedence, and there are varying degrees of power and might among God's ministers.

5. The lion of the tribe of Juda] "Christ is the Lion of the Tribe of Judah. (Rev. 5:5.) When Father Jacob gave Judah his patriarchal blessing, Judah was likened both to a lion's whelp and to an old lion and was promised that the sceptre should not depart from his descendants until the coming of Christ. (Gen. 49:8-12.) Accordingly, to denominate our Lord as the Lion of the Tribe of Judah is to point to his position as a descendant of Judah, to his membership in that tribe from which kings were chosen to reign, and also to show his status as the most pre-eminent of all that house, as the one who bore the banner of the tribe so to speak." (*Mormon Doctrine*, 2nd ed., p. 449.)

The Root of David] "Christ is the Root of David. (Rev. 5:5; 22:16.) This designation signifies that he who was the Son of David was also before David, was pre-eminent above him, and was the root or source from which the great king in Israel gained his kingdom and power." (*Mormon Doctrine*, 2nd ed., p. 657.)

6. A Lamb as it had been slain] "Christ is 'the Lamb of God, which taketh away the sin of the world.' (John 1:29, 36; D. & C. 76:85; 88:106; 1 Ne. 13.) He is 'the Lamb slain from the foundation of the world' (Rev. 13:8), the 'lamb without blemish and without spot: Who verily was foreordained before the foundation of the world' (1 Pet. 1:19) to be the Savior and Redeemer, the One who would work out the infinite and eternal atonement. As a Lamb, he was sacrificed for men, and salvation comes because of the shedding of his blood. (Mosiah 3:18.) Those who gain salvation are the ones who 'have washed their robes, and made them white in the blood of the Lamb.' (Rev. 7:14; 12:11; 1 Ne. 12:11; Alma 13:11; 34:36; 3 Ne. 27:19; Morm. 9:6; Ether 13:10-11.)" (*Mormon Doctrine*, 2nd ed., p. 429.) See Heb. 10:1-18.

I. V. 6. Twelve horns . . . twelve eyes . . . twelve servants] Clearly the allusion here is to the Twelve Apostles of the Lamb who are sent forth "into all the earth" as special witnesses of his name and as the chief administrators of his earthly kingdom.

K. J. 8. Fell down before the Lamb] 12. Worthy is the Lamb] 13. Him that sitteth upon the throne, and unto the Lamb] 14. Worshipped him that liveth for ever and ever] True saints worship the Father, in the name of the Son, by the power of the Spirit. The Father is the object and center of all true devotions; it is to him that we pray; he is not only our God, but the God of the Son (John 20:17) and will be so forever. (D. & C. 88:75.) And yet there are no words to describe, no language to use, no rhetoric to employ, which can begin to praise and glorify the Son for all that he has done for us. The words here sung by the myriads of myriads who praise his holy name perhaps come as close as anything in holy writ.

Of him whom the Father "hath anointed . . . with the oil of gladness" above his fellows, the command is: "He is thy Lord; and worship thou him." (Psalm 45:7-11.) Perhaps Nephi stated this same truth as succinctly and persuasively as it has ever been done in these words: "Believe in Christ, and deny him not; and Christ is the Holy One of Israel; wherefore ye must bow down before him, and worship him with all your might, mind, and strength, and your whole soul; and if ye do this ye shall in nowise be cast out." (2 Ne. 25:29.) See *Commentary II*, pp. 533-534.

9. Thou . . . hast redeemed us] "Redemption is of two kinds: conditional and unconditional. Conditional redemption is synonymous with exaltation or eternal life. It comes by the grace of God coupled with good works and includes redemption from the effects of both the temporal and spiritual fall. Those so redeemed become sons and daughters in the Lord's kingdom and inherit all things And this is the chief sense in which the term redemption is used in the scriptures. (*Doctrines of Salvation*, vol. 2, pp. 9-13.)

"Thus: Lehi taught that 'redemption cometh in and through the Holy Messiah, . . . unto all those who have a broken heart and a contrite spirit.' (2 Ne. 2:6-7.) Alma said that Christ 'cometh to redeem those who will be baptized unto repentance, through faith on his name.' (Alma 9:27.) Nephi explained that though 'the Lord surely should come to redeem his people,' yet 'he should not come to redeem them in their sins, but to redeem them from their sins. And he hath power given unto him from the Father to redeem them from their sins because of repentance; therefore he hath sent his angels to declare the tidings of the conditions of repentance, which bringeth unto the power of the Redeemer, unto the salvation of their souls.' (Hela. 5:10-11.) Mormon said that the redeemed, being 'found guiltless' would 'sing ceaseless praises with the choirs above.' (Morm. 7:7.) Abinadi explained that those who 'dwell with God . . . have eternal life, being redeemed by the Lord.' (Mosiah 15:21-25.)

"The Lord says that the unbelieving 'cannot be redeemed from their spiritual fall, because they repent not' (D. & C. 29:42-45), and the Brother of Jared, because of his righteousness, was told by the Lord: 'Ye are redeemed from the fall; therefore ye are brought back into my presence; therefore I show myself unto you. Behold, I am he who was prepared from the foundation of the world to redeem my people. Behold, I am Jesus Christ.' (Ether 3:13-14.) Full redemption is a blessing reserved for the saints. (D. & C. 35:26; 45:46; 133:52.)

"Unconditional redemption is redemption from the effects of the temporal but not the spiritual fall. It consists in obtaining the free gift of immortality but being denied 'the eternal life which God giveth unto all the obedient.' (Moses 5:11.) It comes by grace alone without works. Speaking in this sense, the Lord says, 'The resurrection from the dead is the redemption of the soul.' (D. & C. 88:14-17, 99; Alma 12:25; Morm. 9:12-14.) It is in this sense that the Lord redeems or 'saves all the works of his hands, except those sons of perdition who deny the Son after the Father has revealed him.' (D. & C. 76:43.)" (*Mormon Doctrine*, 2nd ed., pp. 623-624.)

Redeemed . . . out of every kindred, and tongue, and people, and nation] How universal is the appeal of eternal truth! "There is one God and one Shepherd over all the earth." (1 Ne. 13:41.) Not only shall the gospel be preached "to every nation, and kindred, and tongue, and people" (Rev. 14:6), but converts shall be made among them all; and these newborn saints, alive in Christ, shall advance and progress in spiritual things until they qualify, through the ordinances of the house of the Lord, to rule and reign as kings and priests with Christ on earth a thousand years. When the Lord comes, he shall find "the saints of God . . . upon all the face of the earth"; they shall be "among all nations, kindreds, tongues, and people" (1 Ne. 14:11-14) — all of which indicates that there is yet much to be done to spread truth and righteousness over the earth before the coming of the Son of Man.

10. King and priests] See Rev. 1:1-6.

We shall reign on the earth] See Rev. 20:4-6.

11-14. In his sermon about the resurrection and salvation of all forms of life the Prophet said: "John saw curious looking beasts in heaven; he saw every creature that was in heaven—all the beasts, fowls and fish in heaven—actually there, giving glory to God. How do you prove it?" He then quoted Rev. 5:13, and continued:

"I suppose John saw beings there of a thousand forms, that had been saved from ten thousand times ten thousand earths like this—strange beasts of which we have no conception: all might be seen in heaven. The grand secret was to show John what there was in heaven. John learned that God glorified himself by saving all that his hands had made, whether beasts, fowls, fishes or men; and he will glorify himself with them.

"Says one, 'I cannot believe in the salvation of beasts.' Any man who would tell you that this could not be, would tell you that the revelations are not true. John heard the words of the beasts giving glory to God, and understood them. God who made the beasts could understand every language spoken by them. The four beasts were four of the most noble animals that had filled the measure of their creation, and had been saved from other worlds, because they were perfect; they were like angels in their sphere. We are not told where they came from, and I do not know; but they were seen and heard by John praising and glorifying God." (*Teachings*, pp. 291-292.)

Ten thousand times ten thousand, and thousands of thousands] "Lord, are there few that be saved" or many (Luke 13:23), is the query in the hearts of many disciples. The answer: Few as compared to the hosts of men in our present worldly society (Matt. 7:13-14), but many when all who so obtain are counted together. Here John sees 100,000,000, plus thousands of thousands. Later he shall see "a great multitude [of saved persons], which no man could number." (Rev. 7:9.) The expansion of world population being what it is, we can suppose that the billions who live on earth during the Millennium—and who "grow up without sin unto salvation' (D. & C. 45:58)—shall far exceed in number the total hosts of men who have lived during the preceding six thousand years. Truly, in the aggregate, there are many who shall be saved!

ENOCH MINISTERS DURING FIRST SEAL

REVELATION 6:1-2.

1 And I saw when the Lamb opened one of the seals, and I heard, as it were the noise of thunder, one of the four beasts saying, Come and see.

2 And I saw, and behold a white horse: and he that sat on him had a bow; and a crown was given unto him: and he went forth conquering, and to conquer.

I.V. REVELATION 6:1.

1 And I saw when the Lamb opened one of the seals, **one of the four beasts,** and I heard, as it were, the noise of thunder, saying, Come and see.

When the first seal was opened, what was shown forth of "the revealed will, mysteries, and works of God — the hidden things of his economy concerning this earth" during the first one thousand years of "its temporal existence"? (D. & C. 77:6.)

The period involved is from 4000 B. C. to 3000 B. C. It extends from (or rather, after) the fall of Adam, which according to Ussher's chronology was 4004 B.C., to shortly after the translation of Enoch and his city in 3017 B.C.

What are the events pertaining to the Lord's work on earth which occurred in that period of time and which we might expect to find recorded in the book held "in the right hand of him that sat on the throne." (Rev. 5:1.)

Such of these events as John saw pertained to someone on a white horse (the emblem of victory); who had a bow (weapons of war); wore a crown (the garland or wreath of a conqueror); and who went forth conquering and to conquer (that is, was victorious in war).

Insofar as we know, the actual events of this first millennium-long period included the following:

1. The creation of Adam and Eve; the fall of man, of the earth, and of all forms of life; and the beginning of the peopling of the earth — all of which, however, strictly and properly speaking, preceded the actual period covered by the seal and so may be

excluded from our considerations. As set forth in Section 77, the period covered was part of the earth's "temporal existence" (Verse 5), that is the earth's existence after the edenic or paradisiacal state, its existence after the fall.

2. The revelation of the gospel to Adam and his posterity and the setting up of the initial earthly kingdom of God among men.

3. The murder of Abel, the cursing of Cain, and the beginning of apostasy by many of the sons and daughters of the first man.

4. The populating of the earth and the development of nations, kingdoms, and governments.

5. And finally, the temporal and spiritual ministry of Enoch, which included prophecies, visions, wars of a kind and nature never since duplicated, and the final translation and taking up into heaven of the whole city of Zion.

From the foregoing, excluding, as we necessarily must, the events surrounding the creation and the fall, it is clear that the most transcendent happenings involved Enoch and his ministry. And it is interesting to note that what John saw was not the establishment of Zion and its removal to heavenly spheres, but the unparalleled wars in which Enoch, as a general over the armies of the saints, "went forth conquering and to conquer." Of these wars our revelations recite:

"And so great was the faith of Enoch, that he led the people of God, and their enemies came to battle against them; and he spake the word of the Lord, and the earth trembled, and the mountains fled, even according to his command; and the rivers of water were turned out of their course; and the roar of the lions was heard out of the wilderness; and all nations feared greatly, so powerful was the word of Enoch, and so great was the power of the language which God had given him. There also came up a land out of the depth of the sea, and so great was the fear of the enemies of the people of God, that they fled and stood afar off and went upon the land which came up out of the depth of the sea. And the giants of the land, also, stood afar off; and there went forth a curse upon all people that fought against God; And from that time forth there were wars and bloodshed among them; but the Lord came and dwelt with his people, and they dwelt in righteousness. The fear of the Lord was upon all nations, so great was the glory of the Lord, which was upon his people." (Moses 7:13-17.)

Truly, never was there a ministry such as Enoch's, and never a conqueror and general who was his equal! How appropriate that he should ride the white horse of victory in John's apocalyptic vision!

WAR RAGETH DURING SECOND SEAL

REVELATION 6:3-4.

3 And when he had opened the second seal, I heard the second beast say, Come and see.

4 And there went out another horse *that was* red: and *power* was given to him that sat thereon to take peace from the earth, and that they should kill one another: and there was given unto him a great sword.

Who rode the red horse, the red horse of war and bloodshed and a sword, during the second seal? Perhaps it was the devil himself, for surely that was the great day of his power, a day of such gross wickedness that every living soul (save eight only) was found worthy of death by drowning, which wickedness caused the Lord God of Heaven to bring in the floods upon them.

Or if it was not Lucifer, perhaps it was a man of blood, or a person representing many murdering warriors, of whom we have no record. Suffice it to say that the era from 3000 B.C. to 2000 B.C., was one of war and destruction, these being the favorite weapons of Satan for creating those social conditions in which men lose their souls.

Of the wickedness and abominations of Noah's day, the revealed word says: "And God saw that the wickedness of men had become great in the earth; and every man was lifted up in the imagination of the thoughts of his heart, being only evil continually. . . . The earth was corrupt before God, and it was filled with violence. And God looked upon the earth, and, behold, it was corrupt, for all flesh had corrupted its way upon the earth." (Moses 8:22, 28-29.)

In our day peace has been "taken from the earth and the devil" has "power over his own dominion" (D. & C. 1:35), with the result that soon the vineyard shall be cleansed by fire. Need we suppose it was any different in Noah's day, when the devil raging in the hearts of men, caused the Lord in his anger to cleanse the vineyard with water? And so he did in 2348 B.C.

FAMINE STALKS THE EARTH DURING THIRD SEAL

REVELATION 6:5-6.

5 And when he had opened the third seal, I heard the third beast say, Come and see. And I beheld, and lo a black horse; and he that sat on him had a pair of balances in his hand.

6 And I heard a voice in the midst of the four beasts say, A measure of wheat for a penny, and three measures of barley for a penny; and *see* thou hurt not the oil and the wine.

As famine follows the sword, so the pangs of hunger gnawed in the bellies of the Lord's people during the third seal. From 2000 B. C. to 1000 B. C., as never in any other age of the earth's history, the black horse of hunger influenced the whole history of God's dealings with his people.

In the beginning years of this seal, the famine in Ur of the Chaldees was so severe that Abraham's brother, Haran, starved to death, while the father of the faithful was commanded by God to take his family to Canaan. (Abra. 1:29-30; 2:15.) Of his struggle to gain sufficient food to keep alive, Abraham said: "Now I, Abraham, built an altar in the land of Jershon, and made an offering unto the Lord, and prayed that the famine might be turned away from my father's house, that they might not perish." Later he even had to leave Canaan in search of food. "And I, Abraham, journeyed, going on still towards the south; and there was a continuation of a famine in the land; and I, Abraham, concluded to go down into Egypt, to sojourn there, for the famine became very grievous." (Abra. 2:17, 21.)

This search for sustenance was yet burdening the Lord's people in the days of Jacob, who sent his sons to Egypt to buy corn from the granaries of Joseph his son. In that day "the famine was over all the face of the earth," and it was only through divine intervention that Jacob and the beginning members of the house of Israel were saved from the fate of Haran. (Gen. 41:53-57; 42; 43; and 44.) And in the days of their sojourn in the wilderness, the millions of Jacob's seed who had followed Moses out of Egyptian bondage, lest they perish for want of bread, were fed for forty years with manna from heaven. (Ex. 16.)

Abraham's tenure in mortality was from 1996 to 1822 B. C.; the seven years of famine foretold in Pharaoh's dream commenced in 1709 B. C.; and the exodus from Egypt was in 1491 B. C. Truly the third seal was a millennium in which hunger among men affected the whole course of God's dealings with his people.

5. A pair of balances] "The symbol of scarcity of provisions, the bread being doled out by weight." (*Jamieson*, p. 568.)

6. A measure of wheat] About two pints.

A penny] A day's wages. (Matt. 20:2.)

Three measures of barley for a penny] "The cheaper and less nutritious grain, bought by the laborer who could not buy enough wheat for his family with his day's wages." (*Jamieson*, p. 568.)

Hurt not the oil and the wine] Preserve enough of the fruit of the earth so that man shall not utterly perish and cease to be.

DEATH, HELL, WAR, FAMINE PREVAIL DURING FOURTH SEAL

REVELATION 6:7-8.

7 And when he had opened the fourth seal, I heard the voice of the fourth beast say, Come and see.

8 And I looked, and beheld a pale horse: and his name that sat on him was Death, and Hell followed with him. And power was given unto them over the fourth part of the earth, to kill with sword, and with hunger, and with death, and with the beasts of the earth.

DEATH, HELL, WAR, FAMINE PREVAIL IN FOURTH SEAL

During the fourth seal, from 1000 B. C. to the coming of our Lord, death rode roughshod through the nations of men, and hell was at his heels. Thus, the slain among the ungodly in this age of bloodshed — whether by sword or by famine or by pestilence or by wild beasts — were, at their death, cast down to hell. This is the millennium of those great kingdoms and nations whose wars and treacheries tormented and overran, again and again, the people whom Jehovah had chosen to bear his name. This is also the general era in which the Lord's own people warred among themselves and sent countless numbers of their own brethren to untimely graves.

In 1095 B. C. Saul, the warrior-king, assumed the reins of power in Israel; it was in 1063 that David, a man of blood, slew Goliath and soon thereafter that he was recognized as king over all Israel. At Solomon's death in 975 B.C. the kingdom was divided with Israel and Judah for hundreds of years thereafter engaging in wars with each other and their neighboring kingdoms.

In the early days of this seal, the mighty Assyrian empire held imperial sway over much of the "civilized" world and came again and again against the citizens of Canaan, taking the tribes and hosts of Israel into captivity some 760 years before Christ and again 40 or so years later.

The Babylonian empire, known as the First World-Kingdom, sat in the spotlight of history from 605 to 538 B. C.; the Medo-Persian empire, as the Second World-Kingdom, ruled from 538 to 333 B. C.; it was in 332 that Alexander the Great conquered Persia; and in 60 B. C. that Julius Caesar formed the first triumvirate, with Imperial Rome rising to dominate the kingdoms of the world.

It was Nebuchadnezzar of Babylon who took Jerusalem and made Judah captive shortly after Lehi and his family and friends left for their promised land. And it was in the days of this empire that Shadrach, Meshach, and Abednego were cast unharmed into the fiery furnace, and under the rule of the Medes and the Persians that Daniel found himself in the lion's den. It was in 536 B. C. that the exiled of Israel began to return to Jerusalem to rebuild their temple, and then, after half a millennium of war and trouble, it was 63 B. C. when Pompey subjugated Judea and the Roman yoke began to weigh as an unmerciful burden upon the necks of the Jews and later upon the followers of the lowly Nazarene. It was, of course, in 600 B. C. that Lehi left Jerusalem to father a mighty civilization in the Americas which, following the pattern of their old world kinsmen, soon divided into nations which opposed and slew their fellow American Hebrews in intra-Israelitish wars for hundreds of years.

8. **Hell]** See Rev. 20:11-15.

To kill . . . with death] To slay with pestilence.

CHRISTIAN MARTYRS SLAIN DURING FIFTH SEAL

REVELATION 6:9-11.

9 And when he had opened the fifth seal, I saw under the altar the souls of them that were slain for the word of God, and for the testimony which they held:

10 And they cried with a loud voice, saying, How long, O Lord, holy and true, dost thou not judge and avenge our blood on them that dwell on the earth?

11 And white robes were given unto every one of them; and it was said unto them, that they should rest yet for a little season, until their fellowservants also and their brethren, that should be killed as they *were*, should be fulfilled.

Where the Lord's people are concerned, the events of the fifth seal, that period from our Lord's birth down to 1000 A. D., which are of unspeakable worth are:

1. The birth into mortality of God's only Son; his ministry among men; and the atoning sacrifice which he wrought by the shedding of his own blood.

2. The spread and perfection of the Church which was set up by Him whose Church it is, and the unbelievable fanaticism among unbelievers that made acceptance of martyrdom almost synonymous with acceptance of the gospel.

3. And then, of course, the complete falling away from true and perfect Christianity, which sad eventuality ushered in the long night of apostate darkness on all the face of the earth.

Our Lord's work and ministry are everywhere taught in holy writ; the facts relative to the post-meridian apostasy and the perversion of the saving truths and powers are also abundantly taught in other sacred writings. And so what is more natural than to find the Lord revealing here, that portion of the sealed book which deals with the doctrine of martyrdom. Among the ancient saints martyrdom was an ever present possibility, one which completely occupied their thoughts and feelings. They knew that by forsaking all to follow Christ, they might, if fate so decreed, be called to lay down their lives for Him who had laid down his life for them. In an almost death-inviting sense, the meridian of time was the dispensation of martyrdom.

9. Under the altar] "As the blood of the sacrificial victims slain on the altar was poured at the bottom of the altar, so the souls of those sacrificed for Christ's testimony are symbolically represented as under the altar in heaven." (*Jamieson*, p. 568.)

Slain for the word of God] Among them were James the brother of John (Acts 12:2) and Antipas. (Rev. 6:13.) "In the gospel sense, martyrdom is the voluntary acceptance of death at the hands of wicked men rather than to forsake Christ and his holy gospel. It is the supreme earthly sacrifice in which a man certifies to his absolute faith and to the desires for righteousness and for eternal life which are in his heart.

"Martyrs of religion are found in every age in which there have been both righteous and wicked people on earth. Christ himself was a martyr who voluntarily laid down his life, according to the Father's plan, that immortality and eternal life might become available for his brethren. (John 10:10-18.) 'Greater love hath no man than this, that a man lay down his life for his friends.' (John 15:13.) . . . True martyrs of religion receive eternal life. 'Whoso layeth down his life in my cause, for my name's sake, shall find it again, even life eternal.' (D. & C. 98:13; Mark 8:35; John 12:25; Rev. 2:10.) But the mere laying down of one's life standing alone is not gospel martyrdom. Both the righteous and the wicked have and do sacrifice their lives for friends or country without gaining thereby any hope or assurance of exaltation. Those on the other hand who have the truth and who could escape death by denying it are the martyrs who shall receive a martyr's reward — eternal life. When they seal their testimony with their blood, they are honored and their murderers are condemned. (D. & C. 136:39.)" (*Mormon Doctrine*, 2nd ed., pp. 469-470.)

10. Avenge our blood] 'Our life on earth was cut short; some of us, as Abel (Gen. 4:10), have been denied mortal seed; pour out thy judgments upon the wicked and ungodly who took our lives.'

11. White robes] "Indicative of light, joy, and triumphant victory over their foes." (*Jamieson*, p. 568.)

Rest yet for a little season] Like "the four and twenty elders" whom John saw, sitting with God on his throne (Rev. 4:1-11), but who in fact "were then in the paradise of God" (D. & C. 77:5), these martyrs had also been "received into a state of happiness, which is called paradise, a state of rest, a state of peace, where they shall rest from all their troubles and from all care, and sorrow." (Alma 40:12.)

Until their fellowservants also and their brethren . . . should be killed] "Many apostles, prophets, and saints have been martyred for the gospel cause. (Matt. 23:29-33; Luke 11:47-51; Acts 7; 22:20; Hela. 13:24-28; D. & C. 135.) The Prophet and Patriarch of this dispensation laid down their lives in the gospel cause, as literally thousands of others have done. Men, women, and children, young and old, weak and strong, sick and well, were driven by the thousands from Missouri and Illinois, many to early and untimely deaths as a direct result of the persecutions and diseases thus heaped upon them. Is a saint any less a martyr who is driven from a sick bed into blizzards to freeze and die than he would have been had an assassin's bullet brought merciful death in a brief destroying moment? . . .

"Martyrdom is not a thing of the past only, but of the present and of the future, for Satan has not yet been bound, and the servants of the Lord will not be silenced in this final age of warning and judgment. There are forces and powers in the world today, which would silence the tongue and shed the blood of every true witness of Christ in the world, if they had the power and the means to do it. There are those who would destroy every prophet of God, if they could. Martyrs of true religion are yet to have their blood shed in Jerusalem. 'And their dead bodies shall lie in the street of the great city, which spiritually is called Sodom and Egypt, where also our Lord was crucified.' (Rev. 11:1-12.) True it is that 'the woman,' of whom John wrote is and shall be 'drunken with the blood of the saints, and with the blood of the martyrs of Jesus.' (Rev. 17:6.)" (*Mormon Doctrine*, 2nd ed., p. 470.)

SIGNS OF THE TIMES MANIFEST IN SIXTH SEAL

REVELATION 6:12-17.

12 And I beheld when he had opened the sixth seal, and, lo, there was a great earthquake; and the sun became black as sackcloth of hair, and the moon became as blood;

13 And the stars of heaven fell unto the earth, even as a fig tree casteth her untimely figs, when she is shaken of a mighty wind.

14 And the heaven departed as a scroll when it is rolled together; and every mountain and island were moved out of their places.

15 And the kings of the earth, and the great men, and the rich men, and the chief captains, and the mighty men, and every bondman, and every free man, hid themselves in the dens and in the rocks of the mountains;

16 And said to the mountains and rocks, Fall on us, and hide us from the face of him that sitteth on the throne, and from the wrath of the Lamb:

17 For the great day of his wrath is come; and who shall be able to stand?

I.V. REVELATION 6:14.

14 And the **heavens opened** as a scroll **is opened** when it is rolled together; and every mountain, and island, **was** moved out of **its place.**

We are now living during the final years of the sixth seal, that thousand year period which began in 1000 A.D. and will continue through the Saturday night of time and until just before the

Sabbatical era when Christ shall reign personally on earth, when all of the blessings of the Great Millennium shall be poured out upon this planet. This, accordingly, is the era when the signs of the times shall be shown forth, and they are in fact everywhere to be seen. See *Mormon Doctrine*, 2nd ed., pp. 715-734.

12-13. Speaking of events destined to occur near the close of the sixth seal, the Lord, on December 27, 1832, said to Joseph Smith: "Not many days hence and the earth shall tremble and reel to and fro as a drunken man; and the sun shall hide his face, and shall refuse to give light; and the moon shall be bathed in blood; and the stars shall become exceedingly angry, and shall cast themselves down as a fig that falleth from off a fig-tree." (D. & C. 88:87.)

12. A great earthquake] 14. Every mountain and island were moved] See Rev. 16:17-21.

12. The sun became black . . . and the moon . . . as blood] 13. The stars of heaven fell unto the earth] As a prelude to our Lord's glorious return, such transcendent events shall occur, both in heaven and on earth, that there is no language known to mortals, nor any imagery or illustration, which can convey to them the wonders of that dreadful day.

"The earth shall reel to and fro like a drunkard" (Isa. 24:20), causing such an earthquake as has never before been known (Rev. 16:17-21), and it shall appear to man on earth as though the stars in the sidereal heavens are falling. And in addition, as here recorded, some heavenly meteors or other objects, appearing as stars, will fall "unto the earth." Indeed, the events of that day shall be so unprecedented and so beyond human experience, that the prophets are and have been at an almost total loss for words to describe those realities pressed in upon them by the spirit of revelation. And we can envision only in small measure the great events which they saw and understood by the power of the Spirit; that is, we are so limited unless and until we enjoy the same Spirit and see the same things which that God who is no respecter of persons revealed to them.

This much, however, we do know: Toward the end of the sixth seal the everlasting gospel has been restored, and it is now being preached to the nations of the earth. Soon that universal war and desolation destined to usher in and accompany the Second Coming itself shall commence. "And immediately after the tribulation of those days, the sun shall be darkened, and the moon shall not give her light, and the stars shall fall from heaven, and the powers of heaven shall be shaken . . . . Then shall appear the sign of the Son of Man in heaven, and then shall all the tribes of the earth mourn; and they shall see the Son of Man coming in the clouds of heaven, with power and great glory." (Jos. Smith 1:33-36; Matt. 24:29.)

In the midst of a recitation of the woes that shall befall the world, Isaiah inserts a similar assertion: "For the stars of heaven and the constellations thereof shall not give their light; the sun shall be darkened in his going forth, and the moon shall not cause her light to shine." (Isa. 13:10; 24:23.) And speaking of the events to precede his coming, and of the glorious resurrection which shall attend it, the Lord by latter-day revelation gives us this confirmation of the same events: "Before this great day shall come the sun shall be darkened, and the moon shall be turned into blood, and the stars shall fall from heaven, and there shall be greater signs in heaven above and in the earth beneath." (D. & C. 29:14; 133:49.)

14. The heavens departed as a scroll when it is rolled together] As with all scripture dealing with the events to precede and attend the Second Coming, there is not a perfect chronological recitation of events. That which is to occur in one seal must be related to the things in another, and to give an over-all perspective, things widely separated in time are often spoken of in the same sentence. Here John seems to be seeing that new heaven and new earth which will be when the Lord actually comes, for the old ones are to be dissolved; they "shall melt with fervent heat" (2 Pet. 3:10); and all things shall become new. See Rev. 21:1-6a.

Isaiah speaks of the same events in these words: "And all the host of heaven shall be dissolved, and the heavens shall be rolled together as a scroll: and all their host shall fall down, as the leaf falleth off from the vine, and as a falling fig from the fig tree." (Isa. 34:4.)

15-16. As Jesus carried his cross to Calvary, he also spoke of this day of desolation, saying: "Then shall they begin to say to the mountains, Fall on us; and to the hills, Cover us." (Luke 23:30; Isa. 2:19; Hosea 10:8; D. & C. 88:88-92.)

16. The wrath of the Lamb] 17. The great day of his wrath is come] Precedent to our Lord's return, wars and desolations beyond our present ability to envision shall sweep the earth. What could be more descriptive of these events than such inspired utterances as these?

"Howl ye; for the day of the Lord is at hand; it shall come as a destruction from the Almighty. Therefore shall all hands be faint, and every man's heart shall melt: And they shall be afraid: pangs and sorrows shall take hold of them; they shall be in pain as a woman that travaileth: they shall be amazed one at another; their faces shall be as flames. Behold, the day of the Lord cometh, cruel both with wrath and fierce anger, to lay the land desolate: and he shall destroy the sinners thereof out of it . . . . And I will punish the world for their evil, and the wicked for their iniquity; and I will cause the arrogancy of the proud to cease, and I will lay low the haughtiness of the terrible . . . . Therefore I will shake the heavens, and the earth shall remove out of her place, in the wrath of the Lord of hosts, and in the day of his fierce anger." (Isa. 13:6-9, 11, 13.)

"For the indignation of the Lord is upon all nations, and his fury upon all their armies: he hath utterly destroyed them, he hath delivered them to the slaughter. Their slain also shall be cast out, and their stink shall come up out of their carcases, and the mountains shall be melted with their blood . . . . For it is the day of the Lord's vengeance, and the year of recompences for the controversy of Zion." (Isa. 34:2-3, 8.) "For this was the day of vengeance which was in my heart." (D. & C. 133:51; Isa. 63:4.)

17. Who shall be able to stand?] Before the Lord comes, the wicked and ungodly shall be slain by plague and by pestilence and by the sword; and when he descends with his chariots of fire, the remainder of those who are living a telestial law shall be consumed by the glory of his presence.

Isaiah describes it this way: "For, behold, the Lord will come with fire, and with his chariots like a whirlwind, to render his anger with fury, and his rebuke with flames of fire. For by fire and by his sword will the Lord plead with all flesh: and the slain of the Lord shall be many." (Isa. 66:15-16.) And Malachi, having more particular reference to the actual hour of his return, asks: "Who may abide the day of his coming? and who shall stand when he appeareth?" (Mal. 3:2), and then answers: "The day cometh, that shall burn as an oven; and all the proud, yea, and all that do wickedly, shall be stubble: and the day that cometh shall burn them up, saith the Lord of hosts, that it shall leave them neither root nor branch." (Mal. 4:1.) See 2 Pet. 3:10-18.

GOSPEL RESTORED DURING SIXTH SEAL

REVELATION 7:1.

1 And after these things I saw four angels standing on the four corners of the earth, holding the four winds of the earth, that the wind should not blow on the earth, nor on the sea, nor on any tree.

God be praised, his gospel is here! It was restored in all its everlasting fulness in the closing days of the sixth seal. This restoration commenced in the Spring of 1820 with the appearance of the Father and the Son and was completed sometime before June 27, 1844, when Joseph Smith, the Prophet, and Hyrum Smith, the Patriarch, sealed their testimony with their own blood and went on to join the martyrs of all dispensations in the realms of eternal glory. (D. & C. 135.)

Thus we read in the revealed word: "Q. What are we to understand by the four angels, spoken of in the 7th chapter and 1st verse of Revelation? A. We are to understand that they are four angels sent forth from God, to whom is given power over the four parts of the earth, to save life and to destroy; these are they who have the everlasting gospel to commit to every nation, kindred, tongue, and people; having power to shut up the heavens, to seal up unto life, or to cast down to the regions of darkness . . . . Q. What time are the things spoken of in this chapter to be accomplished? A. They are to be accomplished in the sixth thousand years, or the opening of the sixth seal." (D. & C. 77:8, 10.)

Restoration of the gospel] See Rev. 14:6-7.

ELIAS TO SEAL 144,000 DURING SIXTH SEAL

REVELATION 7:2-8.

2 And I saw another angel ascending from the east, having the seal of the living God: and he cried with a loud voice to the four angels, to whom it was given to hurt the earth and the sea,

3 Saying, Hurt not the earth, neither the sea, nor the trees, till we have sealed the servants of our God in their foreheads.

4 And I heard the number of them which were sealed: *and there were* sealed an hundred *and* forty *and* four thousand of all the tribes of the children of Israel.

5 Of the tribe of Juda *were* sealed twelve thousand. Of the tribe of Reuben *were* sealed twelve thousand. Of the tribe of Gad *were* sealed twelve thousand.

6 Of the tribe of Aser *were* sealed twelve thousand. Of the tribe of Nepthalim *were* sealed twelve thousand. Of the tribe of Manasses *were* sealed twelve thousand.

7 Of the tribe of Simeon *were* sealed twelve thousand. Of the tribe of Levi *were* sealed twelve thousand. Of the tribe of Issachar *were* sealed twelve thousand.

8 Of the tribe of Zabulon *were* sealed twelve thousand. Of the tribe of Joseph *were* sealed twelve thousand. Of the tribe of Benjamin *were* sealed twelve thousand.

I.V. REVELATION 7:2, 4.

2 And I saw another angel ascending from the east, having the seal of the living God; and **I heard him cry** with a loud voice to the four angels, to whom it was given to hurt the earth and the sea,

4 And the number of them **who** were sealed, were an hundred and forty and four thousand of all the tribes of the children of Israel.

"The everlasting gospel," as restored through Joseph Smith and his associates, is to be preached "to every nation, kindred, tongue, and people," during the sixth seal. (D. & C. 77:8, 10.) See Rev. 7:1.

But the preaching of the restored gospel in all the world is not by any means the whole story. Converts are to be made everywhere. The same things here shown to John had been revealed more than six centuries before to Nephi. That Hebrew prophet beheld that in the last days the church of the devil would have "dominion over all the earth, among all nations, kindreds, tongues, and people," and that "the church of the Lamb, who were the saints of god, were also upon all the face of the earth." (1 Ne. 14:9-27).

And now we learn that after the converts are made, after there kindreds of the earth, there will be those among them who advance and progress until they become kings and priests. See Rev. 1:1-6; 5:1-14; 20:4-6. John here sees 144,000 of these kings and priests, 12,000 from each tribe, converted, baptized, endowed, married for eternity, and finally sealed up unto eternal life, having their calling and election made sure. See 2 Pet. 1:1-19.

2-3. "Q. What are we to understand by the angel ascending from the east, Revelation 7th chapter and 2nd verse? A. We are to understand that the angel ascending from the east is he to whom is given the seal of the living God over the twelve tribes of Israel; wherefore, he crieth unto the four angels having the everlasting gospel, saying: Hurt not the earth, neither the sea, nor the trees, till we have sealed the servants of our God in their foreheads. And, if you will receive it, this is Elias which was to come to gather together the tribes of Israel and restore all things." (D. & C. 77:9.)

"According to the plan and program of the Lord, the dispensation of the fulness of times is 'the times of restitution of all things, which God hath spoken by the mouth of all his holy prophets since the world began.' (Acts 3:21.) This restoration is to be effected by Elias. Before the winding up of the Lord's work, the promise is: 'Elias truly shall first come, and restore all things.' (Matt. 17:11.) With these ancient scriptures before us, these questions arise: Who is the promised Elias who was to come and restore all things? Has the work of restoration taken place? Or is it something that is yet future?

"Correcting the Bible by the spirit of revelation, the Prophet restored a statement of John the Baptist which says that Christ is the Elias who was to restore all things. (*Inspired Version*, John 1:21-28.) By revelation we are also informed that the Elias who was to restore all things is the angel Gabriel who was known in mortality as Noah. (D. & C. 27:6-7; Luke 1:5-25; *Teachings*, p. 157.) From the same authentic source we also learn that the promised Elias is John the Revelator. (D. & C. 77:9, 14.) Thus there are three different revelations which name Elias as being three different persons. What are we to conclude?

"By finding answer to the question, by whom has the restoration been effected, we shall find who Elias is and find there is no problem in harmonizing these apparently contradictory revelations. Who has restored all things? Was it one man? Certainly not. Many angelic ministrants have been sent from the courts of glory to confer keys and powers, to commit their dispensations and glories again to men on earth. At least the following have come: Moroni, John the Baptist, Peter, James and John, Moses, Elijah, Elias, Gabriel, Raphael, and Michael. (D. & C. 13; 110; 128:19-21.) Since it is apparent that no one messenger has carried the whole burden of the restoration, but rather that each has come with a specific endowment from on high, it becomes clear that Elias is a composite personage. The expression must be understood to be a name and a title for those whose mission it was to commit keys and powers to men in this final dispensation. (*Doctrines of Salvation*, vol. 1, pp. 170-174.)" (*Mormon Doctrine*, 2nd ed., p. 221.)

3. Sealed the servants of our God in their foreheads] Of this sealing the Prophet Joseph Smith said: "Four destroying angels holding power over the four quarters of the earth until the servants of God are sealed in their foreheads, which signifies sealing the blessing upon their heads, meaning the everlasting covenant, thereby making their calling and election sure. When a seal is put upon the father and mother, it secures their posterity, so that they cannot be lost, but will be saved by virtue of the covenant of their father and mother." (*Teachings*, p. 321.) Thus if both parents and children have their calling and election made sure, none so involved shall be lost; all shall come forth to an inheritance of glory and exaltation in the kingdom of God.

4-8. "Q. What are we to understand by sealing the one hundred and forty-four thousand, out of all the tribes of Israel—twelve thousand out of every tribe? A. We are to understand that those who are sealed are high priests, ordained unto the holy order of God, to administer the everlasting gospel; for they are they who are ordained out of every nation, kindred, tongue, and people, by the angels to whom is given power over the nations of the earth, to bring as many as will come to the church of the Firstborn." (D. & C. 77:11.) See Rev. 14:1-5.

5-8. What groups of Jacob's descendants make up the tribes of Israel? This depends upon the day and age involved and upon what aspect of Israel's history and destiny is being considered. The house of Israel was, of course, a distinct and chosen people in pre-existence, with great hosts of our Father's favored and faithful children being foreordained to receive mortal birth through this elect lineage. (Deut. 32:7-9.) In this mortal sphere, Father Jacob had twelve sons. Leah bore him Reuben (his firstborn), Simeon, Levi, Judah, Issachar, and Zebulun; Rachel gave him Joseph and Benjamin; Bilhah was the mother of Dan and Naphtali; and Zilpah of Gad and Asher. (Gen. 35:24-26.) In the original and strict sense of the word, these twelve sons became the heads of the Twelve Tribes of Israel.

But the Lord and Jacob favored Joseph above his brethren (Gen. 37), and Jacob took Ephraim and Manasseh (the sons of Joseph) as his own, thereby giving Joseph a double portion in Israel. (Gen. 48:1-6.) This made thirteen tribes.

In their journeyings to the promised land, the Levites distinguished themselves above all the tribes of Israel (Ex. 32), and were chosen for special ministerial service. (Num. 3 and 8.) When the promised land was divided by lot among the tribes of Israel, Ephraim and Manasseh were counted as two tribes and the Levites were scattered among all the tribes. (Num. 14 to 19.) This left twelve tribes to receive an inheritance in their promised land.

Because of sin, Reuben lost, for himself and his posterity, his patriarchal pre-eminence as the firstborn (Gen. 35:22; 49:2-3), and

Ephraim was chosen to inherit this favored status. (1 Chron. 5:1-2; Jer. 31:9.) In consequence, it is Ephraim who is being gathered first in this dispensation, and it is he to whom the other gathered tribes will come in due course to receive their blessings. (D. & C. 133:26-34.)

At the death of Solomon, the Lord divided his people into two kingdoms. Judah remained with Solomon's son, Rehoboam, and the other ten tribes (counting Joseph as one tribe and not counting Levi at all) became the kingdom of Ephraim, under the rule of Jeroboam. (1 Kings 11:26-43.) The Ten Tribes were carried into Assyrian captivity in about 721 B. C., were later delivered therefrom by miraculous intervention, and have since been lost to the knowledge of men. (*Mormon Doctrine*, 2nd ed., pp. 455-458.)

The keys and power to restore the Ten Tribes to their former high status in Israel, and to lead them from their unknown places of lodgement in the lands north of Canaan and Assyria, were given by Moses to Joseph Smith and Oliver Cowdery on April 3, 1836. (D. & C. 110:11.) These keys now reside in the President of The Church of Jesus Christ of Latter-day Saints. That the remnants of Israel shall be restored before the Second Coming of the Son of Man is evident from the fact that 12,000 from each tribe are to receive the restored gospel, and that through the ordinances of the Lord's house they are to become kings and priests, who shall administer the blessings of the everlasting gospel to the Lord's elect. (D. & C. 77:9-11.)

The tribes listed by John include Levi, count Ephraim (Joseph) and Manasseh separately, and omit Dan. Why Dan should lose his inheritance is not clear. Perhaps it is forecast in the patriarchal blessings given by Jacob to the head of the tribe: "Dan shall be a serpent by the way, an adder in the path." (Gen. 49:17.) Or perhaps it is because a long course of idolatry and warlike conduct dissipated the strength of the Danites and left them less powerful and numerous than their fellows in Israel. (Judges 18; Jer. 8:16; Amos 8:11-14.)

JOHN SEETH THE HOSTS OF THE EXALTED FROM ALL NATIONS

REVELATION 7:9-17.

9 After this I beheld, and, lo, a great multitude, which no man could number, of all nations, and kindreds, and people, and tongues, stood before the throne, and before the Lamb, clothed with white robes, and palms in their hands;

10 And cried with a loud voice, saying, Salvation to our God which sitteth upon the throne, and unto the Lamb.

11 And all the angels stood round about the throne, and *about* the elders and the four beasts, and fell before the throne on their faces, and worshipped God,

12 Saying, Amen: Blessing, and glory, and wisdom, and thanksgiving, and honour, and power, and might, *be* unto our God for ever and ever. Amen.

13 And one of the elders answered, saying unto me, What are these which are arrayed in white robes? and whence came they?

14 And I said unto him, Sir, thou knowest. And he said to me, These are they which came out of great tribulation, and have washed their robes, and made them white in the blood of the Lamb.

15 Therefore are they before the throne of God, and serve him day and night in his temple: and he that sitteth on the throne shall dwell among them.

16 They shall hunger no more, neither thirst any more; neither shall the sun light on them, nor any heat.

17 For the Lamb which is in the midst of the throne shall feed them, and shall lead them unto living fountains of waters: and God shall wipe away all tears from their eyes.

As John views the sealing up unto eternal life of the 144,000, during the sixth seal, the vision extends out endlessly, and he now sees an innumerable multitude of exalted beings from all nations — all worshipping God and the Lamb, both in Millennial splendor and in celestial glory.

9. A great multitude] See Rev. 5:1-14. **Before the throne]** In the celestial kingdom of God.

Palms in their hands] "The antitype to Christ's entry into Jerusalem amidst the palm-bearing multitude . . . . The palm branch is the symbol of joy and triumph. It was used at the feast of Tabernacles, on the fifteenth day of the seventh month, when they kept feast to God in thanksgiving for the ingathered fruits. The antitype shall be the completed gathering in of the harvest of the elect redeemed here described." (*Jamieson*, p. 570.)

10-12. See Rev. 4:1-11; 5:1-14.

13-14. Whence come saved beings? "Out of great tribulation!" "For whom the Lord loveth he chasteneth, and scourgeth every son whom he receiveth." (Heb. 12:6.) "And no unclean thing can enter into his kingdom; therefore nothing entereth into his rest save it be those who have washed their garments in my blood, because of their faith, and the repentance of all their sins, and their faithfulness unto the end." (3 Ne. 27:19.)

15. Those who serve the Lord, "day and night in his temple," that is, who keep the commandments in this life, shall rise as kings and priests to dwell with him on earth during the Millennial Era; and they are the ones who shall serve him eternally in that kingdom where he and his Father shall dwell with them forever.

Serve him day and night in his temple] Serve him forever in his kingdom, where, in the literal sense, there is neither night nor a temple. See Rev. 21:9-27.

16-17. As used by Isaiah, substantially this same language applies to the latter-day gathering of Israel. Speaking of those who "shall come from far," he says: "They shall not hunger nor thirst; neither shall the heat nor sun smite them: for he that hath mercy on them shall lead them, even by the springs of water shall be guide them." (Isa. 49:9-12.) Isaiah's clear meaning is that the spiritual famine of centuries shall cease; Israel shall now have the gospel; they shall feast again upon the good word of God; once again shall they drink from the fountains of living waters; and in their new found joy, all their sufferings of the past (even the heat of the sun!) shall be forgotten. As pertaining to their eventual inheritance in the celestial kingdom, the promise begins to take upon itself a degree of literal fulfilment.

17. Living fountains of waters] See Rev. 22:1-5.

God shall wipe away all tears] See Rev. 21:1-6a.

Exaltation] See 1 John 3:1-3.

FIRE AND DESOLATION POURED OUT DURING SEVENTH SEAL

REVELATION 8:1-13.

1 And when he had opened the seventh seal, there was silence in heaven about the space of half an hour.

2 And I saw the seven angels which stood before God; and to them were given seven trumpets.

3 And another angel came and stood at the altar, having a golden censer; and there was given unto him much incense, that he should offer *it* with the prayers of all saints upon the golden altar which was before the throne.

4 And the smoke of the incense, *which came* with the prayers of the saints, ascended up before God out of the angel's hand.

5 And the angel took the censer, and filled it with fire of the altar, and cast *it* unto the earth: and there were voices, and thunderings, and lightnings, and an earthquake.

6 And the seven angels which had the seven trumpets prepared themselves to sound.

7 The first angel sounded, and there followed hail and fire mingled with blood, and they were cast upon the earth: and the third part of trees was burnt up, and all green grass was burnt up.

8 And the second angel sounded, and as it were a great mountain burning with fire was cast into the sea: and the third part of the sea became blood;

9 And the third part of the creatures which were in the sea, and had life, died; and the third part of the ships were destroyed.

10 And the third angel sounded, and there fell a great star from heaven, burning as it were a lamp, and it fell upon the third part of the rivers, and upon the fountains of waters;

11 And the name of the star is called Wormwood: and the third part of the waters became wormwood; and many men died of the waters, because they were made bitter.

12 And the fourth angel sounded, and the third part of the sun was smitten, and the third part of the moon, and the third part of the stars; so as the third part of them was darkened, and the day shone not for a third part of it, and the night likewise.

13 And I beheld, and heard an angel flying through the midst of heaven, saying with a loud voice, Woe, woe, woe, to the inhabiters of the earth by reason of the other voices of the trumpet of the three angels, which are yet to sound!

"Q. What are we to understand by the sounding of the trumpets, mentioned in the 8th chapter of Revelation? A. We are to understand that as God made the world in six days, and on the seventh day he finished his work, and sanctified it, and also formed man out of the dust of the earth, even so, in the beginning of the seventh thousand years will the Lord God sanctify the earth, and complete the salvation of man, and judge all things, and shall redeem all things, except that which he hath not put into his power, when he shall have sealed all things, unto the end of all things; and the sounding of the trumpets of the seven angels are the preparing and finishing of his work, in the beginning of the seventh thousand years — the preparing of the way before the time of his coming." (D. & C. 77:12.)

Thus our Lord is not destined to return when the seventh thousand years first commences. Plagues, destruction, fire, bloodshed, war, and desolation — all of incomparable power and degree — are to sweep the earth after the opening of the seventh seal and before the Second Coming. These are announced in the 8th and 9th chapters of Revelation.

1. According to the apparent chronology set forth in Section 88 of the Doctrine and Covenants, there shall be a great sign in heaven (verse 93); then shall come the destruction of the great and abominable church (verse 94); and then: "There shall be silence in heaven for the space of half an hour; and immediately after shall the curtain of heaven be unfolded, as a scroll is unfolded after it is rolled up, and the face of the Lord shall be unveiled; And the saints that are upon the earth, who are alive, shall be quickened and be caught up to meet him." (D. & C. 88:93-96.)

What is meant by the half hour of silence has not yet been revealed. If it is to be reckoned on the basis of "the Lord's time" of 1000 years to a day, the duration would be some 21 of our years. (Abra. 3:4; 2 Pet. 3:8.)

2-4. The saints on both sides of the veil join in worshipping the Lord. The saints on earth pray, while the angels burn incense on a golden altar before the throne of God, an act of devotion patterned after similar rites in ancient Israel. (Lev. 16:12-13; Num. 16:36-40.)

2. The seven angels] An apocryphal statement speaks similarly: "I am Raphael, one of the seven holy angels which present the prayers of the saints, and which go in and out before the glory of the Holy One." (Tobit 12:15.)

5. The hot coals, taken from the altar and cast down to earth, symbolize the judgments of God to be rained down upon the wicked during the opening part of the seventh seal.

7-12; (and chapter 9)] Most of the plagues and destructions, here announced for the early days of the seventh seal, are of such a nature that they (speculatively!) could be brought to pass in large part through atomic warfare.

7. Hail and fire mingled with blood] Of the nation that shall rise to fight his people in that day, the Lord says: "And I will plead against him with pestilence and with blood; and I will rain upon him, and upon his bands, and upon the many people that are with him, an overflowing rain, and great hailstones, fire, and brimstone." (Ezek. 38:22.) By these means a third of all the trees and green grass on earth are to be destroyed. The plague of hail and fire rained upon Pharaoh's Egypt, in the days of the deliverance of Israel from bondage, was perhaps symbolical of this greater deliverance of the Lord's people by the forces of nature in the latter-days. (Ex. 9:22-26.)

8-9. Unbelievable upheavals of nature and the unloosing of near unlimited power shall bring to pass the destruction of a third part of all life in and on the oceans of the world! (Jer. 51:25; Amos 7:4.) Perhaps the turning of the waters of Egypt to blood was in similitude of this great latter-day plague. (Ex. 7:19-25.)

10-11. Could this be atomic fallout which shall poison a third of the drinking water of the earth?

12. As, perhaps, symbolized by the "thick darkness in all the land of Egypt" (Ex. 10:21-23), some forces of man or nature will blot out a third of the light of the luminaries of heaven.

13. And these are but the beginning of that which is to be as wickedness is swept away to prepare the Lord's footstool for his personal habitation.

WAR AND PLAGUES POURED OUT DURING SEVENTH SEAL

REVELATION 9:1-21.

1 And the fifth angel sounded, and I saw a star fall from heaven unto the earth: and to him was given the key of the bottomless pit.

2 And he opened the bottomless pit; and there arose a smoke out of the pit, as the smoke of a great furnace; and the sun and the air were darkened by reason of the smoke of the pit.

3 And there came out of the smoke locusts upon the earth: and unto them was given power, as the scorpions of the earth have power.

4 And it was commanded them that they should not hurt the grass of the earth, neither any green thing, neither any tree; but only those men which have not the seal of God in their foreheads.

5 And to them it was given that they should not kill them, but that they should be tormented five months: and their torment *was* as the torment of a scorpion, when he striketh a man.

6 And in those days shall men seek death, and shall not find it; and shall desire to die, and death shall flee from them.

7 And the shapes of the locusts *were* like unto horses prepared unto battle; and on their heads *were* as it were crowns like gold, and their faces *were* as the faces of men.

8 And they had hair as the hair of women, and their teeth were as *the teeth* of lions.

9 And they had breastplates, as it were breastplates of iron; and the sound of their wings *was* as the sound of chariots of many horses running to battle.

10 And they had tails like unto scorpions, and there were stings in their tails: and their power *was* to hurt men five months.

11 And they had a king over them, *which is* the angel of the bottomless pit, whose name in the Hebrew tongue *is* Abaddon, but in the Greek tongue hath *his* name Apollyon.

12 One woe is past; and, behold, there come two woes more hereafter.

13 And the sixth angel sounded, and I heard a voice from the four horns of the golden altar which is before God,

14 Saying to the sixth angel which had the trumpet, Loose the four angels which are bound in the great river Euphrates.

15 And the four angels were loosed, which were prepared for an hour, and a day, and a month, and a year, for to slay the third part of men.

16 And the number of the army of the horsemen *were* two hundred thousand thousand: and I heard the number of them.

17 And thus I saw the horses in the vision, and them that sat on them, having breastplates of fire, and of jacinth, and brimstone: and the heads of the horses *were* as the heads of lions; and out of their mouths issued fire and smoke and brimstone.

18 By these three was the third part of men killed, by the fire, and by the smoke, and by the brimstone, which issued out of their mouths.

19 For their power is in their mouth, and in their tails: for their tails *were* like unto serpents, and had heads, and with them they do hurt.

20 And the rest of the men which were not killed by these plagues yet repented not of the works of their hands, that they should not worship devils, and idols of gold, and silver, and brass, and stone, and of wood: which neither can see, nor hear, nor walk:

21 Neither repented they of their murders, nor of their sorceries, nor of their fornication, nor of their thefts.

I.V. REVELATION 9:14, 16.

14 Saying to the sixth angel which had the trumpet, Loose the four angels which are bound in the **bottomless pit.**

16 And the number of the army of the horsemen were two hundred thousand thousand; and I **saw** the number of them.

This chapter announces and describes the events of the last great war on earth, the war which ushers in the coming of the Son of Man. All of its events "are to be accomplished after the opening of the seventh seal, before the coming of Christ." (D. & C. 77:13.)

1. A star fall from heaven] Lucifer. See Rev. 12:1-17.

Key of the bottomless pit] Power and dominion over that hell where the devil's angels bow before their master's will.

2. Lucifer opened the depths of hell and every evil influence, symbolized by smoke of a great furnace, arose therefrom.

3. Influenced by the temptations of the devil wicked men (locusts) began their warfare.

4-6. During this particular period of the war and desolation the evil forces will be directed against all men, save those sealed up unto eternal life, for those in Zion shall be preserved. The plagues and torments of this era shall so afflict men that they shall desire to die rather than to suffer more. Perhaps John is seeing such things as the effects of poisonous gas, or bacteriological warfare, or atomic fallout, which disable but do not kill.

4. Seal of God] See Rev. 7:2-8.

7-10. In prophetic imagery John here seeks to describe a war fought with weapons and under circumstances entirely foreign to any experience of his own or of the people of that day. Joel, subject to the same limitations of descriptive ability, attempted to portray the same scenes in these words: "The day of the Lord cometh, for it is nigh at hand; A day of darkness and of gloominess, a day of clouds and of thick darkness, as the morning spread upon the mountains: a great people and a strong; there hath not been ever the like, neither shall be any more after it, even to the years of many generations. A fire devoureth before them; and behind them a flame burneth: the land is as the garden of Eden before them, and behind them a desolate wilderness; yea, and nothing shall escape them. The appearance of them is as the appearance of horses; and as horsemen, so shall they run. Like the noise of chariots on the tops of mountains shall they leap, like the noise of a flame of fire that devoureth the stubble, as a strong people set in battle array. Before their face the people shall be much pained: all faces shall gather blackness. They shall run like mighty men; they shall climb the wall like men of war; and they shall march every one on his ways, and they shall not break their ranks: Neither shall one thrust another; they shall walk every one in his path: and when they fall upon the sword, they shall not be wounded. They shall run to and fro in the city; they shall run upon the wall, they shall climb up upon the houses; they shall enter in at the windows like a thief. The earth shall quake before them; the heavens shall tremble: the sun and the moon shall be dark, and the stars shall withdraw their shining: And the Lord shall utter his voice before his army: for his camp is very great: for he is strong that executeth his word: for the day of the Lord is great and very terrible; and who can abide it?" (Joel 2:1-11.)

It is not improbable that these ancient prophets were seeing such things as men wearing or protected by strong armor; as troops of cavalry and companies of tanks and flame throwers; as airplanes and airborn missiles which explode, fire shells and drop bombs; and even other weapons yet to be devised in an age when warfare is the desire and love of wicked men.

11. Satan is the unseen head of the armies of men as they fight in the last great battles of earth.

Angel of the bottomless pit, . . . Abaddon, . . . Apollyon] Satan, the destroyer.

14-15. Four of Satan's mighty angels are loosed to influence and lead men in that final war which shall slay the third part of men.

16. Armies totalling 200,000,000 warriors!

17-19. Using all the weapons of modern warfare, one-third of the population of the earth shall be slain in the final great war. Assuming, simply for purposes of illustration, that when this day arrives the population of the earth is, say, 12,000,000,000 people, a not improbable possibility, this would mean that more persons shall be slain than now dwell upon this benighted planet.

20-21. Men do not forsake the world and turn to the Lord because of plagues, desolation, and war. Pharaoh's heart was hardened by the plagues of Egypt. The Jaredites and the Nephites fought to their utter destruction as nations rather than open their hearts to Him who would have removed the cause of their sufferings and suicidal course.

20. The rest of men] The remaining two-thirds of the population of the earth which had not been slain by the sword and the plagues.

Repented not] Repentance is a gift of God; it follows faith in the Lord Jesus Christ. It is a philosophical impossibility for those who cleave unto false religions to repent. Repentance is reserved for those who seek the true and living God and who desire to worship him in Spirit and truth. See *Commentary II*, pp. 108-110.

Worship devils, and idols] See Rev. 17:1-18.

21. Sorceries] See Rev. 18:1-24.

JOHN TO PARTICIPATE IN RESTORATION OF ALL THINGS

REVELATION 10:1-11.

1 And I saw another mighty angel come down from heaven, clothed with a cloud: and a rainbow *was* upon his head, and his face *was* as it were the sun, and his feet as pillars of fire:

2 And he had in his hand a little book open: and he set his right foot upon the sea, and *his* left *foot* on the earth,

3 And cried with a loud voice, as *when* a lion roareth: and when he had cried, seven thunders uttered their voices.

4 And when the seven thunders had uttered their voices, I was about to write: and I heard a voice from heaven saying unto me, Seal up those things which the seven thunders uttered, and write them not.

5 And the angel which I saw stand upon the sea and upon the earth lifted up his hand to heaven,

6 And sware by him that liveth for ever and ever, who created heaven, and the things that therein are, and the earth, and the things that therein are, and the sea, and the things which are therein, that there should be time no longer:

7 But in the days of the voice of the seventh angel, when he shall begin to sound, the mystery of God should be finished, as he hath declared to his servants the prophets.

8 And the voice which I heard from heaven spake unto me again, and said, Go *and* take the little book which is open in the hand of the angel which standeth upon the sea and upon the earth.

9 And I went unto the angel, and said unto him, Give me the little book. And he said unto me, Take *it*, and eat it up; and it shall make thy belly bitter, but it shall be in thy mouth sweet as honey.

10 And I took the little book

out of the angel's hand, and ate it up; and it was in my mouth sweet as honey: and as soon as I had eaten it, my belly was bitter.

11 And he said unto me, Thou must prophesy again before many peoples, and nations, and tongues, and kings.

I.V. REVELATION 10:4.

4 And when the seven thunders had uttered their voices, I was about to write; and I heard a voice from heaven saying unto me, **Those things are sealed up** which the seven thunders uttered, and write them not.

1-3. An angelic ministrant — majestic, mighty, one like unto the Son of God himself — whose face was as the sun and his feet as pillars of fire, brought a little book to John. Compare Rev. 1:12-20.

1. Mighty angel] See Rev. 5:1-14.

2-7. From the lips of the angel comes the great pronouncement — sworn with an oath in God's holy name — that the time of sorrow and wickedness, and of the persecution and death of the saints, is now fulfilled; that there shall be no more delay; that the "finishing," of the Lord's "work, in the beginning of the seventh thousand years" (D. & C. 77:12) is at hand; that the Millennial Era of peace and righteousness, when the Prince of Peace dwells among men, is now at long last to begin.

It appears from the added and clarifying knowledge revealed to Joseph Smith that the seven thunders which here utter their voices are the seven angels reciting in some detail that which is to be in each of the thousand year periods of the earth's temporal continance. In the very nature of things, lest men become as God, knowing the end from the beginning, John was forbidden to record these hidden things.

It also appears that John's vision prefigured what is to be when the events occur and that the promised proclamations shall yet be made when the hour for Millennial peace actually arrives. "And then shall the first angel again sound his trump in the ears of all living," the revelation recites, "and reveal the secret acts of men, and the mighty works of God in the first thousand years. And then shall the second angel sound his trump, and reveal the secret acts of men, and the thoughts and intents of their hearts, and the mighty works of God in the second thousand years — And so on, until the seventh angel shall sound his trump; and he shall stand forth upon the land and upon the sea, and swear in the name of him who sitteth upon the throne, that there shall be time no longer; and Satan shall be bound, that old serpent, who is called the devil, and shall not be loosed for the space of a thousand years." (D. & C. 88:108-110.)

6. That there should be time no longer] That there should be no more delay — not that time as such should end and eternity begin, for the Millennial Era is still ahead — but, as shown in D. & C. 88:110, that "Satan shall be bound," thus ending the "time" (it "shall be no longer"!) when persecution prevails. "The martyrs shall have no longer a time to wait for the accomplishment of their prayers for the purgation of the earth by the judgments which shall remove their and God's foes from it (Rev. 6:11). The appointed season or time of delay is at an end." (*Jamieson*, p. 574.)

7. The mystery of God should be finished] "The revealed will, mysteries, and the works of God; the hidden things of his economy concerning this earth"; that portion of his work that pertains to the first six thousand years "of its continuance, or its temporal existence." (D. & C. 77:6.)

8-11. "The little book which was eaten by John . . . was a mission, and an ordinance, for him to gather the tribes of Israel; behold, this is Elias, who, as it is written, must come and restore all things." (D. & C. 77:14.) That John labors in fulfilment of this commission is evident from the statement of the Prophet Joseph Smith, made by the spirit of inspiration in June, 1831, "that John the Revelator was then among the Ten Tribes of Israel who had been led away by Shalmaneser, king of Assyria, to prepare them for their return from their long dispersion, to again possess the land of their fathers." (*History of the Church*, vol. 1, p. 176.)

John, also, fulfilled his mission as Elias when, in company with Peter and James, he participated in the restoration of the Melchizedek Priesthood and the conferral of the keys of the kingdom of God upon Joseph Smith and Oliver Cowdery. (D. & C. 27:12-13; 128:20.)

Elias of the restoration] See Rev. 7:2-8.

9-10. John's act of eating a book containing the word of God to him was in keeping with the custom and tradition of ancient Israel. The act signified that he was eating the bread of life, that he was partaking of the good word of God, that he was feasting upon the word of Christ—which was in his "mouth sweet as honey." But it made his "belly bitter"; that is, the judgments and plagues promised those to whom the Lord's word was sent caused him to despair and have sorrow of soul. "How sweet are thy words unto my taste! yea, sweeter than honey to my mouth!" (Psalm 119:103.) Such is the exulting cry of the Psalmist. And, conversely, how bitter is the penalty for rebellion and disobedience. Ezekiel had a similar experience. He was commanded to eat a roll (a book), which was in his mouth "as honey for sweetness," but in the writing itself there was "lamentations, and mourning, and woe." (Ezek. 2:6-10; 3:1-3.)

11. John was translated. He has been made "as flaming fire and a ministering angel," and "he shall minister for those who shall be heirs of salvation who dwell on the earth." To him the Lord said: "Thou shalt tarry until I come in my glory, and shalt prophesy before nations, kindreds, tongues and people." (D. & C. 7:1-8.) Except for his work among the lost tribes of Israel, the "nations, and tongues, and kings" to whom he has and shall prophesy have not yet been made known.

Translated beings] See Heb. 11:5-6.

TWO PROPHETS SHALL BE SLAIN IN JERUSALEM

REVELATION 11:1-14.

1 And there was given me a reed like unto a rod: and the angel stood, saying, Rise, and measure the temple of God, and the altar, and them that worship therein.

2 But the court which is without the temple leave out, and measure it not; for it is given unto the Gentiles: and the holy city shall they tread under foot forty *and* two months.

3 And I will give *power* unto my two witnesses, and they shall prophesy a thousand two hundred *and* three score days, clothed in sackcloth.

4 These are the two olive trees, and the two candlesticks standing before the God of the earth.

5 And if any man will hurt them, fire proceedeth out of their mouth, and devoureth their enemies: and if any man will hurt them, he must in this manner be killed.

6 These have power to shut heaven, that it rain not in the days of their prophecy: and have power over waters to turn them to blood, and to smite the earth with all plagues, as often as they will.

7 And when they shall have finished their testimony, the beast that ascendeth out of the bottomless pit shall make war against them, and shall overcome them, and kill them.

8 And their dead bodies *shall lie* in the street of the great city, which spiritually is called Sodom and Egypt, where also our Lord was crucified.

9 And they of the people and kindreds and tongues and nations shall see their dead bodies three days and an half, and shall not suffer their dead bodies to be put in graves.

10 And they that dwell upon the earth shall rejoice over them, and make merry, and shall send gifts one to another; because these two prophets tormented them that dwelt on the earth.

11 And after three days and an half the Spirit of life from God entered into them, and they stood upon their feet; and great fear fell upon them which saw them.

12 And they heard a great voice from heaven saying unto them, Come up hither. And they ascended up to heaven in a cloud: and their enemies beheld them.

13 And the same hour was there a great earthquake, and the tenth part of the city fell, and in the earthquake were slain of men seven thousand; and the remnant were affrighted, and gave glory to the God of heaven.

14 The second woe is past: *and*, behold, the third woe cometh quickly.

Having received a divine commission to "prophesy again before many peoples, and nations, and tongues, and kings" (Rev. 10:11); and knowing that he is to remain on earth, as a mortal witness of his Lord until that holy Being comes again to dwell among men (Rev. 10:1-11); John is now commanded to be with and strengthen the Church in his day (verse 1); he is made aware of the long night of apostate darkness ahead (verse 2); he learns of latter-day witnesses who shall bear testimony at the very hour of the coming of the Son of Man (verses 3-14); and he hears the angelic pronouncement that the King of earth and heaven shall reign again among mortals. (Verse 15.)

1. John is an apostle of the Lord Jesus Christ. He holds the keys of the kingdom of God on earth, and as such — and as the last of the apostles left on earth! — he is here commanded to study the conditions of the Church and all its members so he can give proper direction to their worship.

2. But the Church is not to remain among mortal men. For a specified period darkness shall cover the earth and gross darkness the minds of the people. The Gentiles, as it were, shall prevail over the chosen seed.

The holy city shall they tread under foot forty and two months] This is the period of universal apostasy. It began when apostles and prophets ceased to minister among men, and it ended with the opening of the heavens in the Spring of 1820. The Lord's promise was: "Jerusalem shall be trodden down of the Gentiles, until the times of the Gentiles be fulfilled." (Luke 21:24.) The detailed application of the 42 months to this period is yet to be revealed.

3-14. As a prelude to being gathered into the true fold of Christ and of receiving again a knowledge of their Messiah and King, the Jews are now returning to Jerusalem and their ancient homeland. "The two witnesses" here described "are two prophets that are to be raised up to the Jewish nation in the last days, at the time of the restoration, and to prophesy to the Jews after they are gathered and have built the city of Jerusalem in the land of their fathers." (D. & C. 77:15.)

3. Two witnesses] "In the mouth of two or three witnesses shall every word be established." (2 Cor. 13:1.) Such is God's eternal law. And these two shall be followers of that humble man, Joseph Smith, through whom the Lord of Heaven restored the fulness of his everlasting gospel in this final dispensation of grace. No doubt they will be members of the Council of the Twelve or of the First Presidency of the Church. Their prophetic ministry to rebellious Jewry shall be the same in length as was our Lord's personal ministry among their rebellious forebears.

4. The two olive trees, and the two candlesticks] Symbols of the two witnesses; meaning, perhaps, that as olive trees, they shall provide oil for the lamps of those who go forth to meet the Bridegroom (*Commentary I*, pp. 683-686); and that as lamp stands they shall reflect to men that light which comes from Him who is the Light of the World. (*Commentary I*, pp. 452-453.) Similar imagery was used by Zechariah to describe Joshua and Zerubbabel who ministered to the saints in their day. (Zech. 3 and 4.)

5-6. They shall have power like Elijah who called down fire from heaven to consume his enemies, and who sealed the heavens that it rained not in all Israel for the space of three and a half years (1 Kings 17 and 18; 2 Kings 1), and like Moses by whose word blood and plagues lay heavily upon the Egyptians. (Ex. 7, 8, 9, and 10.)

7. Satan shall slay them, by the hands of those in his employ, even as he slew their Lord and the prophets who were before them.

8. Jerusalem — the city of wickedness! "It cannot be that a prophet perish out of Jerusalem. O Jerusalem, Jerusalem, which killest the prophets, and stonest them that are sent unto thee." (Luke 13:33-34.)

The great city] Here it is Jerusalem; elsewhere it is Rome; in principle it is any and all of the cities of world — cities where the gospel is rejected, where the saints are slain, where wickedness reigns. "Babylon marks its idolatry, Egypt its tyranny, Sodom its desperate corruption, Jerusalem its pretensions to sanctity on the ground of spiritual privileges, whilst all the while it is the murderer of Christ in the person of his members." (*Jamieson*, p. 577.)

10. The level of spiritual debauchery is shown forth by the fact that the wicked not only slay the prophets of God, but boast of their deeds and glory in them. Such people, as the Jaredites and Nephites before them, are ripened in iniquity and are ready for that destruction and burning which shall cleanse the vineyard of corruption when Jesus descends with his chariots of fire.

11-12. On the third day, the slain witnesses are resurrected and ascend into heaven, as did He before them who laid down His life that they and all men shall rise from death's dark door to a state of light and immortality.

13. A great earthquake] See Rev. 16:17-21.

14. After showing John the woes that would befall mankind before the Second Coming (Rev. 6:9-17; 7; 8:1-13), the Lord by an angelic ministrant promised three more woes, which were to attend and usher in the reign of the Great King. (Rev. 8:13.) The first of these was the unbelievably destructive series of wars leading up to the final great holocaust. (Rev. 9:1-12.) The second was the final great war itself in which one-third of the hosts of men should be slain. (Rev. 9:12-21; 10; 11:1-14.) And now the third woe is to be the destruction of the remainder of the wicked when the vineyard is burned by divine power and the earth changes from its telestial to its terrestrial state. In destructive power and effect this woe is to surpass all others many times over.

CHRIST SHALL REIGN OVER ALL THE EARTH

REVELATION 11:15-19.

15 And the seventh angel sounded; and there were great voices in heaven, saying, The kingdoms of this world are become *the kingdoms* of our Lord, and of his Christ; and he shall reign for ever and ever.

16 And the four and twenty elders, which sat before God on their seats, fell upon their faces, and worshipped God,

17 Saying, We give thee thanks, O Lord God Almighty, which art, and wast, and art to come; because thou hast taken to thee thy great power, and hast reigned.

18 And the nations were angry, and thy wrath is come, and the time of the dead, that they should be judged, and that thou shouldest give reward unto thy servants the prophets, and to the saints, and them that fear thy name, small and great; and shouldest destroy them which destroy the earth.

19 And the temple of God was opened in heaven, and there was seen in his temple the ark of his testament: and there were lightnings, and voices, and thunderings, and an earthquake, and great hail.

15. Lo, the Great Millennium cometh! And Christ reigneth! "And the Lord shall be king over all the earth: in that day shall there be one Lord, and his name one." (Zech. 14:9.) In that day he shall make "a full end of all nations" (D. & C. 87:6), as he said: "I will be your ruler when I come" (D. & C. 41:4); and, "Ye shall have no laws but my laws when I come, for I am your lawgiver." (D. & C. 38:22.) In that day, "Out of Zion shall go forth the law, and the word of the Lord from Jerusalem." (Isa. 2:3.)

He shall reign for ever and ever] Daniel spoke similarly of the same day. "I beheld till the thrones were cast down," he said, and that to the Son of Man "there was given . . . dominion, and glory, and a kingdom, that all people, nations, and languages, should serve him: his dominion is an everlasting dominion, which shall not pass away, and his kingdom that which shall not be destroyed." (Dan. 7:9-14.) See Rev. 20:4-6.

16-17. See Rev. 4:1-11.

17. Thou . . . hast reigned] During the Millennium the Lord shall reign personally upon the earth, and through him his Father shall reign in the hearts of men.

18. The nations were angry] Before the Lord comes there shall be such anger, hate and enmity among and between nations as has never before been known, and out of it shall come the most devastating wars of history. "The Lord reigneth; let the people tremble." (Ps. 99:1.)

Thy wrath is come] See Rev. 6:12-17.

The time of the dead] The first resurrection when the faithful saints shall rise in glorious immortality. "For the day cometh that the Lord shall utter his voice out of heaven; the heavens shall shake and the earth shall tremble, and the trump of God shall sound both long and loud, and shall say to the sleeping nations: Ye saints arise and live; ye sinners stay and sleep until I shall call again." (D. & C. 43:18.) See Rev. 20:4-6.

That they should be judged] The righteous dead, the prophets, the saints of God, those both "small and great" who have kept his commandments shall come forth from their graves when the Lord comes; their resurrection shall be a judgment for they shall have celestial bodies; and ever thereafter shall they live and reign as kings and priests. (Rev. 20:4-6; D. & C. 29:12-13.)

Destroy them which destroy the earth] When the Lord comes the wicked shall be destroyed. "For I will reveal myself from heaven," he says, "with power and great glory, with all the hosts thereof, and dwell in righteousness with men on earth a thousand years, and the wicked shall not stand." (D. & C. 29:11.) "And every corruptible thing, both of man, or of the beasts of the field, or of the fowls of the heavens, or of the fish of the sea, that dwells upon all the face of the earth, shall be consumed." (D. & C. 101:24.) See Rev. 6:12-17; 2 Pet. 3:10-18.

19. In Israel's temple the ark of the covenant rested behind the veil in the Holy of Holies, which was entered by "the high priest alone once every year." (Heb. 9:7.) Here John sees that ark in the temple in heaven, signifying as Paul had taught aforetime, that all the faithful saints may now enter the Lord's eternal Holy of Holies and there receive celestial rest. See Heb. 9:1-14. Actually there is no temple in heaven, for heaven itself is a temple, and "the Lord God Almighty and the Lamb are the temple of it." (Rev. 21:22.) See *Commentary II*, pp. 73-77.

SATAN MAKETH WAR IN HEAVEN AND ON EARTH

REVELATION 12:1-17.

1 And there appeared a great wonder in heaven; a woman clothed with the sun, and the moon under her feet, and upon her head a crown of twelve stars:

2 And she being with child cried, travailing in birth, and pained to be delivered.

3 And there appeared another wonder in heaven; and behold a great red dragon, having seven heads and ten horns, and seven crowns upon his heads.

4 And his tail drew the third part of the stars of heaven, and did cast them to the earth: and the dragon stood before the woman which was ready to be delivered, for to devour her child as soon as it was born.

5 And she brought forth a man child, who was to rule all nations with a rod of iron: and her child

was caught up unto God, and *to* his throne.

6 And the woman fled into the wilderness, where she hath a place prepared of God, that they should feed her there a thousand two hundred *and* threescore days.

7 And there was war in heaven: Michael and his angels fought against the dragon; and the dragon fought and his angels,

8 And prevailed not; neither was their place found any more in heaven.

9 And the great dragon was cast out, that old serpent, called the Devil, and Satan, which deceiveth the whole world: he was cast out into the earth, and his angels were cast out with him.

10 And I heard a loud voice saying in heaven, Now is come salvation, and strength, and the kingdom of our God, and the power of his Christ: for the accuser of our brethren is cast down, which accused them before our God day and night.

11 And they overcame him by the blood of the Lamb, and by the word of their testimony; and they loved not their lives unto the death.

12 Therefore rejoice, *ye* heavens, and ye that dwell in them. Woe to the inhabiters of the earth and of the sea! for the devil is come down unto you, having great wrath, because he knoweth that he hath but a short time.

13 And when the dragon saw that he was cast unto the earth, he persecuted the woman which brought forth the man *child.*

14 And to the woman were given two wings of a great eagle, that she might fly into the wilderness, into her place, where she is nourished for a time, and times, and half a time, from the face of the serpent.

15 And the serpent cast out of his mouth water as a flood after the woman, that he might cause her to be carried away of the flood.

16 And the earth helped the woman, and the earth opened her mouth, and swallowed up the flood which the dragon cast out of his mouth.

17 And the dragon was wroth with the woman, and went to make war with the remnant of her seed, which keep the commandments of God, and have the testimony of Jesus Christ.

I.V. REVELATION 12:1-17.

1 And there appeared a great **sign** in heaven, **in the likeness of things on the earth;** a woman clothed with the sun, and the moon under her feet, and upon her head a crown of twelve stars.

2 And **the woman** being with child, cried, travailing in birth, and pained to be delivered.

3 And she brought forth a man
child, who was to rule all nations
with a rod of iron; and her child
was caught up unto God and his
throne.

4 And there appeared another
sign in heaven; and behold, a
great red dragon, having seven
heads and ten horns, and seven
crowns upon his heads. And his
tail drew the third part of the
stars of heaven, and did cast them
to the earth. And the dragon
stood before the woman which was
delivered, **ready** to devour her
child **after** it was born.

5 And the woman fled into the
wilderness, where she had a place
prepared of God, that they should
feed her there a thousand two
hundred and three score **years.**

6 And there was war in heaven;
Michael and his angels fought
against the dragon; and the
dragon **and his angels** fought
against Michael;

7 And **the dragon** prevailed not
against Michael, neither the child,
nor the woman which was the
church of God, who had been de-
livered of her pains, and brought
forth the kingdom of our God and
his Christ.

8 Neither was there place
found in heaven **for** the great
dragon, **who** was cast out; that
old serpent called the devil, and
also called Satan, which deceiveth
the whole world; he was cast out
into the earth; and his angels were
cast out with him.

9 And I heard a loud voice saying in heaven, Now is come salvation, and strength, and the kingdom of our God, and the power of
his Christ;

10 For the accuser of our
brethren is cast down, which
accused them before our God day
and night.

11 **For they have overcome** him
by the blood of the Lamb, and
by the word of their testimony;
for they loved not their own lives,
but kept the testimony even unto
death. Therefore, rejoice **O** heavens, and ye that dwell in them.

12 **And after these things I**
heard another voice saying, Woe
to the inhabiters of the earth, **yea,**
and they who dwell upon the is-
lands of the sea! for the devil is
come down unto you, having great
wrath, because he knoweth that
he hath but a short time.

13 For when the dragon saw
that he was cast unto the earth,
he persecuted the woman which
brought forth the man child.

14 **Therefore,** to the woman
were given two wings of a great
eagle, that she might flee into the
wilderness, into her place, where
she is nourished for a time, and
times, and half a time, from the
face of the serpent.

15 And the serpent **casteth** out of his mouth water as a flood after the woman, that he might cause her to be carried away of the flood.

16 And the earth **helpeth** the woman, and the earth **openeth** her mouth, and **swalloweth** up the flood which the dragon **casteth** out of his mouth.

17 **Therefore,** the dragon was wroth with the woman, and went to make war with the remnant of her seed, which keep the commandments of God, and have the testimony of Jesus Christ.

John now sees the organization of the Church in the meridian dispensation and the attempt to create the Millennial Kingdom by the saints of that day. He sees the inevitable and destined failure of that attempt, the full restoration of the kingdom to Israel being reserved for a later dispensation. See *Commentary II*, pp. 21-27. Then the day of universal apostasy and spiritual darkness is revealed; the great warfare of Satan with earth's inhabitants is shown forth; the restoration of the gospel is alluded to; and some events, probably in this dispensation, in which the Church is preserved are named.

I. V. 1-3, 7. A woman ("the church of God"!) gives birth to a man child ("the kingdom of our God and his Christ" which shall hold sway during the Millennial Era, the kingdom John has just seen in vision!). See Rev. 11:14-19. Such is the Prophet's inspired interpretation. Among Biblical scholars of the world, the man child is presumed to be Christ, a speculative conclusion which, though seemingly persuasive, is refuted by the obvious fact that the Church did not bring forth Christ; he is the Creator of the Church. Among Latter-day Saint scriptural exegetes, it is not uncommon to say that the man child is the priesthood, a seemingly persuasive speculation, which again however must be rejected by the same line of reasoning. The Church did not bring forth the priesthood, but the priesthood is the power that brought the Church into being.

K. J. 1. A woman clothed with the sun] The Church in all its glory, beauty, power and perfection — a glory like the sun in the firmament; the Church in which there is power to prepare men to attain that celestial world whose glory is typified by the brightness of that same heavenly luminary. (D. & C. 76:70.)

The moon under her feet] As the moon shines by reflected light, so do all earthly churches and kingdoms. They are under, beneath and lower than the true Church. The highest eternal reward they can offer is the terrestrial kingdom, whose glory is like the moon. (1 Cor. 15:40-41.)

Upon her head a crown of twelve stars] The twelve apostles of the Lamb, who are at the head and preside over the Church, and who with "the saints, . . . small and great" (Rev. 11:18), shall have place in the promised kingdom.

3. John saw Lucifer (the great red dragon), who appears in various forms (having seven heads and ten horns), and who rules over many nations and kingdoms (wearing seven crowns).

4, 7-10. The whole chapter deals with warfare between the saints and the devil. These five verses are parenthetical interpolations; they are inserted to show that this war on earth (note verse 17) actually commenced in heaven and is but a continuation of the confict commenced there.

4. The third part] One-third of that great host of spirit children destined to receive a mortal probation on this planet rebelled and followed Lucifer. (D. & C. 29:36.)

The stars of heaven] Figurative language describing the spirit children of the Father, among whom were "the morning stars" who sang together at the prospect of gaining mortal bodies and the experiences of an earthly probation. (Job 38:4-7.)

Cast them to the earth] The rebellious spirits, denied bodies, were cast down to earth. "I beheld Satan as lightning fall from heaven," Jesus said. (Luke 10:18.) And so it was also with all those who followed him.

5. A rod of iron] The gospel, the priesthood, the laws and power of God. In Lehi's dream, seen later by Nephi, "the rod of iron . . . was the word of God" which led to eternal life. (1 Ne. 11:25.)

6, 14. In the war on earth, Satan prevailed over the meridian saints, and the Church of God was taken away; dire and universal apostasy prevailed until the day of restoration.

7. And there was war in heaven] What kind of war? The same kind that prevails on earth; the only kind Satan and spirit beings can wage — a war of words, a tumult of opinions, a conflict of ideologies; a war between truth and error, between light and darkness, between the gospel of Jesus Christ, with all its saving power, and the false religions of the world, which have a form of godliness but are devoid of saving grace. And the battle lines are still drawn. It is now on earth as it was then in heaven; every man must choose which general he will follow.

Michael] See Jude 7-13.

9. The Devil] "The devil (literally meaning slanderer) is a spirit son of God who was born in the morning of pre-existence. (D. & C. 76:25-26.) Endowed with agency, the free power of choice, he chose the evil part from the beginning, thus placing himself in eternal opposition to the divine will. He was 'a liar from the beginning.' (D. & C. 93:25.)" (*Mormon Doctrine*, 2nd ed., p. 192.) See *Commentary I*, pp. 166-169; 266-269; 307-314; 416-417.

Satan] "Satan is a formal Hebrew name for the devil and means adversary, signifying that he wages open war with the truth and all who obey its principles." (*Mormon Doctrine*, 2nd ed., p. 677.)

10. Now is the time and the day when salvation may be won because Satan has been cast down to earth. He and his followers are here in opposition to all righteousness. It is only by resisting his wiles and rising above his carnal way of life that men can pass the test of mortality which assures them of salvation. Without opposition there could be no salvation; "it must needs be, that there is an opposition in all things. If not so, . . . righteousness could not be brought to pass, neither wickedness, neither holiness nor misery, neither good nor bad." (2 Ne. 2:11.)

11. Overcame him by the blood of the lamb] If there had been no atonement of Christ, Satan's designs for men would have prevailed. In that event, there would have been neither immortality nor eternal life, and all men would have remained forever in "the grasp of this awful monster . . . death and hell." (2 Ne. 9:6-26.)

Except for the shedding of the blood of Christ there is no way to overcome the world and gain salvation.

12-13. Satan makes war with the saints in the meridian of time.

14. He prevails; the Church is taken from the earth — for a specified period, for the age of spiritual darkness and universal apostasy.

15-17. Again the Church is found among men; there has been a restoration of the everlasting gospel. Satan continues his warfare, but the Lord preserves his latter-day kingdom. As Satan centers his opposition upon the gathered remnants of a once glorious people, the especial targets of his fiery darts are those who arc obedient and faithful.

SATAN GOVERNS EARTHLY KINGDOMS

REVELATION 13:1-10.

1 And I stood upon the sand of the sea, and saw a beast rise up out of the sea, having seven heads and ten horns, and upon his horns ten crowns, and upon his heads the name of blasphemy.

2 And the beast which I saw was like unto a leopard, and his feet were as *the feet* of a bear, and his mouth as the mouth of a lion: and the dragon gave him his power, and his seat, and great authority.

3 And I saw one of his heads as it were wounded to death; and his deadly wound was healed: and all the world wondered after the beast.

4 And they worshipped the dragon which gave power unto the beast: and they worshipped the beast, saying,Who *is* like unto the beast? who is able to make war with him?

5 And there was given unto him a mouth speaking great things and blasphemies; and power was given unto him to continue forty *and* two months.

6 And he opened his mouth in blasphemy against God, to blaspheme his name, and his tabernacle, and them that dwell in heaven.

7 And it was given unto him to make war with the saints, and to overcome them: and power was

given him over all kindreds, and tongues, and nations.

8 And all that dwell upon the earth shall worship him, whose names are not written in the book of life of the Lamb slain from the foundation of the world.

9 If any man have an ear, let him hear.

10 He that leadeth into captivity shall go into captivity: he that killeth with the sword must be killed with the sword. Here is the patience and the faith of the saints.

I.V. REVELATION 13:1.

1 And **I saw another sign, in the likeness of the kingdoms of the earth;** a beast rise up out of the sea, **and he stood upon the sand of the sea,** having seven heads and ten horns; and upon his horns ten crowns; and upon his heads the name of blasphemy.

The Prophet Joseph Smith gave this counsel to missionaries: "Declare the first principles, and let mysteries alone, lest ye be overthrown. Never meddle with the visions of beasts and subjects you do not understand." (*Teachings*, p. 292.) He then read Rev. 13:1-8 as an illustration of scriptural passages which should not be used in presenting the message of the restoration to the world. With reference to this passage, he named some of the speculative interpretations found in the sectarian world; said pointedly that they are "not true"; gave some explanations which show the general concept involved; but refrained from identifying those nations and kingdoms whose acts and course are set forth in the imagery revealed to John. (*Teachings*, pp. 292-293.)

John is here seeing a beast in heaven, which is "in the likeness of the kingdoms of the earth" (I.V. verse 1), that is, the beast is being used to symbolize certain unnamed kingdoms on earth and to show their dealings toward the saints and the cause of righteousness.

1-3. Various kingdoms (whether civic or ecclesiastical or both is not stated) shall receive power from Satan to blaspheme the God of heaven and to fight his work. See Rev. 17:1-18.

1. Blasphemy] "Blasphemy consists in either or both of the following: 1. Speaking irreverently, evilly, abusively, or scurrilously against God or sacred things; or 2. Speaking profanely or falsely about Deity." (*Mormon Doctrine*, 2nd ed., p. 90.) It is blasphemous to worship an idol, an emperor, a so-called saint, or for that matter even a true prophet or an angel of God in heaven. True worship is reserved for God alone, as the angel giving this very revelation to John is soon to tell him. (Rev. 19:9-10.)

2. **The dragon gave him his power]** The devil gives power, positions of influence, and great authority to those kingdoms which follow him. "There is a mistranslation of the word dragon" in this verse, the Prophet says. "It ought to be translated devil in this case and not dragon." (*Teachings*, p. 293.)

3. "Some spiritualizers say the beast that received the wound was Nebuchadnezzar, some Constantine, some Mohammed, and others the Roman Catholic Church; but we will look at what John saw in relation to this beast. Now for the wasp's nest. The translators have used the term 'dragon' for devil. Now it was a beast that John saw in heaven, and he was then speaking of 'things which must shortly come to pass;' and consequently the beast that John saw could not be Nebuchadnezzar. The beast John saw was an actual beast, and an actual intelligent being gives him his power, and his seat, and great authority. It was not to represent a beast in heaven: it was an angel in heaven who has power in the last days to do a work.

" 'All the world wondered after the beast,' Nebuchadnezzar and Constantine the Great not excepted. And if the beast was all the world, how could the world wonder after the beast? It must have been a wonderful beast to cause all human beings to wonder after it; and I will venture to say that when God allows the old devil to give power to the beast to destroy the inhabitants of the earth, all will wonder." (*Teachings*, p. 293.)

4. That the beast does not represent all the world, but only selected "kingdoms of the earth" (I. V. verse 1), is evident from this explanation of the Prophet: "Some say it means the kingdom of the world. One thing is sure, it does not mean the kingdom of the Saints. Suppose we admit that it means the kingdoms of the world, what propriety would there be in saying, Who is able to

make war with my great big self? If these spiritualized interpretations are true, the book contradicts itself in almost every verse. But they are not true." (*Teachings*, p. 293.)

4. They worshipped the dragon] Who worships the devil? An immediate and superficial reaction is: Why, no one, or at least scarcely anyone. But more mature reflection leads to the realization that just as the true worship of God consists in keeping his commandments, and in emulating those characteristics and attributes which he possesses, so to pursue a Godless course of rebellion against the truth, to revel in wickedness, and to live carnal and unclean lives is, in the very nature of things, to worship Satan.

They worshipped the beast] Even the kingdoms, which follow Satan's course, shall inspire awe, reverence, and worship on the part of Godless men. In this connection, here is a point to ponder: Do those who espouse Godless communism, substitute the worship of the state for the worship of God?

Who is able to make war with him?] The kingdom (or kingdoms) involved will be a world power (or powers). Wealth, weapons, armies, a ruthless nature and a warlike stance will strike terror into other hearts.

5-6. The beast holds sway and rules with blasphemy and wickedness among apostate peoples for the appointed time.

7-8. "In the last days" (*Teachings*, p. 293), the beast shall have power over every nation, and shall make war with the saints and prevail over all except those who are true and faithful to the standards of the restored gospel.

8. Book of life] See Rev. 3:1-6; 20:11-15.

The Lamb slain from the foundation of the world] See Rev. 5:1-14.

9. Those who have revelation, whose ears are attuned to the whisperings of the Spirit, shall understand the message John is recording.

10. 'Those who lead men into the captivity of sin shall themselves become captives in hell. Those who slay the saints shall themselves be slain spiritually by the sword of the Lord. And in God's own time the patience and faith of his saints shall be rewarded.'

Church of the devil] See Rev. 17:1-18.

CHURCH OF DEVIL WORKETH MIRACLES

REVELATION 13:11-18.

11 And I beheld another beast coming up out of the earth; and he had two horns like a lamb, and he spake as a dragon.

12 And he exerciseth all the power of the first beast before him, and causeth the earth and them which dwell therein to worship the first beast, whose deadly wound was healed.

13 And he doeth great wonders, so that he maketh fire come down from heaven on the earth in the sight of men.

14 And deceiveth them that dwell on the earth by *the means of* those miracles which he had power to do in the sight of the beast; saying to them that dwell on the earth, that they should make an image to the beast, which had the wound by a sword, and did live.

15 And he had power to give life unto the image of the beast, that the image of the beast should both speak, and cause that as many as would not worship the image of the beast should be killed.

16 And he causeth all, both small and great, rich and poor, free and bond, to receive a mark in their right hand, or in their foreheads:

17 And that no man might buy or sell, save he that had the mark, or the name of the beast, or the number of his name.

18 Here is wisdom. Let him that hath understanding count the number of the beast: for it is the number of a man; and his number *is* Six hundred threescore *and* six.

11-12. Other evil and devil-led powers arise to exercise dominion over man in his fallen and spiritually degenerate state. The identity of these powers remains to be revealed.

13-15. Lucifer is the Great Imitator. He patterns his kingdom after that of God the Lord. The Lord proclaims a plan of salvation; Satan sponsors a plan of damnation. Signs follow those who believe and obey the law of the gospel, and false signs, false wonders, false miracles attend the ministry of the Master of Sin. Knowledge is power, and because he knows more about many things than mortal men, the Great Imitator is able to blind the eyes and deceive the hearts of men and to put his own seal of verity, that of false miracles, on his damning philosophies. Thus those who place themselves wholly at his disposal have power to imitate the deeds of the prophets, as the magicians of Egypt imitated the miracles of Moses and as Simon the scorcerer sought to duplicate the works of Peter.

16-18. As the servants of God have their calling and election made sure when they are "sealed . . . in their foreheads" (Rev. 7:2-8), so the Great Imitator places a mark in the right hand or foreheads of those who follow him. Figuratively, this means they receive blessings — if his rewards lawfully may be so named — from under his hands. In the literal sense, we have, of course, seen marks and signs which identify and set apart those who adhere to religious systems that are not of God and which use economic sanctions as a tool to force adherence to their system of worship. It will be interesting — interesting? nay, fascinating! — to see what the future holds as the full meaning of this passage unfolds and the identity of the actual "beast" is revealed.

"THE LAMB SHALL STAND UPON MOUNT ZION"

REVELATION 14:1-5.

1 And I looked, and, lo, a Lamb stood on the mount Sion, and with him an hundred forty *and* four thousand, having his Father's name written in their foreheads.

2 And I heard a voice from heaven, as the voice of many waters, and as the voice of a great thunder: and I heard the voice of harpers harping with their harps:

3 And they sung as it were a new song before the throne, and before the four beasts, and the elders: and no man could learn that song but the hundred *and* forty *and* four thousand, which were redeemed from the earth.

4 These are they which were not defiled with women; for they are virgins. These are they which follow the Lamb whithersoever he goeth. These were redeemed from among men, *being* the firstfruits unto God and to the Lamb.

5 And in their mouth was found no guile: for they are without fault before the throne of God.

There are two Jerusalems and two Mount Zions. The old city and mount are in Canaan, the holy land of ancient times; the new city and mount are in America, the Zion and choice land of latter-days.

Mount Zion of old, adjacent to Jerusalem, was a sacred site in ancient Israel (Ps. 48:1-3; 74:2; 78:68; 125:1; Isa. 8:18), and the new Mount Zion, which shall yet flourish on the American continent in heaven-borne splendor, shall stand as a holy place in the worship of modern Israel. (Ps. 48:1-3; Isa. 4:5; 18:7; 24:23; 29:8; 31:4; Joel 2:32; Obad. 17, 21; Mic. 4:7.)

Our hope is centered, not in the ashes of what once was, but in the majestic grandeur of what is to be. Our affirmation of hope is: "We believe . . . that Zion will be built upon this [the American] continent." (Tenth Article of Faith.) What concerns us is: "The word of the Lord concerning his church, established in the last days for the restoration of his people, as he has spoken by the mouth of his prophets, and for the gathering of his saints to stand upon Mount Zion, which shall be the city of New Jerusalem." This word of revelation from the Almighty includes the fact that the New Jerusalem "shall be built beginning at the temple lot, which is appointed by the finger of the Lord, in the western boundaries of the State of Missouri, and dedicated by the hand of Joseph Smith, Jun., and others with whom the Lord was well pleased. Verily, this is the word of the Lord, that the city New Jerusalem shall be built by the gathering of the saints, beginning at this place, even the place of the temple." It is in this temple that "the sons of Moses and of Aaron shall be filled with the glory of the Lord, upon Mount Zion in the Lord's house." (D. & C. 84:2-4, 32.)

1. A lamb stood on the mount Sion] Which Mount Zion? All of the references to Mount Zion which talk of the Second

Coming and related latter-day events appear to have in mind the new Mount Zion in Jackson County, Missouri. Thus we read: "Prepare ye the way of the Lord, and make his paths straight, for the hour of his coming is nigh — When the Lamb shall stand upon Mount Zion, and with him a hundred and forty-four thousand, having his Father's name written on their foreheads."

Then comes this explanatory comment which shows the Lord will appear many places at his coming: "For behold, he shall stand upon the mount of Olivet, and upon the mighty ocean, even the great deep, and upon the islands of the sea, and upon the land of Zion." And then, using some language borrowed from Rev. 14:2, the revelation continues: "And he shall utter his voice out of Zion, and he shall speak from Jerusalem, and his voice shall be heard among all people; And it shall be a voice as the voice of many waters, and as the voice of a great thunder, which shall break down the mountains, and the valleys shall not be found." (D. & C. 133:17-22.)

It seems clear that the Lord and his exalted associates shall stand in glory upon the American Mount Zion, although it may well be that in his numerous other appearances, including that on the Mount of Olivet, which is itself but a few stones' throw from old Mount Zion, he shall also be accompanied by the 144,000 high priests, "for they follow the Lamb whithersoever he goeth." (Verse 4.)

An hundred forty and four thousand] See Rev. 7:2-8.

Having his Father's name written in their foreheads] See Rev. 3:7-13.

2. The voice of many waters] The sound created by oceans of water as He who created both earth and sea drives "the great deep . . . back into the north countries, and the islands shall become one land." (D. & C. 133:23.)

3. A new song] A song of victory and triumph; a song hailing Christ's Millennial reign, a song proclaiming that the kingdoms of this world are swept away, and that the true King of Earth now dwells with men; a song of redemption and glory and honor; a song that cannot be sung until the promised day of peace and righteousness arrives.

The four beasts, and the elders] See Rev. 4:1-11.

4-5. A perfect description of all exalted beings! For, as with the 144,000, so with all of whom the glorified Lord says, "Ye shall be even as I am." (3 Ne. 28:10.)

4. They are virgins] They are pure and undefiled. Also: "Their not being defiled with women, means they were not led astray from Christian faithfulness by the tempters who jointly constitute the spiritual 'harlot.'" (*Jamieson*, p. 585.)

GOSPEL RESTORED BY ANGELIC MINISTRANTS

REVELATION 14:6-7.

6 And I saw another angel fly in the midst of heaven, having the everlasting gospel to preach unto them that dwell on the earth, and to every nation, and kindred, and tongue, and people,

7 Saying with a loud voice, Fear God, and give glory to him; for the hour of his judgment is come: and worship him that made heaven, and earth, and the sea, and the fountains of waters.

This announcement of the restoration of the gospel — glorious in its import — testifies of at least eight great and wonderous realities:

1. There is to be revelation after the day of John, after New Testament times, after the gospel given by Jesus has been lost; the heavens once again shall rain down righteousness as in days of old. See Rev. 1:1-6.

2. It is the gospel, the plan of salvation, the power of God unto salvation, the very thing preached by Jesus and John, by Peter and Paul and all the holy apostles, which shall be revealed by the angel. See *Commentary II*, pp. 213-216.

3. This gospel is everlasting; it is without beginning of days or end of years; it is the same plan of salvation always and for-

ever. It was had anciently; it shall continue to all eternity. Its terms and conditions apply on this earth and on all the creations of God. It saved Adam and Enoch; it guided Abraham and Moses; it was the standard heralded by John and Matthew; and its truths were to come again to Joseph Smith and latter-day Israel. See *Commentary II*, pp. 491-493.

4. It shall come by angelic ministration. Holy beings shall come from God's presence to bring again his eternal truths. The heavens, long sealed, shall be opened. See *Commentary II*, pp. 96-98.

5. There is to be absolute, total, complete apostasy after John's day and before the angelic ministrations commence. The falling away shall be complete, the apostasy universal. Gross darkness shall be everywhere. The gospel shall not be found in any nation, among any kindred; no tongue shall teach its truths, and no people rejoice in its blessings, for all these shall receive it as a result of the angelic ministrations. See 2 Thess. 2:1-12; 2 Tim. 3:1-13.

6. The knowledge of God shall be restored so that men once again can worship their Creator, rather than the idols of the pagans, the ill-defined nothingness described in the creeds of Christendom, or the laws and forces of the universe. See *Commentary II*, pp. 154-162; Jas. 1:1-7.

7. All this shall transpire after John's day and before the Second Coming of the Son of Man; it shall precede the hour of his judgment, the hour when he returns to assemble all nations before him, with the sheep on his right hand and the goats on his left. See *Commentary I*, pp. 689-695.

8. And it shall result in the fall of Babylon (verse 8), for the onrush of truth cannot and will not be stayed. Truth will prevail! Such is an eternal verity. See Rev. 17:1-18.

Now, as to the actual work of restoration — what angel performed this mighty deed, this work which involves the salvation of all men on earth in these latter-days? Who restored the everlasting gospel? Was it one angel or many?

It is traditional (and true!) to reply: 'Moroni, son of Mormon, the now resurrected Nephite prophet, who holds the keys of "the stick of Ephraim" (D. & C. 27:5), the one through whose ministry the Book of Mormon was again brought to light.' The reasoning is that the Book of Mormon contains "the fulness of the everlasting gospel" (D. & C. 135:3); that therein is God's message of salvation for all of earth's inhabitants; and that this gospel message is now being taken by the Lord's witnesses to one nation, and kindred, and tongue, and people after another.

The Book of Mormon, revealed to man by angelic ministration, was first published to the world in 1830; thereafter, on November 3, 1831, the Lord himself both confirmed and expanded the interpretation of the vision seen by John. On that day he revealed to Joseph Smith a number of great truths about his Second Coming which are not found in the Book of Mormon. (D. & C. 133:1-35.) Then came this pronouncement:

"And now, verily saith the Lord, that these things might be known among you, O inhabitants of the earth, I have sent forth mine angel flying through the midst of heaven, having the everlasting gospel, who hath appeared unto some and hath committed it unto man, who shall appear unto many that dwell on the earth. And this gospel shall be preached unto every nation, and kindred, and tongue, and people. And the servants of God shall go forth, saying with a loud voice: Fear God and give glory to him, for the hour of his judgment is come; And worship him that made heaven, and earth, and the sea, and the fountains of waters — Calling upon the name of the Lord day and night, saying: O that thou wouldst rend the heavens, that thou wouldst come down, that the mountains might flow down at thy presence." (D. & C. 133:36-40.)

From this revelation we learn two things relative to the identity of the angel John saw "fly in the midst of heaven":

1. The angel (Moroni) had by that date already come, and the gospel message in the Book of Mormon was then on earth and would without fail go forth to all of its inhabitants; and

2. The angel of the restoration was yet, in the future, to "appear unto many that dwell on the earth."

Paul makes the apt statement that the gospel consists of two parts: the word and the power. (1 Thess. 1:5.) Thus Moroni brought the word, or at least that portion found in the Book of Mormon, for that record summarizes and teaches, in large part, what men must do to be saved. It records the terms and conditions of the plan of salvation. Also, before November 3, 1831, John the Baptist, and Peter, James, and John, as angelic ministrants, had brought keys and powers. But other angels were yet to come — Moses, Elias, Elijah, Gabriel, Raphael, and "divers angels, . . . all declaring their dispensation, their rights, their keys, their honors, their majesty and glory, and the power of their priesthood; giving line upon line, precept upon precept; here a little, and there a little." (D. & C. 128:21.)

Thus the angel Moroni brought the message, that is, the word; but other angels brought the keys and priesthood, the power. And in the final analysis the fulness of the everlasting gospel consists of all of the truths and powers needed to enable men to gain a fulness of salvation in the celestial heaven.

But one of the most interesting things about John's record of his vision is that it is one of those great prophetic utterances destined to have dual fulfillment. Just as many of the Messianic prophecies deal with both comings of the Lord, so this proclamation relative to an angel committing the everlasting gospel speaks of two widely separated occurrences. One is past, the other is future. The gospel has been restored both in word and in power. And yet there is a future day when the angel of the restoration shall fly again.

In a post-millennial setting; in a recitation of what is to be after the last man, including the sons of perdition, has been resurrected; in fact at the final great day when all things preceding the celestializing of the earth are past, then: "Another trump shall sound, which is the fifth trump, which is the fifth angel who committeth the everlasting gospel — flying through the midst of heaven, unto all nations, kindreds, tongues, and people; And this shall be the sound of his trump, saying to all people, both in heaven and in earth, and that are under the earth — for every ear shall hear it, and every knee shall bow, and every tongue shall confess, while they hear the sound of the trump, saying: Fear God, and give glory to him who sitteth upon the throne, forever and ever; for the hour of his judgment is come." (D. & C. 88:103-104.)

And so, as we ponder upon the identity, mission and ministry of the angel appointed to commit the everlasting gospel to men in latter-days, we are led to exclaim — 'What wonders of eternal truth are found in one short sentence of the revealed word!'

Gospel restored during the sixth seal] See Rev. 7:1.

ETERNAL TORMENT AWAITS THE WICKED

REVELATION 14:8-11.

8 And there followed another angel, saying, Babylon is fallen, is fallen, that great city, because she made all nations drink of the wine of the wrath of her fornication.

9 And the third angel followed them, saying with a loud voice, If any man worship the beast and his image, and receive *his* mark in his forehead, or in his hand,

10 The same shall drink of the wine of the wrath of God, which is poured out without mixture into the cup of his indignation; and he shall be tormented with fire and brimstone in the presence of the holy angels, and in the presence of the Lamb:

11 And the smoke of their torment ascendeth up for ever and ever: and they have no rest day nor night, who worship the beast and his image, and whosoever receiveth the mark of his name.

8. The fall of Babylon shall occur after the restoration of the gospel in this dispensation. See Rev. 14:6-7; 18:1-24.

The wine of the wrath of her fornication] "The wine of the wrath of God, the consequence of her fornication. As she made the nations drunk with the wine of her fornication, so she herself shall be made drunk with the wine of God's wrath." (*Jamieson*, p. 586.)

Fornication] Literally, sex immorality; figuratively, the worship of false gods; that is, false religious worship.

9-11. Eternal damnation, in the full and unlimited sense of the word, is meted out only to the sons of perdition. (*Mormon Doctrine*, 2nd ed., pp. 234-236.) They are the ones who choose to worship the devil; they sell themselves to Satan with the full knowledge that the Lord is God and beside him there is no Savior. To their torment there is no end. See Heb. 6:4-9. Also: Those who do not obey the law of the gospel, and who therefore inherit a lesser place in the mansions that are prepared, shall suffer the fires of eternal torment in the sense of having eternal regret for lost opportunities. See *Commentary I*, pp. 434-436; *Commentary II*, pp. 337-340.

9. See Rev. 13:11-18.

10. The wine . . . of God] "In the hand of the Lord there is a cup, and the wine is red; it is full of mixture; and he poureth out of the same: but the dregs thereof, all the wicked of the earth shall wring them out, and drink them." (Psalm 75:8.)

The wrath of God] "Deity manifests wrath as one of his attributes. It is an accompaniment of anger; indignation is its emotional basis; inherent in it is the purpose and intent of meting out a just punishment upon those whose acts have caused it to be aroused. The wrath of God does not fall upon the righteous, but upon the wicked. (D. & C. 1:9; 59:21.) 'Instead of blessings, ye, by your own works, bring cursings, wrath, indignation, and judgments upon your own heads, by your follies, and by all your abominations, which you practise before me, saith the Lord.' (D. & C. 124:48.)

"When men are 'ripened in iniquity,' then the fulness of the Lord's wrath comes upon them, and they are destroyed in the flesh. (Ether 2:8-9; 14:25.) Such was the case with the Jaredites, the Nephites, and the inhabitants of Sodom and Gomorrah, for instance; such will be the case with the wicked at the Second Coming. The 'fiery indignation of the wrath of God' will continue to be poured out upon the wicked in hell until the day of their resurrection. (Alma 40:14; Rev. 14:10; D. & C. 19:15; 76:106-

107.) Then, to all eternity, those subject to the second death shall be 'vessels of wrath, doomed to suffer the wrath of God, with the devil and his angels in eternity.' (D. & C. 76:33, 38.)" (*Mormon Doctrine*, 2nd ed., p. 851.)

Poured out without mixture] "Wine was so commonly mixed with water that to mix wine is used in Greek for to pour out wine; this wine of God's wrath is undiluted; there is no drop of water to cool its heat." (*Jamieson*, p. 586.) It is justice, not mercy, which the Lord will pour out upon the ungodly. "The wrath of God shall be poured out upon the wicked without measure." (D. & C. 1:9; 103:1-3.)

Tormented with fire and brimstone] See Rev. 20:7-10.

11. See Rev. 13:11-18; 20:7-10.

"BLESSED ARE THE DEAD WHICH DIE IN THE LORD"

REVELATION 14:12-13.

12 Here is the patience of the saints: here *are* they that keep the commandments of God, and the faith of Jesus.

13 And I heard a voice from heaven saying unto me, Write, Blessed *are* the dead which die in the Lord from henceforth: Yea, saith the Spirit, that they may rest from their labours; and their works do follow them.

12. The patience of the saints] See Jas. 5:7-11.

They that keep the commandments of God] As the Lord lives, none else shall be saved! How can it be stated more plainly? It is not the grace of God standing alone; it is not confessing the Lord Jesus with our lips and stopping there; it is not mere belief; it is not church membership as such; it is not a position of prominence or dignity in the Church; it is not any one or all of the thousand winds of doctrine that blow through the sectarian world. It is plain, simple obedience to the laws and ordinances of the gospel. "Ye cannot be saved in your sins." (Alma 11:37.)

The faith of Jesus] The gospel of the Lord Jesus Christ; the identical truths which he believed; the way of life that he lived — nothing short of this will save any man.

13. A voice from heaven . . . Yea, saith the Spirit] Gods and angels speak from heaven; words of eternal truth flow from their lips; and the Holy Spirit of God, dwelling in the hearts of the saints, echoes and re-echoes the endless verity of their divine words.

The dead which die in the Lord] The saints of God who have been true and faithful to every trust, who have kept the faith, who have endured to the end, who at their passing are prepared for an inheritance in the paradise of peace. In that revealed passage universally known as, "The Law of the Mourner," the Lord says of them: "Thou shalt live together in love, insomuch that thou shalt weep for the loss of them that die, and more especially for those that have not hope of a glorious resurrection. And it shall come to pass that those that die in me shall not taste of death, for it shall be sweet unto them." (D. & C. 42:45-46.)

They . . . rest from their labors] "And then shall it come to pass, that the spirits of those who are righteous are received into a state of happiness, which is called paradise, a state of rest, a state of peace, where they shall rest from all their troubles and from all care, and sorrow." (Alma 40:12.)

Their works do follow them] Nothing else is ever taken by anyone when he departs this mortal sphere. "That same spirit which doth possess your bodies at the time that ye go out of this life, that same spirit will have power to possess your body in that eternal world." (Alma 34:34.)

Resurrection] See *Commentary II*, pp. 388-390.

SON OF MAN HARVESTS THE EARTH

REVELATION 14:14-20.

14 And I looked, and behold a white cloud, and upon the cloud *one* sat like unto the Son of man, having on his head a golden crown, and in his hand a sharp sickle.

15 And another angel came out of the temple, crying with a loud voice to him that sat on the cloud, Thrust in thy sickle, and reap: for the time is come for thee to reap; for the harvest of the earth is ripe.

16 And he that sat on the cloud thrust in his sickle on the earth; and the earth was reaped.

17 And another angel came out of the temple which is in heaven, he also having a sharp sickle.

18 And another angel came out from the altar, which had power over fire; and cried with a loud cry to him that had the sharp sickle, saying, Thrust in thy sharp sickle, and gather the clusters of the vine of the earth; for her grapes are fully ripe.

19 And the angel thrust in his sickle into the earth, and gathered the vine of the earth, and cast *it* into the great winepress of the wrath of God.

20 And the winepress was trodden without the city, and blood came out of the winepress, even unto the horse bridles, by the space of a thousand *and* six hundred furlongs.

John now sees the harvest of the whole earth both the righteous and the wicked.

First, as recorded in verses 14-16, he sees the Son of Man harvest his saints. This is now in process, as the laborers in the Lord's vineyard, at his express command, thrust in their sickles and gather in the sheaves of precious grain. (D. & C. 4:4; 6:3-4; 31:3-5.)

Then, as recorded in verses 17-20, he sees the harvest-havoc wrought among the wicked and ungodly when the vintage grapes are slashed from their vines with a sharp sickle and trampled in the wine-press of the wrath of Him whose vineyard they have desecrated.

14. One like unto the Son of man] See Rev. 1:12-20.

15. An angel came out of the temple] Angelic ministrants from heaven itself were to restore the everlasting gospel and announce to the Lord's servants his decree that they should go forth and harvest the earth.

Out of the temple] See Rev. 11:15-19.

The harvest of the earth is ripe] "Behold, the field is white already to harvest; therefore, whoso desireth to reap, let him thrust in his sickle with his might, and reap while the day lasts, that he may treasure up for his soul everlasting salvation in the kingdom of God." (D. & C. 6:3.)

16. The earth was reaped] The harvest is sure. "None of them that my Father hath given me shall be lost." (D. & C. 50:42.)

17. Angelic ministrants shall also have part in the destruction of the wicked at the Second Coming, "for they that come shall burn them, saith the Lord of Hosts, that it shall leave them neither root nor branch." (Jos. Smith 2:37.)

18. Him that had the sharp sickle] The Son of Man; the Lord himself, who personally is to tread in the wine-vat.

19-20. In the day of harvest, "it shall be said: Who is this that cometh down from God in heaven with dyed garments; yea, from the regions which are not known, clothed in his glorious apparel, traveling in the greatness of his strength? And he shall say: I am he who spake in righteousness, mighty to save. And the Lord shall be red in his apparel, and his garments like him that treadeth in the wine-vat. . . . And his voice shall be heard: I have trodden the wine-press alone, and have brought judgment upon all people; and none were with me; And I have trampled them in my fury, and I did tread upon them in mine anger, and their blood have I sprinkled upon my garments, and stained all my raiment; for this was the day of vengeance which was in my heart." (D. & C. 133:46-51.)

And then in the day when all things are accomplished relative to the salvation of men, the angelic trumpet shall proclaim: "It is finished; it is finished! The Lamb of God hath overcome and trodden the wine-press alone, even the wine-press of the fierceness of the wrath of Almighty God." (D. & C. 88:106.) Indeed, in that day, the Son of Man himself, having delivered up the kingdom and presented it unto the Father, spotless, shall say: "I have overcome and have trodden the wine-press alone, even the wine-press of the fierceness of the wrath of Almighty God." (D. & C. 76:107.)

19. Winepress of the wrath of God] See Rev. 14:8-11.

20. The winepress was trodden without the city] The great destructions of Armageddon shall take place outside the city of

Jerusalem, in what Joel calls the Valley of Jehoshaphat, "for there will I sit to judge all the heathen round about," the Lord says. "Put ye in the sickle, for the harvest is ripe: come, get you down; for the press is full, the fats overflow; for their wickedness is great. Multitudes, multitudes in the valley of decision: for the day of the Lord is near in the valley of decision." (Joel 3:12-14.) See Rev. 16:12-16.

EXALTED SAINTS PRAISE GOD FOREVER

REVELATION 15:1-4.

1 And I saw another sign in heaven, great and marvellous, seven angels having the seven last plagues; for in them is filled up the wrath of God.

2 And I saw as it were a sea of glass mingled with fire: and them that had gotten the victory over the beast, and over his image, and over his mark, *and* over the number of his name, stand on the sea of glass, having the harps of God.

3 And they sing the song of Moses the servant of God, and the song of the Lamb, saying, Great and marvellous *are* thy works, Lord God Almighty; just and true *are* thy ways, thou King of saints.

4 Who shall not fear thee, O Lord, and glorify thy name? for *thou* only *art* holy: for all nations shall come and worship before thee; for thy judgments are made manifest.

15. The seven last plagues] These are set forth in Rev. 16, 17, and 18.

The wrath of God] See Rev. 14:8-11.

2. A sea of glass mingled with fire] See Rev. 4:1-11.

The beast etc.] See Rev. 13:11-18.

3-4. Moses and all the prophets of all the ages, as guided by the power of the Holy Spirit, have and do sing songs of everlasting praise unto God and the Lamb. How many are the revelations; how numerous are the inspired utterances; how abundant are the psalms of praise that fall from the lips of those who have seen and heard and felt the things of God. How many, like Lehi, have seen God, "sitting upon his throne, surrounded with numberless concourses of angels in the attitude of singing and praising their God." And how many, with him, have felt to exclaim: "Great and marvelous are thy works, O Lord God Almighty! Thy throne is high in the heavens, and thy power, and goodness, and mercy are over all the inhabitants of the earth; and, because thou art merciful, thou wilt not suffer those who come unto thee that they shall perish!" (1 Ne. 1:8, 14.)

3. Song of the Lamb] All the righteous saints of all the ages shall sing this song in celestial glory forevermore. "And the graves of the saints shall be opened; and they shall come forth and stand on the right hand of the Lamb, when he shall stand upon Mount Zion, and upon the holy city, the New Jerusalem; and they shall sing the song of the Lamb, day and night forever and ever." (D. & C. 133:56.) See Rev. 14:1-5.

GOD POURETH OUT PLAGUES UPON THE WICKED

REVELATION 15:5-8; 16:1-12.

5 And after that I looked, and, behold, the temple of the tabernacle of the testimony in heaven was opened:

6 And the seven angels came out of the temple, having the seven plagues, clothed in pure and white linen, and having their breasts girded with golden girdles.

7 And one of the four beasts gave unto the seven angels seven golden vials full of the wrath of God, who liveth for ever and ever.

8 And the temple was filled with smoke from the glory of God, and from his power; and no man was able to enter into the temple, till the seven plagues of the seven angels were fulfilled.

1 And I heard a great voice out of the temple saying to the seven angels, Go your ways, and pour out the vials of the wrath of God upon the earth.

2 And the first went, and poured out his vial upon the earth; and there fell a noisome and grievous sore upon the men which had the mark of the beast, and *upon* them which worshipped his image.

3 And the second angel poured out his vial upon the sea; and it became as the blood of a dead *man:* and every living soul died in the sea.

4 And the third angel poured out his vial upon the rivers and fountains of waters; and they became blood.

5 And I heard the angel of the waters say, Thou art righteous, O Lord, which art, and wast, and shalt be, because thou hast judged thus.

6 For they have shed the blood of saints and prophets, and thou hast given them blood to drink; for they are worthy.

7 And I heard another out of the altar say, Even so, Lord God Almighty, true and righteous *are* thy judgments.

8 And the fourth angel poured out his vial upon the sun; and power was given unto him to scorch men with fire.

9 And men were scorched with great heat, and blasphemed the name of God, which hath power over these plagues: and they repented not to give him glory.

10 And the fifth angel poured out his vial upon the seat of the beast; and his kingdom was full of darkness; and they gnawed their tongues for pain,

11 And blasphemed the God of heaven because of their pains and their sores, and repented not of their deeds.

12 And the sixth angel poured out his vial upon the great river Euphrates; and the water thereof was dried up, that the way of the kings of the east might be prepared.

I.V. REVELATION 16:7.

7 And I heard another **angel who came** out **from** the altar saying, Even so, Lord God Almighty, true and righteous are thy judgments.

God in his mercy shall pour out destructive plagues upon the wicked and ungodly in the last days. These diseases and calamities shall sweep great hosts of men from the face of the earth, preparatory to that final Millennial cleansing which shall prepare our planet as an abode for the righteous. As shown to John, the seven last plagues are:

1. A noisome and grievous sore. (Rev. 16:2.)

Could this be the plague spoken of by Zechariah in these words: "And this shall be the plague wherewith the Lord will smite all the people that have fought against Jerusalem; Their flesh shall consume away while they stand upon their feet, and their eyes shall consume away in their holes, and their tongue shall consume away in their mouth." (Zech. 14:12.) And is the Lord referring to it in these words of latter-day revelation: "And their flesh shall fall from off their bones, and their eyes from their sockets"? (D. & C. 29:19.)

2. Turning the waters of the sea to blood with the consequent death of the life therein. (V. 3.)

Could this be the curse to which the Lord was referring when he said: "Behold, I, the Lord, in the beginning blessed the waters; but in the last days, by the mouth of my servant John, I cursed the waters. Wherefore, the days will come that no flesh shall be safe upon the waters"? (D. & C. 61: 14-15.)

3. Turning of the rivers and fountains to blood so that all drinking water is diseased. (Vs. 4-7.)

Could this be the result of atomic fallout or other seemingly natural occurrences?

4. Changes in the effects of the sun so that men are scorched with fire and great heat. (Vs. 8-9.)

5. Spread of darkness (probably spiritual darkness) and pain and sores in the kingdoms of the world. (Vs. 10-11.)

6. Waters of the Euphrates, the river of Babylon, dry up; false miracles abound, and the armies of the world prepare for Armageddon. (Vs. 12-16.)

7. War and upheavals of nature lead to overthrow of Babylon itself. (Vs. 17-21, and chapters 17 and 18.)

15:5; 16:1. The Temple] See Rev. 11:15-19.

15:5. The tabernacle of the testimony in heaven] The courts of heavenly glory from which spiritual truth is dispensed, even as the earthly tabernacle (itself a temple) was the place from which light and knowledge was dispensed to the faithful in Israel.

7. Vials] Bowls; small vessels for liquids.

16:1. Pour out the vials of the wrath of God upon the earth] Pour out vengeance, anger, and plagues upon the earth and its inhabitants.

5-7. Men receive what they merit. The plagues of latter-days are a just retribution heaped upon those whose lives have been such as to reap the very harvest of pain, sorrow, and damnation which they receive.

5. The angel of the waters] Not a figurative expression, but the angel who poured out his vial upon the rivers and fountains of waters.

7. "The judgments of the Lord are true and righteous altogether." (Psalm 19:9.) How true it is, from everlasting to everlasting! What the Lord does is right! In "the day of judgment," the wicked shall "shrink with awful fear . . . and be constrained to exclaim: Holy, holy are thy judgments, O Lord God Almighty — but I know my guilt; I transgressed thy law, and my transgressions are mine; and the devil hath obtained me, that I am a prey to his awful misery." (2 Ne. 9:46.)

NATIONS ASSEMBLE FOR ARMAGEDDON

REVELATION 16:13-16.

13 And I saw three unclean spirits like frogs *come* out of the mouth of the dragon, and out of the mouth of the beast, and out of the mouth of the false prophet.

14 For they are the spirits of devils, working miracles, *which* go forth unto the kings of the earth and of the whole world, to gather them to the battle of that great day of God Almighty.

15 Behold, I come as a thief. Blessed *is* he that watcheth, and keepeth his garments, lest he walk naked, and they see his shame.

16 And he gathered them together into a place called in the Hebrew tongue Armageddon.

"Some 60 air miles north of Jerusalem lies the ancient city of Megiddo (now called Tell el-Mutesellim). In its north-central Palestinian location, Megiddo overlooks the great plain of Esdraelon, an area of some 20 by 14 miles in which many great battles took place anciently. Megiddo is the older Hebrew form of Armageddon or Har-Magedon meaning the Mount or Hill of Megiddo, or the Hill of Battles; it is 'the valley of Megiddon' mentioned in Zechariah. (Zech. 12:11.)

"At the very moment of the Second Coming of our Lord, 'all nations' shall be gathered 'against Jerusalem to battle' (Zech. 11; 12; 13; 14), and the battle of Armageddon (obviously covering the entire area from Jerusalem to Megiddo, and perhaps more) will be in progress. As John expressed it, 'the kings of the earth and of the whole world' will be gathered 'to the battle of that great day of God Almighty, . . . into a place called in the Hebrew tongue Armageddon.' Then Christ will 'come as a thief,' meaning unexpectedly, and the dramatic upheavals promised to accompany his return will take place. (Rev. 16:14-21.) It is incident to this battle of Armageddon that the Supper of the Great God shall take place (Rev. 19:11-18), and it is the same battle described by Ezekiel as the war with Gog and Magog. (Ezek. 38; 39; *Doctrines of Salvation*, vol. 3, p. 45.)" (*Mormon Doctrine*, 2nd ed., p. 74.)

13. Unclean spirits like frogs] Frogs are here used to typify the unclean spirits who have power to work miracles. The figure is taken from the experience of Moses and Aaron in Egypt. Even as they, by the power of God, brought forth a plague of frogs upon Pharaoh's land, so did the magicians, by the power of the devil, bring forth a similar plague. (Ex. 8:5-15.)

14. The spirits of devils, working miracles] Perhaps the greatest miracle wrought by these evil spirits will be the indoctrination of the hosts of men with that hate and avarice which will cause them to assemble — in an age of atomic warfare! — with a view to the utter destruction of civilization. See Rev. 13:11-18.

15. I come as a thief] See 1 Thess. 5:1-11; *Commentary I*, pp. 634-686.

Garments] See Rev. 3:1-6.

CHRIST COMES, ISLANDS FLEE, MOUNTAINS CEASE

REVELATION 16:17-21.

17 And the seventh angel poured out his vial into the air; and there came a great voice out of the temple of heaven, from the throne, saying, It is done.

18 And there were voices, and thunders, and lightnings; and

there was a great earthquake, such as was not since men were upon the earth, so mighty an earthquake, *and* so great.

19 And the great city was divided into three parts, and the cities of the nations fell: and great Babylon came in remembrance before God, to give unto her the cup of the wine of the fierceness of his wrath.

20 And every island fled away, and the mountains were not found.

21 And there fell upon men a great hail out of heaven, *every stone* about the weight of a talent: and men blasphemed God because of the plague of the hail; for the plague thereof was exceeding great.

Three natural changes in the earth — all apparently growing out of one transcendent happening — are here named as attending our Lord's Second Coming. They are:

1. Earth's land masses shall unite; islands and continents shall become one land.

2. Every valley shall be exalted and every mountain shall be made low; the rugged terrain of today shall level out into a millennial garden.

3. Such an earthquake as has never been known since man's foot was planted on this planet shall attend these changes in the earth's surface and appearance.

And, fourthly, as recorded elsewhere, the great deep — presumably the Atlantic ocean — shall return to its place in the north, "and the earth shall be like as it was in the days before it was divided." (D. & C. 133:21-24.)

18. A great earthquake] The rearrangement of mountains, valleys, islands, continents, and oceans — in the very nature of things — will cause the greatest earthquake of the ages. When the Lord at his coming, for instance, sets his feet "upon the mount of Olives," that holy mount "shall cleave in the midst thereof toward the east and toward the west, and there shall be a very great valley; and half of the mountain shall remove toward the north, and half of it toward the south." Of those in Jerusalem, in that day, the revealed record recites: "And ye shall flee to the valley of the mountains; for the valley of the mountains shall reach unto Azal: yea, ye shall flee, like as ye fled from before the earthquake in the days of Uzziah king of Judah: and the Lord my God shall come, and all the saints with thee." (Zech. 14:4-5.)

19. The cities of the nations fell] All worldly kingdoms shall be destroyed; none shall remain; the Lord shall make "a full end of all nations." (D. & C. 87:6.)

Babylon came in remembrance] See Rev. 18:1-24.

20. Every island fled away] "He shall command the great deep, and it shall be driven back into the north countries, and the islands shall become one land; And the land of Jerusalem and the land of Zion shall be turned back into their own place, and the earth shall be like as it was in the days before it was divided." (D. & C. 133:23-24.)

The mountains were not found] He "shall break down the mountains and the valleys shall not be found." (D. & C. 133:22.) The mountains shall flow down at his presence. (Isa. 64:1; D. & C. 133:40, 44.) "Every valley shall be exalted, and every mountain and hill shall be made low: and the crooked shall be made straight, and the rough places plain." (Isa. 40:4.) See Rev. 6:12-17.

21. Hail out of heaven] See Rev. 8:1-13.

DEVIL FORMETH A GREAT AND ABOMINABLE CHURCH

REVELATION 17:1-18.

1 And there came one of the seven angels which had the seven vials, and talked with me, saying, unto me, Come hither; I will show unto thee the judgment of the great whore that sitteth upon many waters:

2 With whom the kings of the earth have committed fornication, and the inhabitants of the earth have been made drunk with the wine of her fornication.

3 So he carried me away in the spirit into the wilderness: and I saw a woman sit upon a scarlet coloured beast, full of names of blasphemy, having seven heads and ten horns.

4 And the woman was arrayed in purple and scarlet colour, and decked with gold and precious

stones and pearls, having a golden cup in her hand full of abominations and filthiness of her fornication:

5 And upon her forehead *was* a name written, MYSTERY, BABYLON THE GREAT, THE MOTHER OF HARLOTS AND ABOMINATIONS OF THE EARTH.

6 And I saw the woman drunken with the blood of the saints, and with the blood of the martyrs of Jesus: and when I saw her, I wondered with great admiration.

7 And the angel said unto me, Wherefore didst thou marvel? I will tell thee the mystery of the woman, and of the beast that carrieth her, which hath the seven heads and ten horns.

8 The beast that thou sawest was, and is not; and shall ascend out of the bottomless pit, and go into perdition: and they that dwell on the earth shall wonder, whose names were not written in the book of life from the foundation of the world, when they behold the beast that was, and is not, and yet is.

9 And here *is* the mind which hath wisdom. The seven heads are seven mountains on which the woman sitteth.

10 And there are seven kings: five are fallen, and one is, *and* the other is not yet come; and when he cometh, he must continue a short space.

11 And the beast that was, and is not, even he is the eighth, and is of the seven, and goeth into perdition.

12 And the ten horns which thou sawest are ten kings, which have received no kingdom as yet; but receive power as kings one hour with the beast.

13 These have one mind, and shall give their power and strength unto the beast.

14 These shall make war with the Lamb, and the Lamb shall overcome them: for he is Lord of lords, and Kings of kings: and they that are with him *are* called, and chosen, and faithful.

15 And he saith unto me, The waters which thou sawest, where the whore sitteth, are peoples, and multitudes, and nations, and tongues.

16 And the ten horns which thou sawest upon the beast, these shall hate the whore, and shall make her desolate and naked, and shall eat her flesh, and burn her with fire.

17 For God hath put in their hearts to fulfil his will, and to agree, and give their kingdom unto the beasts, until the words of God shall be fulfilled.

18 And the woman which thou sawest is that great city, which reigneth over the kings of the earth.

Lo, Lucifer formeth his own church over which he reigneth from eternity to eternity!

And from time to time the Lord giveth those with understanding a glimpse of one part or another of this great and abominable church — this church founded, guided, and upheld by that fallen angel whose misery is complete and who seeketh to make all men miserable like unto himself.

But the views seen and the visions unfolded are not always the same; nor do the revelations poured forth always relate to the same portion of that kingdom which is designed to destroy the souls of men and lead them carefully down to hell.

Nor are all parts of the devil's kingdom equally evil; one part is more abominable than another; and the degeneracy and wickedness of the various, shall we say, stakes of Satan, varies from age to age. What the Lord unfolds and what his prophets proclaim at one time or another is what mankind of that era needs to know. The warning voice always identifies those evils from which the hearers must flee.

Let us, then, treading lightly and carefully, and walking in the course set by revelation, learn what the Lord has revealed about the church of the enemy of all righteousness.

The Church and the Plan of Salvation

To know what is meant by the church of the devil, we must first believe that God is our Father; that he ordained and established the plan of salvation whereby his spirit offspring might advance and progress and become like him; that his plan called for an infinite and eternal atoning sacrifice to be made by the Son of God; and that those who believe and obey shall gain eternal life.

The plan of salvation is the gospel of Jesus Christ, and it alone enables man to return to the presence of God and be like him. This plan is administered by the Church of Jesus Christ and includes all of the laws, rites, ordinances, truths and powers by conformity to which salvation is gained. Thus the Lord's Church is the repository of the laws and powers whereby salvation comes.

To know what is meant by the church of the devil, we must also known that Satan stands in opposition to God; that he sought to change the Father's plan of salvation so as to force salvation upon all mankind; that his offer was rejected; that he then rebelled and led one-third of the hosts of heaven in a war against God; that he was cast down to earth, where he continues his war of rebellion, and seeks to lead men away from salvation and to damnation with him in his kingdom. His plan (if such it may be called) is administered by the church of the devil and consists of any and every course which keeps men from being saved and therefore prepares them to be damned. There was thus a church of the devil in pre-existence. Lucifer was its head, and at that day many followed after him.

The Church of the Devil from Adam to Christ

There has always been a church of the devil on earth. Speaking of the Church as the kingdom of God on earth, the Prophet Joseph Smith said: "In relation to the kingdom of God, the devil always sets up his kingdom at the very same time in opposition to God." (*Teachings*, p. 365.) Thus when Adam and Eve taught the gospel to their children, "Satan came among them, saying: I am also a son of God; and he commanded them, saying: Believe it not; and they believed it not, and they loved Satan more than God. And men began from that time forth to be carnal, sensual, and devilish." As a consequence, Cain said: "Who is the Lord that I should know him? . . . And Cain loved Satan more than God. And Satan commanded him, saying: Make an offering unto the Lord." (Moses 5:13-18.)

And thus it was from Adam to Christ. Indeed, was it not one of the most wicked branches of the church of unrighteousness that brought about the crucifixion of Him whose Church is the sole repository of saving truth and power? Surely the church of the evil one has exerted a great influence in the world! And it is not strange to find Paul speaking of sacrifices made "to devils, and not to God" (1 Cor. 10:20), and of the Beloved Revelator himself writing of the "worship" of devils. (Rev. 9:20.)

The Church of the Devil after Our Lord's Ministry

It is easier for us to use divine standards in measuring the churches and systems of the past than to apply the same rules of judgment to those organizations which touch our lives. Providentially Nephi recorded in a plain and clear manner much of the same data summarized by John in his vision of the church of the devil. Nearly 600 years before the Christian Era that Nephite seer saw in vision the mortal ministry of Christ, including his death upon the cross. (1 Ne. 11:26-33.) Then he beheld "the world"— all of it, including "the house of Israel"— in its warfare against "the twelve apostles of the Lamb," and the Church of Jesus Christ over which they presided. (1 Ne. 11:34-36.)

Then Nephi was shown the events destined to occur among the ancient inhabitants of America from about 600 B.C. to 34 A.D. — that is, until the time of the crucifixion of our Lord and of his resurrected ministry among the Nephites. (1 Ne. 12:1-10.) Then he beheld the next three generations of Father Lehi's descendants, and part of the fourth, dwelling in righteousness upon their promised land (1 Ne. 12:11-12), which brings us in point of time to 200 A.D. (4 Ne. 24.)

In 201 A.D., following a glorious era of near perfect righteousness, the Nephite people "began to be divided into classes; and they began to build up churches unto themselves to get gain, and began to deny the true church of Christ. And it came to pass that when two hundred and ten years had passed away there were many churches in the land; yea, there were many churches which professed to know the Christ, and yet they did deny the more parts of his gospel, insomuch that they did receive all manner of wickedness, and did administer that which was sacred unto him to whom it had been forbidden because of unworthiness. And this church did multiply exceedingly because of iniquity, and because of the power of Satan who did get hold upon their hearts. And again, there was another church which denied the Christ; and they did persecute the true church of Christ, because of their humility and their belief in Christ; and they did despise them because of the many miracles which were wrought among them." (4 Ne. 26-29.)

Thus, apostasy, rebellion, wickedness, and great abominations of every manner and form overran the Nephite people and became part of their worship. Satan, in other words, was setting up his church again among them. And he did the same thing, in manner and form, in the Old World when the descendants of the saints of Jesus' day began to depart from the revealed moorings.

With apostasy comes war and destruction; and so, continuing the divine chronology, Nephi was shown the destruction of the people who bore his name, and the dwindling in unbelief of his Lamanite kin, until they became "a filthy people, full of idleness and all manner of abominations." (1 Ne. 12:13-23.)

This brings us, historically speaking, to the day when the American continent was to be again discovered, as it were, by the people of the Old World. At this point, the angelic ministrant who was opening the future to the Nephite seer, turned the scene back again to the Old World. Nephi saw the Gentile nations among whom the apostles from Jerusalem ministered. He even had John the Revelator identified for him by name, and was told that John and he would see these same things in vision; and Nephi was given instructions as to the things both he and John should record and as to the other parts of the vision left to the literary devices of each of them individually. (1 Ne. 14:18-28.)

Thereupon Nephi saw — and we are following a chronological series of events! — the formation of that church of the devil which grew out of the apostasy in the Old World. (1 Ne. 13:1-3.) And as it was with the apostasy on the American continent, there were many churches comprising Lucifer's earthly kingdom, one of which churches was more abominable than all the rest. Indeed, the mere fact that there are more churches than one in the kingdom of the enemy of all righteousness is of itself sufficient proof that all are not equal and that some are better, some worse, than others.

In its chronological setting, 1 Ne. 13:4-9 covers events from the day of Peter and Paul to the discovery of America by Columbus. The church of the devil there described is the same one shown to John, and both revelators record their visions in substantially the same language, except that clarifying phrases inserted by

Nephi, coupled with the chronological data set forth so well in the Book of Mormon account, enable us to understand with certainty the true meaning of John's accounts.

It should be noted that during this period of the dark ages; this era of about a millennium and a half; this succession of generations that looped down to and included the discovery of America by Columbus; during all these centuries; during all this expanse of time; though there were many apostate churches, there was one in particular that troubled Nephi (and John).

And so Nephi speaks of "the foundation" — the founding, the creating, the originating — of "a great church" "among the nations of the Gentiles." This specific church was "most abominable above all other churches," and Satan "was the foundation" of "this great and abominable church." (1 Ne. 13:4-8.)

Next comes the vision of the discovery of America by Columbus, as he was guided by the light of Christ; of the peopling of this New World; and of the Revolutionary War that freed its inhabitants from the dominion of "their mother Gentiles." (1 Ne. 13:10-19.)

Our inspired author then sees the Bible brought from Europe to America, and the angel tells him this sacred book once "contained the plainness of the gospel of the Lord"; that it had been written "in purity"; and that thereafter — after the whole Bible was written! — there came into existence "a great and abominable church, which is most abominable above all other churches," which church then deleted from and made changes in the Bible. (1 Ne. 13:20-28.)

This incomplete and inaccurate Bible "goeth forth unto all the nations of the Gentiles," and is brought to America to the seed of Lehi, and "because of the many plain and precious things which have been taken out of the book, . . . an exceeding great many do stumble, yea, insomuch that Satan hath great power over them." (1 Ne. 13:29.)

Now Nephi's vision comes to the Spring of 1820 and the ushering in of a new and glorious gospel dispensation. He is told that "because of the most plain and precious parts of the gospel of the Lamb which have been kept back by that abominable church, which is the mother of harlots," that the Lord "will be merciful unto the Gentiles in that day," insomuch that he "will bring forth unto them" his gospel, "which shall be plain and precious." (1 Ne. 13:30-34.) The great restoration takes place; truth is restored; the Lord's work rolls on, and the power of "that great and abominable church, which was founded by the devil and his children" begins to wane. (1 Ne. 13:35-42; 14:1-9.)

Truly Nephi saw and described "that great and abominable church, which is the mother of abominations, whose foundation is the devil," as that organization existed during the dark ages. (1 Ne. 14:9.) But now the scene changes. He views our day; the restoration is past; the great day is at hand for the restored gospel to be preached in all the world for a witness unto all nations. Now the entire concept of the church of the devil changes; now the great and abominable church is not one among many, but it is all the forces of evil linked together; as the scene is set for the final warfare between the saints and the world, we find "there are save two churches only" — the Lord's and the devil's. All men are in one camp or the other; those who are not for the Lord are against him.

In other words, the church of the devil is the world; it is all the carnality and evil to which fallen man is heir; it is every unholy and wicked practice; it is every false religion, every supposed system of salvation which does not actually save and exalt man in the highest heaven of the celestial world. It is every church except the true church, whether parading under a Christian or a pagan banner. As Moroni will say in a later era of Nephite history, and as we shall ascertain in our evaluation of Rev. 18:1-24, it is "secret combinations," oath-bound societies, and the great world force of Godless communism. (Ether 8:14-26.)

And in these last days it is spread upon all the earth — the Americas, Europe, Asia, India, the islands of the seas. It is the combined forces of the ungodly. It is Babylon the great which shall fall. "I beheld the church of the Lamb of God, and its numbers were few," Nephi says of our day, "because of the wickedness and abominations of the whore who sat upon many waters; nevertheless, I beheld that the church of the Lamb, who were the saints of God, were also upon all the face of the earth; and their dominions upon the face of the earth were small, because of the wickedness of the great whore whom I saw." (1 Ne. 14:12.)

1, 15. In Rev. 12:1 the woman (a faithful wife living in lawful wedlock) is "the church of God"; here the great whore (an unfaithful woman living the life of a harlot, in lust and debauchery) is the church of the devil. "Behold there are save two churches only," the angel said to Nephi, "the one is the church of the Lamb of God, and the other is the church of the devil; wherefore, whoso belongeth not to the church of the Lamb of God belongeth to that great church, which is the mother of abominations; and she is the whore of all the earth. And it came to pass that I looked and beheld the whore of all the earth, and she sat upon many waters; and she had dominion over all the earth, among all nations, kindreds, tongues, and people." (1 Ne. 14:10-11.)

1. The judgment of the great whore] The fall of Babylon. See Rev. 18:1-24.

2. With whom the kings of the earth have committed fornication] To a greater or lesser degree, as the case may be, all of the governments of the earth are in league with the great whore in that, from time to time, they do such things as:

Prohibit the worship of God;

Enact laws defining religious beliefs and prescribing forms of worship;

Maintain state-supported, false systems of religion;

Deny freedom of religious belief to all their citizens;

Impose the religious beliefs of conquerors upon conquered people;

Permit the mingling of religious influence with civil government;

Foster one religious society and proscribe another;

Deny to men their inherent and inalienable rights;

Fail to guarantee the free exercise of conscience, the right and control of property, and the protection of life;

Enact laws which curtail the agency of man;

Require the teaching of false principles in their educational systems;

Deny the representatives of certain churches the right to teach their doctrines or proselyte among their people; and

Fail to punish crime and protect the rights of their citizens, particularly unpopular minority groups.

The inhabitants of the earth have been made drunk] There is apostasy from the truth everywhere. "They are drunken, but not with wine; they stagger, but not with strong drink. For the Lord hath poured out upon you the spirit of deep sleep, and hath closed your eyes: the prophets and your rulers, the seers hath he covered." (Isa. 29:9-10.)

3-4. "And I also saw gold, and silver, and silks, and scarlets, and fine-twined linen, and all manner of precious clothing; and I saw many harlots," Nephi said. "And the angel spake unto me, saying: Behold the gold, and the silver, and the silks, and the scarlets, and the fine-twined linen, and the precious clothing, and the harlots, are the desires of this great and abominable church." (1 Ne. 13:7-8.)

3, 7-18. These passages dealing with the beast upon which the woman sat, and of the relationship of various kingdoms to the events seen, is a perfect illustration of what the Prophet had in mind when he said: "Whenever God gives a vision of an image, or beast, or figure of any kind, he always holds himself responsible to give a revelation or interpretation of the meaning thereof, otherwise we are not responsible or accountable for our belief in it. Don't be afraid of being damned for not knowing the meaning of a vision or figure, if God has not given a revelation or interpretation of the subject." (*Teachings*, p. 291.) Until such time as further revelation is received it is fruitless to speculate on the detailed meaning of these things. Brief commentary will be made only of those portions where an inspired interpretation has been made or where the meaning is clear because of other revealed truths.

3. He carried me away in the spirit] See Rev. 21:9-27.

5. To Nephi the angel said: "Look, and behold that great and abominable church, which is the mother of abominations, whose foundation is the devil." (1 Ne. 14:9.) Also: "Behold, the wrath of God is upon the mother of harlots." (1 Ne. 14:16.)

5. MYSTERY] How much of false religion is deliberately designed to be an unknown mystery, and to leave men with the idea they have neither the need nor the ability to comprehend the things of God, as for instance the nature and kind of Being he is!

BABYLON THE GREAT] The church of the devil; the world with all its false doctrines and carnal lusts. See Rev. 18:1-24.

THE MOTHER OF HARLOTS AND ABOMINATIONS OF THE EARTH] It seems clear that if the great whore, which is the church of the devil, has daughters who are harlots, the interpretation of this expression is that false churches beget false churches, that the sponsor of one set of abominations begets sponsors of others.

6. "And the angel said unto me: Behold the foundation of a church which is most abominable above all other churches, which slayeth the saints of God, yea, and tortureth them and bindeth them down, and yoketh them with a yoke of iron, and bringeth them down into captivity. . . . And also for the praise of the world do they destroy the saints of God, and bring them down into captivity." (1 Ne. 13:5-9.) See Rev. 6:9-11.

8. Book of Life] See Rev. 3:1-6; 20:11-15.

9. The seven heads are seven mountains, on which the woman sitteth] This seems to be a clear allusion to Rome, the city founded on seven hills, as the headquarters of that branch of Satan's kingdom which was persecuting and slaying the saints in John's day.

14. "And it came to pass that I beheld that the great mother of abominations did gather together multitudes upon the face of all the earth, among all the nations of the Gentiles, to fight against the Lamb of God. And it came to pass that I, Nephi, beheld the power of the Lamb of God, that it descended upon the saints of the church of the Lamb, and upon the covenant people of the Lord, who were scattered upon all the face of the earth; and they were armed with righteousness and with the power of God in great glory. And it came to pass that I beheld that the wrath of God was poured out upon the great and abominable church, insomuch that there were wars and rumors of wars among all the nations and kindreds of the earth. And as there began to be wars and rumors of wars among all the nations which belonged to the mother of abominations, the angel spake unto me, saying: Behold, the wrath of God is upon the mother of harlots; and behold, thou seest all these things — And when the day cometh that the wrath of God is poured out upon the mother of harlots, which is the great and abominable church of all the earth, whose foundation is the devil, then, at that day, the work of the Father shall commence, in preparing the way for the fulfilling of his covenants, which he hath made to his people who are of the house of Israel." (1 Ne. 14:13-17.)

Lord of lords, and King of kings] See Rev. 19:11-16.

18. That great city, which reigneth over the kings of the earth] Again this seems to be a clear allusion to Rome, the capital city and center of civil autocracy, social degeneracy, and spiritual disease and death. "The state of society at Rome, at the time of the Revelation," Dummelow says, "was probably the worst the world had ever seen." This conclusion is, of course, an exaggeration since the most degenerate social circumstances were those of Noah's day. But Dummelow's description is apt in pointing up the difficulties facing the meridian saints. He continues: "The aristocracy, which alone had any voice in public affairs, was, with few exceptions, utterly given over to the most shameless wickedness. Vast wealth was in their hands, which was spent in unbridled luxury and debauchery. Their continual craving for new sensations was ministered to by foreign parasites, who introduced new vices and flagrant superstitions. With no feeling for others, their cruelty was appalling. With their appetite for life jaded by the pursuit of pleasure, suicide became common. The herded masses of the people were sunk in ignorance and pauperism. The public distribution of corn confirmed them in idleness, and the public shows helped to harden their hearts and to corrupt their feelings. The state religion was not believed in by the educated, while it had no moral teaching to provide for those who did believe in it, and there was no system of public education." (*Dummelow*. p. 1086.)

"BABYLON THE GREAT IS FALLEN, IS FALLEN"

REVELATION 18:1-24.

1 And after these things I saw another angel come down from heaven, having great power; and the earth was lightened with his glory.

2 And he cried mightily with a strong voice, saying, Babylon the great is fallen, is fallen, and is become the habitation of devils, and the hold of every foul spirit, and a cage of every unclean and hateful bird.

3 For all nations have drunk of the wine of the wrath of her fornication, and the kings of the earth have committed fornication with her, and the merchants of the earth are waxed rich through the abundance of her delicacies.

4 And I heard another voice from heaven, saying, Come out of her, my people, that ye be not partakers of her sins, and that ye receive not of her plagues.

5 For her sins have reached unto heaven, and God hath remembered her iniquities.

6 Reward her even as she rewarded you, and double unto her double according to her works: in the cup which she hath filled fill to her double.

7 How much she hath glorified herself, and lived deliciously, so much torment and sorrow give her: for she saith in her heart, I sit a queen, and am no widow, and shall see no sorrow.

8 Therefore shall her plagues come in one day, death, and mourning, and famine; and she shall be utterly burned with fire: for strong *is* the Lord God who judgeth her.

9 And the kings of the earth, who have committed fornication and lived deliciously with her, shall bewail her, and lament for her, when they shall see the smoke of her burning,

10 Standing afar off for the fear of her torment, saying, Alas, alas, that great city Babylon, that mighty city! for in one hour is thy judgment come.

11 And the merchants of the earth shall weep and mourn over her; for no man buyeth their merchandise any more:

12 The merchandise of gold, and silver, and precious stones, and of pearls, and fine linen, and purple, and silk, and scarlet, and all thyine wood, and all manner vessels of ivory, and all manner vessels of most precious wood, and of brass, and iron, and marble,

13 And cinnamon, and odours, and ointments, and frankincense, and wine, and oil, and fine flour, and wheat, and beasts, and sheep, and horses, and chariots, and slaves, and souls of men.

14 And the fruits that thy soul lusted after are departed from thee, and all things which were dainty and goodly are departed from thee, and thou shalt find them no more at all.

15 The merchants of these things, which were made rich by her, shall stand afar off for the fear of her torment, weeping and wailing,

16 And saying, Alas, alas that great city, that was clothed in fine linen, and purple, and scarlet, and decked with gold and precious stones, and pearls!

17 For in one hour so great riches is come to nought. And every shipmaster, and all the company in ships, and sailors, and as many as trade by sea, stood afar off,

18 And cried when they saw the smoke of her burning, saying, What *city is* like unto this great city!

19 And they cast dust on their heads, and cried, weeping and wailing, saying, Alas, alas that great city, wherein were made rich all that had ships in the sea by reason of her costliness! for in one hour is she made desolate.

20 Rejoice over her, *thou* heaven, and *ye* holy apostles and prophets; for God hath avenged you on her.

21 And a mighty angel took up a stone like a great millstone, and cast *it* into the sea, saying, Thus with violence shall that great city Babylon be thrown down, and shall be found no more at all.

22 And the voice of harpers, and musicians, and of pipers, and trumpeters, shall be heard no more at all in thee; and no craftsman, of whatsoever craft *he be*, shall be found any more in thee; and the sound of a millstone shall be heard no more at all in thee;

23 And the light of a candle shall shine no more at all in thee; and the voice of the bridegroom and of the bride shall be heard no more at all in thee: for thy merchants were the great men of the earth; for by thy sorceries were all nations deceived.

24 And in her was found the blood of prophets, and of saints, and of all that were slain upon the earth.

As we have seen in Rev. 17:1-18, Babylon the great is the church of the devil; it is the world with all its evil and carnality; it is every organization of very kind, sort and form — whether religious, civic, political, fraternal, or otherwise — which espouses a philosophy or promotes a cause which leads men away from salvation and toward the kingdoms of lesser glory in the eternal world.

Now we shall see the fall of that great church, or in other words "the destruction of the wicked, which is the end of the world." (Jos. Sm. 1:4.)

Be it remembered that John's particular concern is the fall and destruction of that branch of the great and abominable church of the devil which swept over the earth following his mortal ministry, and which thereby destroyed the continuing blessings that otherwise would have been shown forth to mankind through the ministry of the ancient apostles. In effect, John is describing the fall of a particular part of the devil's earthly kingdom and is illustrating the fall of that whole realm, as our analysis of the whole chapter will show. In this setting, note the Lord's interpretation of the parable of the wheat and the tares: "Behold, verily I say, the field was the world, and the apostles were the sowers of the seed; And after they have fallen asleep, the great persecutor of the church, the apostate, the whore, even Babylon, that maketh all nations to drink of her cup, in whose hearts the enemy, even Satan, sitteth to reign — behold he soweth the tares; wherefore, the tares choke the wheat and drive the church into the wilderness." (D. & C. 86:2-3.)

Ezekiel describes the wars, plagues and desolations which would cover the earth at the very hour of the Second Coming. He tells of nations combining to fight in the holy land; of pestilence, great hailstones, and of fire and brimstone being rained upon the earth; and of the beasts of the forest and the fowls of the air devouring the dead. Chapters 38 and 39 of his writings set forth many of the details. After confirming that these very desolations are to precede and attend his Second Coming, the Lord said: "And the great and abominable church, which is the whore of all the earth, shall be cast down by devouring fire, according as it is spoken by the mouth of Ezekiel the prophet, who spoke of these things, which have not come to pass but surely must, as I live, for abominations shall not reign." (D. & C. 29:21.) That is, among other things, the kingdoms of this world are all included within the great Babylon whose destruction is both soon and certain.

1-3. Few things ever befell ancient Israel which were so burdensome, so wholly loathed by the people, and so destructive of the Israelitish way of life as the Babylonian captivity. (Jer. 20:4.) The Lord led Lehi and his family out of Jerusalem to preserve a branch of his people from the evils that were to befall so many of them in the land of the Chaldeans, and 600 years later Matthew was still using those tragic days as a division point in his historical recitations. (Matt. 1:17.) Both Isaiah and Jeremiah spoke at length of the devastations of that day and of the cursings and destruction that would come upon Babylon as a result. (Isa. 13 and 21; Jer. 50 and 51.) Babylon was truly the great enemy of the Lord's people anciently, and her overthrow and the destruction of her worldliness and wickedness was one of the things of greatest interest and concern to them.

What was more natural, then, than for John and all the prophets to use Babylon as the symbol of sin, and her destruction as the overthrow of wickedness on earth. Thus, for instance, we find Isaiah telling of the future destruction of Babylon and likening it unto the Second Coming, the day when the Lord "shall destroy the sinners," and "punish the world for their evil, and the wicked for their iniquity." (Isa. 13.)

This same imagery was used by the Lord in revealing to Joseph Smith why the wicked "shall be cut off from among the people" at his Second Coming. "They have strayed from mine ordinances and have broken mine everlasting covenant," he said. "They seek not the Lord to establish his righteousness, but every man walketh in his own way, and after the image of his own God, whose image is in the likeness of the world, and whose substance is that of an idol, which waxeth old and shall perish in Babylon, even Babylon the great, which shall fall." (D. & C. 1:14-16.)

Also: "Without faith shall not anything be shown forth except desolations upon Babylon, the same which has made all nations drink of the wine of the wrath of her fornication." (D. & C. 35:11.)

2. **Babylon]** Capital of the Chaldean empire, located astride the Euphrates river, this unbelievably magnificent and mighty city of old, is said to have included 100 square miles within its lofty walls. Manifestly it was the center of worldliness and all the might and power that opposes God and his cause.

Babylon the great is fallen] How aptly Isaiah described the literal fall of the mightiest city of antiquity in these words: "And Babylon, the glory of kingdoms, the beauty of the Chaldees excellency, shall be as when God overthrew Sodom and Gomorrah. It shall never be inhabited, neither shall it be dwelt in from generation to generation: neither shall the Arabian pitch tent there; neither shall the shepherds make their fold there. But wild beasts of the desert shall lie there; and their houses shall be full of doleful creatures; and owls shall dwell there, and satyrs shall dance there. And the wild beasts of the islands shall cry in their desolate houses, and dragons in their pleasant palaces: and her time is near to come, and her days shall not be prolonged." (Isa. 13:19-22; 14:22-23; Jer. 51:37-43.) And how aptly this downfall describes that of "Babylon the great, the mother of harlots and abominations of the earth." (Rev. 17:5.) "That great church, the mother of abominations, that made all nations drink of the wine of the wrath of her fornication, that persecuteth the saints of God, that shed their blood — she who sitteth upon many waters, and upon the islands of the sea — behold, she is the tares of the earth; she is bound in bundles; her bands are made strong, no man can loose them; therefore, she is ready to be burned. . . . She is fallen who made all nations drink of the wine of the wrath of her fornication; she is fallen, is fallen!" (D. & C. 88:94, 105.)

4. The Lord's promise to ancient Israel was that after 70 years of Babylonian captivity they should return to the land of their true inheritance and live there again as his chosen people. (Jer. 25:11; 29:10.) "By the rivers of Babylon," they intoned, "there we sat down, yea, we wept, when we remembered Zion."

(Ps. 137:1.) There they looked forward to the day when Isaiah's prophecy would be fulfilled: "Go ye forth of Babylon, flee ye from the Chaldeans, with a voice of singing declare ye, tell this, utter it even to the end of the earth; say ye, The Lord hath redeemed his servant Jacob." (Isa. 48:20.)

And so, also, the Lord, in November 1831, commanded latter-day Israel: "Go ye out of Babylon; gather ye out from among the nations, from the four winds, from one end of heaven to the other. . . . Go ye out from among the nations, even from Babylon, from the midst of wickedness, which is spiritual Babylon." (D. & C. 133:7, 14.)

6-8. The greater the wickedness, the more intense the suffering. "The wrath of God shall be poured out upon the wicked without measure." (D. & C. 1:9.)

7. Lived deliciously] Waxed wanton. "Men's carnal mind relishes a religion like that of the apostate Church, which gives an opiate to conscience, whilst leaving the sinner license to indulge his lusts." (*Jamieson*, p. 594.)

8. She shall be utterly burned with fire] Babylon shall be burned! "All the proud and they that do wickedly shall be as stubble; and I will burn them up, for I am the Lord of Hosts; and I will not spare any that remain in Babylon." (D. & C. 64:24; 86:7.)

9-19. Dirge of all those who have been made rich through the wickedness and wantonness of the great whore.

10. In one hour is thy judgment come] When the Lord comes it will be as a thief in the night, suddenly and unexpectedly, without warning to the wicked; and in a single day, as it were, the whole social structure of the earth will be changed.

11. No man buyeth their merchandise any more] How much of false and apostate worship is tied in with the sale of special items of religious significance!

12. Merchandise of . . . 13. Souls of men] For sale — the souls of men! What is this but a fulfilment of Moroni's prophecy: "There shall be churches built up that shall say: Come unto me, and for your money you shall be forgiven of your sins"? (Morm. 8:32.) What is it but granting, for a price, freedom from sins yet to be committed? What is it but paying for the performance of ordinances which save the dead from whatever fate they are assumed to inherit? What is it but selling religion in any form? Of paying to hear preaching? Of making salvation available on the basis of wealth, or power, or influence?

20-21. God Almighty overthrows Babylon. Until the Prince of Peace comes in power wickedness shall prevail on earth.

21. A mighty angel] See Rev. 5:1-14.

22. Musicians] Not all music is of God. Lucifer has his harpers, pipers and trumpeters. Some singing is sensuous and evil and lust-inciting.

23. Sorceries] "Use of power gained from the assistance or control of evil spirits is called sorcery. Frequently this power is used in divination, necromancy, and witchcraft. In effect a sorcerer worships Satan rather than God and uses such power as Satan can give him in a vain attempt to imitate the power of God." (*Mormon Doctrine*, 2nd ed., p. 747.) At his coming and incident to the overthrow of Babylon, the Lord himself "will be a swift witness against the sorcerers." (Mal. 3:5.)

24. See Rev. 17:1-18.

COME UNTO THE MARRIAGE SUPPER OF THE LAMB

REVELATION 19:1-9a.

1 And after these things I heard a great voice of much people in heaven, saying, Alleluia; Salvation, and glory, and honour, and power, unto the Lord our God:

2 For true and righteous *are* his judgments: for he hath judged the great whore, which did corrupt the earth with her fornication, and hath avenged the blood of his servants at her hand.

3 And again they said, Alleluia. And her smoke rose up for ever and ever.

4 And the four and twenty elders and the four beasts fell down and worshipped God that sat on the throne, saying, Amen; Alleluia.

5 And a voice came out of the throne, saying, Praise our God, all ye his servants, and ye that fear him, both small and great.

6 And I heard as it were the voice of a great multitude, and as the voice of many waters, and as the voice of mighty thunderings, saying, Alleluia: for the Lord God omnipotent reigneth.

7 Let us be glad and rejoice, and give honour to him: for the marriage of the Lamb is come, and his wife hath made herself ready.

8 And to her was granted that she should be arrayed in fine linen, clean and white: for the fine linen is the righteousness of saints.

9a And he saith unto me, Write, Blessed are they which are called unto the marriage supper of the Lamb.

I.V. REVELATION 19:2, 5.

2 For true and righteous are his judgments; for he hath judged the great whore, which did corrupt the earth with her fornication, and hath avenged the blood of his **saints** at her hand.

5 And a voice came out of the throne, saying, Praise our God, all ye his **saints,** and ye that fear him, both small and great.

1-6. With the fall of Babylon and the end of wickedness on earth, songs of praise and glory and thanksgiving burst forth from heaven's hosts. See Rev. 4:1-11; 5:1-14; 7:9-17; 15:1-4.

1. Alleluia] Hallelujah, meaning praise ye the Lord; that is, praise ye Jah or Jehovah: Hallelu-Jah.

6. Alleluia: for the Lord God omnipotent reigneth] Praise Jehovah, "the Lord Omnipotent who reigneth, who was, and is from all eternity to all eternity" (Mosiah 3:5), and who now as Christ the Lord reigns "personally upon the earth." (Tenth Article of Faith.)

7-9a. "In this dispensation the Bridegroom, who is the Lamb of God, shall come to claim his bride, which is the Church composed of the faithful saints who have watched for his return. As he taught in the parable of the marriage of the king's son, the great marriage supper of the Lamb shall then be celebrated." (*Mormon Doctrine*, 2nd ed., p. 469.) The elders of Israel are now issuing the invitations to the marriage supper of the Lord; those who believe and obey the gospel thereby accept the invitation and shall sit in due course with the King's Son at the marriage feast. See *Commentary I*, pp. 596-599.

"THE TESTIMONY OF JESUS IS THE SPIRIT OF PROPHECY"

REVELATION 19:9b-10.

9b And he saith unto me,
These are the true sayings of God.
10 And I fell at his feet to worship him. And he said unto me,
See *thou do it* not: I am thy fellowservant, and of thy brethren that have the testimony of Jesus: worship God: for the testimony of Jesus is the spirit of prophecy.

9b. He saith unto me] Who is speaking to John? It is none other than the angel sent of God to stand in the place and stead of the Lord Jesus Christ in giving the Beloved Revelator all those things recorded in the Book of Revelation. See Rev. 1:1-6, 12-20; 22:6-16.

In their epistle of June 30, 1916, setting forth the relationship of the Father and the Son to each other and man's relationship to each of them, the First Presidency and the Council of the Twelve, having first quoted various scriptures bearing upon the point, say this: "Thus the Father placed his name upon the Son; and Jesus Christ spoke and ministered in and through the Father's name; and so far as power, authority and Godship are concerned his words and acts were and are those of the Father.

"We read, by way of analogy, that God placed his name upon or in the Angel who was assigned to special ministry unto the people of Israel during the exodus. Of that Angel the Lord said: 'Beware of him, and obey his voice, provoke him not; for he will not pardon your transgressions: for my name is in him.' (Exodus 23:21.)

"The ancient apostle, John, was visited by an angel who ministered and spoke in the name of Jesus Christ." Here they quote Revelation 1:1, and then say: "John was about to worship the angelic being who spoke in the name of the Lord Jesus Christ, but was forbidden." Revelation 22:8-9 is then quoted, in which the angel says he is John's fellow servant and one of his brethren among the prophets. "And then the angel continued to speak as though he were the Lord himself: 'And, behold, I come quickly; and my reward is with me, to give every man according as his work shall be. I am Alpha and Omega, the beginning and the end, the first and the last.' (Rev. 22:12-13.) The resurrected Lord, Jesus Christ, who had been exalted to the right hand of God his Father, had placed his name upon the angel sent to John, and the angel spoke in the first person, saying, 'I come quickly,' 'I am Alpha and Omega,' though he meant that Jesus Christ would come, and that Jesus Christ was Alpha and Omega." (Cited, Joseph Fielding Smith, *Man: His Origin and Destiny*, pp. 117-129; James E. Talmage, *Articles of Faith*, pp. 465-473.)

These are the true sayings of God] The angel, in the Lord's name, bears testimony of the truth and divinity of his teachings and ministerial acts — setting a perfect example of testimony bearing for all the Lord's agents in all ages.

10. Thy fellowservant . . . thy brethren] The Lord's servants in every state and stage of eternal progression — those yet in pre-existence; those dwelling as mortals on earth; those in the paradise of God; those who have been translated; and those who have come forth in the resurrection — all the Lord's servants in all spheres of existence are brethren, fellow laborers, fellow servants.

The testimony of Jesus] The revealed knowledge of the divinity of the Lord and his work. See 2 Tim. 1:1-12.

The spirit of prophecy] Since the greatest and most important revealed truth in all eternity is that Jesus Christ is the Son of the living God and that he was crucified for the sins of the world; since this truth is and can be known only by revelation from the Holy Ghost; since prophecy consists of what holy men speak when they are moved upon by the Holy Ghost (2 Pet. 1:20-21); it follows that any person who has a testimony is a prophet, as Joseph Smith, citing this very passage declared. See *Commentary I*, pp. 251-253; *Commentary II*, pp. 381-388.

CHRIST IS KING OF KINGS AND LORD OF LORDS

REVELATION 19:11-16.

11 And I saw heaven opened, and behold a white horse; and he that sat upon him *was* called Faithful and True, and in righteousness he doth judge and make war.

12 His eyes *were* as a flame of fire, and on his head *were* many crowns; and he had a name written, that no man knew, but he himself.

13 And he *was* clothed with a vesture dipped in blood: and his name is called The Word of God.

14 And the armies *which were* in heaven followed him upon white horses, clothed in fine linen, white and clean.

15 And out of his mouth goeth a sharp sword, that with it he should smite the nations: and he shall rule them with a rod of iron: and he treadeth the winepress of the fierceness and wrath of Almighty God.

16 And he hath on *his* vesture and on his thigh a name written, KING OF KINGS, AND LORD OF LORDS.

I.V. REVELATION 19:11-13, 15.

11 And I saw heaven opened, and behold a white horse; and he that sat upon him **is** called Faithful and True, and in righteousness he doth judge and make war;

12 His eyes as a flame of fire; and **he had** on his head many crowns; and a name written, that no man knew, but himself.

13 And he **is** clothed with a vesture dipped in blood; and his name is called The Word of God.

15 And out of his mouth **proceedeth the word of God, and with it he will** smite the nations; and he **will** rule them with **the word of his mouth;** and he treadeth the wine-press **in the** fierceness and wrath of Almighty God.

11. Faithful and True] Names of Christ, which signify that he is the embodiment and personification of these godly attributes. Above all his fellows, he was obedient to the will of the Father and true to every trust imposed upon him.

In righteousness he doth judge] "The Father judgeth no man, but hath committed all judgment unto the Son." (John 5:22.) "The judgments of the Lord are true and righteous altogether."

(Psalm 19:9.) "Holy, holy are thy judgments, O Lord God Almighty." (2 Ne. 9:46.)

Make war] "The Lord is a man of war" (Ex. 15:3), and the promise is that when he comes again, he will fight the battles of his saints, "as when he fought in the day of battle." (Zech. 14:1-5.) Also: "I have sworn in my wrath, and decreed wars upon the face of the earth." (D. & C. 63:33.)

12. His eyes were as a flame of fire] See Rev. 1:12-20.

On his head were many crowns] Christ reigneth over many kingdoms! He is above all kingdoms, dominions, principalities and powers. (Col. 1:16; 2:10.) He is "far above all principality, and power, and might, and dominion, and every name that is named, not only in this world, but also in that which is to come." (Eph. 1:21.) All things are subject unto him.

A name written, that no man knew] As with all glorified beings, our Lord has a new name in celestial exaltation, a name known to and comprehended by those only who know God in the sense that they have become as he is and have eternal life. See Rev. 2:12-17. Thus, Christ's "new name" shall be written upon all those who are joint-heirs with him (Rev. 3:12), and shall signify that they have become even as he is and he is even as the Father. (3 Ne. 28:10.)

13-15. When the God of Battles comes to overthrow the wicked and bring peace to the earth, he "shall be red in his apparel, and his garments like him that treadeth in the wine-vat. . . . And his voice shall be heard: I have trodden the wine-press alone, and have brought judgment upon all people; and none were with me; And I have trampled them in my fury, and I did tread upon them in mine anger, and their blood have I sprinkled upon my garments, and stained all my raiment; for this was the day of vengeance which was in my heart." (D. & C. 133:48-51; Isa. 63:1-6.) It is noteworthy that the armies of heaven who return with him shall be "white and clean," for in that day all victory and glory shall be attained by the word of his power.

13. The Word of God] Christ, the Lord. See *Commentary I*, pp. 70-71.

16. All men of whatever rank, status or position are now and everlastingly shall be subject to Christ our Lord who is King over all. But in the great and eternal plan of salvation, as joint-heirs with the Father's natural Son, all exalted beings shall become kings, priests, lords and gods. Christ thus becomes a King of Kings, a Priest of Priests, a Lord of Lords, a God of Gods. (*Mormon Doctrine*, 2nd ed., pp. 322-323; 424; 451.)

"COME . . . UNTO THE SUPPER OF THE GREAT GOD"

REVELATION 19:17-21.

17 And I saw an angel standing in the sun; and he cried with a loud voice, saying to all the fowls that fly in the midst of heaven, Come and gather yourselves together unto the supper of the great God;

18 That ye may eat the flesh of kings, and the flesh of captains, and the flesh of mighty men, and the flesh of horses, and of them that sit on them, and the flesh of all *men, both* free and bond, both small and great.

19 And I saw the beast, and the kings of the earth, and their armies, gathered together to make war against him that sat on the horse, and against his army.

20 And the beast was taken, and with him the false prophet that wrought miracles before him, with which he deceived them that had received the mark of the beast, and them that worshipped his image. These both were cast alive into a lake of fire burning with brimstone.

21 And the remnant were slain with the sword of him that sat upon the horse, which *sword* proceeded out of his mouth: and all the fowls were filled with their flesh.

I.V. REVELATION 19:18, 21.

18 That ye may eat the flesh of kings, and the flesh of captains, and the flesh of mighty men, and the flesh of horses, and of them that sit on them, and the flesh of all **who fight against the Lamb,** both **bond** and **free,** both small and great.

21 And the remnant were slain with the **word** of him that sat upon the horse, which **word** proceeded out of his mouth; and all the fowls were filled with their flesh.

"Those with refined senses find it difficult to conceive of the desolation, destruction, and death that will prevail during the final great battles ushering in Christ's reign of peace. So great shall be the slaughter and mass murder, the carnage and gore, the butchery and violent death of warring men, that their decaying bodies 'shall stop the noses of the passengers,' and it shall be a task of mammoth proportions merely to dispose of them. Then shall Ezekiel's prophecy be fulfilled that every feathered fowl and every beast of the field shall assemble to 'eat the flesh of the mighty, and drink the blood of the princes of the earth.' (Ezek. 39.) . . . That all this is an actual, literal supper, an horrible but real event yet to be, has been specifically confirmed in latter-day revelation. (D. & C. 29:18-21.)" (*Mormon Doctrine*, 2nd ed., p. 772.)

19. Armies, gathered together to make war] All the nations of the earth shall be engaged in the final great war during which the God of Battles shall return to overthrow and destroy the wicked and bring peace on earth for those who remain. (Zech. 12 and 14; Joel 3.)

20. The false prophet that wrought miracles] See Rev. 13:11-18; 16:3-16.

A lake burning with brimstone] See Rev. 20:7-10.

21. The wicked and ungodly who are not slain in the earth-covering war that attends our Lord's return shall be consumed by the fire that accompanies that transcendent event. "They that come shall burn them, saith the Lord of Hosts, that it shall leave them neither root nor branch." (Jos. Sm. 2:37.)

SATAN BOUND DURING MILLENNIUM

REVELATION 20:1-3.

1 And I saw an angel come down from heaven, having the key of the bottomless pit and a great chain in his hand.

2 And he laid hold on the dragon, that old serpent, which is the Devil, and Satan, and bound him a thousand years,

3 And cast him into the bottomless pit, and shut him up, and set a seal upon him, that he should deceive the nations no more, till the thousand years should be fulfilled: and after that he must be loosed a little season.

1. The bottomless pit] "In an attempt to convey in imperfect, mortal language the infinite intensity of the sufferings of those cast into the pit (that is, into hell), John spoke not simply of the pit, but of the bottomless pit. (Rev. 9:1-2, 11; 11:7; 17:8; 20:1-3.) The bottomless pit is the depths of hell. It is not a literal pit without a bottom, for such is a contradiction in terms. But it is a pit or prison where the inhabitants suffer, as mortals view suffering, to an infinite, unlimited, or bottomless extent. Referring to finite inability to comprehend the vastness of the suffering of those reaping the full measure of this status, the revelation says: 'The end, the width, the height, the depth, and the misery thereof, they understand not, neither any man except those who are ordained unto this condemnation.' (D. & C. 76:48.)" (*Mormon Doctrine*, 2nd ed., pp. 101-102.)

2-3. "When we speak of the binding of Satan in connection with the millennium, we mean that he will be bound during that era, that his powers will be limited after that day commences, and not that men will turn to righteousness so as to tie the hands of Satan, thereby bringing millennial conditions to pass. The plan does not call for men to turn voluntarily to righteousness thereby causing the thousand year era of peace to commence. Rather, the millennium will be brought about by power; the wicked will be destroyed; and those only will remain on earth who are sufficiently righteous to abide the day of the Lord's coming (Mal. 3; 4), a day when the elements shall melt with fervent heat and all things become new.

"However, Satan shall be bound (D. & C. 43:31; 45:55; 84:100; 88:110-111; Rev. 20:1-3, 7), and for a thousand years he 'shall not have power to tempt any man.' (D. & C. 101:28.) Accordingly, 'children shall grow up without sin unto salvation' (D. & C. 45:58), and righteousness and peace be everywhere present. It was this concept that caused Nephi to write, speaking of the period after the commencement of the millennium, that: 'Because of the righteousness of his people, Satan has no power; wherefore, he cannot be loosed for the space of many years; for he hath no power over the hearts of the people, for they dwell in righteousness, and the

Holy One of Israel reigneth.' (1 Ne. 22:26.)" (*Mormon Doctrine*, 2nd ed., pp. 495-496.)

3. Set a seal upon him] Sealed up the door of the abyss or bottomless pit where he shall dwell for the thousand millennial years.

Loosed a little season] "For Satan shall be bound, and when he is loosed again he shall only reign for a little season, and then cometh the end of the earth." (D. & C. 43:31.) How long will the little season be? President Joseph Fielding Smith suggests it may last about 1000 years. His reasoning is that Christ came in the meridian or midday of time; that from the fall to his coming was 4000 years; that from then until now is another 2000; that the millenium itself will be 1000; and that to make the time of his coming the actual meridian of earth's temporal continuance needs the the added 1000 years of postmillennial existence. (*Doctrines of Salvation*, vol. 1, p. 81.)

Satan] See Rev. 12:1-17.

Millennium] See Rev. 11:15-19; 20:4-6.

SAINTS LIVE AND REIGN DURING MILLENNIUM

REVELATION 20:4-6.

4 And I saw thrones, and they sat upon them, and judgment was given unto them: and *I saw* the souls of them that were beheaded for the witness of Jesus, and for the word of God, and which had not worshipped the beast, neither his image, neither had received *his* mark upon their foreheads, or in their hands; and they lived and reigned with Christ a thousand years.

5 But the rest of the dead lived not again until the thousand years were finished. This *is* the first resurrection.

6 Blessed and holy *is* he that hath part in the first resurrection: on such the second death hath no power, but they shall be priests of God and of Christ, and shall reign with him a thousand years.

4. Thrones] Only those who gain eternal life, which is exaltation, shall sit upon thrones.

Judgment was given unto them] "Christ is the great and eternal Judge of all. (John 5:22; Acts 10:42.) 'Ye must all stand before the judgment-seat of Christ,' Mormon wrote, 'yea, every soul who belongs to the whole human family of Adam; and ye must stand to be judged of your works, whether they be good or evil.' (Morm. 3:20.)

"Under Christ, selected agents and representatives shall sit in judgment upon specified peoples and nations. Scriptural intimations indicate that there will be a great judicial hierarchy, each judge acting in his own sphere of appointment and in conformity with the eternal principles of judgment which are in Christ. . . .

"Our Lord promised his 12 apostolic ministers in Jerusalem that when he came in glory, they also should 'sit upon twelve thrones, judging the twelve tribes of Israel.' (Matt. 19:28; Luke 22:30.) 'It hath gone forth in a firm decree, by the will of the Father, that mine apostles, the Twelve which were with me in my ministry at Jerusalem, shall stand at my right hand at the day of my coming in a pillar of fire, being clothed with robes of righteousness, with crowns upon their heads, in glory even as I am, to judge the whole house of Israel, even as many as have loved me and kept my commandments, and none else.' (D. & C. 29:12.)

"Some 600 years before the first coming of our Lord, an angel told Nephi, 'The twelve apostles of the Lamb . . . are they who shall judge the twelve tribes of Israel; wherefore, the twelve ministers of thy seed shall be judged of them; for ye are of the house of Israel. And these twelve ministers whom thou beholdest shall judge thy seed.' (1 Ne. 12:9-10.) Then to those 12 Nephite ministers, the resurrected Lord said: 'Ye shall be judges of this people, according to the judgment which I shall give unto you, which shall be just. Therefore, what manner of men ought ye to be? Verily I say unto you, even as I am.' (3 Ne. 27:27; Morm. 3:19.)

"Nor is this principle of placing eternal judgment in the hands of the Lord's agents, who have undergone the testing of mortality along with those who are to be judged, limited to the Jewish and Nephite Twelves. Paul said that the saints should judge both the world and angels (1 Cor. 6:2-3); and the faithful elders have this promise relative to those who reject their testimony, 'Know this, that in the day of judgment you shall be judges of that house, and condemn them; And it shall be more tolerable for the heathen in the day of judgment, than for that house.' (D. & C. 75:21-22; Matt. 10:14-15.) Daniel has left us the assurance that when the Ancient of Days sits in that great council at Adam-ondi-Ahman that then judgment will be given to the saints of the Most High. (Dan. 7:22.)

"We have every reason to expect that the saints and the world will be judged by the apostles and prophets sent to carry the message of salvation to them; and that the great hierarchal chain of judgment with Christ at the head, will include Adam and the prophets of all ages, Peter and the apostles of all ages, and all the elders of the kingdom of all ages who have kept their covenants, died in the faith, and who are entitled therefore, as the Lord said, 'to receive a crown of righteousness, and to be clothed upon, even as I am, to be with me, that we may be one.' (D. & C. 29:13.)" (*Mormon Doctrine*, 2nd ed., pp. 398-399.)

The souls of them that were beheaded] "And whoso layeth down his life in my cause, for my name's sake, shall find it again, even life eternal." (D. & C. 98:13.)

They lived and reigned with Christ a thousand years] "Christ will reign personally upon the earth" (Tenth Article of Faith), and with him, in like glory, exercising rule and dominion, each in his appointed sphere, shall be all those who, through righteousness, have become kings and priests. "In mine own due time will I come upon the earth in judgment, and my people shall be redeemed and shall reign with me on earth. For the great Millennium, of which I have spoken by the mouth of my servants, shall come." (D. & C. 43:29-30.)

5-6. See *Commentary II*, pp. 388-404.

6. The second death] See Rev. 21:8.

DEVIL AND HIS ARMIES CAST OUT ETERNALLY

REVELATION 20:7-10.

7 And when the thousand years are expired, Satan shall be loosed out of his prison,

8 And shall go out to deceive the nations which are in the four quarters of the earth, Gog and Magog, to gather them together to battle: the number of whom *is* as the sand of the sea.

9 And they went up on the breadth of the earth, and compassed the camp of the saints about, and the beloved city: and fire came down from God out of heaven, and devoured them.

10 And the devil that deceived them was cast into the lake of fire and brimstone, where the beast and the false prophet *are*, and shall be tormented day and night for ever and ever.

7-9. Before the millennium, Gog and Magog— that combination of nations from the lands of the north, who opposed the Lord and his purposes and people — were overthrown by the coming of the God of Battles to reign personally upon the earth. (Ezek. 38 and 39.) After the millennium — plus a little season to allow the forces of evil to gather their numberless hosts, this time from the four quarters of the earth — Gog and Magog again shall array themselves against the Lord and his saints; and then shall come the final overthrow of the devil and all his evil devices.

"When the thousand years are ended, and men again begin to deny their God, then will I spare the earth but for a little season; And the end shall come, and the heaven and the earth shall be consumed and pass away, and there shall be a new heaven and a new earth." (D. & C. 29:22-23.)

"Satan shall be bound, that old serpent, who is called the devil, and shall not be loosed for the space of a thousand years. And then he shall be loosed for a little season, that he may gather together his armies. And Michael, the seventh angel, even the archangel, shall gather together his armies, even the hosts of heaven. And the devil shall gather together his armies; even the hosts of hell, and shall come up to battle against Michael and his armies. And then cometh the battle of the great God; and the devil and his armies shall be cast away into their own place, that they shall not have power over the saints any more at all. For Michael shall fight their battles, and shall overcome him who seeketh the throne of him who sitteth upon the throne, even the Lamb. This is the glory of God, and the sanctified; and they shall not any more see death." (D. & C. 88:110-116.)

10. "They who are righteous shall be righteous still, and they who are filthy shall be filthy still; wherefore, they who are filthy are the devil and his angels; and they shall go away into everlasting fire; prepared for them; and their torment is as a lake of fire and brimstone, whose flame ascendeth up forever and ever and has no end." (2 Ne. 9:16.)

DEAD ARE JUDGED ACCORDING TO THEIR WORKS

REVELATION 20:11-15

11 And I saw a great white throne, and him that sat on it, from whose face the earth and the heaven fled away; and there was found no place for them.

12 And I saw the dead, small and great, stand before God; and the books were opened: and another book was opened, which is *the book* of life: and the dead were judged out of those things which were written in the books, according to their works.

13 And the sea gave up the dead which were in it; and death and hell delivered up the dead which were in them: and they were judged every man according to their works.

14 And death and hell were cast into the lake of fire. This is the second death.

15 And whosoever was not found written in the book of life was cast into the lake of fire.

11. A great white throne] Emblematic of purity and justice.

Him that sat on it] Christ our Lord, the Great Eternal Judge, "For the Father judgeth no man, but hath committed all judgment unto the Son." (John 5:22.)

The earth and the heaven fled away] This is truly the end of the earth and of the atmospheric heaven which surrounds it. This is the day when there shall be new earth — a celestial sphere

— "For all old things shall pass away, and all things shall become new, even the heaven and the earth, and all the fulness thereof, both men and beasts, the fowls of the air, and the fishes of the sea; And not one hair, neither mote, shall be lost, for it is the workmanship of mine hand." (D. & C. 29:24-25.)

12. The dead, small and great, stand before God] Essentially this is the judgment of the wicked dead. True all men, both the righteous and the wicked, shall be present; all shall hear the decrees; "we shall all stand before the judgment seat of Christ," Paul says. "For it is written, As I live, saith the Lord, every knee shall bow to me, and every tongue shall confess to God. So then every one of us shall give account of himself to God." (Rom. 14:10-12.)

This is the day of which Jacob wrote: "And it shall come to pass that when all men shall have passed from this first death unto life, insomuch as they have become immortal, they must appear before the judgment-seat of the Holy One of Israel; and then cometh the judgment, and then must they be judgd according to the holy judgment of God." (2 Ne. 9:15.)

And it is the day of which the Lord himself says: "Before the earth shall pass away, Michael, mine archangel, shall sound his trump, and then shall all the dead awake, for their graves shall be opened, and they shall come forth — yea, even all. And the righteous shall be gathered on my right hand unto eternal life; and the wicked on my left hand will I be ashamed to own before the Father; Wherefore I will say unto them — Depart from me, ye cursed, into everlasting fire, prepared for the devil and his angels." (D. & C. 29:26-28.)

But, at this late date, the judgment of the righteous dead is in fact a thing of the past. It long antedates this formal occasion when all men shall stand before the judgment bar to hear confirmed what has already been established.

The godfearing and the righteous from Adam to Christ were with our Lord in his resurrection; they came forth with him in the day he burst the bands of death; and they all then received their reward of eternal life. Of this group, speaking in about 148 B. C. — that is, "of those that have been, and who are, and who shall be, even until the resurrection of Christ" — Abinadi says: "All the prophets, and all those that have believed in their words, or all those that have kept the commandments of God" shall come forth with Christ. "These are they that have died before Christ came," he says. "They are raised to dwell with God who has redeemed them; thus they have eternal life through Christ, who has broken the bands of death." (Mosiah 15:21-25.) Numbered with this group, by way of illustration, are Abraham, Isaac and Jacob, of whom the scripture saith: "They have entered into their exaltation, according to the promises, and sit upon thrones, and are not angels but are gods." (D. & C. 132:37.)

When Christ comes again, hosts of others of high spiritual caliber shall come forth with celestial bodies to inherit eternal life. John has in fact just seen these faithful saints upon their "thrones" and described them as living and reigning "with Christ a thousand years." (Rev. 20:4.) And of course, during the millennium the righteous, having attained "the age of a tree, . . . shall be changed in the twinkling of an eye, and shall be caught up, and his rest shall be glorious" (D. & C. 101:30-31), whereas "the sinner being an hundred years old shall be accursed." (Isa. 65:20.)

Thus when the Great God sits upon the white throne, the righteous having been judged, having received eternal life, having entered into a glorious rest, having lived and reigned during the millennium, and having been judged by those appointed so to do — all these shall now stand before the bar of the Great Jehovah to have that judgment confirmed. But the wicked and ungodly shall then be judged according to the deeds done in the flesh; they shall be judged, not by the Lord's agents — not for instance by the Twelve who shall judge the faithful in the house of Israel, "and none else" (D. & C. 29:12) — but by the Lord Jesus Christ himself. He it is who shall assign them their places in the lesser mansions that are prepared. In the first resurrection there are many judges; in the second, one alone, him to whom the Father hath committed all judgment.

Degrees of glory] See *Commentary I*, pp. 727-730; *Commentary II*, pp. 397-400.

The books were opened] What books? The Standard Works of the Church, the holy scriptures wherein the law of the Lord is recorded and the instruction given as to how men should walk in this mortal probation; also, the records of the Church wherein are recorded the faith and good works of the saints — the records of their baptism, celestial marriage, tithe paying, missionary service, and their acts of devotion and worship.

The book of life] What is it? Figuratively, it is our own life, and being, the record of our acts transcribed in our souls, an account of our obedience or disobedience written in our bodies. Literally, it is the record kept in heaven of the names and righteous deeds of the faithful. (*Mormon Doctrine*, 2nd ed., p. 97.)

Judged out of . . . the books, according to their works] In presenting the doctrine of salvation for the dead, the Prophet Joseph Smith quoted Rev. 20:12, and then said: "You will discover in this quotation that the books were opened; and another book was opened, which was the book of life; but the dead were judged out of those things which were written in the books, according to their works; consequently, the books spoken of must be the books which contained the record of their works, and refer to the records which are kept on the earth. And the book which was the book of life is the record which is kept in heaven; the principle agreeing precisely with the doctrine which is commanded you in the revelation contained in the letter which I wrote to you previous to my leaving my place — that in all your recordings it may be recorded in heaven." Then he spoke of binding and sealing on earth and in heaven and explained: "Or, in other words, taking a different view of the translation, whatsoever you record on earth shall be recorded in heaven, and whatsoever you do not record on earth shall not be recorded in heaven; for out of the books shall your dead be judged, according to their own works." (D. & C. 128:7-8.)

13. There shall be an end to death and an end to hell. "Jesus Christ . . . hath abolished death" (2 Tim. 1:10); he gained the victory over the grave; and every living soul shall come forth in the resurrection. And when the wicked and ungodly come forth out of hell to be judged according to their works and receive their inheritance in a telestial kingdom, hell itself ends (D. & C. 76:81-106); it no longer exists; all of its captive spirits are freed from their prison. Thus Jacob says: "O how great the goodness of our God, who prepareth a way for our escape from the grasp of this awful monster; yea, that monster, death and hell, which I call the death of the body, and also the death of the spirit. And because of the way of deliverance of our God, the Holy One of Israel, this death, of which I have spoken, which is the temporal, shall deliver up its dead; which death is the grave. And this death of which I have spoken, which is the spiritual death, shall deliver up its dead; which spiritual death is hell; wherefore, death and hell must deliver up their dead, and hell must deliver up its captive spirits, and the grave must deliver up its captive bodies, and the bodies and the spirits of men will be restored one to the other; and it is by the power of the resurrection of the Holy One of Israel." (2 Ne. 9:10-12.)

Paradise] See *Commentary I*, pp. 823-825.

13. "After death and hell have delivered up the bodies and captive spirits which were in them, then, as John foresaw, 'death and hell were cast into the lake of fire.' (Rev. 20:14.) This lake of fire, a figure symbolic of eternal anguish and wo, is also called hell, but is a hell reserved exclusively for the devil and his angels which includes the sons of perdition. (D. & C. 29:38; 88:113; 2 Pet. 2:4.) . . .

"Thus, for those who are heirs of some salvation, which includes all except the sons of perdition (D. & C. 76:44), hell has an end, but for those who have wholly given themselves over to satanic purposes there is no redemption from the consuming fires and torment of conscience. They go on forever in the hell that is prepared for them." (*Mormon Doctrine*, 2nd ed., p. 351.)

Second death] See Rev. 21:8.

15. See Rev. 21:8.

EARTH RECEIVETH ITS PARADISIACAL GLORY

REVELATION 21:1-6a.

1 And I saw a new heaven and a new earth: for the first heaven and the first earth were passed away; and there was no more sea.

2 And I John saw the holy city, new Jerusalem, coming down from God out of heaven, prepared as a bride adorned for her husband.

3 And I heard a great voice out of heaven saying, Behold, the tabernacle of God *is* with men, and he will dwell with them, and they shall be his people, and God himself shall be with them, *and be* their God.

4 And God shall wipe away all tears from their eyes; and there shall be no more death, neither sorrow, nor crying, neither shall there be any more pain: for the former things are passed away.

5 And he that sat upon the throne said, Behold, I make all things new. And he said unto me, Write: for these words are true and faithful.

6a And he said unto me, It is done.

1. A new heaven and a new earth] "This earth was created in a new or paradisiacal state; then, incident to Adam's transgression, it fell to its present telestial state. At the Second Coming of our Lord, it will be renewed, regenerated, refreshed, transfigured, become again a new earth, a paradisiacal earth. Its millennial status will be a return to its pristine state of beauty and glory, the state that existed before the fall." (*Mormon Doctrine*, 2nd ed., p. 796; Tenth Article of Faith; Isa. 65:17-25; 66:22-24; Matt. 19:28; D. & C. 63:20-21; 101:23-31.) This same designation applies also "to the celestial heaven and earth that will prevail in the day when the Father and the Son make this planet their habitation." (*Mormon Doctrine*, 2nd ed., p. 531; D. & C. 29:22-25; 77:1; 88:16-32; Rev. 21:10-27.)

There was no more sea] Seas shall no longer separate islands and continents as at present. All the land surface of the earth shall be united into one body "like as it was in the days before it was divided." (D. & C. 133:23-24.) See Rev. 16:17-21.

2. New Jerusalem] To envision what is meant by this title, we must know these five facts:

EARTH RECEIVETH ITS PARADISIACAL GLORY

1. Ancient Jerusalem, the city of much of our Lord's personal ministry among men, shall be rebuilt in the last days and become one of the two great world capitals, a millennial city from which the word of the Lord shall go forth.

2. A New Jerusalem, a new Zion, a city of God shall be built on the American continent.

3. Enoch's city, the original Zion, "the City of Holiness, . . . was taken up into heaven." (Moses 7:13-21.)

4. Enoch's city, with its translated inhabitants now in their resurrected state, shall return, as a New Jerusalem, to join with the city of the same name which has been built upon the American continent.

5. When this earth becomes a celestial sphere "that great city, the holy Jerusalem," shall again descend "out of heaven from God," as this earth becomes the abode of celestial beings forever. (Rev. 21:10-27.)

Ministering among the Nephites, the resurrected Lord told them that the American continent was to be the site of a city, to be built by latter-day Israel, "called the New Jerusalem." (3 Ne. 20:22; 21:23-24.) Ether told the Jaredites that this continent "was the place of the New Jerusalem, which should come down out of heaven." (Ether 13:3.)

In recording Ether's teachings, Moroni wrote that a "remnant of the house of Joseph shall be built upon this land; and it shall be a land of their inheritance; and they shall build up a holy city unto the Lord, like unto the Jerusalem of old; and they shall no more be confounded, until the end come when the earth shall pass away. And there shall be a new heaven and a new earth; and they shall be like unto the old save the old have passed away, and all things have become new. And then cometh the New Jerusalem; and blessed are they who dwell therein, for it is they whose garments are white through the blood of the Lamb; and they are they who are numbered among the remnant of the seed of Joseph, who were of the house of Israel. And then also cometh the Jerusalem of old; and the inhabitants thereof, blessed are they, for they have been washed in the blood of the Lamb; and they are they who were scattered and gathered in from the four quarters of the earth, and from the north countries, and are partakers of the fulfilling of the covenant which God made with their father, Abraham." (Ether 13:8-11.)

It was of this American Zion that Isaiah spoke when he recorded these words from the Lord: "For, behold, I create new heavens and a new earth: and the former shall not be remembered, nor come into mind. But be ye glad and rejoice for ever in that which I create: for, behold, I create Jerusalem a rejoicing, and her people a joy. And I will rejoice in Jerusalem, and joy in my people: and the voice of weeping shall be no more heard in her, nor the voice of crying." (Isa. 65:17-19.)

To Enoch the Lord revealed that the gospel would be restored in the latter-days. "Righteousnes and truth will I cause to sweep the earth as with a flood," he said, "to gather out mine elect from the four quarters of the earth, unto a place which I shall prepare, an Holy City, that my people may gird up their loins, and be looking forth for the time of my coming; for there shall be my tabernacle, and it shall be called Zion, a New Jerusalem. And the Lord said unto Enoch: Then shalt thou and all thy city meet them there, and we will receive them into our bosom, and they shall see us; and we will fall upon their necks, and they shall fall upon our necks, and we will kiss each other; And there shall be mine abode, and it shall be Zion, which shall come forth out of all the creations which I have made; and for the space of a thousand years the earth shall rest." (Moses 7:62-64.)

3. **The tabernacle of God is with men]** God's house is established; his temple is erected; the New Jerusalem has been built on earth and Enoch's city has been joined thereto; the center of pure and perfect worship is now among men.

God himself shall be with them] "Christ will reign personally upon the earth." (Tenth Article of Faith.)

4. "And there shall be no sorrow because there is no death. In that day an infant shall not die until he is old; and his life

shall be as the age of a tree; And when he dies he shall not sleep, that is to say in the earth, but shall be changed in the twinkling of an eye, and shall be caught up, and his rest shall be glorious." (D. & C. 101:29-31; Isa. 65:19-20.)

OVERCOME AND BECOME A SON OF GOD

REVELATION 21:6b-7.

6b I am Alpha and Omega, the beginning and the end. I will give unto him that is athirst of the fountain of the water of life freely.

7 He that overcometh shall inherit all things; and I will be his God, and he shall be my son.

6b. Alpha and Omega] See Rev. 1:7-8.

Waters of life] See *Commentary I*, pp. 150-152.

7. He that overcometh] See Rev. 2:1-7, 8-11, 12-17, 18-29; 3:1-6, 7-13, 14-22.

Inherit all things] They have exaltation. "They are gods, even the sons of God — Wherefore, all things are theirs, whether life or death, or things present, or things to come, all are theirs and they are Christ's, and Christ is God's. And they shall overcome all things." (D. & C. 76:58-60.)

Sons of God] See *Commentary II*, pp. 474-475.

WHAT IS THE SECOND DEATH?

REVELATION 21:8.

8 But the fearful, and unbelieving, and the abominable, and murderers, and whoremongers, and sorcerers, and idolaters, and all liars, shall have their part in the lake which burneth with fire and brimstone: which is the second death.

After the separation of body and spirit, which is the natural death, the wicked and ungodly die a second death, a spiritual death, meaning they are cast out of the presence of the Lord and are dead as pertaining to the things of righteousness, which are the things of the Spirit. "I, the Lord, have said that the fearful, and the unbelieving, and all liars, and whosoever loveth and maketh a lie, and the whoremonger, and the sorcerer, shall have their part in that lake which burneth with fire and brimstone, which is the second death. Verily I say, that they shall not have part in the first resurrection." (D. & C. 63:17-18.)

But when those here designated have suffered for their own sins, after they have paid the utmost farthing in hell, after they have suffered "the wrath of Almighty God, until the fulness of times," they shall come forth in the second resurrection and receive their inheritance in the telestial kingdom. (D. & C. 76:103-106.) That is, the allotted period of their spiritual death shall cease; death and hell shall deliver up the dead which are in them; and all men, except the sons of perdition, shall receive their part in the kingdoms which are prepared. Thus these vessels of wrath are "the only ones on whom the second death shall have any power" after the resurrection. (D. & C. 76:37.)

Murderers] When the Lord paraphrases the language of Rev. 21:8 in latter-day revelation (D. & C. 63:17-18 and 76:103-106) he omits murderers from the list of evil persons. Their inclusion here by John, however, coupled with the fact that only those who deny the truth after receiving a perfect knowledge of it shall become sons of perdition, is a clear indication that murderers shall eventually go to the telestial kingdom, unless of course there are some among those destined to be sons of perdition who are also murderers.

EARTH ATTAINS ITS CELESTIAL GLORY

REVELATION 21:9-27.

9 And there came unto me one of the seven angels which had the seven vials full of the seven plagues, and talked with me, saying, Come hither, I will show thee the bride, the Lamb's wife.

10 And he carried me away in the spirit to a great and high mountain, and showed me that great city, the holy Jerusalem, descending out of heaven from God,

11 Having the glory of God: and her light *was* like unto a stone

most precious, even like a jasper stone, clear as crystal;

12 And had a wall great and high, *and* had twelve gates, and at the gates twelve angels, and names written thereon, which are *the names* of the twelve tribes of the children of Israel:

13 On the east three gates; on the north three gates; on the south three gates; and on the west three gates.

14 And the wall of the city had twelve foundations, and in them the names of the twelve apostles of the Lamb.

15 And he that talked with me had a golden reed to measure the city, and the gates thereof, and the wall thereof.

16 And the city lieth four-square, and the length is as large as the breadth: and he measured the city with the reed, twelve thousand furlongs. The length and the breadth and the height of it are equal.

17 And he measured the wall thereof, an hundred *and* forty *and* four cubits, *according to* the measure of a man, that is, of the angel.

18 And the building of the wall of it was *of* jasper: and the city *was* pure gold, like unto clear glass.

19 And the foundations of the wall of the city *were* garnished with all manner of precious stones. The first foundation *was* jasper; the second, sapphire; the third, a chalcedony; the fourth, an emerald;

20 The fifth, sardonyx; the sixth, sardius; the seventh, chrysolyte; the eighth, beryl; the ninth, a topaz; the tenth, a chrysoprasus; the eleventh, a jacinth; the twelfth, an amethyst.

21 And the twelve gates *were* twelve pearls; every several gate was of one pearl: and the street of the city *was* pure gold, as it were transparent glass.

22 And I saw no temple therein: for the Lord God Almighty and the Lamb are the temple of it.

23 And the city had no need of the sun, neither of the moon, to shine in it: for the glory of God did lighten it, and the Lamb *is* the light thereof.

24 And the nations of them which are saved shall walk in the light of it: and the kings of the earth do bring their glory and honour into it.

25 And the gates of it shall not be shut at all by day: for there shall be no night there.

26 And they shall bring the glory and honour of the nations into it.

27 And there shall in no wise enter into it any thing that defileth, neither *whatsoever* worketh abomination, or *maketh* a lie: but they which are written in the Lamb's book of life.

10. He carried me away in the spirit to a great and high mountain] This is literal; John was transported bodily to the appointed vantage point from which the vision was to be seen. Nephi had a similar experience. "I was caught away in the Spirit of the Lord," he said, "yea, into an exceeding high mountain, which I never had before seen, and upon which I never had before set my foot." (1 Ne. 11:1.) And a similar thing occurred to Ezekiel. (Ezek. 40:1-2.)

The holy Jerusalem, descending out of heaven from God] The earth becomes a celestial sphere, with its capital city coming down from celestial spheres, to stand as a type of life and conditions everywhere on the new heaven, for such this earth will then be.

11. Having the glory of God] This earth is now in its fallen or telestial state, in which condition wickedness prevails on its surface. When our Lord comes to usher in the millennial era, there will be a new heaven and a new earth. See Rev. 21:1-6a. The earth will be renewed and receive its paradisiacal glory; it will return to that edenic state which prevailed before the fall. The wicked, meaning those who live a telestial law, shall either be destroyed before the Second Coming or be burned at that time. None will remain who do not live at least a terrestrial law.

Then at the end of the millennium, plus the appointed little season, this planet will change again. Once more there shall be a new heaven and a new earth, but this time our globe will become a celestial sphere, and none shall remain on its surface unless they are living a celestial law. In that day, "the poor and the meek of the earth shall inherit it" (D. & C. 88:17), meaning that the godfearing and the righteous, those who have lived a celestial law, the law of the gospel, shall be the sole inhabitants of this planet.

To prepare the earth itself for that glorious day, the Lord says of our planet, of the very elements which compose it: "Therefore, it must needs be sanctified from all unrighteousness, that it may be prepared for the celestial glory; For after it hath filled the measure of its creation, it shall be crowned with glory, even with the presence of God the Father; That bodies who are of the celestial kingdom may possess it forever and ever; for, for this intent was it made and created, and for this intent are they sanctified. . . . And again, verily I say unto you, the earth abideth the law of a celestial kingdom, for it filleth the measure of its creation, and transgresseth not the law — Wherefore, it shall be sanctified; yea, notwithstanding it shall die, it shall be quickened again, and shall abide the power by which it is quickened, and the righteous shall inherit it." (D. & C. 88:18-26.)

Her light was like unto a stone most precious, . . . clear as crystal] Descriptive of conditions in the holy Jerusalem, which is now in heaven, where God is, our revelation recites: "The angels do not reside on a planet like this earth; But they reside in the presence of God, on a globe like a sea of glass and fire, where all things for their glory are manifest, past, present, and future, and are continually before the Lord. The place where God resides is a great Urim and Thummim." Then, as to conditions on this planet as they shall be after the holy city descends out of heaven from God, the record continues: "This earth, in its sanctified and immortal state, will be made like unto crystal and will be a Urim and Thummim to the inhabitants who dwell thereon, whereby all things pertaining to an inferior kingdom or all kingdoms of a lower order, will be manifest to those who dwell on it; and this earth will be Christ's." (D. & C. 130:6-9.)

12. A wall great and high] Signifying the perfect security and peace enjoyed by all who dwell therein, and also that "there shall in no wise enter into it any thing that defileth, neither whatsoever worketh abomination, or maketh a lie." (Verse 27.)

The names of the twelve tribes of the children of Israel] Signifying that those who dwell in Israel's capital city shall be the saved and exalted remnant of that chosen people, those who as the 144,000 high priests "follow the Lamb whithersoever he goeth." (Rev. 14:4.)

14. The names of the twelve apostles of the Lamb] Signifying that their names — as well as those of all who endure valiantly in the cause of truth and righteousness — shall be had in honorable and everlasting remembrance in the presence of God and his saints.

15-21. Here is a city, in size and dimensions, in splendor and glory, which is so far beyond human experience or comprehension that there is no way to convey to the finite mind what the eternal reality is. Hence, expressions relative to precious stones, to streets of gold, and to pearly gates. It is noteworthy that the city is cubic in shape. Calculated on the basis of 606 feet, 9 inches to the furlong, its outer limits will stretch nearly 1400 miles in length and breadth and height. This means there will be approaching 2,744,000,000 cubic miles of dwelling space within its sacred portals.

18. Clear glass] 21. Transparent glass] See Rev. 4:1-11.

22. Temples, now and during the millennium, are to prepare men for a celestial inheritance. When that glorious goal is gained, heaven itself becomes a temple. The holy of holies in the Lord's earthly houses are symbols and types of the Eternal Holy of Holies which is the highest heaven of the celestial world.

27. The Lamb's book of life] See Rev. 3:1-6; 20:11-15.

SAINTS REIGN AS GODS IN CELESTIAL SPLENDOR

REVELATION 22:1-5.

1 And he showed me a pure river of water of life, clear as crystal, proceeding out of the throne of God and of the Lamb.

2 In the midst of the street of it, and on either side of the river, *was there* the tree of life, which bare twelve *manner of* fruits, *and* yielded her fruit every month: and the leaves of the tree *were* for the healing of the nations.

3 And there shall be no more curse: but the throne of God and of the Lamb shall be in it; and his servants shall serve him:

4 And they shall see his face; and his name *shall be* in their foreheads.

5 And there shall be no night there; and they need no candle, neither light of the sun; for the Lord God giveth them light: and they shall reign for ever and ever.

1. **Water of life]** See *Commentary I*, pp. 150-152.

2. **Tree of life]** See Rev. 2:1-7.

3. **There shall be no more curse]** In the beginning the Lord cursed the ground; decreed that Adam should eat of its fruits in sorrow all his days; and placed Cherubim and a flaming sword to keep him from eating of the tree of life while yet in his sins. (Gen. 3.) Now the curse is removed; all men who attain celestial glory have free access to the tree of life and partake of all the goodness of God.

4. **They shall see his face]** They shall dwell in the presence of God and the Lamb and have personal communion and intercourse with them. Man shall converse with God, as when "a man speaketh unto his friend." (Ex. 33:11.)

His name shall be in their foreheads] See Rev. 3:7-13; 7:2-8; 14:1-5.

5. **They shall reign for ever and ever]** "Then shall they be gods." (D. & C. 132:20.) "Every man who reigns in celestial glory is a God to his dominions." (*Teachings*, p. 374.)

The celestial city] See Rev. 21:9-27.

Exaltation] See 1 John 3:1-3.

CHRIST COMETH AND HIS REWARD IS WITH HIM

REVELATION 22:6-16.

6 And he said unto me, These sayings *are* faithful and true: and the Lord God of the holy prophets sent his angel to show unto his servants the things which must shortly be done.

7 Behold, I come quickly: blessed *is* he that keepeth the sayings of the prophecy of this book.

8 And I John saw these things, and heard *them*. And when I had heard and seen, I fell down to worship before the feet of the angel which showed me these things.

9 Then saith he unto me, See *thou do it* not: for I am thy fellowservant, and of thy brethren the prophets, and of them which keep the sayings of this book: worship God.

10 And he saith unto me, Seal not the sayings of the prophecy of this book: for the time is at hand.

11 He that is unjust, let him be unjust still: and he which is filthy, let him be filthy still: and he that is righteous, let him be righteous still: and he that is holy, let him be holy still.

12 And, behold, I come quickly; and my reward *is* with me, to give every man according as his works shall be.

13 I am Alpha and Omega, the beginning and the end, the first and the last.

14 Blessed *are* they that do his commandments, that they may have right to the tree of life, and may enter in through the gates into the city.

15 For without *are* dogs, and sorcerers, and whoremongers, and murderers, and idolaters, and whosoever loveth and maketh a lie.

16 I Jesus have sent mine angel to testify unto you these things in the churches. I am the root and the offspring of David, *and* the bright and morning star.

6-16. The Lord Jesus placed his own name on a highly favored angel, directed him to speak in the first person as though he were the Lord God himself, and then sent him to reveal to John all that is in the Book of Revelation. See Rev. 19:9b-10.

6. These sayings are faithful and true] When the Lord's agents speak by the power of his Holy Spirit — and, "Angels speak by the power of the Holy Ghost; wherefore, they speak the words of Christ" (2 Ne. 32:3) — they can (and do!) bear that perfect testimony which includes the solemn proclamation that the doctrines they have taught and the words they have spoken are true.

The Lord God of the holy prophets] The Lord Jesus Christ, the God of Israel, the Almighty Jehovah, the One of whom all the prophets bear witness — such act on their part being the very thing that establishes their standings as prophets. See 2 Pet. 1:20-21; Rev. 19:9b-10.

The things which must shortly be done] See Rev. 1:1-6.

7. I come quickly] Not soon, but in a quick manner; that is, with speed and suddenness after all of the promised conditions precedent have occurred. "I am Jesus Christ, who cometh quickly, in an hour you think not." (D. & C. 51:20.)

He that keepeth the sayings of the prophecy of this book] "This book" is the Book of Revelation. All who keep its sayings shall, for instance, know that revelation is to continue after New Testament times; that the gospel was destined to come again in the latter-days by angelic ministration; that glory and honor and exaltation await those who overcome the world and are true and faithful in all things; and that Christ the Lord shall receive glory and honor, power and might, now and forever.

9. **Worship God]** "Thou shalt worship the Lord thy God, and him only shalt thou serve." (Luke 4:8.)

10. **Seal not . . . this book]** It is the divine will that men should know the truths revealed to John and recorded in the Book of Revelation.

11. How true it is that men get what they earn and keep what they have acquired! "They who are righteous shall be righteous still, and they who are filthy shall be filthy still." (2 Ne. 9:16.) So shall it be in the day of judgment. What was earned in this life shall remain with each person as his forever. The effect of the resurrection is "to bring back again evil for evil, or carnal for carnal, or devilish for devilish — good for that which is good; righteous for that which is righteous; just for that which is just; merciful for that which is merciful." (Alma 41:13.) "Neither can filthiness or anything which is unclean be received into the kingdom of God; therefore I say unto you the time shall come, yea, and it shall be at the last day, that he who is filthy shall remain in his filthiness." (Alma 7:21.)

12. **My reward is with me]** All who dwell on earth shall face a day of judgment when Christ comes — not the final and formal occasion set forth in Rev. 20:11-15 — but a day when the wicked shall be burned and the righteous exalted to thrones from which they shall live and reign with Christ a thousand years, as set forth in Rev. 20:4-6.

13. **Alpha and Omega]** See Rev. 1:7-8.

14. **Blessed are they that do his commandments]** There is no language too strong and no repetition too frequent to thunder into

the ears of all who dwell upon the earth that salvation comes to those and those only who keep the commandments.

Right to the tree of life] Those who keep the commandments earn the right to receive the blessings of the Lord; he, the Almighty, has ordained that blessings do and shall follow obedience to law.

15. See Rev. 21:8.

16. The root and the offspring of David] The Son of David was also David's Lord. Christ established David and was the source of his power; and through David's lineage the Great God received his mortal body. See *Commentary I*, pp. 611-612; Rev. 5:1-14. **The bright and morning star]** "Christ is the Bright and Morning Star. (Rev. 22:16.) In speaking of a man as a star the meaning is that he is a person of brilliant qualities, who stands out pre-eminently among his fellows. Thus to single out our Lord as the Bright and Morning Star, the last bright luminary of the night to give way before the rising sun, is to testify that he is pre-eminent over all his brethren, that he is the Son of God in whom all fulness and perfection dwell." (*Mormon Doctrine*, 2nd ed., p. 106.)

"COME UNTO CHRIST"

REVELATION 22:17-21.

17 And the Spirit and the bride say, Come. And let him that heareth say, Come. And let him that is athirst come. And whosoever will, let him take the water of life freely.

18 For I testify unto every man that heareth the words of the prophecy of this book, If any man shall add unto these things, God shall add unto him the plagues that are written in this book:

19 And if any man shall take away from the words of the book of this prophecy, God shall take away his part out of the book of life, and out of the holy city, and *from* the things which are written in this book.

20 He which testifieth these things saith, Surely I come quickly. Amen. Even so, come, Lord Jesus.

21 The grace of our Lord Jesus Christ *be* with you all. Amen.

17. The Beloved Revelator ended his gospel by testifying to all men that his words were written, "that ye might believe that Jesus is the Christ, the Son of God; and that believing ye might have life through his name." (John 20:31.)

Now he bears anew the same testimony and issues anew the same glorious invitation to all men to come unto that being in whom salvation is found.

Moroni felt the same surge of testimony and was filled with the same desire for the welfare of all men as he finished the Book of Mormon account. "Come unto Christ," he pleaded, "and lay hold upon every good gift, and touch not the evil gift, nor the unclean thing. . . . Yea, come unto Christ, and be perfected in him, and deny yourselves of all ungodliness; and if ye shall deny yourselves of all ungodliness and love God with all your might, mind and strength, then is his grace sufficient for you, that by his grace ye may be perfect in Christ; and if by the grace of God ye are perfect in Christ, ye can in nowise deny the power of God. And again, if ye by the grace of God are perfect in Christ, and deny not his power, then are ye sanctified in Christ by the grace of God, through the shedding of the blood of Christ, which is in the covenant of the Father unto the remission of your sins, that ye become holy, without spot." (Moro. 10:30-33.)

18-19. Moses issued the same decree relative to his teachings: "Ye shall not add unto the word which I command you, neither shall ye diminish ought from it, that ye may keep the commandments of the Lord your God which I command you." (Deut. 4:2; 12:32.) God alone can add to or diminish from holy writ. What he has spoken, he has spoken, and none but he can alter. When a prophet speaks by the power of the Holy Ghost, it is the voice of God; and none can change it without suffering the penalty prescribed for perverting the pronouncements of Deity.

19. Book of life] See Rev. 3:1-6; 20:11-15.

20. I come quickly] See Rev. 22:6-16.

Even so, come, Lord Jesus] 'Come even as thou hast said. Let all things be done according to thy mind and purposes. Thy will, O God, is perfect; thy will be done, as in heaven, so on earth.'

21. 'May the manifest love, mercy and condescension of Christ — who redeems all those who believe on his name and who keep his commandments — abide in the hearts of his saints forever.'

And so endeth John's record of what the Lord Jesus Christ, by his angel, revealed on Patmos.

And so endeth that glorious and inspired collection of revealed writ known to men as the New Testament.

How wondrous it is that this brief New Testament account has preserved for us so much of that everlasting truth which enables fallen man to return to his high state with the Gods of Heaven and there, with them, sit down in eternal glory!

One thing only remains to complete this work — and that is the seal of testimony. May I, therefore, quote my own words, poetically expressed as follows:

I BELIEVE IN CHRIST

I believe in Christ, he is my king;
With all my heart to him I'll sing;
I'll raise my voice in praise and joy,
In grand amens my tongue employ.

I believe in Christ, he is God's Son;
On earth to dwell his soul did come;
He healed the sick, the dead he raised,
Good works were his, his name be praised.

I believe in Christ, O blessed name,
As Mary's Son he came to reign
Mid mortal men, his earthly kin,
To save them from the woes of sin.

I believe in Christ, who marked the path,
Who did gain all his Father hath,
Who said to men: "Come follow me,
That ye, my friends, with God may be."

I believe in Christ — my Lord, my God —
My feet he plants on gospel sod;
I'll worship him with all my might;
He is the source of truth and light.

"COME UNTO CHRIST"

I believe in Christ, he ransoms me;
From Satan's grasp he sets me free,
And I shall live with joy and love
In his eternal courts above.

I believe in Christ, he stands supreme;
From him I'll gain my fondest dream;
And while I strive through grief and pain,
His voice is heard: "Ye shall obtain."

I believe in Christ; so come what may,
With him I'll stand in that great day,
When on this earth he comes again,
To rule among the sons of men.

May I also renew the witness borne at the conclusion of Volume One of this work:

"Let it now be written once again — and it is the testimony of all the prophets of all the ages — that he is the Son of God, the Only Begotten of the Father, the promised Messiah, the Lord God of Israel, our Redeemer and Savior; that he came into the world to manifest the Father, to reveal anew the gospel, to be the great Exemplar, to work out the infinite and eternal atonement; and that not many days hence he shall come again to reign personally upon the earth and to save and redeem those who love and serve him.

"And now let it also be written, both on earth and in heaven, that this disciple, who has prepared this work, does himself also know of the truth of those things of which the prophets have testified. For these things have been revealed unto him by the Holy Spirit of God, and he therefore testifies that Jesus is Lord of all, the Son of God, through whose name salvation comes." (*Commentary I*, p. 876.)

END OF VOLUME THREE